Tourism Development
Principles, Processes, and Policies

Tourism
Development

Principles, Processes, and Policies

William C. Gartner

VNR

Van Nostrand Reinhold

I(T)P® A Division of International Thomson Publishing Inc.

New York • Albany • Bonn • Boston • Detroit • London • Madrid • Melbourne
Mexico City • Paris • San Francisco • Singapore • Tokyo • Toronto

5918662O
62023568

I(T)P® an International Thomson Publishing Company
The ITP logo is a registered trademark used herein under license

Printed in the United States of America

For more information, contact:

Van Nostrand Reinhold
115 Fifth Avenue
New York, NY 10003

Chapman & Hall GmbH
Pappelallee 3
69469 Weinheim
Germany

Chapman & Hall
2-6 Boundary Row
London
SE1 8HN
United Kingdom

International Thomson Publishing Asia
221 Henderson Road #05-10
Henderson Building
Singapore 0315

Thomas Nelson Australia
102 Dodds Street
South Melbourne, 3205
Victoria, Australia

International Thomson Publishing Japan
Hirakawacho Kyowa Building, 3F
2-2-1 Hirakawacho
Chiyoda-ku, 102 Tokyo
Japan

Nelson Canada
1120 Birchmount Road
Scarborough, Ontario
Canada M1K 5G4

International Thomson Editores
Seneca 53
Col. Polanco
11560 Mexico D.F. Mexico

2 3 4 5 6 7 8 9 10   QEB-FF   01 00 99 98 97

Library of Congress Cataloging-in-Publication Data

Gartner, William C.
    Tourism development: principles, processes, and policies / William C. Gartner.
        p. cm.
    Includes bibliographical references and index.
    ISBN 0-442-00893-7
    1. Tourist trade.   I. Title.
G155.A1G295 1996   96-33757
338.4'791——dc20   CIP

Richard (Hoagy) Gartner (1959–1994)

Contents

Acknowledgments

No book is written by a single author. Many people have contributed their time and expertise to this effort. While it is not possible to mention everyone by name here, some are too important not to identify. First and foremost my family. Hank and Adele, my parents, have always provided support, encouragement, and, too important to ignore, a quality education. My wife, Carolyn, and children, Molli, Peter, and Hunter, put up with an absentee husband and parent who, when present, was often a cranky one when nothing seemed to come together. Professionally, many colleagues should be mentioned, but none were more prominent than Jafar Jafari. Besides being a friend and someone I could bounce ideas off of, he allowed me open use of his extensive tourism library which surpasses many university collections. Staff of the Tourism Center, especially Eileen, pulled everything together to meet numerous deadlines and made it possible for me to get my other work done while I was finishing up this manuscript. Finally, this book would not have been possible without a mind enriched and recharged every year by forays into the marshlands of North America. The sight of an untiring, overgrown Black Lab swimming in the frigid water to retrieve a Drake Mallard, and overjoyed to do it, does a whole lot to restore one's psychological balance.

Preface

There is no longer any doubt regarding the importance of tourism in today's world. Its ascendancy to the world's largest industry has been a rapid one. What has not kept pace with the increasing amount of tourists and growth in areas devoted to tourism has been knowledge about the phenomenon itself and its consequences. Within the last few years, that trend has changed. Numerous tourism texts are appearing to fill some of the knowledge gaps. Governments and private sector operations are more willing to finance tourism related research. Academic institutions are beginning to offer more courses in tourism and include the name in degree programs. What this all means is that tourism is no longer the private domain of the wealthy, but is enjoyed, studied, and integrated into the daily lives of many people throughout the world. Obviously, one could argue that pleasure tourism is not enjoyed by even a majority of the world's populations, especially those in developing countries, but then neither is adequate health care. Simply because one doesn't have the wherewithal to travel does not preclude being affected by tourism. It is the sheer number of travelers and the even larger group of willing and unwilling hosts that require that more attention be paid to the consequences of tourism. This book is an attempt to add to the increasing level of knowledge regarding tourism.

Tourism development can be defined in many different ways. This book discusses development as a process. That is, it focuses on the factors affecting development. It begins with a discussion of the foundations of tourism and development along with a historical overview of forces that have led to modern-day tourism. It then moves into the impacts, both positive and negative, resulting from the movement of people around the globe. The third part discusses the organizational structures and policies that make tourism development possible, and then moves into demand and supply factors underlying tourism development. Finally, the concluding section reviews techniques and principles that make possible the successful implementation of a tourism development strategy.

As the reader progresses through the chapters he/she will generally find that the material becomes more complex and theoretical toward the end of each chapter. This is done purposefully as a means of both reinforcing some of the material learned in an introductory course or book on tourism and adding new information to that foundation. This is a book intended for a graduate class but with applications useful to practitioners.

Since the study of tourism is a multidisciplinary field, different authors approach the subject from different perspectives. In this book, the disciplines of economics and recreation are represented more than others. This, of course, reflects the author's own academic and professional background. Since economic theory is used throughout the book, it is recommended that the reader have taken some introductory courses or have a professional background in economics. Yet this is not a book on tourism economics. Economic theory is simply used to support many of the author's statements and recommendations. It is possible to ignore the economic theory utilized in this text and still appreciate the range and scope of tourism development issues discussed.

As society approaches the next millennium, tourism will become an even more important part of the world economy. The momentous events of the last part of the twentieth century almost guarantee this will happen. Yes, wars will still rage, poverty will persist, and social injustice will continue, but so will the expansion of a global economy. More than anything else, mutually beneficial economic linkages between businesses and countries will fuel an expanding tourism industry. Even if, as some experts predict, the level of business travel declines as a result of communication technology, there will remain an overwhelming need for people to travel. Throughout history people have exhibited a unquenchable need to travel. The motivations may have changed, but the end result has always been the same. Every so often there is a need to change place and pace. This book is an attempt to more fully understand that "wanderlust" and the development process that makes it possible.

Tourism Development
Principles, Processes, and Policies

Foundations

The first part of this book is an introductory or survey discourse on tourism as field of study, development as a process, and an overview of historical events related to the evolution of modern-day tourism. Tourism development is a largely undefined concept with much disagreement among the academic and professional community about how the subject should be defined, studied, and applied. Part I does not solve this dilemma for the reader, but instead attempts to offer some of the more classic definitions about what it is we are dealing with, and sets the stage for more focused material appearing in later chapters.

Tourism began definitively when humans settled in one area and began to call it home. Whether earlier nomadic tribes practiced tourism is still debatable. What is new is the study of tourism as a societal phenomenon and the development process associated with it. Part I exposes the reader to different schools of thought about what tourism is, what it means, and what constitutes modern-day tourism's antecedents. It would be surprising if all students, instructors, and members of the tourism industry that read this book agreed with what is presented not only in Part I but throughout the text. That outcome is neither expected nor encouraged. Development of the human intellect is no different than the process of tourism development, and advances come through disagreement and the search for solutions to problems and questions. Those of us who make a living in some way through tourism argue constantly about what the concept means (e.g., is it travel or tourism?; is it a discipline?), what constitutes appropriate development, and the extent to which tourism has been shaped by past events and continues to shape the future. Part I addresses these questions but does not answer them. It is up to the reader to assimilate the material, revisit the questions, and formulate his/her own answer. Just as the tourism product is an individualized experience, so will be the answers to these questions.

Tourism and Development

Roman architecture in the city center of Split, Croatia.
Photo by the author

Learning Objectives

Understand that there is no universally accepted definition of tourism or tourism development, yet there is no shortage of proposed definitions.

•

Look for similarities between the various definitions that have been offered.

•

Realize that tourism and development take on many diverse forms.

•

Review significant trends and constraints affecting tourism development.

•

Follow the evolution of the study of tourism utilizing a historic platform approach.

INTRODUCTION

Conceptualize tourism. Do images of white sandy beaches, palm trees, and turquoise seas come to mind, or are visions of mountain trekking more likely to appear? What does a cramped seat in an airplane, a taxi darting through traffic, the loss of a sale because you're late, and learning that your hotel has been overbooked have in common with the first set of images? Is one tourism because it conjures up pleasant images and the other work because it brings forth images of unpleasant experiences? What is tourism?

Now conceptualize development. Do images of championship golf courses, tennis courts, and resort hotels spring to mind or do pictures of starving children outside thatched huts appear to remind you of the economic differences that exist throughout the world? Is development represented through physical structures or is it something that can be compared? What is development?

A rational person would expect that by now, someone had figured out the answers to these questions. After all, tourism is widely touted as the world's largest industry, and that alone should mean that thousands of scientists are studying the phenomenon. Unfortunately, there are not thousands studying tourism and those that are have been doing it for only a relatively short period of time. No clear-cut definition exists of what tourism is.

There is no shortage of physical developments which one could claim were built solely for tourists. Many of these are economically successful. But simply because some developments provide economic benefits, does it follow that these are appropriate or could serve as models for future development? Do they serve to protect the environment on which development relies? Do they provide opportunities for non-intrusive integration into the host community?

This book explores some of the issues surrounding tourism and the development which makes hosting visitors possible. It also offers suggestions for change when development does not serve to protect the interests of developers, host communities, and the environment in which development takes place. However, to fully understand the nature of tourism and development, we must begin with some proffered definitions of tourism and the process (development) that makes the phenomenon possible.

TOURISM DEFINED

Early definitions of tourism focused on the spatial dimension. A person was considered to be a tourist when he moved a specified distance away from his home. If a passenger was picked up along the way, the first traveler became a tourist before the second one. No physical changes were noticeable for either traveler, but in an economic balance sheet only one person's expenditures were related to tourism. Compounding the problem of who is and who is not a tourist, the "magic" distance changed from place to place and from organization to organization.

The United States National Tourism Resources Review Commission presented one of the early spatial definitions of the domestic tourist. The distance used was 50 miles, and all types of travel except commuting to work were included; length of stay and a minimum expenditure were irrelevant (National Tourism Resources Review Commission, 1973). The U.S. Census Bureau, which conducted a national travel survey every five years, used a 100 mileage figure plus the requirement of one or more nights away from home, a criterion dropped in the last few surveys conducted. Currently, the most widely accepted definition of a domestic traveler in the United States is: "any resident of the United States, regardless of nationality, who travels to a place 100 miles or more away from home within the United States or who stays away from home one or more nights in paid accommodations" (U.S. Travel Data Center, 1989). This latest definition has both distance and expenditure elements. Other governments use different definitions for the domestic tourist; Canada has a 25-mile requirement.

A definition of the tourist which can be used for statistical purposes becomes even more complex when international travel is considered. McIntosh et al. (1995) have traced the definition of an international tourist, termed "foreign tourist," to the League of Nations Committee of Statistical Experts. This 1937 definition required someone to visit a country in which they did not reside for at least 24 hours before they became a "foreign tourist." Those people staying in a country less than 24 hours were labeled "excursionists." This definition is still in use today.

Consider the following conundrum. A person living in Detroit, Michigan, travels to Windsor, Ontario, to take advantage of a weekend vacation package offered by one of the urban hotels. Detroit is separated from Windsor by the two-mile-wide Detroit river. Using the above international definition, the person from Detroit is a tourist for Canada and all his/her expenditures should be included in that country's tourism accounts ledger. On the same weekend, the person's neighbor decides to buy a similar weekend vacation package at a hotel within the Detroit metropolitan area. Motivations for selecting a hotel package are the same for each person. Activities engaged in (e.g., dining, dancing) are remarkably similar, yet one person is a tourist while the other is not. Does this make sense?

The reason spatial definitions are accepted, regardless of their faults, is because they provide economic and statistical legitimacy to the tourism phenomenon. Once sectorialized, a phenomenon becomes an industry and it is given equal status with all other legitimate economic pursuits.

Spatial definitions alone cannot define tourism. They are demand-side definitions and ignore the supply aspect of tourism. As such, they only attempt to define what a tourist is rather than what tourism is. If tourism is to be analyzed from an industry perspective (i.e., all supply/demand components considered), then more inclusive definitions of the activity are needed. McIntosh et al. (1995) define tourism as "the sum of the phenomena and relationships arising from the interaction of tourists, business suppliers, host governments, and host communities in the process of attracting and hosting these tourists and other visitors." This definition recognizes four important elements of tourism: the tourists, businesses providing travel related services, governments (at all levels) which exert policy control over tourism, and the people who live in an area visited by tourists.

Leiper's (1981) definition of tourism includes all the elements of McIntosh et al.'s with slightly more specificity. He defines tourism as

> an open system of five elements interacting with broader
> environments, the human element, tourists; three geographical
> elements: generating region, transit route and destination region; and
> an economic element, the tourist industry. The five are arranged in
> functional and spatial connection, interacting with physical,
> technological, social, cultural, economic and political factors. The dy-
> namic element comprises persons undertaking travel which is, to
> some extent, leisure-based and which involves a temporary stay away
> from home of at least one night" (1981:74).

This definition, which appears broad enough to include almost anything leading to or happening as a result of travel away from home, does place some specific limits on what tourism can be. The addition of leisure excludes business travelers who do not consider their trip to have a pleasurable component. Anyone who has spent hours in airports, taxis, uncomfortable but cheap motels, while missing his/her spouse's fortieth birthday knows travel is not always leisure-based. But is it tourism? The addition of at least a one-night stay also limits the extent of tourism.

There are probably as many definitions of tourism as the number of people addressing the issue. In an attempt to survey tourism definitions, Cook (1975) summarizes them into the following categories: those that deal with geographical dimensions (e.g., international vs. domestic); time away from home; mode of transportation; purpose of trip; miles traveled; and a combination of the above.

One of the simplest yet most inclusive definitions is offered by Jafari

(1977:8): "tourism is a study of man away from his usual habitat, of the industry which responds to his needs and of the impacts that both he and the industry have on the host sociocultural, economic and physical environment." This definition is not offered so much as a means to define tourism as to define what an academic tourism discipline would do. The definition is succinct yet broad enough to fully explain what tourism is all about. When someone leaves home they can become a tourist; there are no spatially delimiting factors. Chapter 8 presents a model showing the various psychological changes someone may experience while traveling. The important point is that one can become a tourist without traveling a significant physical distance. Jafari's definition also recognizes that tourism creates economic, sociocultural and environmental impacts, discussed more fully in Part II of this book. Finally, it recognizes that tourism providers constitute an industry group, essential not only for statistical purposes but also in establishing an identity for the phenomenon. Rather than considering the accommodations or restaurant industry individually, this definition allows us to view the group as a holistic, integrated, interconnected tourism industry comprised of many sub-industries.

One of the problems not only in defining tourism but in recognizing it as a discipline is a general disdain in viewing leisure or pleasure as a legitimate activity. Veblen (1912), in one of the earliest works on tourism, characterizes the leisure class as exempt from all useful employment. This is not a new insight, as similar feelings have their roots in early Judeo-Christian theology:

> "The Bible legend tells us that the absence of labour—idleness—was a condition of man's first blessedness before the Fall. Fallen man has retained a love for idleness, but the curse weighs on the race not only because we have to seek our bread in the sweat of our brows, but because our moral nature is such that we cannot be both idle and at ease. An inner voice tells us we are wrong if we are idle" (Tolstoy, [1865] 1981:657).

An industry that relies on the idle or leisure class to provide it legitimacy has to overcome problems of moral acceptance before it can be treated as a viable economic activity.

Given that all the above definitions have their proponents and opponents, it is not necessary to attempt to add one more. However, if only the common elements of each are retained, tourism could be defined as occurring when an individual changes physiological place and psychological pace. Simply put, tourism is a change of place and pace.

DEVELOPMENT DEFINED

Development is an even more elusive term to define than tourism. It can be viewed as either a process or a state (Goulet, 1968, from Pearce, 1989). Development as a state refers to the relative condition of the object of interest. For example, "third world" or "underdeveloped world" refers to the economic condition of a group of nations. Defining development as a condition or state of being requires the acceptance of a unit of measurement. Gross National Product, per capita income, or some other economic value measurement can be used to measure the relative economic condition of nations. Similarly, reading comprehension scores can be used to measure an individual's reading development state. Measurements of the state of development are always relative and only relevant for a particular point in time.

Development can also be viewed as a process. Tourism development is often viewed as a process of physical change. Noronha (1976) identified three stages of tourism development. The first begins with the discovery of an area by tourists. As word of the discovery spreads, tourist flows to the area increase and host societies respond to this new economic activity, usually by beginning to construct facilities and offering services in demand by tourists. If tourism continues to expand, it enters the last stage of development in which it is fully institutionalized. It becomes a formal business activity complete with attractions, service facilities and organizations dedicated to supporting and promoting tourism to the area. The risk of major sociocultural and environmental change accelerates as development evolves into the institutionalized state.

Butler (1980) describes the evolution of tourism development as consisting of six stages (Figure 1.1). The first stage, exploration, is similar to discovery in the sense that initially small numbers of tourists choose to visit a particular place. Once significant numbers of tourists have arrived, the stage of involvement commences. The appearance of small facilities or businesses catering to tourists are the first signs that the destination is beginning to enter the involvement stage. The third stage is development, referring to a condition of extensive facility construction to either provide attractions to tourists or service their needs. The development stage is the one most critical when addressing the impacts resulting from tourism development. That is, impacts are most likely to occur during this stage when a destination evolves from a small scale provider of tourist services to one dominated by the tourism industry. Advertising and promotion are now necessary to maintain the size of the created industry.

Eventually, the early influx of tourists begins to level off and the destination enters the consolidation stage. If significant negative sociocultural

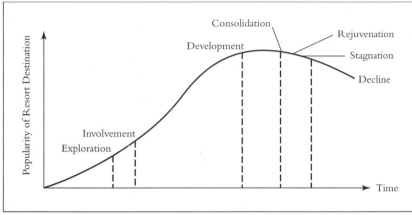

Figure 1.1 Hypothetical Model
of Resort Life Cycle

Source: Butler, 1980

and environmental impacts occurred during the development stage, it is in
the consolidation stage that they begin to be recognized by larger segments of the host society. As tourist flow slows to the point where there is
no growth in new arrivals, the destination enters the stagnation stage. One
of two things has happened. Either physical capacity has been reached or
tourist interest has declined. The destination now has two choices. It can
enter a stage of decline as tourists move to newer or more appealing destinations, or it can begin a period of rejuvenation. Rejuvenation can occur
in two dissimilar ways. If the facilities constructed to accommodate tourist
needs have reached capacity, another round of development can begin. If
tourists are no longer interested in the destination, the product line may
have to be changed.

Miossec (1976) also models tourism development with respect to
physical change (Figure 1.2). The original impetus for change begins with
the development of facilities (e.g., resorts) dedicated to serving tourist
needs. The earliest developers make tourists aware of the destination.
These efforts constitute an induced form of image formation (see Chapter
11) and rely on the promotional abilities of developers to entice tourists to
visit. If the promotion is successful and tourists become aware of the destination, the process of change begins to accelerate. Reacting to the success
achieved by pioneer developments, other facilities are built. Infrastructure
needs, including transportation networks, are simultaneously constructed.
Land-use patterns change as the area becomes increasingly saturated with
new tourist facilities. Eventually, more organically based information
sources replace the reliance on induced image formation. In other words,
tourists themselves become the promoters of the area. The destination, if
allowed to develop at will, establishes a hierarchy of facilities catering to

Evolution of Tourism Development

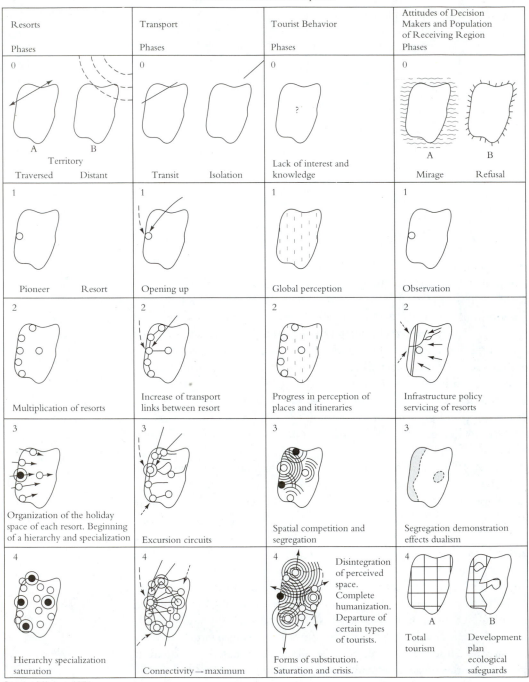

Source: Miossec, 1976

Figure 1.2 *Evolution of Tourism Development*

different income and psychographic market segments. When the area reaches this point, lack of planning controls will result in increasing environmental and sociocultural impacts.

Both Miossec and Butler's models presuppose that development is a physical process. As areas physically transform, original resource values drastically change. While this has, for the most part, proved true of tourism development in the past, it does not have to be the model of the future. Development should not be viewed solely as a physical phenomenon. It is simply an evolutionary process encompassing noticeable economic, physical, or social restructuring. In that respect, appropriate tourism development should be defined as the process of increasing the quality of life for tourists and host societies alike. The key is determining a measurable unit for quality of life. What it is, how to measure it, and when it has been achieved are highly subjective judgments. For the purpose of this text, tourism development is defined simply as an evolutionary process related to tourist activity. Whether that change process is good or evil is something that has to be determined by the people directly involved in the tourism industry. Host governments, host societies, tourists, and tourist service providers are equally important in determining the type and level of change that is acceptable. Since they often have conflicting goals, each group must try to understand what development means to each other. There is no predetermined destiny when it comes to tourism development. Change brought on by tourism development can be directed.

TOURISM TRENDS *Conclusion*

What does the future hold for tourism? This question cannot be addressed with total certainty due to the inability of any one person, think tank, etc., to accurately predict the future. However, forecasts or statements about what we expect to happen can be made based on historical data and trends. In some cases, there are no historical antecedents on which to base trends as new forces arise which are so powerful that in a matter of years they completely change the way things were done in the past. Recently this has been the case with communications technology. What follows is an overview of tourism travel trends in general, followed by a review of some of the more significant trends affecting the big picture.

Travel Flows

Some of the trends expected to occur, if world conditions change at approximately the same rate they have in the immediate past, can be found in the World Tourism Organization's most recent publications (see reference list at the end of the chapter). Most of the trends are reported for in-ternational tourism. There are many reasons for this, most significantly that data on domestic tourism are not readily available for many countries in the world.

However, there is a strong relationship between international and do-mestic tourism. If a country increases its share of international arrivals, it should benefit domestic tourism by increasing the earning power of peo-ple in the host country allowing them to use some discretionary income for their own domestic travel. Domestic and international tourism com-plement each other in that the same infrastructure, facilities, and services can generally be used for both types of travel.

If travel is considered one product with a downward sloping demand curve, international and domestic tourism are affected differently. Interna-tional travel, especially the long haul variety, is more expensive than do-mestic travel. The demand for international travel would be located in the upper, more elastic portion of the demand curve. Economic factors (e.g., recession, oil shortage) which increase the relative cost of travel should have a greater impact on products such as international travel, located in that upper end. This appears to be true, as the World Tourism Organiza-tion estimates that worldwide, domestic tourism arrivals are ten times those for international tourism, with expenditure levels higher by a factor of seven. Therefore, the following international travel trends should be viewed as only a small part of total travel throughout the world.

International tourism arrivals are expected to increase at an annual rate of 4% throughout the 1990s, a small decrease from growth rates of 4.5% annually through the 1980s (Table 1.1) and a decrease from growth rates experienced in the three previous decades. Tourism receipts, on the other hand, grew at a rate of approximately 9.5% during the 1980s (Table 1.2). Receipts, considered to a better indicator of tourism's economic worth, continue to outpace tourist arrivals in terms of percentage increases (Fig-ure 1.3). However, data on receipts should be viewed with a degree of skepticism as real increases are not separated from those occurring as a re-sult of inflationary pressures.

Not all increases in arrivals or expenditures are proportionally distrib-uted throughout the receiving regions of the world. The biggest gainers in the last thirty years, with most of the increases recorded in the last ten, are the East Asian and Pacific Rim nations (Table 1.3). Europe shows a net decrease in arrivals over the last twenty years, with the Americas relatively stable. The only exceptions to this are the United States and Mexico, which record recent increases in tourism receipts of 19% (1988–89) and 18% (1989–90) respectively (Waters, 1991).

The major tourist-generating countries are generally the same as the major receiving countries. The United States tops the list for total receipts

TABLE 1.1 World Top Tourism Destinations

International Tourist Arrivals

Rank 1990	Country	Tourist Arrivals (Thousands)		Rank 1980	Average Annual Growth Rate (%) 1980/90	% Share of Arrivals Worldwide	
		1990	1980			1990	1980
1	France	51,462	30,100	1	5.5	11.60	10.57
2	USA	39,772	22,500	3	5.9	8.97	7.90
3	Spain	34,300	23,403	2	3.9	7.73	8.22
4	Italy	26,679	22,087	4	1.9	6.02	7.75
5	Hungary	20,510	9,413	9	8.1	4.62	3.30
6	Austria	19,011	13,879	5	3.2	4.29	4.87
7	UK	18,021	12,420	7	3.8	4.06	4.36
8	Germany	17,045	11,122	8	4.4	3.84	3.90
9	Canada	15,258	12,876	6	1.7	3.44	4.52
10	Switzerland	13,200	8,873	10	4.1	2.98	3.12
11	China	10,484	5,703	12	6.3	2.36	2.00
12	Greece	8,873	4,796	14	6.3	2.00	1.68
13	Czechoslovakia	8,100	5,055	13	4.8	1.83	1.77
14	Portugal	8,020	2,708	15	11.5	1.81	0.95
15	Yugoslavia	7,880	6,410	11	2.1	1.78	2.25
World Total		443,477	284,841		4.5	100.00	100.00

Source: World Tourism Organization (WTO), 1991

and is also the world's largest travel spender (Table 1.4). Only three countries besides the U.S. and those in Western Europe (Japan, Mexico, and Australia) show up in the list of the top fifteen tourism spenders.

Social

What trends have fueled the constant increases in tourism? What trends are likely to affect future travel patterns? World population continues to increase at the rate of 170 persons per minute, which over a three-month period is equivalent to the population of Canada (Villeneuve, 1991:19). The highest rates of growth are occurring in developing countries, accounting for approximately 95% of all new additions to world population (Godbey, 1995). With few exceptions, these countries are neither the major receivers nor generators of tourists. However, they are the source for most of the world's immigrants and there is evidence to suggest that diversity and multi-culturalism are affecting both supply and demand factors of tourism. Different lifestyles, customs, and traditions are powerful

TABLE 1.2 World's Top Tourism Earners

International Tourism Receipts

Rank 1990	Country	Tourism Receipts (Million US$) 1990	Tourism Receipts (Million US$) 1980	Rank 1980	Average Annual Growth Rate (%) 1980/90	% Share of Receipts Worldwide 1990	% Share of Receipts Worldwide 1980
1	USA	40,579	10,058	1	15.0	15.93	9.82
2	France	20,187	8,235	2	9.4	7.92	8.04
3	Italy	19,738	8,213	3	9.2	7.75	8.02
4	Spain	18,593	6,968	4	10.3	7.30	6.81
5	UK	15,000	6,893	5	8.1	5.89	6.73
6	Austria	13,017	6,442	7	7.3	5.11	6.29
7	Germany	10,683	6,566	6	5.0	4.19	6.41
8	Switzerland	6,839	3,149	9	8.1	2.68	3.08
9	Canada	6,374	2,284	10	10.8	2.50	2.23
10	Mexico	5,324	5,393	8	−0.1	2.09	5.27
11	Hong Kong	5,032	1,317	13	14.3	1.98	1.29
12	Singapore	4,362	1,433	12	11.8	1.71	1.40
13	Thailand	4,326	867	15	17.4	1.70	0.85
14	Australia	3,797	967	14	14.7	1.49	0.94
15	Netherlands	3,615	1,668	11	8.0	1.42	1.63
World Total		254,767	102,372		9.5	100.00	100.00

Source: World Tourism Organization (WTO), 1991

Figure 1.3 *Development of International Tourism Arrivals and Receipts Worldwide (1950–1991)*

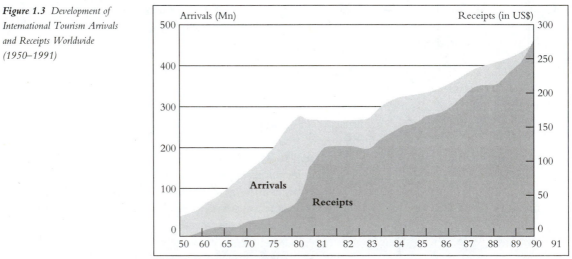

(1) Excluding international fare receipts
Source: World Tourism Organization (WTO), 1991

TABLE 1.3 Percent Share of Each Region in World Tourism

	Arrivals						Receipts					
	1960	1970	1980	1990	1991	1995	1960	1970	1980	1990	1991	1995
World	100.00	100.00	100.00	100.00	100.00	100.00	100.00	100.00	100.00	100.00	100.00	100.00
Africa	1.08	1.51	2.48	3.40	2.88	3.31	2.59	2.23	2.65	1.88	1.58	1.86
Americas	24.11	22.95	18.85	18.79	19.20	19.74	35.71	26.81	24.91	26.10	25.89	25.62
East Asia/Pacific	0.98	3.04	7.01	11.45	12.01	14.75	2.84	6.15	7.31	14.40	14.75	18.66
Europe	72.54	70.50	68.42	63.47	63.82	59.47	56.82	61.99	59.34	54.36	55.76	51.07
Middle East	1.03	1.43	2.44	2.16	1.52	1.95	1.53	2.26	4.28	2.49	1.44	1.79
South Asia	0.26	0.57	0.80	0.73	0.57	0.77	0.51	0.56	1.51	0.77	0.58	1.00

Source: World Tourism Organization (WTO), 1991 and 1993

TABLE 1.4   World's Top Tourism Spenders

International Tourism Expenditures

Rank 1990	Country	Tourism Expenditures (Million US$)		Rank 1980	Average Annual Growth Rate (%) 1980/90	% Share of Expenditures Worldwide	
		1990	1980			1990	1980
1	USA	38,671	10,385	2	14.1	16.02	10.47
2	Germany	29,836	20,599	1	3.8	12.36	20.78
3	Japan	24,928	4,593	6	18.4	10.33	4.63
4	UK	19,106	6,893	3	10.7	7.91	6.95
5	Italy	13,826	1,907	13	21.9	5.73	1.92
6	France	12,424	6,027	4	7.5	5.15	6.08
7	Canada	8,390	3,122	9	10.4	3.48	3.15
8	Austria	7,476	2,847	10	10.1	3.10	2.87
9	Netherlands	7,340	4,664	5	4.6	3.04	4.70
10	Sweden	6,066	2,235	12	10.5	2.51	2.25
11	Switzerland	5,989	2,357	11	9.8	2.48	2.38
12	Belgium	5,664	3,272	8	5.6	2.35	3.30
13	Mexico	5,379	4,174	7	2.6	2.23	4.21
14	Spain	4,254	1,229	15	13.2	1.76	1.24
15	Australia	4,120	1,749	14	8.9	1.71	1.76
World Total		241,433	99,143		9.3	100.00	100.00

Source: World Tourism Organization (WTO), 1991

demand attractors. At the same time, newly found economic power on the part of a previously ignored ethnic group leads to product change (supply) to meet the new group's tastes and desires (Dwyer, 1995; Nickerson and Uysal, 1995).

One noticeable social trend is the aging of the population in developed countries. The Post World War II or "baby boom" generation (as it is known in the U.S.) is getting older and possesses significant disposable income. The mature market age category is the one with the highest propensity and financial ability to travel. It is also in better health than previous generations at the same age, leading to a steady growth in the senior market (Crandall and Fay, 1995).

Other social trends in the major tourist-generating countries likely to affect future travel include smaller family sizes, both spouses working outside the home, the growing proportion of single adults, increasingly urban lifestyles, higher education levels, earlier retirement, and more experience with travel and awareness of the opportunities. On the other hand, the average number of hours worked per week is on the rise, more children are being raised in single parent households, and there is more wealth being accumulated by relatively fewer people (Godbey, 1995; Crandall and Fay, 1995). These trends may restrict individual travel, at least temporarily.

Business travel, at least in the U.S. and Europe, changed dramatically in the 1980's. Women comprised less than one percent of all U.S. business travelers in 1970; today, they account for almost one-third of all business travelers. The average female business traveler is 40 years old with an annual income of $30,000 to $40,000, and has a mid-level management position (United States Travel Data Center, 1991). Firms catering to the business traveler must adjust their product offering to serve this new segment of the market.

There is a growing trend toward shorter vacations. Whether this is due primarily to family and career life cycles of the baby boom generation, (longer hours at the office) or whether it reflects a change in tastes and preferences is not entirely known. Most probably, it is a combination of many factors. Regardless of the cause, vacation trips appear to be decreasing in length. In 1989, over 55% of all vacation trips in the U.S. were less than three nights. From 1984 to 1989 the number of weekend vacation trips increased 28% (United States Travel Data Center, 1990). This trend has implications for destination locations, as those in close proximity to large urban areas are most likely to reap the benefits from the shift to shorter vacations.

Increased experience and awareness are important trends with respect to vacation destinations. The growth in the numbers of travelers from developed countries has outpaced population growth rates in those same countries. This means that the increases are not fueled by population growth, but through an increased propensity and ability to travel. The demand for international travel is partially a function of cultural distance or the relative difference between host's and guest's way of living (McIntosh et al., 1995). The lesser the cultural difference, the higher the propensity to travel. Each successive trip builds experience and helps reduce future cultural distance factors. Thus, the future bodes well for non-traditional trips, which might help explain the increased popularity of "ecotourism" and other "alternative forms of tourism." Preplanned and complete package trips to familiar destinations are likely to lose market share in favor of customized trips to more exotic destinations.

Demand for ecotourism or nature-based trips is increasing, due in part to increased urbanization. As more people concentrate in urban areas, the experience of traveling to a place relatively unspoiled by major physical development provides psychological balance. "The preservation of a certain amount of unpolluted, natural space of high quality appears essential so as to maintain general ecological balance and enable city dwellers to relax in a healthy natural environment" (OECD, 1980:22). This direction, identified by the Organization for Economic Co-operation and Development (OECD) in 1980, is not new. In 1921, Aldo Leopold expressed similar sentiments in support of official wilderness land designation in the United States. Leopold was upset that recreation areas were being "spoiled by tourists" and argued that there was a need for land that would remain undeveloped even if it only served a minority of the population (Leopold, 1921). Increasing levels of urbanization and alienation from the land are more severe today than in Leopold's time. One could argue that the need for unspoiled natural land is more critical today than ever before. It is becoming less a trend and more a requirement for all life.

Political

The doomsday clock, which measures the threat of wholesale nuclear war, is now set back to a level unachieved since the advent of the Cold War. With the threat of global nuclear holocaust receding and old enemies becoming new friends, a global economy has a chance of becoming a reality. This will lead not only to increased international business travel, but new destinations will become available as the emerging democracies of eastern Europe and the old Soviet Union openly embrace tourism as a means of economic development while they struggle to implement market-based systems. A similar situation can be expected in the Middle East as centuries-old enemies attempt to create a structure for peace.

The European Community plan is also expected to increase travel not only from the west to the east, but the deregulation of air transportation will lead to more competition and possibly lower prices for people traveling throughout Europe. Reduced or eliminated border controls will also accelerate the movement of people throughout Europe.

At the same time that new destinations are realized through a warming of relations, some traditional tourist destinations are experiencing rapid decline. The most prominent of these is former Yugoslavia, which, in the last few years, has fractured into smaller and smaller units.

Heightened environmental and social concerns will lead to a redefinition of tourism development. Changes both structural and behavioral will become more frequently a part of the tourism development planning process. Government policy, already implemented in some countries by the requirement to file environmental impact statements before physical development occurs, will become increasingly a means to direct development. Already, more than a few voices are demanding that social impact statements be required as well before major projects are started.

Technological

"Science and Technology are often the wildcards in the tourism strategic planning game" (Shafer, 1989). Although the future is uncertain, some science and technology trends affecting tourism are expected to continue.

TOURISM AND DISEASE

Health concerns may present an obstacle to tourism development in many parts of the world. To be sure, health problems can happen to anyone anywhere in the world, but some regions have more than their share of diseases or ancillary health concerns which serve to keep many people away. Most international travelers have experienced a bout of traveler's diarrhea, but this is only a minor inconvenience, easily treatable, and usually not a deterrent to travel. Other diseases are significant deterrents. The region of the world most affected by health and safety issues for travelers lies between the Tropic of Cancer and the Tropic of Capricorn and is known simply as the tropics. The tropics are home to half the world's population and a host of dangerous diseases. By far the most serious of these for travelers is malaria.

Malaria, which means bad air, was once thought to be caused by breathing the unhealthy air of swamps. This is not an unreasonable deduction since mosquitoes, carriers of the malarial parasite, frequent the naturally stagnant water conditions found in some tropical swamps. Today, stagnant water is even more prevalent given man-made problems such as poverty and increasing urbanization, which leads to pools of untreated, polluted waste water found throughout major population centers. Since the malarial protozoan parasite is spread through the bite of a female Anopheline mosquito, conditions which favor mosquito breeding in close proximity to large numbers of people will surely increase the incidence of contracting the disease.

During the 1950s and 60s a single strategy of spraying likely breeding grounds, primarily with DDT, was considered a sure way of eradicating the disease. While this strategy worked in large areas of North America, the old Soviet Union, and parts of Latin America, it was not economically feasible in Africa. An alternate strategy of using drugs to kill the parasite was the second major weapon used against the parasite. The most common drugs, chloroquine derivatives, were effective at first but have recently been proven ineffective in large parts of Africa, Asia, and South America. The incidence of malaria is so high and it spreads so quickly that the parasite is evolving resistant strains faster than medical science can come up with new treatments. Melfloquine, a new drug with unknown long range side effects, has replaced cholorquine as the drug of choice in many areas, but in Thailand more than 50% of malarial cases are not responding to Melfloquine treatment. Recent reports hint at a possible vaccine for malaria, but at the moment the disease is once again causing enormous economic problems in large parts of the tropics, notably acting as a barrier to tourism development and foreign exchange needed for improving living conditions which, in the absence of an effective vaccine, is the only sure way to control the disease.

Schistosomiasis (or Bilharziasis) is the second most prevalent disease found in the tropics. It is most common in Africa. Similar to malaria, it is a parasitic disease but it is spread by contact with polluted fresh water. The parasite is actually one of five types of flatworm which finds a host in a freshwater snail. Once in the snail it divides, producing thousands of clones. The flatworm is excreted by the snail and finds a human host where it can penetrate

(continued on next page)

the skin in a matter of a few seconds. Depending on the type of flatworm, it may attach itself to blood vessels, the intestinal lining, or the bladder. In all cases, the eggs it lays cause bleeding and swelling to occur, often leading to death. Some of the eggs excreted by an infected person, once in contact with fresh water, hatch into a flatworm which finds a host snail to begin the cycle again.

Schistosomiasis is easily prevented by cleaning up water supplies, but lack of funds for proper sanitation and education of the populace has rendered most efforts unsuccessful. Recent movements of refugees, accelerating urbanization, and adventure tourism to "off the beaten path" places are the most common transmission vectors. Advice to tourists entering areas where Schistosomiasis is likely to be encountered includes avoiding bodily contact with fresh water and boiling or otherwise sterilizing all water for human consumption. While this advice is definitely worth taking, it virtually eliminates the possibility of water sports activities in areas that have opportunities to develop tourism around some freshwater natural resources.

Finally, the last disease to be discussed here is Dengue Haemorraghic Fever (DHF) and the closely related Dengue. Although not a new disease, it has recently received media attention as the incidence of DHF appears to be increasing. DHF is spread by mosquitoes primarily of the Aedes Aegypti variety. The same conditions (i.e., rapid urbanization, untreated sewage) that have led to a resurgence in malaria are responsible for the increase in DHF. One big difference is that while malaria is caused by a parasite, DHF is a virus and there is no known treatment. DHF symptoms are similar to the flu and include severe joint aches. While not usually fatal, the symptoms are painful enough to cause one a great deal of concern, especially for the young or old. Prevention is to avoid mosquito bites. Recent outbreaks of DHF in Latin America that have received extensive media attention will undoubtedly slow travel to affected parts of the world if they continue to occur.

Diseases, regardless of the likelihood of contraction, can be a real deterrent to travel. The relatively small numbers of tourists out of the world total that travel to Africa can be blamed on many causes including unstable political situations, poor service levels, and fear of physical harm. Undoubtedly, one of the main causes is fear of contracting a tropical disease. The above discussion has only mentioned a few, but there are many more including Chagas, Yellow Fever, Typhoid Fever, Cholera, Ebola, HIV infection, etc. Many travelers throughout the world are not yet ready to take the risks associated with visiting some of the world's more exotic locations. Yet with proper precautions the probability of contracting any one of the debilitating diseases found in the tropics is still relatively slim. However, until the traveling population receives the proper education and is convinced that the risk is small, the threat of contracting one of the tropical diseases will keep levels of tourism development much below those found in other parts of the world.

Source: World Health Organization web site accessed through the Center for Disease Control home page (http://www.cdc.gov)

The major advances in air transportation technology experienced during the 1970s and 1980s will continue, but at a slower rate. Larger aircraft with increased flight distances will be developed, which should lower travel costs. The picture is clouded, however, by the impacts of deregulation. A reduction in carriers can result in a move away from a competitive market into an oligopolistic one, with prices controlled by a few major airlines. Deregulation, apart from competition, has already had one major effect in the United States. The Air Transport Association (1991) estimates that over 74% of Americans have flown on a commercial airline. Since travel is a learned activity, prior personal experience with air travel should serve to reinforce the continuation of this mode of travel as a preferred transportation option.

Communications and data processing technology will continue to improve, increasing the efficiency of those businesses able to afford and adopt the latest equipment. By the turn of the century, a single microchip will contain the central processing unit of today's most sophisticated computers, and will cost approximately 10% of what a computer costs today (Godbey, 1995). More advanced visual teleconferencing and virtual reality technology is viewed by some as decreasing the need for business and pleasure travel. Advances in communication technology are so rapid and critical to how all business will be conducted in the future that an entire section in Chapter 10 (Marketing) is devoted to this issue. However, as long as personal relationships continue to be important in business negotiations and status, prestige, and self-actualization motives drive pleasure travel, the desire to travel will remain high. A move toward a global society, which begins with trade, is expected to accelerate with the demand for business travel worldwide continuing to expand.

Constraints

Crowded skies over airports and the continuing threat of terrorism are two main problems facing tourism in the foreseeable future. Transport infrastructure (e.g., roads, airports, rail) in many parts of the world is deteriorating. This is especially apparent in parts of West Africa which saw large-scale infrastructure projects in the 1970s fueled by foreign exchange earnings from cocoa, gold, timber, and tropical oils. With worldwide demand for all but timber decreasing, and that commodity becoming increasingly scarce, the 1970s infrastructure has largely crumbled. As travel increases pressure to renovate and expand, the infrastructure network will increase.

The inability of governments to stop terrorism directed at tourists will also affect travel at least regionally. Although reported incidents of terrorist activity have decreased during the early 1990s, there is no guarantee this trend will continue. Many terrorist groups target tourists as a means of destabilizing the political system when tourism becomes a significant foreign exchange earner for the country. Egypt is a case in point.

Crime, or the concern over becoming a victim of crime, will continue to pose problems for destination promoters, especially in urban areas. Media reports about violence and crime can affect destination images and reduce the propensity to travel to perceived crime-ridden areas. Demos (1992), studying tourists' perception of crime in Washington, D.C., concludes that increasing crime rates and declining tourist arrivals are related. Visitors to the city are clearly concerned for their safety. The results of this micro-study should be viewed as a warning sign that tourists will react to increasing levels of destination violence in a market fashion. That is, they will vote with their pocketbooks to travel elsewhere or spend disposable income on other consumer goods. Miami, Florida has recently seen foreign visitors targeted by criminals, not to destabilize the government, but because tourists make easy victims owing to their unfamiliarity with the city. History has shown that it does not take many incidents of the kind experienced in Miami to significantly reduce travel to the area, at least in the short run.

Health concerns will affect primarily developing countries. Malaria, a constant problem in the tropics, is once again becoming a major health concern. Chloroquine, the most common prophylactic drug prescribed for travelers to the tropics, is no longer effective against new strains of malaria. Cholera is also experiencing a comeback as waste treatment programs are unable to keep pace with population increases in developing countries. Hepatitis outbreaks have also received some press. Fear of AIDS is expected to have an effect on travel. Regions of the world with a higher-than-average incidence of the disease may be regarded by potential travelers as unsafe travel destinations.

Even though travelers may be at little risk of contracting these illnesses, especially if proper precautions are followed, the less experienced traveler will react more to perception than reality when making a travel choice. Two-pronged efforts are needed to counter these constraints. Medical technology will continue to develop new prophylactic treatments for these diseases, but the travel trade must mount educational programs to inform travelers not only of the risks but of the precautions that should be taken.

Artificial barriers erected by governments can present constraints, especially with respect to international travel. Restrictive visa regulations, entry and exit taxes, passport approval difficulties, currency exchange controls affecting the amount of money that can be taken out of country by its residents or the amount that must be spent by visitors all serve to limit the amount of international travel. Numerous rules governing international trade have been negotiated by governments interested in increasing the flow of manufactured products, but relatively few have been negotiated for trade in services (Edgell, 1988). Countries wishing to increase international travel receipts should review their travel policy regulations and reduce any unnecessary barriers.

STUDY OF TOURISM AND NEED FOR THIS BOOK

This book is a product of the increasing attention being paid to the study of tourism. Tourism as a field of study is a rather recent development. Figure 1.3 shows a rapid increase in the number of international tourists from the early 1950s to the early 1980s. This trend closely parallels that for domestic tourism as well. Tourism as a significant force in society is a product of the technological advances, and indirectly, policy decisions made after World War II. Even today, with tourism becoming recognized as the world's largest industry, very few institutes of higher learning recognize tourism as a distinct discipline. Most of the research and teaching conducted on tourism is of a multidisciplinary nature. That is, it usually originates as a topic of interest for an academician and reflects that individual's disciplinary background. Tourism programs or emphasis areas can be found in departments or schools of business, economics, anthropology, geography, planning, hospitality management, sociology, recreation and natural resources, among others. A model of the multidisciplinary approach to the study of tourism is found in Figure 1.4.

Acknowledgment of tourism as a beneficial pursuit is centuries old. Generally, it appears in popular writing and reflects personal viewpoints. Scholarly treatment of tourism is rather new and for the most part did not begin until the 1950s when unprecedented numbers of travelers began to discover not only their own country but also the world. Jafari (1988) has analyzed the evolution of the study of tourism and organized it into what he refers to as "tourism platforms."

Advocacy Platform

After World War II, the tourism industry was seen primarily as a means of economic development. Early scholarly and popular treatments of this development are generally supportive of the phenomenon, concentrating on the economic benefits derived from tourists. Among the numerous economic benefits attributed to tourism included: it can generate substantial foreign exchange earnings; it is labor-intensive and therefore can provide

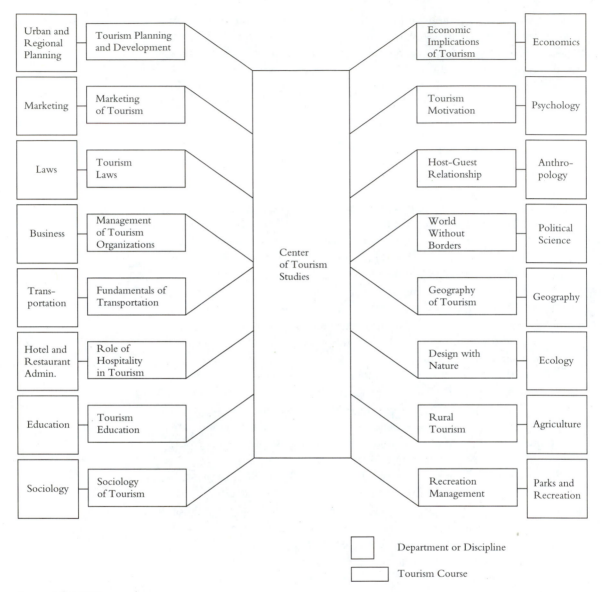

Source: Jafari, 1977

Figure 1.4 *Study of Tourism Choice of Discipline and Approach*

numerous employment opportunities; it can be developed almost anywhere and areas or countries in short supply of trade commodities can use
their resources for tourism development; it stimulates development in
other sectors. Advocates of tourism development extolled more than its
economic benefits. Tourism was claimed to preserve and protect the envi-

ronment as well as preserve and revive cultural traditions. This advocacy platform is a product of scholarly writings of the 1950s and 60s which provided the necessary supportive foundation and justification for tourism development. Much of this early work has been internalized by developers, governments, members of the travel trade, and others who today continue to glorify the virtues of tourism development and disregard its dark side.

Cautionary Platform

Experience with tourism development revealed that not all the claims in favor of it, espoused by subscribers to the advocacy platform, actually materialized. Contributors to the cautionary platform began to counter almost every claim emanating from the advocacy platform. Tourism did provide significant economic benefits, but they primarily accrued to large corporations, with relatively small amounts remaining to benefit indigenous populations. This problem was more severe in developing countries, as most of the large corporations were owned by multinational firms located in the tourist-generating markets. It became even worse when the distribution of jobs was analyzed. Low paid, servile positions with little if any upward mobility were the norm for members of the host society, while managerial positions were reserved for expatriates. Counter claims to the advocacy platform extended beyond basic economic impacts. Tourism was blamed for destroying or seriously degrading ecosystems, commoditizing local cultures, and disrupting community social structures.

The cautionary platform is generally a product of the 1970s, although examples continue to appear today not only in scholarly writings but in popular culture as witnessed by a segment on the U.S. television program "60 Minutes" (January 19, 1992) which represented much of what the cautionary platform challenged. Debate between members of the advocacy and cautionary platform continues, with each claim supported by a real-life example countered by another claim using another example. Some of the claims and counter-claims between the two platforms are presented in Figure 1.5.

Adaptancy Platform

Alternative forms of tourism, sometimes referred to as ecotourism, green tourism, soft tourism, small-scale tourism, appropriate tourism, and so on, result from the polarized debate between members of the advocacy and cautionary platforms. Subscribers to the adaptancy platform recognize that tourism is not all good, nor is it all bad. They propose a form of tourism that is responsive to the needs of the host community, protects while it uses environmental resources, improves and encourages social exchange

Advocacy Platform		Cautionary Platform	
Economic	*Sociocultural*	*Economic*	*Sociocultural*
Examples	Examples	Examples:	Examples:
• Tourism is labor intensive –full time –seasonal –unskilled	• Tourism broadens education	• Tourism causes inflation	• Tourism contributes to misunderstanding
	• Promotes international peace and understanding	• Results in high leakage	• Generates stereotypes of the host and guest
• Generates foreign exchange		• Has seasonality and contributes to unemployment	• Leads to xenophobia
• Can be built on existing infrastructure	• Breaks down: –language barriers –sociocultural barriers –class barriers –racial barriers –political barriers –religious barriers –sex barriers	• Is susceptible to change, rumor, spread of disease, economic fluctuation	• Results in social pollution
• Can be developed with local products and resources			• Commercializes culture, religion, and the arts
• Spreads development		• Results in unbalanced economic development	• Threatens family structure
• Complements production of other economic activities	• Reinforces preservation of heritage and tradition	• Leads to extraneous dependency	• Contributes to prostitution
• Has high multiplier effect	• Promotes worldview/ membership in the global community	• Increases demonstration effects	• Increases instances of crime
	• Enhances appreciation of ones culture	• Destroys resources and creates visual pollution	• Conduces conflicts in the host society

Source: Jafari, 1988

Figure 1.5 *Positions of Advocacy and Cautionary Platforms on Tourism's Impacts*

between hosts and guests, and still provides rewarding experiences for tourists. In a sense, the adaptancy platform accepts the touted benefits of tourism, but only when the problems exposed by the cautionary platform can be dealt with in a manner sensitive to the host community. Tourism development, to be acceptable to subscribers to the adaptancy platform, must be community-focused, provide a wide range of responsible positions for community residents, protect and enhance the cultural and environmental resources of the destination, and strive to enhance social exchange between host and guest. Mass tourism, with its emphasis on volume, would not be an option supported by members of the adaptancy community.

The adaptancy platform appeared in the scholarly writings of academics primarily in the late 1970s and early 80s. Its supporters include community developers, consultants, religious groups, academicians, and conservationists. Although the goals of the adaptancy platform are altruistic and defensible, the present state of tourism development has not embraced a complete alternative forms approach.

Knowledge-Base Platform

The advocacy and cautionary platforms deal with the impacts of tourism. Adaptancy addresses preferred forms of development. The present state of tourism is a global phenomenon, with millions of people moving between destinations daily, and it will not, nor should it, go away. The knowledge-base platform addresses tourism holistically. Any type of tourism creates desirable and undesirable impacts. Once this is accepted, the study of tourism can move beyond analyzing each impact independently of every other one, and assess the trade-offs and relationships between impacts. The study of tourism should focus on understanding the structural and functional relationships between hosts, guests, environments, businesses, governments, and every other entity involved in producing and consuming touristic products. The main goal of the knowledge-base platform is to develop a scientific body of knowledge on tourism. This is somewhat hampered by the multidisciplinary models that have been employed to study tourism. What is needed is an interdisciplinary approach where scholars from all the other disciplines related to tourism are brought together to study how their home discipline fits into tourism rather than how tourism fits into their home discipline. It also requires that tourism related businesses recognize that the industry group to which they belong is only a sub-group of a larger tourism industry. This can only be accomplished if the ethnocentrism which we all bring to our professional activities is redefined into a much broader and more holistic view of tourism.

CONCLUSION

Tourism development is a difficult term to define. Without attempting to add any more definitions to those already offered, the remainder of the text simply explores the process of development related to the tourism phenomenon. It attempts to embrace the knowledge-base platform and utilizes existing literature as a foundation for discussion.

Tourism, with all its ramifications, is not a passing fad. It is of such global importance that almost everyone born today will in some way be affected by it. How it is planned and managed will not only determine economic success for businesses involved in providing touristic products and services, but will define in large part how humanity shapes its future. How tourist service providers and tourists themselves view the environment, unique cultures, and interpersonal relationships between hosts and guests will become apparent through the types of developments which prosper long-term. Even though tourism as a field of study is a relatively new endeavor, its impacts as the world's premier industry require immediate attention from academics, governments, private business, and others to make sure the process of tourism development is based on new knowledge. It is easy to criticize and simply explore the dark side of any industrial venture, and tourism is no exception. While this text does criticize, hopefully it also provides direction. The premise on which this text is based is that tourism is beneficial but its full potential as a beneficial change agent can only be realized through the acquisition and application of knowledge. This text endeavors to synthesize some of that knowledge in a form that can be applied to development projects which, while proving economically successful, have societal benefits that transcend economics.

EXECUTIVE SUMMARY

Tourism has never been adequately defined, which has hampered its acceptance as an industry group.

Tourism as defined in this text includes both business and leisure travel, and can be described as occurring when someone (the tourist) changes place and pace.

Development can be viewed as either a state (relative present condition) or a process with observable stages.

Appropriate tourism development can best be defined as a process which, when observed at any stage, has served to increase the quality of life for the tourist and host culture alike.

Tourism development often attaches itself to the infrastructure built for domestic commerce and travel.

Domestic tourism numbers are estimated to exceed international tourism by a factor of 10:1 with relative expenditures estimated at 7:1.

Tourism growth rates in the 1990s are averaging around 4 percent, which is a decrease over those experienced in the 1970s and 80s.

Social trends influencing travel include in-creased levels of disposable income, especially for the mature market in developed countries which is enjoying increasing life expectancy in relatively better health than previous generations.

There is a noticeable trend for shorter trips focused increasingly on nature based activities.

Political landscapes are in flux, with more travel expected to Eastern Europe, parts of the former Soviet Union, and the Middle East.

Relatively small technological changes in airline transportation will increase travel, but the most significant changes affecting how we live and travel is taking place in communications and information processing.

Some of the constraints affecting travel include deteriorating infrastructure, terrorist attacks directed against tourists, crime directed at tourists, and health concerns, especially in the developing world.

The study of tourism is relatively new and can be viewed from an early position of advocacy, giving way to a cautionary or questioning perspective, leading to an argument of adaptancy where new types of tourism development are proposed, and finally to a holistic approach where decisions are based on more thorough understanding and knowledge of the phenomenon.

REFERENCES

Air Transport Association. *Newsletter*. June 20, 1991. Washington, D.C.: ATA.

Butler, R. 1980. The Concept of a Tourist Area Life Cycle of Evolution: Implications for Management of Resources. *Canadian Geographer* 19(1):5–12.

Cook, S. 1975. *A Survey of Definitions in U.S. Domestic Tourism Studies*. Washington, D.C.: USTDC.

Crandall, D. and B. Fay. 1995. Recreation's Role in 21st Century Lifestyles. *Trend Trackers, 4th International Outdoor Recreation and Tourism Trends Symposium,* 19. St. Paul, Minn.: Tourism Center, University of Minnesota.

Demos, E. 1992. Concern for Safety: A Potential Problem in the Tourist Industry. *Journal of Travel and Tourism Marketing* 1(1):81–86.

Dwyer, J. 1995. Multicultural Values: Responding to Leisure Customers and Employees. *Trend Trackers—4th International Outdoor Recreation and Tourism Trends Symposium,* 23. St. Paul, Minn.: Tourism Center, University of Minnesota.

Edgell, D. 1988. Barriers to International Travel. *Tourism Management* 9(1):63–66.

Godbey. J. 1995. Things Will Never be the Same—Prospects for Recreation and Tourism in an Era of Exponential Change. *Trend Trackers, 4th International Outdoor Recreation and Tourism Trends Symposium,* 79. St. Paul, Minn.: Tourism Center, University of Minnesota.

Goulet, G. 1968. On the Goals of Development. *Cross Currents* 18:387–405.

Jafari, J. 1977. Editor's Page. *Annals of Tourism Research* 5(Sp. No.):6–11.

Jafari, J. 1988. Retrospective and Prospective Views on Tourism as Field of Study. Paper presented at the 1988 Meeting of the Academy of Leisure Sciences, Indianapolis, Indiana.

Leiper, N. 1981. Towards a Cohesive Curriculum in Tourism: The Case for a Distinct Discipline. *Annals of Tourism Research* 8(1):69–84.

Leopold, A. 1921. The Wilderness and Its Place in Forest Recreation Policy. *Journal of Forestry* 19(7):718–721.

McIntosh, R., C. Goeldner, and B. Ritchie. 1994. *Tourism: Principles, Practice and Philosophies*. 7th ed. New York: John Wiley and Sons, Inc.

Miossec, J. 1976. Eléments pour une theorie de l'espace touristique. *Les Cahiers du Tourisme*. Aix-en-Provence: C.H.E.T. quoted in Pearce, 1990.

National Tourism Resources Review Commission. 1973. *Destination U.S.A.* Vol. 2. Washington, D.C.: Government Printing Office.

Nickerson, N., and M. Uysal. 1995. Economic and Social Determinants of Travel. *Trend Trackers, 4th International Outdoor Recreation and Tourism Trends Symposium,* 11. St. Paul, Minn.: Tourism Center, University of Minnesota.

Noronha, R. 1976. *Review of the Sociological Literature on Tourism*. New York: World Bank.

Organization for Economic Co-operation and Development. 1980. *The Impact of Tourism on the Environment*. Paris: OECD.

Pearce, D. 1989. *Tourist Development*. New York: Longman Scientific and Technical.

Pearce, D. 1990. *Tourism Today. A Geographical Analysis*. New York: Longman Scientific and Technical.

Shafer, E. 1989. Future Encounters with Science and Technology. *Journal of Travel Research* 27(4):2–7.

Tolstoy, L. [1865] 1981. *War and Peace*. Norwalk, Conn.: Easton Press.

U.S. Travel Data Center. 1989. *The 1988–89 Economic Review of Travel in America*. Washington, D.C.: USTDC.

U.S. Travel Data Center. 1990. *Weekend Travel: America's Growing Trend*. Travel Printout, June.

U.S. Travel Data Center. 1991. *Women Business Travelers Increase in 1990*. Travel Printout, September.

Veblen, T. 1912. *The Theory of the Leisure Class: An Economic Study of Institutions*. New York: B.W. Huebsch.

Villeneuve, C. 1991. The Citizen and the Environment. *The Unesco Courier* (November).

Waters, S. 1991. *Travel Industry World Yearbook: The Big Picture—1991*. New York: Child and Waters Inc.

World Tourism Organization. 1988. *Tourism Development Report: Policy and Trends*. Madrid: WTO.

World Tourism Organization. 1990. *Tourism to the Year 2000: Qualitative Aspects Affecting Global Growth*. Madrid: WTO.

World Tourism Organization. 1991. *Tourism Market Profile*. Madrid: WTO.

World Tourism Organization. 1991. *Travel and Tourism Barometer*. Madrid: WTO.

CHAPTER TWO

History of Tourism Development

Pictographs in southern Utah from the Anasazi Period.
Photo by the author

Learning Objectives

Trace the history of mankind, paying special attention to significant events which, either because of a philosophical or physical occurrence, can be viewed as the antecedents of modern–day travel.

•

Understand that non–European civilizations contributed to today's tourism industry through their beliefs and physical accomplishments.

•

Understand what conditions were necessary for a shift from a hospitality– or transportation–based industry to an integrated tourism industry.

INTRODUCTION

Attempting to write the history of tourism development is tantamount to writing the history of humanity. Since no universally accepted definition of tourism exists, at what point did the movement of people constitute migration as opposed to what we may define as tourism? Compounding the problem is the difficulty of defining development. If we accept the working definition used in the previous chapter that development is a process leading to noticeable economic, physical, or social change, then historical events are as much a part of development as the bricks and mortar of a new resort. Events are only important in so much as they affect us today, and since tourism has become such an important part of modern life, the trick is to select the most significant periods or events from human history and describe their implications for contemporary life.

What historians are comfortable in reporting are milestone events. They are fairly certain that particular events took place and of the time period in which they occurred even if they do not fully understand why they occurred. Thus, it is possible to view each event in sequence and hypothesize its impact on future events. From that perspective, it is possible to formulate a history of tourism and discuss implications for modern-day tourism. Some events simply describe movements of individuals or people. Others describe wholesale changes in social structures, resulting in the way people view their role in the universe. All have implications for tourism. The following discussion reviews some periods or events selected for their historical importance to what is known as the tourism industry in the late 20th century. Many of the dates or general time frames derive from books describing history's evolution or significant periods. Only a few are referenced in the body of this chapter to reduce the repetition of citations. All sources are listed at the end of the chapter. Whenever possible, dates of events are cross referenced for accuracy. What is important is the sequence of events. Through this process, an understanding of an event's contribution to types of tourism practiced today can be discussed. Even if a date listed is not exactly accurate, as long as the event sequence remains valid, an interpretation of history and its implications to tourism can be provided. A historical timeline of significant events in the history of tourism development is in Figure 2.1.

A common criticism of historical overviews of tourism is that they are Eurocentric. This is understandable since the majority of written histories are of European origin. Some of the earliest accounts of life from other parts of the world were passed on as folktales and eventually committed to paper primarily by European scholars. Even the meaning of the few accounts of early life recorded by humans (e.g., cave petroglyphs and

8000 B.C.	*3000–2175 B.C.*	*1200 B.C.*
Agricultural development in Middle East leads to formation of communities. Sense of place results, which is a prerequisite for tourism. Travelers must return to a home.	Pharaonic Egypt. Pyramids, Sphinx, temples, and tombs combine into major tourism attraction for later generations.	Phoenicians use sailing vessels extensively for transportation. Vessels also used throughout South Pacific.

776 B.C.	*500–400 B.C.*	*200 B.C.*
First Olympiad; beginning of sport tourism.	Greek and Mayan civilizations. Advances in mathematics, sciences and philosophy; construction of temples.	Roman Empire grows, Chinese civilization focuses on arts, builds Great Wall to keep out invaders.

100 B.C.–Birth of Christ	*400 A.D.*	*600–900 A.D.*
Roman expansion and civilization. Road network connects the empire. Travel possible for others besides the ruling class. Trade becomes a major motive for travel.	Disintegration of the Roman Empire. Europe plunged into Dark Ages. Most traveling is done by sea as land travel is too dangerous. Pilgrimages are a major reason for individual travel.	Xian in China becomes a major international trading center. Caravanserai which serve as rest stops/hotels for caravans on the way to/from Xian are built to accommodate traders' needs. Great Silk Route (trade route to Xian) is now focus of a World Tourism Organization initiative.

1076 A.D.	*1096–1270 A.D.*	*1100–1300 A.D.*
Fall of Ghana Empire and rise of Mali Empire in Africa. African slave trade with Arabs to the north begins in earnest. Center of trade is Timbuktu.	Crusades begun ostensibly to protect Christians in the Holy Land. Unstated purpose to protect trade routes.	Roman Catholic Church controls most of Europe's arts and spirituality. In partnership with kings and barons, the church supports the feudal system. In the process acquires enough wealth to engage in large-scale cathedral building and heavily subsidizes the arts. This period's output forms the attraction base for the Grand Tour.

1215 A.D.	*1295 A.D.*	*1347–1351 A.D.*
King John signs the Magna Carta. It includes the right to travel.	Marco Polo the first recognized travel writer whose acounts of China lead to expanding trade.	Plague, imported from the East, spreads throughout Europe. Loss of life is so great among serfs that the feudal system loses its foundation and collapses.

Late 1400s A.D.	*1500s A.D.*	*1600s A.D.*
Europe erects first white settlements in Africa, building castles along the coast which will eventually be used to house cargo destined for Europe and the Americas.	Renaissance period known for its art treasures. Roman Catholic Church remains a major sponsor of the arts and further adds to attraction base for Grand Tour.	White settlers colonize North America. Spanish conquer Mayans and move through Latin America.

Figure 2.1 *Historical Timeline for Tourism Development*

1700–1825 A.D.	*1841* A.D.	*1903* A.D.
Beginning of industrial revolution. Steam engine replaces sails on ships, rail travel develops, air travel using hot air balloons is attempted. Height of Grand Tour for Europe's elite. Hotels, rental carriages, and restaurants in European capitals flourish.	Thomas Cook forms the world's first travel agency and organizes group tours.	Mass production of automobiles begins. A large middle class forms in the United States. Wright brothers successfully fly a motor-powered plane at Kitty Hawk, North Carolina.
1914–1919 A.D.	*1930–1939* A.D.	*1939–1945* A.D.
World War I leads to numerous technological advances and recognition of the beginning of a global society. League of Nations is formed. First scheduled air service between London and Paris.	Great Depression, travel declines dramatically, mass migration of people, U.S. becomes a mobile society.	World War II. Major technological changes. Nuclear age dawns and Cold War begins. National boundaries redrawn. Tourism builds on the reconstruction in the aftermath of World War II. Dawn of mass tourism.
1944 A.D.	*1957* A.D.	*1961* A.D.
U.S. Federal Highway act begins development of world's largest infrastructure of roads, the backbone of the world's largest domestic tourism industry.	Space Age begins with successful launch of Sputnik.	Yuri Gagarin becomes first earthling to venture into space.
1969 A.D.	*1970* A.D.	*1980's* A.D.
Astronauts land on the moon, the first extraterrestrial body explored by humans.	Jumbo jets arrive. Mass tourism begins an unprecedented rise to eventually become the world's largest industry within 25 years.	Tourism impacts detailed. Mass tourism splinters slightly resulting in new (to some) forms of tourism called alternative forms of tourism (e.g. ecotourism, green tourism).
1990s A.D.		
Information and Communication Age. Mature market exerts its buying power which, coupled with business travel, vaults tourism into the world's largest industry.		

Figure 2.1 *Historical Timeline for Tourism Development (cont.)*

pictographs), is subject to widespread interpretation and speculation. Obviously, these limitations provide for only a piecemeal approach to history and even less of an understanding of the importance and magnitude of travel. In this chapter, an attempt is made to include examples from and about non-European cultures. Although it can be stated without too much argument that European and American cultures have had more to do with developing the type of tourism practiced throughout the world today, much of tourism's richness is due to cultural diversity.

PREHISTORY (40,000 B.C.–10,000 B.C.)

The prehistoric period is the longest in terms of the existence of human-like creatures on earth. It is also the period modern man knows the least about. Due to the lack of written material, it is simply referred to as pre-history. The period extends from about 40,000 B.C. to 10,000 B.C. The earliest archeological records trace travel (migration?) to 40,000 B.C. when Cro-Magnon man moved westward into Europe. Evidence of Cro-Magnon Man in modern-day France can be found in cave paintings dated to about 20,000 B.C. in Lascaux. Very little is known about why early peoples traveled since no written records exist from this period. It can only be surmised that travel was undertaken for survival purposes. Most likely a combination of reasons, including escape from more powerful tribes and the search for food, motivated travel. However, simply because no written records exist, an inherent *wanderlust* cannot be ruled out as a travel motivator.

EARLY CIVILIZATIONS (10,000 B.C.–500 B.C.)

Early civilizations are a product of the Neolithic period. It is also the first major period in the history of tourism development (Figure 2.2). Around 10,000 B.C., there is evidence that man's view of his role in the universe began to change. In the Prehistoric period, man's survival was determined by natural events. If drought reduced the number of prey animals, man suffered the consequences. Eventually, man reached a state of intelligence (or lack thereof) where he began to assert control over nature. The earliest evidence of this is the domestication of animals. Domesticated dogs were used by Indians in Idaho (northwestern U.S.) as early as 8400 B.C. Most likely, dogs were used to aid in the hunt or for food but other domesticated animals could have been used for transportation.

The most significant event spurring civilization's rise was the advent of farming. In 8000 B.C., agriculture developed in the Middle East. This phenomenon gave rise to early civilizations between the Tigris and Euphrates rivers (Mesopotamia), now modern-day Iraq. It was not until approximately 5000 B.C. that the Sumerians settled in this area. Eventually they became the first civilization credited with forming an urban life even though a walled settlement existed at Jericho in 7000 B.C. Sumerian civilization consisted of city-states with water transportation systems constructed for urban dwellers and used for irrigation by farmers. Farming

Civilization Period	Trade Period	Industrial & Technological Period	Tourism's Adolescent Years	Mass Tourism— Rapid Growth Years	Tourism Matures
8000 B.C.– Birth of Christ	Birth of Christ– 1700s A.D.	1700s–1900s A.D.	1910–1945 A.D.	1946–1990 A.D.	1990s A.D.
Sense of place forms as civilizations create ethnic, spiritual, and national identities which become tied to a piece of land.	As civilizations rise and fall, trade begins to flourish between the old and new. Travel is for elite who can afford bodyguards or for traders who travel together for protection. New areas are colonized expanding trade.	Industrial revolution, demise of feudal system, and new technology leads to new and/or more efficient transport. Upper class, as evidenced by Grand Tour, beginning to travel in large numbers. Travel services are offered. Mass tourism begins to take fledgling steps.	World War I brings technological advances but Great Depression slows that. Economic, political, social, and legal systems have not matured to the point where they can utilize the advances as a foundation for societal growth.	Mass tourism flourishes as societal systems develop to make full use of new science and technology.	Although growth is still fairly rapid, the percentage increases in travel experienced during the 1970s and 1980s are no longer registered. Value added takes on increased importance. Focus on service and alternative travel experiences.

Figure 2.2 Historical Periods of Tourism Development

allowed one person to produce food for many, freeing time for other pursuits such as social administration, production of trade goods, and scholarship. The first known writings, on clay tablets, are of Sumerian origin (3100 B.C.). The Sumerians are also credited with the invention of money, which was necessary to purchase the goods of craftsmen.

Civilizations were also developing at the same time in other parts of the world, most notably in China, India, and Egypt. Again, agriculture allowed people to permanently locate in one area and produce enough food to devote time to other pursuits.

Two other notable events occurred from around 3500 B.C. to 3000 B.C. The wheel was invented by the Sumerians and used to move military hardware and supplies. The second achievement was the use of bricks by the Egyptian and Assyrian civilizations. The Egyptian Pharaohs were such prolific users of bricks and laborers that between 2800–2175 B.C. (Old Kingdom), they built the Sphinx and all the major pyramids.

As man began to discover how much control he had over nature, and how he could fashion tools and weapons of destruction, the perception of his role in the universe began to take another evolutionary step. Where early civilizations had been made possible by man's belief that he was meant to control nature, he now believed he could also subjugate and dominate other peoples. The worth of a civilization was now measured by the control it could exert over others. In that respect, the Persian Empire was one of the greatest ever built. Within a 25-year period, 550–525 B.C., Cyrus, and later his son, were able to unite the various Persian tribes and conquer a land extending from India to the Mediterranean. Also during this time, the Roman Empire was beginning to extend from the capital city of Rome, which was founded during the 700s B.C. and the Greek civilization was beginning to form the world's first democracy (ca. 508 B.C.).

Civilization created one of the most important requirements for travel and one of the major reasons for modern-day travel. When large numbers of people decided to band together in a particular area, a "sense of place" began to develop. For the first time, a piece of land was known as home. Tourism requires a movement of people from, and a return to, home. Secondly, concentrations of people all calling the same area home allow for the evolution of a culture. Experiencing cultural diversity, a major outcome of travel, is a direct product of this period of expanding civilizations.

It was during the Early Civilizations period that the first signs of a tourism industry were noticeable. Crude inns located at trade centers were the first manifestations of a hospitality-based industry. The appearance of a hospitality industry points out some of the conditions necessary for tourism to grow, such as relative political stability and a mobile population.

EVOLUTION OF WESTERN SOCIETY (500 B.C.–500 A.D.)

The evolution of western society has it roots in the civilizations of Greece and Rome. The Age of Pericles in Athens (460–429 B.C.) is notable for the refinement of democratic principles of government. Pericles is often referred to as the "Father of Democracy" because of his belief in rule by and for the people. Democratic rule allowed for the open and free discussion of ideas, with philosophers and scientists becoming respected citizens. The Periclean Age of Democracy is the time in which scientific reasoning and method began to evolve. Socrates, Plato, Aristotle, Euclid, Herodotus, and Hipparchus, considered the fathers and refiners of philosophy, mathematics, history and medicine, were all products of the democratic movement started in Greece in 508 B.C. and refined by Pericles in the 400s B.C. Many of the ancient temples (e.g., the Parthenon) were also started during the Periclean Age.

Although other civilizations (e.g., Mayans) were to develop their own line of scientific reasoning which is apparent in their structures built in accordance with the seasons or used to study the heavens, it is the Greeks who left behind a written record which is used as the foundation for the sciences of today.

The other significant civilization with respect to Western evolution is the Roman Empire. Rome began its expansion in 241 B.C. when it assumed control over Sicily. The greatest period of growth took place during the last 100 years B.C. when Julius Caesar was in power. The Roman conquest, extending as far north as Britain and southeast to Egypt, was made possible by an efficient division of labor, an unprecedented transportation and communication network, an agricultural revolution, and a belief in a superior way of life. The Roman Empire meant oppression to groups of conquered people, but it also represented relative security from invasion. The masses of people appeared less interested in individual freedom and more interested in survival. Trade between peoples, who prior to the Roman Empire were more interested in stealing each other's land, flourished. The road system built for military purposes began to accommodate business tourism, and for the wealthy, pleasure tourism. Inns were built along the roads and the business of renting horses, carts, and other means of transportation began to thrive.

That war, or the threat of war, brings peace is one of the classic arguments throughout history. It has also been alleged that tourism brings peace as it fosters an exchange of ideas between people. Finally, it can be argued that war brings tourism development, not in the sense that the movement of soldiers constitutes a form of tourism, but because tourism attaches itself to the infrastructure of war. The extensive network of roads, bridges, and aqueducts for urban as well as rural development that the Romans built for military purposes became the primary tourism support network of the Empire.

Modern forms of tourism have their beginnings in the Greek and Roman civilizations. Because of the excellent (for the time) system of transportation and the relative security afforded by the Empire's size, wealthy Greeks and Romans traveled to the Oracles to pay homage to their numerous gods and journeyed to Athens, Rome, and other cities to attend performing arts events and engage in sporting competitions, both as participants and observers. Travel was beginning to take on new dimensions. The Roman civilization made possible the production and transportation of basic goods (i.e., food) and offered security to its citizens. Travel for purposes other than basic survival was possible and it began to assume its place as a meaningful societal activity. Leisure was increasingly recognized as an important element of life. In Greece, this concept found support in the lectures and writings of Plato and Aristotle.

OTHER CIVILIZATIONS

While the roots of western civilization were developing in the Greek and Roman world, other groups of people were establishing sophisticated civilizations which later contributed in some significant ways to modern tourism. The Pacific Islands were being explored, and civilizations were founded by seafaring travelers. Mayan civilization (ca. 400 B.C.) was spreading throughout Central America and eventually into Mexico. The Mayans built extensive road systems to connect their centers of civilization. Many of these centers have been restored and today attract millions of tourists. The famous ruins of Chichen Itza and Tikal have observatories, sports fields, and temples indicating that leisure, science, and religion were important elements of Mayan life. The famous temple of Chichen Itza annually attracts thousands of visitors during the vernal and autumnal equinox to watch a snake deity descend from the top of the temple and connect with its head at the base. The Mayan civilization was primarily landbound, although one site (Tulum) on the Caribbean side of the Yucatan Peninsula, has a structure which, when a torch was situated in a specific spot, would guide seafarers through a dangerous reef. The ancient road system developed by the Mayans was later used by Spanish explorers in their move north.

The Ch'in Dynasty (221–207 B.C.) in China is credited with being the first to unify the country although it was in existence less than 14 years. The Chinese civilization contrasts sharply with that forming in the

Rebuilt portion of the Great Wall outside Beijing.
Photo by the author

West, as it lacked the philosophy of dominion over others. Instead of extending its borders, it preferred to live within a set space. The construction of the Great Wall (beginning in 214 B.C.) was to keep invaders out and was purely a defensive structure. This live-and-let-live philosophy was responsible for major technological advances and scientific discoveries which occurred at the same time that western civilization entered into a period of decline known as the Middle or Dark Ages.

MIDDLE AGES

It is generally alleged that the Middle Ages began with the overthrow of the last Roman emperor, Romulus Augustus, by the Goths in 476 A.D. In fact, the disintegration of the Roman Empire started much earlier. Travel which flourished when the Empire was at its zenith began to decline as it unraveled. Any travel was perilous and was undertaken only by the adventurous or the dispossessed.

Much of the travel that occurred throughout Europe during the Middle Ages was for trade, and sea or river travel was the preferred option. Overland travel used the remains of the Roman road system which consisted of rutted gravel and mud. Caravans of traders were formed for protection and travel was primarily a daytime activity. Trade fairs were established at main crossroads, with some held annually and lasting over a month. Inns and other elements of a hospitality industry appeared at these major crossroads to serve traders.

National governments were nascent and warlords became the dominant controlling power. During the early Middle Ages, a form of government, the feudal system, dominated life. The feudal system relied on the granting of power from one strong person to those less powerful in exchange for a particular service. As a result of the feudal system, life centered around the manors of the lords which, for the most part, were self-supporting, reducing the need for travel.

While the nations of Europe were being slowly formed through the feudal system, a more powerful force was actually in control of the continent's ideology and politics. The Roman Church, built on the teachings of Jesus Christ, had its center of power in Rome and built monasteries, with support of the barons, throughout Europe. Since the Church was the only unifying force in Europe at the time, it was able to establish a powerful spiritual and political power base. Monasteries became the cultural centers of Europe and also afforded travelers shelter, in a sense becoming guest houses. The unifying power of the Church and the spiritual control it exerted over the continent's people made pilgrimages the dominant form of non-business (trade) travel.

The Church between the 12th and 14th centuries embarked on a program of cathedral building which today provides one of the distinctive features of the European travel product. The cathedrals of Notre Dame, Paris, Chartres, Le Mans, and others were all built during this time. Cathedrals, and the cities in which they were built, became destinations for pilgrims on their way to the seat of the Holy Roman Empire in Rome or to the Holy Land. Some of the first recorded attraction promotion occurred during this period. Many of the cathedrals relied on travelers' money for support, and to induce them to stop along the way it was not unusual to advertise the opportunity to see relics of the saints, pieces of the True Cross or the crown of thorns. By some estimates, all the pieces of the True Cross on exhibit would equal a small forest of trees. One cathedral was even so bold as to claim it had the foreskin of Jesus on display (Feifer, 1985)!

One of the most significant documents affecting the development of Western-style democratic political systems to come out of the Middle Ages was the Magna Carta (1215). This document, which set the basis for legal taxation, a legal system of justice, and the right of the accused to a fair trial, also included the right to travel.

The bubonic plague was to have a great effect on the history of Europe during the Middle Ages. Travel was partly responsible for spreading the plague, as it is generally believed to have started in China and traveled via fleas on rats which stowed away on caravans coming from there to the West. From 1347 to 1351, the plague killed over 25 million people, fully one quarter of Europe's population. The cause of the plague was originally thought to be the bad air of the crowded cities. In fact, it was more likely to occur in cities than in the rural areas as more rats bred in city squalor than in uncrowded rural outposts. People with resources fled the cities and traveled primarily to the seaside to breathe the fresh ocean air. Early seaside resorts developed in response to this phenomenon. Another outcome of the plague was a reduction in the labor force. Laborers did not have the means to flee the city, and consequently were most likely to acquire the plague. As a result, a severe shortage of labor ensued, wages were raised, and with the increase in income the shackles of the feudal system were cast off. The base of the feudal pyramid began to erode, bringing down the entire system.

The Middle Ages may have been the Dark Ages for much of Europe and an evolving western society, but it was a period of growth in the sciences, technology, and spirituality in other parts of the world. In 570, Muhammad was born at Mecca. His history, including expulsion from

Mecca, writing the Koran, and triumphant return to Mecca, has resulted in one of the most powerful religious movements in the world today. Annually thousands of pilgrims journey to Mecca to visit the home of Muhammad which is prohibited from visitation to all but the faithful.

Africa was to see its first great civilization develop in ancient Ghana (northeast of present-day Ghana). The empire was built on its vast resources of gold, which was a much-sought-after trade good to civilizations to the north. When the kingdom of Ghana collapsed in 1076, it was replaced by the Mali Empire, the rulers of which were Muslim immigrants from the north. A trading and cultural center was established at Timbuktu, and extensive contact with North Africa ensued. Eventually, Arab traders journeyed to this part of the world and started the first organized African slave trade.

The Chinese civilization during the Middle Ages reached its zenith under the T'ang Dynasty. The Chinese civilization had developed in relative isolation for most of its history, but under the T'ang Dynasty, extensive sojourns to India, Rome, and other parts of the world were undertaken for trade and to acquire wisdom. They brought back from India the philosophy of Buddha, which they combined with the philosophy of Confucius to form a civilization based on enlightenment and wisdom. The arts flourished during the T'ang Dynasty and Xian became an international city, with dancers from Persia performing in the theaters. In his book Marco Polo describes the Chinese civilization as the greatest in the world, having established extensive systems of navigable waterways and overland roads including the Great Silk Road leading to the famous trading center at Xian. The Great Silk Road is now the focus of an international tourism development effort supported by the World Tourism Organization. From 1368 to 1644, the Ming Dynasty ruled China. During this time, the Great Wall was rebuilt and many of the palaces in Beijing were erected. Much of what was constructed during the Ming Dynasty, including subterranean tombs, attracts visitors to China today.

It was also during this period that the first recorded civilizations in the United States were reaching their zenith. In what is now the southwest United States, the Anasazi (the ancient ones) developed a civilization which encompassed parts of four states. Spiritual and trade centers at Chaco Canyon and Mesa Verde were connected by a system of trails to outlying villages. The Anasazi originally lived on the upland, farming for sustenance, but around 1000 they moved into the canyon country, constructing cliff dwellings and food storage shelters (granaries) on seemingly inaccessible cliffs. Around 1300, the Anasazi vanished, leaving behind the material remnants (e.g., pottery, ruins) of a culture which today attracts millions of tourists to the area annually.

EUROPEAN RENAISSANCE

During the Middle Ages, the Church in Europe was a patron of the arts and the center of scholarly activity. While this allowed for some advances in learning, any activity considered by the Church to be heretical was suppressed. The Renaissance, or rebirth, was a period of change and divergent thinking. New ideas, independent of Church doctrine and quickly spread via books, a product of the printing press, ushered in a period of philosophical change.

The Church, even though losing substantial power as a result of the Reformation movement, continued to be a patron of the arts, sponsoring such famous Italian artists as Michelangelo, Leonardo da Vinci, and Raphael during the 1500s. Their legacies, represented by their famous works, inspired the Grand Tour, which reached its height of popularity in the 1700s. The artistic accomplishments of this period continue to form part of the European travel experience today.

The collapse of the feudal system and establishment of national borders allowed resources of the independent states to be used for purposes other than military expeditions, even though wars were still waged. The shift of resources allowed for the financing of explorations. Portuguese seamen were the principal early explorers, although some were financed by the King of Spain. Trade was still the primary motivation for the early expeditions, but an ancillary benefit was the discovery and subsequent claim of new lands. Portuguese explorers Bartolomeu and Vasco da Gama explored the western coast of Africa in the late 1400s in an attempt to establish trade routes with India. The resources of West Africa (e.g., gold) were in such abundance that the Portuguese built the first European structure in West Africa, a castle, in what is now Elmina, Ghana. This castle, along with others built or captured by the Swedish, Dutch, and British in later years, was to become the center of the African diaspora to the Americas in the 17th and 18th centuries.

GRAND TOUR

The Grand Tour is English in origin, and it was primarily a finishing school for the sons of the British elite. The purpose of the Grand Tour, which for some lasted over three years, was exposure to the cultural attractions of the European mainland. While the primary reasons for travel during the Middle Ages were trade and religious pilgrimage, the focus now shifted to attaining cultural enrichment. Tour participants were accompanied by a mentor and guardian, and were expected not only to observe the arts, literature, music, science, and other cultural refinements of Europe, but were expected to return home with an increased ability to utilize the knowledge gained in their travels. The purpose of the Grand Tour eventually evolved from one of learning for the young to one of sensual pleasure for all ages. Some maintain that the Grand Tour continues to exist today as evidenced by the pilgrimage of North American travelers to the cultural centers of Europe.

The origins of a modern tourism industry are believed to have begun with the Grand Tour. Many of the major cities of Europe (e.g., Paris, Milan, Rome) developed superior hotels and services for their guests. Stays in each capital were long by today's standards, as travel was still relatively risky and laborious. Rural stays were viewed as a necessary evil rather than as a sought-after pleasure. As the number of tourists from England increased, reaching a peak in the 1700s, many companies renting carriages, bodyguards, and other travel services were formed. The French Revolution of 1789 and later the Napoleonic Wars of the early 1800s effectively ended the Grand Tour for the English elite. A resurgence after the Napoleonic Wars more closely resembled the tourism of today, with all ages and classes participating in shorter stays (Towner, 1985).

AGE OF REVOLUTION

European New World colonialism, which was developing on the heels of exploration during the 1500s and 1600s, began to unravel during the 1700s. Social revolutions, which gave people the right to govern themselves and determine their own destiny, were actually preceded by another form of revolution—the industrial revolution. The industrial revolution began in Britain in the middle 1700s and has accelerated and spread throughout the world ever since. The shift from hand to machine labor freed time for many other pursuits, including self-government. The strength of a country's ideology was soon to be entwined with the strength of its industry and technology. The products of the industrial revolution changed the face of tourism forever and ushered in what is referred to today as mass tourism. However, for the industrial revolution to generate the products needed for mass tourism to develop, it required an ideological base. That base can be found in the writings of Thomas Paine, appearing in pamphlets and articles prior to the American Revolutionary War. These principles, which were later published in the *Rights of Man* (1791), influenced American Revolutionaries who drafted the Declaration of Independence (1776), and the Constitution of the United States (1787).

The American Revolution and Paine's writings also provided the impetus for the French Revolution of 1789. Other forms of government were soon to follow, but throughout the western world, even though monarchies were still revered, they had a collective root—rule by the people.

Common individuals were now freer to direct their own destiny. Although the promises embodied in the American Revolution with respect to individual rights were not offered to all segments of American society in the late 1700s—and some contend they are still not today—enough change took place to set the world on an unprecedented course of development. Free choice resulted in a free enterprise system with a common denominator for measuring success—the accumulation of wealth.

One of the first products of the Age of Revolution to affect tourism was the development of the steam engine. Crude steam engines had been around since the 1600s but it wasn't until James Watt devised the first practical one in 1769 that they became part of the industrial scene. Steam engines were first used to move people by sea. People had been moved by wind power for centuries, and as colonial empires grew throughout the world, there was increasing demand for safe and dependable transportation for people and goods.

The first locomotive steam engine was in use in Britain by 1813. It was used to haul coal, and in 1825 enough refinements had been made that the first passenger railway was built. The use of the locomotive steam engine spread throughout Europe and America by 1835. The passenger locomotive was a necessary step to connect what were becoming industrially based urban centers. However, rail travel, although it could be undertaken for pleasurable purposes (e.g., to visit family, the seacoast, etc.), was not set up for leisure travel. Thomas Cook, while walking down a rail line to a temperance meeting in 1840, decided he could use the convenience afforded by rail travel to increase attendance at the meetings and garner more support for his cause. The experience gained from using rail transportation in this way eventually led to the development of a large-scale travel agency. Package tours were arranged by establishing networks with travel service providers (e.g., hotels). Cook also made it easier for people to purchase a complete travel package by offering reduced rates and coupons or tickets which could be used to purchase meals, in effect establishing the first travelers' check. Cook's tours were more like adventure travels of today, as he arranged the first organized excursions into Africa using steamers to cruise up the Nile or rail, steamer, and foot travel to traverse the entire continent (*Time Traveller*, n.d.). Many of Thomas Cook's innovations are still in use today, even if the original impetus for his business, temperance, was never fully realized.

Rail travel, with its ability to move large numbers of people at relatively low cost, permitted the first form of mass travel to develop. No longer was travel considered an activity only for the elite. Travel began to take on a new dimension. Prior to the advent of mass tourism, the ability to travel was considered prestigious and carried with it certain social status. Now that travel was available to more people, status, through travel, became associated with different classes of travelers (Urry, 1990). How people traveled, and where, became more important than just simply the act of traveling. This status distinction continues today, and may be one of the reasons for the burgeoning growth in market niches such as ecotourism and adventure travel.

Rail is still used extensively today for travel by many millions of people. It is much more important to the travel industry in some parts of the world (e.g., Europe) than in others. Where it is not an important mover of people, it has begun to take on a new form. Instead of being viewed as a means of transportation, it is increasingly being marketed as an experience in itself. Rail lines through scenic areas, used for short excursions and offering gourmet meals and/or theater, are becoming more commonplace. Even abandoned rail lines are being reclaimed by rural communities as part of a bike/hike trail system affording old rail towns a type of tourism not previously available.

AUTOMOBILE

Automobiles are generally regarded as the technological advance which allowed people to move at will. The number of passenger miles accounted for by automobiles far exceeds the miles of any other form of transportation. However, the invention of the automobile in and of itself was not sufficient to make it the mover of tourists that it has become today.

The industrial revolution, with all its technological advances, did not protect the people who made it possible. Factories for the most part were unsafe, miserable places to work. Wages were low and the hours long. Many workers were paid in script which could only be used to purchase goods, at highly inflated prices, in the factory store.

Henry Ford is credited with adopting the assembly line approach to automobile production. This process allowed for the mass production of automobiles at low prices. However, even at a relatively low price, factory work still did not produce sufficient income for the purchase of luxury goods such as an automobile. What made the purchase of an automobile possible was the five dollars per day wage (unheard of at the time) paid by Ford Motor Company. Workers now had enough disposable income to purchase automobiles, and as other factories followed suit, the formation of a middle class in the United States was underway (Iacocca, 1984). It is this middle class throughout the world which today constitutes the majority of travelers.

TRANSATLANTIC PASSENGER TRAVEL

Life before World War I throughout Europe and in the United States was one of splendor for members of the privileged class. Servants, leisure time, and a standard of living unequaled at the time was available to those who understood and were able to exploit the opportunities brought on by the industrial revolution. Nowhere was the opulence so apparent as in the luxury liners which crossed the Atlantic. The services and comfort available to passengers on those luxury liners surpass many of the finer resorts of today.

The first transatlantic pleasure party voyage was the Quaker City journey embarking from New York in 1867. Mark Twain was a passenger on the ship and his memories are chronicled in *The Innocents Abroad*. Early promotions for the voyage stated that General Tecumseh Sherman and Henry Ward Beecher would be featured passengers. They never made it, but as soon as Mark Twain booked passage, he was included in the list of notable personalities who would accompany the guests (Wagenknecht, 1962). Twain's story of the adventure was so well received that transatlantic steamship travel became a desired form of transportation.

> I have no fault to find with the manner in which our excursion was conducted. Its program was faithfully carried out—a thing which surprised me, for great enterprises usually promise vastly more than they perform. It would be well if such an excursion could be gotten up every year and the system regularly inaugurated. Travel is fatal to prejudice, bigotry, and narrow-mindedness, and many of our people need it sorely on these accounts. Broad, wholesome, charitable views of men and things can not be acquired by vegetating in one little corner of the earth all one's lifetime. (Twain, 1869; EP edition, 1962:498).

Transatlantic cruises were set back for a period of time when the "unsinkable" Titanic struck an iceberg in the North Atlantic in 1912 and lost 1,513 of its 2,224 passengers. Still, luxury liners dominated travel between North America and Europe until the outbreak of World War I in 1914.

WORLD WAR I

World War I started after Archduke Franz Ferdinand of Austria was assassinated in June, 1914, but a major cause of the war was rivalry over trade and colonial possessions. Major European countries formed alliances which threw them into war when one member of the alliance was attacked. The industrial revolution had made it possible to establish effective military powers, allowing for the destruction of human life and property on an unprecedented scale. As a result of the war, vast amounts of resources were devoted to producing even more effective military hardware. Research and development led to advances in radio communication and ground and air transport. These advances would later be used by a developing tourism industry.

The end of World War I ushered in prosperity throughout Europe and the United States. This period is commonly referred to as the "roaring twenties." Transatlantic travel on luxury liners returned, and wealth generated through the technological advances made during World War I fueled an increase in pleasure travel. Advances in automobile transportation led to the development of a more efficient transportation infrastructure. Camping became a popular activity, and small-scale lodging properties along transportation networks began to appear. Resort operations in close proximity to major urban areas began to develop along the coastal, mountainous, and lake areas of the United States. More people were acquiring the wealth and leisure time to pursue pleasure tourism.

GREAT DEPRESSION

The "roaring twenties" came to a abrupt halt with the collapse of world financial markets, starting in New York, in 1930. The tourism of the "roaring twenties," built on high levels of conspicuous consumption, came to a virtual standstill. Businesses catering to the high-rolling tourists, especially upscale hotels, virtually disappeared. There was a mass migration of people from one region of a country to another in search of any type of employment. This movement in the U.S. is chronicled in the fictional but still accurate book, *The Grapes of Wrath* by John Steinbeck. As a result of the mass migration, people left family and friends behind; this translated into future travel to renew interpersonal relationships. Reforms and government programs were beginning to restore a measure of economic stability in the late 1930s when World War II began.

WORLD WAR II

World War II began when Germany invaded Poland in 1939 and ended with the surrender of Japan in 1945. Technology accelerated rapidly within the six-year period of World War II and was never so noticeable as when the nuclear age was ushered in with the detonation of an atomic bomb at Hiroshima in 1945. The war effectively ended the Great Depression throughout the Western world as industry expanded to produce the weapons of war. This industrial expansion continued after World War II as the technological advances became the building blocks for the consumer age. The United States, except for the human toll, was relatively untouched by World War II, and its industry made it the dominant Western power. Wartime industry was converted after 1945 to producing consumer goods such as automobiles, which, when coupled with a government interstate highway building program, connected most parts of the U.S. with an efficient highway system. The wealth created through the production of consumer goods translated into a growing middle class in the United States with the means, and, with advances won by labor unions, the time to become the world's largest producer of tourists. Mass tourism was fully underway.

AIR TRAVEL

Air travel was started by the French in 1783 when they began experimenting with hot air balloons. The first motorized flight by a heavier-than-air machine was achieved by the Wright brothers at Kitty Hawk, North Carolina in 1903. Technology developed during the World Wars made motorized flight possible at a much faster rate than would have been possible in a peacetime economy. Shortly after World War I (1919), the first international airline went into service, shuttling passengers on a daily basis between London and Paris. World War II brought even greater advancements in aerospace technology.

Early air travel was decidedly for the adventurous. Unscheduled stopovers, which today irritate the consumer, were the norm rather than the exception. With the relative stability brought on by government regulation, service could be expanded. In-flight meals, flight attendants and, on some long-distance flights, sleeping berths were offered. Still, the price of air travel made it impossible for the masses. The use of jet engines in 1958 reduced travel time and the use of larger aircraft lowered the relative price of air transportation. When wide-body jumbo jets arrived in 1970, the world had become a much smaller place. After World War II, air technology continued to advance, partly because a large industry had been created but also because of the advent of another war—the Cold War.

COLD WAR

The Cold War had its roots in the ideology espoused by Friedrich Engels (1820–1895) and Karl Marx (1818–1883). In 1848 they co-authored the Communist Manifesto in which they reacted to the abuses of the proletariat or workers by capitalists and urged a social revolution. Although Marx was expelled from Germany for his heretical views, they were taken up by the proletariat, led by Vladimir Lenin, in Russia in 1917. Russia at the time was suffering through World War I, which claimed millions of Russian lives. Partly because of this human toll, there was much discontent with the poor government of Tsar Nicholas II. Although the new Russia, which through land acquisition evolved into the Soviet Union, was to enter World War II on the side of the Allies, it came out of the war a sworn enemy of the capitalistic powers. The Cold War had begun.

Technology developed during the Cold War eventually found its way into consumer goods and assisted the development of a worldwide tourism industry. One area of technology which received a boost from the Cold War is communications. In 1957, the Soviet Union sent the satellite Sputnik into orbit. The space race was on. Yuri Gagarin became the first citizen of earth to enter space in 1961. By the time man reached the moon in 1969, space was crowded with satellites and space flight debris. The technological advances accomplished during the space race resulted in a satellite supported global communication system, allowing almost every point of the world to be in contact with every other point. The tourism industry of today has been made possible by advances in telecommunication. From airline reservation systems to an expanding awareness of the world through alternative cable television programming, to international weather reports, and lately "fast" information via the internet, more parts of the world are known and accessible to more people than ever before.

The end of the Cold War, which occurred when the Soviet Union dissolved at the end of 1991, has interesting implications for tourism. Larger areas of the world are now beginning to develop a tourism industry. A western curiosity to see life behind the "Iron Curtain" has led to increased travel to parts of the old Soviet Union and Eastern Europe. However, in the haste to throw off the chains of communism, historic sites, which are important tourist attractions, are being dismantled. The Berlin Wall, which more than any other object exemplified the Cold War, is almost gone, having been torn down and sold piece by piece to souvenir seekers. Statues of communist leaders, including Lenin, have been removed from their pedestals and presumably destroyed. New democracies, which until their manufacturing base catches up after fifty years of neglect, will rely partly on tourism for needed foreign exchange. Care must be exercised in order that hatred of past rule does not destroy part of the base of tomorrow's tourism industry.

LEISURE TIME

Leisure time is essential to a tourism industry. The Roman civilization probably had the largest amount of leisure time for elite members of the ruling class, as near its end almost one-third of the days in a year were considered holidays. This amount of leisure time is not likely to be repeated as the economic structure on which market-based systems are built cannot accommodate that much leisure time. During the early period of the industrial revolution, the majority of workers had only enough time off work to recover from the drudgery of their occupations. Even though laws were passed which regulated the amount of time children could work, it was not until labor unions were organized, accepted, and supported by government legislation that the blue collar worker began to experience an increase in the amount of leisure time. Gradually, the average work week shrunk from

The Temple of Kukulkan at Chichen Itza, showing the snake descending (shadow) from the top and visible during the autumnal or spring equinox.
Photo by John Archer

MATURE MARKET

Increasing levels of travel, such as that experienced during the 1970s and 1980s, depend on increasing numbers of travelers who possess sufficient discretionary income to engage in the activity. There are many different reasons for the large growth in tourism. However, one remains predominant: the expanding population in what has been referred to as the mature market (>50 years), coupled with corresponding increases in its disposable income. Although the mature market is a diverse one (some would argue too diverse to be grouped together as one segment), a broad overview of the background characteristics of this market is helpful both in understanding how the travel industry has reached its present state of development, as well as future travel demand.

The mature market in the U.S. counts more than 65 million people and is expected to rise to over 75 million by the year 2000. These people have enormous buying power, holding the majority of wealth in the U.S. It is estimated that they control 75% of the nation's assets and account for almost 70% of discretionary spending. They also account for over 80% of all leisure travel. The mature market is expected to maintain its standing as the fastest growing segment of the travel industry for at least the next 20 years. Once the "baby boomers" reach retirement age (approximately 2010), the percentage of the mature market over 65 will double from what it is today. It will rise from approximately 29 million to over 65 million or 21+% of the population. An increasing life expectancy promises to swell these numbers considerably. History shows that the number of women seniors will greatly exceed that of men, with a ratio of 1.5:1, or one-and-a-half times as many women as men in the mature market segment.

What are all these people going to do? First, it appears that they will continue to travel, with many opting for international experiences. Over 50% of passport applications today in the U.S. are issued to members of the mature market. Research indicates that escorted tour groups are rising in popularity because of the security, convenience, and companionship tours offer. Cruise ship and motorcoach travel are very popular with this group, with over 70% of cruise and motorcoach customers considered part of the mature market. Natural attractions and/or historical sites are most popular, and are visited during warm weather. Special attractions such as seasonal color tours or festivals and special events are also high on the list.

The mature market is already a major factor in the increasing popularity of travel as a preferred consumer good. It will continue to exert significant influence in the future as the market increases in size and the amount of discretionary income grows ever larger. Due to the mature markets' desire to experience natural and historical attractions in a controlled environment, mass travel, which is supported by the group tour concept, will continue to be a major force shaping industry operations at both ends of the tourism supply/demand equation.

Source: National Tour Foundation; Davidson-Peterson Associates, Inc.

over 70 hours per week to less than 40 during the 1970s. Increases in leisure time, through a reduction in hours of work per week, paid vacations, and increasing disposable income won through collective bargaining agreements, were responsible for the increases in leisure time appearing after World War II. However, through the 1980s and extending into the early 1990s, the average work week has started to increase.

While certain segments of the population may experience less leisure time today, there are other segments with plenty of leisure time and the means to travel. In the United States, the over-50 age group is the fastest growing segment of the population. While leisure time for workers is not expected to decline much in the future, more people reaching retirement age with pensions, social security, and savings will continue to exert a strong influence on travel demand.

CONCLUSION

The process of tourism development is a product of historical events, and these antecedents have led to the tourism industry of the 1990s. A detailed account of these events along with an interpretation is found in Figure 2.3. Throughout history, some form of tourism development has been a part of the world's social and economic system. Whether it was crude inns and restaurants along major trade routes or luxury hotels built to serve participants of the "Grand Tour," some form of an industry developed to serve the needs of travelers. Some purists may argue that the study of tourism and tourism development should confine itself strictly to pleasure travel, and development associated with trade is another subject area. Others argue, including the author, that pleasure is just as much a commodity as gold. If we accept that line of reasoning, then a review of history's important events is a valid starting point for discussing the ramifications of tourism development. Equally important is recognizing many of the contributions to modern-day tourism that non-European civilizations have left, and continue to offer, the world.

The history of tourism is still being written. With the threat of a major nuclear war diminished and powerful enemies becoming more interdependent, mass tourism is poised to reach new heights. History tells us that human beings have always found reasons and ways to travel. It took literally thousands of years for the number of tourists to equal the number we now record traveling each year. The next chapter to be written in the history of tourism development will most surely concentrate on the management of the phenomenon rather than the antecedents of growth. The rest of this book is the foundation for that future chapter.

Date	Event	Tourism Significance
40,000 B.C.	Cro-Magnon man moves westward into Europe	Beginning of human-like existence in Europe
28,000	Early humans cross into North Amerca (Bering Strait)	Beginning of human existence in North America
20,000	Period of cave painting in Lascaux	First known human written record
8400	Dated fossil remains of domesticated dog	Domestication of animals for human use
8000	Agriculture develops in Middle East	Man begins evolution from hunter/gatherer to controller of nature.
5000–3000	Sumerian civilization in Mesopotamia	Invention of money, wheel, and written records on clay tablets (3100)
3100	King Menes unites Upper and Lower Egypt	Beginning of Egyptian civilization
2800–2175	Age of Pharaoh in Egypt	Sphinx and most pyramids built
2697	Huang-Ti (Yellow Emperor) of China	First record of Chinese civilization
2500	Indus valley civilization	Beginning of Bronze Age
2100	Aryans from Northwest invade Indus valley	Possible transfer of Bronze Age technology
2000	Bronze Age in Europe	Implements fashioned of metal
1860	Druids	Stonehenge built
1400	Iron Age in India and Asia	Advancements in metal technology
1200–800	Phoenician civilization in Middle East	Use of sailing vessels for transportation
776	First Olympiad in Greece	Beginning of organized sports tourism
563	Birth of Prince Siddhartha (Buddha)	Ideology and culture formation
551	Birth of Confucius	Ideology and culture formation
550–525	Persian Empire under Cyrus	Large tracts of land and divergent cultures brought under one rule
508	Beginning of Greek civilization	Beginning of experiment in democracy
400	Mayan civilization begins expansion north	Road system developed, stars studied, sports organized
460	Age of Pericles in Athens	Democracy refined; scientific method and reasoning evolves; Age of Philosophy begins with Aristotle; leisure recognized as important element of society in writings of Plato, student of Socrates, and later in writings of Aristotle
241	Rome controls Sicily	Beginning of Roman civilization
221–207	Ch'in dynasty in China	Dynasty gives China its name, arts flourish
214	Great Wall built	Major tourist attraction today
60–44	Age of Roman expansion under Caesar	System of roads, aqueducts; travel for nobles; Egypt becomes a popular destination, largest and most organized civilization yet; trade routes through Empire established

Figure 2.3 *History of Tourism Development*

Date	Event	Tourism Significance
5	Birth of Jesus of Nazareth	Beginning of one of the world's most powerful political and spiritual powers
476 A.D.	Overthrow of Roman Empire	Beginning of Middle or Dark ages for Europe; start of feudal system; travel dangerous; most travel for trade or religious pilgrimage throughout Europe
570	Muhammad born in Mecca	Powerful ideologic movement created; Mecca is to become a major pilgrimage site
618–907	T'ang Dynasty in China	Chinese begin to travel to other parts of the world; Xian becomes an international city; silk trade, arts flourish
900	Myan Empire extends into Yucatan	Extensive road system established throughout Central America; ruins at Chichen Itza and Tikal are major tourist attractors;
920	Height of the Empire of Ghana	Trade, primarily gold, with Arabs of North Africa
960–1275	Sung Dynasty in China	Block printing, paper money, and newspapers
962	Holy Roman Empire established by King Otto I	Church controls spiritual and political power through Europe until Refomation; sponsor of arts and architecture, religious pilgrimage to Rome or Jerusalem
1002	Leif Ericson explores North North American coast	First known European explorer in the Americas
1076	Fall of Empire of Ghana and rise of Mali Empire	Islamic Arabs found Mali Empire and begin the African slave trade; Timbuktu becomes a center of Muslim culture and trade
1096–1270	Crusades	Military expeditions by Christians to the Holy Land ostensibly to protect Christian pilgrims, more likely to protect trade routes
1100–1300	Period of cathedral building in Europe	Church builds cathedrals that form part of present–day European travel experience
1215	King John signs Magna Carta	Foundation for justice system, includes right to travel
1232	Gunpowder used to propel rockets	Principles of propulsion tested
1295	Marco Polo returns to Venice	Experiences of Far East are chronicled in book of Marco Polo
?–1300	Anasazi culture in Southwest U. S.	Construction of cliff dwellings, trails connecting major population centers, wall art; ruins are major tourist attractions today

Figure 2.3 *History of Tourism Development (cont.)*

Date	Event	Tourism Significance
1347–1351	Plague	Plague spread by fleas on rats carried on caravans from China; one quarter of European population dies; many flee to seaside to escape "bad air" of cities, erosion of feudal system
1368–1644	Ming Dynasty in China	Great Wall rebuilt, most of the ancient palaces built, subterranean tombs built, recently discovered
1438	Inca Empire established in Peru	Communication between settlements with trained runners using stone roads
1454	Guttenberg invents movable type	Learning and divergent philosophies easily spread
Late 1400s	Portuguese explore West Africa on their way to India	Establishment of forts and castles in West Africa later to become important in slave trade with Americas
1492	Columbus discovers West Indies	Routes to the Americas are established
1502	Vespucci follows Columbus's path	New World acknowledged
1507	First World Map	America is named on the first map
1517	Start of Reformation	New thoughts and ideas proposed
1500s	Michelangelo, Da Vinci, Raphael	Church-sponsored art continues to attract millions of tourists to cultural centers of Europe
1531	Spanish exploration and colonization of Americas	End of Inca Empire and beginning of European influence in Americas
Late 1500s–early 1600s	Brahe, Kepler, Galileo	Scientific observations redefine man's role in the universe
1607	Jamestown settlement	First English colony in North America
1600s–1700s	African Diaspora to Americas	Mass forced movement of people to a new Continent
1700s	Height of Grand Tour	Travel for learning, development of transportation rental companies, rise of elegant hotels, importance of the arts reinforced
mid 1700s	Industrial Revolution	Machines do the work of many men; later advancement and social reforms set the stage for increases in leisure time and development of a middle class
1776	Declaration of Independence	Democratic ideals with their roots in ancient Greek civilization which, when coupled with the Industrial revolution, have formed modern-day Western society
1787	Constitution of the United States	
1789	French Revolution	
1791	Thomas Pain publishes Rights of Man	
1769	Steam engine	First practical steam engine invented by Watt
1783	Hot air balloon used in France	First successful attempt at air travel

Figure 2.3 History of Tourism Development (cont.)

Date	Event	Tourism Significance
1818	Birth of Karl Marx	Fathers of major ideological movement which
1820	Birth of Friedrich Engels	shapes the history of the world througout the 1900s
1825	First steam-powered locomotive transportation	Replaces horse drawn trains, more efficient and faster
1841	Thomas Cook tours	Use of rails for mass transportation, established package tour business
1800s	New Colonialism	European colonies established throughout Africa and Asia, extensive business travel to colonies, system of exploitive dependency established
1903	Mass production of automobiles	Affordable automobiles produced by workers well paid for the time, beginning of a middle class in U.S.
1903	Wright brothers fly at Kitty Hawk	First successful motorized flight
Early 1900s	Age of the Luxury Liner	Ocean travel for the wealthy
1912	Titanic sinks	Luxury ocean travel is set back
1914–1919	World War I	Technological advances, age of rapid growth ensues as a result of wartime production
1917	Russian Revolution	Beginning of the Soviet Union
1919	League of Nations	First attempt to recognize a community of nations and a global society
1919	First international flight	Air passenger service inaugurated between London and Paris
1919	First transatlantic flight	Crossing of the Atlantic by two RAF officers
1927	First transatlantic solo flight	Lingbergh flies from New York to Paris
1930–1939	Great Depression	Stock market collapse ushers in a period of major unemployment, travel declines, migration resulting in later travel to renew relationships occurs on a major scale
1938	Civil Aeronautics Board (CAB)	Act of U.S. Congress establishes the CAB to ensure a competitive airline industry develops in the U.S.
1939–1945	World War II	Major technological advances; national boundaries redefined; Nuclear Age begins; Cold War begins; mass tourism originates in developed world; rebuilding of Japan results in major economic power in the 1980s and new tourism market
1944	U.S. Federal Highway Act	Origination of U.S. Interstate Highway system; major boon for domestic tourism in U.S.

Figure 2.3 History of Tourism Development (cont.)

Date	Event	Tourism Significance
1945	Cold War	Conflict between capitalism and communism; major technological advances
1957	Sputnik sent into orbit	Space race begins, development of a global communication network
1961	Yuri Gagarin sent into orbit	First earth space traveler, beginning of manned space exploration
1969	Man lands on moon	First exploration of an extraterrestrial body
1970	Jumbo jets	Lower fares, more travelers per plane, major growth in international travel
1978	Cannon Kennedy Pearson Act	Derugulation of the U.S. airline industry, lower travel costs increase air travel
1980s–?	Rise of Asian ecomony	New economic power in asia, tourism to and from Pacific Rim nations increases

Figure 2.3 *History of Tourism Development (cont.)*

EXECUTIVE SUMMARY

Early tourism developed in response to civilization and its formation of communities with a "sense of place."

Early travelers were for the most part traders, and a crude hospitality industry (inns) developed at major trade centers to accommodate their needs.

Travel and the growth of the hospitality industry began to accelerate rapidly during the Greek and Roman civilizations due in large part to stable political systems and respect for science and democracy.

With the collapse of the Roman civilization commenced the Middle Ages, where travel was risky and only undertaken for high rewards associated with trade or religious pilgrimage (spiritual salvation).

While the Middle Ages enveloped Europe for hundreds of years, civilizations in other parts of the world flourished, their physical remains becoming major tourist attractions today.

The bubonic plague, brought to Europe by traders from China, led to a sizeable reduction in the labor force, allowing the feudal system to be overthrown.

The industrial revolution made possible mass production of consumer goods, including those related to travel, which when combined with the purchasing power of a newly emerging middle class, set the stage for the creation of a tourism industry .

Thomas Cook, using the products of the industrial revolution, packaged travel products (e.g. transportation and lodging), leading to the formation of a tourism industry .

Two World Wars and the Cold War accelerated technological advances in transportation and communications, allowing a mass tourism industry to evolve in a short period of time.

REFERENCES

Cook, J., A. Kramer, and T. Rowland-Entwistle. 1981. *History's Timeline*. London: Grisewood and Dempsey Ltd.

Feifer, M. 1986. *Tourism in History: From Imperial Rome to the Present*. New York: Stein and Day.

Fridgen, J. 1991. *Dimensions of Tourism*. East Lansing, Mich.: Educational Institute of the Hotel and Motel Association.

Grun, B. 1975. *The Timetables of History: A Horizontal Linkage of People and Events, based on Werner Stein's* Kulturfahrplan. New York: Simon and Schuster.

Iacocca, L. with W. Novak. 1984. *Iacocca: An Autobiography*. New York: Bantam Books.

Steinberg, S. 1979. *Historical Tables, 58 B.C.–A.D. 1978*. New York: St. Martins Press.

Early Tours in Unknown Africa. *Time Traveller*, n.d. 4:2.

Towner, J. 1985. The Grand Tour: A Key Phase in the History of Tourism. *Annals of Tourism Research* 12(3):297–334.

Trajer, J. 1979. *The People's Chronology: A Year by Year Record of Human Events from Prehistory to the Present*. New York: Holt, Rinehart and Winston.

Twain, M. [1869] 1962. *The Innocents Abroad*. Norwalk, Conn.: Easton Press.

Urry, J. 1990. The "Consumption" of Tourism. *Sociology* 24(1):23–34.

Wagenknecht, E. 1962. Introduction to M. Twain, *The Innocents Abroad*. Norwalk, Conn.: Easton Press.

II

Impacts

The process of writing this book included many different stages. First came submission of an outline for review. After considering reviewers' comments, a first draft was completed and another round of reviews was conducted by the publisher. After changes were made based on reviewers' comments came the finished product which you are now reading. During each stage, one frequent comment was that the ordering of chapters was unusual and the section on impacts should appear at the end of the book. Obviously the author ignored those comments. Experience as a practitioner led to that decision. Often impacts are ignored or are not given serious consideration (except for positive economic projections) during development planning. Yet impacts are often serious enough that they determine the long term viability of development projects and/or the quality of life for host communities. Because of its importance, this section on impacts has, by design, been situated in the beginning of the book.

The author may be accused of a biased presentation through the ordering of chapters in this book. That charge is accepted as the ordering is indeed intentional.

Tourism development invariably causes change. Some of those changes are beneficial; others are not. Whether change is considered good or bad depends on the individual and the interest group with which he/she is aligned. Part II contains a review of some of the changes that may result from tourism development. "Impacts" is used to describe these changes.

Since the author is a product of a market-based economy, the first impact to be discussed is economic Not all economic impacts are beneficial, but if the economic ramifications of tourism development are understood, managers, planners and individuals can consider the trade-offs. Although tourism does not fit neatly into definitions used by many governments to define and describe an industry group, numerous attempts have been made to identify tourism's economic impacts and its contributions to economic development. Some of those attempts at classification are included in Chapter 3, Economic Impacts.

The second impact to be discussed is environmental or physical. The inclusion of a chapter on environmental impacts has to do with the author's academic background as well as the anxiety statements such as "tourism protects the environment" bring to the author. While this assertion can be true, it is not always so. Therefore, this chapter aims at presenting a balanced approach to the subject of environmental impacts. Whether that goal has been achieved is left up to the reader to decide.

Finally, Chapter 5 examines the sociocultural impacts brought by tourism development. Interest in this subject evolved from the author's attempts at "touristhood" and his relationship with host communities, and in a different context from work in international tourism development. Chapter 5 proved the most difficult to write in Part II due to two factors. First, most of the literature on tourism development has a strong marketing focus. How to increase the flow of tourists to an area dominates the tourism scientific literature. Secondly, sociocultural impacts are not easy to quantify, which makes impact comparison a difficult, if not impossible, task. Only recently have the discussions and research into sociocultural impacts resulting from tourism development received academic and government attention.

CHAPTER THREE

Economic Impacts

Waikiki Beach, Hawaii, where tourism's economic impacts are visibly apparent.
Photo by the author

Learning Objectives

Explore some of the claims and counterclaims made about tourism's economic impact.

•

Understand how regional economies are defined and the criteria used to delineate a region based on the "area of influence" requirement.

•

Understand how economic impacts can be measured and the advantages/disadvantages of the various methods used for measurement.

•

Discuss economic impact multipliers, how they are derived, and their possible uses and abuses.

•

Examine the influence different "tourist types" have on economic impact.

INTRODUCTION

It was Ben Franklin, in *Poor Richard's Almanac*, who said visitors and fish stink after three days. Tourism involves hosting and opening up one's community to guests. It is no wonder that with increasing levels of tourism in an area, tourists begin to be perceived in the same light that Ben Franklin viewed visitors. Why do people wish to share their community with tourists throughout the year? One could argue that community pride is enhanced through the act of hosting, but the answer, even if not openly expressed, is invariably economic benefit. The money brought into an area through the process of hosting tourists provides more economic return than simply the sum of the expenditures accruing to the few businesses that come in direct contact with tourists. Almost all sectors of an economy benefit economically from tourism. All sectors also pay a price for tourism development, although that impact may not be as quantifiable as the economic impacts that result from tourism expenditures. Chapters 4 and 5 detail some of those hard-to-quantify impacts, but in this chapter the focus is on economics.

The shift to a service-oriented economy in the United States and in other parts of the developed world began in earnest during the 1960s and continues today. Recently, this service trend has begun to appear in the developing world, mostly tied to an increase in tourism. It is this growth in service and its resulting economic contributions that led to more intensive study of the travel phenomenon.

As discussed in Chapter 1, early tourism studies focused almost exclusively on the economic benefits derived from tourism. Since tourism was a rather new field of study without widespread acceptance within the academic or business community, early works extolled the economic virtues of tourism development. This approach justified the industry's public and political acceptance at a time when it was a growing economic force.

The first studies validated this newly recognized industry by comparing it to more established fields such as agriculture and manufacturing. Problems that resulted from tourism development were generally ignored or not considered as a focus of study. Many of the beneficial claims made in the early days have since been debunked or toned down. This is not meant to imply that economic benefits as a result of tourism development are not real or substantial, but rather that some of the economic costs which were not considered are just as real and tend to temper the benefits.

This chapter begins by exploring some of the economic benefits and costs of tourism development. It then discusses economics from a regional perspective, including the elements needed to create an economic area of influence, and discusses some of the different types of economic impacts that can be measured and multipliers that can be derived. Finally, this chapter reviews methods to measure the benefits derived from tourist activity and finishes with a discussion of how different types of tourists have different effects on regional economic benefits.

FOREIGN EXCHANGE

Keynesian economic theory identifies a country's wealth in terms of its Gross National Product (GNP). The formula used to derive GNP is

$$GNP(Y) = C+I+G+(X-M).$$

A student of introductory economics will recognize C as consumer expenditures, I as investment, G as government expenditures, and (X–M) as exports minus imports. Tourism is considered an export for a country. The larger the share of tourism expenditures, the larger a country's GNP, as the difference between X–M increases if there is a positive trade balance or is smaller if there is a negative trade balance. Foreign exchange provides more purchasing power in the international market, and if a country has a nonconvertible currency, foreign currency may be the only means to purchase goods that cannot be produced locally.

Obviously, there are different opportunities to acquire foreign currency. The traditional means is through the exportation of domestically produced goods. In the developing world these goods are primarily agricultural or mined products. Because of the easy substitutability of these products and intense competition, which depresses prices, many of the agricultural and extractive industries operate at exploitive rates, thereby depleting resources needed to maintain increasing populations and provide for economic growth. Tourism, with its ability to generate foreign exchange, and possibly protect resources needed to sustain the tourism industry, has been embraced as a new industry in many developing countries. Unfortunately, misconceptions exist about the tourism industry's ability to generate sufficient foreign exchange and provide enough income to sustain an area's economy and a government's social programs. There are exceptions where tourism has proved the backbone of a developing country's economy, but generally long-term economic health depends more on establishing a diversified economic base rather than reliance on one industry.

One way to understand some of the perceptions related to tourism and its impacts on a country's economy is through popular literature. Perceptions eventually become rooted in reality and are expressed as distinct possibilities in popular writings. For example, Bishop's (1982) protagonist in the award winning novel *No Enemy But Time* eventually becomes the Minister of Tourism in a fictional third world African country. Revenues from development of a major casino/resort are expected to "fund schools, agricultural programs, cultural exchanges and technological progress for everyone in East Africa" (1982:382) and help put an African on the moon! This example is not meant to suggest that the author believes tourism can accomplish the above stated economic goals, as the novel is definitely science fiction, however enormous claims for the riches brought by tourism, still commonly heard today, should also be considered science fiction.

One reason for tourism's inability to provide as much foreign exchange as desired has to do with the highly competitive nature of the industry. Although tourism growth has been substantial during the last twenty years, competition for travelers has also been intense. The People's Republic of China (PRC) is a case in point. In 1978, the PRC officially opened its doors to the outside world after being closed since World War II, and experienced what has been termed a "tourist tidal wave" (Dunn, 1986). In the early years the country had difficulty meeting travelers' needs, especially with hotel rooms, guides, and inland transportation. Visitors accepted the lack of services as part of the travel adventure, but the novelty quickly wore off (Choy and Gee, 1985). Although the number of international visitors increased during the 1980s, percentage increases began to decline (Table 3.1). As a result of the Tiananmen Square conflict in 1989, international visitation to the PRC almost came to a virtual halt. Even before Tiananmen Square the PRC, which by all accounts is a destination with high recognition value, had trouble maintaining an economy built on high levels of tourism. Today the PRC has regained much of the lost tourist market share from the Tiananmen Square conflict and service levels have improved, but the country's overall economic growth is due more to a highly diversified economy led by a strong manufacturing sector than to the return of the tourist.

The problems experienced by the PRC are also felt by other developing countries in their quest for foreign exchange. To have long-term success, the level of services and facilities must be of tourist-class quality. Many developing countries do not have the capital or expertise to develop a tourism industry from scratch. Instead, they rely on multinational companies through direct foreign ownership or joint venture relationships to provide not only the capital needed for construction but also the expertise needed for management. These types of arrangements increase leakage (a concept to be developed later) and reduce the amount of foreign exchange remaining in the host country.

Compounding the leakage problem is the provision of quality service, which is a function of the host country's educational system. Without

TABLE 3.1   Growth in Tourist Arrivals to China 1978–88

| Year | Total Arrivals | | Foreign Arrivals | | |
	No. (000)	Annual Growth %	No. (000)	%	Annual Growth %
1978	1,809		230	12.7	
1979	4,203	132.3	362	8.6	57.4
1980	5,702	35.7	529	9.3	46.1
1981	7,667	34.5	675	8.8	27.6
1982	7,924	3.4	765	9.7	13.3
1983	9,477	19.2	872	9.2	14.0
1984	12,852	35.6	1,134	8.8	30.0
1985	17,833	38.8	1,370	7.7	20.8
1986	22,810	27.9	1,480	6.5	8.0
1987	26,900	17.9	1,728	6.4	16.8
1988	31,700	17.8	1,840	5.8	6.5
AVG.	13,534	36.3	999	7.4	24.1

Source: China National Tourism Administration

basic grounding in tourist's needs and requirements, service levels are apt to be less than desirable, resulting in declining visitation over time. Many developing countries do not have the technical expertise or educational programs in place to provide international standard service training for their citizens who wish to be involved in the tourism industry.

The above discussion is not intended to belittle the importance of foreign exchange earnings generated through tourism for developing countries. Tourism is indeed a means of acquiring needed foreign currency but in many cases, because of the obstacles in place, the amount of foreign exchange earned is less than expected or desired. Developed countries, on the other hand, have many of the systems in place required to retain a substantial percentage of international expenditures resulting from visitation, thereby allowing needed reinvestment and boosting local earnings.

The statement that tourism is an excellent earner of foreign exchange is not axiomatic but rather circumstantial. Tourism may actually benefit the developed world more than the developing world. The reason for this is economic diversification. Countries or regions with one industry experience more volatile economic swings than those with multiple industries. It is not unusual for policy makers to embrace tourism when their predominant industry turns sour and major unemployment results. Developing countries may put too much reliance on tourism as their major industry and suffer major economic setbacks and social unrest when the touted benefits of tourism do not materialize. The safest way to approach tourism development is through a carefully thought out and planned process integrating tourism into existing or planned industrial growth. In this way, economic downturns will be less damaging as more than one industry is available to offset declines in others. Obviously, it is not always possible to diversify the economic base of a region. Many factors are involved in industrial location decisions and some regions will benefit more from diversification than others. However, if the emphasis is on diversification rather than a one industry economy, there is a greater opportunity for long-term sustainable growth (this line of reasoning is explored in more depth in the last chapter). It is unfair to the people of a host society to promote tourism as an economic savior. There is no evidence to suggest that it is a panacea for all economic ills but rather works as a prophylactic when managed properly.

INFRASTRUCTURE DEVELOPMENT

Proponents of tourism development claim that tourism utilizes an existing infrastructure. To an extent, this claim is valid. If sufficient excess infrastructure capacity exists, then tourism can be developed with little additional cost. However, this requires that infrastructure capacity be known and that tourism does not expand beyond capacity levels. It is difficult to control the number of visitors, and large increases may require new infrastructure development. Infrastructure investment is costly and is usually subject to indivisibility constraints. Adding an additional sewage treatment system to handle the waste from only five hundred extra tourists is difficult. Generally, the treatment plant would be built to handle thousands of new visitors and the level of tourism required to justify the expense may not occur. Planned tourism development should consider present infrastructure levels and project costs associated with exceeding present capacity.

When sufficient infrastructure is not available to handle the present needs of a community, tourism may be the economic agent responsible for developing one. Witt (1991) credits the impressive performance of the tourism sector for considerable infrastructure improvements in Cyprus. New roads, airports, seaports, electrical plants, and improvements in telecommunications resulted from tourism development on the island. These improvements, as a result of meeting the needs of the tourism industry, benefit all members of the host community as well.

TAXES AND INFLATION

As with any type of development, new business will have an impact on local resource prices and labor supply. Changes in land prices are often the first indicators of the economic effects of tourism. While a rise in land value benefits those investing in land, there is usually a concurrent rise in property taxes. Land speculation rarely benefits local populations, as they generally enjoy only a small share of land value increases (Thurot, 1975).

Other land users, such as agricultural producers, are often forced to sell because they are unable to pay inflated property taxes. Some areas have enacted farmland preservation acts to ensure that productive farmland is taxed at a lower rate. However, this legislation does not protect residents on fixed incomes without active farming interests. While these residents can reap the benefits of inflated land values, they often forego the quality of life aspects which attracted them to the area.

On the positive side, taxes generated through tourism development can help reduce local tax burdens. If an area institutes a local sales tax, then money tourists spend can help offset local property tax burdens. In areas where extensive seasonal home development occurs, property taxes paid by these home owners can significantly reduce local tax burdens. Gartner's study (1987) comparing permanent and seasonal home owners finds that permanent home owners are more likely to favor increased development and fewer restrictions on land use than seasonal home owners. Seasonal home owners are also more likely to purchase rural property located a substantial distance away from incorporated cities and towns, whereas the permanent home owners live for the most part within incorporated cities and villages. One of the reasons for the difference in attitude toward future development is the lower property tax burdens for permanent home owners, offset by the increase in local tax revenues provided by seasonal home owners. However, what appears to be an economic benefit to the community can turn into an economic disadvantage in the long run. This happens when and if a large percentage of seasonal home owners choose to convert their residences to permanent dwellings upon retirement. At that time, taxes paid by the previous seasonal home owners may not cover increased services that must now be provided on a year-round basis (e.g., police and fire protection, road maintenance). What initially appears to be a tax advantage to community residents can become a tax liability, with higher property taxes for all residents to pay for increased costs of services to outlying areas.

Seasonal home owners' location preference can also pose environmental problems. This impact is hard to quantify and therefore does not appear in a balance of payments account, but it can significantly reduce the quality of life for all residents. The next chapter addresses the subject of environmental impacts in more detail.

The effect of tourism on taxes has not been sufficiently studied to determine at what point a tax advantage may in actuality become a tax liability. For the most part, researchers and decision makers accept tourism as a tax revenue generator. If there is no taxation of tourists, either through local sales, accommodations, or some other type of tourist-specific tax, then imposing such a tax would be considered a revenue generator. If taxes received from tourists are used simply to offset local tax burdens and not to plan for tourism development, tourism is more likely to become a tax liability.

Increasing levels of tourism also affect labor. Tourism can create jobs, but it can also lead to inflation. The level of inflation depends on the available labor supply in the area. Figures 3.1 and 3.2 depict two different labor situations. In Figure 3.1, an excess supply of labor exists; in other words, there are high levels of unemployment or underemployment within the area. Tourism development, like any other industrial expansion, moves the demand for labor outward. With a relatively abundant supply of labor such as that depicted in Figure 3.1, inflationary impacts on wages will be minimal.

Labor demand in Figure 3.1 is depicted by the demand curve DL. Labor supply is depicted by the supply curve SL. Equilibrium is at the point of P0, where the quantity of labor demanded is Q0. As mentioned above, tourism development shifts the demand curve for labor outward (in Figure 3.1 this is the line DL1). Once a new equilibrium point is reached, the quantity of labor demanded will be at Q1, with the price paid at P1. The proportional increase in quantity demanded (Q1-Q0) is more than the proportional increase in price paid (P1-P0). The relatively horizontal slope of the labor supply curve indicates that there is an excess supply of labor, labor is elastic, and inflation does not pose a problem.

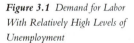

Figure 3.1 *Demand for Labor With Relatively High Levels of Unemployment*

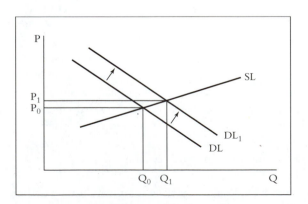

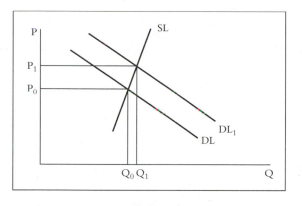

Figure 3.2 Demand for Labor
With Relatively High Levels of
Employment

In Figure 3.2, there is relatively full employment before tourism development. In this case, the inflationary impact on wages is much higher. Again, the equilibrium point before tourism development is at Q0 and P0. However, the labor supply curve, SL, has a much steeper, almost vertical slope reflecting conditions approximating full employment. Shifts in the demand curve for labor from DL to DL1 reset the equilibrium point to Q1, P1. The proportional increase in quantity demanded (Q1–Q0) is less than the proportional increase in wages paid (P1–P0). In this situation, the labor supply is relatively inelastic, resulting in higher wage inflation. The impacts of wage inflation will be felt throughout the rest of the economy, raising prices for all goods and services, including those for residents not directly benefiting from any tourism-related salary increases. Obviously, if one must choose between two areas for tourism development investment, choosing the one with an excess supply of labor will have less of an inflationary impact on the area's economy. Unfortunately, it is not always possible to pick areas for their respective labor supply conditions as for other characteristics (e.g., natural resource attractions) that make one area more appealing than another for development.

Tourism-related businesses can offset labor shortage problem and resulting wage inflation by importing labor, thereby increasing the size of the labor pool. This scenario is more likely in areas subject to seasonal tourism. Workers can be hired only for the duration of the season, keeping labor costs low. On the other hand, businesses may not have to import labor if high levels of unemployment exist throughout the region or country. Tourism development can alter established employment patterns, with a labor shift from high unemployment rural areas to more densely populated tourism centers (Tangi, 1979). This migration of labor increases supply and tends to keep labor costs low. Unfortunately, keeping labor costs low does not necessarily mean that other goods and services in the area remain moderately priced.

Tourism development produces higher prices for consumer goods more often than does other types of industrial development. The reason for this is the amount of discretionary income in the hands of visitors. Travel, especially pleasure travel, is still a luxury good. The majority of people travel only after the necessities of life (e.g., rent, food, transportation) are paid. People pay higher prices for products while traveling than they would at home. Businesses that cater to tourists as well as locals price their products to receive the highest return. Whenever product demand increases, prices rise. Locals are often forced to pay increased prices simply because they live in an area experiencing higher product demand due to increased tourist flows (Din, 1995). Although this type of economic impact has not been extensively studied, it is clearly observable. It is often easy to differentiate tourists from residents in grocery stores simply by observing shopping behavior. Residents find it less expensive to buy what is on sale rather than what they prefer. Tourists, on the other hand, prefer to purchase what they want rather than what is on sale, rarely using coupons. This trend is most noticeable in areas which are highly tourism-dependent (e.g., Hawaiian Islands).

OTHER ECONOMIC DEVELOPMENT

Tourism is often touted as an economic stimulus agent for regional development. Any industry that creates employment opportunities and brings money into an area is an economic development stimulus. As services increase and further infrastructure development proceeds due to tourism, other economic development activities can take advantage of existing transportation networks, expanding populations, and available sources of capital. The reverse also holds. Economic development brought by other industries can stimulate tourism. This is especially true for business-related travel.

In some instances, tourism development actually hinders new industrial activity. Often tourism develops in an area because of the attractiveness of the natural resource base. Even with expanding markets in the area, some forms of industrial activity may not be perceived as compatible with tourism. Arguments over highest and best use of resources continue to rage. For example, in the mid 1980s, the U.S. Federal Department of Energy studied an area on the border of Canyonlands National Park in the state of Utah for use as a nuclear waste repository. Many local residents were in favor of not only the study phase of the project, but also site designation. The lure of relatively high paid employment at the nuclear waste site was a powerful inducement. Canyonlands National Park, on the other hand, provided limited employment opportunity due to its relatively un-developed resource base as a hiking/jeep trail park with few facilities for tourism. Although the nuclear waste study site was not in Canyonlands National Park, opposition to the site focused on the visual impact of the proposed activity as well as inappropriate use of buffer zones surrounding the park. Eventually, the agencies involved in site selection dropped the site from further study. Although the agencies disseminated public state-ments indicating that the decision was based on problems not directly tied to park issues, it was still clear, based on public hearing transcripts, that the proximity of Canyonlands National Park to a proposed nuclear waste site posed obstacles.

This case shows that even though tourism is often claimed to act as an impetus for other types of economic development, it may actually be the opposite. Published newspaper stories also provide accounts of how forms of economic development can negatively impact an area's tourism indus-try. For example, at the time this section was first drafted, unrelated news stories on successive days raised concern over potential damage to the tourism industry from industries wishing to operate within environmen-tally sensitive areas. Opponents of a proposed mining operation along the state of Wisconsin's Flambeau flowage claimed that mining operations would seriously damage present levels of tourism (St. Paul Pioneer Press, 1991). Oil drilling opponents used similar arguments to try to prevent ex-ploratory drilling in another area of Wisconsin that "touts its outdoors ap-peal to tourists" (Saint Paul Pioneer Press, 1991). These two stories are not isolated instances, as similar accounts appear on a regular basis wherever natural-resource-based tourism is a strong economic force. In these in-stances, tourism does not act as an impetus to further economic develop-ment, but instead may exclude other industries from developing. Obvi-ously, industrial compatibility needs to be addressed before any industry can be considered a means of fostering further economic development.

REGIONAL ECONOMIES

One of the primary purposes of regional economics is to better understand how tourism affects an economy. This is only possible if an economic area of influence is defined; if there is an impact, it must be on something or somebody. Tourism is generally discussed in terms of its impacts on some recognized community, which then becomes the region of economic in-fluence. However, a community defined by political boundaries may not be the best representation of an area of influence, and assuming that eco-nomic impacts are best measured at the community level injects a parochial view that often prevents successful tourism development from occurring. Communities are only one sub-system in a set of sub-systems that define regional economies. They may be large enough to be considered regions in and of themselves, but more often they provide the essential ingredients for a larger functioning region. Davis and Kennedy (1980) identify four sub-systems that, when combined, form a region of economic influence: economic, political, social/cultural and environmental/natural resources.

Economic

Interrelationships between the factors of production form the economic sub-system of an area. For example, a resort operation may require goods and services from a variety of support businesses to adequately serve its guests. It must obtain liability insurance, identify sources of capital, locate food suppliers, contract for energy services, and so on. It is the interrelationships between the final providers of tourism goods and services and their suppliers that define an economic sub-system. Obviously, a large economic sub-system can make delineating regional boundaries only by economic interrelationships problematic. Therefore, regions based on an economic area of influence also include the other regional delineators as a means of reducing the complexity inherent in using economic interrelationships as the sole determining factor.

Political

The political sub-system allows the economic sub-system to function according to prescribed conditions. Issuing liquor licenses and hours of operation, providing highway maintenance, regulating architectural design, publicly funding promotions, and making other decisions that affect a business' operation are the responsibility of the political sub-system. The political sub-system includes managing the network of publicly provided resources that attract travelers to a region. The maintenance and management of public parks, campgrounds, forests, scenic overlooks and other public areas frequented by tourists form part of the total attraction package for an area. The political sub-system should be viewed not only in terms of controlling the economic sub-system, but as a functioning part of it.

Social/Cultural

The social/cultural sub-system consists of people. Permanent as well as seasonal residents of a region fuel the engine of the economic and political sub-systems. They provide a labor pool for businesses and determine how residents and visitors view the region. How people organize themselves and their community projects their culture.

Environmental/Natural Resources

The fourth sub-system comprises environmental/natural resources. It consists of the land and water base of a region, prevailing climatic conditions, and geologic resources. Natural resources often overwhelm the other sub-systems in determining how a region develops. Regions with outstanding scenic natural resources will ultimately develop some form of a tourism industry. In some cases, the political sub-system may not consider tourism an acceptable activity, which makes it more difficult for the economic system to function, but with few exceptions tourism asserts itself as a dominant use of these unique natural resources.

Successful tourism development in a region depends on the recognition of the four sub-systems, their interrelationships, and functions. None of the sub-systems is static. Change in one activates change in another. To more fully understand the nature of economic impacts on a region, it is necessary to define how regional systems are delineated.

REGIONAL DELINEATION

In the preceding section, a region is defined as four distinct sub-systems which combine to form an area of influence (i.e., containing all four sub-systems). However, most regions chosen for economic impact analysis are not defined by the area of influence criterion, but by other, more convenient and easily identified characteristics. Regional boundaries are usually set according to one of the following criteria.

1. Political boundaries define a governmental unit. Townships, cities, boroughs, etc., are formed in order to establish rules for those residing within the governmental unit's borders.

2. Sociocultural distinctions are based on the predominant societal characteristics of the area. Ethnic communities within large cities may form distinct sociocultural regions. Chinatown in San Francisco and Greektown in Detroit (U.S.), and the Ashanti region in Ghana, West Africa are some examples. These regions may develop as major tourist attractions because of their unique sociocultural characteristics.

3. Economic regions are usually delineated according to their primary products. The Grain Belt refers to the group of states in the upper Midwest and the Great Plains of the United States which annually

produces over 90 percent of the grain products in the country. Similarly, Silicon Valley refers to an area in California where a large portion of the U.S. semiconductor industry is located. The Champagne region of France grows all of that country's grapes used to produce Champagne sparkling wines. There are no established boundaries for an economic region, but when referred to by their economic name most people have a basic understanding of the region's location.

4. Natural resource characteristics commonly define regions. Many political regions were initially delineated according to some predominant natural feature. Major river systems form the boundaries for many states in the U.S. and countries throughout the world. The Mississippi river is responsible for defining, in whole or in part, the eastern or western boundary of ten states. Natural features also help establish an area's tourism identity. The state of Arizona bills itself as the Grand Canyon State in order to establish a brand image built on one of the world's natural wonders. The Intermountain West is a name given to the area in the U.S. between the Rocky Mountains to the east and the Sierra Nevada range to the west. Although boundaries for this region are not well defined and the region covers parts of a few states, the name has significance for area residents. It not only describes a particular land base but also infers certain climatic characteristics.

When does the struggle for economic gain border on poor taste? Photo by the author

Why should a tourism professional be concerned about how regions are defined? To a large extent, the boundaries of a region determine economic impact. For example, the closing of a national park which annually hosts over one million visitors will have only minimal economic impact if the region is defined only by the land within the politically established boundaries of the park. If the park has limited or no concessionaire facilities, local communities provide the bulk of tourism goods and services. Revenue loss due to park closure will be minimal unless the region is defined according to the area of influence criterion.

In one case (Davis and Kennedy, 1980), a proposed 25-percent reduction in timber harvest was determined to have no economic impact on a region. In this case, the region was defined solely according to natural resource characteristics (i.e., tracts of harvestable timber). No communities or factors of production (e.g., sawmills) were located within the delineated region. Thus, the statement that a reduction in logging activity would have no economic impact is valid but nonsensical, since the regional limits are not determined by area of economic influence, but rather arbitrarily by location of the raw product. Therefore, the process of regional delineation is an important determinant of economic impact.

Before discussing how to trace tourist expenditure flows and derive regional economic impact, it is important to understand the different types of industries that generate revenues within a region.

BASIC AND NON-BASIC INDUSTRIES

Businesses can be separated into two types, basic or non-basic. A basic business is one that sells the majority of its products outside the region. It can be considered an exporter of goods and services, resulting in positive currency flows to the region.

Non-basic businesses provide goods and services to other businesses within the region or to the region's residents. For a business to be considered non-basic, money received for its products originates primarily within the region. Non-basic businesses exist because basic industries create employment and spur community growth. Suppliers of components to other companies, which in turn export their finished products, would be considered vertically linked basic support entities. They exist because the primary basic businesses exist.

Very few businesses can be considered solely basic or non-basic. The concept is best conceived on a continuum, with 100-percent pure basic regional industries anchoring one end, and 100-percent pure non-basic industries at the other. For example, champagne production is considered a basic industry for the Champagne region of northern France. However, some champagne produced in the area is also purchased by regional residents. The criterion used for classification of a business is the percentage of sales received from outside sources. If more than fifty percent of sales are to individuals or businesses located outside of the region, the business is classified as basic. Conversely, if more than fifty percent of sales are generated within the region, the business classification is non-basic.

Business classification takes on greater value when industrial investment strategy is discussed. Tax abatements, subsidized land purchases, and relaxed zoning regulations are a few of the incentives often used to lure basic businesses to an area. The economic advantages to be gained—new jobs, a higher standard of living for residents, and further industrial growth and development—are easily recognized. Exporting industries create a support system of businesses for a region that provides increased opportunities and products for its residents.

Tourism is an industry that defies easy classification. Many tourists purchase goods and services also purchased by regional residents. Seasonal home owners may buy groceries or hardware items in the area where their seasonal home is located. Generally, supermarkets and hardware stores are considered support businesses and classified as non-basic. Similarly, day visitors may eat at local restaurants and purchase sundry items from the local drugstore, both of which are considered non-basic businesses. The value of these types of tourism expenditures is often overlooked, as they are not seen as providing basic income to a region. However, tourism is a basic industry for a region using the criterion of percentage of sales derived from outside sources. Purchases are made with money brought in from outside the region and the individual's experience becomes the exported product. However, since not all tourism purchases are made at basic businesses, the importance of this industry to a region is not often perceived.

ECONOMIC IMPACT TYPES

Tracing the flow of tourist dollars through a regional economy helps elucidate the importance of industrial classification. Sales made to tourists result in basic income for a region, termed "direct economic impact." However, direct economic impact calculations do not accurately measure the overall importance of tourism to a region. It is possible for one region to receive more money directly from tourists than another, yet benefit less from those expenditures. For example, mega-festivals and -events of short duration may have less overall economic impact on a region than numerous small events occurring throughout the year, even though the direct economic impact from the mega-event is larger than the combined direct economic impact from all the smaller events (Gartner and Holecek, 1983). The reason for this lies in the nature of indirect economic impacts and a region's economic base. Sustained levels of tourism in a region provide a greater opportunity to capture and retain tourist revenue due to the supporting businesses which develop in response to predictable and steady flows of tourists. Large inflows of revenue for a short time do not provide the base needed for business growth; hence, a large share of expenditures may leave the region with the transient businesses that appear only in response to the mega-event.

A front-line tourist-dependent business is supported by many backward-linked businesses. A hotel must purchase liability and property insurance, secure investment capital, purchase the services of local labor, locate a steady supplier of food products for its in-house food service operations, and contract for a host of other products and services for successful management of the operation. These backward-linked businesses do not interact directly with visitors but cannot exist at the same level without them. Purchases the hotel makes from these businesses constitute some of the indirect economic impacts in a region. The backward-linked businesses also purchase goods and services and continue the cycle of indirect impacts. Indirect impacts continue as long as money is re-spent within the region. Re-spending money at support businesses located outside of the region is termed "leakage," and acts to reduce the total economic impact within the region. Figure 3.3 presents a model of the flow of tourism expenditures through a regional economy. Notice that leakages ("import leakages") occur during each round of spending.

MULTIPLIERS

The sum of direct economic impact, often referred to as first-round spending, plus indirect economic impact, equals total economic impact. This relationship gives rise to what is referred to as an economic impact multiplier or the amount of money that stays in a region as a result of outside money being used to purchase goods and services locally produced. One type of economic impact multiplier, a ratio multiplier, is derived by dividing total economic impact by direct economic impact. If the purchase of $1 worth of goods and services could be traced through a regional economy using expenditure breakdowns shown in Figure 3.3, direct and indirect expenditure levels could be calculated. The sum of these expenditures, minus any leakages, would be divided by direct economic impact to derive an economic-impact ratio-type multiplier.

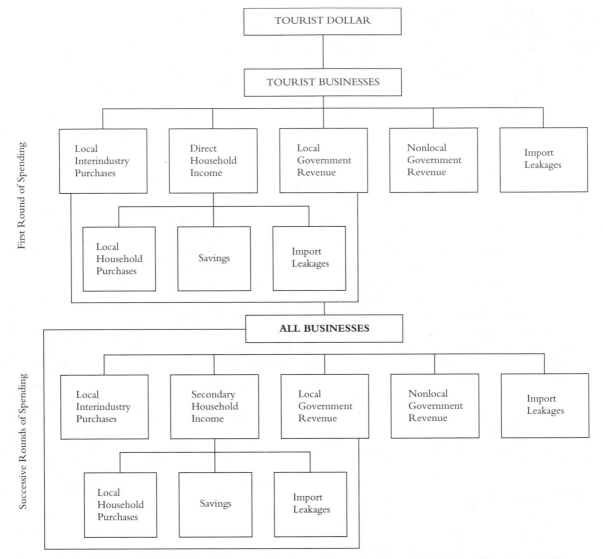

First Round of Spending

Successive Rounds of Spending

Source: Liu, J. and T. Var. 1983, The Economic Impact of Tourism in Metropolitan Victoria, B.C., *Journal of Travel Research* 22 (2), Fall.

Figure 3.3 *Flow of the Tourist Dollar in the Local Economy*

The ratio-variety economic-impact multiplier is also termed a dependency or transactions multiplier, as it reflects total purchases within a region due to an increase of $1.00 (or any other currency unit) in spending originating with or from an outside source. An economic impact multiplier of 2.4 indicates that for every $1.00 increase in visitor spending, an additional $1.40 in sales are generated within the region. Richardson

(1972) terms this type of ratio multiplier a "type 1 income multiplier." A type 2 income multiplier can also be computed. It is higher than the type 1 because it takes into account direct, indirect, and induced income changes resulting from an increase in final demand (spending from outside sources). The induced changes come about because of an increase in consumer spending resulting from inter-industry transactions. Both type 1 and type 2 multipliers are ratio-derived in that direct, indirect, and for type 2, induced, transactions are summed and divided by the direct impact.

Archer (1984) argues that ratio-type multipliers are meaningless when calculating income derived from tourist spending. That is, they do not accurately measure the amount of income that accrues to local residents. Further, they are not grounded in economic theory. Their only use is in examining the degree of internal linkages between sectors in a region. Archer (1976) proposes using a Keynesian-type multiplier to measure income generated from tourism spending. This multiplier rarely approaches unity unless the region is large with an extremely developed economic base. Calculating a personal-income multiplier of the type proposed by Archer requires estimating the amount of each dollar in tourist sales that ends up as personal income through wages and salary.

McIntosh et al. (1995) use a simple Keynesian ratio-type personal-income multiplier to measure economic impact. It is of the form:

$$\text{Multiplier} = 1/1-\text{MPC}$$

where

M = Marginal (extra),
P = Propensity (inclination),
C = Consume (spending).

Alternatively, the same multiplier can be expressed as $1/\text{MPS}$ where S = Savings. Either multiplier will give the same result. Macintosh et al. include any money taken out of the regional economy through savings, not available for reinvestment, or through the purchase of imported goods and services in the calculation of the MPS. Since savings are often reinvested by local banks it is necessary to determine the amount of savings held in reserve and the amount available for local reinvestment. One way of determining the amount of money available for reinvestment, at least in the United States, is by using the Federal Reserve Board's reserve requirement, which is a percentage of total demand deposits held by banks. Another multiplier calculation would be:

$$\text{Multiplier} = 1/1-\text{MPC}\star$$

where

MPC⋆= Marginal Propensity to Consume Locally and includes
all business consumption, including local lenders
purchases of security instruments.

Liu (1986) offers a more detailed equation to represent income multipliers. It is of the form:

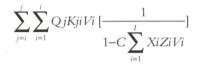

$$\sum_{j=i}^{j} \sum_{i=1}^{i} Q_j K_{ji} V_i \left[\frac{1}{1-C\sum_{i=1}^{I} X_i Z_i V_i}\right]$$

where:

j represents a different category of tourist;

i is a different category of business;

Q_j represents the proportion of total expenditure by the jth type
of tourist;

K_{ji} represents the proportion of total expenditures by the jth type
of tourist in each ith type of business;

V_i is direct plus indirect income generated per $1 of tourist
revenue received by the ith type of business;

C represents propensity to consume;

X_i represents the proportion of total consumer spending by
residents of the region in the ith type of business;

and Z_i represents the proportion of consumer spending by
residents in the ith type of business in the region. This type of
formula not only produces normal (i.e., not ratio) income
multipliers but can produce them for each different type of
tourist group (e.g., Japanese versus Australian), region, and different business category (e.g., accommodation types). It is a much
more refined model which can help direct marketing strategy if a
primary objective is to concentrate on groups contributing the
most in terms of regional income generation.

The majority of income multipliers encountered in the literature are
actually sales or transactions (i.e., ratio type) multipliers. This is primarily
due to ease of calculation. The more refined multipliers such as the one
proposed by Liu require a greater degree of data specificity, which is both

time-consuming and costly. If the purpose is simply to compare performance characteristics across industry groups, ratio multipliers are adequate and usually available, with slight modification, from data maintained at national levels.

Employment multipliers can also be calculated. The number of jobs created by the tourism industry depends on many factors. The level of leakage within a regional economy affects local employment, as it does transactions and income. Wage rates and the degree of automation also affect employment. Employment multipliers are generally based on productivity. The simple functional form used to illustrate this relationship is:

$$E_i = a + bX_i,$$

where

E_i is employment in industry i and X_i is output of industry i.

This employment production function can then be used to derive the employment multiplier. The direct employment change is the slope of the production function, represented by b in the linear regression equation above, which is used to estimate employment as a function of production. Calculate the multiplier by summing the direct employment change plus indirect, and dividing by direct. This ratio-type multiplier is similar to the sales or transaction multiplier discussed above. Indirect changes are determined by summing the direct and indirect changes in industry i for each unit change in demand for any other industry in the region. The sum of all changes in final demand is direct plus all indirect employment changes due to a change in final demand. This value is then divided by direct employment change, calculated by the production function, to derive the employment multiplier.

Employment multipliers may appear to be more difficult to derive than simple ratio type sales or transaction multipliers. However, computer algorithms make the steps outlined above easy to compute. The increasingly scarce public resources available for industry assistance underscore the need to derive employment multipliers. More public investment decisions are being based on the number of jobs created rather than the amount of income generated. However, the two types of multipliers (i.e., income and employment) are directly related. Industries which are labor intensive, such as tourism, generally have both relatively high income and employment multipliers. Note that high is a relative term with both an income and employment multiplier usually less than 1 and a transactions (ratio) multiplier less than 3.

ECONOMIC IMPACT ESTIMATION

A number of methods are available to determine the relative economic importance of any industry to a region. One of the simplest is to calculate the total value of products sold. For example, agricultural products have either a market-determined or government-supported price. Summing the price paid for all agricultural goods produced within a region provides a simple measure of the value of the agricultural enterprise to that region. Comparing across industry groups allows for analysts to determine the relative importance of each industry to a region. However, this type of analysis does not take into account cost of production or possible linkages between industries or between public resources (e.g., water supplies) and production. Determining tourism's value to a region is even more problematic. Since tourism is a basic regional industry but tourists purchase goods and services from many non-basic industries in a region, how does an analyst determine the value of the tourism products consumed? Various methods have been borrowed or developed to deal with this issue. What follows are some models, starting with the more complex, which, if appropriately constructed, can provide a wealth of information about regional industry relationships.

Input–Output Analysis

Input–output analysis generally requires collecting primary data on interindustry flows. Analyzing these flows provides a basis for determining the various multipliers discussed above. Although input–output analysis is not required for deriving multipliers, it greatly facilitates the task.

Purchases and sales from one industry to another form the basis for constructing an interindustry flows matrix. Although the task of collecting detailed primary data poses operational problems, designating industry groups can be more difficult, especially if the focus is on linkages between the different components of the tourism industry. Industries, also referred to as sectors, are formed by grouping businesses that produce a similar product together. Businesses that produce more than one product or those serving both local residents and tourists create special problems. The general rule for overcoming this problem is to lump businesses by their primary product. If the same company produces two or more dissimilar products, the product earning the highest revenue for the firm becomes the product used for industry grouping. What if a business sells to both visitors (tourists) and residents? Is this business selling a tourist product, which would make it a basic industry, or providing a local service, which would make it non-basic? One way to overcome the problem of differentiating between visitor and local resident expenditures is to create a visitor sector and a separate households sector in an input-output table. In this way, an industry's dependency on tourists versus local residents can be analyzed. Unfortunately, creating visitor and household sectors increases data collection efforts, as a sample of tourists and local households is required to estimate expenditure patterns and magnitude.

There are short cuts available when grouping businesses into sectors. Most governments group businesses by Standard Industrial Classification (SIC) codes. In the United States, there are over seven levels of industry groupings from which to choose. Level one has the highest degree of aggregation, and level seven the lowest. Depending on the degree of aggregation or disaggregation required, SIC codes may be useful in assigning industry groups to sectors within a region.

Once industries or sectors are identified, data is collected from a sample representing each sector within the region. If the region is a large political unit (e.g., a province), it may be possible to utilize previously constructed input-output models and bypass the primary data collection stage. For example, Gartner and Holecek (1984) use a statewide model to estimate the economic impact of a short-term tourism exposition on the city of Detroit, Michigan. However, the level of aggregation for the state model prohibits a close examination of visitor impacts. The only sectors remotely related to tourism are labeled retail and wholesale trade. This level of aggregation does not provide for a close examination of tourism-related industry linkages.

If the intent is simply to assess the total impact of travel on regional economies, shortcuts may be available. Mak (1989) uses the U.S. Department of Commerce, Bureau of Economic Analysis' Regional Input-Output Modeling System (RIMS II) (U.S. Department of Commerce, 1986), which adapts national input-output tables to state tables in order to measure travel's impact on state economies. In this case, secondary data such as that produced by the United States Travel Data Center's annual survey of direct expenditure impacts on state economies must be available. Using these data, it is possible to apply direct expenditure estimates to multipliers for the transportation, hotels/lodging and amusement, food service, and general retail trade sectors in the RIMS II model, to derive total economic impact on state economies from travel. While this method represents an improvement over other regional input-output models, which are generally not specific enough for investigating tourism linkages, it is still a rough approximation of total economic impact. To be useful, secondary data must be accurate enough to capture the magnitude and patterns of total spending. Also, the RIMS II sectors must be sufficiently disaggregated for the analyst to feel comfortable in applying certain expenditures to sector multipliers. For example, the general retail trade sector does not adequately differentiate between retail businesses patronized more frequently by tourists (e.g., specialty crafts shops) and those utilized by residents (e.g., hardware stores). Still, if the focus is on regional economic impact, this shortcut approach is less costly than constructing more data intensive models. However, if the focus is on economic impact occurring to smaller regions within the model defined region, or linkages between regions, then neither the approach used by Gartner and Holecek (1984) or Mak (1989) is adequate.

The following discussion provides a better understanding of how input-output models work to uncover interindustry linkages. Assuming that sectors have been identified and data on sales and expenditures collected for each sector, an interindustry flows table similar to that displayed in Table 3.3 can be constructed. This is also called a transactions matrix. Sectors 1 through 7 are endogenous or located within the region. Sectors 8 and 9 are exogenous and represent leakage (imports) from the region or sales to sectors outside the region (exports). The matrix is diagonal in that all identified row sectors are the same for those identified only by numbers in each column. Reading down a column shows annual gross PURCHASES by that particular sector from every other sector in the region and also from external sectors. Reading across each row shows each sector's annual gross SALES to every other sector. Table 3.2 provides a crude estimate of interindustry linkages, indicating whether one sector is forward- or backward-linked to another. For example, sector 3, commercial fishing, is forward-linked to sector 7, manufacturing, which processes the commercial fishing product. Commercial fishing depends heavily on other industries which generate basic income through processing the commercial fishing product. Sector 8, tourists, is not forward-linked to any other sector since tourists do not sell any products within the region. However, the tourist sector is backward-linked to many other sectors since tourists purchase products within the region. Table 3.3 can also be used to identify the region's basic industries and their relative strength. Reading down sector 9, exports, reveals revenues generated for each sector from extraregional sales. Sector 8, tourists, has no export value since the tourist sector is exogenous (i.e., located outside the region) and does not sell products but rather purchases them from other sectors. Sector 7, manufacturing, is the region's largest basic industry, generating over $10 million in export sales annually. However, if the figures in column 8 are added together, the total tourist expenditures ($29.3 million) exceed the dollar value of manufacturing exports. Therefore, tourism, based on tourist expenditures, is actually the region's largest basic industry. Since tourism is not a traditional industry with clearly defined products, its impact on a region is often overlooked. Input-output analysis, given its rigid operational characteristics, tends to mask the importance of tourism unless the analyst specifically investigates tourism's linkages with all other sectors.

TABLE 3.2 A Transaction Matrix (in $)

Sector	(1)	(2)	(3)	(4)	(5)	(6)	(7)	(8)	(9) (exports)	Total Gross Output
(1) Households	8	1,500	2,000	3,200	500	2,200	8,000	0	7,327	24,735
(2) Law Enforcement	300	300	1	2	2	1.5	7	0	1,295.5	1,909
(3) Commercial Fishing	27	0	50	0	0	0	4,000	1,300	0	5,377
(4) Restaurants	8,000	90	5	9	0	0	0	6,800	0	14,904
(5) Lodging	1,400	1	0	0	0	0	50	12,600	0	14,051
(6) Service Stations	11,000	18	3	4	0	700	0	8,200	0	19,925
(7) Manufacturing	700	0	0	400	15	72	200	400	10,470	12,257
(8) Tourism	0	0	0	0	0	0	0	0	0	0
(9) Imports	3,300	0	3,318	11,289	13,534	16,951.5	0	0	0	48,392.5
Total Gross Outlay	24,735	1,909	5,377	14,904	14,051	19,925	12,257	29,300	19,092.5	141,550.5

Table 3.2 is useful in grasping linkages between sectors and the value of their exports; however, since it displays raw data, it is not always easy to interpret. Table 3.3, the Direct Coefficients Matrix, is based on Table 3.2 and is constructed by taking the entry in each column for each internal sector and dividing by the total expenditures for that sector (column total). The total for each column in Table 3.3 equals approximately one. Each column entry shows how each sector spends each dollar, and linkages become much clearer. Column entries measure the direct economic impact of a sector on every other sector in the region. For example, manufacturing spends over 32 cents of every dollar on commercial fishing products. It also spends almost 65 cents of every dollar on labor, possibly indicating an industry with low technology inputs and high labor dependencies. This forward linkage indicates that any decline in fishing stocks or labor unrest will significantly impact manufacturing. Reading down column 8 (tourists) easily identifies tourism sensitive businesses. In this hypothetical example, tourists spend almost 28 cents of every dollar at service stations (e.g., gas, oil) and 43 cents on lodging. There could be many reasons for the high percentage spent on lodging, including proximity to major attractions, lack of lower priced accommodations (e.g., campgrounds), or positioning as an upscale destination area with concomitant high prices for lodging. The Direct Coefficients Matrix (Table 3.3) does not provide reasons for expenditure patterns, but it helps the analyst understand present industry linkages, and with an assessment of a community's tourism potential, it can provide direction for future development efforts.

TABLE 3.3   Direct Coeffcient Matrix (in $000)

Sector	(1)	(2)	(3)	(4)	(5)	(6)	(7)	(8)	(9) (exports)
(1) Households	.00032	.78575	.37195	.21471	.03559	.11041	.65269	0	.3837
(2) Law Enforcement	.01213	.15715	.00018	.00013	.00014	.00007	.00057	0	.06785
(3) Commercial Fishing	.00109	0	.00930	0	0	0	.32634	.04437	0
(4) Restaurants	.32343	.04714	.00093	.0006	0	0	0	.23208	0
(5) Lodging	.05660	.00052	0	0	0	0	.00408	.43003	0
(6) Service Stations	.44471	.00943	.00056	.00027	0	.03513	0	.27986	0
(7) Manufacturing	.02829	0	0	.02684	.00107	.00361	.01632	.01365	.54838
(8) Tourists	0	0	0	0	0	0	0	0	0
(9) Imports	.13341	0	.61707	.75745	.9632	.85076	0	0	0

Table 3.4, Direct and Indirect Business Coefficient Matrix, reveals the direct plus indirect economic impacts of every dollar of outside sales. For any model with a large number of sectors, a computer is indispensable for deriving this matrix. The sum of each column in this matrix gives the transactions multiplier for each sector. The value of this information is that sectors can now be compared based on their relative contribution to sales and ultimately income in the region. For example, a $1.00 increase in final demand for manufacturing results in a total of $2.5918 in sales to the region. This is not viewed by some as an income multiplier (Archer, 1984), although others argue that if households are included as an endogenous sector (#1), the multiplier is a true income multiplier of the type 1 variety (Richardson, 1972). In either case, the transactions multiplier is a proxy for the income multiplier, as sectors that are heavily labor dependent (e.g., law enforcement) also have high transaction multipliers, representing a large proportion of industry purchases going directly to labor. This "sales to labor" results in income which is then available for re-spending within the region. In other words, leakage is reduced. Tourism, therefore, should have relatively high multipliers when compared to other industries because many tourism-sensitive businesses are labor dependent. However, Table 3.4 does not provide a tourism multiplier because the tourism sector is exogenous and reflects a type of export. Only endogenous or internal sectors are represented in the Direct and Indirect Business Coefficient Matrix, and the tourism multiplier is contained within the multipliers for other sectors (e.g., lodging, restaurants) that cater to tourists.

TABLE 3.4   Direct and Indirect Coefficient Matrix with an Additional $1 Change in Final Demand

Sector	(1)	(2)	(3)	(4)	(5)	(6)	(7)
(1) Households	1.00041	.83461	.42222	.24391	.04112	.13602	.68252
(2) Law Enforcement	.01453	1.17412	.00024	.00021	.00016	.00009	.00061
(3) Commercial Fishing	.00111	.00002	1.00931	.00012	.00023	.00014	.3652
(4) Restaurants	.36917	.05271	.00118	1.00021	.00017	.00025	.00019
(5) Lodging	.06772	.00262	.01098	.02971	1.00327	.00047	.0066
(6) Service Stations	.51451	.01256	.00062	.00392	.12971	1.05212	.3215
(7) Manufacturers	.04966	.00199	.02563	.04921	.01137	.04397	1.2150
Total (Transaction Multiplier)	2.01711	2.07863	1.97017	1.32729	1.18603	1.23366	2.5918

Some aspects of tourism do affect multiplier size for the tourism industry as a whole and for each of its dependent sectors. Important ones include seasonality and ownership of establishments. Seasonal tourist areas often use temporary labor pools during peak season. For example, if students are employed as temporary labor, their tendency to save for school would reduce the amount of re-spending within the area. This saving represents a form of leakage if money earned by a resident labor pool is transferred outside the area. Ownership can also be problematic, especially if multinational companies own and/or operate local businesses and repatriate a high percentage of the profits. This situation is often a problem in developing countries that do not have sufficient capital (public or private) for development, but rely heavily on foreign ownership or joint venture operations. If a significant percentage of the profits are not available for local reinvestment, then the tourism multiplier may be lower than for other industry types.

Table 3.4 contains one other important finding. Tables 3.2 and 3.3 have zero entries in some of the cells. A zero entry indicates that there is no direct relationship between the two sectors. For example, restaurants (sector 4) purchase nothing directly from lodging (sector 5); thus, both Tables 3.2 and 3.3 have a zero entry for the column cell. In Table 3.4, however this same cell has a value of .02971, indicating that as a result of a change in final demand, such as in an increase of $1.00 to restaurants, the induced spending effect resulted in a sales increase to lodging. This is an important point, since it often seems that only a few businesses benefit economically from tourism, while another group bears the social costs (e.g., crowding). While some groups do benefit at a higher rate, Table 3.4 reveals economic linkages between all sectors. (Note: Although Tables 3.2, 3.3, and 3.4 are hypothetical, they are based on relationships contained in Darr and Fight (1974), and therefore reflect actual linkages. The original study which contained 35 sectors, has been drastically modified for presentation here.)

Employment multipliers can also be calculated from the information collected to develop Tables 3.2, 3.3 and 3.4. Data collection on interindustry purchases can also yield information on employment. Using the simple linear regression model described above, employment's relationship to output for each sector can be calculated.

Advantages of Input-Output Models

Proponents of input-output models use three main arguments to support their use:

1. At the present time, they provide the closest approximation to a regional general equilibrium model. General equilibrium models

assume that for each action, there is an equal reaction. When there is a change in final demand to any sector in the regional economy, other sectors are also impacted. The input-output model describes those changes in terms of monetary values and employment.

2. The model is easily computable. Once data are collected, the model lends itself to easy computation, especially with a computer. Simulations and projections are likewise easy to perform. Once the initial calculations are completed, many different scenarios can be analyzed. For example, if a recession is expected to reduce travel expenditures to a region by fifteen percent, this information can be entered into the model to identify impacted sectors.

3. The model is descriptive (Bendavis-Va, 1983), with outputs in the form of easily interpretable tables. Transactions can be identified in absolute value terms, direct coefficients describe transactions in terms of individual monetary units, and multipliers or outputs can describe the overall change in a region, from an increase or decrease in final demand. All of these outputs are sector or industry specific.

4. Currently, input-output models are the most comprehensive available for describing interindustry linkages (Chappelle, 1989; Briassoulis, 1991). Depending on the degree of aggregation, they have the potential for providing the most detailed view possible of a region's economic structure.

Disadvantages of Input-Output Models

Input-output requires the acceptance of many assumptions for it to be considered a valid model depicting regional industrial activity. It is these assumptions, inherent in its design and application, that form the basis for criticisms leveled against it:

1. Any forecasts using input-output are questionable due to time lags. Even though every action provokes a reaction, changes are not always immediate. Other changes in the interim may make it impossible to accurately predict the consequence of any action.

2. The production function used to derive employment multipliers, because it is based on a simple linear regression, may be a naive and rudimentary type of estimation. Economies of scale, separation into fixed and variable costs, and indivisibilities are not taken into consideration.

3. The assumption that excess capacity exists for the inputs used in production may not be realistic. The model assumes that increased

tourism can be simply absorbed by the economic system, and does not consider resource depletion as a limiting factor.

4. There may be a problem with sectorization or assigning a multiproduct firm to a specific sector. This problem can sometimes be handled through sector aggregation, but valuable information can also be lost through this process.

5. Since input-output is a static model which requires some time to construct, it provides only a snapshot view of a specific period in a region's economic history. If technology dramatically changes an industry's production function, the static input-output model cannot describe the impacts of that change.

6. Input-output cannot reveal interindustry linkages as a result of a new industry entering the region. If an industry not already represented in the region chooses to locate there, any previously constructed input-output model will be unable to predict the impacts on other sectors in the region.

7. Time and money required to construct an input-output model, especially if primary data are collected, may be prohibitive for a region without a large economic base. Although using previously developed models is one option to reduce time and cost, unfortunately few of these models are useful for tourism development purposes because the level of aggregation is too high, or tourists are not represented as an exogenous sector. Costs can be reduced by using non-survey-based input-output models or hybrid models (i.e., survey and non-survey combined). Many of these have been developed, and a summary of their advantages and disadvantages is provided in Erkkila and Penney (1992).

More sophisticated models using an input-output framework have been developed for measuring tourism's economic impact. The most promising of these is the Tourism Satellite Account (Campbell and Lapierre, 1991). This model seeks to establish a means to measure tourism's economic contribution to a region, identify the structure of the tourism industry, and assess tourism's impacts on the demographic, social, economic, and environmental resources of a region. Although this model promises to extend the use of input-output modeling beyond simple economic analysis, its data requirements, cost, and time involved in constructing such a model are prohibitive for many regions or countries. However, the reader who wishes to learn more about input-output advances for measuring tourism's quantifiable impacts is encouraged to review the literature on satellite account systems.

Economic Base

Early regional economic impact models were generally of the economic base variety. The implicit assumption behind this type of study is that exports fuel the economy and form the basis for regional economic growth. The analysis uses only two sectors, basic (EB) and non-basic (ENB). Employment in each sector is calculated, and the ratio of non-basic to basic employment determined (ENB/EB). Regional population (P) to total employment (E) is also calculated (P/E). At this point, future scenarios can be analyzed. Once a change in future basic employment (EB) is estimated, then future total employment ($^\wedge$E) and regional population ($^\wedge$P) can also be determined.

With the introduction of input-output models, economic base studies became generally ignored. They do not provide insights into industrial linkages within a regional economy, multipliers are not industry-specific as the analysis considers only two sectors (basic and non-basic), and the assumption that exports are the only means to increase regional income is invalid. However, economic base studies may be useful if the region is heavily dependent on one exporting industry. They are also easier and less expensive to calculate if employment data are available. The change predicted in employment is not always tied to expenditures, although one can imply a relationship between employment and expenditures.

Linkages between tourism and other regional industries are difficult to quantify. Although input-output analysis is one of the best models currently used to reveal interindustry linkages, it does not adequately handle an industry that exports experiences rather than tangible products. One could argue that because of tourism's uniqueness, that is, its different production and consumption patterns, it has been neglected as a true basic regional industry. This neglect has led to a search for methods that identify the economic importance of tourism as an industry and allow comparisons between it and other industries. Most studies focus on tourist expenditures; the amount of money tourists spend in an area is calculated and compared to money brought in through other industrial activity.

Diary Method

A commonly used method to collect expenditure information is the analysis of trip diaries. First, a sample of visitors is selected. Visitors are provided with a diary instrument and are asked to maintain a record of expenditures by day and purpose. After the trip is completed, the respondent returns the completed diary, usually by post. In addition to collecting expenditure information, diary data are often used to identify market origin, activity preference, and demographic characteristics of visitors. Although other sources and methods provide a simple estimate of expenditures in a region (e.g., tax information), ancillary information gleaned about the market makes diary instruments particulary advantageous.

Diary surveys also reduce the incidence of recall bias, or the inability of people to remember what they did and spent during a preceding time period (Howard et al., 1992; Perdue and Botkin, 1988). On the other hand, they have been criticized for increasing non-response bias, or people's unwillingness to complete or return diary surveys. The daily log or diary format usually produces low return rates which rarely exceed 30 percent of the sample (Perdue, 1985). When a majority of the sample choose not to respond, the risk is that non-respondent characteristics and expenditure patterns differ significantly from the respondent population. Any conclusions or recommendations based on these results may be seriously flawed. Low response may be partly attributed to asking people to record detailed information during their discretionary time. If completing the diary poses an intrusion into free time or if it asks for personal information, low response rates can be expected. Another criticism of the diary method is cost. Gartner and Hunt (1988) estimate the cost of each return at $10.58, very high compared to other forms of data collection.

Non-response and excessive cost problems can be significantly reduced through the use of front-end analysis (FE) (Gartner and Hunt, 1988). FE analysis utilizes a simple personal interview during diary distribution. If the sample population consists of visitors entering a region, four key questions are all that is necessary to complete the FE portion of the study. Questions are selected for the FE based on the probability of obtaining accurate answers. For example, if the sample population consists of visitors entering a region in private motor vehicles, answers to questions about party size (easily discernable by interviewer), type of vehicle (recorded by interviewer while approaching vehicle), expected length of stay (reported by the driver of vehicle), and purpose of trip (reported by driver) can be easily obtained. The FE information is then analyzed separately from diary results. To use the FE successfully, the diary instrument must contain the same questions used in the FE personal interview. FE results are then used to adjust diary results. The process is relatively straightforward. For example, FE results reveal how many people are traveling through the area for business purposes. If diary results reveal that business travelers have different expenditure patterns than pleasure travelers, FE data can provide the true proportion of business to vacation travelers, and diary results can be adjusted to reflect true sample proportions. This weighting procedure can be further used to adjust diary results by party size, type of vehicle, and length of stay.

Questions to include on the FE survey are based on two criteria. First, the expected random and systematic errors from question responses must be very low. Easily identifiable characteristics that can be recorded by the interviewer such as vehicle type and party size reduce the chance of erroneous data collection. The second criterion for selecting FE questions is the known or expected degree of variability for travel behavior between different groups of travelers. If previous research has revealed that business travelers differ in their expenditure patterns from pleasure travelers, then a question regarding purpose of trip is appropriate. An overview of how different types of tourists differ in their expenditure patterns is found later in this chapter, and provides support for utilization of a form of FE analysis whenever low survey response rates are expected.

The FE method also greatly reduces cost per response. Since data are collected from the entire sample, cost per response can be as low as $2.50, very competitive with other types of survey techniques. The FE method combined with a diary survey instrument can be used to collect detailed expenditure information, profile visitors, identify attractions, and at the same time greatly reduce recall and non-response bias at competitive data collection rates.

Although there is great political pressure to quantify the impact of every industry and rank each one in terms of its relative regional importance, in some cases there is less of a need to justify the industry than to monitor its progress. This may occur if the political system has already recognized the industry as valuable and one of the leading income producers. If the focus shifts from one of justification to one of monitoring for investment and policy purposes, then collecting detailed expenditure information or uncovering interindustry linkages may no longer be critical. In that case, indirect means of monitoring an industry's economic health may prove more important.

Barometers

A travel barometer is no more than an index of tourism activity. One widely known barometer used by the U.S. government is the Consumer Price Index (CPI), which measures the price change in a typical market basket of goods and services from one period to another. A travel barometer's primary purpose is to measure change in variables directly or indirectly related to tourism flows. In other words, it provides an index which, when viewed over time, measures increases or decreases in the level of tourism in an area. Travel barometers have been developed by the province of Nova Scotia (Nova Scotia Department of Tourism, 1975), as well as the states of Arizona (Bond and McDonald, 1978), Minnesota (Minnesota Department of Economic Development, 1975), and Michigan (Holecek et al., 1983). Advantages of developing travel barometers include:

INTERNATIONAL TOURISM TAXATION

The World Travel and Tourism Council estimated that by the end of 1995, international travel and tourism would account for approximately 10 percent of global Gross Domestic Product (GDP), 11.4 percent of global investment, and would generate over $655 billion in taxes. With an estimated output of $3.4 trillion, international travel and tourism ranks as one of the world's largest employers and industries. The political treatment of travel and tourism varies widely throughout the world. Fiscal policies can encourage or discourage travel volume and tourism development. Analyzing the way commonly consumed tourism services are taxed yields insight into the political and economic climate of a given tourism market.

Consumption taxes of the type discussed here are just one of many policy vehicles available to governments to raise revenue or modify behavior. Others such as personal and corporate income taxes, tariffs, and production based excise taxes, are equally important in developing a complete profile of fiscal policy as it relates to tourism.

Two types of consumption taxes typically apply to tourism services:

1. General consumption taxes such as the European value-added tax (VAT) and the North American sales tax apply to a wide variety of goods and services, and provide a primary source of government revenue. Throughout Europe, most of the Pacific Rim, and South America, general consumption taxes are administered at the national level. The United States government relies more heavily on

national income taxes for revenue; there is no national general consumption tax in the U.S. Sales tax collected in the U.S. is typically administered at the state and county level, though some larger cities such as New York levy their own general sales tax.

2. Selective consumption taxes are applied to a specific product or groups of products. Examples include an excise tax on sporting goods purchases whose proceeds help acquire additional public lands, or a tax on hotel rooms earmarked for tourism development. Selective taxation is generally established in order to:

    a. correct for externalities (e.g., infrastructure improvements) associated with the product's consumption or production.
    b. provide a collective (public) good that market exchange would not otherwise provide.
    c. erect barriers to consumption of internationally competitive goods and services (i.e., tariffs).

CONSTRUCTING A TRAVEL AND TOURISM TAX INDEX

A number of approaches and techniques may be employed in analyzing tax policy; the objectives of the analysis generally determine what tools to use. When analyzing the potential impact of a tax increase on demand, econometric techniques are often employed to estimate price elasticity of demand. When considering tax incidence and more normative issues, a combination of econometrics and case-study approaches may be used. Indices (barometers) are econometric tools used to describe changes in the level of a data series.

The World Travel and Tourism Tax Barometer (Tax Barometer) is a form of composite index. The composite elements may be characterized as a standardized trip consisting of standardized purchases, with prices and exchange rates fixed at the base year level (1994). The "trip" consists of an international arrival and departure from the airport, a four-night stay in a hotel room, a five-day car rental, and twelve full meals. The price data for the composite elements are either bought or derived from other secondary sources for each of 51 cities. The tax rate data are collected by survey from both the local Convention and Visitor Bureaus or the American Express Travel Service Office (TSO) in the destination.

To establish a base value, the tax rates are applied to the adjusted prices, providing an estimate of the total tax paid on the composite trip. The tax estimates are converted into U.S. dollar values, using exchange rates effective August 1, 1994. An estimate of each individual component of the index (lodging, car rental, meals, and air transport) and the composite is simply the sum of the estimated tax paid on each component.

CALCULATING CHANGES IN THE BAROMETER

In June of 1995, a second round of surveys was distributed to the 1994 sample. Respondents were asked to identify any changes in the tax rates that had occurred in the previous year.

The new rates could then be applied to the respective component price and a new tax amount in U.S. dollars estimated using the 1994 exchange rates. Dividing the new estimate by the base year estimate, then multiplying by 100, produces an index value for the city of interest. The general equation of the index is:

$$\frac{\sum \{(P_{ijt} \times T_{ijt}) + F_{ijt}\}}{\sum \{(P_{ij1994} \times T_{ij1994}) + F_{ij1994}\}} \times 100$$

P = price $\qquad$ T = tax rate $\quad$ F = fee

i = component $\quad$ j = city $\qquad$ t = time
good

Example:

1) In Mexico City, the prices in U.S. dollars, excluding taxes, for each of the components of the index in 1994 were:

Five-day car rental = $222.11

Four nights lodging = $662.19

12 meals = $128.97

These dollar values are based on an exchange rate of 1USD=3.40 MXP

2) The value-added tax rate on each of these services was 10 percent. Calculating the tax on each service yields:

Car rental:

$222.11 \times .10 = 22.21$

Lodging:

$662.19 \times .10 = 66.22$

Meals:

$128.97 \times .10 = 12.90$

(continued on next page)

In 1994, the Mexican government collected departure and arrival taxes totalling $11.85 per "trip."

3) The total tax estimate for the base year of 1994 is the sum of these values:

22.21+66.22+12.90+11.85 = 113.18

The tax index number for 1994 is

(113.18/113.18)×100 = 100

4) In 1995, the value-added tax rate was raised to 15%. To calculate the index value for 1995, the tax rate is applied to the 1994 prices at 1994 exchange rates:

Car rental:

222.11×.15 = 33.32

Lodging:

662.19×.15 = 99.33

Meals:

128.97×.15 = 19.35

In 1995, the Mexican government raised the international departure tax, bringing the total air passenger tax component of the index to $12.16.

5) The total estimated tax for 1995 is the sum of these values:

33.32+99.33+19.35+12.16 = 164.16

6) The tax index number for 1995 is
(164.16/113.18) × 100 = 145

The index number indicates that the total travel and tourism tax, holding exchange rates and prices constant, has increased by 45 percent from 1994 to 1995 in Mexico City.

Source: James Myers, Travel, Tourism and Recreation Resource Center, Michigan State University

1. The barometer concept provides a convenient grouping of diverse tourism related variables.

2. Barometers are ideally suited to measure the range and interactions of variables related to tourism activity. Once the relative importance of each variable is determined, it can be weighted to reflect its contribution in tourism activity.

3. Indices can be used to assess short-term changes as long as they cover a representative base period and recognize seasonality. For example, an increase or decrease from a previous period can be measured by comparing the index value for the two periods. The period for which change is to be measured is subject to available data.

4. Barometers, because they are an index, can be expressed in real

terms. For example, since expenditure estimates are reported in percentages, they can be easily adjusted for inflation. Assuming a 10-percent increase has occurred during the same period that 5-percent inflation was recorded, the real increase would be 5-percent.

5. Barometers can be published at periodic intervals. The only limiting factor is data availability (Bond and McDonald, 1978).

Variables used to construct a travel barometer can be grouped by those that measure tourism flows or those that measure tourist-related economic activity.

Tourism flow variables measure the movement of people into and through an area. For example, tourism flow variables record hotel/motel occupancy rates, passenger-vehicle traffic, attraction attendance, and information inquiries. Barometers using only tourism flow variables may provide misleading estimates of the magnitude of tourism increases/decreases in an area. For example, if visitation is up at national parks, one would naturally assume that tourism-sensitive economic activity would also be up. However, if national park visitors had reduced their length of stay significantly, this fact would not register in the barometer reading. Visitation may be up but economic returns could still be down. If there is more interest in social experience impacts, such as crowding and congestion than in levels of tourist generated economic activity, tourism flow variables may be the best indicators for measuring change. If, as is most often the case, the focus is on economic activity, then converting flow variables to economic impact changes remains troublesome.

Economic activity variables are appropriate if monitoring economic impact fluctuations is a high priority. They directly measure economic change in a region since they are sensitive to tourist spending. Examples of economic activity variables are special lodging taxes, sales tax receipts, admission fees, gasoline taxes, and tourism-sensitive businesses' gross sales receipts. The problem is that data pertaining to economic activity variables are not always available. Often, local governments choose whether and how much to charge for lodging taxes. A region comprising many municipalities often has difficulty determining an average room tax rate, if indeed one exists. To effectively use sales tax receipts requires breaking down local and tourist spending. A similar problem exists when using gross sales or taxes generated by tourism-sensitive businesses, although one could argue that once properly identified, percent of sales should remain relatively constant among residents and tourists patronizing these businesses. This relationship would only need to be reassessed if prevailing conditions change dramatically. Admission fees are appropriate if the bulk of tourist activity in a region is tied to attractions requiring them. Gasoline taxes may be a good indicator if one can rightly assume that local purchases remain constant over time at various price levels. Assuming some or all of the economic activity variables are relevant, they may better indicate economic change than the tourism flow variables discussed above.

Univariate Travel Barometers

Univariate, or one-variable travel barometers are the easiest to construct. They consist of a single variable that can be consistently measured, using it as a proxy to monitor overall tourism increases or decreases. Bond and McDonald (1978) construct a univariate barometer for the state of Arizona using a tourism flow variable based on attendance data for public and private tourism attractions. Unfortunately, univariate models measure only one facet of tourism. In the case of Arizona, tourism activity related to business travel, conventions, visiting friends and relatives, and any other form of tourism which does not appear in attendance data is not measured. Therefore, univariate barometers potentially introduce significant bias in estimating tourism change unless ratios between the measured variable and other important unmeasured variables remain the same.

A unique univariate travel barometer which avoids some of the above problems has been employed by Ocean City, Maryland since 1972. Called the "Demoflush," it measures the amount of sewage generated during a specific period, subtracts that number from what would be expected from the resident population, and divides the remainder by 36.04, which is the amount of estimated sewage generated each day by a tourist. The result is the number of tourists during the period under study (St. Paul Pioneer Press, June 1, 1991). Tourism barometers similar to the "Demoflush" model can provide accurate estimates of visitors, but still must be adjusted to derive expenditure information. No information yet exists on the economic impact of a "flush."

Multivariate Barometers

Multivariate models, as their name implies, employ more than one variable when attempting to measure tourism related increases or decreases. Monitoring more than one variable has the advantage of capturing changes in the different types of tourism in an area. Wyoming was the first state in the U.S. to employ a multivariate travel barometer (Phillips, 1977). Their approach, in existence since 1972, uses traffic counts (a tourism flow variable) and sales tax collections (an economic activity variable) for three tourism-sensitive businesses (gasoline service stations, commercial lodging, and campgrounds) as indicators of tourism within the state. Using 1970 data as the base year, annual tourism changes are calculated by subtracting the percentage increase or decrease for each variable in succeeding years, then averaging the change between the two variables. Sales tax data are also adjusted for inflation in order to reflect real change rather than inflationary change. The state is also divided into four regions, with separate barometers constructed for each one. Although this approach has merit in that it attempts to capture as much tourism activity as possible, it suffers from assuming that changes in two distinctly different variables are comparable, and that a composite change index can be developed by calculating an average change between the two.

The Michigan barometer model uses multiple regression techniques to estimate tourism change (Holecek, Slana, and Verbyla, 1983). The dependent variable, lodging sales and use taxes, is of the economic activity type, and the independent variables are of the tourism flow type. Tourism flow variables include traffic counts at selected locations, attendance at parks and campgrounds, and visitor counts at highway information centers. Although the dependent variable does not capture economic activity from travelers purchasing non-lodging goods or services, if the ratio of tourists using lodging establishments to those not using them remains constant, then the model will accurately predict change.

Criticisms of Barometer-type Models

Barometers are not intended to estimate economic impact, but rather to monitor industry changes on a periodic basis. A major criticism of barometer models is that they do not measure all touristic activity taking place within a region. While this criticism is valid, the development of barometers based on relationships and dependencies as in the Michigan model, indicate that direct measurement of all types of tourism do not have to be made in order to monitor change. This assumes that the proportions of different types of tourism activity within an area remain relatively constant. Obviously, this assumption is questionable, especially in the long run, since different sectors of the tourism industry adjust to market trends. Periodic research on the changing mix of tourism activity within an area can help analysts adjust barometer models in order to provide credible industry change information.

Another criticism of barometer models is their reliance on secondary data. Techniques utilized to collect data on attendance, traffic counts, lodging taxes, and other aspects have often been criticized for their lack of rigidity. For example, the USDA-Forest Service has historically used Resource Inventory Management (RIM) data for figures on use. Since actual monitoring of use is rarely undertaken, primarily due to cost constraints, RIM data are often a "best guess" estimate. Other publicly provided tourist attractions without staffed entrance booths may also be forced to guess attendance. Even mechanical devices such as traffic counters are subject to counting error, and in some cases close lightning strikes have erroneously recorded thousands more vehicles passing a certain point than actually did.

Almost every variable estimate, whether based on primary or secondary data, has some bias problem. The difference is that a researcher using secondary data stands the risk of inheriting unknown bias problems. However, these problems, even if potentially severe, do not render barometer models unusable if the errors inherent in data collection are consistent throughout each sampling period. RIM estimates, although questionable, are completely acceptable as barometers if the methods used to arrive at the "best guess" are constant for each estimating period. Barometers are indices and not measurements of actual tourism expenditures. Therefore, errors, if they occur on a predictable basis with constant magnitude, will not affect the calculation of percentage changes from one period to another.

One major advantage of tourism barometer models is that they allow tourism to be compared to any other industry which employs models to estimate changes in production. Travel barometers, therefore, provide one more means of economic measurement for an industry that has proven difficult at best to quantify and compare to other industries.

TOURIST TYPES AFFECTING ECONOMIC IMPACT

Tourists come in different shapes and sizes, and have different reasons for traveling. The type of tourist activity found in an area, where tourists come from, and how long they stay are likely to affect the magnitude of total economic impact. People from parts of the world with a strong currency (e.g., Japan) may engage in more shopping activity while traveling simply because the relative price of goods encountered during their trip represents a price saving over similar products at home. This, combined with cultural traditions which require gifts be brought back to friends and relatives, may make one group of tourists more economically important to a region than another. Reasons for a trip are also important indicators of economic impact.

PURPOSE OF TRIP

Trip purpose affects the level of tourist spending. Business travelers not only spend at different rates than pleasure travelers, but also demonstrate

different expenditure patterns. Broadbent (1989) reports that business travelers spend at twice the rate of pleasure travelers. Meeting and Convention
magazine (1990) asserts that the rate is closer to three to one in favor of
business travelers.

For many years, the Institute of Outdoor Recreation and Tourism at
Utah State University conducted surveys of visitors to the state of Utah.
Some of the findings revealed interesting expenditure patterns for different
types of tourists. Motor vehicle pleasure travelers, although accounting for
more expenditures in the state, actually spent less per person per visit than
business travelers. Percentage breakdowns by expenditure category indicated that for each dollar spent by the business traveler, almost 45 cents
went to retail goods and services. Pleasure travelers reported that only 16
cents of their dollar went to this category. Pleasure travelers were more
likely to spend a higher portion of their dollar for food, lodging, transportation, and entertainment.

Differences in expenditure patterns were also related to mode of
transportation used to enter the state. Tourists entering Utah via commercial air transportation spent, on a per-visit per-person basis, substantially
more than motor vehicle travelers. Expenditure categories were also much
different. Business travelers flying into the state spent a higher percentage
of each dollar for food, lodging, and transportation than pleasure travelers.
Pleasure travelers spent a higher percentage of each dollar for retail
goods, services, and entertainment than business travelers. These results
indicate almost a complete reversal of expenditure patterns between
purpose of trip for tourists driving versus those flying into the state (Table
3.5). One explanation for this reversal in expenditure patterns related
to the type of activities in which visitors flying into the state engaged.
The only major airport in Utah is in Salt Lake City, in close proximity
to major destination ski resorts. Further analysis of commercial air travelers to the state revealed that skiers spent almost twice as much as nonskiers.

The disparity in expenditures by mode of transportation and purpose
of trip reveals how economic impacts can fluctuate widely depending on
the type of tourists surveyed. Some of the differences can be accounted for
by area visited, as travelers into and out of Salt Lake City have a greater
opportunity to spend money in this heavily diversified economic region,
versus travelers to less populated rural areas where expenditure opportunities are more limited. The point of this discussion is simply to show that
whatever methods are used to derive economic impact or assess tourist related economic activity over time, there are bound to be major differences
in estimates unless the full range of activities, area of visitation, purpose of
trip, length of stay and mode of transportation are considered.

TABLE 3.5   **Expenditure Patterns by Mode of Transportation and Tourist Type**

| | Pleasure Travelers | | | |
| | Private Motor Vehicle | | Commercial Air | |
	Dollars (1980)	Percentage	Dollars (1979)	Percentage
Food	45,264,700	26.0	13,569,300	25.0
Lodging	40,544,400	22.5	14,025,900	25.9
Transportation	58,503,700	32.5	9,759,200	18.0
Retail and Services	29,566,600	16.4	11,681,200	21.6
Entertainment	5,834,000	3.2	5,153,400	9.5
Total Per Person/Per Visit	39.95	NA	177.03	NA
	Business Travelers			
Food	28,576,400	19.3	14,067,300	19.3
Lodging	19,944,300	13.5	16,439,400	13.5
Transportation	30,939,700	20.9	13,065,100	13.5
Retail and Services	67,361,800	45.6	5,797,300	45.6
Entertainment	1,021,300	0.7	481,100	0.7
Total Per Person/Per Visit	47.92	NA	106.36	NA

Source: Hunt, J. and G. Cadez. *Utah Tourism Motor Vehicle Travel Annual Report 1980–81* and *Utah Tourism Commercial Air Travel Annual Report 1979–80*. Institute of Outdoor Recreation and Tourism, Utah State University.

CONCLUSION

The purpose of this chapter is to provide a more detailed review of the different economic impacts that result from tourism development, and discuss methods and problems in estimating tourism's economic benefits. As mentioned in Chapter 1 and the introduction to this chapter, early studies attempted to justify tourism activity and development from an economic gains perspective. Later studies refuted many of the supposed benefits, and countered them with arguments identifying economic costs. One way of putting this chapter in perspective is to synthesize it in benefit/cost terms.

A benefit/cost ratio is simply a comparison of the economic benefits of an activity and the costs of providing that activity. A value greater than one indicates a positive flow of benefits, more than needed to offset costs of providing the activity. A benefit/cost analysis is usually conducted at the micro or firm level, as is the case when this subject is broached again in Chapter 9. At the macro level, larger than an individual property, benefit/cost analysis is prone to a great deal of unknowns and subjective interpretation. The problem rests primarily on the cost side of the ratio, although decisions must also be made about which benefits to count.

For the purpose of this conclusion, benefits are defined as local income (including taxes, wages, and profits to owners) generated from tourism activity in the region. Using some of the models or techniques discussed above (e.g., input–output, barometers) can help define either absolute magnitude or relative change in benefits. Depending on the degree of model complexity, benefit increases/decreases from a change in the present economic base of a region can also be estimated.

Costs are determined by calculating expenses borne by the region where the tourism activity takes place. Individual business costs of construction and operation are not used in the calculations, as they are not region-specific costs, but rather individual operation costs. Regional costs include infrastructure development, land purchase expenses, any monetary concessions made to entice new businesses, and costs of additional services. These costs can be estimated and amortized. The amortization process, also explained in Chapter 9, is important in that many communities or regions will issue bonds to pay for additional infrastructure improvements. The interest rate for those obligations is market determined and can be easily calculated.

Complicating the cost side of the equation is how non-monetary costs are estimated. What most regionally specific benefit/cost calculations do not consider are the environmental or social costs of increased development activity. The next two chapters demonstrate that environmental and social costs are often not easily quantifiable. They are also not immediately discernible, but subject to considerable lag effects. Due in part to the problem of assigning monetary values to many of these difficult to quantify costs, there are no valid regional benefit/cost analyses in the literature. Researchers have been able to develop different techniques to determine benefits, the more relevant of which are discussed in this chapter. Although the research community, fueled by interest group demand, continues to experiment with new techniques or spends time and money using existing techniques to estimate tourism's economic benefits, the cost side has been left to politicians and interest groups to debate. Because costs of tourism development do not explicitly recognize environmental or social costs, the political process is often relied on to determine those values. Having made this rather broad and, one could argue, inflammatory statement, the next two chapters attempt to synthesize what is known about tourism development's externalities.

EXECUTIVE SUMMARY

Tourism is a "basic" or export industry for a region, as it serves to bring in money for goods or services (including the tourist's experience) sold to non-residents.

Very few generalizations are valid when considering the economic benefits and costs of tourism development. Almost every beneficial claim has its negative counterpart. Each case must be decided on its own merits.

Rules used to delineate regions for economic analysis greatly affect the ultimate size of economic impact estimates.

An effective region contains political, sociocultural, economic, and physical features which interrelate to form a functioning system or "area of influence."

Different techniques, all with their own peculiar requirements, can be utilized to determine economic impact. The most commonly used are input-output models which produce different types of multipliers and allow for the examination of interindustry linkages.

Multipliers can be produced to show how much additional income, employment, or sales an additional unit of sales in a region will produce.

Univariate or multivariate barometers are appropriate when the focus shifts from estimating the total economic impact of tourism to indicating the direction (percentage up or down) the activity has taken.

Different types of tourists (e.g., business vs. pleasure) have different expenditure patterns, and as researchers need more detailed information, different techniques such as the Front End Diary Method become more important.

REFERENCES

Archer, B. 1976. The Anatomy of a Multiplier. *Regional Studies* 10:71-77.

Archer, B. 1984. Economic Impact: Misleading Multipliers. *Annals of Tourism Research* 11(3): 517-518.

Bendavis-Va, A. 1983. *Regional and Local Economic Analysis for Practitioners*. New York: Praeger Publishers.

Bishop, M. [1982] 1991. *No Enemy but Time*. Norwalk, Conn.: Easton Press.

Bond, M., and B. McDonald. 1978, Tourism Barometers: The Arizona Case. *Journal of Travel Research* 17(2):14-17.

Briassoulis, H. 1991. Methodological Issues: Tourism Input-Output Analysis. *Annals of Tourism Research* 18(3):485-495.

Broadbent, J. 1989. Business Travel, in S. Witt, ed. *Tourism Marketing and Management Handbook*. 104-105. New York: Prentice Hall.

Campbell, K. and J. Lapierre. 1991. Developing a Satellite Account and Information System for Tourism. *Tourism: Building Credibility for a Credible Industry*. Proceedings of the Travel and Tourism Research Association Annual Conference. Long Beach Calif.: Travel and Tourism Research Association.

Chappelle, D. 1989. Strategies for Developing Multipliers Useful in Assessing Economic Impacts of Recreation and Tourism. In *Assessing* the *Economic Impacts of Recreation and Tourism*. D. Propst, compiler. Asheville, N.C.: Southeastern Forest Experiment Station.

Choy, D. and C. Gee. 1985. Tourism in China: Five Years after China Opens its Gates. *Tourism Management* 4(2):85-93.

Darr, D. and R. Fight. 1974. *Douglas County Oregon: Potential Economic Impacts of a Changing Timber Resource Base*. Portland, Ore.: USDA-FS Pacific Forest and Range Experiment Station.

Davis, L. and J. Kennedy. 1980. *Economic Analysis for Forest Planning*. Logan, Utah: Utah State University.

Din, K. 1995. Tourism Development: Still in Search of a More Equitable Mode of Local Involvement. Paper presented at the June, 1995 meeting of the International Academy for the Study of Tourism, Cairo, Egypt.

Dunn, C. 1986, *A Guide to All China*. Lincolnwood, Ill.: Passport Book.

Erkkila, D. and C. Penney. 1992. *Tourism Impact Estimation Methods: A Literature Review*. St. Paul, Minn: Tourism Center, University of Minnesota.

Gartner, W. 1987. Environmental Impacts of Recreational Home Developments. *Annals of Tourism Research* 14(1):38-57.

Gartner, W. and D. Holecek. 1983. Economic Impact of an Annual Tourism Industry Exposition. *Annals of Tourism Research* 10(2):199-212.

Gartner, W. and J. Hunt. 1988. A Method to Collect Detailed Tourist Flow Information. *Annals of Tourism Research* 15(1):159-165.

Holecek, D., R. Slana, and D. Verbyla. 1983. Developing a Travel Activity Monitoring System for Michigan. East Lansing, Mich.: Parks and Recreation Resources, Michigan State University.

Howard, D., M. Havitz, S. Lankford, and F. Dimanche, 1992. Panel Survey Assessment of Elapsed Time Response Error in Travel Spending Measurement. *Journal of Hospitality and Leisure Marketing* 1(1):39-50.

Liu, J. 1986. Relative Economic Contributions of Visitor Groups in Hawaii. *Journal of Travel Research* 25(1):2-9.

Mak, J. 1989. The Economic Contribution of Travel to State Economies. *Journal of Travel Research* 28(2):3-5.

McIntosh, R., C. Goeldner, and J.R. Ritchie. 1994. *Tourism Principles, Practices and Philosophies*. 7th ed. New York: John Wiley and Sons, Inc.

Minnesota Department of Economic Development. 1975. The Economic Distribution of Tourism Travel Expenditures in Minnesota by Regions and Counties. *Research Bulletin 06*. St. Paul, Minn.: Department of Economic Development.

1990 Market Study. *Meeting and Convention Magazine* 11(1990):21-33.

Nova Scotia Department of Tourism. 1975. *Statistical Indicators Relating to Nova Scotia's Travel Industry 1973–74*. Halifax, Nova Scotia: Nova Scotia Department of Tourism.

Perdue, R. 1985. The 1983 Nebraska Visitor Survey: Achieving a High Response Rate with a Diary Questionnaire. *Journal of Travel Research* 24(2):23-26.

Perdue, R. and M. Botkin. 1988. Visitor Survey versus Conversion Study. *Annals of Tourism Research* 15(1):88-105.

Phillips, C. 1977. Barometer Increase Indicated. *Wyoming Travel Commission Travel Log* 17(6):1.

Richardson, H. 1972. *Input-Output and Regional Economics*. London: World University Press.

Mine opponents plan to be arrested at rally in Ladysmith. *St. Paul Pioneer Press*. July 6, 1991, 1A.

Stakes high over proposed test oil well. *St. Paul Pioneer Press*. July 7, 1991, 1B.

Tangi, M. 1979. Tourism and the Environment, in *Further Case Studies in Tourism*. London: Barrie and Jenkins.

Thurot, J. 1975. *Impact of Tourism in Socio-cultural Values*. Aix-en-Provence: Center for Tourism Studies.

U.S. Department of Commerce, Bureau of Economic Analysis. 1986. *Regional Multipliers: A Users Handbook for the Regional Input-Output Modeling System (RIMS II)*. Washington, D.C.: U.S. Government Printing Office.

Witt, S. 1991. Tourism in Cyprus: Balancing the Benefits and Costs. *Tourism Management* 12(1):37-46.

Environmental Impacts

Winter concentration of elk in Hardware Ranch, Utah,
has become a tourist attraction.
Photo by the author

Learning Objectives

Examine the factors affecting environmental change.

•

Examine different ecosystem types and the
impact of tourism development on the
environment in those areas.

•

Examine methods used to mitigate environmental
damage, with special emphasis on the concepts of
carrying capacity and Limits of Acceptable Change.

•

Explore the concept of ecotourism as a tourism
development alternative.

INTRODUCTION

Tourism protects the environment. Tourism destroys the environment. Which statement is true? Both statements are correct and defensible. African elephants, rhinos, mountain gorillas, lions, and other indigenous species are being protected and actively managed as an economic resource for tourism development. Each lion is estimated to be worth $27,000 annually, and an elephant herd's value is estimated at $610,000 per year (McNeely, 1988). Some believe that without tourism, many African animal species would be extinct from poaching and detrimental land settlement practices. While critics of tourism development concede that tourism does occasionally play a beneficial role in conserving certain species and ecosystems, they maintain that only those species with high aesthetic appeal to citizens of the developed world, such as the "charismatic megafauna" of Africa, are protected. Less appealing species are neglected and do not receive even token protection.

Those who oppose tourism development on ecological grounds cite examples of visitor overuse in the Mediterranean, the Adriatic, and other popular tourism destinations, resulting in declining water quality. Even in the managed African game parks, some have expressed concern over large numbers of visitors forcing certain predator species to switch from diurnal to nocturnal hunts to catch prey. One could argue that any form of tourism development negatively impacts the environment. If development requires any modification to the landscape, such as lodging construction or infrastructure development (e.g., roads), then the environment changes, most often permanently.

It is not the intent of this chapter to pass judgment on whether tourism is harmful or beneficial to the environment. Rather, it seeks to identify the forces behind environmental change, some of its impacts, and the measures undertaken to mitigate environmental degradation.

SOCIETAL FORCES AFFECTING ENVIRONMENTAL CHANGE

One of the primary tourism attractions is natural resources. Land, water, flora, and fauna are all included in this category. Travelers have always been attracted, physically or vicariously, to natural resources. In designating national parks and wilderness areas, society recognizes special natural resources deserving protected status. However, even designation as a unique ecosystem does not always ensure protection. As discussed in

Chapter 6, the United States Park Service is mandated to preserve, but at the same time allow public use of the parks. Prior to the advent of forces which unleashed mass tourism, this may not have been a difficult task. Today, natural areas all over the world are increasingly accessible to more and more people. The question of how to allow use while maintaining resource integrity has generated much debate. Restricting use is an option. Opponents of use restrictions argue that limiting use will lead to a situation where only the wealthy will be able to buy a natural experience. They argue that tourism based on natural resource use will become an elitist activity. Others argue that education focusing on people/land relationships is needed to ensure wise use and enjoyment of the resource. Numerous solutions have been proposed and tried with varying measures of success.

It is important to understand some of the root causes of environmental impacts before solutions can be proposed. Filani (1975) cites three societal changes that have drastically affected environmental integrity. Although this study was conducted over 20 years ago, the forces affecting environmental quality remain largely unchanged:

1. Rapid population growth, which has led to an ever-increasing demand for further exploitation of renewable and non-renewable resources;

2. Increasing industrial growth, which has accelerated the rate of air and water pollution;

3. The general lack of public awareness of the value of natural resources, especially fauna and flora, and man's limited knowledge of the complex system of interacting processes and interdependent components of the environment.

Environmental impacts result from two forces often acting in concert. The first cause lays the blame on the tourist and the second on the industry serving the tourist.

Tourist-Generated Impacts

Hardin (1968) describes the communal use of grazing lands for livestock production, a situation where a finite amount of resources is used to provide a livelihood for many members of a community. The assumption under which all users of the resource operate is that the land base can only support a limited number of animals and still maintain its viability. Any one individual using communal grazing lands knows the value of the livestock he/she owns. The price of each animal is market determined. An individual may choose to add an additional animal, enjoying the economic gain but also understanding that any increase will negatively impact communal grazing lands (assuming they are now being used to capacity). The individual gains, but all users of the resource bear the cost. Assuming that the additional animal can be sold for $100, that will be the gain which accrues to the individual; the loss resulting from overuse of the resource may not be immediately apparent, but will be shared by all. Therefore, the individual reaps the economic reward from this detrimental activity but only has to pay a portion of the costs. The economic incentive is in place for all resource users to act in a similar manner, resulting in resource depletion and eventual destruction of the resource on which all depend for survival. Hardin calls this behavior the "tragedy of the commons." Pursuit of individual gain results in total loss for all.

Although this example applies to communal grazing lands, the extension to tourism is direct. Snorkeling and diving on coral reefs is a popular activity for many "sunlust" tourists. Coral reefs are living ecosystems. The coral themselves are part of the invertebrate family of organisms. They exude a calcium-based substance which forms the reef and protects the coral animal which lives inside this exoskeleton. It takes years for a coral ecosystem to form. Standing on a coral reef while swimming or diving can break coral into pieces. While this impact may not appear too severe to casual tourists (after all, they are only there for one week), the thousands of tourists who do the same thing can cause the entire ecosystem to collapse. Tourists may also wish to take some of the beautiful coral pieces home as souvenirs. Unfortunately, in some instances members of the host society have dynamited reefs to collect coral for the tourist trade. Again, the tourist perceives no harm in buying one piece of coral, forgetting the thousands of other tourists who feel the same way. Eventually, the coral reef is fully exploited, reducing the quality of the experience for all. Similar environmental damage occurs in other ecosystems. Camping in nondesignated areas may result in soil compaction, vegetation damage, and other visible scars on the land. Continued use of the same site only exacerbates the situation.

Tourists may be blamed for the "tragedy of the commons," but they often differ from the group in Hardin's example in a very important way. Whereas the users of the communal grazing land know a biological carrying capacity exists, tourists may not be aware of the environmental consequences of their actions. One time or occasional visitors may have no historical frame of reference from which to evaluate change. For all they know, their actions have no effect on the environment. What they see is what exists and has existed. Only when the ecosystem shows serious signs of destruction does a problem become apparent. In many cases it may be too late to save the resource. Assuming that every area has a carrying capacity, a concept that will be discussed in more detail later in this chapter, it is only when capacity has been exceeded that major environmental damage results. In natural environments, damage may only appear after carrying capacity has been greatly exceeded.

Anyone who has raised tropical fish can understand this argument. A closed ecosystem such as a fish tank has to process waste from the living organisms it contains. Under normal conditions, a complex process involving beneficial bacteria breaks down noxious wastes into harmless by-products. If too many fish are added to the tank, the beneficial bacteria cannot keep up with the nutrient load. After a period of time some of the beneficial bacteria die, contributing even more pollution to the tank and setting off a chain reaction often resulting in the overnight death of all tank inhabitants. In the morning, the tropical fish enthusiast realizes the tank's carrying capacity has been exceeded, but it is too late to take corrective action.

To an extent, tourism also operates in a closed environment. Once infrastructure and superstructure are in place it is almost impossible to reverse the direction of development. The level of development may greatly exceed the area's carrying capacity, but negative impacts may not appear in some ecosystems until after a few years of operation. Even when there is no indication of potential environmental change, a naturally occurring phenomenon can unleash disastrous results. In the Lake Pepin area, located on the Mississippi River between the states of Minnesota and Wisconsin, phosphate discharge levels from municipal sewage treatment and agricultural runoff collected for years in the soil sediment at the bottom of the lake. In 1988, a severe drought reduced the flow of water through the lake. In normal years, water takes nine days to make its way through the lake and down the river, but during the drought year, it took 60 days. This slow movement of water, coupled with winds which stirred up the sediment in the lake, resulted in an algae bloom, reducing oxygen levels and killing large amounts of fish and vegetation (Laszewski, 1992). It also made the lake, an important recreation area supporting the tourism industry of many small towns, an unsightly place to visit and use.

Environmental carrying capacity has clearly been exceeded when tourists are no longer attracted to the natural resource base of the area. At that point, the area has two choices. First, it can reverse the flow of development, but, as previously mentioned, this rarely happens. More often, a concerted effort is undertaken to transform the attraction base from one dependent on natural resources to one dependent on manmade attractions.

Often environmental damage is accepted as a consequence of tourists' actions. Instead of correcting environmental problems by imposing use limits, technical solutions are usually sought. Hardin (1968:16) defines a technical solution as "one that requires a change only in the techniques of the natural sciences, demanding little or nothing in the way of changes in human values or ideas in morality." Lakes entering the eutrophic stage of their life cycle due to excessive nutrient loads brought on prematurely by lakeshore developments and subsequent septic tank seepage generally produce large amounts of weeds. Weeds can be temporarily eradicated through harvesting or herbicide treatment, both technical solutions. Chemical treatment or mechanical harvesting does not eliminate the systemic problem of too much shoreline development; it just treats the symptoms. While some technical solutions such as sewage treatment plants have the potential to extend environmental carrying capacity, others only postpone the inevitable.

Some argue that tourists should be absolved from environmental damage on the grounds of ignorance. After all, unless the tourist is a frequent visitor, he/she will probably not notice a deteriorating condition. This is not true of destination residents, however. They not only see deteriorating conditions but they are negatively impacted by them. Why don't they act? In some cases, those impacted are not part of the political process. Others may be trapped in an economic vise. Liu and Var (1986), studying residents of Hawaii, found that for the most part they regard environmental protection as more critical than economic growth. However, they are unwilling to reduce their standard of living in order to protect their environmental surroundings—another example of the "tragedy of the commons." When residents do not act to prevent environmental damage simply because action may compromise a source of income, it poses an interesting question. How much blame should be placed on the shoulders of tourists and tourism development for negative environmental change versus the level of responsibility borne by local residents? This question has no clear-cut answer, but it does drive the issues surrounding methods, presented later, that can be used to mitigate negative environmental impacts.

Industry–Generated Impacts

It is assumed that businesses operate in an environment of uncertainty. Exogenous forces such as economic recessions, government policy shifts, or changes in consumer tastes and preferences affect business operations. Three assumptions underlie the "tragedy of the commons." First, individuals operate in their own best interest, disregarding the consequences of their action on the community. Second, when faced with an opportunity to maximize utility (in the case of a business enterprise, profit maximization is the rule) individuals will choose the course of action that results in utility maximization. Third, the consequences of the above two actions bring ruin to all. Fife (1971) argues that the first two assumptions are valid, especially as regards business operations, but the third assumption must be relaxed. Some businesses are aware of product and destination life cycles (see Chapters 1 and 10 for more discussion on product life cycles). Because they operate in an uncertain business environment and they do not know when the area will enter the maturation stage of the life cycle, they choose to operate their business in a manner that maximizes profits. Even though the area itself may suffer from environmental degradation, the businesses that feed off the tourist expenditures profit. Any slowdown in activity intended to lessen environmental impact will be opposed on economic grounds. Those businesses with the ability to foresee the "tragedy of the commons" will sell and move on shortly before the damage is serious enough to reduce revenues.

Gartner (1987) describes a case, termed keyhole access, in recreational home subdivisions in northern Michigan. Recreational home developers, reacting to market demand for seasonal homes, purchased undeveloped land along inland lake shorelines. Prices for homes with lake access greatly exceeded prices charged for land without lake access. Initially, homes were developed around the lake and sold. Since these homes were located in rural areas, septic tank systems were installed to handle waste. Gradually, nutrient seepage from septic systems migrated to the lake and accelerated the process of lake aging. Eutrophication of the lake systems was the inevitable outcome. However, since this process is slow to occur, the lakes were still in the oligotrophic or mesotrophic stage when the lake homes were sold. Developers, understanding the market demand for homes with lake access, withheld some lake access lots from sale. When all lake access lots were developed or sold, the developers cut canals into the lake where the retained lots were located. They cut canals perpendicular to the main canal, and additional homes were constructed along these feeder canals. This arrangement is known as keyhole access (see Figure 4.1). Homes located on the canals did not command as much market value as similar homes constructed directly on lake shoreline, but they were considerably more expensive than those without some type of lake access. Each additional home along the canals contributed nutrients to the lake, thus further accelerating the process of eutrophication. By the time environmental problem became a noticeable nuisance, the developers had finished with the project, leaving the community and second homeowners to contend with the negative impacts. Thus, operating a business to maximize short-run profits can prove beneficial to the owner of the business, and detrimental to those who have to deal with the consequences. Market based economies that ignore external costs and businesses that are operated irresponsibly (e.g., exacerbating environmental impacts) contribute to the "tragedy of the commons," but only for those unable to perceive the long-term consequences of a course of action.

This discussion of industry generated impacts has focused, almost exclusively, on businesses operating in the destination area. The distribution system for tourism is large and complex, including diverse businesses such

Figure 4.1 *Keyhole Access*

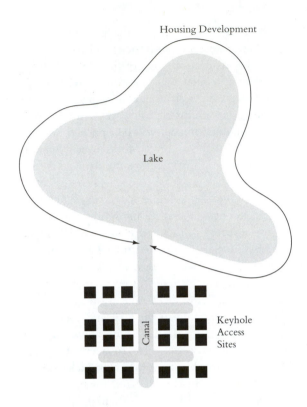

as tourisiers (e.g., wholesalers, brokers), transportation, (e.g., airlines), and so on. Each element in the distribution chain benefits from increased business. While environmental impacts do concern many of those working in tourism, it is not much of a concern when they occur somewhere else. For example, an airline company's primary concern is to move people to where they want to go, assuming the company has obtained landing rights in the destination. This chapter began with a discussion of the economic value of African elephants. Those values are partly derived from tourist demand for viewing elephants. Should it concern the airline company if overuse threatens the biological diversity needed to sustain an elephant herd? One could argue that environmental change may eventually result in fewer tourists to the African savannah parks, but if airline A eliminates flights to reduce an overcapacity situation, airline B will pick up the slack. The same damage occurs, but airline A pays a price for its altruistic stand through lost revenues. Obviously, the above scenario is not realistic. Most reasonable people would argue that it is the responsibility of the host society represented through its political process to make decisions about how much tourism is enough. This is difficult enough in developed countries, but is compounded by conditions existing in the developing world, especially where overpopulation and a lack of other income generating industries prevail. Any curtailment of tourism to protect an environmental resource may also reduce the flow of much needed foreign exchange. This discussion could continue along these lines indefinitely, but the point is that industry-generated impacts are not confined to just those businesses located on site, but are intensified by all those businesses operating in the distribution chain.

FACTORS AFFECTING ENVIRONMENTAL IMPACTS

A variety of factors affects ecosystem viability. Not all ecosystems react to change in the same way. The unique qualities of each ecosystem in part determine the level of environmental degradation associated with use. Some types of use affect some ecosystems more than others. Cohen (1978) has identified four factors contributing to the environmental impact of tourism developments:

1. The intensity of tourist site use and development;

2. The resiliency of the ecosystem;

3. The time perspective of the developer;

4. The transformational character of tourist development.

Intensity of Site Use

Intensity of site use is determined by the number of tourists visiting an area, their length of stay, what they do, and the level of development in place to meet tourists' needs. The level of physical development required to accommodate tourists increases at an accelerating rate after critical mass has been reached. In physics, critical mass is the amount of radioactive material required to start a chain reaction. In tourism, it can be defined as the number of tourists required to start site transformation. Almost any ecosystem can accommodate a certain number of visitors before existing facilities and infrastructure prove inadequate. Once an area reaches critical mass, it undergoes a rapid and unidirectional transformation that accelerates the environmental impacts concurrently with this increase in development.

Studies comparing regional tourist statistics often use the number of visitors as their common denominator. However, the number of visitors times the average length of visit provides a better measure of environmental pressure, since the potential for environmental damage is a function of how many people visit a site coupled with how long they stay. If two areas host the same number of tourists, but length of stay in one area is double that of the other, then intensity of site use for the two areas is not the same. Some tourist groups have been known to fly into an area, take pictures, and fly out; total time on site may be only a few hours. Most tourist statistics are based on entry/exit counts. For example, it is easy to calculate the total number of visitors if a visa is needed to enter a country or an exit tax is collected. Similarly, if an attraction charges entrance fees, total attendance numbers are readily available. However, determining how long tourists stay within an area is slightly more difficult and usually requires that the tourist complete some form of survey.

Even when total visitation adjusted for length of stay is known, potential environmental impact must be modified by the types of activities in which the tourists engage. Passive activities (e.g., birdwatching) are usually less damaging to an area than activities which require major land transformation such as building a golf course. Passive activities also provide a greater opportunity to manage environmental values. If too much birdwatching activity proves detrimental to nesting success, controls can be implemented to allow only so many people to visit during specific periods. On the other hand, if the new golf course drastically reduces water quality through pesticide and fertilizer run-off, it is almost impossible to return the land to its natural state. Economic factors alone prevent this from happening. Even when attempts are made to restore an area to a natural state, the site may not be restorable. Transformation may have changed the previous ecosystem relationships dramatically and irreversibly.

Certain ecosystems lend themselves to certain types of activities. Tropical islands, warm climates and beaches invariably lend themselves to "sunlust" tourism. Developers in these areas recognize these attractions

Disregard for natural processes has led to improper development and subsequent property loss in environmentally sensitive areas. Photographer unknown

and locate facilities in close proximity to the beach. "Sunlust" tourists are generally not as sensitive to the presence of other tourists as in some different types of activities. Therefore, the large number of tourists which can be accommodated before friction between tourists themselves becomes problematic allows for greater facility development. If the area has a powerful draw, sometimes supported by major marketing campaigns, there will be pressure to increase facility development, resulting in greater site use. The only constraint on use may be the lack of land available for further facility development. When this happens, development radiates outward along the coast from the original staging area (see Chapter 12).

In addition to spreading outward, development may also spread upward. High-rise hotels maximize the use of small beach frontage. More people can be accommodated on less land, increasing the intensity of site use. For years, beach frontage on Waikiki, Honolulu, was touted as the most expensive property in the world. That claim is now made for the Ginza strip in Tokyo, but visitors to Waikiki can readily see why land is so expensive along the beach; high-rise hotels dominate the coastal view. High-rise developments shift land value, increasing it for properties on the beach and reducing it for those located behind them. This claim may seem hard to substantiate if anyone has ever inquired about purchasing a hotel in Waikiki, but one can measure land values indirectly by comparing room rates of hotels on and off the beach. Environmental impacts of high-rise developments appear in the form of land transformation and visual impairment. Ocean views are blocked for all local residents and hotel guests who can not afford the cost of a room in a high-rise beach front hotel.

Development may also determine the type of activities engaged in by tourists. In this case, planners assess the attraction potential of the area, determine activity opportunities, and select a scale of development which encourages certain activities and discourages others. This is the approach advocated by proponents of ecotourism developments, and will be discussed later in this chapter.

Resiliency of the Ecosystem

Each ecosystem is different. Some can withstand enormous pressure without showing signs of deterioration. In others, small changes result in major disruption. In the western United States, a horse trail used by mail carriers (pony express) for only two years (1860–61) is still visible as it cuts across the plains of Wyoming; historical markers commemorate this early form of mail service. The climate in that part of the United States is arid, with less than ten inches of precipitation annually. Any type of development in this region has the potential to drastically change the character of the ecosystem for centuries. Other parts of the United States receive over thirty inches of precipitation a year, that, coupled with a moderate climate and loamy soil, quickly erases the remains of any prior land use. This discussion is not meant to discourage tourism development in areas with low resiliency. Those areas may have natural resource attractions which are in demand by tourists and can be developed appropriately. In the development planning stage, ecosystem resiliency must be considered and action taken to prevent undesirable changes that in some cases may be permanent.

Resiliency is also a function of scarcity. The less abundant a resource or ecosystem, the more valuable it is, and the more likely it is to be viewed as less resilient to any change. Grandeur often determines scarcity. For example, the Grand Canyon or the gothic cathedrals cannot be replaced or replicated, and their unique status guarantees them governmental protection. Some may argue that national park or historic site designation puts resources at risk from overuse, but without formal protection, they are more likely to be transformed forever. Resources at risk from all forms of development are small villages, fragile coastal zones, or minor architecture which do not have the grandeur or perceived scarcity to receive formal protection (Tarr, 1987).

Since ecosystems differ in their level of resiliency, the rest of this section discusses the types of environmental impacts which certain activities create in particular ecosystems. However, it is not meant to be inclusive of all possible environmental impacts resulting from tourism development.

Islands

Tropical island environments are depicted as paradise in the paintings of Gauguin and the writings of 19th-century novelists such as Melville (*Typee*) and Hudson (*Green Mansions*). The climatic conditions which they found so appealing (the native inhabitants are not so pleasantly portrayed) are the same that attract New World tourists. "In economic terms those countries in which tourism contributes to the highest share of gross domestic product and are therefore most dependent on tourism are, almost without exception, islands" (Shackleford, 1995).

The types of activities many tropical island visitors enjoy lend themselves to mass tourism. Sun-, sea-, sand-, and sex-focused advertising has been a staple of tropical island destination promotion for years. Swimming and sunbathing are activities that many people crowded together in relatively little space can enjoy. This type of mass tourism has the potential to create numerous environmental problems. Tourists in tropical island resorts use large quantities of fresh water for bathing, both to remove salt residue from ocean swimming and as a refreshing, cooling respite from the tropical climate. Studies show that tourists' use of fresh water at tropical island resorts greatly exceeds the per capita consumption of local people. In Barbados, tourist per capita consumption of water is between six and ten times higher than that of the local population (Gajraj, 1989). Fresh water is not generally found in abundant supply in island ecosystems. Large-scale desalinization plants or excessive consumption of local sources of fresh water not only increase the expense of providing fresh water, but may actually exclude other forms of industrial activity from developing. If the tropical resort offers other activities such as golfing, fresh water consumption can increase dramatically during dry seasons. Obtaining fresh water from wells drilled into aquifers can cause cones of depression to develop, resulting in salt water intrusion or sinkholes.

Adequate sewage treatment also requires fresh water. The large number of people attracted to tropical island resorts generates great amounts of waste. The use of salt water in septic systems prevents adequate biological breakdown of waste, and when discharged into a marine environment, may cause detrimental impacts on marine life (Clare, 1971; from Mathieson and Wall, 1982:115). Many of the early tropical island resorts did not even bother to treat sewage, choosing instead to dump it directly into the ocean. If the discharge location is poorly chosen, massive amounts of sewage remain in one location, drastically reducing biological diversity. Swimming areas can be polluted through indiscriminate sewage dumping, raising fecal coliform counts beyond accepted standards and causing health problems for swimmers.

Other types of environmental impacts associated with tropical island resort developments include the destruction of protective sand dune barriers. Facility construction or even excessive walking on barrier dunes can destroy the vegetation which anchors the dune, resulting in beach erosion (Lavery and Van Doren, 1990). Sometimes breakwaters (concrete or rock called riprap) which extend out into the ocean are built with the intent of stabilizing coastal ecosystems. These breakwaters not only create visual pollution, but have been shown to shift erosion from one place to another. Solid waste disposal also creates problems. If ground water reserves are located close to the surface of the land, solid waste landfills can leach pollutants into fresh water aquifers. Burning solid waste does not necessarily solve this problem, as it turns one form of pollution into another.

Impacts on animal life are also a concern. Facility construction may destroy sea turtle nesting sites, and excessive human pressure may reduce success in prime nesting areas. The Grafton Resort in Tobago provides an example of a recent development which is trying to coexist with sea turtles. Access to the beach is restricted during early morning hours when sea turtles use the area for nesting. Guests wishing to view the turtles register with the front desk. When a turtle is sighted, guests are paged and a resort staff member accompanies them to the beach to observe the turtles. Flashlights and cameras are used only under restricted conditions in order to disturb the turtles as little as possible. By most accounts, this is a successful program accomplished with few restrictions, an educational program to encourage cooperation, and the expansion of guest services to offer new experiential opportunities for visitors. As the impacts of human activity on native species become more understood, programs of this type will be more widely adopted.

Impacts on coral reefs as a result of human activity are addressed above, but other forms of animal life may also suffer from increased development. Over-fishing certain species to satisfy tourists' desire for local foods may be a problem. Some species of birds may increase in numbers (i.e., seagulls feeding off garbage) and others may decline. Since every animal species reacts to increasing use in different ways, it is almost impossible to predict the extent of environmental damage to an ecosystem without careful study. In many cases, it is only after physical development that detrimental impacts are noted and studied.

A simple solution would be to impose a moratorium on further tourism development until all environmental impacts from any proposed development are known. In fact, many countries and smaller political subdivisions require the completion of environmental impact statements or environmental assessments before they issue permits for development. However, these processes, which can be costly both in terms of money and time, do not provide guarantees against environmental damage. Too much remains unknown about ecosystem dependencies. As a general rule of thumb, the smaller the ecosystem, the higher the risk of environmental change when ecosystem linkages are disrupted. Because of their size, island ecosystems are especially vulnerable to change, and require greater attention to the type of developments proposed. Rather than a moratorium on development before all impacts are understood, an unrealistic expectation, increased emphasis on environmental management, including periodic monitoring, is necessary.

Coastlines

Coastline developments are similar to island developments with respect to the types of impacts created. The main difference is that where islands may only have limited resources (e.g., fresh water) to handle the influx of tourists, coastline developments often have greater access to a larger supply of resources. Coastline developments may be able to use rail service to transport compacted waste to a central location built specifically to deal with solid waste disposal. This central location may serve many areas in the region.

In the Florida Keys, a series of islands connected to the mainland by U.S. Highway 1, over 150 miles of pipelines transport fresh water from the mainland to communities. In the early 1970s, the amount of water that could be transported was insufficient to handle the demand, causing periodic system shutdowns. Some restaurants were unable to wash dishes, forcing unscheduled closures. Residents and tourists were equally inconvenienced. If this problem occurred on a remote island, the impact would be more severe. The problem, however, was resolved through a technical solution, constructing another pipeline to increase supply.

The environmental impacts of coastline tourism developments result from two different types of tourist activity. One is the inherent attractiveness of coastlines, resulting in common forms of beach activities and associated development to accommodate tourist demands. The other is related to access points for tourists. Technological advances in the airline industry make ocean crossing cheaper and faster. Previously, transoceanic travel by passenger or freight ship meant that tourist facilities were constructed at ports of call. Patterns of development similar to those occurring today around airports resulted, although not on the same scale. Environmental impacts included land transformation and raw sewage discharge into the marine environment, increasing the incidence of illness for bathers and causing major algae blooms which spoiled the aesthetic qualities of some areas.

When dealing with water quality issues, not all pollutant sources are easily identifiable. Point sources of pollution are those which discharge directly into the water (e.g., sewage outflows, industrial waste discharge). Non-point sources are more difficult to identify and control, stemming from homes, businesses (e.g., resorts), and farm fertilizer and pesticide use. Excess nutrients or pesticides can move through the watershed into rivers, streams, or groundwater, ending up in a lake or sea. Non-point pollution, because it is difficult to identify, poses more of a long-term threat to water quality than point sources. Coastal areas generally have sandy soils which transport fertilizer and pesticide residue more readily into ground or surface water supplies. Tourism developments which place a high premium on aesthetic surroundings (e.g., landscaped lawns and gardens) and developed recreation facilities (e.g., golf courses), and require high and constant applications of fertilizer and pesticides may be prime contributors to non-point source pollution problems.

Coastal areas, especially in warm humid regions, were uninhabited for years because they were considered unhealthy environments. Malaria and yellow fever were more often associated with the "bad air" of coastal marshes than the mosquitos that carry disease. When mosquitos were identified as the culprit, chemical pesticides were applied to control the problem (another technical solution). Coastal marshes throughout the world were then drained, or filled and developed for other uses such as tourism. In some cases, certain animal and vegetative species were completely eradicated. It wasn't until the publication of Rachel Carson's *Silent Spring* in 1962 that the environmental consequences on wildlife populations resulting from widespread pesticide application became a public concern in the United States. Thirty years later, new forms of pesticides are being used to control resistant strains of mosquitos and other undesirable insects. Meanwhile, marshes continue to be drained for all types of development. The beneficial qualities of marshes, usually considered wasteland and easily filled or drained for development, are becoming more understood. It is increasingly evident that marshes are efficient biological filters able to neutralize many of the harmful substances humans have haphazardly and cavalierly dumped into the environment. They also possess significant flood control properties. Various local, regional, and national governments throughout the world are now beginning to address marshland development policies.

Two specific environmental benefits result from tourism development in coastal areas. First, where private ownership of the coastline occurs, very little public access to the resources is possible. Tourism development can open up part of the coastline for public use. This is not always the case, as some private developments exclude public use of the resource. To counter this practice, some countries have enacted legislation which prohibits any coastal development from restricting beach access. Secondly, tourism development gives the resource political and economic value. This is especially important for fragile or otherwise endangered ecosystems. It helps make conservation and preservation politically defensible (Hudman, 1980).

High Elevations

High elevations include mountainous areas as well as expansive plains. Climatic extremes are characteristic of high altitude areas, making them quality tourism development areas but also rendering them susceptible to environmental damage. Mountainous areas in close proximity to urban centers are prime ski resort locations, and large amounts of snowfall and low average temperatures for long periods provide opportunities for the development of a ski industry. Obvious environmental impacts are the construction of ski trails and ski lifts needed to move people up the mountain. Trees must be cut, leaving visible scars on the land which become most noticeable during the summer season. If care is not exercised in the construction of the lifts or trails, erosion may result. Removing trees also increases the incidence of avalanches. If a development is abandoned, the area may not be able to be restored without careful and expensive attention. The long winter climate, which makes mountainous areas prime for ski development, also reduces their ability to regenerate quickly.

Many facilities servicing skiers are located in mountain valley areas. Mountain valleys are susceptible to air inversions, especially during winter months. Inversions are caused when a high pressure weather system locates over a valley which is surrounded by mountains. The high pressure prevents airborne pollutants from escaping into the upper atmosphere and being dispersed by the jet stream. Normal human activity such as driving an automobile, using a fireplace, or heating buildings contributes to airborne pollutants. Winter periods, when inversions are most likely to occur, coincide with high use periods at mountain ski resorts. The resulting smog created by an inversion has visible aesthetic as well as invisible health implications.

Wildlife migratory patterns can also be disrupted by development in high elevation areas. Certain wildlife species have summer and winter ranges. Winter ranges are found in the lower elevations as snow cover reduces food stocks higher up. Development often concentrates in lower elevations, thus reducing the amount of winter range available for wildlife. Man/wildlife conflicts are common in the winter range zone, with the wildlife population usually ending up on the short end of any solution.

Skiing is not the only activity in high elevation areas. Hiking is also common, and in some areas an extensive road system accommodates tourists who prefer to view scenic areas from behind a windshield. Again, because of the inability of high elevation areas to restore themselves quickly, development scars are long-lasting. Road construction can contribute to erosion, and rains wash oil and other residue from highways into streams and rivers. Hikers may leave waste behind, and depending on the prevailing microclimate, it could remain intact for archaeologists centuries from now to ponder over the slovenly practices of 20th-century humans. Areas in the Himalayas have accumulated so much trash (e.g., human feces and other solid waste) that expeditions have to be arranged to clean up the garbage piles.

High plains are also susceptible to long-lasting environmental damage. The example of the pony express trail mentioned above demonstrates how even short-term uses can result in long-term consequences. Many consider high plains to be similar to marsh environments—that is, wasteland with few redeeming qualities. Because high plains experience extreme climatic conditions, the flora and fauna in these environments have adapted specialized survival features. Certain plant species may constitute the majority of a particular animal's diet. Development in these areas may introduce exotic species into the environment, upsetting the ecological balance. Agricultural development in the plains of Canada and the northern United States has been credited with creating environments conducive to raccoon and fox populations. Since these species are not native to these regions, certain animals such as waterfowl have not evolved effective coping behavior making them easy prey.

Tourism developments, although historically not common throughout high plains regions, are becoming increasingly viewed as economic opportunities. Dude ranches in the United States are one example. Very little information exists to document the environmental impacts of tourism in high plains regions, but the fragility of these ecosystems indicates that any type of development is bound to have significant impacts.

Deserts

Deserts are preferred tourism development areas for many reasons. Depending on their location with respect to latitude and elevation, many deserts have warm climates year-round, low average annual precipitation, and due to the paucity of vegetative life, present relatively few allergy problems for people. The population growth in the southwestern United States, especially in Arizona and southern California, attests to the attractive potential of deserts. Technology and massive infrastructure development make it possible to bring water to deserts. Resorts and retirement communities have developed in response to the increased supply of water. One of the attractions for desert resorts is the opportunity to play golf almost on a year-round basis. The amount of water use for golf courses, coupled with water use for lawns and gardens in new resort communities, has been implicated in microclimate change. Increased humidity levels, much higher than long-term averages, have decreased comfort levels and heightened energy demand for indoor climate control devices (e.g., air conditioners, swamp coolers).

Agricultural enterprises serving new desert communities and providing excess supply for export have also developed in response to increasing water supplies. Farming the desert is now common practice. Lack of water is the primary reason deserts did not witness much development until the last quarter of this century. Bringing water to deserts usually involves damming rivers to form large supply reservoirs which are also used to generate hydroelectric power for new developments. Reducing natural river flows has resulted in habitat destruction for certain river fish (e.g., Colorado chub), putting them on the endangered species list. Also, small, naturally occurring ponds in the deserts of southwestern North America are home to the desert pup fish, a very small fish with unique ecosystem requirements. The transformation which development brings to the desert has severely impacted this species.

Deserts, like other ecosystems with extreme climatic conditions, have developed unique plant and animal species. Some species, like the desert tortoise in southern California, are region specific. The growth in southern California's population has resulted in home development and recreational playgrounds in desert areas. Threats to the desert tortoise population include the development of recreational vehicle campgrounds (habitat loss) and the increasing use of off-road vehicles (habitat loss and death by contact). Concern over the desert tortoise's long-term survival has forced land management agencies, which control much of the land in some parts of the southwestern U.S. desert, to severely restrict previously accepted activities. For example, a major off-road vehicle race across the deserts of southern California and Nevada has been permanently cancelled because of its detrimental impact on desert tortoise populations.

Fire also plays a role in desert environments. Certain species of plants require periodic burning to release seeds. In a natural desert ecosystem, fires occur on a regular basis, usually started by lighting. Suppressing fires to protect developments changes this natural processes. Since periodic burning is no longer the norm, large quantities of fuel build. When fire does strike through natural or manmade causes, the result is much more intense and destructive. As desert environments are increasingly transformed into housing subdivisions and recreational playgrounds, the intensity of environmental impacts will rise.

Polar

Polar areas have not been actively developed for tourism, primarily due to their harsh climatic environments. The arctic polar region, however, contains stocks of mineral resources, the most valuable of these being oil. Currently, oil exploration and extraction is the primary threat to the arctic ecosystem. On the other hand, development in Antarctica is prohibited except for scientific research stations under the Antarctic Treaty signed by 39 nations. Prohibiting physical development, however, does not prohibit use. In the late 1950s, the first institutionalized tourists traveled to Antarctica by ship. Until the late 1970s, Argentine and Spanish companies organized most Antarctic cruises. In the mid 1970s, approximately 3,700 tourists went to Antarctica. In the 1991–92 season, over 40 cruises escorted over 5,600 tourists to the continent. Travel to Antarctica is expensive, costing between $3,500–4,000 per person excluding airfare. Demand, however, is increasing. Antarctica is arguably one of the last unexplored wilderness areas left in the world; it is certainly the largest. The quest for a discovery and/or challenge experience may be a prime motivator fueling demand. In recent years, expeditions across the continent on dogsled or cross country skis have received a great deal of press. These news accounts reinforce the discovery/challenge image of the continent and focus attention on it as a destination. As mass tourism services represented by cruise lines become increasingly available, visitation should continue to rise.

Although the Antarctic Treaty prohibits waste or oil discharges into Antarctic waters, accidents are bound to occur, and the increasing number of cruise ships poses a threat to the fragile and complex ecosystem of the continent. Penguins, seabirds, seals, and other wildlife live in an interrelationship that is not fully understood. The impacts of human interference on wildlife populations are not known. Because of the increasing demand for travel to the continent, certain temporary controls are in place to protect and monitor the consequences of tourism activity. In addition, educational programs are being organized and implemented. A visitor code of ethics is distributed to all passengers aboard U.S. cruise ships operating in Antarctic waters (Figure 4.2). Additionally, visitors watch a video program

---

Antarctica, the world's last pristine wilderness, is particularly vulnerable to human presence. Not only must life in the Antarctic contend with one of the harshest environments on earth, but an ever-increasing human presence is adding a greater amount of stress to the fragile and unique ecosystem.

Recognizing this, the following Visitor Guidelines have been adopted by all of the U.S. ship tour operators and will be made available to all visitors traveling with them to Antarctica. With your cooperation we will be able to operate environmentally-conscious expeditions which will protect and preserve Antarctica, leaving the continent unimpaired for future generations. We ask you to thoroughly study and follow these guidelines. By doing so, you will make an important contribution towards the conservation of the Antarctic ecosystem, and avoid potentially harmful and long-lasting damage.

1. **Maintain a distance of at least 15–20 feet from penguins, nesting birds and crawling seals, and 50 feet from fur seals.** Most Antarctica species exhibit a lack of fear which allows you to approach closely; however, please remember that the austral summer is a time of courting, mating, nesting and rearing young. If you approach the animals or birds too closely you may startle and disturb them sufficiently that they will abandon the nesting site, leaving eggs or chicks vulnerable to predators. And even from the recommended distance you will be able to obtain fantastic photographs.

   You should also remember that wild animals, especially seals, are extremely sensitive to movement and a person's height above the ground in relation to their size. Approach wildlife slowly when preparing to take photographs. And it is important to remember that your photography is not over when the shutter clicks—make your retreat from the subject in the same way you approach. The key point to remember is not to cause the animals any distress. You should be careful to avod altering their natural behavior.

2. **Be alert while you are ashore!** Watch your step in order not to stumble upon an aggerssive fur seal or a nesting bird that is unaware of your presence. And pay attention to the behavior of flying birds, as well as those on the ground. For example, when a tern or skua becomes excited or agitated and starts "dive-bombing" you, it is a good indication that you are walking too close to its nest, though you may have not spotted it.

3. **Do not get between a marine animal and its path to the water, nor between a parent and its young.** Never surround a single animal, nor a group of animals, and always leave them room to retreat. Animals always have the right-of-way!

4. **Be aware of the periphery of a rookery or seal colony, and remain outside it.** Follow the instructions given by your leaders.

Figure 4.2 *Antarctica Visitor Guidelines. Source: U.S. Ship Tour Operators*

5. **Do not touch the wildlife.** the bond between parent and young can be disrupted, and the survival of the young jeopardized.

6. **Never harass wildlife for the sake of photgraphy.** Our intention is to observe wildlife in its natural state.

7. **Keep all noise to a minimum in order not to stress the animals.**

8. **Avoid walking on, stepping on, or damaging the fragile mosses and lichens.** Regeneration is extremely slow and the scars from human damage last for decades.

9. **Take away only memories and photographs.** Do not remove anything, not even rocks or limpet shells. This includes historical evidence of man's presence in Antarctica, such as whale bones seen at some sites, which resulted from the whaling industry's activities.

10. **Return all litter to the ship for proper disposal.** This includes litter of all types, such as film containers, wrappers, and tissues. Garbage takes decades to break down in this harsh environment.

11. **Do not bring food of any kind ashore.**

12. **Do not enter buildings at the research stations unless instructed to do so.** Remember that scientific research is going on, and any intrusion could affect the scientist's data. Be respectful of their work.

13. **Historic huts can only be entered when accompanied by a specially-designated governmental representative or properly authorized ship's leader.**

14. **Smoking is prohibited when ashore!**

15. **When ashore stay with the group and/or one of the ship's leaders.** For your own safety, do not wander off on your own.

16. **Listen to the Expedition Leader, Lecturers and Naturalists.** They are experienced and knowledgeable about Antarctica. If you are not sure about something, please don't hesitate to ask your leaders and guides.

Figure 4.2   *(continued) Antarctica Visitor Guidelines. Source: U.S. Ship Tour Operators*

produced jointly by the U.S. Park Service and the National Science Foundation, explaining the increasing awareness of the Antarctic Conservation Act. Because the Antarctic Treaty designates the continent as a special conservation area, continual monitoring of visitor impacts will be required.

Rain Forests

Public interest in rain forests has accelerated as the rate of rain forest destruction has increased. Concern over rain forest destruction has focused primarily on the Amazon river basin, the largest rain forest ecosystem in the world, although rain forests exist all over the world in different climatic zones. Rain forests have been exploited for timber, cut down for agricultural use, mined for valuable minerals, and developed for human settlements. All of these practices bring short-term economic gains at the expense of long-term environmental consequences. The lush vegetative growth in rain forests masks the fact of low soil nutrient levels. Slash and burn agriculture practices provide only a few years of decent growing conditions, as crop production quickly depletes the soil of its nutrients.

Logging in tropical rain forests.
Photo by the author

Once abandoned, the area cannot revert back to its original condition. Forestry requires new reforestation practices, since techniques developed for temperate climates are not easily transferred to rain forest ecosystems. Mining for precious minerals, especially gold, often requires large amounts of water with mercury added to assist in the extraction process. Mercury-contaminated water is discharged back into the ecosystem and works its way through the food chain into the diets of indigenous peoples. Removing mercury from the ecosystem is more expensive than extracting the gold.

Due to increasing public awareness of rain forest destruction, tourism development is being touted as a possible preservation agent. Rain forests contain the greatest diversity of plant and animal species in the world. However, individual species populations are not considered large compared to species indigenous to temperate zones. This diversity of species forms part of the attraction potential for tourism development in rain forests. Unfortunately, the interrelationships between species is not well understood. Because of the complexity of the ecosystem, tourism development must be well planned, managed, and monitored so as not to contribute to the destructive effects of other rain forest uses. At the present time, little is known about tourism's impact, beneficial or harmful, on rain forest systems.

One example where tourism appears to be rewarding rain forest conservation and protection policies is in Costa Rica. Almost one-quarter of the country's land base enjoys protected status either through national park designation or through biological and private preserves. In 1992, the country received the Golden Compass Award (voting restricted to 35 travel writers in the U.S.) as the world's premier ecotourism destination (Baez, 1992). Income from tourists continues to climb faster than visitor numbers, with much of the income benefitting rural areas, but while the increases are impressive, there remains cause for concern. Budgets to manage the protected areas have not kept pace with increases in use. By some accounts, less than $1.00 per visitor is plowed back into resource management. Some areas such as Tortuguero, which recorded almost 50,000 visitors in 1991, over 90 percent foreign, saw only 18 percent of tourist revenues available for park management and less than 6 percent staying within the Tortuguero community (Baez, 1992). Obviously, the last chapter of Costa Rica's success with ecosystem protection tied to tourism has yet to be written.

One common thread linking the above discussions on various ecosystem types is that we know very little about the natural processes in place. This ignorance is partly due to the perception that most of these areas are wasteland with little development potential. Increasingly transportation technology allows people to move freely to all parts of the world, and expanding populations to search for new wealth in neglected places. Other technological advances allow for comfortable living in previously inhospitable places. All of this has led to increased development pressure on the earth's reserve resources. In one generation, people have begun to realize that a global community does exist. We also have the means to access it. What has not kept pace with our ability to exploit new areas is our knowledge of how life has developed there for eons, with little or no human influence. If the reader detects a bias towards a conservative approach to development in these areas, its presence is by design. What we don't know about life's processes may be much more valuable than what we do know.

Built Environments

The discussion of tourism's environmental impacts has so far concentrated on what occurs as a result of tourism development in natural settings. However, the majority of tourist activity takes place in built environments. The built environment includes concentrated population centers as well as remains of past settlements or civilizations. Tourism was not the initial impetus for development of built environments, but it exerts a powerful influence in the patterns of daily life in these environments. It is generally accepted that tourism is not the primary cause of environmental transformation in urban areas. The infrastructure of cities is usually designed to handle large amounts of people, but where the infrastructure is insufficient to handle the demands of residents, tourism can

COSTA RICA AND SUSTAINABLE DEVELOPMENT

Costa Rica, located in Central America, is a land of many contrasts. A relatively small country (approximately 20,000 square miles) with respect to land base, it is bordered on the east by the Caribbean and the west by the Pacific Ocean. In between, mountain slopes rise to over 12,000 feet (3,800 meters). The country is well known, at least in the Americas, for having taken enormous steps to protect its land base; over 12 percent is reserved in national parks or other private and public resource protection areas. Yet Costa Rica has one of the world's highest rates of deforestation. Once covered with forest, less than 30 percent of the land base is still considered in a forested state. In spite of Costa Rica's reputation as the Switzerland of Latin America, maintaining no standing army (constitutional decree) and one of the highest literacy rates in the world, rapid population growth and escalating debt continue to challenge the country. Since the early 1960s, the country's population has almost tripled to over 3 million. Population increases due to new births and immigrants seeking refuge from surrounding war-torn countries have led to massive government borrowing to finance new infrastructure development and provide social services.

Tourism is one of the top three export earners for Costa Rica. Since 1988, total arrivals have doubled from approximately 329,000 to over 650,000. Most of the growth is in the North American market. Given the importance of tourism as a foreign exchange earner and the value of the natural resource base to Costa Ricans themselves, be they farmers, loggers, or regular citizens that enjoy out-door recreation in the species-rich and diverse forested areas, it became obvious that the country needed national policy to guide its future use of land. The Costa Rican government developed the Costa Rican Conservation for Sustainable Development (ECODES) to provide that policy guidance.

Concerns about environmental degradation in Costa Rica had been raised as early as 1974, when the First Congress on Natural Resources was held. After the same issues were continually raised at the national level a working group formed in 1986 to draft the ECODES framework. Eventually ECODES, with its emphasis on sustainable development, expanded from a historic focus on the environment to become a planning framework for the entire country. Task forces convened with the intent of developing sustainable development strategies for 19 sectors including tourism, agriculture, government, energy, mining, science and technology, the legal system, etc. Each sectoral working group provided strategies for making its sector more responsive to constituent needs and made policy recommendations for sustainable growth (see Figure 12.9 in Chapter 12).

What has been the result of ECODES with respect to tourism? One of the sustainable development recommendations was to discourage mass tourism and promote more profitable alternative forms of tourism such as science and conference tourism. While alternative tourism development strategies appear to have been successful, social, economic, and political forces in the country have not been able to discourage mass tourism. The beaches and national parks continue to attract all types of tourists. The need for foreign exchange is real, and grows as the national debt increases.

One can argue about whether Costa Rica has achieved sustainable development when it comes to tourism. At the moment the answer would appear to be no. However, what has been accomplished by the ECODES process is a series of action steps for almost every viable sector in the nation. This framework will provide the basis for future policy debates, and within it is the potential for long-term utilization of the country's last remaining wild areas. The ECODES process will surely be noted for

linking the various sectors of the nation's political, social, and economic systems together to deal with immediate and long-term threats to the natural inherited wealth of the county.

Sources: Embassy of Costa Rica, Ottawa, Ontario, Canada
Hill, C. 1990. The Paradox of Tourism in Costa Rica.
Cultural Survival Quarterly 14(1):14-19.
Quesada-Mateo, C. and V. Solis-Rivera 1990. "Costa
Rica's National Strategy for Sustainable Development: A
Summary. Futures 22(4):396-416.
Thanks to Charlotte Echtner for compiling and making much
of the information available.

contribute to environmental damage. For example, air pollution in Mexico City has reached dangerous levels. Causes of the problem include too many vehicles, factories with lax pollution controls, and a burgeoning population. Tourism is not the cause of the air pollution problem, but it does contribute to it. Whenever the population of a built environment exceeds infrastructure capacity, any other industrial activity, including tourism, only exacerbates the problem.

Problems caused by tourism prove more severe in historical built environments. Early civilizations and historical events have left monuments to their existence. The pyramids of Egyptian and Mayan civilizations and the temples of Greece not only recall ancient civilizations, but have become major tourism attractions. Threats to these built structures include products of modern civilizations such as acid rain, air pollution, and overuse from tourism. Mark Twain's chronicles (*The Innocents Abroad*) of a trip to Egypt in the late 1800s contain accounts of American tourists carving their name into the base of the Sphinx. Similar evidence of graffiti vandalism can be found on almost any prehistoric structure. Even ancient graffiti (pictographs and petroglyphs) are in danger of destruction by modern-day amateur artists who think nothing of adding their message to that of their ancestors. Damage to ancient structures occurs even when there is no malice intended. Sections of the Great Wall of China are reportedly crumbling under the weight of all the tourists who take a short stroll on it. Officials in urban built environments can always initiate policies to address infrastructure overload. On the other hand, ancient relics cannot be replaced and any environmental damage that occurs to them is permanent.

Not all tourist-instigated environmental damage to historic built environments is physical. Ashworth and Tunbridge (1990) cite the use of traffic lights to control pedestrian circulation in heavily visited cathedrals as an example of how the medieval piety values for which the monument was preserved have been transformed. One can argue that an environment extends beyond physical transformation and includes a holistic set of characteristics that must be present for the environment to remain intact. In the same sense that a wetland is transformed if contiguous upland habitat is changed, causing certain species of wildlife that used the wetland to vanish, the environment of historic sites changes once preservation values are lost. "No longer is it sufficient to preserve monuments; areas must be planned for conservation" (Ashworth and Tunbridge, 1990:15).

Time Perspective of the Developer

This subject is addressed above as one of the societal causes of environmental impacts. As long as short-term profits dominate the decision process for businesses providing tourism goods and services, environmental impacts will result. Sustainable development, discussed in more depth in Chapter 12, is a concept intended to reduce the reliance on short-term profits and shift it to long-term returns by protecting the resources which originally attracted tourists to the area.

Transformational Character of Development

Physical development, whether for tourism or some other purpose, inevitably transforms the environment. Tourists may originally be attracted to an area because of the presence of unique or aesthetically pleasing natural resources. As tourist numbers increase, the scale of development required to accommodate them also increases—more lodging, more food service operations, and eventually more attractions to extend length of stay. In the absence of any limiting regulations or policies, visitors can shift their focus from natural attractions to contrived or manmade attractions. The Dells, Wisconsin provides an example of this transformation. The Dells is located approximately two hours from Chicago, Illinois, a major market for Wisconsin tourism. Visitors to the area were originally attracted to the sandstone cliff formations along the banks of the Wisconsin river. Eventually, the focus shifted from the sandstone formations to contrived attractions in the community. Today the area contains numerous contrived attractions, including Western World, Robot World, ski shows, water parks, and a greyhound racing track. Visitors wishing to see the sandstone formations can journey down the river in World War II amphibious vehicles called "ducks," which some view as more of an attraction than the natural resources they take people to see. Because of the major transformation that has taken place over time, the majority of visitors to The Dells no longer visit, or are even aware of the natural attractions.

Areas without especially unique natural resources can develop their own brand of tourism based solely on contrived attractions. Disney properties in the United States, Japan, and France are examples of this form of transformation. Las Vegas, Nevada is another. Obviously, contrived attractions exert a strong pull; Disney's success outside of Europe supports this statement. Transformation is not always an environmental evil. The sandstone formations along the Wisconsin river remain intact, while the community extracts tourist money in other ways. Large expanses of Nevada desert, similar to the site selected for Las Vegas, remain undeveloped. However, large-scale transformation should be carefully monitored, as it may eventually result in peripheral developments feeding off the attraction power of the originally contrived attractions.

Transformation is most commonly associated with increasing development. However, transformation can also occur when foreign flora and fauna are introduced into ecosystems. The importation of rabbits to Australia, carp to North America, and lampreys, alewife, and zebra mussels to the Great Lakes ecosystems in the U.S. are some of the more notable cases of exotic species introduction which have dramatically transformed existing ecosystem complexity. Some of these introductions were intentional, others by-products of development activities. Romeril (1989) cites the introduction of foreign seeds to Tenerife National Park as a major threat to the park's native vegetation. These seeds were carried in on the shoes of tourists who unknowingly became the agents of distribution.

Two types of tourism developments are especially noteworthy for their tendency to initiate major transformational forces. These are resorts and second home developments.

Resorts

Resort development, as part of attraction development, is covered in depth in Chapter 9. However, that chapter focuses on location and investment concerns, and only lightly touches on impacts created through development. The resort concept is based on providing leisure and recreation opportunities. Many resorts are self-contained destinations providing accommodations, food service, shopping, and developed recreation opportunities. Some resorts rely on the natural resource base of the area for access to recreational opportunities. In either case, development results in major land transformation. Resorts can be classified according to the recreational opportunities they provide. Seaside resorts offer sun based activities (e.g., swimming, sunbathing), mountain resorts offer skiing or access to wildland recreation, health resorts offer programs for weight reduction and substance dependency treatment, and so on.

Butler (1980), using product life-cycle analysis, models the evolution of resorts (see Chapter 1, Figure 1.1). In the early stages of the life cycle, few people visit the area and most services are locally provided. As the area increases in popularity, major physical development takes place. Multinational corporations come to the area during the development stage as visitor numbers reach the level where large-scale developments can be supported. During the development stage, the focus may shift from the natural resource base to one of contrived attractions. Eventually, resort areas reach a point of maturation depicted by the stagnation stage. Different options are available at this stage. Further transformation can result in rejuvenation, increasing visitor numbers and level of physical development. As development increases, infrastructure keeps pace with the rising level of visitors. More activity options are also added. Environmental impacts result not only from facility development, but from accompanying infrastructure development. Roads may be built into scenic areas to offer more sightseeing options. Seaside resorts may experience a spread of development along the coastline, with negative impacts on wetland and dune ecosystems. Ski resorts may expand the number of trails, further changing the environmental integrity of mountain hillsides. Additional roads, further opening up previously inaccessible areas, provide access to all new developments.

Mathieson and Wall (1982:121) identify four types of transformation that occur during the development stage; all of them directly affect the environmental quality of an area:

1. Architectural Pollution

    The inability to integrate resort design and infrastructure development into the inherent characteristics of the natural environment constitutes architectural pollution. Poorly or inappropriately designed facilities can clash with their environmental surroundings, creating aesthetically unappealing facilities. The importance of architectural design standards can be recognized in areas that have imposed them. Mackinac Island, Michigan is designed as a late 1800s community. Authentic street lamps, hanging signboards (termed shingles), and no motor vehicle transportation all support the thematic design appeal of the community. Since the island is located in the Straits of Mackinac, store fronts and local housing all replicate a seaside resort community.

2. Ribbon Development and Sprawl

Ribbon development results from the perceived need to be close to certain resources. In coastal areas, development proceeds along the beach from its origination at a coastal community. New roads link developments. Eventually, a ribbon of development extends outward from the original tourist staging area. Ribbon development also occurs up mountain valleys, allowing access to more mountainous terrain. The extent of sprawl is a function of land values. As development proceeds away from the center of activity, land value generally decreases. Eventually, the center may deteriorate and the value of what used to be marginal land increases, resulting in even more spread outward from the new center of activity. This tendency, termed by some as development spread, is discussed in more detail in Chapter 12.

3. Infrastructure Overload

Infrastructure development is often all or nothing. As resort areas increase in popularity, new infrastructure replaces the old. The cost of a new sewage treatment plant may not be justified based on annual use levels. However, the amount of sewage generated during high use periods may overload the present system, resulting in poorly treated sewage being dumped directly into water bodies. Overloaded power systems can result in periodic outages. Local power supplies may not be sufficient to handle the demands of air conditioning and other electrical needs of visitors during seasonal demand peaks. Insufficient infrastructure occurs when development proceeds at too fast a rate, or seasonal demand peaks concentrate visitors in the area for a relatively short period of time.

4. Traffic Congestion

Some areas are incapable of handling large amounts of traffic. Sometimes the infrastructure is not sufficient for efficient traffic control, and other times the type of environment in which the resort area is located traps automobile pollutants, leading to climatic inversions. This phenomenon is discussed above under the High Elevations section.

Resort areas, because of the large economic impacts occurring in a relatively small area, are difficult to manage from an environmental perspective. Often, it is only when the stagnation stage of the life cycle is reached that environmental impacts are recognized as negative. Before that stage, the prevailing philosophy is that natural resources should be used for their highest and best purpose, defined simply as the amount of money they can generate through development. It is not suggested that resort areas be de-emphasized; the market demand for resorts indicates a need for this type of development. However, effective planning and management is required for assuring environmentally sensitive resort development. Later in this chapter, a process termed "Limits of Acceptable Change" is offered as a method for planning tourism development by designating development opportunity zones. If done properly, impacts can be concentrated to what some call a "sacrifice area." Only in the absence of any development controls do resort areas expand beyond the ability of the area to absorb additional use without widespread environmental damage. A planned approach may extend Butler's resort life cycle, and forestall the advent of the stagnation and decline stages.

Seasonal Homes

Seasonal home developments are more common in North America and Europe where disposable income levels afford this type of tourism. In the United States, the highest percentage of seasonal homes is in the Great Lakes states of Michigan, Wisconsin, and Minnesota. The numerous inland lakes in those areas, in close proximity to major urban areas, make them attractive seasonal home locations. Environmental impacts associated with seasonal home development include flooding, siltation of water bodies, and infrastructure damage through the filling and dredging of wetlands and flood plains (Stroud, 1983). Wildlife patterns may be disrupted and vehicle/animal collisions increase in areas with high seasonal home density. If located in a forested environment, the additional human activity increases the likelihood of wildfire ignition. Lake eutrophication is also a problem, as discussed earlier in this chapter.

Initially, most seasonal home settlements were located near urban areas. As road systems and transportation corridors have developed, seasonal homes have moved further away from the urban center. The limiting factor is travel time, as most seasonal homes are used for short visits such as weekends. However, the growth of time-share developments has opened up more inaccessible areas for seasonal homes and condominiums, often purchased for their investment potential as well as their leisure appeal. Seasonal homes exhibit patterns of development similar to those of resorts; ribbon and sprawl developments are common. Additional seasonal home owners attracted to the area demand more facilities and services. There is a further linkage between resort destinations and seasonal home development. In northern Wisconsin, the decline in resource-dependent resorts corresponds to an increase in seasonal homes. Often resort lodges and cabins convert to seasonal home use. Resort developments, because of their dependence on an area's natural resource base, may also initiate infrastructure needed for seasonal home developments.

Many home owners purchase seasonal homes with the intent of converting them to permanent residences upon retirement. Depending on the concentration of seasonal homes, some areas have become small-scale approximations of the urban area where the seasonal home owners originated, complete with the types of services (e.g. health facilities, shopping centers, etc.) demanded by urban residents.

METHODS TO MITIGATE ENVIRONMENTAL IMPACTS

As mentioned, any physical transformation, regardless of the primary reason for development, can impact the environment. Although development impacts appear to occur over time, in reality they occur in moments. Key hole access, cited earlier as a way to describe how seasonal home construction can accelerate the process of lake aging, is a prime example. While environmental impacts began at the moment the lake's carrying capacity for seasonal homes was exceeded, those impacts appeared some time after the event which caused them. Therefore, mitigating environmental impacts requires attention to specific developmental events which set in motion the process of environmental change. Carrying capacity is the concept often used to determine at what point developmental changes initiate environmental impacts.

Carrying Capacity

Carrying capacity implies that some use or development limit exists which, when exceeded, begins the process of environmental degradation. Any use or development level below carrying capacity, and the environment remains relatively unchanged. No magic use number can be applied to all situations, since different ecosystems have different resiliencies. Environments change even in the absence of human activity, and natural processes must be considered when establishing carrying capacity limits. Therefore, any carrying capacity number is site specific.

Carrying capacity also includes a social component with both physical and perceptual elements (Walter, 1982). Physical carrying capacity is the natural resource's ability to accommodate the use for which it was designed. Perceptual carrying capacity refers to the social experience values originally inherent in the site; these may be eclipsed before physical carrying capacity becomes problematic. Perceptual carrying capacity can occur to both tourists and destination residents, and is discussed in the next chapter.

The concept of carrying capacity has its roots in wildlife and range management. It was not until the early 1960s that recreation researchers began to apply the concept to human impacts on ecosystems. Many studies (over 2,000 by some accounts; Drogin et al., 1986) documenting environmental damage to resources through use led to a search for methods to control these problems.

Six basic principles underlie the concept of carrying capacity:

1. Carrying capacity can only be defined in light of management objectives for the area in question. In other words, there must be a delineated geographical area with an acknowledged management authority if carrying capacity controls are to be utilized.

2. A variety of carrying-capacity planning frameworks have been applied. All specify indicators and standards, and monitor whether or not acceptable conditions are exceeded.

3. Obtaining the opinions and preferences of recreation users and nonusers can help administrators set objectives (indicators and standards) and suggest changes to current policy.

4. A full range of recreational opportunities should be available to satisfy the diversity of tastes.

5. Since many techniques are available to manage an area for its carrying capacity, the ones selected should match management objectives and the significance of the area.

6. Ultimately, the management authority decides appropriate levels of use for an area (Lime, 1995).

Operationalizing carrying capacity requires four steps:

1. Determine management objectives by weighing information concerning people's preferences, resource capabilities, institutional directives, and the existing situation. Developing management objectives based in part on people's preferences means recognizing the social element of carrying capacity.

2. Inventory the area's physical capacity to withstand use.

3. Use the inventory as a base to determine what areas are acceptable for use.

4. Calculate carrying capacity by estimating the number of people that can use each area (Greene, 1976, from Brown et al., 1985).

Carrying capacity is a concept ideally suited to designated natural areas such as parks or wilderness areas. In those cases, boundaries are established and a managing authority can implement policies to restrict or redistribute use. When applied to a tourism destination area, the process is not so straightforward. Different interest groups hold different opinions about the level of use that can be sustained. Destination areas often overlap political boundaries, raising the question of who has authority to establish any use limits. There are other problems with carrying capacity. Stankey and Schreyer (1985) argue that there is no such thing as a finite carrying capacity for an area; many possible carrying capacities exist depending on managements goals, microsystem resiliency and type of activity. Cole (1985) contends that environmental damage normally occurs at low use levels, as marginal damage declines with increasing levels of use. For example, it does not take much hiking to destroy all the vegetation on a trail. After the vegetation is gone, large numbers of extra users do relatively little additional damage.

The process of establishing a carrying capacity for an ecosystem inevitably encounters political, social and economic forces which may serve to override environmental concerns. The Galapagos Islands, controlled by Ecuador, are a case in point. In 1982, the Ecuadorian government established an annual limit of 25,000 visitors to the islands. Despite this carrying capacity number, nearly 50,000 visitors toured the islands in 1990. In addition, new tour boat permits were issued and hotel construction was being considered. Because of the economic benefits derived from serving tourists, the islands are becoming home for many Ecuadorans choosing to relocate their permanent settlements. Understandably, these forces are contributing to an unprecedented environmental decline for the islands (Miller, 1991). Carrying capacity numbers applied in this way are nothing more than a first step in recognizing that overuse can destroy ecosystems. They do not prevent it from happening.

Some economists argue that a market system can restrict use, as the following analysis illustrates. Assuming a single management authority determines a carrying capacity number for a particular ecosystem, it can either arbitrarily restrict use or charge an entrance fee. Even if an entrance fee is currently assessed, it may not be sufficient to restrict use to the carrying capacity level. Any visitor use beyond carrying capacity raises total cost, as shown in Figure 4.3. As use increases beyond the point N1, marginal benefits for users decline. Congestion and crowding reduce user satisfaction, and due to these same factors, marginal costs increase proportionately. The maximization point is N1, where the distance between benefits and costs is greatest (this is also where parallel lives are tangential to the PC and TB curves). In the absence of any economic controls, use

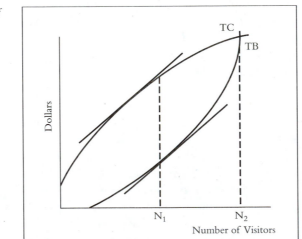

Figure 4.3 Benefits and Costs of Visitation at a Nature Tourism Attraction

will increase beyond the point where total benefits equal total costs (set at N_2 in Figure 4.3). When this happens, user benefits are less than user costs (including entrance fees) associated with traveling to the site. Using one of the methods described in Chapter 11 under amenity valuation, it is possible to determine what the economic value of a visit is to an individual. A fee can then be assessed which will restrict use to the level of N_1 (Figure 4.4). A new total cost curve, TC_2, results. With the new user fee, total costs equal total benefits, limiting use through economic constraints rather than any arbitrarily imposed use limit.

This economic solution does not address questions of equity or policy. Should domestic tourists, who support the natural areas through general taxes, pay the same for visitation as international visitors? What does the decline in use do to local enterprises located on the park periphery and dependent on visitors for economic survival? Should additional monies collected through a higher entrance fee be used for improving park management, providing local assistance, or be returned to the general treasury?

As mentioned, a number of planning/management frameworks have been offered to operationalize the concept of carrying capacity, including: Limits of Acceptable Change (LAC), Visitor Impact Management (VIM), Visitor Experience and Resource Protection (VERP), and Carrying Capacity Assessment Process (CCAP) (Lime, 1995; Manning et al., 1995) An example of one proposed process is contained in Figure 4.5. Since the techniques are similar in operation, LAC, one of the first to be developed, will serve as a guide in the discussion that follows.

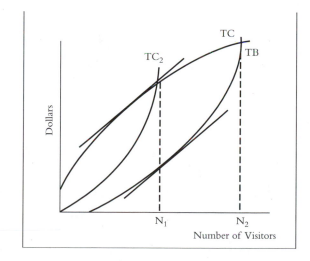

Figure 4.4 *Using a Tourist Levy to Reduce Visitation by Raising Cost*

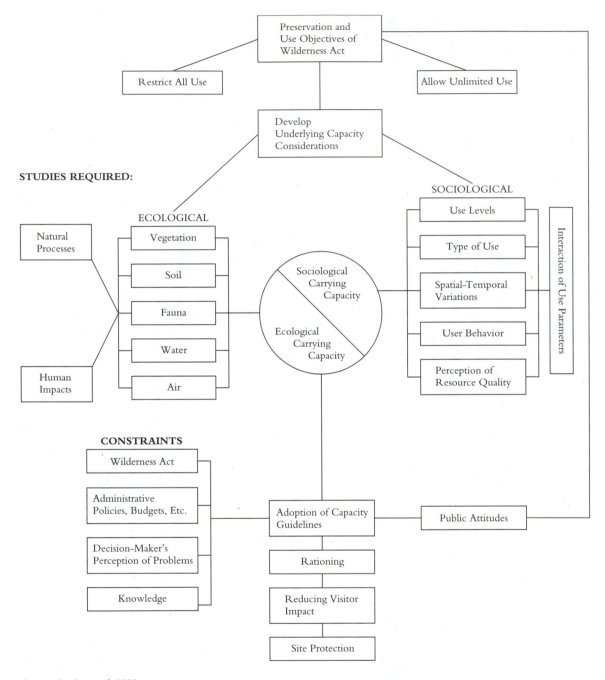

Source: Stankey et al, 1985

Figure 4.5 *Stankey Carrying Capacity Model*

LIMITS OF ACCEPTABLE CHANGE

Destinations without the power to impose use limits often do not even bother to calculate a carrying capacity number. Problems of implementation render the exercise academic. The Limits of Acceptable Change concept shifts the focus from how much use is acceptable to how much change is acceptable. Stankey et al. (1985) propose a nine step process for implementing Limits of Acceptable Change. Although this process was developed for recreation management, it is appropriate for tourism management through minor modifications in the various steps.

1. Identify area issues and concerns.

    This initial step allows the host community and its visitors to help decide the types of tourist activity and level of development considered appropriate for the area. Government policies affecting the level of development are also considered at this point. Information on issues and concerns can be collected through surveys of visitors and hosts, public meetings, and discussions with interested parties. Data on wildlife populations, air and water quality, and cultural and historic sites must also be assembled.

2. Define and describe tourist activity opportunity classes.

    Any area can support a diversity of potential tourist experiences. Attention should be directed at determining appropriate activities for specific ecosystems or zones within the destination area. Certain activities may not be acceptable. For example, off-road vehicle use or large-scale resort development may not be appropriate in a designated scenic zone. As previously mentioned, a coastline or littoral zone may attract high-rise accommodations. However, development in this zone may damage the visual qualities of the site. Each identified use zone should have different social, managerial, and resource conditions associated with it. Since tourists differ in their choice of activities, a variety of experiences should be made available but not necessarily within each zone.

3. Select indicators of resource change.

    Probably the most difficult step in the LAC process is determining indicators of change, be they biological or social. For example, water quality indicators may include bacteria counts, suspended solids, nutrient levels or social perceptions of shoreline development. Indicators selected to measure change must be quantifiable, reliable, and cost effective to monitor. Usually more than one indicator is necessary to accurately assess an area's condition.

Several indicators should be used to provide an overall report on the health of an area.

4. Inventory existing conditions.

Existing conditions are measured with respect to the indicators chosen in Step three. Baseline data is necessary to measure the direction and magnitude of any change to the ecosystem. The inventory is also necessary to complete the next step, where acceptable standards are determined.

5. Specify standards for resources and social conditions.

Standards form the heart of the Limits of Acceptable Change framework. In essence, standards set the tolerable limits of change for each indicator. Each identified use zone has its own set of indicators and related standards. Standards are not objectives or goals in the sense of something that the area is striving to attain; rather, they are limits of change which, once exceeded, change the activity opportunities available in a specific zone. Only in areas where limits are already exceeded do standards become objectives. In this case, active management is required to return the area to its previous condition.

6. Identify alternative opportunity class allocations reflecting area issues and concerns and existing resource and social conditions.

Any area can be managed in a variety of ways to provide desired user experiences and host benefits. This step provides for the reassessment of the types of activities or development allowed in each zone to determine if the needs of visitors, hosts, businesses, and other interested parties are being met. This is accomplished by reviewing the collected information and the decisions made in Steps one through four, and revising zone opportunity classes if needed.

7. Identify actions needed for each alternative.

The next step is to determine different actions for each opportunity zone and the costs associated with them. Costs include not only money and time, but also social costs resulting from exclusion of certain activities or developments. In areas where measured indicators show that standards have been exceeded, costs represent what it would take to bring the area within the Limits of Acceptable Change.

8. Evaluate and select a preferred alternative.

After the benefits and costs of each alternative set of activities and development for each zone are evaluated, a preferred alternative is selected. Establishing a preferred alternative requires the groups providing initial input in step one to once again contribute to the dialog.

9. Implement the preferred alternative and monitor conditions.

Once a preferred alternative for each opportunity zone is established, it can be implemented. If certain zones are reserved for accommodation development, the private sector can begin constructing hotels, motels, or resorts. In addition to implementing the preferred alternative, a monitoring plan is devised. Indicators of change must be assessed on a scheduled periodic basis and compared to standards established in Step five. Adjustments can be made by selecting new indicators, revising standards or implementing new preferred alternatives for each opportunity zone. Establishing a monitoring program should make the Limits of Acceptable Change process dynamic and responsive to the needs of all affected parties.

Obviously, "Limits of Acceptable Change" is more applicable to an area with a single management authority. This is due to its historical roots, as researchers developed the process public recreation managers use. The concept, however, is transferable to tourism destination areas if the host society assumes control over tourism development. In certain areas where the prevailing philosophy is laissez–faire, many of the environmental problems identified as part of the tourism development process will not be solvable. The Limits of Acceptable Change process allows everyone affected by tourism development to be involved in deciding the scale and type of development wanted in a destination area. Accepting LAC or a similar development process is in keeping with the philosophy of liberal democratic principles. Inherent in the process is also a recognition of a "go slow" approach to tourism development. The amount of information required to implement LAC make it time- and money-intensive. However, in the absence of any planned approach to deal with the environmental impacts of tourism development, the unidirectional flow of development inevitably results in increasingly unacceptable levels of environmental degradation.

LAC and its variations are management-driven techniques. That is, they operate best when a single management authority exerts control. Since most tourism areas have at least one community base with private operations supplying services, carrying capacity may not be an appropriate concept. When this is the case there may be a tendency for the private sector to operate along the lines suggested by Fife (1971). However there is a noticeable private sector movement, sometimes called "Green Tourism," that is based on "Best Practice" principles which melds environmental stewardship without sacrificing financial profitability.

GREEN TOURISM

"Best practice," which is the basis for green tourism, follows guiding principles that help a company change and adjust to market pressures to continually produce the best product. In the past, producing the best product often meant ignoring the environmental consequences of the production process, but current "best practice" principles include "the integration of environmental management into all operations of the business" (Pigram, 1995). How this is done is primarily left up to the individual business.

The World Travel and Tourism Council (WTTC) has been offering a Green Globe program for member companies since 1994. It consists of a manual listing environmental and cost-saving practices that can be easily initiated. The program also makes available a number of consultants on a fee basis to members who wish to more thoroughly review their operations, followed by environmentally based recommendations. Member companies that sign up for the Green Globe program receive the manual and a list of consultant services and are listed as part of the Green Globe program. Compliance with Green Globe guidelines is voluntary.

Other companies such as Canadian Pacific Hotels and Resorts, Inter-Continental Hotels Groups, and the Prince of Wales Business Leaders Forum also produce environmental guidelines for hotel operations. Some hotel companies have begun to involve customers in their program by asking them, for example, to reuse towels (Figure 4.6).

The greening of tourism is a relatively new phenomenon in the private sector. It is based partly on demand from customers, and on the recognition that the future of tourism greatly depends on the environmen-

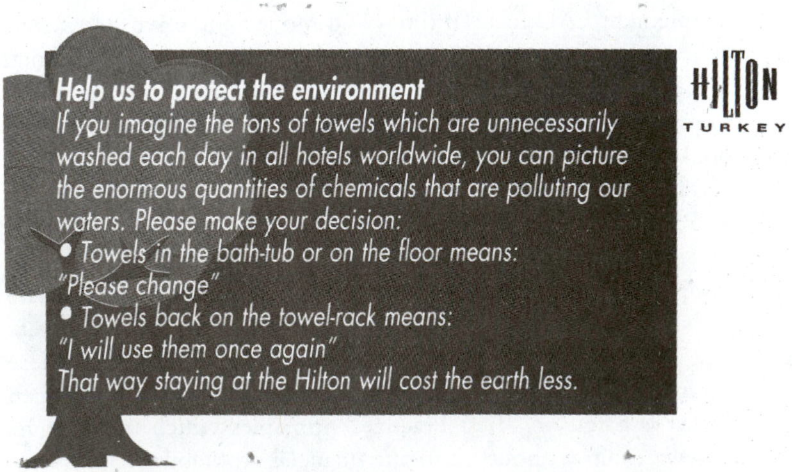

Figure 4.6 *Corporate Response to Enviornmental Issues: Reduce Pollution/Save Money*

Help us to protect the environment
If you imagine the tons of towels which are unnecessarily washed each day in all hotels worldwide, you can picture the enormous quantities of chemicals that are polluting our waters. Please make your decision:
• Towels in the bath-tub or on the floor means: "Please change"
• Towels back on the towel-rack means: "I will use them once again"
That way staying at the Hilton will cost the earth less.

HILTON
TURKEY

tal quality where the activity takes place, and environmental considerations can improve operating efficiencies through programs that reduce waste.

Many critics of the Green programs have appeared in the last few years, pointing most significantly to the voluntary compliance requirements and the inability of the small operator to take advantage of programs based on economies of scale. For example, a waste management program may only be economically feasible once a certain amount of waste is recycled. The cost of equipment and refitting may not make the same program feasible for a ten unit resort. Since most tourism businesses are classified as small businesses, best management practices, including limited scale technology, must be extended to the small operator before any significant differences will be noticed.

The private sector stands to benefit from environmental "best practices" since tourists are now demanding experiences that involve a healthy environmental component. Many people classify all nature/environmentally based travel as ecotourism. While this is not correct, a review of ecotourism provides an interesting perspective on where the increasing demand for environmentally based tourism originated.

Ecotourism

Alternative forms of tourism, discussed in Chapter 1, include ecotourism. However, the attention it receives as a type of tourism sensitive to the environment and host society needs separates ecotourism from other alternative forms as worthy of discussion on its own merits. Ecotourism springs from the increasing market demand for adventure tourism or outdoor travel (Ingram and Durst, 1989). The importance of ecotourism is underscored by Whelan (1988), who claims that this market transferred over $25 billion from developed to developing countries in 1987.

The Ecotourism Society (1991) argues that "ecotourism is less a word that needs defining than a concept in search of content." Nevertheless, it defines ecotourism as: "Purposeful travel to natural areas, . . . to understand the culture and natural history of the environment, . . . taking care not to alter the integrity of the ecosystem, while . . . producing economic opportunities that make the conservation of natural resources beneficial to local people." Accepting this definition recognizes that ecotourism includes more than visits to study or learn about an area's indigenous plants and animals. It also includes learning about the cultural history of an area. In that sense, travel to Tikal to visit the ancient Mayan city is ecotourism.

Koth (1991), reviewing the literature in an attempt to define ecotourism, assembles the following list of attributes common to those definitions:

1. The *setting* where ecotourism takes place

2. The type of *activity* taking place

3. The *impact* of activities and behavior

4. The resulting *psychological outcome* of the activity

5. The *economic linkage* between tourism and conservation in a specified development model

6. *Site management* for ecotourism destinations

7. A *philosophical* or *ethical* component

Setting

Ecotourism is assumed to take place in some exotic, remote, undisturbed natural area. Most of these natural areas are protected parks or forest reserves, and the type of activity associated with visiting these areas is limited by the regulations governing use of the designated area. Most recently, ecotourism has been viewed as travel to any natural area that differs from one in close proximity to the tourist's home. This is a function of increasing demand for ecotourism travel accompanied by the rush to sell ecotourism experiences as part of a travel package.

Activity

Almost any non-consumptive activity that relies on a natural resource base for achieving desired experiences is included as ecotourism. Both "hard" and "soft" dimensions of activities, based on physical rigor required, are included. Since most ecotourism definitions include a historic or cultural resources element, visits to historical sites or to local villages with the intent of learning more about a different culture are included as ecotourism activities.

Impact

An assumption about ecotourism is that it is purposeful travel which minimizes negative environmental and social impacts. Activities are intended to be pursued in an environmentally responsible manner. Visitors rely more heavily on local lodging, transportation, and locally made products. Operators are expected to minimize waste through proper disposal and recycling methods, and initiate environmental policies for their clients which are based on responsible behavior.

Psychological Outcome

The psychological outcome is related to an increased awareness of environmental issues. The primary tourism motive is increasing knowledge and involvement in conservation issues. In a sense, ecotourism motives address Maslow's highest order needs of self-actualization rather than the simple pursuit of pleasure. Fennell and Eagles (1991) argue that the ecotourism experience is highly personal, involving educational pursuits and personal responsibilities.

Economic Linkages

Ecotourism attempts to link economic and environmental impacts in a model which promotes community development activities while protecting and preserving local resources. This economic facet is one of the primary differences between what has been called nature tourism, which includes mass tourism that relies on a natural setting (e.g., beaches) and ecotourism. Economic leakages from tourism activity, especially in developing countries, is usually high due to heavy reliance on multinational enterprises. Ecotourism's intent is to establish a strong linkage between local industries and tourism development.

Site Management

Uncontrolled access to sensitive natural areas can destroy the integrity of the resources. Ecotourism is characterized by intensive planning for development. The Limits of Acceptable Change framework is most applicable to site management for ecotourism development. Formal policies and regulations directing both visitors' and developers' use of resources are necessary.

Philosophy

Ecotourism is less a tangible construct, and more an ethic or philosophical approach to tourism development. The establishment of guidelines and a code of responsible behavior for Antarctic tourism is an attempt to import ethics into travel experiences. Ecotourism is a reaction to many of the abuses cited for mass tourism. Many of the early arguments in support of tourism (e.g., clean industry) are slowly being rejected as the literature citing tourism's negative impacts continues to grow. Many travelers and operators are searching for an ethic which can guide tourism. Ecotourism is a beginning attempt to provide some ethical basis for travel to natural areas.

Ecotourism Benefits

Arguments in support of ecotourism as opposed to mass tourism appear almost daily. Arguments in favor of ecotourism are remarkably similar to those offered in support of tourism in general (e.g., provides employment, economic growth, etc.). However, most of the advantages ascribed to ecotourism have not yet been substantiated by long-term studies. The following lists some of the purported advantages of ecotourism over traditional mass tourism.

1. Higher daily expenditures and a longer average length of stay than mass tourism

2. Fewer capital requirements since ecotourists demand simpler services supplied by local societies

3. Fewer economic leakages as more local spending is generated

4. Increases in rural employment as local resources (e.g., capital and labor) are more heavily utilized

5. Education for both locals and guests is supported. If there is a heavy reliance on an area's natural resource base and local involvement in tourism development is supported, this should lead to a greater awareness of environmental and conservation issues for both hosts and guests

6. Less detrimental environmental impacts as resources are protected for long-term tourism development

7. Fewer social impacts as hosts and guests are more interactive

Ecotourism Costs

Since the concept of ecotourism is relatively new, it remains in the advocacy stage of study. In other words, it has numerous proponents and few opponents. Little is known about its costs, yet there is still room for concern. Ecotourism remains a concept driven by altruistic values. How it is operationalized and the slant different people put on its core values will determine whether it eventually becomes an accepted development option or simply a marketing niche for an increasingly fragmented tourism industry. For example, it is unlikely that any development option will ensure that economic benefits accrue almost entirely to the host society. Economic leakage occurs in the most highly diversified regional economies—why should ecotourism be any different? Even if economic leakage is accepted, as most tourism development professionals would agree is inevitable, how much is acceptable before ecotourism fails to be an alternative form of tourism? Is ecotourism really a sustainable development option or is it simply an evolutionary step in what ultimately will become mass tourism? Answers to these questions, along with a host of others, are critical to determining what the costs may be.

DEVELOPED/DEVELOPING COUNTRIES

Most of the recent scientific and popular literature addressing tourism's environmental impacts centers on developing countries. This is due in part to the desire of developing countries to increase their foreign exchange earnings through tourism development, and because of the demand from developed countries for the types of tourist products offered by developing countries. Developing countries also have most of the undeveloped wildland left in the world. Many developed countries' ecosystems have already been drastically transformed through industrial expansion. For example, outdoor sports enthusiasts in developed countries are aware of the extent of environmental degradation that has already occurred in their own country. In the United States, every state requires a license be purchased before fish and game can be harvested. Booklets listing harvest regulations contain warnings regarding fish and game consumption. The presence of PCBs, mercury, and other dangerous poisons found in the tissue of the nation's fish and game provide ample evidence of the extent of environmental degradation that has already occurred. Developing countries counter developed countries' claims of impending environmental degradation from development by pointing out that clean development practices were not and are not being practiced by citizens, businesses, and governments of those countries most concerned about what happens in the developing world. For wide-scale environmental damage to be avoided throughout the world, a consensus must be reached about what constitutes safe development practices. Tourism development should be viewed in terms of long-run returns on investment rather than exploitation of resources for short-term gain. The concern over environmental degradation from any type of development is being increasingly recognized as one of the major international political issues of the last decade of the 20th century, extending into the next century. Romeril (1989) identifies at least five major international agreements which specifically identify environmental protection as a major component of tourism development. His list includes:

1. World Conservation Strategy (1980)—sustainable use of natural resources

2. Brandt Commission Report (1980)—development must include "care of the environment"

3. WTO Manila Declaration (1980)—all resources are a common heritage

4. UNEP/WTO Accord (1982)—to promote environmentally sound tourism development

5. Bruntland Report (1987)—sustainable development with economic growth

To this list should be added the Earth Summit Conference held in Brazil in 1992. With one notable exception (United States), world leaders affixed their name to a document recognizing much of the environmental damage done to the world today and attempted to outline a plan to deal with present and future global environmental threats. The conference was not intended to single out any one country or industry as the environmental culprit but the message was clear—development activity of all types poses significant environmental threats to the world's resources. It is the responsibility of people, industries, and governments to mitigate those threats and instead strive to support long-term sustained environmental health. As one of the leading world industries, tourism and its development consequences should be at the forefront of assuring economic gain through environmental protection.

CONCLUSION

Tourism does destroy and protect natural environments. As tourism continues to expand and access to remote areas of the world increases, there will be a greater search for new areas which can support tourism development. Tourism should be viewed in the same light as other industries. Goods and services production has as one of its by-products pollution. How this pollution is managed will determine if tourism serves to destroy or protect an ecosystem. Much has been learned about the different types of environmental impacts resulting from tourism development. Certain ecosystems are more capable of supporting tourism than others. Those less capable of supporting major tourism development and those most susceptible to significant environmental change are in areas of the world that have been left relatively untouched by human development. Often it is the harsh and sometimes hostile environment of these areas which has precluded any significant human settlement; now, increasing levels of technology and the search for exploitable resources is affecting these previously untouched areas. Tourism is often cited as the type of industry which can bring long-term, sustainable development to them. For this to happen, tourism development will have to be intensively planned and managed. This chapter explores some methods for accomplishing that objective. Complete recognition of tourism's costs and benefits underlies any planning intended to maximize economic benefits and, at the same time, maintain resource integrity.

EXECUTIVE SUMMARY

Much environmental change is not industry specific but can be traced to societal causes including worldwide population increases, increasing levels of industrialization, and ignorance of environmental change processes.

Environmental change as a result of tourism development can be either tourist-specific, as when the tourist only perceives the consequence of his/her individual actions and ignores the cumulative effect of all tourists, or industry-generated, which happens when industry responds to demand without regard for the long-term environmental consequences of their action.

Four main factors contribute to the extent of environmental damage: intensity of site use, resiliency of the ecosystem where use and development are occurring, time perspective of the developer, and the transformational character of the development.

Two types of development noted for their propensity to exert strong transformational change are resorts and seasonal home developments.

Carrying capacity has been offered as a means to limit use and protect the integrity of the environment. There are two components to carrying capacity: physical and social. Most carrying capacity numbers, when used, are based on political considerations and are easily changed to accommodate new political views.

Limits of Acceptable Change is another method often cited as a means of protecting environments from excessive development. It has been most often used in protected areas operating with a single management authority.

Green tourism, as an industry initiative, has its roots in "best management" practices that include an environmental principle. While much has been accomplished with these programs, critics point out that they are voluntary and only focus on large operators.

Ecotourism has received a great deal of attention recently as a kinder type of "sustainable" tourism. Little research has been undertaken on ecotourism's costs or benefits to support or refute the claims made on its behalf.

REFERENCES

Ashworth, G. and J. Turnbridge, 1990. *The Tourist-Historic City*. London: Belhaven Press.

Baez, A. 1992. Ecotourism in Costa Rica: The Tough Road for Remaining Number One.

Newsletter of the Adventure Travel Society Fall, 1992.

Brown, P., S. McCool, and M. Manfredo. 1985. Evolving Concepts and Tools for Recreation User Management in Wilderness: A State-of-Knowledge Review. *Proceedings—National Wilderness Research Conference: Issues, State-of-Knowledge, Future Directions.* Ogden, Utah: Intermountain Research Station, USDA Forest Service. 320–346.

Butler, R. 1980. The Concept of a Tourist Area Cycle of Evolution: Implications for Management of Resources. *Canadian Geographer* 24 (1): 5–12.

Clare, P. 1971, *The Struggle for the Great Barrier Reef.* London: Collins.

Cohen, E. 1978. The Impact of Tourism on the Physical Environment. *Annals of Tourism Research* 5(2):215–237.

Cole, D. 1985. Management of Ecological Impacts of Wilderness Areas in the United States. 138–154. In Bayfield, N., and G. Barrow, eds. *The Ecological Impacts of Outdoor Recreation on Mountain Areas in Europe and North America.* R.E.R.G. Report No. 9. Wye, England: Recreation Ecology Research Group.

Drogin, E., A. Graefe, and J. Vaske. 1986. *A Citation Index for the Recreation Impact/Carrying Capacity Literature: A Descriptive Analysis and Demonstration.* Maryland: College Park, Department of Recreation, University of Maryland.

Fennell, D. and P. Eagles. 1991. Ecotourism In Costa Rica: A Conceptual Framework. *Journal of Park and Recreation Administration* 8(1):23–34.

Fife, D. 1971. Killing the Goose. *Environment* 13(3):20–27.

Filani, M. 1975. The Role of National Tourist Associations in the Preserving of the Environ-ment in Africa. *Journal of Travel Research* 13(4): 7–12.

Gajraj, M. 1989. Warning Signs. *Tourism Management* 10(3):202–203.

Gartner, W. 1987. Environmental Impacts of Recreational Home Developments. *Annals of Tourism Research* 14(1):38–57.

Greene, P. 1976. Calculating Carrying Capacity in Wilderness Areas. M.S. Thesis. Colorado State University.

Hardin, G. 1968. The Tragedy of the Commons. *Science* 162:1243–1248.

Hudman, L. 1980. *Tourism: A Shrinking World.* Columbus, Ohio: Grid Publishing.

Ingram, D. and P. Durst, 1989. Nature-Oriented Tour Operators: Travel to Developing Countries. *Journal of Travel Research* 28(2):11–15.

Koth, B. 1991. Ecotourism: Definition, Costs and Benefits, and Major Players. Unpublished paper. St. Paul, Minn: Tourism Center, University of Minnesota.

Laszewski, C. Treatment Plant may not be Source of Pepin Problems. *Pioneer Press* August, 3:5–6A.

Lavery, P. and C. Van Doren. 1990. *Travel and Tourism: A North American-European Perspective.* Suffolk: St. Edmunsbury Press.

Lime, D. 1995. Principles of Carrying Capacity for Parks and Outdoor Recreation Areas. Paper presented at the Conference on Carrying Capacity, Slovakia.

Lindberg, K. 1991. *Policies for Maximizing Nature Tourism's Ecological and Economic Benefits.* Washington, D.C.: World Resources Institute.

Liu, J. and T. Var. 1986. Residents' Attitudes Toward Tourism Impacts in Hawaii. *Annals of Tourism Research* 13(1):193–214.

Manning, B., A. Graefe, and S. McCool. 1995. Trends in Carrying Capacity Planning and Management, 38. *Trend Tracker, 4th International Outdoor Recreation and Tourism Trends Symposium*. St. Paul, Minn.: Tourism Center, University of Minnesota.

Mathieson, A. and G. Wall. 1982. *Tourism: Economic, Physical and Social Impacts*. New York: Longman Scientific and Technical.

McNeely, J. 1988. *Economics and Biological Diversity*. Gland, Switzerland: IUCN. Cited in Lindberg, 1991.

Miller, A. 1991. Galapagos at the Crossroads. *The Ecotourism Society Newsletter* Spring:1–2.

Pigram, J. 1995. Best Practice Environmental Management and the Tourism Industry. Paper presented at the International Academy for the Study of Tourism, biennial meeting, Cairo, Egypt.

Romeril, M. 1989. Tourism and the Environment—Accord or Discord. *Tourism Management* 10(3):204.

Shackleford, P. 1995. Excerpts from a speech presented at the World Conference on Sustainable Tourism, 27–28 April, Lanzarote, Canary Islands. *WTO NEWS* 3 (May):4.

Stankey, G., D. Cole, R. Lucas, M. Peterson, and S. Frissell. 1985. The Limits of Acceptable Change (LAC) System for Wilderness Planning. *General Technical Report INT-176*. Ogden, Utah: USDA Forest Service, Intermountain Forest and Range Experiment Station.

Stankey, G., and R. Schreyer. 1985. Attitudes Toward Wilderness and Factors Affecting Visitor Behavior: A State-of-Knowledge Review, 246–293. *Proceedings—National Wilderness Research Conference: Issues, State-of-Knowledge, Future Directions*. Ogden, Utah: Intermountain Forest Range and Experiment Station, USDA Forest Service.

Stroud, H. 1983. Environmental Problems Associated with Large Recreational Subdivisions. *Professional Geographer* 35:303–313.

Tarr, J. 1987. The Case for Cultural Tourism in the Caribbean. *Place*, May/June. Washington, D.C: Partners for Livable Places.

The Ecotourism Society. The Quest to Define Ecotourism. *Newsletter* Editorial, Spring 1991.

Walter, J. 1982. Social Limits to Tourism. *Leisure Studies* 1(1982):295–304.

Whelan, H. 1988. Nature Tourism. *Environmental Conservation* 15:182. Cited in Romeril, 1989.

CHAPTER 5

Social Impacts

Cultural expression through dress, illustrated by a market woman in Zagreb, Croatia.
Photo by the author

Learning Objectives

Recognize the different cultures involved in tourism.

•

Examine the various types of social impacts and benefits related to tourism.

•

Examine social-impact mitigation strategies.

•

Identify the types of social indicators that can be used to address sociocultural change.

•

Review a multicountry longitudinal case study of social-impact analysis.

INTRODUCTION

When the study of tourism moved from the advocacy to the cautionary platform (see Chapter 1), negative impacts related to development became the focus of discussion. The first spate of studies were concerned primarily with environmental issues. A few reports, especially case studies, dealt with possible sociocultural impacts, due in large part, to the difficulty of quantifying sociocultural impacts. Economic impacts have a worldwide common denominator (money), environmental impacts can be measured using some accepted parameters (e.g., vegetation loss), but sociocultural impacts, with some exceptions, are rarely measured. They are most often observed. In fact, sociocultural is a hybrid term which, used in the context of impacts, encompasses changes to the social organization of a group of people as well as more fundamental reorganization of a society's culture. Social change does not necessarily indicate cultural change but it is a precursor to it. The point where social change results in cultural change is not easily determined; thus, most studies review impacts from a sociocultural perspective.

Not all sociocultural impacts are negative. New revenue from tourism can result in increasing incomes and improve quality of life for local residents. Tourism employment can provide entry level positions for youths or other seasonal employment for a family's second wage earner. Infrastructure improvements benefit tourists as well as local residents. Services and attractions unavailable before tourism development (e.g. sports facilities, theater) may need the support of tourists to exist. Community residents also benefit from these additions to the attraction and service base.

In addition to increasing the quality of life for local residents through economic impacts, tourism may be responsible for protecting and preserving cultural traditions. Examples where tourism has helped preserve the cultural heritage of a people can be found in Esman (1984), Witt (1991), and Din (1988). The influx of tourists may also be a source of pride and can improve the self-esteem of the host society (Boissevain, 1979).

Sociocultural impacts result whenever different cultures come into contact. They are most noticeable when two distinctly different cultures interact, as occurs when Western tourists visit developing countries. However, they also occur when tourists from one region of a country visit other regions. To more fully understand sociocultural impacts, it is necessary to define culture. According to Greenwood (1989), culture is an integrated system of meanings, known to members of a specific culture, and from which reality is established. Culture may also be defined as the sharing of common beliefs, resulting in predictable patterns of behavior. In this sense, cultures exist throughout all levels of what appears to be a singular society. A local community may be said to possess a different culture from neighboring communities, most noticeable through celebrations and festivals which serve to reinforce cultural identity.

The degree of cultural difference between people may be seen as a function of interaction. The more interaction between groups of people, the less noticeable the different patterns of behavior. The assimilation of one culture into another is called acculturation. Certain aspects of one culture are adopted by another, resulting in the emergence of a new culture based more on the patterns of behavior of the strong or dominant culture. It is the reactions to acculturation which results in sociocultural impacts.

This chapter discusses the different types of cultures that come into contact through tourism. It also explores the different types of impacts, both positive and negative, that may result from this interaction. A model depicts when change is most likely to be perceived, related to stages in the development process, and is followed by coping strategies to deal with change. Finally, a time series case study of sociocultural change associated with tourism in different countries is presented to more fully understand the nature and scope of sociocultural impacts.

CULTURE AND TOURISM

Jafari (1987) recognizes three different types of cultures related to tourism: host, tourist, and residual. In addition, businesses involved in the movement of tourists influence the tourist culture. These different cultures are discussed below.

Host

Regardless of the reason(s) for tourist travel to an area, a host society is expected to provide tourist services. In some cases, the host society provides more than a service function, as they may be part of the attraction base of the area. The types of services provided may be no more than the construction of a road through a village, allowing access to a historical site. In other cases, the level of services may be intensive and include use of land for facility construction, employment within the facilities, sharing of natural areas, and increased infrastructure development. The more a local economy becomes dependent on tourism, the greater the degree of local involvement in the tourism industry becomes. This is not to say that host societies will always be able to control the direction of tourism development within their community, as the opposite is often true, but that host societies will find it harder to ignore the consequences of a tourist-based economy.

Host cultures are not static or interchangeable. Cultures evolve, and a specific host culture encountered by tourists may have already been changed through prior contact with tourists, adoption of new agrarian practices, internal changes of the country the host society is part of, migration resulting from war in neighboring countries, regional economic chaos, or a host of other causes unrelated to tourism development. Anthropologists often describe specific host cultures in terms of their historical traditions which may have developed in relative isolation for centuries but are now being changed by global forces which redefine and shape everyone's life. Tourism is only one of those forces which makes the identification of sociocultural impacts resulting from development a difficult process. Nonetheless, a host culture can be described as one which possesses certain norms and standards directing daily life for members of the host society. When those norms and standards differ from those of another culture that comes into contact with it, changes and sociocultural impacts can result.

Host cultures are susceptible to sociocultural impacts since tourism takes place within their home environment. If tourists are not comfortable with the experience of visiting a particular area, they can leave. Members of a host society are often unable to leave due to lack of financial resources, or may be unwilling because of ties that bind them to the host culture.

Tourist

Tourists form their own culture based on the activities they pursue at the destination. Most often these activities have a high play component as pleasure travel is still one of the primary reasons for mass tourism. Destinations developed for scientific tourism, such as in Costa Rica (Laarman and Perdue, 1989), where visitors focus on acquiring knowledge according to the scientific method, have an entirely different tourist culture. However, when pleasure activities dominate, the probability of sociocultural impacts on the host culture increases. According to Jafari (1987), tourists exist in a non-ordinary world at the destination, while host societies remain in their own ordinary world. This differentiation is in reality a clash of cultures. Tourist cultures are formed by observing the behavior of other tourists similarly instructed in the ways of the culture by tourists who preceded them. If the tourist culture is based on play, pleasure, and the free spending of money which makes it all possible, then the degree of difference between the tourist's non-ordinary world and the ordinary world of the hosts is high. The tourist culture may be viewed as the dominant culture, as it exemplifies a sense of freedom from the constraints of ordinary life. The inability of host societies to become a part of the tourist culture, to free themselves from ordinary life, can cause negative reactions throughout the host society. Some of the reactions resulting from this clash of cultures are reviewed later in this chapter.

Residual

Tourists who adopt a tourist culture from observing other tourists at the destination are still constrained from total abandonment of their own ordinary life culture by the extent to which a residual culture remains. A residual culture consists of the norms and standards operational in the tourist's ordinary life which may not be totally rejected when he/she becomes a member of the tourist culture. Some tourist activities may be viewed as unethical or immoral to new initiates to the culture. Rejection of those activities constitutes a denial of some aspects of the tourist culture. The residual culture also serves as a reminder of how far the tourist has come, psychologically, from ordinary life. The responsible behavior guidelines for Antarctica tourists and tour operators in Figure 4.2 (Chapter 4), for example, are an attempt to instill travel ethics in the residual culture of tourists. Education of this type, which takes place in the tourist's ordinary life, is intended to reduce the psychological distance between the tourist's non-ordinary life and the host culture's ordinary life.

Transitional Companies

Companies which direct the flow of tourists to an area are known as tourisiers or transitional companies (Jafari, 1989). These companies make up yet a different culture which impacts the host society. The majority of these companies are located outside the destination, usually promoting and encouraging the tourist culture. In many cases, they provide the cues of behavior which form the tourist culture even before the tourist arrives at the destination. Opportunities do exist for the host society to influence the tourism business culture as, especially for international tourism, regulations and controls can be imposed on business operations. Even so, the types of destination images the tourisiers project are not always compatible with those members of the host communities desire. Britton (1979) and a report by International Union of Official Travel Organizations (IUOTO, 1976) contend that foreign companies influence the image of a destination through their advertising, which often leads to unjustified expectations. When the transitional company is in the business of hosting tourists (e.g., destination resorts), they control not only the types of activities offered but the extent of host society involvement in the tourism industry.

Cultural cross dressing. Photo by the author.

LAND TENURE

It is an oversimplification to state that land is needed for most tourism development projects. Developers must consider the location, quality, and physical attributes of the land before entering into an agreement to acquire control of the land. While land assessment may seem an onerous task, acquisition itself may make the assessment process seem like child's play. Acquisition becomes extremely complicated when various land tenure systems must be recognized and dealt with at the same time. Such is the case in Ghana.

Ghana has a history rich in tradition and culture. Located in West Africa, its land tenure system was formed centuries ago, for the most part based on tribal traditions. Prior to colonial rule, disputes over land were often settled by force. Boundaries were rarely recognized and changed with the fortunes of the various tribes. Colonial powers often left traditional land tenure systems in place unless they required the land for their own purposes. Upon independence in 1957, the new national government inherited a system of land tenure which needed codification and registration if development of all types was to proceed on a somewhat stable course.

Currently, three historical claims to land are recognized by the national government: family, quarter, and stool. Family lands are those controlled by one family and which have been passed down through generations. Family lands were acquired when a family left a tribe and settled land that was not claimed by any other tribal entity. Similarly, quarter lands are those controlled by descendants of one family with some loose affiliation binding all descen-dants together. The largest share of the country's land base is controlled by tribes or villages with a recognized chief. These are called stool lands because the chief, symbolically, receives his authority from a golden stool. When made a chief, he is enstooled, and if village elders strip his authority in concurrence with the Queen Mother, he is destooled. As in small city-states, a village chief owes his allegiance to a paramount chief, who in turn recognizes the authority of, in the case of the Ashanti people, a king or Ashantehene.

In 1962, Ghana's national government passed the Lands Act, an attempt to bring order to the confusing system of land tenure in place. Provisions of the act require that all classes of land be subject to registration. Boundaries must be submitted to the national government for registration and adjudication of those in dispute. This system has been resisted and is still far from complete. Secondly, foreign ownership of land is prohibited, but leases are allowed. At the present time, land can be leased from a chief for development, but the lease arrangement must be submitted to the national government for review. In keeping with tradition, lands are owned by ancestors, the living, and the yet to be born. Any lease arrangement must respect the ancestors who passed on the land to the living, must not unduly damage the rights of the living, and must provide for the welfare of the unborn. The chief is not to benefit directly from the lease arrangement, but is required to represent all three classes of people. If the lease is deemed satisfactory, a libation is poured to the ancestors in a tradition-rich cer-

(continued on next page)

emony in order to obtain their blessings. Leases are set at 99 years for domestic use, and 50 years for commercial.

The Lands Act also sets the requirements for government purchase of land for its own use. It follows the colonial model, where in the case of family and quarter lands, eminent domain is practiced, but the government leases stool lands in perpetuity at a yearly rate. For example, the colonial government established Kakum National Park in the Central Region in 1920 as a forest reserve by leasing stool lands. As long as proceeds from logging were available, the stool was paid an annual rent. Now that it is a national park prohibiting logging and trespass, annual rents have ceased even though the land remains, technically, stool land. Traditional authorities are petitioning the national government to reinstate annual rents, especially since the park is beginning to receive substantial revenue from user fees.

Since 1962, other acts have been passed which allow family lands to be sold to individuals, a freehold situation thus creating another form of land tenure, but prohibiting quarter and stool land holders from disposing of their lands in a similar manner. In 1982, outright sale of family lands was prohibited, but the right to sell was returned to family lands in 1993.

Currently, in the lower third of the country, land registration required in the 1962 act is making some progress. Anyone purchasing or leasing land must publish a notice of the sale in various newspapers, with a one-month reserve time for counterclaims to be heard. If disputes are entered, an adjudication committee hears the case and renders a decision. This, however, does not prohibit a future claim from someone who may have been unable to receive adequate notice of the pending land sale or lease.

If the above account of the land tenure system in Ghana appears confusing to the reader, it is equally so to the developer. Many rely on national government assistance to secure development rights to a piece of property. Whenever land-tenure systems are based on historical, traditional, and cultural rights, the issue of land transfers for development purposes adds cost and risk to the procedure and is sure to keep numerous lawyers in practice.

Source: Ghana Ministry of Lands and Forestry

CULTURE MIX

Figure 5.1 encapsulates the impacts of different cultures existing in a tourist destination. The tourist culture, residual culture, and tourism business culture (transitional companies) to a large extent determine the state of development, local and national policies, local business environment, and natural habitat. These impacts in turn affect the host culture. How a host culture changes or reacts to increasing levels of tourism is a function of how divergent the extraneous cultures are from the host culture, and the changes that take place in the destination. Some of the more commonly observed or measured sociocultural impacts are discussed below.

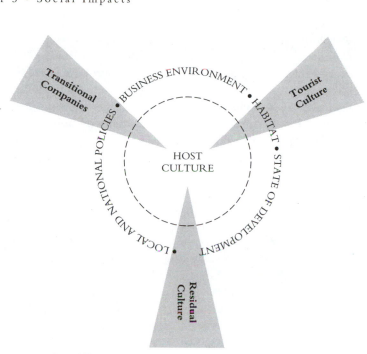

Figure 5.1 Compounded Cultural and Operational Forces

Source: Jafari, 1989

SOCIOCULTURAL IMPACTS

Tourism's sociocultural impacts can be grouped into two categories, qualitative and quantitative. Qualitative impacts are not easily measured. They can be observed, but the magnitude of their effects are rarely examined with respect to what population segments are most susceptible to the impact, how many people are affected, and when in the development process they are most likely to occur. Quantitative impacts, on the other hand, are measurable (e.g., crime). There is some debate as to whether quantitative and qualitative sociocultural impacts are distinctively different, or whether the quantitative impacts are simply indicators for the qualitative impacts. What follows is an examination of these impacts beginning with the qualitative types.

Demonstration Effect

Acculturation theory assumes that when two cultures interact, the dominant culture overpowers the weaker one, resulting in changes within the weaker culture. The demonstration effect is another name for this process of acculturation. It is most apparent where economic class differences between hosts and guests are greatest. Free-spending tourists engaging in pleasurable activities exert a powerful influence on host societies. Members of the host society are drawn to the tourist culture because of the emphasis on pleasure and the seemingly endless supply of money which to many represents a modern way of life (Smith, 1982). Younger members of the host society are most susceptible to the demonstration effect (Murphy, 1985). Some of the indicators of the demonstration effect include the abandonment of traditional enterprises (e.g. agriculture) to join the labor force catering to tourists, adoption of tourist dress and language, change in societal values and roles, and migration from rural areas to tourist destinations. It is not unusual for young members of a society to earn more money from tourists by pandering and prostitution than their parents, who are engaged in producing culturally reinforcing handicrafts which may be sold to tourists at unbelievably low prices. In addition to the decline in moral values, the demonstration effect can result in the loss of artistic skills, as young members of the host society reject the low paying, long apprenticeship periods required to learn traditional skills. The demonstration effect is also observable when members of the host society try to fully assimilate themselves into the tourist culture. Examples of this can be seen on tropical islands where locals have become part of the beach bum crowd. Whereas the tourists can return home and recharge themselves financially and emotionally, the local beach bum finds that he has adopted a monoculture with few psychologically counterbalancing opportunities. The demonstration effect does not only affect residents of developing countries. Gambling meccas (e.g., Las Vegas, Monte Carlo) have their own segments of society which can not resist the bright lights and party atmosphere of the casinos. Paychecks lost at the table translate into severe emotional and economic problems. Because of the strong gambling culture, many areas throughout the world restrict gambling to tourists, prohibiting it for local residents. However, this may result in another aspect of the demonstration effect, resentment over preferential treatment of foreigners.

It should not be assumed that all demonstration effect impacts are inherently bad. Rural economies may not be able to support an increasing population, and tourism may offer employment opportunities that were not previously available in the local community. Changing societal roles may give more decision-making power to women and younger members of the society who, prior to tourism development, held subservient and dependent positions within the household. Herein lies one of the problems in analyzing the sociocultural impacts of tourism: Who determines whether changes are detrimental or beneficial? If the interpreter of change assumes that any modification to the traditional culture is unacceptable, then the demonstration effect will be seen as negative sociocultural impact.

However, if one assumes that cultural change is inevitable and it is accompanied by other opportunities (e.g., development of an educational system) related to tourism development, then the demonstration effect need not always be something to avoid.

Marginal Man

Associated with the demonstration effect is the phenomenon known as the marginal man. When members of a host society attempt to fully assimilate themselves into the tourist culture, they reject some or all of the values of the host society. This rejection constitutes a removal from one culture, with the expectation of acceptance by another. However, because the tourist culture is often based on excessive play behavior made possible by large amounts of money, full assimilation is not probable. Tourists always have the option of returning to ordinary life to build the financial resources needed for another round of touristic experience. The marginal man does not have this option as he has rejected his ordinary life. When it dawns on the marginal man that he cannot continue his pursuit of pleasure, he finds that it is impossible to assimilate back into the original culture. Not only did he reject his original culture, but it in turn has rejected him. Marginal refers then to a person who is living on the outside boundaries of both the host and tourist culture, with full assimilation into either one impossible (Smith, 1982). The marginal man has not adopted a set of norms and standards acceptable to either culture, and his behavior is considered deviant by both groups, further separating the marginal man from either culture. One of the only options left for the marginal man is to physically move to another place and attempt the process of assimilation into a new culture.

Culture Shock

Culture shock can be defined as the anxiety which results from losing the physical and psychological markers of one's home environment (Oberg, 1960). Culture shock is one of the few sociocultural impacts of tourism which affects tourists. Most of the literature on tourism's impacts centers on the effects of tourism on host societies. This phenomenon is understandable since tourists choose where and what they want to visit, while members of the host society are often unable to choose if they even want tourists. However, culture shock is one of the few identified sociocultural impacts that affects both hosts and guests.

Culture shock manifests itself in different ways. For the tourists, it appears when they adjust to different languages, lifestyles, dress, and other aspects of behavior acceptable in the destination but different from the home environment. The extent of culture shock is a function of cultural distance. The greater the difference in the culture of the tourist's home environment and what he or she encounters at the destination, the greater the cultural distance and hence culture shock. Culture shock for host societies is also related to cultural difference, but in this case it refers more to the difference between the prevailing tourist culture and the host culture than to any specific culture existing within a particular market. Tourists can and do insulate themselves against culture shock by traveling in groups or purchasing a package tour. Traveling within the "environmental bubble" of a package tour allows an exotic culture to be observed without having to be experienced. Enclave developments exclusively for tourists also erect a protective culture shock barrier. Unfortunately for host societies, enclaves or travel within an "environmental bubble" only serve to widen the gap between tourist and host cultures, thereby increasing culture shock for hosts. Host societies are reduced to the level of objects which can be collected on film or in the mind as souvenirs of the trip. The methods used to eliminate or reduce culture shock for tourists in turn increase the extent of culture shock for host societies.

Cultural Commodization

In the last chapter, environmental impacts are linked to the transformational character of tourism development; as the natural beauty of an area attracts tourists, facilities are constructed to meet their needs. Cultures also exert a strong draw, especially if they are considered exotic or differ markedly from the tourist's home environment. Because of the attractive potential of culture, attempts are made to package them for sale. This packaging is often referred to as cultural commodization. Dances or rituals with religious or culturally reinforcing properties for a host culture, may not be viewed with the same sense of importance by tourists, but they are nonetheless sought after as cultural experiences. Some rituals may take days to perform, too long to maintain a heightened arousal level for most tourists. However, the dances or costumes used in the ritual may seem exotic expressions worthy of purchase. When rituals are staged to fit into the tourist's time frame, cultural commodization results. Adams (1990) describes an attempt by Indonesian government officials to designate a "tradition-free" zone in which rituals and dances of life and death could be presented to tourists at the same time, even though this is forbidden by Toraja tradition. This "tradition-free" zone permits tradition to be ignored and exotic elements of the culture to be sold to tourists.

Cultural commodization also occurs when members of a host society mass produce handicrafts to sell to tourists, bypassing traditional methods of manufacture, or when they offer their bodies as photo opportunities to tourists at a price. If economic forces prevail, strong traditions are ignored and eventually lost as they become modified products for sale. Further modification of traditions occurs as marketing concepts of target markets and product positioning replace the fundamental reasons for the existence of the traditions.

Greenwood (1989) argues that cultural commodization occurs whenever local cultures are used as part of the pull component for destination promotion. It is more profound when local cultures are not compensated for the attraction embodied in their culture, but can also occur if tourists pay for the privilege of viewing elements (e.g., dances) of a culture and in the process of viewing somehow alter the meaning of the activities presented.

Relocation and Displacement

Relocation is an accepted phenomenon in western society. People move freely within their country in pursuit of employment opportunities or in search of a better quality of life, most frequently in European or American cultures, as people from all regions mix and share cultural values. In other societies, free relocation is not commonly practiced or accepted. The economic forces of tourism development can result in population shifts. New tourism developments can provide employment opportunities for local people as well as immigrants to the area. New immigrants to an area can bring in new cultural values. Cultural changes not only arise from mixing cultures with different values, but also through legislative or policy shifts. In democratic societies where all residents of a community express their opinion by voting, immigration can shift the balance of power, resulting in changing norms and standards supported by legislative language. For example, extended hours for establishments serving alcoholic beverages may be a reaction to the importance of a local tourism industry. Without the tourism development stimulus generating employment opportunities for new residents, local liquor laws may have remained unchanged. Consequently, any resulting negative impacts (e.g., increase in alcohol-related traffic accidents) would not have occurred. Political power bases for rural communities can shift dramatically in a short period of time, especially if the area is small to begin with and tourism development is rapid.

Displacement occurs whenever people move from the area because a tourism industry develops. People on fixed incomes may not be able to afford the higher property taxes which accompany an increase in assessed value. Other local long-term residents may not like what the area has become and seek a different living environment. Forced displacement also occurs when governments exercise their authoritative power, in some countries called rights of eminent domain, to force people off land designated for tourism development. Displacement causes culture change, since cultures are built on the traditions of a group of people. When people move, their traditions move with them. New people moving into an area bring their own traditions, resulting in wholesale cultural change. Any sociocultural impact of displacement or relocation is often difficult to quantify since these events may occur gradually over time. If a sociocultural assessment occurs after significant relocation or displacement has already occurred, it may not be possible to reconstruct the culture that existed in the area prior to tourism development; hence, there is no base from which to measure change.

As mentioned, governmental powers, using the concept of eminent domain, may force relocation. Eminent domain requires that land owners be compensated at a price commensurate with market value. While this "land taking" is constitutionally legal in many countries, some societies do not practice fee simple ownership practices. For example, the Melanesian people's cultural identity derives from social group membership attached to specific geographical settings. Private land ownership is not legal, nor is land perceived as an economic asset (Bonnemaison, 1985). There is no universally accepted system of land tenure. Depending on the society, property rights may be subject to residence, or current usage and inheritance customs, among others (Crocombe, 1972; Lane, 1971). Obviously, the use of land and the transfer of rights to developers or governments can impose major social impacts on societies which view land as anything but an economic asset to be bought and sold.

Dependency

When tourism supplants traditional economic enterprises or creates a strong, new economic system, dependency relationships can result. This is most likely in developing countries which do not have the capital or expertise to develop their own tourism industry. Instead, they rely on businesses from the developed world to bring tourists into the area, build facilities, and manage the industry. The result is high leakage, as tourist money does not stay in the local area for respending and income generation, but is returned to the headquarters of the multinational firms which operate tourist facilities and provide transportation services. Mathieson and Wall (1982) refer to this dependency as neo-colonialism. Dependency relationships can contribute to cultural commodization as entrepreneurs from the developed world decide what tourists want and repackage cultures for presentation and sale to tourists. Because of the loss of traditional enterprises, local residents accept tourism as the only means of employment and income. At the extreme, neo-colonialism provides very few additional economic gains from tourism, and developing countries find themselves being viewed as pleasure colonies for the elite of the developed world.

Murphy (1985) relates dependency to the demonstration effect. He argues that tourism induced social change can lead to development and socioeconomic advantages (e.g., employment), but can also result in a dependency relationship if a host society is unable to fully capture the socioeconomic benefits. While some members of the host society capitalize on increased development, many other members do not fully benefit or gain from development, remaining dependent on multinational firms which direct the development process. Small-scale operations such as guest houses or local restaurants find it difficult to prosper without linkages to the multinational firms which are more interested in directing the flow of tourists to their own operations rather than spreading business throughout the community. One way the demonstration effect occurs is when the prosperity created by and for the multinationals attracts immigrants from non-touristic areas to new tourist "meccas" in the hope of sharing in tourist-induced wealth. For many, the dream of wealth is illusory as the emulation of tourist lifestyles remains elusive, and resentment toward tourists and the development which brought them is the only lasting result.

Crime

One of the few quantifiable sociocultural impacts is the type and magnitude of crime associated with tourism. Crime statistics are routinely maintained, allowing for an analysis of change over time. Tourism contributes to crime increases in an couple of ways. First, as the level of development increases, there is a corresponding increase in people attracted to the area for employment. As local populations increase, the potential for criminal activity increases. In this case, tourism should not be viewed as the cause of crime any more than an increase in any other industrial activity which contributes to population growth causes crime. Secondly, tourists are often easy prey for criminal activity. The majority of crimes against tourists are robbery, larceny, and burglary. Tourists are generally concentrated in an area (e.g., hotels) which make them easy to locate. They are often free spenders, which reinforces the income differential existing between them and local residents. They are also less likely to return for any legal trials if the crime is not major (e.g., loss of jewelry) and losses are covered by insurance. Resorts and hotels attempt to reduce the incidence of criminal activity by instituting security programs for guests which may include increasing the number of security personnel on the premises, offering safe storage for valuables, use of surveillance cameras in high crime areas, or publishing recommendations for areas to avoid during certain periods of the day. Some destinations also have victim-compensation programs, including covering expenses associated with a return visit for testifying during any subsequent court case.

One of the reasons frequently mentioned for increases in criminal activity directed at tourists is the perceived gap between the wealth of visitors and residents. If only a small portion of the host population economically benefits from tourism, negative attitudes about tourism and tourist wealth are common. When local inhabitants are not allowed to enter tourist facilities, this increases the level of resentment against the privileged class (Dogan, 1989). In extreme cases, large-scale social uprisings result when the level of resentment reaches the boiling point, as happened in Trinidad in 1970 (Wall and Ali, 1977).

Prostitution

Prostitution is not included in the above crime category, although it is illegal in many countries. In other areas, it can be considered part of the attraction package. Prostitution is legal in the state of Nevada, and when one of the more well known brothels was unable to maintain its mortgage payment, ownership reverted to the mortgager, in this case the United States government. In other areas of the world, prostitution is a tourist attraction (e.g., Asian sex tours). The tourist culture, based on non-ordinary life and the pursuit of pleasure, supports the types of activities not normally pursued in one's home environment; prostitution may be one of those activities. Since local standards differ in their acceptance of prostitution, there is no evidence based on statistical data of tourism's role in increasing prostitution. However, tourism is conducive to perpetuating and supporting activities outside the bounds of ordinary life. It is generally assumed that the nature of tourism contributes to prostitution (Jud and Krause, 1976). Even when tourism may not be the cause of prostitution and other illicit activities such as drug trafficking and smuggling, host communities may still perceive that it is the reason for increases in these activities (Belisle and Hoy, 1980). Certain tourism activities, such as casino gambling, may be more susceptible to this criticism than others (Pizam and Pokela, 1985).

Other

The use of stimulants, mind-expanding hallucinogenic, and other sense altering drugs have been around probably as long as prostitution. Because travel provides physical and psychological escape, drug use is viewed as contributing to the enhancement of psychological escape. Jamaica may be famous for its beach resorts, but many returning travelers also tell stories of the wonderful "ganja," a local idiom for marijuana. Hashish use in India, although illegal, is accepted as part of daily life for many people and is commonly made available to tourists. Tourism's contribution to increasing drug use by local residents has not been thoroughly studied, but its influence can be viewed as one of the manifestations of the demonstration effect.

Religious value changes have also been addressed as a product of a strong tourist culture. The powerful influence of the tourist culture manifested in the demonstration effect has the potential to overthrow strong moral conduct values inherent in different religions. Religious experiences, important to tourists on a pilgrimage, can also be affected by increasing levels of tourism. The presence of non-believers mixing with serious religious pilgrims at a holy site can reduce the spiritual experience for true believers. Inappropriate behavior (e.g., photography of holy shrines), based on ignorance rather than malice, can degrade the quality of the religious experience for pilgrims who may only be able to make the pilgrimage once in their life.

Language changes are also noted as a consequence of tourism. Loss of native languages occurs when host societies adopt the language of their visitors, usually as a result of the tourists' inability to communicate in the language of their hosts. Societies with a language difficult to learn or one that is regionally limited are most at risk. Language changes also occur from the importation of slang or phrases that are not translatable into the native tongue. Language changes may be an indicator of acculturation and can be used to study the effects of tourist contact with local societies.

Diseases can be transmitted from touristic contact. The spread of AIDS in North America has been linked to a flight attendant employed by an international airline. Similarly, the spread of other sexually transmitted diseases, resulting in widespread decimation of insulated societies, has been linked to the establishment of new settlements. While modern tourism is not blamed for these cases of unintentional genocide, it is still responsible for the movement of disease vectors between regions of the world. Some countries deal with the spread of disease by requiring specific immunizations (e.g., yellow fever) before tourists are issued visas in an attempt to protect susceptible members of the population.

Social structures frequently redefine themselves after tourism becomes a significant economic force. Young people may decide to forego traditional skills training, opting for jobs, including illicit occupations, in the tourism industry. In patriarchal societies with clearly defined roles, women working outside the home may upset traditional family members' roles (Kousis, 1989). While some may feel that this eventually leads to economic emancipation for women in societies which place little value on their intellectual abilities, there is nonetheless a change occurring whose long-term consequences are debatable.

SOCIOCULTURAL BENEFITS

Not all sociocultural impacts are detrimental to host societies. The process of development provides opportunities for an improved quality of life. Increased employment opportunities, possibly allowing for multiple income households, enhances purchasing power and the acquisition of goods previously considered cost prohibitive. Increasing levels of tourism can also result in improvements of basic social services (e.g., medical, security). Determining what constitutes beneficial change is based on subjective value judgments. Acquisition of material goods may be viewed as a move to secularization and away from spiritually reinforcing traditional values. Alternately, it can be viewed as an improvement in living standards and quality of life. What constitutes sociocultural benefits and costs remains a controversial topic. In spite of this difficulty, some non-quantifiable sociocultural benefits are assumed to be associated with tourism development.

Peace and Understanding

Cultural differences between groups of people result primarily from the formation of complex social relationships which develop in relative isolation from each other. Misunderstanding between social groups can be reduced by sharing and learning from each other what is important to each group's value system. Tourism provides an opportunity for this sharing and learning to take place.

Young children apparently happy with tourists at Cape Coast, Ghana.
Photo by the author

Dann (1988) describes some of the classic arguments against tourism, including tourism as a form of imperialism, capitalist exploitation, and promoter of master/servant relationships. He counters each argument against tourism with equally compelling evidence supporting tourism as a means of promoting understanding and exchange (social and economic). Although no substantial evidence exists to support the statement that tourism is a force for peace, it is clear that peace is not attainable without tourism. People-to-people interaction is necessary for understanding and discovery of common ground, and tourism provides the stage for social exchange to occur.

Where tourism involves more than a cursory interaction between hosts and guests, there is some evidence to indicate that it has beneficial consequences. Stringer (1981) describes how tourists and owners of bed and breakfast operations in Great Britain saw cross-national contact as the center of the transaction, with the tourist viewing the exchange as an authentic tourism experience. Similarly, Gamper (1981) describes how increased contact between hosts and guests in two communities in Austria led to the removal of ethnic barriers which had been in place centuries before the arrival of tourism. The main feature of these examples is close personal contact between hosts and guests. If tourism is seen and presented only as a touring experience with little or no social contact fostered between hosts and guests, peace and understanding between different cultures will not result.

Cultural Pride

The process of hosting guests implies a sharing of resources, both environmental and social. If tourism development is sensitive to the needs and desires of a host society, the type of tourism created will project a sense of place. A sense of place can be defined as "...the subtle, intangible, but soul-deep mix of landscape, smells, sounds, history, neighbors, and friends that constitute a place, a homeland" (Wilkinson, 1990: 75). Although developing a sense of place and a local tourism industry at the same time may not be an easy task, the rewards are substantial. Not only does the community benefit from an active tourism industry, but community pride in what it has been able to accomplish is enhanced. Instead of leaving town during the height of the tourist season, local residents exhibit pride in showcasing their community for visitors. Similar to the feeling of hosting friends in one's house, community pride is exhibited in the type of development created, and extends into the quality of service delivered to visitors. In the absence of any strong sense of place, tourism can easily overwhelm a community and result in some of the negative social impacts discussed above.

One of the sociocultural impacts discussed above, cultural commodization, is difficult to identify since there is a fine line between a benefit
and a cost. For example, Esman (1984) describes a situation in Louisiana
where the Cajuns have constructed a tourist stage

> "which permits them to act out aspects of their culture for their own
> and their visitor's edification. This tourism stage, stimulated by a
> general interest in ethnic identity and a desire to maintain an ethnic
> boundary, has helped to preserve aspects of traditional culture that
> might otherwise have died" (1984:464).

Cultural pride and preservation may be reinforced for one group of people
in one particular situation, and viewed as cultural commodization by another group in a similar situation.

Education

Education and learning can be acquired through formal instruction or
through life experience. Education through tourism is similar to the understanding that occurs when members of different cultures interact. Learning
about each other's way of life, values, and traditions is a form of educational
enrichment. Both hosts and guests gain the opportunity to learn from each
other. Critics of tourism development, especially the forms of development
often occurring in developing countries, argue that enclave, packaged types
of tourism erects barriers and does not stimulate social interaction. While
this does occur, it is not true of all types of tourism. Embedded in the value
system that underpins "alternative forms of tourism" is a focus on education. For many travelers, especially those with experience, education is replacing simple "site collecting" as a benefit to be earned from tourism.

Educational benefits from travel are more heavily weighted in favor of
the traveler. Although the host society can learn about different ways of
life from its visitors, this type of educational enrichment is most likely to
occur when hosts and guests meet as equals. When members of the host
society fill subservient roles (e.g., wait staff), little opportunity for meaningful social exchange results. In this case, the educational benefits to a
host society are more related to the type of skills acquired which are necessary to be employed in the tourism industry.

SOCIOCULTURAL IMPACT MODEL

As mentioned, it is difficult to determine what constitutes a sociocultural
benefit or cost. When a benefit crosses the line and becomes a cost may be
a function of an individual's perception or may be related to stages in the

development process. The magnitude and types of sociocultural impacts depend on the intensity and speed with which tourism development occurs. Doxey (1976) identifies four stages in the development process which help determine when social impacts are most likely to occur. The first stage he terms euphoria, which occurs during the discovery or initial tourism development phase for a destination. Each succeeding stage is characterized by increasing levels of facility development. The next section outlines the different stages and their relationship to sociocultural impacts.

Euphoria

In the euphoric stage, local residents support tourism development and are willing and eager to share their community with visitors. New employment opportunities, increased incomes, and escalating property values are often cited as positive benefits. Rapid development is frequently associated with higher levels of euphoria. Development opponents are few in number and generally dismissed as part of a radical fringe element.

The euphoria stage is most likely to occur when local economies have been in a dormant stage for a period of time and tourism brings new opportunities for growth and expansion. They also occur when existing industry leaves, unemployment results, and tourism is viewed as a replacement industry. Local support for the tourism industry is based on economic projections that ignore or downplay social costs. Most likely, few

Tourists enjoying a form of indigenous transportation. Photo by the author.

local residents have had any experience with an economic tourism boom and are unaware of the potential negative consequences.

Apathy

Eventually, the growth which fueled rapid tourism development begins to slow. Land values and business expansion, although continuing their upward rise, are no longer increasing at the same rate as during the tourism boom period. The level of tourism reaches a point where the novelty of arriving visitors gives way to the acceptance of tourism as part of the community's economic base. The social structure of the area most likely changes with new migrants arriving in search of jobs, and family roles change as different members (e.g., youths) find employment within the industry. The promise of economic "good times" which pervaded the euphoria stage is now viewed as accruing to only a limited number of residents, with the rest not realizing or believing the potential.

Irritation

If the level of tourism activity continues to expand, either through increases in arrivals or season extension, a stage of irritation may occur. Most likely, tourism development has been unplanned and has spread into environmentally sensitive areas. Locals must now share with outsiders what used to be their own recreation areas. Concurrently, prices of staple goods (e.g., food) rise at a much faster rate than local incomes. Income growth realized in earlier stages vanishes as inflation takes back earlier gains. If the environment or the attractiveness of the local area is drastically modified through development, visitor numbers may decrease, resulting in an overabundance of facilities and eventually economic decline. During the irritation stage, the social and environmental impacts of unplanned tourism development begin to receive attention. Local residents perceive a loss of "place" and blame tourism for it.

Antagonism

As a sense of loss of "place" becomes more profound, residents blame tourists for the changes rather than the unplanned and uncontrolled developments. Most likely, the type of tourist that arrived when the area was in the euphoria stage has been replaced with an entirely new type of visitor that is less interested in local customs and traditions and more drawn to specific physical attractions. Local residents manifest their antagonism through the passive aggressive types of behavior they exhibit toward tourists, for example, through angry letters to the local newspaper editor complaining about different types of tourist behavior. They may come up with names for tourists which have a derogatory connotation understood only by the locals. Passive aggressive behavior may shift to overtly aggressive actions, as when automobiles with out-of-state license plates are chosen as objects for criminal activity.

Antagonistic activity can occur in any area, but it is more apparent where a wide gap between the lifestyle of the tourists and locals exists. In developing countries, it may occur after local residents realize that the tourism industry does not offer the type of jobs desired. If development is of an enclave, "environmental bubble" nature, very little social exchange between locals and tourists occurs, in contrast to the first tourists who arrived when the area was relatively undeveloped and mixing between the groups was necessary and desired. The stage of antagonism can occur whenever either group, and most likely both, is perceived as a commodity to be exploited rather than as a guest or host.

The different stages discussed above are graphically represented in Figure 5.2. Even though tourist arrivals increase from point A to point B, social impacts decrease; this is the stage of euphoria. The dashed horizontal line AD depicts social impact levels which existed prior to tourism development. With the euphoric feeling that accompanies rapid growth and development, the aggregate perceived level of social impacts experiences a decline. As tourists continue to arrive and facility development increases, the nature of host/guest interactions begins to change. Eventually euphoria gives way to apathy, and the level of social impacts begins to move upward (point B). The types of social impacts may be entirely different than

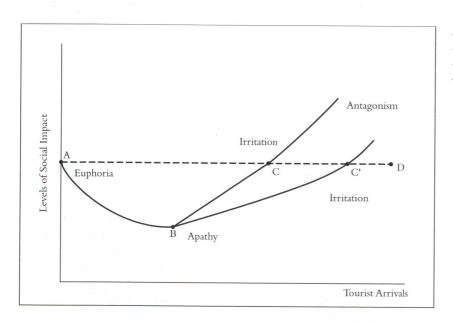

Figure 5.2 Level of Social Impacts With Relationship to Doxey's Euphoria/Antagonism Model

those that existed prior to tourism development. Discontent with the type of development or the level of tourism that the area now experiences begins to pervade the social consciousness. Even though it is not entirely possible to compare the different types of social impacts of pre- and post-tourism development, certain indicators show that the level of impacts increases. Eventually, a point (C) is reached where apathy gives way to irritation. If a social carrying capacity for tourism could be determined, it would be somewhere between point B and C, or where the level of social impacts is less than that existing before tourism growth and development. Anything beyond point C results in an even greater level of social impacts than before development, and if put in economic terms, would be beyond the point of diminishing returns. If tourism continues to expand, irritation changes to antagonism. At this point, it is too late to turn back the level of tourism development and recapture the sense of "place" that previously existed.

The process outlined by Doxey is not *fait accompli*. It can be directed, but to do so requires the active involvement of community residents and businesses. Methods of coping behavior or sociocultural impact mitigation strategies must be adopted.

SOCIOCULTURAL IMPACT MITIGATION

The time it takes to proceed through each of Doxey's stages depends on various factors, including the types of development, number of tourists, preferred tourist activities, and extent of development planning. There is no set social carrying capacity for any area, as various techniques can forestall the advent of the irritation stage and at least hold the line on the level of perceived sociocultural impacts. In Figure 5.2 the curve ABC′ depicts the stage where additional tourist arrivals can be accommodated without reaching the irritation stage as quickly.

Numerous methods can be employed to deal with the onset of the irritation stage. A brief overview of some of these follows. Most are revisited in subsequent chapters of this text when they become integral components of other concepts that are related to the development process.

1. Inform residents of the advantages and costs of tourism development. Too often, residents are not familiar with the concept of economic multipliers. Explaining how tourism expenditures are distributed throughout the local economy should be one of the primary objectives of a resident education program. Information on some of the

consequences of increased levels of tourism should also be addressed in order to avoid "surprises."

2. Plan tourism based on goals and priorities identified by local residents. Obviously, this is much easier to recommend than it is to implement. There are many ways to obtain public input including public meetings, opinion polls, studies of perceptions and attitudes, and referenda. The main idea is to allow local people to feel a part of the development planning process. Development plans proceed more smoothly when local residents sense they have ownership of the resources used for tourism development.

3. Involve both public and private sectors in the development process with the intent of maintaining the integrity and quality of local natural resources. Many local residents find the same resources which attracted them to the area attract tourists. Crowding and congestion can seriously affect local residents' perceptions of the benefits of tourism development. If resources are used wisely and their integrity is maintained, most residents do not oppose or begrudge visitors' use of the resources.

4. Provide opportunities for minority groups or native peoples to become involved in the tourism industry. Tourism development benefits from diversity. Minority or native peoples have a unique sociocultural resource which, if developed properly, adds to the local attraction package.

5. Utilize local capital, expertise, and labor whenever possible. Local ownership of the tourism industry is an important ingredient for obtaining support. It may not be always possible to utilize local capital, as in small rural communities or developing countries it is not always readily available. Similarly, local expertise may not exist for the types of management positions required. Whenever these resources are found in short supply, development must proceed at a slow enough pace to allow for local capital accumulation and expertise to be acquired before the next phase of growth begins. Rapid growth and development tends to exclude local investment and participation in the industry, leading to a feeling of alienation.

6. Provide opportunities for community participation in local events and festivals. One of the advantages gained from festivals and event is community pride. Inviting visitors to participate in events that reinforce community identity and values is the basis on which a strong host recognition can be built.

7. Deal with present problems before proceeding with increased

tourism development. Once negative sociocultural impacts are recognized, the community must deal directly with resolving those problems. Further development at this time will only create new problems and exacerbate present ones.

8. If thematic development is chosen, it should reflect the area's historical, lifestyle, or geographic setting. Disney-type themes are suited to created attractions. Communities are living attractions and should project development themes that have relevance to local residents. Fantasy theme parks may be wonderful places to visit but they do not make acceptable places to live. Well-planned "sacrifice areas" for major contrived attractions are necessary in order to manage some of the sociocultural impacts.

9. Promotional programs should reflect images supported by and subject to the endorsement of local residents. Again, this involves a concerted effort to involve local residents in the tourism industry. The extent of involvement will determine the point at which apathy changes to irritation.

Even when the above methods become part of the strategic planning process for tourism development, there will still be debates over what constitutes a benefit and cost and how important each one is. There will be forces pushing for increased levels of development at the same time that other groups claim too much development has already occurred. Ultimately, the final decision about acceptable levels of development finds its way into the political arena. Political decisions can be simply a power struggle between different interest groups, or they can proceed based on a defined process which includes collecting factual data to guide the decision. The Limits of Acceptable Change strategy, first discussed in the preceding chapter, combines data with politics to achieve this goal. With slight modifications, the strategy can incorporate sociocultural elements into the development process.

LIMITS OF ACCEPTABLE CHANGE

Although the Limits of Acceptable Change (LAC) framework has a social component, it has been for the most part restricted to users of the resources and not providers. Since it is a planning framework, with slight modifications it can be applied to providers as well, and used as a community tourism planning model. A brief review of the LAC steps modified to fit a community planning framework follows.

1. Identify Area Issues and Concerns. What special conditions currently exist in the area which may be changed via growth in tourism? Are there certain traditions, local events, or customs which reinforce resident values and are susceptible to change if tourism development proceeds too rapidly?

2. Define or Describe Opportunity Classes. While this step was developed to protect a certain type of user experience, it can also be used to identify opportunities for local residents who wish to participate in the tourism industry. What social conditions represent opportunities that may appeal to visitors but should also be protected for residents? Some opportunities may be identified which can improve the quality of life for certain segments of the local population. For example, if further tourism development is being supported as a means of employment, one of the opportunity classes would be for employment to increase within a certain socioeconomic group of the population.

3. Select Indicators of Social Conditions. Indicators should be measurable and relate to identified opportunities. Again, if employment is used as an indicator, there must be some way to track employment effects on targeted socioeconomic groups. Other indicators of social conditions may include perceptions of crowding and congestion at local recreation areas. Perceptual studies using similar instruments and designs conducted on a regular basis can provide a barometer type measure of change for selected indicators. The barometer concept, using multiple indicators, is appealing as individual indicators may portray a biased view of change. A "bundle" of indicators provides a more comprehensive view of change.

4. Inventory Social Conditions. What social conditions exist right now that should be protected? What social indicators are available to assess the current situation?

5. Specify Standards for Social Conditions. This step identifies the range of conditions considered appropriate and acceptable. In a sense, it acknowledges the existence of an initial carrying capacity. Standards become the carrying capacity, and can be readjusted to shift carrying capacity, allowing flexibility in the type and level of development preferred.

6. Identify Alternative Opportunity Class Allocations. This step forces a decision-making body to determine the type and scale of development acceptable. How many new jobs are desired? How much pressure on local infrastructure is tolerable? These questions should

be answered when standards are initially identified. In this step, it is important to identify developments (i.e., alternatives) that can be accommodated without exceeding pre-selected standards, or that have the best chance of reaching minimum standards (e.g., new jobs).

7. Identify Actions Required for Each Alternative. What type of policies, regulations or planning requirements are needed to make each alternative feasible? Who does what and how it is done are addressed during this stage. Public and private sector roles are defined and outlined.

8. Evaluate and Select an Alternative. After each alternative development strategy is fully analyzed, each one is compared and evaluated with respect to expected outcomes. During this stage, the alternative expected to provide the greatest economic contribution to the local community without exceeding critical social or environmental standards is selected.

9. Implement and Monitor. Once a preferred alternative is implemented, a social monitoring scheme should be implemented concurrently.

The entire LAC process may take some time to implement, but if integrated with the techniques that extend the onset of the irritation stage, more tourists can be accommodated, thereby increasing economic impact without exceeding an area's theoretical social carrying capacity for tourism development. Opponents of the process may object on the grounds that private capital, land, and other resources should not be controlled by what appears to be a bureaucratic, socialized planning framework. Countering this position is the argument that bureaucratic development controls already exist (e.g., zoning) and these regulations must be implemented to protect social welfare. As discussed in Chapter 7, different types of community development strategies (or lack thereof) can lead to different levels of perceived social impacts. If a "sense of place" is altered it affects all community residents. Therefore, planning for community tourism development requires a process that involves as many people who are concerned about a "sense of place" as possible. The tourism product is a combination of different goods and services sold or available free of charge at a destination. Local resident cultures often supply as much of the total product as private sector vendors. Community involvement does not thwart capitalistic, free enterprise, but directs it into a long-run strategy that benefits as many providers of the total touristic experience as possible.

Social Indicators

One of the key elements of the LAC framework is the selection and monitoring of social indicators. Much of the early work on social indicators utilized secondary sources (e.g., census data) and focused on socioeconomic characteristics. Unemployment levels, median family incomes, and other indicators of economic well-being were the primary indices monitored to assess quality of life changes. Relatively little, if any, primary data was used, most likely because of cost and time constraints. Fitzsimmons and Ferb (1977) were among the first to develop small sample primary data collection instruments, which had the advantage of relatively low cost and assessed attitudinal dimensions of community life which went beyond socioeconomic characteristics. Their approach, termed Community Attitude Assessment Scale, used Likert type scales to determine the relative importance to individuals of diverse items such as schools, health services, recreation and leisure activities, social services, and so on. After collecting baseline information, the scale identified and monitored important dimensions of community life with periodic population sampling.

A criticism of any type of attitude or perceptual estimation scale is that the items evaluated may not reflect the important characteristics of community life. One method to overcome this objection is to assemble community focus groups and determine directly from local residents community characteristics important to their quality of life. This obviously increases data collection cost by adding a step.

Hetherington (1992, 1989) offers an alternative approach to determining social indicators, which asks community leaders to identify as many different groups as possible, assemble representatives from each group, and have them engage in an exercise termed "finding the heart and soul of the community." Workshop attendees split into small groups and are asked to draw a picture of what they believe represents the heart of the community, defined as the thing most critical to maintaining a functional community system. A similar exercise determines a community's soul, defined as the element(s) which gives a community its uniqueness or sense of place. Each small group presents its picture to the whole group and discusses the implications of what has been drawn. This process is intended to help community residents identify values which must be maintained or enhanced as development proceeds. It can also be used to identify sensitive social indicators which, when monitored over time, can determine whether important community values persist intact or have eroded.

An important question remains. How many social indicators should be monitored and how important is each one? A partial answer to this question may be found in the theory of salient beliefs. When any new information only serves to reinforce information already acquired, the point of salient beliefs is reached (Stutman and Newell, 1984). The most important social indicators, then, are those identified most frequently by workshop participants. They represent community values embraced by the majority of local residents. However, care must be exercised so that community values minority populations identify are not overwhelmed by those of one dominant culture. In the case where values differ between subcultures, the process of identifying appropriate social indicators to monitor becomes a more complex task which may have no optimal solution.

VIENNA CENTER PROJECT

The Vienna Centre project is the only longitudinal, multicountry study of tourism's sociocultural impacts conducted to date. It began in 1982 with the intent of studying tourism as a factor of sociocultural change. Representatives from six countries (Poland, Hungary, Spain, United States, United Kingdom, The Netherlands) cooperated to establish the research design, develop survey instruments, and compare findings. The primary research question is "whether tourism is an essential factor in social change within the host environment visited by tourists, and if so, what is the character of such change" (Przeclawski and Travis, 1989:8).

Each country representative selected at least one site within her/his home country to study. Sites selected were expected to meet or exceed four criteria:

1. Direct income derived from tourism should be in the range of 5–10 percent with tourism related employment between 5–15 percent of total employment.

2. The number of tourists arriving annually should be in the range of .5–2.5 the number of residents.

3. Small-scale accommodations (e.g., farm stays, guest houses) should account for at least 75 percent of all overnights.

4. Most services should be provided by local enterprises.

Because of the restrictive criteria chosen for site selection, results cannot be generalized to the entire population of the country nor to all types of tourism. The types of sites selected would most likely fit the profile of a community with a diversified economy with tourism not considered the primary sector. Residents from each site would be selected to receive a survey administered by phone or mail, with the minimum sample size set at 250 or 25–35 percent of the local population, whichever was larger.

Pizam and Telisman-Kosuta (1989) report some of the more important results of the study, including that host societies differed with respect to their acceptance of tourists' social behavior. Polish and British respondents were less tolerant of sexual permissiveness. Yugoslavian (at the time the study was conducted there was still a Yugoslavia) respondents were most tolerant of alcohol consumption, especially if it involved "drinking with friends," while the Polish group was less likely to tolerate this type of social interaction. While these results do not include all the sociological differences between these host societies, they indicate that different types of tourism have different effects on different host societies. This serves to reinforce earlier recommendations that host societies take an active role in the type(s) of tourism offered to visitors.

The study also reveals that negative changes appear to take place across all study areas. Honesty, friendliness, sincerity, and confidence among people seem to be declining. These changes, however, appear more related to some overall trend rather than associated with increasing tourism development. Most of the respondents notice sociocultural changes occurring in their community, but are not resisting these changes, especially since many are considered positive and appear to reinforce certain cultural values. The most positive changes noted from tourism are related to economic improvements (e.g., employment opportunities, increasing incomes). Few respondents perceive tourism as a negative influence on social relationships, with the exception of the Bulgarians who perceive that morality has declined as a result of increasing levels of tourism. Additionally, Bulgarians tend to perceive the most problems with tourism, whereas at the other end of the spectrum, Spanish residents view tourism most positively. The Poles are more likely to share the view of the Bulgarians.

The study shows that the major differences between members of a host society and its tourists are the way tourists spend leisure time and their view toward nature. Since leisure is a primary objective of pleasure travel, it is not surprising to find that tourists make different use of their leisure time than residents of the host society. More interesting was the finding that tourists tend to be observers of nature and host societies see themselves as "users" of nature.

Most respondents report high levels of satisfaction with the presence of tourists in their community, yet few want more tourism. Yugoslavs are the exception to this trend, as they tend to support increasing levels of tourism. This is not surprising considering that the study selected sites where tourism was not the dominant economic activity. Research reporting high levels of dissatisfaction with tourism and increasing levels of social impacts generally focus on a destination where tourism is the only or at least the dominant form of economic activity. Some of the findings compared across countries can be found in Tables 5.1, 5.2, and 5.3.

The findings of the Vienna Center project should not be assumed transferable to other areas. The study has many limitations which the project investigators acknowledge. However, there is a dearth of longitudinal

TABLE 5.1 Respondent's Perception of Changes in Social Relationships

Social Relationships*	YU $\overline{X}$(SD)	E $\overline{X}$(SD)	PL $\overline{X}$(SD)	UK $\overline{X}$(SD)	H $\overline{X}$(SD)	USA $\overline{X}$(SD)	BG $\overline{X}$(SD)
- Friendliness and sincerity	1.5(.7)	2.0(.9)	1.6(.7)	1.8(.7)	1.8(.8)	N/A	1.4(.7)
- Theft	2.7(.5)	2.8(.5)	2.5(.7)	2.6(.5)	2.6(.6)	N/A	2.7(.6)
- Hypocrisy	2.6(.6)	2.7(.6)	2.5(.6)	2.4(.5)	2.7(.5)	N/A	2.9(.5)
- Alcoholism	2.4(.7)	2.6(.7)	2.7(.6)	2.6(.5)	2.8(.4)	2.3(.6)	2.7(.6)
- Honesty	1.6(.7)	1.7(.8)	1.4(.6)	1.8(.6)	1.6(.7)	1.9(.5)	1.3(.6)
- Fights	2.2(.7)	2.1(.8)	2.0(.8)	2.3(.6)	2.1(.7)	N/A	2.1(.7)
- Unwillingness to work	2.4(.7)	2.3(.8)	2.3(.7)	2.2(.7)	2.2(.7)	N/A	2.3(.8)
- Drug addiction	2.2(.6)	2.8(.5)	2.4(.6)	2.7(.6)	2.5(.6)	2.3(.5)	2.1(.5)
- Politeness and good manners	2.0(.8)	2.2(.9)	1.8(.7)	1.7(.6)	2.1(.8)	2.0(.7)	1.6(.7)
- Hospitality	2.1(.8)	2.1(.8)	2.1(.7)	2.0(.5)	2.6(.6)	2.2(.7)	1.7(.8)
- Family conflicts	2.1(.6)	2.5(.7)	2.3(.6)	2.3(.5)	2.4(.5)	N/A	2.5(.7)
- Confidence among people	1.5(.7)	1.8(.9)	1.6(.7)	1.9(.6)	2.5(.6)	2.0(.6)	1.3(.6)
- Openness to sexual behavior	2.7(.6)	2.8(.5)	N/A	2.5(.5)	2.8(.4)	1.8(.5)	2.5(.6)
Perceived change in social relationships							
Mean ($\overline{X}$)	27.8	30.5	N/A	28.8	30.4	N/A	26.9
Standard deviation (SD)	3.5	3.3		2.6	2.3		2.6

*Perceived changes in social relationships are measured on a scale: (1) decreasing, (2) no change, (3) increasing.
Source: Pizam and Tellisman—Kosuta, 1989
Key
YU = Yugoslavia   PL = Poland   H = Hungary   BG = Bulgaria
E = Spain   UK = United Kingdom   USA = United States

research on tourism's sociocultural impacts, in contrast to both economic and environmental impact analyses. Even considering the study's limitations, the findings reinforce some of the recommendations discussed earlier for mitigating tourism's negative sociocultural impacts.

One other significant finding is that sociocultural impacts differ depending on the traditions, norms, and standards within each host society. Where tourism is not the dominant form of economic activity in an area, residents are more likely to view its impacts positively and focus on the

TABLE 5.2   Respondents' Perception of Tourism Impacts on Community

Social and Economic Categories*	YU $\bar{X}(SD)$	E $\bar{X}(SD)$	PL $\bar{X}(SD)$	UK $\bar{X}(SD)$	H $\bar{X}(SD)$	USA $\bar{X}(SD)$	BG $\bar{X}(SD)$
- Morality	2.1(.7)	2.1(.8)	1.8(.7)	1.9(.5)	1.9(.7)	1.9(.6)	1.2(.5)
- Income and standard of living	2.7(.5)	2.8(.5)	2.6(.6)	2.5(.6)	2.7(.5)	2.6(.7)	2.7(.6)
- Family life	2.2(.6)	2.3(.7)	2.0(.6)	2.0(.4)	1.9(.4)	N/A	1.7(.6)
- Employment opportunities	2.7(.5)	2.8(.5)	2.6(.6)	2.6(.6)	2.8(.4)	2.7(.6)	2.7(.6)
- Human relationships	2.1(.7)	2.6(.7)	1.9(.7)	2.1(.5)	2.6(.6)	N/A	2.0(.8)
- Opportunities for relaxation and entertainment	2.5(.6)	2.8(.5)	2.2(.7)	2.3(.6)	2.5(.6)	N/A	2.5(.8)
- Housing conditions	2.5(.6)	2.3(.8)	2.0(.7)	2.1(.5)	2.0(.5)	N/A	2.3(.8)
Perceived social and economic impacts of tourism (INDEX) $\bar{X}=$ (SD)=	16.8 2.2	17.7 2.6	15.2 2.3	15.6 2.3	16.6 2.1	N/A	14.4 2.5

*Perceived impacts of tourism on social and economic categories are measured on a scale: (1) worse, (2) no change, (3) better.
Source: Pizam and Tellsman—Kosuta, 1989

TABLE 5.3   Respondents' Attitudes Toward Tourists

Respondents' Attitudes	YU $\bar{X}(SD)$	E $\bar{X}(SD)$	PL $\bar{X}(SD)$	UK $\bar{X}(SD)$	H $\bar{X}(SD)$	USA $\bar{X}(SD)$	BG $\bar{X}(SD)$
- Feelings about presence of tourists*	2.7(.5)	2.6(.5)	2.2(.8)	2.6(.6)	2.6(.6)	2.7(.6)	N/A
- Feelings about numbers of tourists**	2.6(.6)	1.6(.6)	1.8(.8)	1.6(.6)	1.5(.6)	1.5(.7)	N/A
- Resident support for tourism $\bar{X}(SD)$	5.4(.8)	4.2(.1)	4.0(.8)	4.2(.6)	4.2(.6)	4.9(.1)	N/A

*Resident feelings about presence of tourists are measured on a scale: (1) annoyed, (2) indifferent, (3) happy.
**Resident feelings about number of tourists are measured on a scale: (1) decrease, (2) stay same, (3) increase.
Source: Pizam and Tellsman—Kosuta, 1989

beneficial impacts of economic returns. If this study were repeated in destinations with different levels of tourism dependency, it may be possible to determine at what point sociocultural concerns override economic benefits. However, because that point would probably be different for each host society, each resident population must be involved in determining the appropriate type and level of tourism which is right for them.

CONCLUSIONS

Examining the sociocultural impacts related to tourism development is a daunting task. Their identification, categorization, magnitude, and relationship to the development process are not clear. What is clear is that they do occur. While this chapter explores some of the different sociocultural costs and benefits related to tourism development, this list is not all inclusive. There is simply not enough information to identify or quantify each one. Nevertheless, lack of information should not paralyze the tourism development process. Recognizing that sociocultural impacts occur and appear to increase as development increases is sufficient to address and incorporate strategies for dealing with them into any tourism development planning process. Of the mitigation and coping strategies discussed for confronting sociocultural impacts, the common element is the importance of input from residents of the host community. While none of the strategies examined prevents sociocultural impacts from occurring, at least they force decision makers to address the problems as part of an overall management strategy for tourism development.

EXECUTIVE SUMMARY

Four separate cultures interact in most destinations: hosts, tourists (as a group), residual (individual tourist), and transitional companies. The difference between these cultures results in sociocultural impacts.

Most sociocultural impacts are hard to quantify although they can be observed; this problem makes them easy for planners to ignore.

For every sociocultural cost identified as tourism-related, a counter sociocultural benefit can be claimed.

Previous research identifies four stages a

community undergoes as it witnesses increasing levels of tourist numbers and development: euphoria, apathy, irritation, and antagonism.

Social impact mitigation involves active community educational campaigns, community involvement in the planning process, opportunity access for all community groups, and utilization of local labor and capital.

The Limits of Acceptable Change framework can deal with sociocultural impacts but it must be modified to fit into this context.

Identifying social change indicators is an involved process requiring community involvement.

The Vienna Center project is a longitudinal research study addressing social impacts and sociocultural change. Among its important findings is that different cultures have different degrees of tolerance for different types of tourist behavior. Therefore, social indicators are specific to host cultures, and any planning framework must encourage community involvement in the planning process.

REFERENCES

Adams, K. 1990. Cultural Commodization in Tana Toraja Indonesia. *Cultural Survival Quarterly* 14(1):31–34.

Belisle, F., and D. Hoy. 1980. The Perceived Impact of Tourism by Residents: A Case Study in Santa Marta, Columbia. *Annals of Tourism Research* 8(1):83–10.

Boissevain, J. 1979. The Impact of Tourism on a Dependent Island: Gozo, Malta. *Annals of Tourism Research* 6(1):76–90.

Bonnemaison, J. 1985. The Tree and the Canoe: Roots and Mobility in Vanuatu Societies. *Pacific Viewpoint* 26(1):30–62. Cited in de Burlo, 1988.

Britton, R. 1979. The Image of the Third World in Tourism Marketing. *Annals of Tourism Research* 9(3):331–358.

Crocombe, R. 1972. Land Tenure in the South Pacific, 219–251. In R. Ward, ed. *Man in the Islands: Essays on Geographical Change in the Pacific Islands*. Oxford: Clarendon Press. Cited in de Burlo, 1988.

Dann, G. 1988. Tourism, Peace, and the Classical Disputation. *In Tourism—A Vital Force for Peace*. Montreal: L.J. D'Amore and Associates, Ltd.

De Burlo, C. 1988. Land Alienation, Land Tenure, and Tourism in Vanuatu, A Melanesian Island Nation. Paper presented at the IGU Recreation, Leisure and Tourism Working Group, Christchurch, New Zealand.

Dinn, K. 1988. Social and Cultural Impacts of Tourism. *Annals of Tourism Research* 15(4):563–566.

Dogan, H. 1989. Forms of Adjustment: Sociocultural Impacts of Tourism. *Annals of Tourism Research* 16(2):216–229.

Doxey, G. 1976. When Enough's Enough: The Natives are Restless in Old Niagara. *Heritage Canada* 2(2):26–27.

Esman, M. 1984. Tourism and Ethnic Preservation: The Cajuns of Louisiana. *Annals of Tourism Research* 11(1):451–467.

Fitzsimmons, S. and T. Ferb. 1977. Developing a Community Attitude Assessment Scale. *Public Opinion Quarterly (POQ)* 41(1977):356–378.

Gamper, J. 1981. Tourism in Austria: A Case Study of the Influence of Tourism on Ethnic Relations. *Annals of Tourism Research* 8(3):432–446.

Greenwood, D. 1989. Culture by the Pound: An Anthropological Perspective on Tourism as Cultural Commoditization, 171–186. In *Hosts and Guests: The Anthropology of Tourism*. V.

Smith, ed. Philadelphia: University of Pennsylvania Press.

Hetherington, A. 1989. Rural Tourism Development: Finding, Preserving and Sharing Your Community's Heart and Soul. *Pacific Mountain Review* Fall:5–8.

Hetherington, A. 1992. Community Heart and Soul Workshop presented at the Inland Sea Society Meeting. Bayfield, Wisconsin.

International Union of Official Travel Organizations (IUOTO). 1976. *The Impact of International Tourism on the Economic Development of the Developing Countries.* Geneva: World Tourism Organization.

Jafari, J. 1989. Tourism as a Factor of Change: An English Language Literature Review 17–60. In *Tourism as a Factor of Change: A Sociocultural Study.* J. Bystrzanowski, ed. Vienna: European Coordination Centre for Research and Documentation in Social Sciences.

Jud, G., and W. Krause. 1976. Evaluating Tourism in Developing Areas. *Journal of Travel Research* 15(2):1–9.

Kousis, M. 1989. Tourism and the Family in a Rural Cretan Community. *Annals of Tourism Research* 16(3):318–332.

Laarman, J. and R. Perdue. 1989. Science Tourism in Costa Rica. *Annals of Tourism Research* 16(2):205–215.

Lane, R. 1971. The New Herbides: Land Tenure Without Land Policy. In R. Crocombe ed. *Land Tenure in the Pacific.* Melbourne: Oxford University Press. Cited in de Burlo, 1988.

Mathieson, A. and G. Wall. 1982. *Tourism: Economic, Physical and Social Impacts.* New York, N.Y.: Longman Scientific and Technical.

Murphy, P. 1985. *Tourism: A Community Approach.* New York: Methuen.

Oberg, K. 1960. Culture Shock: Adjustment to Neo-Cultural Environments. *Practical Anthropology* 17:177–182.

Pizam, A. and J. Pokela. 1985. The Perceived Impacts of Casino Gambling on a Community. *Annals of Tourism Research* 12(1):147–165.

Pizam, A. and N. Telisman-Kosuta. 1989. Tourism as a Factor of Change: Results and Analysis, 69–94. In *Tourism as a Factor of Change: A Sociocultural Study.* J. Bystrzanowski, ed. European Coordination Centre for Research and Documentation in Social Sciences (Vienna Center).

Przeclawski, K. and A. Travis, 1989. Tourism as a Factor of Change: Introduction, 7–16. In *Tourism as a Factor of Change: A Sociocultural Study.* J. Bystrzanowski, ed. European Coordination Centre for Research and Documentation in Social Sciences, (Vienna Centre). Vienna, Austria

Smith, S. 1982. The State of the Arts of Tourism Research: A Theoretical Perspective, 55–60. In *Michigan Tourism: How Can Research Help?* J. Fridgen and D. Allen, eds. Special Report #6, Agricultural Experiment Station. East Lansing, Mich.: Michigan State University.

Stringer, P. 1981. Hosts and Guests: The Bed and Breakfast Phenomenon. *Annals of Tourism Research* 8(3):357–376.

Stutman, R. and S. Newell, 1984. Beliefs versus Values: Salient Beliefs in Designing Persuasive Messages. *The Western Journal of Speech Communication* 48(Fall):362–372.

Wall, G. and M. Ali. 1977. The Impact of Tourism in Trinidad and Tobago. *Annals of Tourism Research* 4(4):43–49.

Wilkinson, C. 1990. Toward an Ethic of Place. In S. Udall, *Beyond the Mythic West*. Salt Lake City, Utah: Peregrine Smith Books.

Witt, S. 1991. Tourism in Cyprus: Balancing the Benefits and Costs. *Tourism Management* 12(1):37–46.

P A R T

III

Levels of Organization

Many people, whether they are involved directly in the tourism industry or simply tourists on holiday, have witnessed what they perceive as good and bad examples of tourism development. Regardless of how a development is viewed, a system in place allowed it to become reality. Recognizing how organizational systems control, direct, facilitate, or manipulate what is presented to tourists is important to understanding the tourism development process.

Part III consists of two chapters. Chapter 6 addresses tourism development at the national or regional level, reviewing organizational structures and goals. A case is made for including governmental agencies not normally associated with tourism development in the organizational mix providing management for a substantial portion of a country's attraction base. It discusses different methods to analyze, plan, finance, and manage tourism development projects at the national/regional level.

Chapter 7 explores the issues surrounding tourism development at the local or community level. The mission of many national/regional organizations is to increase the level of tourism activity within their borders. Communities are the beneficiaries/victims of those actions. Since tourism-generated impacts first appear at the community level, an entire chapter discusses coping strategies. Coping is defined broadly to include managing as well as surviving tourism development.

Community tourism development has become an active area for research and training within the last decade, especially in rural areas. Throughout the world increasing numbers of people have moved from rural to urban living environments. The lack of economic opportunity in rural areas is often cited as a motivator for the migration to cities. Increasing rural development opportunities lessens the burden placed on cities from burgeoning populations, and allows rural communities to remain viable centers of life. Tourism has been identified as one of the leading economic activities that can still be developed and sustained in rural areas; hence, the focus on and importance of community tourism development strategies.

CHAPTER 6

National/Regional Organization for Tourism Development

定慧中西快餐厅

中餐炒菜　　西式快餐
服务热情　　方便及时

旅游促进社会的繁荣与发展
TOURISM BRINGS PROSPERITY AND PROGRESS

*Part of the government's program in centrally planned economics is
preparing residents for tourism.*
Photo by the author

Learning Objectives

Understand tourism's role in a national economy with reference to
exchange theory.
•
Examine the different ways National Tourism •
Organizations (NTO's) have been structured.
•
Explore the role of other federal agencies in contributing to a
country's tourism attraction base.
•
Examine the different types of regional tourism organizations.
•
Explore funding sources for regional tourism organizations.
•
Review different methods for delineating a functioning tourism
region including supply-side and development-zone models.
•
Examine the processes used, with special emphasis on
funding, for an international development project.

INTRODUCTION

Attractions, facilities, and tourists are the visual signs of tourism development. How they come to be found in any one place is a complex process involving interactions between private businesses and government agencies. In some centrally planned economies, the distinction between a private operation and a government agency is purposefully blurred. Regardless of the type of government structure, if tourism development is a policy goal, public organizations will be dedicated to directing in the development process. Their actions influence the type of development found on site.

Holecek (1981) describes how government agencies influence development, and proposes a tourism system model encompassing private firms, private resources, public agencies, public resources, and tourists (Figure 6.1). The model assumes a consumer orientation, so tourists are the focal point. It replicates a dynamic system whereby an action taken by a member of one component generates change in every other component. For example, a public agency may issue a special use permit for constructing a new downhill ski area on public land. Obviously, this action changes the use patterns on the designated public land, part of the public resource component. Changes within the private firms component may not be as easy to predict. Existing downhill ski operations may either suffer from the increased competition, or benefit from the synergy created by adding another attraction to the mix. Other private sector opportunities may also

Figure 6.1 *Michigan's Tourism System*

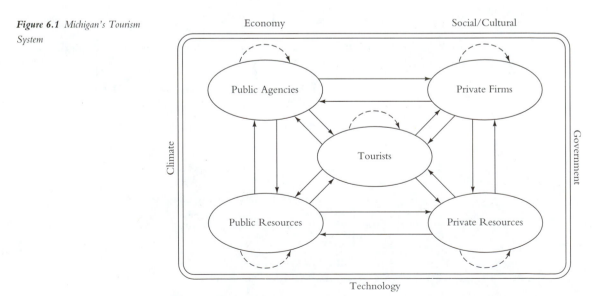

Source: Holocek, 1981

increase such as restaurants, accommodations, equipment rental, and so on. How private firms react to the change authorized by the public agency also affects how private resources (capital, land) are used. Eventually, these changes also affect tourists, providing additional opportunities to engage in downhill skiing, new shopping, eating, and sleeping choices, and altering in a non-quantifiable way the nature of their overall experience.

Interactions also take place within each of the five components. Public agencies may issue contradictory opinions over proposed land use. Using public resources such as land for a different purpose may transform the ecological balance of the entire system. Private firm interactions obviously include competition, but may also take the form of cooperative programs or partnerships. Tourists interaction may affect experiential outcomes through congestion or crowding, or may make the tourist an indirect source of promotion.

The tourism system model is bounded by exogenous factors (e.g., technology, weather) that, while not under direct control of any one component, nonetheless influence each component. Most tourism system models group public agencies under a broad government heading. Yet public agencies affecting tourism development exist at all political levels within a country. This chapter discusses the public sector's role in tourism development. It begins with a discussion of tourism as an earner of foreign exchange, then focuses on national and regional organizations, their purpose, interactions with other agencies, and funding sources. It analyzes the resources required for development, and concludes with a development example of a case study of a project in Ghana. The organizational structure and process for tourism development at the local or community level is not discussed in this chapter. Since most of the impacts generated from tourism development are community-specific, Chapter 7 deals more directly with the development process from that perspective.

TOURISM'S ROLE IN A NATIONAL ECONOMY

Tourism, since it cannot be undertaken without host and guest interaction, has not always been viewed as an acceptable activity by national policy makers. Dogmatic ideology, whose existence relies on suppressing freedom, does not survive in an environment where people are exposed to different lifestyles or schools of thought. Historically, authoritarian regimes have prohibited tourism or controlled it so tightly that cultural exchange did not flourish. Since few countries, regardless of political ideology, are completely self sufficient, they must find ways to accummulate convertible foreign currency, sometimes called hard currency, for international transactions. One way to obtain foreign currency is by exporting locally produced goods. Developing countries often rely on agriculture or extractive industries to produce export products. Since fluctuations in world supply and demand often affect the value of those exports, countries must find additional means of obtaining foreign currency. Tourism is often selected as the export industry of choice. Exchange theory illuminates the ramifications of tourism as an export industry for acquiring hard currency.

EXCHANGE THEORY

Trade between nations can be viewed in terms of a balance of payments or from a social welfare perspective. Balance of payments is an accountant's approach to measuring real dollar flows. All countries use it to measure the inflow and outflow of currency in the purchase or sale of goods across borders. Balance of payments works well when the goods in question are tangible, but when they are more experiential or service-oriented, social welfare considerations become important. Social welfare is a utilitarian approach which includes dollar flows along with intangible benefits derived from sales or purchases of goods. It is especially appropriate for tourism because of its intangible nature.

Balance of Payments

In Chapter 3, tourism receipts are defined as export earnings, and in that sense contribute positively to a country's trade balance. Many factors affect the balance of payments for any industry. Government policies restricting entry or travel abroad influence the size and magnitude of the balance. Governments have historically erected barriers to control or increase the cost of both the inflow and outflow of tourists (Edgell, 1988), including policies restricting the amount of currency a country's residents can take with them when traveling, requiring foreign visitors to exchange a certain amount of hard currency for each day in the host country, entry and exit taxes, and other taxes which may be included in an airline ticket or imposed on services utilized by visitors.

In a free trade situation where travel is unrestricted, the relative value of a country's currency on the world market influences balance of payments. A simple demand analysis serves to illustrate this point. In Figure 6.2, the demand for a country's tourism products is at equilibrium where price P_0 intersects the demand curve, resulting in quantity purchased equal to Q_0. Demand is influenced by the touristic image the country holds in foreign markets, ease of access which includes economic and cultural distance, government policy, and other factors such as safety and security concerns. Holding demand influences constant, the relative value of a country's prices determines the equilibrium point. If country A's currency declines in value relative to other countries, then the purchasing power of people holding foreign currency increases for products purchased in country A, and declines for residents of country A when traveling abroad. This change in purchasing power is reflected in the demand curve by a lowering of price from P_0 to P_1, with an increase in quantity purchased from Q_0 to Q_1. For residents of country A, an opposite movement along the demand curve occurs, depicted in Figure 6.3. The relative price for international travel now increases from P0 to P2, with a resulting decrease in quantity purchased from Q0 to Q2. The balance of payments for each country reflects the magnitude of the shift in currency values.

In the U.S., the balance of payments with respect to tourism in 1984 was a negative $8.119 billion. Almost four million more U.S. residents traveled abroad that year than foreign visitors to the United States. In 1989, for the first time since international travel flow records in the U.S. have been collected, there was a positive U.S. tourism balance of payments. The U.S. received $44.533 billion from foreign travelers, and U.S. residents spent $43.499 billion abroad, resulting in a positive balance of $1.034 billion (U.S. Bureau of Economic Analysis, 1990). In 1994, the U.S. trade balance from tourism increased to over $16 billion.

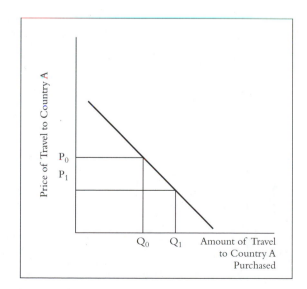

Figure 6.2 Demand Curve for Country A's Tourism Products

At the beginning of 1984, the U.S. dollar bought 231 Japanese yen, .6886 British pounds, and 2.728 West German marks (Wall Street Journal, January 2, 1984). In mid-1995, the U.S. dollar substantially declined in value against most foreign currencies. It was worth only 76 Japanese yen (down 67 percent), .50267 British pounds (down 27 percent), and 1.531 German marks (down 44 percent) (Wall Street Journal, June 1, 1995). One can argue that the U.S. tourism balance of payments increased because of an improving touristic image of the U.S. in foreign markets, but the hard evidence supports currency fluctuations as the primary cause.

Social Welfare

Focusing on a bottom line balance of payments ignores the intangible nature of tourism products. If one were to analyze only net tourism receipts, statements such as: foreign travel is counterproductive to domestic growth because more money leaves the country than is brought in, are valid. Social welfare theory argues that value extends beyond the simple summation of money flows.

Figure 6.4 graphically depicts exchange between two countries using an "Edgeworth Box," originally developed by the British economist Francis Edgeworth in the late 1800s. Each country has an indifference curve, Ia for country A and Ib for country B, where anywhere along the curve each country's residents are equally satisfied with the corresponding quantities of tourism and all other goods that can be purchased at that point. Also,

Figure 6.3 Demand Curve for Other Countries' Tourism Products by Residents of Country A

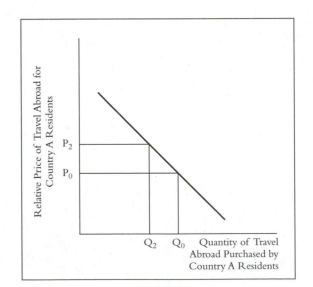

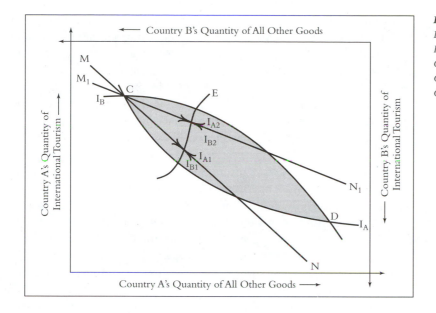

Figure 6.4 "Edgeworth Box" Depicting Trade Maximization Points for Country A and Country B Residents for Two Goods: Tourism and All Other Goods

there are only two points, C and D, where the indifference curves intersect and where residents of both countries are equally satisfied with the amount of tourism and all other goods that can be purchased at those points. However, through trade, residents of both countries can move onto a higher indifference curve, in the shaded area between indifference curves Ia and Ib. For the sake of simplicity we will only assume a budget line passing through the point C, although one passing through D could also be constructed. The budget line MN reflects the relative purchasing power of each country's currency, and determines the amount of tourism and all other goods residents of each country are willing to purchase. Since this line passes through the shaded area, it is possible to find a point where each country's residents are equally satisfied but on higher indifference curves than at C, our original starting point. Country A now moves to indifference curve I_{a1} and country B is at I_{b1}, both higher than I_a and I_b respectively. Trade between the two countries, in this case tourism, benefits residents of each.

If currency values of country A and country B change with respect to each other, then the budget line shifts. Line M_1N_1 in Figure 6.4 depicts this, showing a devaluation of country B's currency, leading to less tourism consumption for country B and more for country A. It is now less expensive for country A's residents to travel in country B than it is for country B's residents to travel in country A. A shift in each country's consumption of the other's tourism goods occurs. New indifference curves,

I_{a2} and I_{b2}, can be located within the shaded area, revealing the new equilibrium point of consumption. The line connecting the different equilibrium points, E, is labeled the contract curve. The contract curve represents the level of exchange that takes place when each country's indifference curves are tangential. It is similar to an individual's Income Expansion Path which shows the amount of each type of good purchased as an individual's purchasing power expands or contracts.

What does this example have to do with social welfare? When trade occurs, residents of both countries are better off, what economists would call a Pareto optimal solution. Some may be better off from the purchase of tangible goods, while others receive benefits from the intangible nature of tourism experiences. Balance of payments is irrelevant in the sense that it does not determine social utility gained from trade. As long as residents from each country gain from the transactions, then social welfare increases.

Obviously, a country's balance of payments affects its domestic economy. When this happens, currency values fluctuate and new budget lines result. Consumption patterns change, reflecting the relative purchasing power of each country's residents. Indifference curves shift and ultimately the balance of payments bottom line changes as well. Market economies based on truly free trade should be able to adjust, allowing residents of each country to be better off in a social welfare context than in the absence of trade.

However, many scholars question whether this is actually the case. High leakages due to multinational operations removing tourism revenues from the local economy reinforce beliefs that third world tourism developments are nothing more than pleasure colonies for citizens of the developed world. When examining the magnitude of sociocultural impacts, it is easy to question if residents of both countries are better off from tourism exchange. Macro-level social-exchange theory simply says that residents of both countries benefit if trade takes place; it does not identify individuals or groups who benefit disproportionally. It is possible, and has often been the case, that only a small group of people stand to benefit from tourism development. However, if decisions as to the nature and extent of tourism development become more of a local issue, host societies are in a better position to manage tourism. In this case, the benefits of tourism are spread throughout a local economy and social welfare improvement through tourism trade becomes an accepted principle rather than a theoretical construct.

Since most countries actively seek the economic benefits of tourism development, they create agencies to deal with these issues. The next section explores the different ways countries organize their national tourism agencies.

NATIONAL TOURISM ORGANIZATIONS

National Tourism Organizations (NTOs) carry out public policy in accordance with the goals of the government. There are four basic forms of NTOs: state tourism secretariats, government agencies within larger departments, quasi-public tourism agencies, and private industry. State tourism secretariats are either independent ministries or form part of a related ministry. Governmental agencies within larger national departments are less powerful than a secretariat position, and reflect a lower priority for tourism development in the country. Quasi-public organizations may be incorporated entities (see Tennessee Valley Authority later in this chapter) with a board of directors. Normally, a quasi-public organization collects part of its operating budget from products sold. Private industry groups may be authorized by a national government to carry out national tourism development goals, and they generally receive an operating subsidy from public revenues, but their administrative structure and mission is similar to a private corporation. Although a majority of the NTOs recognized by the World Tourism Organization are of the secretariat or government department class, with approximately ten percent private or nongovernmental, this mix is beginning to change.

Most NTOs have as their primary goal a mandate to increase the amount of foreign travel to their country. Although programs intended to encourage domestic tourism are sometimes initiated, most NTO mission statements explicitly focus on the need to increase international inbound travel. Only recently have NTOs begun to incorporate in their mission statements the goals of protecting tourist attractions, including environmental and social resources. These goals are viewed as complementing and enhancing marketing goals. Some examples of the environmental, social, and economic goals that may be encountered include:

Economic

increase employment

stimulate investment

improve living standards for country residents

maximize foreign exchange earnings

develop a marketable image

increase off season or shoulder season travel

focus on high yield market segments

market economically depressed regions

enhance long-term economic development through diversification

sponsor marketing workshops

Environmental

promote sustainable tourism development activities

preserve natural areas by creating tourism demand for the resource

Social

maximize social benefits for residents through increased tourism expenditures

protect and preserve cultural heritage

establish service personnel training programs

develop social impact assessment models

Additional goals could be included in each category, but NTOs have historically focused on those in the economic category. Although many nations have environmental and social development policies affecting tourism, they are usually the responsibility of other units of government. Most NTOs still operate simply as a tourism marketing agency. As environmental and social impact goals appear more frequently in NTO mission statements, there is more attention given to planning for tourism development.

Gilbert (1990) proposes a four stage planning process for NTOs (Figure 6.5). Stage one is the establishment of long-range goals related to the mission of the organization. Stage two is an analysis of the current situation. Stage three is setting short-term objectives and appropriate strategies to achieve them; Gilbert refers to this stage as short-term campaigns. The final stage is control, which consists of an evaluation of the short-term campaigns with respect to expected economic, environmental, and social impacts. A fifth stage, although not explicitly identified, is implementation. Once short-term campaigns are acceptable they are implemented and monitored to make sure they are meeting stated objectives. Gilbert's stages are similar to a basic marketing strategy utilized by most companies.

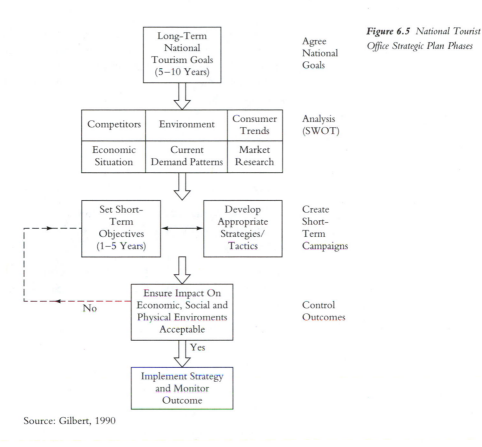

Figure 6.5 National Tourist Office Strategic Plan Phases

Source: Gilbert, 1990

ORGANIZATIONAL STRUCTURE

Countries organize their NTOs differently. It is not the intent of this section to propose an ideal organizational model, but rather to examine a few of the systems in place and discuss implications of the organizational structure. The reader should be aware that by the time they read this section, the model outlined for the U.S. may be a historical overview. The United States Travel and Tourism Administration as currently structured has been the target of budget reduction proponents in Congress, and is preparing to be eliminated in 1996.

United States Travel and Tourism Administration

In 1981 the United States passed the National Tourism Policy Act (NTPA), establishing the United States Travel and Tourism Administration (USTTA). Previously, international travel marketing activities were performed by the United States Travel Service (USTS), established in

1961 as a branch office of the Department of Commerce. The NTPA explicitly identified the mission of USSTA as fostering the growth of the U.S. travel industry by encouraging travel to the U.S. from abroad, leading to a reduction in the U.S. travel deficit. Edgell (1990) specifically identifies the goals of USTTA as defined by the U.S. Secretary of Commerce:

- Develop, plan, and carry out a comprehensive program to stimulate travel to the United States by residents of foreign countries

- Encourage the development of tourist facilities, package tours, and other arrangements within the United States for meeting the requirements of foreign visitors

- Foster and encourage the widest possible distribution of the benefits of travel between foreign countries and the United States with sound economic principles

- Encourage the simplification, reduction, or elimination of barriers to travel and the facilitation of international travel generally

- Collect, publish, and provide for the exchange of statistics and technical information, including schedules of meetings, fairs, and other attractions relating to international travel and tourism

- Establish facilitation services at major U.S. ports of entry

- Consult with foreign governments on travel and tourism matters and . . . represent U.S. tourism interests before international and inter-governmental meetings .

- Develop and administer a comprehensive program relating to travel industry information, data service, training and education, and technical assistance

- Develop a program to seek and receive information on a continuing basis from the tourism industry, including consumer and travel trade associations, regarding needs and interests that should be met by a Federal Agency or program to direct that information to the appropriate agency or program

- Encourage, to the maximum extent feasible, travel to and from the United States on U.S. carriers

- Assure coordination within the Department of Commerce so that, to the extent practicable, all the resources of the Department are used effectively and efficiently to carry out the national tourism policy

• Develop and submit annually to the Congress, within six weeks of transmittal to the Congress of the President's recommended budget. . . . a detailed marketing plan to stimulate and encourage travel to the United States during the fiscal year for which such budget is submitted

The location of USTTA in the U.S. Department of Commerce's organizational chart is significant. It is headed by an Under Secretary of Commerce reporting directly to the Secretary of Commerce. By virtue of USTTA's position in the Department of Commerce and its specific charges identified above, it functions as a marketing organization. Domestic tourism development issues, such as environmental and social impacts, are not within the domain of its responsibilities.

Two advisory boards provide counsel and input to USTTA. The Tourism Policy Council, chaired by the Secretary of Commerce, is comprised of representatives from other U.S. Departments in an effort to coordinate policies that affect international travel to the United States. Permanent membership on the Council is held by the U.S. Departments of Transportation, the primary organization responsible for negotiating international air agreements, especially landing rights; State, responsible for immigration and visa policies; Interior, responsible for major attractions such as national parks and monuments; the Office of Management and Budget, the governments' primary accounting and policy oversight agency; Labor, to deal with employment generated and impacted by tourism; and Energy, to deal with policy issues related to price and tax changes that may have an impact on travel to the U.S. Only recently added to the Tourism Policy Council is a representative from the U.S. Department of Agriculture (USDA). Located within the USDA is the U.S. Forest Service, an agency responsible for administering many of the nation's public lands and, as will be shown later in this chapter, a significant provider of tourism attractions.

Travel and Tourism Advisory Board

In an effort to balance government agencies' influence on U.S. tourism policy direction, the NTPA also provides for the establishment of the Travel and Tourism Advisory Board (TTAB) which is comprised of fifteen members from the private sector. Members of the TTAB must hold senior level positions within the travel and tourism industry, and include members representing organized labor, consumers, academic institutions, and the states. Only eight seats can be held by members representing one political party. The TTAB has two primary functions. The first is to advise the USTTA and through it the Secretary of Commerce on how best to implement the 1981 National Tourism Policy Act. The function is to provide counsel to the USTTA on the development of an annual marketing plan.

EXAMPLES

An NTO's organizational structure identifies its primary functions and responsibilities. The chain of command, identified in an organizational chart, provides information on the relative importance of each unit. The following section discusses the approach to tourism at the national level in three countries (United States, People's Republic of China, Canada).

United States

The USTTA's organizational chart is characterized by simplicity, with only four major units all reporting directly to the Deputy Under Secretary for Commerce who heads USTTA (Figure 6.6). USTTA is not directly involved in the tourism industry, in the sense that they do not engage in packaging tours, initiating sales, or controlling transportation access. The Department of Commerce, the parent organization for USTTA, only provides policy advice with respect to visa regulations and international air agreements which are set by other governmental organizations. The role of USTTA can best be described as providing information on the actual

Figure 6.6 *Organization Chart of the United States Travel and Tourism Administration*

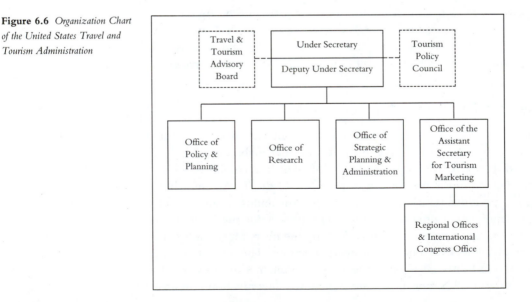

and potential economic benefits of international tourism to both governmental agencies and private-sector tourism-industry organizations.

One of the primary research efforts of USTTA is an in-flight survey of visitors to the United States. With the assistance of 55 U.S. and international carriers, over 82,000 surveys were completed by people departing the U.S. in 1991. Information collected includes sources used to plan the trip, length of stay, places visited, activities, and quality of airline services. Information is made available to participating airlines and U.S. companies or residents who wish to know more about international visitors' U.S. travel patterns.

The United States is not a relatively heavy spender when funding for National Tourism Organizations is compared. The U.S. ranks 45th in per capita spending and 19th in total spending by National Government Tourism Organizations (Ahmed and Krohn, 1990). However, there are many other national level agencies involved in the delivery of tourism products. Focusing only on an NTO budget and efforts does not provide an accurate picture of federal level involvement in tourism development.

People's Republic of China

The People's Republic of China (PRC) has developed a decentralized system of operation which grants a great deal of authority to local travel bureaus. There are very few private-sector tourism-industry operations in the PRC, although small, privately held operations were legalized in 1984 (Choy and Can, 1988). Prior to 1980, all sales and contacts with foreign tour operators were handled by either China International Travel Services (CITS) or China Travel Service (CTS). Since private-sector operations were not legally recognized in the PRC at that time, both CITS and CTS were responsible for arranging all foreign tour packages including lodging, transportation, and associated services. This centralized form of control eventually gave way to a completely decentralized system during the early 1980s, going so far as to grant local travel bureaus the right to issue visas, set prices, develop tour packages, enter into international financial arrangements for facility development, and, for the most part, enter into separate agreements with foreign tour operators (Choy and Can, 1988). This decentralized form of management has led to confusion on the part of foreign tour operators, often promised but never delivered services, and competition among local travel organizations for existing markets rather than ventures into new markets. The PRC continues to experiment with what can best be described as a system that embodies one of the primary elements of a market based economy, competition, without any clear national policy direction to ensure that certain standards of operation are maintained. The complexity of the PRC's approach to national tourism development can be seen by reference to its organizational chart for the delivery of travel services in the country (Figure 6.7). The number of organizations, their relationship to the governing state council as well as to Provincial, City, and County Travel and Tourism Bureaus reveals a government that has yet to design a functioning system able to embrace market economy qualities within the confines of communist idealogy.

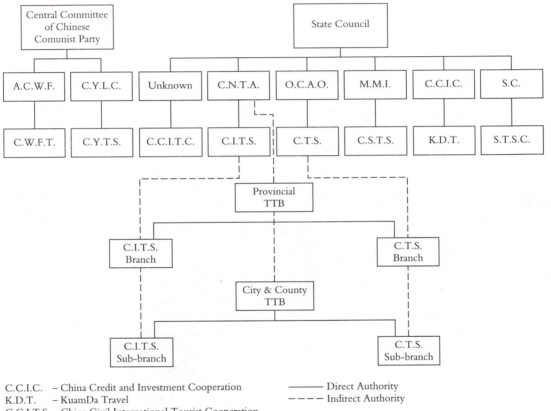

C.C.I.C. – China Credit and Investment Cooperation
K.D.T. – KuamDa Travel
C.C.I.T.S. – China Civil International Tourist Cooperation
C.Y.L.C. – The Communist Youth League of China
C.Y.T.S. – China Youth Travel Service
C.N.T.A. – China National Tourism Administration
C.I.T.S. – China International Travel Service
M.M.I. – The Ministry of Metallurgical Industry
C.S.T.S. – China Swan Travel Service
O.C.A.O. – Overseas Chinese Affairs Office
C.T.S. – China Travel Service
A.C.W.F. – All-China Woman's Federation
C.W.F.T. – China Woman's Federation Travel
S.C. – The Sports Commission
S.T.S.C. – Sports Travel Service Company

——— Direct Authority
– – – – Indirect Authority

Source: Choy and Can, 1988

Figure 6.7 *Organization of Travel Services in China*

Canada

Tourism Canada is the national level organization responsible for implementing tourism policy for Canada. Similar to USTTA, it is a department within the larger national organization of Industry, Science, and Technology Canada, a ministerial agency of the Canadian government. Its organizational chart (Figure 6.8) identifies three main responsibilities: general and information marketing, research and information services, and research. Although Tourism Canada is not actively involved in developing new attractions, it assists both the private and public sector in this venture by providing market-demand information and technical expertise. Tourism Canada can best be characterized as an efficient marketing organization assisting in all aspects of tourism development, including lobbying with respect to policy that benefits the tourism industry, promotion of Canadian tourism products to international markets, conducting research for the industry, conducting seminars and workshops for members of the industry, and coordinating major events in which the private and public sector market their specific products.

Even though the organizational structure outlined above remains in place at the time this section was written, it may not be the case when the reader arrives at this point. In February, 1995, members of a new Canadian Tourism Commission (CTC) were announced. The CTC is a public/private sponsorship intended to guide Tourism Canada. Representatives from the private sector hold the majority of the 26 seats on the commission. Funded with a budget of $50 million, a $35 million increase from the old Tourism Canada budget, it is expected that the private sector will realize the potential of this venture and contribute an additional $50 million for a promotion and marketing budget of $100 million annually. At the time of this writing, no decision has been taken as to how the money will be spent, as there is no strategic plan in place to guide the commission. That should all be worked out after the CTC finishes reorganizing Tourism Canada, a process currently underway. Unfortunately, no information could be obtained from principals involved in the reorganiza-

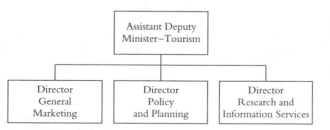

Source: McIntosh, et al., 1995

Figure 6.8 Organization Chart of Tourism Canada

tion that could be used to provide a view of what Tourism Canada may look like after the reorganization is finished.

DEVELOPED/DEVELOPING COUNTRIES

Governments take active or passive roles in tourism development. The extent of involvement is usually related to the development level of the country.

Passive

Jenkins and Henry (1982) define a passive role as one where actions not specifically directed or intended to assist tourism development nonetheless influence it. Passive actions can be mandatory or supportive.

Mandatory involvement results from legislation. Restrictions on employment of foreign nationals, child labor laws, investment programs, bilateral air service agreements, tax reform, and workers compensation programs are examples of legislation which, though not directed at tourism per se, impact how tourism development proceeds. As reference to Holecek's model indicates (Figure 6.1), almost all government-enacted programs have some implications for tourism development.

Supporting involvement is indirect and not regulated by legislation. For example, private sector organizations such as the Travel Industry Association (TIA) in the United States, may receive no government subsidies or assistance in organization, but neither are they prevented from organizing and carrying on an active lobbying program. National or regional educational programs, like those at universities which receive government assistance, may support tourism development. University courses in hospitality and tourism may not directly result from government intervention, but still may be supported by general revenue tax funds collected by regional or federal governments.

Active

Active involvement occurs when a government recognizes the role tourism plays in meeting national policy objectives, and establishes formal participatory programs to accomplish the objectives. Active involvement can be either managerial or developmental.

In managerial involvement, a government sets specific tourism objectives and introduces legislation directed toward meeting those objectives. Negotiating agreements between other countries or multinational corporations with the intent of supporting tourism development is an example of government-provided managerial involvement. Although governments are always entering into agreements with other countries, the difference between active and passive involvement is the extent to which agreements address specific tourism objectives.

Developmental involvement occurs whenever government assumes an active role in planning, managing, or passing legislation that directly affects the tourism industry in a country. The role assumed by government may be driven by ideological justification, such as occurs in centrally planned economies, or may be due to a lack of sufficient expertise, interest or capital. Many countries find themselves owning and managing tourism facilities or providing developmental assistance by initiating training programs intended to improve skill levels of tourism employees. One of the most common forms of developmental assistance that national governments provide is the formation of a national level Tourism Development Corporation (TDC). TDCs have a variety of functions. In some countries they may own tourist facilities, or be a source of guaranteed government loans for small businesses in need of start up capital. Others, such as the London Docklands Development Corporation (LDDC) may become the primary tourism planning agency for an entire region, producing detailed site development plans (Figure 6.9). Whatever their role, TDCs are an active form of government involvement for tourism development.

An example of active legislation-driven government involvement can be found in Egypt, where the national government has enacted a law to allow for a ten-year tax "holiday" for development projects occurring in remote areas of the country. The law also allows full foreign investment in some cases, where the previous legislation limited the amount of foreign investment to 49 percent of invested capital (Wahab, 1995).

Although it is risky to generalize, most developed countries operate their National Tourism Organizations primarily as passive support agencies. That is, they do not own or operate attractions or products, but rather work on behalf of the industry to sell their products. In other words, they market the country's tourism offerings and assist passively in further development of the products. It is analogous to a private sector operation which purchases the exclusive distribution and marketing rights to products made by another company. This is easier to do in a market-based economy with sufficient private sector operations to offer an array of products and services. Many developing countries do not have that advantage.

Developing country economies are often plagued by shortages of capital and expertise needed for tourism development. This may be due to an ideology opposed to market-based systems, political corruption, overpopulation, or simply bad luck in not having sufficient resources to sustain growth. If capital is not available, governments often enter into joint own-

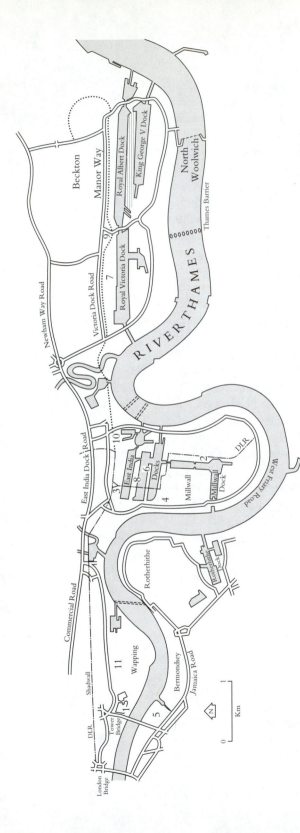

HOTEL DEVELOPMENT
as from January 1988

Existing

		Capacity
1	Lower Thistle Hotel (1973)	

Proposed

		Capacity
2	Brunel Centre	200 Bedrooms
3	Port East	260 Bedrooms
4	Waterside	200 Bedrooms
5	Butlers Wharf	70 Apartments
6	Heron Quay	Unknown
7	Victoria Dock	600 Bedrooms
8	Canary Wharf	Unknown
9	Connaught Centre	400 Bedrooms
10	Poplar Dock	Unknown
11	Saab Site	Unknown

London City Airport

DLR — Dockland Light Railway

.... Proposed Dockland Light Railway Extension

Source: Page, 1989

Figure 6.9 *Hotel Development in London Docklands*

ership and management agreements with multinational firms for facility development, or they may choose to use tax revenues and develop government owned and operated businesses. When this happens, NTOs assume a much broader, active, role.

The role an NTO plays in tourism development varies depending on many factors, but primarily on the level of private sector development already in place. When tourist facilities do not exist and private capital is not available, an NTO may assume a much more integrated development role, sometimes owning and operating a large portion of a country's tourism industry.

OTHER TOURISM ORGANIZATIONS

National Tourism Organizations are the most visible of a country's public sector organizations dedicated to tourism development. Most NTOs are marketing-focused; that is, their efforts concentrate primarily on increasing the number of international arrivals to the country. However, the importance of other federal agencies to tourism development is often more substantial than the role the NTO performs. In the United States, the role these federal agencies fill as providers of tourism attractions is not always recognized. Tourism probably provides more direct and indirect linkages with the largest number of government ministries, agencies, and departments than any other industrial activity (Gajraj, 1989).

Crompton (1990) acknowledges the importance of the private sector in providing essential travel services, but he contends the public sector is a more important provider of attractions. "The Disney Parks may attract over 40 million visitors a year, but this represents only 12 percent of the visitation recorded in the National Parks. . . . The number of visitors to the National Parks, in turn, are minuscule when compared to visitations to state, regional and local parks" (1990:6). Crompton explains that part of the reason for the failure to recognize the value of public attractions is the way in which public agencies represent themselves. They almost always present a financial balance sheet which only lists revenues received and expenses incurred. Local community expenditures as a result of public attraction visitation are ignored. Other public agencies charged with promoting a state or region generally assume the amount of expenditures and tax revenue generated from tourism is due to their promotional efforts. Consequently, high return on investment figures are commonplace. Public land management agencies are subject to budget cuts when they fail to take credit for local tourism revenue from visitors to publicly provided attractions. It is much easier to slash a public agency's budget that is constantly operating in the red rather than to reduce allocations to a revenue generating agency. But as Crompton has pointed out, the role of government as a provider of tourism attractions, and by association employment and business opportunities for the private sector, is immense and cannot be ignored.

The following discussion focuses on U.S. federal agencies and their importance to the tourism industry in the United States. Many of them (Bureau of Land Management, USDA Forest Service, Corps of Engineers, Bureau of Reclamation) are in the process of searching for a new mission as their traditional mandates are no longer needed or have fallen out of favor with society. The new missions will likely place high priorities on recreation (Ridenour, 1995), and consequently tourism.

Similar agencies to those operating at the U.S. federal level exist in almost every state and add another dimension to the importance of public agencies for tourism development. Still others exist at county and municipal levels, adding even more attractions and economic opportunities. Other countries also have similar public agencies in place. Some are more tourism-dedicated than others, but their actions, if Holecek's tourism system model is operational (Figure 6.1), all impact the level of tourism development in their respective country. The following discussion is not intended as support for a larger public lands program, an issue for politicians to debate. However, having a mixture of public and private attractions available creates a balance. The relative proportion of that mix will continue to be a topic of discussion as long as land has value for alternative uses.

U.S. Department of Interior

The U.S. Department of Interior (DOI), created in 1849, has cabinet-level status within the U.S. government, with the Secretary reporting directly to the President. It is also a permanent member of the Tourism Policy Council of USTTA. It has jurisdiction over 500 million acres and trust responsibility for an additional 50 million acres which are principally reservation lands of Native Americans. Through its various agencies, the DOI is charged, inter alia, with:

• Preserving the nation's scenic and historic areas

• Conserving, developing, and utilizing fish and wildlife resources

• Coordinating federal and state recreation programs

• Operating job corps conservation youth camps

• Managing hydroelectric power systems

The department is also responsible for initiating programs to foster social and economic development in the territories of the United States and
in the trust territories of the Pacific Islands, and administering programs
providing services to Native Americans in the contiguous 48 states and to
Alaska natives. Recently, the DOI instituted the Outdoor Recreation Initiative Program, which through it bureaus, intends to provide additional
recreation opportunities to citizens of the United States, and through
tourism initiatives, to increase the supply of natural resource based attractions.

The primary agencies responsible for carrying out the department's
mission, and important to the provision of tourism attractions and services,
are the Fish and Wildlife Service, National Park Service, Bureau of Reclamation, Bureau of Indian Affairs, and Bureau of Land Management (Figure 6.10).

Fish and Wildlife Service

The mission of the Fish and Wildlife Service is to conserve, protect,
and enhance fish and wildlife and their habitats for the continuing benefit
of the American people. Although this mission statement does not address
recreation or tourism specifically, the clause for the "benefit of the American people" includes those activities. Nature-based tourism, as discussed
before, is becoming increasingly popular, and some of the best areas for
these activities are lands administered by the U.S. Fish and Wildlife Service. Some of the tourism activities currently supported on lands and waters under Fish and Wildlife Service jurisdiction include fishing, hunting,
wildlife viewing, other water-based activities (swimming, skiing, diving,
etc.), hiking, and environmental education.

The Fish and Wildlife Service system includes 456 national wildlife
refuges and 150 waterfowl production areas, totalling over 90 million
acres. It also operates 70 fish hatcheries. Primary responsibilities include
management and protection of migratory birds, endangered species, and
certain marine mammals. An extensive research effort supports program
activities. The service operates 25 major fish and wildlife laboratories and
research centers, with cooperative research units at 36 universities. The
system is also responsible for drafting an endangered species list, identifying wildlife products that are banned from import into the U.S., and assisting other countries in their fish and wildlife management efforts.

Although not the most visible of the federal agencies providing
tourism attractions and recreational opportunities, the Fish and Wildlife
Service plays an important tourism role in continuing to protect native fish
and wildlife species. The linkage between man and land continues to be
important as urbanization increases, direct relationships to the nation's

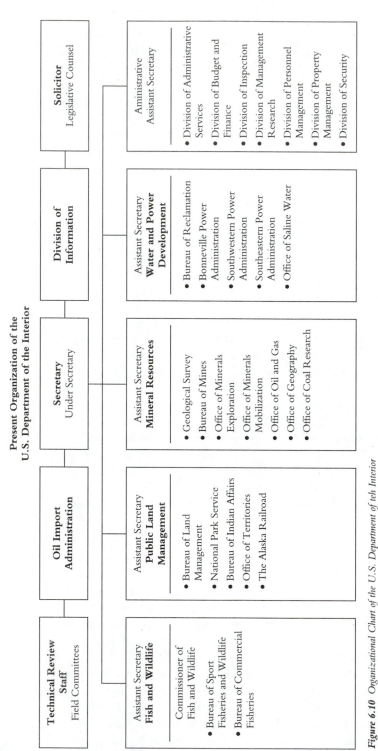

**Present Organization of the
U.S. Department of the Interior**

| **Technical Review Staff** Field Committees | **Oil Import Administration** | **Secretary** Under Secretary | **Division of Information** | **Solicitor** Legislative Counsel |

Assistant Secretary **Fish and Wildlife**

Commissioner of Fish and Wildlife

- Bureau of Sport Fisheries and Wildlife
- Bureau of Commercial Fisheries

Assistant Secretary **Public Land Management**

- Bureau of Land Management
- National Park Service
- Bureau of Indian Affairs
- Office of Territories
- The Alaska Railroad

Assistant Secretary **Mineral Resources**

- Geological Survey
- Bureau of Mines
- Office of Minerals Exploration
- Office of Minerals Mobilization
- Office of Oil and Gas
- Office of Geography
- Office of Coal Research

Assistant Secretary **Water and Power Development**

- Bureau of Reclamation
- Bonneville Power Administration
- Southwestern Power Administration
- Southeastern Power Administration
- Office of Saline Water

Amministrative Assistant Secretary

- Division of Administrative Services
- Division of Budget and Finance
- Division of Inspection
- Division of Management Research
- Division of Personnel Management
- Division of Property Management
- Division of Security

Figure 6.10 Organizational Chart of the U.S. Department of teh Interior

INDIAN GAMING

Casino-style gaming, which includes most types of Native American operated gaming, has become one of the fastest growing industries worldwide. For years, only the state of Nevada allowed casino gaming in the United States. Atlantic City, New Jersey joined Nevada in 1978 as the only other jurisdiction allowing casino gaming, and it wasn't until 1989 that changing social attitudes coupled with a Supreme Court decision favoring Native American tribal sovereignty that casino gaming began a rapid expansion that has yet to slow. Today, over 20 states (14 with Native American operations) allow some type of casino gaming. Casino gaming in the U.S. generates over $300 billion in wagering (handle), an increase exceeding 160 percent since 1994.

Native American gaming resulted from a 1987 Supreme court decision, Cabazon vs. State of California, which established tribal sovereignty on reservation lands and required states to accept, without regulatory authority, Native American gaming operations provided other forms of gaming (e.g. charitable) were allowed in the state. In 1988, the U.S. Congress passed the Indian Gaming Regulatory Act (IGRA), which required states to enter into compacts with Native American tribes for the purpose of allowing gaming operations. Since the passage of the IGRA, Native American casino gaming has spread rapidly, with the largest operation in Connecticut and the greatest density in Minnesota and Wisconsin. Because the increase has been so rapid, with regulatory control lacking, very little substantiated information can accurately identify the impacts of Native American gaming operations. A sampling of some of the identified impacts gleaned from recent studies

follows. Readers should be cautioned that many studies have been either commissioned by the tribes or by parties in opposition to Native American gaming expansion. Whenever possible, studies discussing casino operations in general have been consulted, and impacts were only accepted if they appear in two or more independent studies.

ECONOMIC

Property values experience rapid increases (1,000 percent or more) for some properties in downtown areas after the advent of casino type operations. Since Native American gaming occurs on tribal lands, this is only a concern if tribes purchase additional lands in downtown areas.

Unemployment figures do not always reliably indicate the success of Native American gaming operations. For example, unemployment figures on the Shakopee reservation in Minnesota show no decline (70 percent) before and after gaming. This is due to the tribe's decision to share profits equally with all members (approximately 150). In 1994, each member received a cash payment of $500,000, regardless of employment status.

Some tribes make cash payments directly to members, while others invest heavily in educational programs and drug and alcohol treatment centers.

Native American casino employment is expected to exceed 17,000 by the end of 1996, with an additional 33,000 secondary jobs created.

In Minnesota, average payout in Aid to Families with Dependent Children (AFDC)

(continued on next page)

increased in 1992 except to members of Native American tribes. After casinos have been in operation one or two years, it is not unusual to see AFDC payouts reduced by more than 50 percent.

The annual impact on Minnesota's Gross Domestic Product as a result of Native American gaming exceeded $1.5 billion in 1994.

Wisconsin state government returns from Native American gaming operations are estimated to exceed $52 million from sales, income, and gas taxes. As elsewhere, no direct payments on proceeds from tribal gaming revenues are made to the state.

The growth in casino gaming directly affects other gaming operations. One of the most affected, resulting in a decreased handle, has been pari-mutuel wagering. Combining pari-mutuel with other forms of gaming is now becoming commonplace and has shown some promise in increasing the overall handle from the operation.

SOCIOCULTURAL

The incidence of compulsive gambling behavior has been set at between one and five percent of the adult population. It is higher for youth, estimated at 2-1/2 times that of the adult population. Native American youth in Minnesota have higher levels of problem gambling behavior than in areas without casinos.

Community satisfaction in gambling towns is usually lower than in non-gambling towns.

Alcohol abuse and related crime figures show rapid increases after the introduction of gaming operations.

Educational and other services improve for many Native American as a result of tribal reinvestment of casino profits in its people.

OTHER CONSIDERATIONS

Casinos can be classified as either the exotic (mega-type) or convenience type. Exotic casinos are developed as tourist attractions and serve as destinations. New developments in Nevada are the only ones in the U.S. that fit this category. Most casinos are of the convenience type, attracting people from the local or regional area. Native American casinos fit into this category. Convenience casinos are most at risk from business loss due to casino gaming expansion.

Traffic volume increases dramatically, requiring infrastructure investment to improve safety and ease congestion. Housing and public services may become stressed if people are attracted to an area because of the increase in jobs.

There is no doubt that Native American gaming operations have greatly assisted tribal members economically. For some, the sociocultural costs have offset the economic gains. Whether the benefits outweigh the costs, especially in the long run, is open to debate. As the proliferation of gaming operations reduce effective market area, casino profits may be short lived. Also, in areas that have shown either employment gains or welfare case load decreases, this trend could change as more people are attracted to the area because of the employment opportunities. Native American gaming operations are such a recent phenomenon, as are most other types of legal gaming in the U.S., that very few longitudinal studies have been undertaken. Most experts agree that the market is not yet saturated but it is moving rapidly to a situation where effective market area for any new operation is shrinking

Sources:

Callaway, A., J. Gish, R. Parker, and G. Szychowski. 1992. *Assessing the Social Impacts of Gambling as Perceived by Local Government and Agency Officials, on Permanent Residents of Black Hawk, Colorado. Class research project.* P. Long, Instructor. University of Colorado, Boulder.

Cozzetto, D. 1995. The Economic and Social Implications of Indian Gaming: The Case of Minnesota. American Indian Culture and Research Journal *19(1):119-131.*

Eadington, W. 1995. Casino Gaming-Origins, Trends and Impacts. *Reno: Institute for the Study of Gambling and Commercial Gaming.*

Hanners, D. 1995. The Odds Improve. St. Paul Pioneer Press *September 10.*

Long, P., and Y. Kang. 1994. *Impacts of Limited Stakes Casino Gambling on Resident Satisfaction with Community Life: A Preliminary Report. Presented at the Ninth International Conference on Gambling and Risk Taking, Las Vegas, Nevada.*

Murray, J. 1992. *The Economic Benefits of American Indian Gaming Facilities in Wisconsin. Study Commissioned by the Wisconsin Indian Gaming Association and the University of Wisconsin Cooperative Extension.*

Thalheimer, R. and J. Rovelstad. 1995. *The New Gambling Wave—Its Impacts. Presentation at the 16th Annual CenStates TTRA Conference. Lexington, Kentucky, September 7-8.*

Volberg. R. 1993. Estimating the Prevalence of Pathological Gambling in the United States, 365-384. In W. Eadington, and J. Cornelius, eds. Gambling Behavior and Problem Gambling. *Reno, Nev.: Institute for the Study of Gambling and Commercial Gaming, University of Nevada.*

Zelio, J. 1994. The Fat New Buffalo. State Legislatures *(June).*

wildland base are severed, wildland becomes a scarce commodity, and pressures mount for travel experiences that contrast with everyday life. These examples underscore an important principle of tourism development: preservation is also development if by doing so, society benefits.

National Park Service

Very little explanation is required for the inclusion of the National Park Service in the group of federal agencies providing tourism attractions and programs. As the principal federal agency responsible for the protection of unique natural and historical resources in the United States, the linkage with tourism is direct. Early leaders of the National Park Service movement viewed the nation's outstanding scenic areas as important not only for the mental well-being of people but as major contributors, through tourism development, to the national economy (Sellars, 1992). Although what is an appropriate level of development within a national park continues to be debated, its importance to regional and national economies cannot be ignored.

The U.S. National Park Service was established in 1916 by President Theodore Roosevelt, with the designation of Yellowstone as the first national park. Although Yellowstone is the first national park authorized by Congress and approved by the President, it was actually the fight over construction of Hetch Hetchy dam in the Yosemite valley which aroused public interest over the physical transformation of unique wild areas. (An excellent historical review of the issues that led to the establishment of the National Park Service, its growth, and development can be found in Everhart, 1983).

> The mission of the National Park Service is to "conserve the scenery and the natural and historic objects and the wildlife . . . and provide for the enjoyment of the same in such a manner and by such means as will leave them unimpaired for future generations" (Ridenour, 1991:22).

There are more than 350 designated areas located in 49 states, the District of Columbia, and the territories of Guam, Saipan, Puerto Rico, Virgin Islands and American Samoa (Figure 6.11 and Table 6.1). By the end of the 1980s, over 300 million visitor days were recorded at park system lands annually.

Some of the programs administered by the National Park Service which directly affect tourism include:

- Development and implementation of Park management plans

- Presentation of talks, tours, films, exhibits, publications and other interpretive media for the purpose of environmental or historical education

- Operation of campgrounds and other visitor facilities

- Land and Water Conservation Fund program which provides direct grants to states for recreation facility development

- Supply planning and technical assistance for the National Wild and Scenic Rivers program, National Trails program, and National Register of Historic Places program.

In addition to providing the above services, the NPS enters into negotiated agreements with the private sector for concessionaire management of visitor facilities (e.g., lodges and food service operations within parks). Although the National Park Service is a major provider of tourism attractions within the United States, and directly and indirectly is a major force of tourism development in some areas of the country, it is faced with a serious challenge to its mission statement. Increasing use of park system lands, brought on by population increases and greater mobility, have caused some people to question whether the two main charges embodied in the service's mission statement, preservation and use, are compatible. Overuse threats to National Parks are real, and as discussed in Chapter 4, crowding and congestion can compromise the integrity and values of any

TABLE 6.1 Number and Acreage of National Park Service Units		
Classification	*Number*	*Acreage*[1]
International Historic Site	1	35.39
National Battlefield	11	12,771.90
National Battlefield Park	3	8,767.39
National Battlefield Site	1	1.00
National Capital Park	1	6,468.88
National Historic Site	68	18,467.71
National Historic Park	29	151,632.86
National Lakeshore	4	227,244.37
National Mall	1	146.35
National Memorial	23	7,949.16
National Military Park	9	34,046.72
National Monument	79	4,844,610.12
National Park	50	47,319,321.07
National Parkway	4	168,618.32
National Preserve	14	22,155,497.84
National Recreation Area	18	3,686,923.39
National Rivers[2]	5	360,629.91
National Scenic Trail	3	172,202.61
National Seashore	10	597,096.47
National Wild and Scenic River and Riverway[3]	9	292,596.82
Park (other)	10	40,120.70
White House	1	18.07
Totals	354	79,997,167.05

[1]Acreages as of December 31, 1988.
[2]National Park System units only.
[3]National Park System units and components of the Wild and Scenic Rivers system.

Source: The National Park Index, 1989

natural area. The National Park Service continues to monitor external threats such as air pollution to units in the system, while struggling with questions of how to manage the internal threats such as overuse.

Bureau of Land Management

The Bureau of Land Management (BLM) is usually forgotten when discussing tourism development in the U.S. Founded in 1946 when the

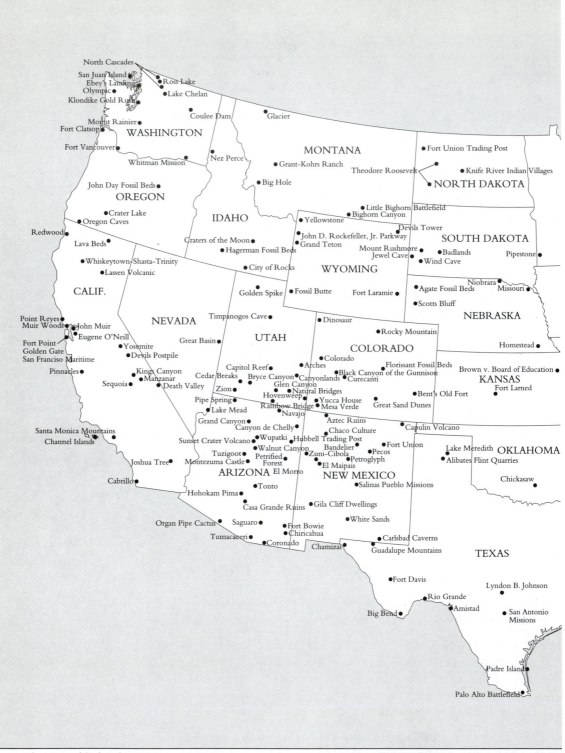

Figure 6.11 *The National Park System*

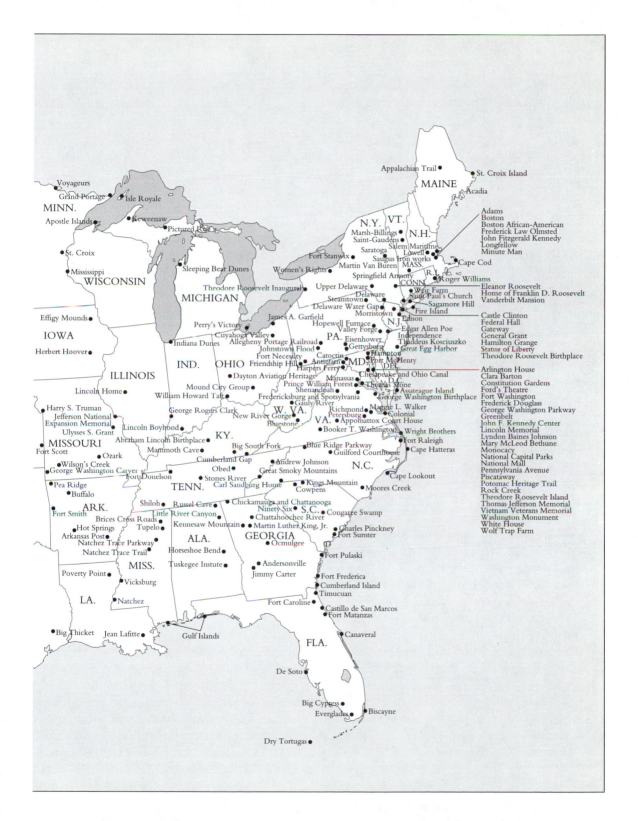

Voyageurs

Grand Portage
Isle Royale
MINN.
Apostle Islands
Keweenaw
Pictured Rocks
St. Croix
Mississippi
WISCONSIN
Sleeping Bear Dunes
MICHIGAN
Effigy Mounds
Perry's Victory
Theodore Roosevelt Inaugural
IOWA
Cuyahoga Valley
James A. Garfield
Herbert Hoover
Indiana Dunes
Allegheny Portage Railroad
ILLINOIS
IND.
OHIO
Johnstown Flood
PA.
Lincoln Home
Dayton Aviation Heritage
Fort Necessity
Mound City Group
Friendship Hill
Harry S. Truman
William Howard Taft
Harpers Ferry
Jefferson National
Expansion Memorial
George Rogers Clark
New River Gorge
W. VA.
Ulysses S. Grant
Lincoln Boyhood
Gauley River
MISSOURI
Abraham Lincoln Birthplace
Bluestone
Fort Scott
Ozark
KY.
Booker T. Washington
Wilson's Creek
Mammoth Cave
Big South Fork
George Washington Carver
Forts Donelson
Cumberland Gap
Obed
Pea Ridge
Buffalo
Stones River
ARK.
TENN.
Carl Sandburg Home
Fort Smith
Shiloh
Russel Cave
Little River Canyon
Brices Cross Roads
Ninety Six
Hot Springs
Tupelo
Kennesaw Mountain
Arkansas Post
Natchez Trace Parkway
ALA.
Natchez Trace Trail
Horseshoe Bend
MISS.
Tuskegee Instute
Poverty Point
GEORGIA
Ocmulgee
Vicksburg
Andersonville
Jimmy Carter
LA.
Natchez
Fort Caroline
Big Thicket
Jean Lafitte
Gulf Islands
FLA.
De Soto
Big Cypress
Everglades
Biscayne
Dry Tortugas

Appalachian Trail
St. Croix Island
MAINE
Acadia
Adams
Boston
Boston African-American
N.Y.
VT.
Frederick Law Olmsted
Marsh-Billings
N.H.
John Fitzgerald Kennedy
Saint-Gaudens
Longfellow
Salem Maritime
Minute Man
Saratoga
Fort Stanwix
Saugus Iron works
Women's Rights
Martin Van Buren
Lowell
Cape Cod
Springfield Armory
MASS.
R.I.
CONN.
Roger Williams
Upper Delaware
Weir Farm
Eleanor Roosevelt
Delaware
Saint Paul's Church
Home of Franklin D. Roosevelt
Steamtown
Sagamore Hill
Vanderbilt Mansion
Delaware Water Gap
Fire Island
Hopewell Furnace
Morristown
Castle Clinton
Valley Forge
Edison
Federal Hall
N.J.
Gateway
Edgar Allen Poe
Independence
General Grant
Eisenhower
Thaddeus Kosciuszko
Hamilton Grange
Gettysburg
Great Egg Harbor
Statue of Liberty
Catoctin
Theodore Roosevelt Birthplace
Antietam
Hampton
MD.
Fort McHenry
DEL.
Chesapeake and Ohio Canal
Arlington House
Manassas
Clara Barton
Prince William Forest
Thomas Stone
Constitution Gardens
Shenandoah
Assateague Island
Ford's Theatre
Fredericksburg and Spotsylvania
George Washington Birthplace
Fort Washington
Gauley River
Frederick Douglass
Richmond
Maggie L. Walker
George Washington Parkway
VA.
Petersburg
Colonial
Greenbelt
Appomattox Court House
John F. Kennedy Center
Booker T. Washington
Wright Brothers
Lincoln Memorial
Fort Raleigh
Lyndon Baines Johnson
Blue Ridge Parkway
Cape Hatteras
Mary McLeod Bethune
Guilford Courthouse
Monocacy
N.C.
National Capital Parks
Cape Lookout
National Mall
Kings Mountain
Pennsylvania Avenue
Cowpens
Moores Creek
Piscataway
S.C.
Potomac Heritage Trail
Chickamauga and Chattanooga
Congaree Swamp
Rock Creek
Chattahoochee River
Theodore Roosevelt Island
Charles Pinckney
Thomas Jefferson Memorial
Martin Luther King, Jr.
Fort Sumter
Vietnam Veterans Memorial
Washington Monument
Fort Pulaski
White House
Wolf Trap Farm
Fort Frederica
Cumberland Island
Timucuan
Castillo de San Marcos
Fort Matanzas
Canaveral

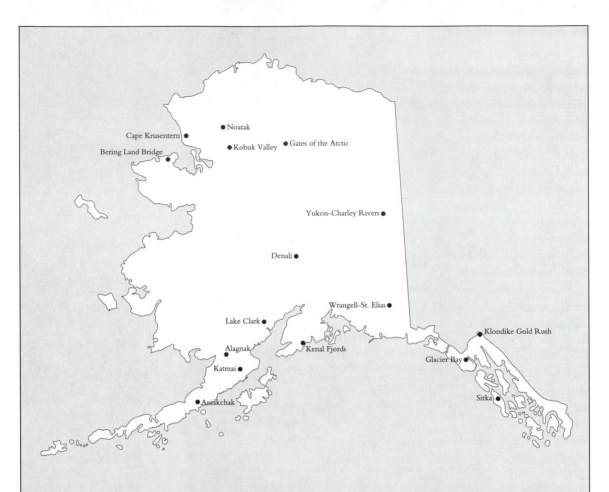

Seven national park areas in Alaska have adjoining national preserves, counted as separate units of the National Park System. They are: Aniakchack, Denali, Gates of the Arctic, Glacier Bay, Katmai, Lake Clark, and Wrangell-St. Elias.

Guam

War in the Pacific

Hawaii

USS Arizona Memorial
Kalaupapa
Haleakala
Puukohola Heiau
Kaloko-Honokohau
Pu'uhonua o Honaunau
Hawaii Volcanoes

Puerto Rico and the Virgin Islands

San Juan
Virgin Islands
Salt River Bay
Buck Island Reef
Christiansted

American Samoa

American Samoa

Figure 6.11 (cont.)

General Land Office and Grazing Service were consolidated, the BLM's principal duties are to manage the nation's public lands for grazing and mining interests. The mission of the BLM is to be:

> ". . . responsible for the balanced management of the public lands and resources and their various values so that they are considered in a combination what will best serve the needs of the American People. Management is based on the principles of multiple use and sustained yield—a combination of uses that takes into account the long-term needs of future generations for renewable and nonrenewable resources. These resources include recreation, range, timber, minerals, watershed, fish and wildlife, wilderness and natural, scenic, scientific and cultural values" (Department of Interior, 1989).

The BLM is the largest land management agency in the U.S., responsible for approximately 270 million acres. Most of these lands are located in the western United States and Alaska. Resources managed by the BLM include timber, solid minerals, oil and gas, geothermal energy, wildlife habitat, endangered plant and animal species, rangeland vegetation, recreation and cultural values, wild and scenic rivers, and designated conservation and wilderness areas. The 1976 Federal Land Policy and Management Act stipulates BLM lands be managed for multiple use. That charge, plus the increasing amount of recreation use on BLM-managed lands (over 60 million visits in 1990 with an economic value exceeding $500 million annually), led to the design of Recreation 2000, a strategic recreation management plan (Ravnikar, 1990). Expected to be operational by 1997, Recreation 2000 seeks to:

- Improve visitor information and interpretation services

- Strengthen resource protection efforts

- Improve access to public lands

- Enter into partnerships with the private sector and other government agencies to increase recreation opportunities

- Develop marketing strategies to increase use of BLM facilities

- Expand volunteer programs to provide additional recreation services

- Review and recommend plans for improving permits and concessionaire operations

- Become active participants in state and local tourism programs

Three major initiatives of the Recreation 2000 strategy intend to accomplish the above goals:

1. Backcountry Byways

    This program identifies a system of backcountry roads for public use. Partnerships with the public and private sector are being sought to assist in developing maps, signs, and roadside exhibits.

2. Adventures in the Past

    This program provides an opportunity for the public to learn how public lands have been used through history. Every state BLM office is encouraged to develop at least one project for the public to learn and experience some exceptional aspect of the nation's cultural heritage.

3. Watchable Wildlife

    This program enhances wildlife viewing opportunities, provides educational programs about wildlife's importance, and fosters support for wildlife conservation and management.

Currently, the BLM is evaluating over 800 areas for inclusion into the nations's wilderness system, and administers 27 designated wilderness areas. The BLM must protect the wilderness character of these lands which have been classified either as a recreational attraction or ecosystem preserves which may be threatened by some form of pollution (Marlatt et al., 1989).

The BLMs current emphasis on recreation management indicates that the values of recreation, and indirectly tourism, are receiving increasing attention within the federal government. Partnerships with other organizations will lead to establishing a larger attraction package, either through increased physical development, or greater awareness of wildland values, for the tourism industry.

Bureau of Reclamation

The Bureau of Reclamation (BOR) originally began as a program within the U.S. Geological Survey Office to provide the arid and semi-arid lands of the western United States with a secure, year-round supply of water for irrigation and domestic use. The program began in 1902, and by 1907 the BOR separated from the U.S. Geological Survey; in 1923 it was renamed the Bureau of Reclamation. The BOR provides water for farms, towns, industry, generation of hydroelectric power, river flow regulation, flood control, enhancement and protection of fish and wildlife habitat, and outdoor recreation opportunities. The BOR is responsible for most of the reservoir and hydroelectric projects throughout 17 western states. BOR facilities include over 350 storage reservoirs, 250 diversion dams, 54 hydroelectric powerplants and thousands of miles of canals and pipelines.

The creation of reservoirs led to a surge in water-based recreation activity, since in most parts of the western United States water is a scarce commodity. Even though the BOR is not primarily responsible for managing recreation activity or providing large recreation facility development, its projects provide tourism attractions by increasing the supply of water-based recreation opportunities in a historically arid region of the country. Once recreation on a BOR project becomes popular, the 1965 Water and Recreation Act requires that the BOR transfer control to either a non-federal agency (state or local government) or another federal agency such as the Forest Service or National Park Service.

Bureau of Indian Affairs

The Department of Interior holds in trust almost 50 million acres of Native American lands. The Indian Self-Determination and Education Assistance Act of 1975 allows tribes to contract with the Bureau of Indian Affairs (BIA) for aid in managing those trust lands. Millions annually use tribal lands for fishing, hunting, camping, rafting, skiing and other related outdoor recreation activities. In 1990 the BIA adopted this goal: Guide and coordinate tourism as an economic resource for tribal nations and Native American entrepreneurs.

Tourism development is not new to Native Americans. However, early projects met limited success, due in part to an inappropriate positioning strategy. Native American tourism developments competed directly with other private sector operations for a domestic tourism market which was not particularly interested in Native American culture or heritage, but was more enthralled with the "cowboy" image rather than the "indian" image (Bureau of Indian Affairs, n.d.). International visitors, especially from Japan and Europe, are considered to be more interested in Native American heritage. The BIA's new tourism strategy reflects this product repositioning.

Major objectives included in BIA's tourism strategy include:

- Developing a memorandum of agreement with USTTA for support and development of a tourism policy subcommittee for Indian affairs.

- Establishing linkages with other federally funded programs, especially Scenic Byways, for tourism development and planning purposes.

- Initiating specific regional market research for Indian tourism in the United States by regions to guide financial institutions and tribal planning.

- Establishing monitoring and evaluation procedures for ongoing tourism projects.

- Developing an advanced international symposium for thematic cultural tourism.

- Initiating a technical assistance program for tourism.

Although not specifically addressed in their tourism strategy, Native Americans have begun to develop casino operations on tribal lands. The Department of Interior holds tribal lands in trust, but all lands belonging to a particular tribe are in theory separate nations. Recent court opinions hold that states must enter into compacts with tribes that allow legal gaming, clearly defining the extent of gaming operations. Originally intended to provide additional income for tribal members, the exponential growth in gaming operations has led to major casino developments. To date, most of the growth has occurred in Connecticut and in the midwestern states of Michigan, Wisconsin, and Minnesota (see case study).

Department of Agriculture (USDA)

The U.S. Department of Agriculture (USDA) was created in 1862 by the Morril Act. It is principally directed to assist agricultural producers through a major program in research and outreach extension activities. The establishment of land grant universities in every state ensures that agricultural research is an important component of the higher education system in the United States. Through the Cooperative Extension Service (CES), programs to transfer research findings to producers, consumers, youth groups, and others have been implemented. In some states, the CES also includes tourism outreach efforts.

Agriculture is an important contributor to the tourism industry. Recreation opportunities on privately held farm and ranch lands are important additions to a community tourism attraction base, and both federal and state programs enhance and encourage public use of private lands. Within the USDA, probably the most visible federal agency responsible for maintaining multiple use public lands is the Forest Service.

USDA Forest Service

The mission of the Forest Service is to provide a sustained flow of renewable resources, goods, and services that help meet the needs of the Nation and to contribute to the needs of the international community. Its guiding principle is to provide the greatest good to the greatest number in the long run. Major objectives include:

- Providing a sustained flow of renewable resources—outdoor recreation, forage, wood, water, wilderness, wildlife, and fish—in a combination that best meets the needs of society now and in the future

- Administering the nonrenewable resources of the National Forest System to help meet the nation's needs for energy and mineral resources

- Promoting a healthy and productive environment for the nation's forests and rangelands

- Developing and making available scientific and technological capabilities to advance renewable natural resource management, use, and protection

- Furthering natural resource conservation through cooperation with other federal agencies and state and local governments

The Forest Service manages over 191 million acres in 44 states, the Virgin Islands, and Puerto Rico. Within the National Forest System are 156 National Forest, 19 National Grasslands and 15 land utilization projects. In addition, 32 million acres are designated wilderness, and 175,000 additional acres are set aside as primitive areas where timber will not be harvested.

The most important new program affecting tourism development initiated by the Forest Service during the last decade is the Recreation Strategy. It is a four-pronged approach which emphasizes the importance of

U.S. Forest Service-managed land available for recreational use in the United States.
Photo by Patricia Irwin

recreation both internally and externally. The four points explicitly addressed by the Recreation Strategy are: rounding out multiple-use management, customer satisfaction, professionalism, and partnerships.

Rounding out multiple-use management means support for implementing forest plans. Forest plans address all functions, including recreation; if implemented, recreation programs receive increasing emphasis. Supporting a goal of customer satisfaction means recognizing the importance of a consumer orientation to the continued provision of forest products, including recreation. Specifically, this goal seeks to force forest planners to identify their customers—who they are, where they come from, and what they want to do. Understanding the customer base assists in providing the types of recreation opportunities in demand. The goal of professionalism is internally directed. By recognizing recreation as a profession, it puts recreation planners and managers on par with other recognized professionals within the Forest Service (e.g., foresters). It is an effort to raise the status of recreation within the organization and provide rewards and recognition for this type of service. Encouraging partnerships is a means of establishing cooperative relationships with private sector operators and local governments. This goal encourages Forest Service managers to become more actively involved in providing recreation opportunities for economic development.

Department of Defense

At first glance, the Department of Defense seems an unlikely candidate for the group of federal organizations responsible for providing recreation and tourism services. Apart from military bases, which can have an enormous impact on local area economies, the Department of Defense through the Army Corps of Engineers is responsible for numerous water development projects which increased the attraction base of many areas.

Army Corps of Engineers

The primary mission of the U.S. Army Corps of Engineers (USACE) is to support environmentally sustainable engineering. It supports commercial navigation on the nation's waterways, and provides flood control and flood area reduction, shore and hurricane protection, hydroelectric generation, water supply, recreation, and conservation. The USACE was formed by General George Washington during the Revolutionary War as the engineering and construction arm of the Continental Army. Since the early 1800s it has been the principal developer of the nation's water resources. The 1944 Flood Control Act authorizes the USACE to construct, maintain, and operate public park and recreational facilities at water resource development projects. It also instructs the USACE to open those projects for public recreation use.

The USACE's annual budget exceeds $9.5 billion, with $3.5 billion spent on civil works projects. Ten regional offices throughout the country support 50 divisions. Many of its construction projects result in major reservoirs with recreation use. To support recreation on USACE-managed areas, campgrounds, cabins, and other recreation user facilities have been developed. Considering the size of USACE's budget allocated to civil works projects, it is safe to assume the agency will continue to be an important provider of natural resource based attractions.

Tennessee Valley Authority

The Tennessee Valley Authority (TVA) is unique for the public sector in the United States. It is a quasi-public/private corporation created by the U.S. Congress in 1933. TVA operates a series of dams on the entire length, 650 miles, of the Tennessee River. The electricity produced by these dams, coal, and nuclear-fueled generating plants are sold to users in seven states at fair market rates. Funds for other projects, which include recreation, are provided by the U.S. Congress. The TVA provides tourism-promotion assistance and works with local communities and groups to develop maximum use of available resources. It operates a demonstration project, Land Between the Lakes, in the western part of Kentucky and Tennessee which emphasizes outdoor recreation, environmental education, and resource management.

The brief review provided above of the various federal agencies' role in attraction development underscores their importance as contributors to the nation's system of recreation and tourism attractions. This relationship is not always recognized. Other countries have similar agencies to these operating within the United States. Complete packaging of a country's tourism products requires close cooperation between all federal agencies providing the attractions. If Holecek's tourism system model is operational (Figure 6.1), and no evidence suggests otherwise, any decision by a federal agency impacts other federal agencies' policies, the private sector, and ultimately tourists. National level tourism development plans and debates should include all tourism attraction providers as key members.

REGIONAL ORGANIZATION FOR TOURISM DEVELOPMENT

The concept of regionalization addressed in Chapter 3 is a question of definition. Whereas political borders define sovereign nations, regions can be delineated based on a number of features. Apart from the "area of influence" criterion used in Chapter 3, for successful tourism development a region must contain all the elements necessary for a tourism industry to function.

Gunn (1988) lists twelve essential elements required for regional tourism development:

1. Natural Resources

2. Cultural Resources

3. Viable Service Communities

4. Access

5. Markets

6. Favorable Development Image

7. Local Acceptance of Tourism

8. Favorable Government Controls

9. Available Land for Development

10. Availability of Entrepreneurs and Managers

11. Availability of Labor

12. Availability of Finance

Regional Organizational Structure

Almost any area containing the above elements can be formed into a tourism region. Reasons for regional organization include:

1. Combining elements necessary for development into a holistic package. Systems work best when they are well organized and managed. Combining various political entities into a tourism region does not guarantee an efficient organizational structure, but it does provide the framework for one to develop.

2. Increasing marketing effectiveness. Marketing cooperatives, such as used for agricultural products, combine the financial resources of many small operators, allowing the development of marketing programs that would not be independently possible. Even if a formal marketing cooperative is not formed, the principle of cooperating to increase marketing effectiveness remains valid and can be accomplished in different ways.

3. Identifying and protecting symbiotic relationships. Many small communities providing tourism services rely on an attraction base

found in other communities or areas. Conversely, areas with attractions may need tourism services found elsewhere. Divergent programs of development may adversely affect each area's ability to become an integral part of a regional tourism industry.

4. **Image Development.** As will be discussed in Chapter 11, a unique or independent tourism image is difficult for small communities to develop. Regional organizations can assist in developing an image which effectively represents all the communities in the region.

5. **Partnerships.** Partnerships arise whenever one or more independent organizations agree to work toward a common goal. Although a regional organization is not necessary for partnerships to form, it facilitates the potential for cooperation. For example, motorcoach touring has increased dramatically within the United States in the last ten years. Motorcoach packages of seven to thirty days are common, with length of stay in any one area minimal. Assembling a tour package which can be sold to motorcoach operators requires a regional organization.

6. **Establishing an identity.** Communities establish a sense of place or home for local residents. Regionalization can establish a tourism identity for communities and their residents within a region.

7. **Assisting public/private cooperation.** Regions comprise many different entities. Public agencies and private operators have an easier time cooperating and working toward common goals when they are all active members of the same organization.

The advantages listed above, plus the resources required for successful tourism development, reinforce the need for forming some type of regional organization dedicated to tourism. Regional organizations do not replace community based tourism organizations, but work closely with them to maximize the potential of planned developments. The next section explores some of the different types of regional organizations throughout the world and how they function.

Types of Regional Organizations

Regional organizations are more common in the public sector, although some private sector examples exist. Private sector regional organizations are usually product specific, focusing on marketing and sales. For example, the private regional organization Circle Wisconsin promotes member communities to motorcoach operators. Since motorcoach tours rarely stop in one area for more than a day, many communities form packages for sale to motorcoach operators through the efforts of the regional organization. Similarly, in New Zealand working farms that wish to accommodate overnight guests can join a regional organization which inspects each property and, if found to meet certain standards, can be promoted by the organization. In this way, many farms in one area come together to form a set of farm stays that can be marketed to large groups on tour buses. Member dues or assessment fees usually finance private sector regional organizations.

Public sector regional organizations are usually established according to preexisting regional boundaries. The three most common are multi-county, state, and multistate. The terms county and state are used simply for brevity; boroughs, republics, provinces, etc., are interchangeable with county and state, and could be substituted without changing the content of the following discussion.

Multicounty

Multi-county tourism organizations are common throughout the United States. Their strength varies by budget size, a product of funding sources. A stable source of funding usually results in a more active and powerful organization. In order to more fully understand the concept of multicounty regional tourism organizations, an example from the state of Utah follows.

Utah is divided into nine tourism regions, each containing more than one county (Figure 6.12). Each region has a descriptive name which forms the basis for establishing regional tourism images. Regional names describe either a historical event, personage, or land feature. For example, Golden Spike Empire is the home of Promontory Point, where the ceremonial golden spike was driven into rail tracks connecting the east and west coast of the United States in 1869. Similarly, Bridgerland is named after Jim Bridger, a famous mountain man and early white explorer of the area. Dinosaurland is named after the prehistoric animals which roamed the area and is home to Dinosaur National Monument, where dinosaur fossils are displayed at a U.S. Park Service visitor center.

Funding for each region is provided primarily from special assessment room tax revenues. Room taxes are county option, and range between one to three percent. All taxes collected within a county, minus a small administrative fee, are rebated to the promotional region in which the county is located. These taxes were originally authorized exclusively for tourism promotion and marketing use, but this has been broadened to include tourism related infrastructure development. The use of a room tax to fund promotional regions does create some inequities. For example, Great Salt Lake county, which has the majority of hotels/motels in the

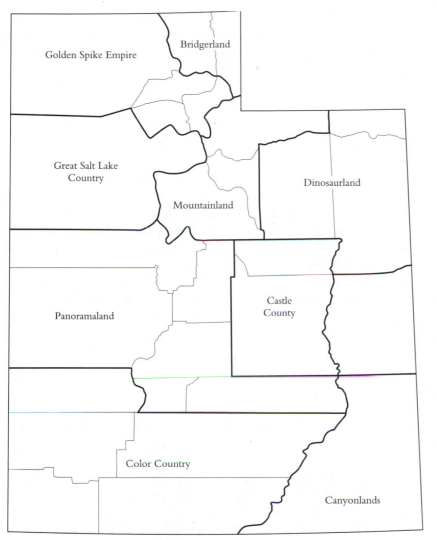

Figure 6.12 *Utah's Promotional Regions*

Source: Institute of Outdoor Recreation and Tourism, Utah State University

state, annually collects almost as much as the state office receives from general revenue appropriations.

Each region also receives approximately $15,000 annually from the state Division of Tourism. This money is available on a matching fund basis for projects that involve two or more regions. Promotional regions primarily focus on in-state programs which complement state programs directed at out-of-state markets. Promotional regions have been in existence since the late 1960s, and have been funded through room taxes since the early 1970s. The delineation of multicounty promotional regions allows for regional organizations to form, more effectively leveraging scarce financial resources. Many states in the U.S. use some form of a multi-county promotional model, although not all are as effective as those in Utah, due primarily to lack of funding.

State Organizations

The division of a country into smaller units such as states allows different political identities to be established. Sometimes a political identity is so strong, it gives rise to nationalistic movements (e.g., Soviet Union, Yugoslavia). It may also result in a tourism identity for each political unit. In the United States, almost every state has a division, department, or agency devoted to tourism development within its governmental structure (Table 6.2). The primary function of these different units is marketing and promotion.

Regional organization can also be set up to represent different countries within a larger political union. In the United Kingdom, separate tourist boards operate in Wales, Scotland, and England, but they are joined by the British Tourism Authority which is responsible for marketing the entire United Kingdom through overseas offices (Wanhill, 1995).

Multistate

Regions of a country may share common characteristics. Differences in geography, climate, political persuasion, touristic image, and many others can be used to divide a country into regions. Often, dividing a country into multistate regions is done to measure tourist flows between regions. For example, for years the United States Travel Data Center has used a four-region partition of the United States to analyze travel flows and economic impact (Figure 6.13). Regionalization along these lines allows for a more accurate representation of travel patterns. The larger the size of the region, the fewer individuals have to be surveyed to collect accurate tourist flow data. In this case regionalization allows for travel flows to be monitored across regional borders. However, as regions become smaller in size, accuracy is sacrificed unless data collection efforts are intensified.

Funding

Funding for regional level programs varies. In the United States, general revenues fund most state tourism offices. However, a majority of the states also collect special taxes from tourism related activities.

Hotel/motel taxes—sometimes referred to as a transient room tax—varying in size from one-tenth of one percent to eight percent, are allowed by 44 of the 50 states (Loyacono, 1991). A transient room tax is the

TABLE 6.2   Placement of State Travel Offices (STOs), 1989

State	STO Part of Larger Dept.?	Which Dept.?	Position Appointed	By Whom?
Alabama	No	—	Yes	Governor
Alaska	Yes	Commerce, Econ. Dev.	Yes	Governor
Arizona	No	—	Yes	Governor
Arkansas	Yes	Parks & Tourism	No	—
California	Yes	Commerce	Yes	Governor
Colorado	Yes	Local Affairs	No	—
Connecticut	Yes	Econ. Dev.	No	—
Delaware	Yes	Dev.	No	—
Washington, DC	—	—	—	—
Florida	Yes	Commerce	Yes	Sec. of Commerce
Georgia	Yes	Industry & Trade	Yes	Dept. Ind. & Trade
Hawaii	Yes	Business, Econ. Dev.	No	—
Idaho	Yes	Commerce	Yes	Dir. of Commerce
Illinois	Yes	Commerce	Yes	Governor
Indiana	Yes	Commerce	Yes	Lt. Governor
Iowa	Yes	Economic Development	No	—
Kansas	Yes	Commerce	Yes	Governor
Kentucky	No	—	Yes	Governor
Louisiana	Yes	Culture/Tourism	Yes	Lt. Governor
Maine	Yes	Economic Development	Yes	Governor
Maryland	Yes	Economic Development	No	—
Massachusetts	Yes	Economic Affairs	Yes	Governor
Michigan	Yes	Commerce	No	—
Minnesota	Yes	Trade/Economic Dev.	Yes	Governor
Mississippi	Yes	Economic Development	Yes	Agency Dir./Gov.
Missouri	Yes	Economic Development	No	—
Montana	Yes	Commerce	No	—
Nebraska	Yes	Economic Development	No	—
Nevada	—	—	Yes	Governor
New Hampshire	Yes	Economic Development	No	—
New Jersey	Yes	Commerce, Energy/Econ. Dev.	Yes	Governor
New Mexico	Yes	Econ. Dev./Tourism	Yes	Governor
New York	Yes	Economic Development	Yes	Econ. Dev. Commission
North Carolina	Yes	Economic Development	Yes	Governor
North Dakota	Yes	Economic Development	Yes	Dir. of Econ. Dev.
Ohio	Yes	Development	Yes	Governor
Oklahoma	Yes	Tourism/Recreation	Yes	Executive Director
Oregon	Yes	Economic Development	Yes	Governor
Pennsylvania	Yes	Commerce	Yes	Secretary of Commerce
Rhode Island	Yes	Econ. Dev.	Yes	Dir. of Econ. Dev.
South Carolina	Yes	Parks, Rec.	No	—

(continued)

		TABLE 6.2 Continued		
State	STO Part of Larger Dept.?	Which Dept.?	Position Appointed	By Whom?
South Dakota	No	—	Yes	Governor
Tennessee	No	—	Yes	Governor
Texas	Yes	Commerce	No	—
Utah	Yes	Community	Yes	Governor
Virginia	Yes	Econ. Dev.	Yes	Dir. of Econ. Dev.
Washington	Yes	Trade/Econ. Development	Yes	Dir. of Trade/Econ. Dev.
West Virginia	Yes	Commerce	Yes	Governor
Wisconsin	Yes	Development	Yes	Governor
Wyoming	No	—	Yes	Bd. of Commission

Source: Loyacono, 1991

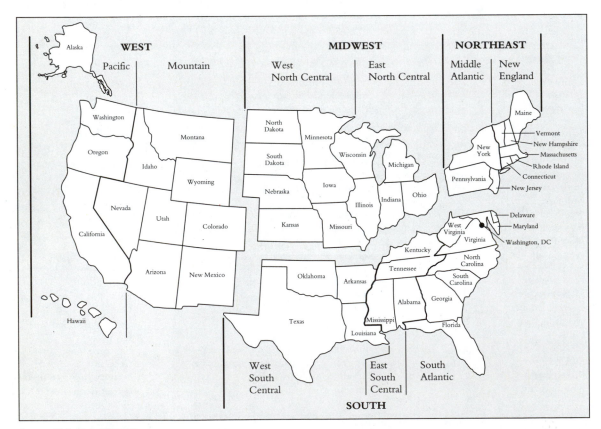

Source: U.S. Travel Data Center

Figure 6.13 U.S. Travel Regions

primary funding source for the Utah multicounty example described above. These special taxes are charged in addition to regular sales tax. A minority of states require all proceeds be used for tourism promotion by local governments. Uses of the tax are as diverse as beach preservation (Delaware) to general fund purposes.

Entrance fees at amusement parks, theater events, or other tourism attractions are taxed at a rate from one-tenth of one percent to ten percent in 32 states. In 1989, the total collected from amusement/admission special taxes was less than for hotel/motel room taxes; Tennessee collected the most at $25 million (Loyacono, 1991). These special taxes are also used for a variety of purposes including education, conservation, local governments, capital improvement bonds, as well as tourism development.

Fourteen states impose special taxes on food and drink. States use the revenue generated from this source for aid to local government, education, and in some instances tourism development programs. Tennessee also generated the most revenue from this source, collecting over $455 million in 1989.

Other forms of tax revenue impact a regional tourism industry. The U.S. federal government, as well as each state, imposes special taxes on the sale of gasoline and other motor fuels. The proceeds from these taxes are primarily used for highway construction and improvement programs. Although none of the states dedicates a portion of fuel taxes directly to tourism, improving the transportation infrastructure directly benefits regional tourism development.

In part, special excise taxes imposed on the purchase of sporting goods fund access to public waterways, public marina construction, public land programs, and natural resource research programs. The Land and Water Conservation Fund (LWCF) and the Pittman Robertson Fund are formula driven federal programs which distribute a percentage of the taxes collected from sporting goods sales to each state for dedicated purposes. These special taxes contribute to tourism development by providing public attractions. Each state also charges special fees primarily used to improve, increase the supply of, or provide access to public attractions. Boat registration fees, purchase of special stamps required to hunt specific game animals, and park entrance fees are examples of funding sources that directly or indirectly contribute to tourism development.

The preceding discussion on types of regional organizations and funding sources is based on the assumption that regions must have some defined political boundaries. However, as discussed in Chapter 3, artificial designation by political boundary does not always determine an effective "area of influence." Regional politics may control tourism development, but tourism does not always respect political boundaries. Basing policy decisions only on a particular political boundary ignores the location of touristic attractions and services. Another way of approaching the concept of regionalization is through a supply-side analysis.

Regionalization through Supply-Side Analysis

A regional supply-side analysis of tourism resources provides an appraisal of each area's ability to attract and host tourists. It assesses the resources necessary to the functioning of a tourism industry, and identifies regions which are or can be considered prime tourism areas. Smith (1987) proposes using supply-side analysis to estimate the importance of tourism to specific areas within a larger region. Six steps are required to conduct the analysis.

1. Identify existing tourism resources. Secondary data sources identify the number and type of tourism resources within a region, including number of golf courses, number of hotel/motel rooms, number of campground sites, number of ski hills, and so on. The resources used are limited by the amount of statistical data available and the manner in which it is reported. Supply-side analysis relies on the existence of politically defined regions, and then combines data for all those regions to determine new ones. Therefore, data must be available at county, multicounty, planning district or some other regional level.

2. Use an appropriate data reduction technique to develop indices. Use as many tourism resources in a region as possible in order to capture the influence of each resource's influence on the strength of the regional tourism industry. Many resources complement each other, and are positively correlated; that is, one resource influences another. The purpose of employing a data reduction technique is to uncover any strong linkages between resources. Many different techniques can be used, and most fall under the category of Factor Analysis (see Kim and Mueller, 1978). Principle Components Analysis (PCA), used by Smith, is a form of Factor Analysis.

3. Reduce variables into dimensions or combine related variables. The output of PCA reduces the number of original variables (tourism resources) into a smaller group which the researcher can then interpret and name. Smith's example identifies four groups of related variables, "urban tourism," "outdoor recreation," "cottaging and boating," and "urban fringe tourism."

4. Identify regional clusters. Some regions may contain relatively high concentrations of more than one set or dimension of tourism resources. Using a hierarchial clustering algorithm (Ward, 1963),

regional clusters can be identified. Each cluster should be distinctively different from every other cluster in order to apply appropriate tourism policy.

5. Map regional clusters. Once distinctive regional clusters are identified, they can be mapped onto the larger region. In Smith's example, the larger region is the province of Ontario, and the smaller regions are counties. Figure 6.14 shows output from the mapping step. Not all clusters are contiguous; in other words, there are areas

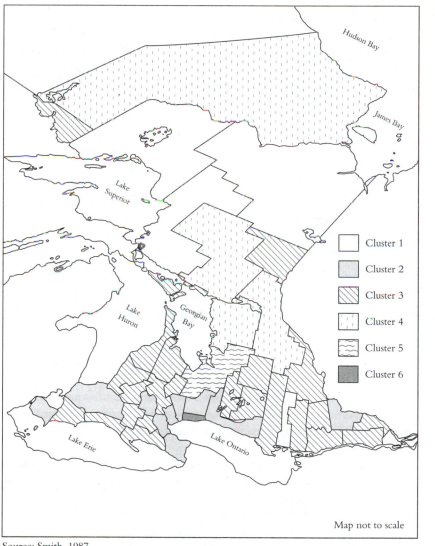

Figure 6.14 Regional Patterns of County Clusters

Source: Smith, 1987

within the region where tourism resources are not abundant or data are unavailable to assess the importance of the resources.

6. Develop policy. The output shows which counties have more of a certain set of tourism resources than others. Appropriate development projects (i.e. those that link with resources currently in place) can be proposed. Smith also investigates the relative importance of each one of the dimensions and concludes that "urban tourism" generates more tourism economic impact than the other three dimensions. This is likely due to the diversified economic base in urban areas, reducing the leakage from visitor expenditures. Lower economic importance is assigned to those regions heavily dependent on rural or outdoor recreation tourism resources. A smaller economic base in rural areas generally results in higher leakages and less local economic impact. However, the populous and economically diverse urban areas may capture the economic leakages from rural areas, resulting in as much total economic impact to the larger region regardless of where tourist expenditures initially took place. Further analysis of regional economic linkages would be necessary to prove this point. However, the type of regional analysis performed by Smith and replicated by Lovingood and Mitchell (1989), and Backman et al. (1991), underscores the importance of a regional analysis approach to understanding differences in the supply of tourism resources, and can greatly assist policy makers to develop regional strategic planning and marketing strategies.

Both Smith (1987) and Lovingood and Mitchell (1989) report that regional assessments do not support the arbitrary aggregation of multicounty tourism regions, as discussed above for the state of Utah. There do not appear to be any strong linkages between regions which are grouped together under a descriptive name and the distribution of resources in each region. Counties arbitrarily grouped together either because they are contiguous or for political expediency may not share any tourism commonalities. However, there is also no reason to suspect that grouping regions by their resource distribution will foster a better working relationship between these similar regions.

The above regional analysis is an example of a supply-side approach to determining regional tourism strengths and weaknesses. It assumes the existence of tourism resources within an area, and the acceptance of Say's law, "supply creates demand." Some of those tourism resources may derive from past development activities that were not undertaken with an understanding of tourism demand. For example, federal water projects initiated for agriculture and domestic water use nonetheless may become tourism development magnets. Similarly, tourism developments may be assisted by the construction of a high speed highway system. Regional assessments of tourism resources using supply-side approaches ignore changing tourism demand, or the impacts of other projects on regions not presently endowed with substantial tourism resources. As long as the status quo remains, supply-side regional analyses can greatly assist planning and marketing efforts. However, it is a poor predictor of future demand and the impact of non-tourism-related development projects on tourism. The next generation of regional analyses may work toward ascertaining tourism demand and proceed to identify regions able to meet the demand with resources either existing or potentially available.

Supply-side analyses such as Smith's can identify areas with the greatest economic contribution potential. However, some significant social concerns may be overlooked. Metropolitan areas almost always appear as major tourist destinations. Business activity in metropolitan areas supply the infrastructure necessary for pleasure tourism to develop. Rural areas rely almost exclusively on a pleasure tourism market, and in the absence of a strong manufacturing base and declining agricultural activity, tourism may be one of the few industries available for rural economic development. The percentage of advertising expenditures directed at increasing rural tourism flows may not be in proportion to the relative economic contributions from this type of tourism. However, from a social welfare perspective, increasing rural tourism activity may actually be directing economic development activity where it has the greatest chance of improving an individual's standard of living (Pearce, 1989).

REGIONALIZATION THROUGH OBSERVATION OF CRITICAL ELEMENTS

Assistance is sometimes provided at the national level in identifying areas of the country which have the resources and infrastructure in place for development. This process of regionalization is called the delineation of development zones. It requires an assessment of resources needed for development to occur, and while it does not require any complex statistical analysis, it does not preclude that type of input. Delineating development zones is more likely in developing countries where the National Tourism Organization often assumes a more extensive and proactive role in development.

The term "development zone" is not uniformly understood in tourism planning. In much of the literature, development zones are linked with marketing and community development (Kaiser and Helber, 1978; Gee et al., 1984; Getz, 1991). Gunn (1982) identifies several terms used interchangeably to describe development zones: administrative zone, marketing zone, and destination zone. Blank (1989) defines a development zone as:

1. A recognizable, definable area with appeal to tourists

2. Containing a tourism industry generating sufficient sales to deserve treatment as a factor in the local economy

3. Having coherence in geography and among its tourist-related features

4. Having political integrity, allowing for effective communications and decisions to be made.

Gunn's definition is simpler, as he defines a tourism development zone as a generalized area possessing some special tourism development qualities unlike other areas.

The above definitions imply that any identified tourism development zone should be attractive to tourists and also operators of tourist related businesses. This is true if development is viewed only in terms of growth. It is possible and often advisable to classify certain areas for little or no development. Lack of development in one zone can greatly enhance development in other zones.

Gunn (1988) identifies four essential elements needed for a primary development zone: attraction clusters, community, a circulation corridor, and linkage corridors.

Attraction Clusters

An attraction cluster consists of resources available for touristic consumption; they can be natural-resource-based, cultural, or manmade structures. Although people travel to areas for purposes other than to visit attractions, such as to visit friends and family, there is no definable tourist area without an attraction base. Attractions provide things to see and do. Attractions can be evaluated according to quality, authenticity, uniqueness, activities offered, and drawing power. These evaluative factors are discussed in greater detail in Chapter 9.

Community

A community can be part of the attraction base, but its primary function is to provide services demanded by tourists. An area can be endowed with an attractive resource base but still suffer from lack of visitation. Accommodation facilities, restaurants, and retail shops are a few of the services necessary for a community to function as a destination area. Lack of these services results in short lengths of stay, low expenditures, and limited opportunities for ancillary attraction development.

Circulation Corridor

Moving people into and out of an area with minimum disruption is a necessary component of a development zone. A primary development zone is usually serviced by more than one type of transportation system. Fly/drive combinations, where a visitor enters an area via commercial air transportation, then rents a car or hires a driver for travel to the attractions, are becoming increasingly popular. Areas which rely on one type of transportation may find themselves limited with respect to the numbers and type of visitors they can attract.

Linkage Corridor

Linkage corridors connect the attraction clusters to the community. Linkages may take the form of a transportation system dedicated to moving people between attractions and the community, or they may be more promotionally oriented to make visitors aware of the various attractions within an area. Some ski resorts in the United States have developed a public transportation system to move skiers from the community to the ski hills. These services reduce the need for further road construction and decrease the amount of automobile pollutants discharged into the atmosphere which may become trapped and hang over the area in the form of smog.

If all four elements exist within an area, it is designated as a primary development zone. Figure 6.15 displays this destination zone concept

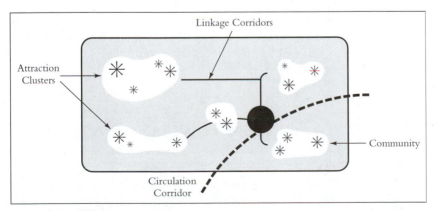

Figure 6.15 Destination Zone Concept

Source: Gunn, 1988

schematically. Remove one of the elements and the destination area becomes dysfunctional. Although attractions may be present, lack of a circulation corridor prevents tourism development from achieving its maximum potential. An area with one element missing or in short supply is considered a secondary development zone. If more than one element is missing the area is designated as a tertiary development zone.

Once primary development zones have been determined, choosing among them for investment consideration requires an analysis of critical inventory elements. Gunn (1982) identifies seven key elements that should be analyzed:

1. The number and quality of each zone's resource characteristics (e.g. natural, historic, cultural)

2. Accessibility with respect to present transportation circulation systems

3. Amount of open land available for facility development

4. Presence of high quality service centers

5. Ease with which each zone can be promoted with similar budgets

6. Level of organization and leadership currently in place

7. Type and strength of existing barriers and inhibitors

A simple comparative assessment of each development zone can be accomplished by constructing a matrix with the critical inventory elements listed in a column and the identified development zones arrayed across the top. Numerical values, using a finite scale, are assigned to each zone according to how much of each element they possess. More sophisticated approaches which prioritize elements and weigh each one accordingly can also be employed. The final product, once all numerical values are assigned and summed, is an investment preference listing for all primary development zones. Even when development zones can be identified, it is not always possible to obtain the needed financing for physical development. This is more of a problem in developing countries that must rely on donor agencies for development support.

FINANCING TOURISM DEVELOPMENT

Capital requirements for tourism development projects can be immense. Capital is needed not only for facility construction but for planning and infrastructure development as well. It becomes more problematic when the needs of developing countries are considered. One of the previously mentioned criticisms of tourism projects in developing countries is that the financing and most of the earnings are contributed and acquired by multinational corporations, increasing leakage and reducing the amount of expenditures left to circulate in the local economy. Local capital is often inadequate to finance the desired level of development. One solution is to develop an alternative form of tourism model requiring less capital. Currently international agencies and organizations still provide most capital for large-scale planning and development. The primary agencies involved in tourism development are the World Bank and its regional offices, federal donor agencies such as the United States Agency for International Development (USAID), the Inter-American Development Bank, The United Nations Development Program (UNDP), The Organization of American States (OAS), the European Community, and the World Tourism Organization. Assistance is provided in three ways:

1. Technical assistance, usually in preparing development plans

2. Loans for infrastructure development or improvement

3. Loans and equity investment in private facilities (Pearce, 1989)

A development project usually begins at the national or regional level. Once a general overview of the plan is prepared, any of the above agencies can be approached for one or more forms of assistance.

Loans to developing countries come in three types. If the originator of the loan is a commercial bank in an industrialized country, then private debt is created. When governments lend other governments money, the debt is termed bilateral official debt. Finally, loans from international financial institutions such as the World Bank result in multilateral official debt. Official debt (bilateral and multilateral) is estimated to be over $450 billion or almost twice that of private debt ($230 billion). Most of the debt of sub-Saharan African countries is official debt (White, 1992). Since most international development projects require some local currency for in-country work, private debt can be purchased from commercial banks, usually at a steep discount, and swapped with the borrower nation for an amount of local currency equal to the face value of the foreign currency debt that is being retired. Variations on this approach include debt-equity swaps, where instead of conversion to local currency, land or buildings are exchanged. Usually, land is exchanged for equity in a newly constructed facility. For example, the New Hyatt hotel in Warsaw was built on land the corporation acquired from the city, in exchange for an equity position in the hotel. The American Bank Security Pacific made other funds available (Frank, 1992).

Conservation organizations were the leaders in swapping land for debt in the 1980s, as many critical conservation zones were obtained from borrower nations in exchange for a buy-down of the foreign debt. When borrower nations are unable to come up with local currency for development projects, equity swaps take on much greater importance. Most debt swaps have been limited to private debt, as official debt has not generally been offered at a discount or for equity purchase.

Local currency for development projects can also be purchased from the private sector. Development agencies purchase local currencies that are not available for expatriation or conversion to foreign currency by other means for a percentage of their face value. By using foreign currency to purchase the private local currency, called "blocked currency," the private sector benefits from swapping to a convertible currency and the development project benefits by having local currency available to pay expenses.

Debt, currency, and equity swaps are appealing to development organizations and the private sector since they create little new debt by leveraging capital and/or assets. Accumulating debt was the norm during the 1980s, while shedding debt has become the focus of the 1990s. Tourism development projects requiring large sources of capital face a credit crunch in the 1990s. Creative financing options that do not accumulate large debt loads are increasingly favored over traditional programs.

DEVELOPMENT EXAMPLE: CENTRAL REGION IN GHANA, WEST AFRICA

Background

The Republic of Ghana is located on the west coast of Africa, approximately 750 kilometers north of the equator. As a tropical country, average temperatures range between 21–32° C, with rainfall in the south averaging 2,030 mm annually. Southern lands are coastal plains with elevations rarely exceeding 200 meters. Northern regions are drier, with predominantly savannah type vegetation. Population is estimated at over 15 million, with the majority concentrated in the southern and central part of the country.

Tourism arrivals average less than 500,000 per year and possibly less than 250,000; with the lack of a functioning data collection and analysis system it is difficult to identify the exact number. By some accounts, pleasure travel constitutes less than ten percent of all arrivals. The absence of a tourism industry of note in the country is due more to historical, political, and economic problems rather than from lack of trying. Teye (1988) notes the many attempts Ghana has undertaken to develop a tourism industry in the past. Due to numerous failed and successful coups, economic development and tourism were set back at least in the short run. The last coup in Ghana occurred in 1981, and currently the country is governed by a president and Parliament, with elections for both branches of government held in late 1992.

While the capital city of Accra has shown some encouraging signs of tourism development within the last few years, evidenced by new four- and five-star hotel properties, most of the country's regions (similar to states or provinces) are only now beginning to position themselves for economic development activity led by tourism. One of those areas is the Central Region, with its capital in the historic city of Cape Coast.

Central Region Development

The Central Region is located on the coast approximately 160 km west of Accra. It has particular historic importance as the first area of contact between European governments and the people of West Africa. The Portuguese were the first Europeans to build a structure in this part of the world, the castle at Elmina in 1482. Other European countries, including Great Britain, expanded into West Africa, building fortifications which were instrumental in the African diaspora to the New World during the slave trade of the 17th and 18th centuries. The remains of these buildings (forts and castles) form a significant part of the tourism potential of this area. Other attractions include a newly designated national park (Kakum), one of the few remaining tropical forests left in West Africa and a five-kilometer stretch of undeveloped beach with rolling hills and lagoons. Kakum has some of the tallest trees in the world, and contains a population of forest elephants and other endangered species, including Bongos and Diana monkeys. The beach area (Brenu) is one of the few areas in West Africa that is not subject to riptides, making it an ideal setting for water-based recreation activity.

In order to organize the Central Region's development efforts, two institutions were created. The lead institution is the Central Region Development Commission (CEDECOM), responsible for formulating policies and programs for an integrated development plan for the entire region. CEDECOM is an organ of the Ministry of Finance and Economic Planning of the central administration. CEDECOM has a fifteen-member commission representing both private and public sector interests in the region, and is administered by an Executive Secretary. Besides developing policy and implementation plans for economic development, CEDECOM is responsible for maintaining relations with central government agencies and ministries as well as international donor and development agencies.

A subsidiary of CEDECOM is the Tourism Development Scheme for the Central Region (TODSCER), responsible for coordinating the region's various tourism projects. Although CEDECOM heads an integrated economic development program which covers agriculture, fishing, and micro enterprise development, tourism is the lead sector for regional development. TODSCER provides the oversight and leadership for tourism development projects.

Financing for CEDECOM and TODSCER projects in Ghana began with the UNDP allocating approximately $3.4 million, to be matched with an equal amount in local currency by the government of Ghana. All the money was to be distributed to CEDECOM through the Ministry of Finance and Economic Planning. This money is considered an expenditure for institutional building, and the majority of it is dedicated to conducting feasibility/design studies and investment proposals. This UNDP funded project could also be considered seed money, as the work conducted interested other donor agencies in the potential for development in the Central Region.

USAID is another donor agency attracted to the Central Region, and the difference in financing between the UNDP and USAID projects reveals how creative international development financing has become. USAID contracts with private and public groups to administer projects it funds. In the case of the Central Region project, USAID contracted with the Midwestern Universities Consortium for International Activities (MUCIA), an agency representing a group of universities in the midwestern United States. MUCIA in turn subcontracted with the Smithsonian Institution, Conservation International, the International Council on Monuments and Sites, and the University of Minnesota (one of its member institutions) to carry out the terms of the contract. In order to complete the USAID funded project as designed, substantial local currency had to be acquired.

Approximately $6 million was available from USAID for a five-year tourism development project in the Central Region. The government of Ghana was not required to provide any additional monetary match, although wages of personnel from the various government agencies involved in the project continued to be covered by the central administration agency. The amount of money available to the project was deemed inadequate to complete it as outlined, especially if local currency had to be obtained without the benefit of any leveraging provided by a debt swap. Debt swap opportunities were then investigated to determine if local currency could be obtained using one of the previously tested methods.

However, due to the scarcity of commercial-bank-sponsored debt in sub-Saharan Africa, new debt swap arrangements had to be explored.

A multinational company was contacted which had "blocked currency," a name given to company owned local currency which can not be converted to foreign currency and repatriated. In this case, the multinational company needed to take out foreign currency from earnings within the country in order to contribute to the retirement fund of its expatriate employees. The legality of withdrawing these funds for a retirement account was disputed by the Ghanaian government, effectively blocking any transfer of funds outside the country. The currency was, however, available for any in-country investment. USAID and MUCIA approached the company, and it was agreed that $250,000 would be transferred to the company in exchange for a contribution equivalent to $1 million in local currency to the Central Region tourism development project. The company received a tax credit equal to the difference between current market value and the discount price, or $750,000. Additional "blocked currency" transactions were attempted, but a general improvement in Ghana's economic climate made local investment more attractive for the company. All other companies contacted that had identified "blocked currency" also declined to participate, citing an improving local investment climate as the reason.

Acquiring additional local currency required a different approach. One possible source was United States Public Law (PL) 480, which addresses Food Aid for Development. Only in extreme cases of need is food from United States agencies provided free of charge to a recipient country's citizens. Free distribution of food has been associated with depressing prices and undermining local market systems. Food is instead provided at no charge to central government agencies who sell it on the open market at prices which are intended to stabilize local markets. The proceeds from the sale of this food is to be used for development projects agreed to by USAID and the central government. After negotiations with the Ministry of Finance and Economic Planning, it was agreed that the PL 480 program would be used to acquire local currency, which was to be allocated to the Central Region tourism development project.

There is one other significant difference between the UNDP and USAID/MUCIA projects. UNDP funds are provided to the central government which then disburses them to CEDECOM and TODSCER for Central Region projects. Although PL 480 money is administered by the Ministry of Finance and Economic Planning, it is the only money on the USAID/MUCIA project under direct control of the central government. This may appear to be a minor point, but it has enormous significance when it comes to completing work components. For example, foreign currency expenditures are initiated by the various project subcontractors and generally follow an annual plan of work developed by the subcontractor in consultation with in-country counterparts. Local currency expenditures must be approved by the CEDECOM executive committee and, in the case of PL 480 money, be released by the Ministry of Finance and Economic Planning. The approval process can take some time, and given the rate of inflation in Ghana, purchasing power can erode while funds are awaiting release and approval to spend is granted.

PROJECT STRATEGY

As mentioned, tourism is the lead sector for Central Region development. Once local currency had been secured, the project could concentrate on developing its attraction base. The International Council on Monuments and Sites provided technical assistance for the renovation of two castles (Elmina and Cape Coast) and one fort (St. Jago) deemed to be the most significant of those remaining intact in the region. Conservation International is responsible for inventorying the resources of Kakum and identifying compatible tourism activities. To date, interpretive trails have been constructed and canopy viewing platforms connected through a canopy trail system have been completed. The Smithsonian Institution is providing interpretive training services and assists in developing museums in Cape Coast and Elmina Castle. UNDP is providing funds for infrastructure development of the beach site. The University of Minnesota is responsible for linking all project components into an integrated tourism development plan. All project subcontractors work closely with Ghanaian counterparts who have ultimate responsibility for the project.

As this discussion is being written, the project has started its fifth year of operation. Without delving into extensive detail, the project is organized according to many of the principles discussed in this book. Training in the areas of marketing, sociocultural assessment, interpretation, site planning, and hospitality services have been initiated. In addition to developing the attraction base, community involvement is a primary concern. Components of the project bring community groups into the planning process. A design team has been hired to integrate attraction development into a wider community planning process. Part of the design team's responsibility is to designate zones for special uses (i.e., transformation, modification, etc.). Already, a draft site plan for beach development has been produced with extensive areas that will remain in agricultural production. This is necessary in order for local residents to choose between occupations that are traditional (i.e., agricultural) or within the newly created tourism industry. Most of the agricultural products will be sold directly to the tourism industry in an attempt to capture more of the economic benefits of tourism development.

Environmental concerns are also being addressed. Poaching is still a serious threat to the wildlife of Kakum. One of Conservation International's primary objectives is to prevent poaching by developing other income-producing opportunities for village residents surrounding the park. Training for local people to serve as guides and the development of camping opportunities operated by local villagers are a couple of the alternative economic development strategies currently being considered.

The success of the Central Region tourism development program is still unknown. The project has contributed to substantial tourism growth in the area. This is planned growth with most of the initial visitor increases coming from local areas (e.g., Accra). Only recently, with the opening of the canopy walkway, museum in Cape Coast Castle, and restoration of Elmina and Cape Coast Castles has the strategy shifted from encouraging local or regional visitation to one focusing more heavily on international visitors.

Tourism development strategies continue to evolve. Financing and investment for projects respond to changing worldwide economic conditions. On-site planning responds to successes and failures of past efforts. The Central Region project is a product of changing economic conditions, new strategies, and old biases. It will not be an unqualified success. New development techniques are being tested, and some show great potential. Others will be discarded as well-intentioned but unworkable. One thing that has been learned from the project is that successful tourism development depends not only on adherence to certain principles, but flexibility in the application of those principles into different cultural contexts. This will be discussed in more detail in the last chapter.

CONCLUSION

Tourism development requires some form of organizational structure. This chapter discusses organization at the national/regional level. Most tourism organizations have as their primary responsibility the orderly growth of a tourism industry, but there are different philosophies about how this growth can be achieved.

A substantial percentage of this chapter deals with the role public land management agencies play in tourism development. Most of the tourism development literature focuses on the official national or regional tourism agency. However, many of a country's attractions are managed by agencies not normally associated with tourism. Although the examples used in this chapter are U.S. agencies, almost every country has counterparts. Kenya could not have achieved its level of tourism development without the involvement of its national park agency. Likewise, land management agencies throughout Latin America are becoming increasingly involved in tourism development as more land is cultivated or otherwise modified for human settlement. The importance of land management agencies in tourism development is slowly being recognized.

Holecek's model integrates public and private agencies and resources into a development mix. Changes in one sector initiate changes in another sector. If the community attraction complex is a viable concept, it must begin with a recognition that there are many different players in tourism development. Understanding each one's role is the first step toward successful development. Of course, there will continue to be examples where private-sector tourism development financed entirely from private capital does not require the involvement of public land management agencies. While these developments are important economic impact generators, they will remain, in total, a small percentage of the world's major attractions.

This chapter also deals with financing for international tourism development projects, using a project in Ghana as a case study. Traditional models have probably become financing dinosaurs. New strategies not only with respect to how tourism development is approached but how it is financed will continue to evolve based on world economic conditions.

EXECUTIVE SUMMARY

Trade or exchange through tourism benefits both countries involved in the transaction although, depending on the internal organizational structure, not all elements of society will benefit equally.

Four types of National Tourism Organizations (NTOs) are discussed, the most common being a department within a larger government agency, although recent public budget cutting decisions are changing the prevailing NTO model.

NTOs are characterized by the role, either active or passive, they play in a country's tourism industry. Passive roles can entail conducting national marketing efforts while an active role may include public ownership of tourism service facilities.

When considering the provision of tourism attractions, the most important resources are often controlled by the national government and administered by agencies not directly linked to the NTO.

Functioning tourism regions must possess certain essential elements including resources (natural, cultural), transportation corridors, and service facilities.

Most regional tourism organizations operate as smaller versions of the NTO in the sense that the majority restrict themselves to marketing the region.

The most common funding sources for regional tourism organizations include special room taxes, special food and beverage taxes, entertainment entrance fee taxes, and excise taxes on sporting goods or fuel.

One way to determine regions with tourism development potential is with a statistical-based supply-side analysis which uses data reduction techniques to group like resources or services.

Another method for regionalization uses inventory analysis to determine development zones. For a region to be considered a primary development zone, it must contain four elements: attraction cluster, community, circulation corridor, and linkage corridor.

Funding for international tourism development projects took on new forms in the 1980s and early 1990s. Some of these are discussed in the case study of Ghana which concludes this chapter.

SOURCES:

Ahmed, Z. and F. Krohn. 1990. Reversing the United States Declining Competitiveness in the Marketing of International Tourism: A Perspective on Future Policy. *Journal of Travel Research* 24(2):23–29.

Backman, S., M. Uysal, and K. Backman, 1991, Regional Analysis of Tourism Resources. *Annals of Tourism Research* 18(2): 323–327.

Blank, E. 1989. *The Community Tourism Industry Imperative: The Necessity, the Opportunity and its Potential.* State College, Pa.: Venture Publishing.

Bureau of Indian Affairs. *Tourism Strategy for Economic Development.* n.d.

Choy, D. and Y. Can. 1988. The Development and Organization of Travel Services in China. *Journal of Travel Research* 27(1):28–34.

Crompton, J. 1990. Tourism Research: Redirection for the Nineties. In Proceedings of the National Outdoor Recreation Trends Symposium III. Indianapolis, Indi., March 29–31, 1990.

Department of Interior. 1989. *Managing the Nation's Public Lands.* Washington, D.C.: Bureau of Land Management, Government Printing Office.

Edgell, D. 1988. Viewpoints: Barriers to International Travel. *Tourism Management* March: 63–66.

Edgell, D., Sr. *International Tourism Policy.* New York: Van Nostrand Reinhold, 1990.

Everhart, W. 1983. *The National Park Service.* Westview Press.

Frank, C. 1992. Tourism Trends: Investing in Tourism in Central and Eastern Europe—Current Status and Outlook. *WTO NEWS* 6(June): 15–16.

Gajraj, M. 1989. Limits to Tourism Development—Warning Signs. *Tourism Management* 10(3):202–203.

Gee, C., D. Choy, and J. Makens. 1984. *The Travel Industry.* Westport, CT: AVI Publishing.

Getz, D. 1991. *Festivals, Special Events and Tourism.* New York: Van Nostrand Reinhold.

Gilbert, D. Strategic Marketing Planning for National Tourism. *The Tourist Review* 1(1990): 18–27.

Gunn, C. 1982. Destination Zone Fallacies and Half Truths. *Tourism Management* 3(4):263–269.

Gunn, C. *Tourism Planning.* New York: Taylor and Francis, 1988.

Holecek, D. 1981. Michigan Tourism: How Can Research Help? *Symposium Proceedings.* J. Fridgen and D. Allen, eds. Michigan State University Parks and Recreation Resources Department: 18.

Jenkins, C. and B. Henry. 1982. Government Involvement in Tourism in Developing Countries. *Annals of Tourism Research* 9(4):500–521.

Kaiser, C. Jr, and L. Helber. 1978. *Tourism Planning and Development.* Boston: CBI Publishing Company, Inc.

Kim, J. and C. Mueller. 1978. Introduction to *Factor Analysis: What It Is and How To Do It,* Newbury Park, Ca.: Sage Publications.

Lovingood, P. and L. Mitchell. 1989. A Regional Analysis of South Carolina Tourism. *Annals of Tourism Research* 16(3):301–317.

Loyacono, L. 1991. *Travel and Tourism: A Legislator's Guide.* Washington, D.C.: National Conference of State Legislators.

Marlatt, W., A. Riebau, W. Erickson, M. Sestak, and L. Smith, 1989. Baseline Wilderness Monitoring in the Bureau of Land Management. Presented at the Wilderness Management Conference, Minneapolis, MN, September 11–14.

McIntosh, R., C. Goeldner and B. Ritchie. 1995. Tourism: Principles, Practices, Philosophies. 7th edition. New York: John Wiley and Sons, Inc.

Mill, R., and A. Morrison. 1985. *The Tourism System.* Englewood Cliffs, N. J.: Prentice Hall.

Page, S. 1988. Tourist Development in London Docklands in the 1980s and 1990s. Paper presented at the IGU Leisure and Tourism Seminar. Christchurch, New Zealand.

Pearce, D. 1989. *Tourist Development.* New York: Longman Scientific and Technical.

Ravnikar, M. 1991. Recreation through the Year 2000. *Parks and Recreation* April:60–64.

Ridenour, J. Building on a Legacy. *National Parks* May/June (1991):22.

Ridenour, J. 1995. Trends in Management and Operations: New Problems, New Solutions. *Trend Tracker, 4th International Outdoor Recreation and Tourism Trends Symposium.* St. Paul Minn.: Tourism Center, University of Minnesota.

Sellars, R. 1992. The Roots of National Park Management. *Journal of Forestry* 90(1):16-19.

Smith, S. 1987. Regional Analysis of Tourism Resources. *Annals of Tourism Research* 14(2): 254–273.

Teye, V. 1988. Coups d'Etat and African Tourism: A Study of Ghana. *Annals of Tourism Research* 15(3):329–356.

U.S. Bureau of Economic Analysis. *Survey of Current Business.* June 1990.

Wahab, S. 1995. Tourism Development in Egypt: Competitive Strategies and Implications. Paper presented at the June 1995 meeting of the International Academy for the Study of Tourism. Cairo, Egypt.

Wall Street Journal. January 2, 1984.

Wall Street Journal. June 1, 1995.

Wanhill, S. 1995. "Encompassing the Social and Environmental Aspects of Tourism within an Institutional Context: A National Tourist Board Perspective. Paper presented at the June, 1995 meeting of the International Academy for the Study of Tourism. Cairo, Egypt.

Ward, J., 1963. Hierarchical Grouping to Optimize an Objective Function. *Journal of the American Statistical Association* 58:236–244.

White, W. 1992. *Debt-For-Development Conversions and the University Role*. Washington, D.C.: Whitman and Ransom.

Community Tourism Development

*Reconstructed 18th-century community in
Philadelphia, Pennsylvania.
Photo by the author*

Learning Objectives

Review examples that identify some basic community
tourism development principles.

•

Examine the functions of a dedicated community
tourism development organization.

•

Examine the requirements for successful community
tourism development.

•

Review different promotion, advertising, and
communication techniques that a local tourism
organization can successfully utilize.

•

Explore funding and development assistance programs
available to people or businesses at the local level.

•

Analyze different community development
models with respect to drawing potential and
impact generation.

INTRODUCTION

Many of the impacts discussed in Chapters 3–5 are community-specific. That is, they occur at the local level and reside most clearly with the hosts or local residents. Negative impacts are magnified when touted economic returns do not materialize or are siphoned off as a result of non-local investment in tourism development. It is imperative, then, that local communities positioning themselves for a piece of the tourism pie spend more time planning and managing their tourism industry. Too often, tourism is viewed at the community level as a means to offset losses in other industrial sectors. When that happens, tourism becomes an expedient remedy rather than a well-planned economic development initiative.

One common characteristic of communities embracing tourism as an economic savior is the almost exclusive reliance on advertising to let people know that they can visit and spend money. More successful communities, however, realize that tourism development is a painstaking business requiring constant attention and management. It also means change, the only constant in tourism development.

Tourism development affects cultures, lifestyles, family structures, and so on. The lazy Sunday afternoon, with free time for family obligations, vanishes. The uncrowded beach or mountain trail is no longer one's private domain, but instead must be shared. The sleepy little town that rolled up the sidewalks at five p.m. is now buzzing with strangers in the evening hours. New residents with different values appear in town. Change that comes with tourism is not always welcome. However, if a community is to reap some of the economic benefits, it must recognize that managed change can be beneficial. This chapter addresses the process of organizing and managing change resulting from tourism development.

Some readers may view this chapter as pro-development, as it deals in part with techniques to increase the flow of visitors. It also examines methods that allow a community's citizenry to become more involved in deciding the type of development appropriate for them. In that sense, the chapter is less pro-development than about coping strategy. Tourism can begin to increase in a community because of the efforts of just one individual. Rarely is there ever a concerted effort to stop tourism development when it is in the beginning stages. Organized efforts usually begin when it reaches a level where negative consequences are being experienced. Therefore, we must accept tourism development as something that all communities may eventually encounter, and develop a coping strategy for managing it so that it provides the benefits we seek.

Requirements for Tourism Development

Before delving into specific community development guidelines, this section offers examples of well-intentioned but nevertheless failed or misdirected efforts as a means of underscoring some of the basic requirements for successful community tourism development. The following examples are real. While the authenticity of each example can be documented, those involved in community tourism development will undoubtedly recognize numerous similar situations.

Accepting Change

A small community in the southwestern United States was doing nicely as a result of uranium mining. However, nuclear reactor accidents at Three Mile Island and Chernobyl resulted in a decreasing demand for uranium, bringing mining activity to a virtual standstill. Employment losses were substantial, and tourism was seen as a means to breathe life back into the community. Natural resource attractions were abundant, as the community was located near two national parks, one national monument, and a major national recreation area. Much of the surrounding countryside was federally managed land with varied topography including alpine areas, steep canyons, and Piñon/Juniper desert land. Cultural resources included a large, aesthetically pleasing Native American reservation. The community had three trading posts specializing in authentic Native American arts and crafts, and a museum with prehistoric Indian ruins on site. Access was somewhat limited as no major transportation corridors came close to the community, although modern two lane highways provided access from the north, south and west.

In an attempt to plan for tourism development, the community requested tourism training programs. These programs were presented on two weekends to front line personnel, city officials, and business owners. Recommendations were presented to a group of city officials after the training programs were completed. Recommended changes included extension of business hours, weekend openings for certain businesses, and a relaxation of liquor laws (no alcoholic beverages were available for sale in the entire community). City officials were unanimous in their support for further tourism development, but they were opposed to any changes. One statement by a city official underscored this resistance to change: "We understand what you are saying we need to do to attract more tourists but how do we do that and maintain the way of life in our community?" In essence, the message that change is inevitable if tourism is to be a major economic force was not internalized.

The tourism industry does not operate in the same manner as other industries; it is not a nine-to-five occupation. The community resisted the move to a tourism based economy because it meant unacceptable social changes. There is nothing wrong with a community deciding that tourism development is not in its best interest. The community that reviews its options and decides against a major tourism push is probably better off for it. The mistake is to believe tourism is possible without accepting some degree of change.

Resource Analysis

One of the basic requirements for all communities embarking on tourism development efforts is to be aware of the resources available to attract tourists to an area before undertaking any marketing efforts. Too often, community development efforts focus on bringing people into an area before understanding why anyone would want to come. Marketing is perceived as the fun part of development, but without adequate planning, including understanding tourism products, marketing is doomed to fail. Our second community example reinforces this point.

A small community in the upper midwestern United States completed an application for a tourism development assistance program. The intent of the program was to assess community potential and recommend opportunities for tourism development. By most accounts, the community appeared to be doing nicely as it had more businesses than a town of its size needed to serve year-round residents. The site visit revealed that the community was primarily a regional shopping center and tourism was not a significant part of its economic activity, but community leaders felt that the tourism potential was high. The community's location in a northern lakes area with significant numbers of seasonal homes and recreation resorts appeared to justify their assessment. The tourism development effort undertaken by the community consisted primarily of marketing the area through advertising a toll free information number in publications available in large population centers. So far, so good. The flaw in the plan was in operations and knowledge of community tourism resources.

The central tourism office servicing the toll-free number was located in a one-room building, also containing a one-chair barber shop and a very small (one table) used baseball card business. The tourism office was staffed by a part-time person (20 hours per week) on a two-month contract (June and July). During the month of August, the heavy use season, the office was unstaffed. When the part-time person was not available, the barber, or occasionally the baseball card dealer, would answer the phone.

There was no record of who called the toll-free number and even if there had been, no information was available for distribution. Personnel conducting the site visit were told that a person from a major metropolitan area had called and requested resort information as they were organizing a week vacation for twenty people. The caller was told that numerous resorts were located in the area but they were unable to provide phone numbers for reservations, maintaining no records of the number of resorts, their locations, or contact personnel in the tourism office. No one knew if the party of twenty ever decided to come to the area.

Two rules of operation were broken. First, there was no information available on area attractions or services that could be presented over the phone or mailed to interested individuals, and secondly, the information center was not adequately staffed. Obviously, a brochure of area attractions would have been helpful, but the mundane task of inventory assessment had never been undertaken. Failure to provide service personnel to answer the phone also negated the effectiveness of the marketing effort. One may term this community's effort to attract tourists de-marketing, as the toll-free number service probably did more to remove the community from people's list of possible destinations than anything else they did.

Community Awareness

Community residents do not often understand the economic benefits derived from tourism, especially if they are not on the receiving end of tourist expenditures. Instead, they tend to focus more on the negative impacts resulting from congestion and overcrowding, inflation, and other ills related to the hosting function. Community tourism development specialists recommend periodic awareness programs to instruct local residents of the benefits of tourism. Failure to do so can result in a loss of tourism market share, as hosting visitors turns from a positive experience to one of open resentment. The next community example helps put the importance of community awareness programs in perspective.

The economic base of our community is agriculture, education, and recreation. Community population is approximately 30,000, with an influx of 11,000 university students for nine months of the year. It is located in the rocky mountain area of the United States, at approximately 4,000 feet in elevation. Summer temperatures rarely exceed ninety degrees, accompanied by very low humidity levels. For years, summer visitors (one- to three-month stays were common) were primarily older residents of the southwestern United States. The attraction was the climate, comparable to winter climates in the U.S. southwest. Living expenses were relatively low, as apartments vacated by students were available for rent by the summer visitors. Over time, negative reaction to the summer visitors began to grow, as evidenced in letters to the editor of the local newspaper. Complaints focused on long lines at local stores, slow driving speeds on city roads, and crowding at local recreation areas. None of the letters were countered by awareness campaigns extolling the benefits of having empty apartments rented year-round, or the multiplier effects of visitors' expenditures. Slowly, the summer visitors relocated to a winter ski community boasting similar summer climatic conditions. Local officials in the skiing community actively courted the summer visitors with a marketing campaign in the areas where the visitors lived for nine months of the year. The impetus for actively seeking this market was the seasonality of the skiing community, with excess room capacity in the summer months.

Our original community has now been in a stagnant growth pattern for over a decade. Very few of the original summer visitors have returned. There is no attempt here to blame the loss of summer visitation for the economic stagnation experienced by our original community, but the absence of a steady summer trade does not improve the situation. There is no way of knowing if an awareness campaign could have offset the marketing efforts undertaken by the ski community, but failure to understand the hosting component of tourism led to a situation where nothing was done to stem the flow of summer visitors away from their traditional summer home. Tourism is not an industry that benefits from neglect. In this case, neglect and antagonism led to an unfriendly situation for a significant group of tourists who chose to exercise the age-old economic ballot by voting with their feet and pocketbooks.

Chamber of Commerce/Visitor Information Center offices in a western U.S. community. The building selection provides thematic design for community development. Photo by the author

Industrial Legitimacy

Tourism differs from other industries. As discussed in later chapters, the product is decidedly different and requires different marketing attention. Government is also involved at many levels. One of the significant governmental functions for communities is information services. A central clearinghouse for meeting visitors and informing them of the different opportunities available in a community is almost a must for effective tourism development.

Often, official information centers are government operations. As such, they tend to operate under governmental guidelines which spell out working conditions, including hours of operation. Failure to provide information at the time information centers are most likely to be frequented by visitors results in lost business. In the next example, our community suffers not only from its failure to recognize the difference between tourism and traditional industries, but also from inadequate funding for operations.

There is nothing spectacular about this community. Its tourism potential is directly tied to a significant war memorial site, and it is located at the crossroads of two major highways. It is termed a travel node, because travelers on the two highways have no choice but to pass through the community. The information center receives its share of visitors who have visited the war memorial and are searching for something else to do in the area. One of those visitors, who happened to be a previous resident of the community, stopped at the information center for advice. The center was closed. This in itself is not unusual, unless it occurs during the busiest weekend of the season. The visit happened to take place on the fifth of July, a Friday that year and part of a long holiday weekend in the United States. The person in charge of the information center was in the park, cleaning up after the Fourth of July celebration the previous evening. Apparently, her job included not only dealing with tourists but park maintenance as well. Obviously, tourism was not considered a legitimate industry for the community as evidenced by inadequate staffing for a vital component of the industry, information-delivery services.

Similarly, another community not far from the one discussed above, for years relied on manufacturing for its industrial base. The community has a substantial population of over 50,000. Within a year, two major plant closings were announced, resulting in major job losses. Predictably, tourism was identified as a source of substantial, quick income, and the process of starting a tourism industry was begun. Monthly meetings were held to identify people belonging to the tourism industry, money was obtained for promotional activities, and marketing efforts were begun. The monthly meetings ended after three months. The research and promotion budget of $6,000 was deemed inadequate, and marketing efforts, consisting of brochure development, ceased. The mistake was believing that tourism requires very little concerted effort, and that the industry pretty much takes care of itself. If this was the case, there would have already been a tourism industry of note operating in the community.

Opportunity Recognition

One of the most difficult things for a community to recognize is the tourism possibilities in their own area. Too often, communities overlook even some of the spectacular attractions available to them. There appears to be a feeling that if it exists in your own backyard, then it must not be a notable attraction. The process of identifying attractions becomes even more difficult when they are not individually impressive, but must be grouped and marketed as a package to lure tourists. Attractions that are not easily recognizable, such as ethnic or sociocultural resources, receive even less attention.

Our next community example is actually a group of small towns adjacent to a beautiful but infrequently visited national park in the U.S. southwest. The national park has no concessionaire operations within its borders. It has a public campground operated by the U.S. Park Service, often full during the season, which encompasses over five months because of the relatively mild climate. The communities adjacent to the park have limited lodging facilities (approximately 25 rooms total in three communities). Some of the lodging facilities are considered less than tourist class and are in need of repair. There is also one tourist-class restaurant, and no crafts or gift shopping businesses. The nearest community where traditional tourist services are abundant is over 70 miles away from the park. Industries currently in the area include agriculture and small-scale mining operations. When queried about the low number of lodging facilities, the most common answer is that present visitation to the park does not justify any further development, and besides the park there are no other tourist attractions. The surrounding countryside contains high mountain areas, spectacular canyons, alpine lakes, and clear streams. Much of the land is in federal ownership, providing easy access to many of the more impressive areas. Community residents fail to recognize the value of the publicly provided resources as significant attractions. Having lived in the area most of their lives, they do not see the area as attractive to tourists. They also fail to recognize that limited park visitation is due more to lack of overnight lodging facilities than to low demand. Many area residents, not having been actively involved in the tourism industry, are unfamiliar with how it operates and opportunities it presents for them. Instead of the park and surrounding federal land being viewed locally as an attraction, they are viewed more as a deterrent to local economic growth.

Cooperation, Communication, and Compromise

It is the nature of business to capitalize as quickly as possible on new economic opportunities. Boom towns are common throughout the world. New sources of mineral wealth, forest products, or any other good for which demand increases sharply is hurriedly extracted, finished, and rushed to market. The resulting development to support the economic activity is often haphazard. In this sense, tourism is no different than any other type of industrial activity. Our final community example is located on the South Island of New Zealand surrounding an alpine lake which for years has seen a steady flow of tourists because of its aesthetic beauty, proximity to a major national park, and high mountain downhill ski areas.

Concerns over the future of the community reached their apex when it became apparent that Japan's economic wealth was beginning to manifest itself in an increasing flow of tourists throughout the Pacific Rim. New Zealand was geographically situated to capture a significant portion of the Japanese tourist migration. Community resident concerns were not centered on whether a tourism industry would be good for the community; after all, it was already a tourism-dependent community. Rather, concern centered on the eventual size and environmental changes that would result from new tourism development initiatives. At an arranged meeting between interest groups, debate was polarized. The business community supported development options that would double the size of the community and extend physical development onto a significant portion of the open land bordering the lake. Environmental groups opposed the extent of development on the grounds that new building would destroy the environmental integrity of the area which had historically been its strong touristic appeal. There did not seem to be any middle ground between the opposing views. The opportunity presented by an increasing Japanese tourist market had split the community into opposing camps with little room for compromise. The question of sustainability was never raised. Today that community has seen further development, but not along the lines proposed in the most aggressive development option. The area along the lakeshore, at the center of the controversy, is still in a natural state. However, the pressure to develop further remains and is given impetus by an ambitious government goal of increasing tourism arrivals to the country. It is left to the local communities to find room for the new tourists the government is able to attract.

The community examples cited above are not exceptions or unusual situations. They probably represent the norm when all communities interested in tourism at one time or another are considered. Tourism as a community industry is difficult to start and even more difficult to maintain. The remainder of this chapter discusses methods that should be employed to either start a community-based tourism industry from scratch or maintain one that is currently operating. The emphasis is on what is workable. Many guidelines published for community tourism development are idealistic and ignore a primary economic axiom—limited means. An attempt is made here to provide the basic requirements for successful community tourism development given means available to most communities. Even so, some community leaders may review the material and decide that a tourism industry is not worth the effort. At least those communities will not proceed to waste resources on efforts destined to fail. Tourism requires a commitment and dedication to an unending task. It is hoped that the communities deciding that tourism is a necessary part of their economic base will place a high priority on its successful implementation and management.

COMMUNITY TOURISM MODEL

Murphy (1985) proposes a model where the objective is to develop a community tourism product that is perceived by residents as a local resource (Figure 7.1). His model outlines the complex components which interact to produce a community-specific tourism product. It includes business and sociocultural considerations, along with the environmental and accessibility considerations that pull people to the area and make their entrance to the community possible. Management is a major component since, ideally, it coordinates various interests and allows for public participation in developing the product presented to tourists. Management is greatly facilitated when a tourism organization is in place as a central organizing body.

Community Tourism Organizations

The tourism industry often lacks organization, especially in rural communities. Small businesses dominate the industry in rural areas, and even though individual businesses may operate efficiently and along defined organizational lines, the tourism industry itself is often left to find its own path of least resistance. A community tourism organization entity is often needed.

Literally thousands of different types of tourism organizations operate throughout the world, classified in many ways. McIntosh et al. (1995) propose five methods for classification. The first is geographical. Organiza-

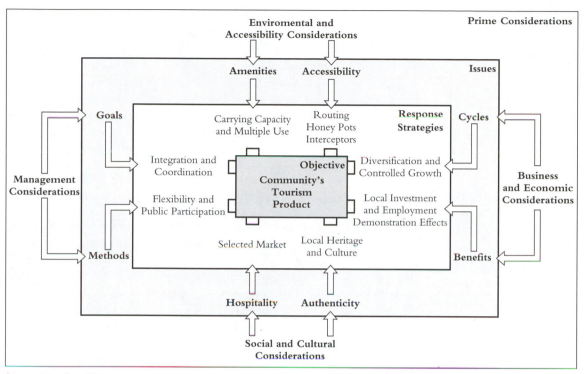

Source: Murphy, 1985

Figure 7.1 *Major Compnents for a Community-Oriented Tourism Strategy*

tions can be classified depending on their geographic influence: international, regional (within the world), national, regional (within a nation), state, republic, or provincial, regional (within a state, republic, or province), and local (community level). Organizations can also be classified by type of ownership (private, public, or quasi-public), function (regulators, suppliers, researchers, consumers, consultants, etc.), industry group (transportation, lodging, recreation, etc.) and motive (profit, non-profit).

Gee et al. (1984) suggest classifying tourism organizations into three levels. The first is direct providers, which include the front-line tourism businesses such as hotels, airlines, rental car agencies, etc. The second level is made up of supporting businesses such as tour brokers and contract food service operations, and the third level is defined as tourism development agencies. Planning offices, local Chambers of Commerce, and universities offering courses in tourism all fall into the third category.

Pearce (1989) contends that a group of associations or organizations indirectly involved in the tourism industry should also be considered. These include cultural and historical societies responsible for the conservation of historic districts and management of art galleries or museums. One may even extend this argument to include organizations or associations dedicated to environmental protection as pursuit of their goals ultimately affect tourism in some manner.

There is no clear-cut definition of what qualifies as a tourism organization. Because tourism is such a complex, fragmented industry, almost every organization or association can lay claim to some aspect of it. The following section focuses on what constitutes a viable tourism organization at the local or community level, its role and function in serving the needs of its citizenry, and its respective constituent groups.

Types of Community Tourism Organizations

Many times a Chamber of Commerce supplies local tourism leadership by operating within its own internal structure to meet the needs of member businesses. In larger communities, the organizational function may be provided by a Convention and Visitor Bureau (CVBs). CVBs are usually non-profit organizations that represent a city or urban area in marketing that destination to all types of travelers. Their main objective is to fill hotel rooms, convention centers, restaurants, and tourist attractions (Levin, 1988). CVBs are not normally in charge of overall planning for an area; instead, their primary goal is to increase travel flows to the area.

Some communities establish a separate organization to deal specifically with the tourism industry. The smaller the community, the smaller the tourism organization. In many communities, the tourism organization begins with a small group of people meeting informally to discuss or advocate tourism development, or in some cases one strong-willed individual assumes a leadership position on the issue (Murphy, 1988).

Whatever the type of organization in place at the community level, there are five key functions necessary to its successful operation. The United States Department of Commerce (1986) identifies these five functions as Communications, Research and Data Collection, Education and Training, Promotion, and Budget and Finance. These five functions are discussed below.

Budget and Finance

Any tourism organization, to be effective, must be adequately funded. In order to carry out the functions discussed above, a budget must be prepared and financial means found to carry out the responsibilities of the organization. There are two types of funding sources: those that provide funds for daily operations and activities, and those that finance special projects. For a long time, local general revenue funds were the main source of support for tourism organizations. Often these funds were inadequate to maintain an organizational staff, let alone allow for carrying out the above-mentioned functions.

Budget and Finance is the most critical function, as the organization is doomed to fail unless it has a budget to carry out the other four functions. There are many methods currently used to acquire a budget for the organization. Special tax levies such as a transient room tax (see Chapter 6) are among the most common. Others may include general tax revenue appropriations, organization dues, fund raising events, and contributions. Usually a mix of the above methods are employed.

Communications

There are two types of communications to consider. One is to the visitor and the other to local residents. Communication to the visitor is often confused with promotion. The main purpose of promotion is to help push the destination into an individual's evoked set of possibilities (see Chapter 8). As such, promotion is directed at potential visitors while they are in their home community. Communication with visitors takes place once they arrive in the community. Essential to the communication function is a well staffed visitor or information center providing information on community attractions, events, and services. Operating a visitor information center requires a substantial budget, and in many small communities information centers are not well maintained, staffed, or located in areas frequented by tourists, due to the inability to rent or purchase prime space and employ full time personnel. However, without some type of information center, a valuable communication linkage with the visitor is missing. In many cases, individual businesses recognize the need to provide this service and establish their own informal information centers. Again, due to lack of resources, information disseminated in this manner is often too limited to adequately serve the community. There may also be resistance to informing visitors of a competitor's services, leading to limited community coverage.

To overcome these problems, a program initiated by the Northwest Regional Planning Commission (1989) in Wisconsin and the University of Wisconsin Extension Service resulted in the compilation of a directory of services available in a ten-county area. The directory was put into a three-ring binder with tabs for reference by county, attractions, and services. Participating businesses receive a copy of the directory and affix a decal to the outside of their establishment. The decal reads "Tourism Spoken Here" (Figure 7.2). Any visitor requesting information can be easily taken care of simply by referring to the directory. This innovative approach shifts the focus of visitor communication to the industry in a way that shares production costs for all participating businesses, making it possi-

Figure 7.2 *Involving Community Businesses in the Dissemination of Tourism Information*
Source: University of Wisconsin Extension and Northwest Regional Planning Commission

ble to produce a quality reference guide for a large region at minimum cost. Participating businesses also expect sales to increase as more potential customers are initially drawn into their store in search of information.

Communication to residents is also an important function of a community tourism organization. Sociocultural impacts, discussed in Chapter 5, are often exacerbated by ignoring the people who bear the brunt of increased tourism but do not readily see increased economic benefits. One of the problems most often cited in studies addressing tourism's impact on communities is the perception that local control over the industry has been lost (Jordan, 1980; Allen et al., 1988). Communicating with residents has the effect of involving them in the development processes and helps form a bridge between a tourism organization and the people it is intended to serve. Problems as well as opportunities that tourism presents should be part of the information made available to local residents.

Education and Training

Education is related to the communication function in the sense that its intent is to provide information directly to local residents. However, where the intent of communications is to keep local residents informed as to the workings of the tourism industry, education and training helps prepare the local work force to better serve the visitor. The importance of friendly and efficient service personnel is increasingly recognized as key to a community's package of tourism goods and services.

Gartner and Shen (1992) theorize that images of service related attributes, which include receptiveness and friendliness of local residents to tourists, may actually be more important in maintaining and increasing travel market share than the image of tourism attractions. Further support for this line of reasoning can be found in Scott et al. (1978), who find that the most important variable influencing a decision to visit Massachusetts is the friendliness of the local people, and in Fridgen (1984), who refers to the importance of the image of destination "social situations" as a powerful factor affecting the travel decision process. It is imperative, then, that a community tourism organization assist local businesses to educate and train front line personnel about the benefits derived from hosting visitors, with the goal of providing not only better but also friendlier service.

Research and Data Collection

One of the perceived problems with research is that it takes too long to complete and it never answers all the questions. Often the need to conduct research is viewed as a means of forestalling decisions. Recognizing that research will not answer all questions it is nevertheless an important function of a tourism organization.

The type of research conducted at the community level for use by area businesses is of an applied nature. Visitor profiles are an example of an appropriate applied type of research for communities. Visitor profile research falls under the heading of an immediate practical concern; it must be completed prior to any major promotional campaigns. Research on the type of education programs needed for front line personnel is also a form of applied research with immediate practical applications. Tracking type research is intended to monitor change. Visitor satisfaction, attractions visited, and image assessment are all subjects that should be considered for periodic review. Research conducted on a regular basis, and compared to baseline data, can help a community predict changes that may affect the level of tourism presently experienced by its visitors. Tracking type research should also be considered as a means to evaluate local resident satisfaction with the tourism industry.

Promotion

Promotion is sometimes viewed as communications, but the distinction between the two is quite clear. Communication is the provision of useful information to tourists who have already selected your community as a destination. Most communication functions take place within the community itself. Promotion is intended to move a community into an individual's awareness or evoked set (see Chapter 8). Promotion can take the form of direct advertising, utilizing a mass audience media source, through direct contact with individuals such as meeting planners or tour brokers, or through special events promoted via second-party sources such as the local news media. The intent of promotion is to protect or increase market share.

COMMUNITY TOURISM DEVELOPMENT REQUIREMENTS

A prerequisite of development is to understand the attraction base and the users of those attractions. Tourists do not visit a community simply to stay in a lodging establishment. They are drawn to the area because the attraction base is expected to provide the types of experiences that satisfy their desires. There are few exceptions to this statement, most noticeably those lodging properties that also function as resorts, but this type of activity is addressed in Chapter 9. If tourists are drawn to a community because of its attraction base, then it makes sense to understand why they are coming and what attractions are responsible for generating the "pull" necessary for development.

Inventory Analysis

Attractions come in all shapes, sizes, colors, and flavors. The ones most often mentioned from a community perspective are natural resources, historic, cultural, man-made, and, in some cases, services. It is possible and often advisable to package two attractions together to form a new, more powerful attraction. For example, an area that is endowed with a natural resource base that is beautiful but nonetheless similar to others in a region can achieve superiority by concentrating on service. The combination of impressive attractions and quality service forms a new type of attraction for the community.

Many inventory assessment guidelines recommend a checklist of all attractions located within the community. For example, under the category natural resources, beaches, lakes, rivers, and so on would be identified. Cultural attractions would encompass the various ethnic groups that live in the area, special events or festivals, museums, and other cultural resources within the community. An attraction checklist makes people aware of all the attractions located in the community. For a more detailed explanation of the different types of attractions that could be considered, refer to Chapter 9. However, simply listing attractions does not identify their strength as a primary, secondary, or support type attraction.

A primary attraction is a pull attraction. Its appeal is strong enough to induce people to visit an area. A secondary attraction may also be termed a spillover attraction, as it receives its visitors from the pulling power of the primary attraction. A example of a primary attraction may be a national park. A secondary attraction which feeds off the primary attraction may be a water park. People visiting the national park may also spend some time at the water park, but without the primary attraction in place, very few people would come specifically to visit the water park. Supporting type attractions rely on the primary and secondary type attractions for success. They have limited pulling power, but instead serve to supplement the major attractions by providing alternative sources of enjoyment. They are important primarily because if developed properly, they have the potential to increase length of stay in an area.

Visitor Profiles

Concurrent with attraction inventory assessment, a visitor-profile analysis should be undertaken. Although the eventual marketing effort may focus on a market segment that is not presently represented in the community, it is important to understand the visitor currently attracted to the community. Current visitors can reveal a great deal of information about not only the quality of present attractions, but services present or lacking, and the need for additional attractions. Information most often sought from visitors includes basic demographics (e.g. age, gender, income, family size), attractions visited, activities engaged in, length of stay, origin, frequency of visitation, and expenditures. Obviously, much more information can be acquired from current visitors, but depending on budget considerations, it may not be feasible to collect too much at once. Only data deemed critical to understanding the current visitor should be ascertained and collected at the start of the visitor profile effort. Many different techniques and methods may be utilized to collect necessary information. The most frequently used are: intercept method, sample of all visitors, or a modified Delphi technique.

Intercept

The intercept method involves contacting visitors and administering visitor profile surveys at sites selected based on the known or expected probability of encountering an adequate number of visitors to make the effort worthwhile. The problem with intercept methods is that they often interject a systematic bias into the research design, especially if attractions are chosen as sites. Contacting individuals at attractions provides a biased estimate for certain variables such as length of stay and expenditures. The pass-through visitor is not counted as is the visitor frequenting attractions not on the site selection list. Intercept methods perform well if the researcher is only interested in visitation at specific sites. For example, Ehrlich (1970) uses an intercept method to develop a gravity model for regional park visitation with respect to certain location characteristics. Using observational techniques, researchers recorded automobile license plate numbers and determined future park visitation by estimating expected visitation within a specific radius of a new park's location. While this type of approach works well for specific sites, if the purpose is to generalize to visitation within an entire community, then intercept methods may not be appropriate.

Systematic Sampling

Systematic sampling at community entry and exit points provides an opportunity to collect more accurate information than that provided through intercept techniques. Systematic sampling implies that surveys be distributed to a sample of travelers passing through the selected entry/exit points. The advantage of systematic sampling at entry/exit points is that all travelers, regardless of time spent in the area, have an equal chance of being selected. This reduces bias inherent from only selecting travelers at known attractions. A more detailed explanation of this data collection technique is provided in Chapter 3, in the section on diary methodology.

Modified Delphi

A modified Delphi technique to collect visitor profile information involves a survey, or alternatively a focus group discussion, of individuals within the community assumed to be most knowledgeable of visitors. Lodging operators, attraction managers, and information center personnel would all be likely candidates for a Delphi type analysis. A major drawback to this approach is that precision estimates for certain variables would not be possible. Only informed guess-type data would be collected, but depending on the size of the community this information may be sufficient to begin understanding the visitor market. At the very least, organizing the Delphi group would serve the purpose of identifying tourism as an activity worth investigating and the various actors that may take a more involved role in other community tourism development efforts.

Use Zones

Zoning is concept that is understood and applied, although loosely, throughout the world. Basically, it is a technique to designate a specific area for a specific activity. For example, a zoning designation of single-family housing implies that apartments or multi-family dwellings are not allowed to be constructed in the area. Tourism development does not have its own zoning designation, but fits within those applied to all other uses. This does not mean that a community would not benefit from a specific set of criteria for tourism development zoning, but examples where it has been applied are not common.

Rosenow and Pulsipher (1979) identify four steps in what they term a community's personality planning process. Application of these steps would be a form of tourism development zoning:

1. Delineate Distinctive Features

2. Plot Critical Zones

3. Establish Use Objectives

4. Formulate Specific Action Programs

Step 1 should be handled during the inventory process discussed above. Distinctive features refer to the community's resources that are important for tourism development. Critical zones are those areas where tourists are often found. These may be transportation corridors, city centers, recreation sites, or any area where degradation of the resource will reduce its attractive power. Once critical zones are identified, use objectives can be applied. At this stage, the development zone concept becomes fully operational. Use objectives suggested by Rosenow and Pulsipher are: preservation, retention, modification, or enhancement. Preservation use objectives are applied to areas that are presently considered aesthetically appealing, are of significant environmental or historic significance, or where any modification will degrade its present value. Preservation as a use objective for a development zone is perfectly acceptable as it identifies those areas that contribute economically to other areas because of their intrinsic values. For example, official wilderness designation for a tract of land is a preservation use objective that enhances economic benefits to a community located in close proximity to the wilderness area. Wilderness designation in the United States often precludes other types of uses (e.g., logging, road construction) from occurring. Often local communities view this use exclusion as a negative economic impact, eliminating jobs and causing other related economic hardship. However, an attractive area for recreationists may result in longer-term economic benefits for the community than short-term profits from exploitative industries that decline as soon as the resource is exhausted. In the long term, a preservation use objective may indeed be a form of economic development.

Retention objectives are applied to areas in need of improvement but not requiring drastic modification. Retention implies maintaining the essential character of the area but improving it in a way that expands its appeal. Generally, large-scale development would not be appropriate in a retention zone.

Modification objectives are applied to areas that could benefit from additional facilities or services. New lodging facilities, increased shopping outlets, and different attractions would all be acceptable in a modification zone. Modification means change not only to the character of the area but to the attraction package as well. For example, an abandoned warehouse district may benefit from redevelopment activities that focus on shopping and restaurants. Modification in this sense changes the nature of the area to one more appealing to visitors.

Enhancement is usually applied to areas in need of renovation. Historic districts that are in disrepair may benefit from programs that restore the area to its original appearance. Main transportation corridors may benefit from landscaping or even re-routing that takes visitors through areas with more touristic appeal (e.g., along coastlines). Enhancement is different than modification in that the basic appeal or atmosphere of the area is not changed but improved.

The application of use objectives forms distinctive development zones, each with their own long-term objectives. It provides communities with their own character and a focus for development planning. Zones are now identified for specific uses and new developments can be clustered together in areas where the principle of organic bunching (see Chapter 9) can be utilized, resulting in a planned and organized development.

Murphy (1985), citing Pearce (1981) and Clarke (1981), describes the application of tourism development zoning on a regional scale in the Languedoc-Roussillon area of France (Figure 7.3). Identified zones include areas for reforestation, protected natural areas, sanitation, coastal industry, ecological protection, and tourism development. Although this scheme does not follow that proposed by Rosenow and Pulsipher, it is an

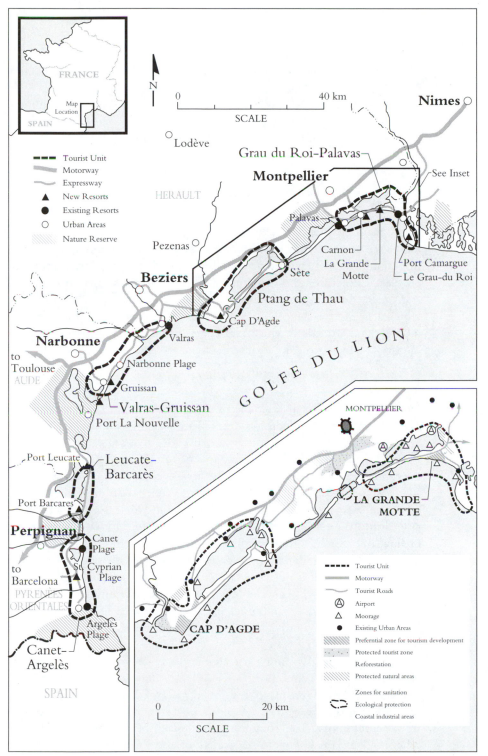

Source: Murphy, 1985, from Clarke, 1981 and Pearce, 1981

Figure 7.3 *Regional Zoning Recognizing Tourism Development*

attempt to apply the concept of zoning, using region specific characteristics as criteria, to the broader issue of how tourism development fits into overall regional planning.

Once the above requirements have been addressed, the community is ready to begin assembling the parts. What results is one strong component that becomes part of the community attraction complex.

COMMUNITY ATTRACTION COMPLEX

Three main elements are inherent in successful destinations: the community, a set of travel attractors, and a market. The community must be able to tie into a set of travel attractors which appeals to a significant group of travelers. Sometimes the community itself forms the attraction complex, and other times the attraction complex is located near the community, which acts as a service center for the tourist. In other cases, the community relies on attractions which it doesn't control, and develops its own set of travel attractors to complement the main attractors.

Examples

Dorset, Minnesota is an example of a community that has developed its own set of attractors. Dorset is located in a resort community of north central Minnesota. The community consists of five separate food service establishments serving ethnic cuisine in a novel setting (e.g., old malt shop, tea room). People are attracted to the area because of the number of resorts and inland lakes found there. With the concentration of food service establishments and opportunities for shopping in Dorset, it has successfully tapped into the resort market for its customer base. Dorset is an example of how one community has utilized a secondary market, one that is attracted to the area initially for some other reason, to develop its own brand of tourism. It is not necessary to always consider the origin of visitors when planning for development. Symbiotic relationships should also be considered, as one can argue that the resort area also benefits from Dorset's existence by providing an expanded menu of activities for its visitors.

Jackson Hole, Wyoming, because of its close proximity to Yellowstone and Grand Teton National Parks, is often considered a gateway community. However, it has developed a set of attractions (e.g., skiing, shopping) utilizing a western development theme to increase length of stay in the community. The community has established its own identity and relies not only on visitors to the parks but also those seeking the type of attractions offered independently of the park system.

DORSET, MINNESOTA

Dorset, Minnesota is a small community, population 25–32 depending on who you talk to, located in the north central portion of the state. The area is a known resort destination. What makes Dorset unique is its evolution from a typical small town into a tourist center based on food service.

Dorset's early life was tied to area resorts. It was a drop off point on the Blueberry Special Train operated by the Great Northern Railroad. The Blueberry Special refers to the fruit found in abundance throughout the area during mid to late summer which many people strolled through the woods picking. Shortly after World War II, new highways replaced the Great Northern Railroad as the primary mover of tourists into northern Minnesota. In the 1950s, the Great Northern Railroad ceased operating altogether. At about the same time many area resorts closed. Even though most of the resorts offered the American plan (three meals included), meaning that Dorset's food service operations were not geared to resorters but rather catered to a local clientele, the tourist decline affected all local businesses. In fact, the only restaurant that survived the decline years was the Dorset Cafe, which met its demise in 1980 when a runaway truck crashed into the cafe, causing much structural damage. What wasn't realized at the time was that the death of the cafe meant a rebirth for Dorset.

The Dorset Cafe was resurrected from the scrap heap when new owners rebuilt the restaurant. At the same time, the old Great Northern Rail line was converted into a partially paved major recreational bike trail. Soon, the old general store was converted into an old fashioned soda fountain and pizza parlor. Two years later, the lumber yard was converted by the new owners into a Mexican restaurant. During this same period, an Italian restaurant was built, and the bank was converted into a gift shop with a tea room. The resurrection of Dorset was well underway.

The decision to become a center of ethnic cuisine in northern Minnesota was part genius and part luck. New resorts without the American Plan were springing up throughout the area. Resort customers could choose from a large number of area restaurants which, for the most part, served the same menu items, or they could journey to Dorset and sample dishes from around the world. The genius part was that local entrepreneurs recognized their clientele's needs and took steps to cater to their customers. The luck part was that owners with imagination bought up the old properties and were willing to take a risk on something new.

Today Dorset has grown to 12 businesses. The success of the restaurants has given rise to a bed and breakfast, stained glass shop, antique emporium, book store, campground, boat and marine supplies establishment, and an additional gift shop. Even though population remains somewhere between 25–32, community businesses employ over 300 people. Its market comprises about 40% resorters, 40% second home owners/visitors, and 20% local. Dorset has not forgotten the roots of the second renaissance period. To celebrate its recent history, it stages the "Taste of Dorset" festival the first weekend in August.

(continued on next page)

Dorset's success story also includes some innovative marketing. There is an annual newspaper which, tongue in cheek, represents Dorset as a major metropolitan area. Its big city spoof has earned it numerous marketing awards. To pay for publication and distribution of the newspaper, each business is assessed $50 annually. There are also special assessments if the local marketing committee decides other advertisements are in order. This may cost each business up to $100 per year, prorated to the size of the business. The marketing committee also develops programs to increase customer involvement in the community. Each year customers can vote for a mayor. Each vote costs $1, and all contributions support local charities. The "elected" mayor does not have to come from Dorset and does not have to be present to serve.

From the above profile, a few lessons in community development can be gleaned. A community does not have to be big to succeed. In Dorset's case, it was the creative juices of a few people in a purely entrepreneurial spirit which made it happen. Another major lesson is to constantly improve the product in some way. The newspaper, food festival, and mayoral vote are a few creative programs which have made Dorset a fun place to spend some time.

Source:
Tom and Lorren Wood, Fremont Point Resort

Pella, Iowa depends almost entirely on its own set of attractions to entice visitors. Located in east central Iowa, surrounded by vast expanses of agricultural land, the community has embraced a Dutch theme as its primary draw. Authentic restaurants and shops support this theme, which is further sustained by a Glockenspiel in the center of town donated by the Pella Window Company in memory of one of their employees. Pella is an example of a community which does not fully rely on tourism for its entire economic base, but works closely with its major manufacturer in a cooperative effort to diversify its economic base through tourism.

Ugrup, Turkey has fully integrated tourist service facilities and natural resources into a successful tourism industry. Located in the Cappodocia region, it is known for its ancient underground cities, and cone-shaped houses and churches carved entirely out of tuff, a soft volcanic deposit rock. Local businesses include inns, restaurants, folk centers, and craft factories (e.g., pottery) built in the tuff formations to provide the visitor opportunities to see and experience what living within some of the rock formations might have been like.

Linkages Between Community and Markets

Once a community has established its ties to certain attractions and identifies appropriate markets, linkages between the market and the attraction complex must be developed. The most common linkage with the market is advertising and promotion of its attractions, although the transportation

Local restaurant represents regional products in Detroit, Michigan. Photo by the author

linkage must also be considered. Advertising and promotion linkages take three forms:

1. Marketing directly to a concentration of potential tourists. Generally this is the potential tourist's home community but as shown above, marketing to tourists already concentrated in an attraction area may also prove beneficial.

2. Impulse marketing involving outdoor advertising at a destination or official community information centers that stimulate interest, resulting in unplanned side excursions into and through the community.

3. Enroute marketing through outdoor advertising or radio directed at travelers as they approach the community.

Most communities focus on marketing to concentrations of tourists rather than using either impulse or en-route strategies, even though these efforts can result in high returns.

Impulse Communication

The intent of impulse advertising is to alter a traveler's plans, ending in an unscheduled stop in the community. The most common form of impulse advertising is the brochure. Although brochures are not solely used for impulse advertising, as very often they are contained in other advertising packages, they are often distributed at numerous points surrounding a community and in that way act to induce impulse purchasing. Stringer (1984) find that many tourists criticize brochures but use them in making purchase decisions. A major problem with the use of brochures is that there are often too many of them and the time required to search through all the possibilities consumes more time than many people are willing to allocate.

Gartner and Verbyla (1986) experiment with impulse information delivered through a microcomputer system housed in a tourism information center. Visitors to the center were presented with a computer screen listing over twenty-five attraction/activity options ranging from the most recognized attractions, such as state parks, to the less obvious activities, such as rockhounding. One of the main advantages of this approach is the reduction in time required to find something of interest. Once an activity is selected, information regarding the activity, including location, is presented. Users can receive a hard copy of the information, including directions to the various sites. The program was first-generation in the sense that it required users to input requests on a standard keyboard. This tended to limit use to those familiar with personal computer systems, which was not as widespread in 1985 as it is today. Recommendations for future systems included employing touch-sensitive equipment in an effort to make the program more user-friendly. These systems are now receiving attention as a means of distributing information in a more efficient manner. Many computers now have display text plus graphic and audio (voice simulation) capabilities. These systems are useful for serving individuals unable or unwilling to read all of the information presented on the screen (Hultsman, 1988). With recent advances in computer technology, making systems more accessible (e.g., available on hotel-room televisions) and easier to put together, these "fast information" systems may be the answer to increasing impulse buying behavior as more information is available to users, requiring less time than it takes to browse through brochures.

En Route

Travelers are exposed to several sources of information en route, including outdoor advertising, road maps that also function as travel guides, and radio advertising. The importance of en route information dissemination should not be overlooked. Perdue (1986) finds that almost 10% of all visitors to Nebraska entering the state with no intention of visiting any attractions actually changed their plans and made one or more impulse stops. En route communication provides an important source of information for impulse travel purchases.

Outdoor advertising differs from most other forms of advertising media, as the message is not delivered to people but rather relies on the traveler to pass by it. An important criterion for outdoor advertising to be effective is location. Its main drawback is that it normally holds an individual's attention for a very short time; therefore the amount of information that can be conveyed is rather limited. Outdoor advertising on an interstate system will receive widespread exposure, as thousands of people drive by it each day; however the generally fast speeds associated with interstate driving greatly reduce exposure time. Much of the communication in outdoor advertising is through symbols or pictures rather than words.

Outdoor advertising is not without its detractors. Claims of visual pollution are common. The United States attempted to address this issue with the passage of the Highway Beautification Act in 1965. The law limited billboards in non-urban, non-commercial zones. Some states promptly responded by designating all their road corridors as commercial zones. The law also allowed billboards to increase in size from 672 square feet to 2,500 square feet. The end result is that there are now twice as many billboards in the U.S. than when the law was passed. Recently there have been attempts to enforce and strengthen the act in order to provide a pleasing landscape for the road bound traveling public.

Radio advertising is also effective en route communication, with potential visitors as long as their radio is tuned to the right frequency. This may not be much of a problem in rural areas where there are only a few stations operating, but in more populated areas the number of stations may seriously reduce the probability a traveler has tuned in. Experiments with all-travel news stations are currently underway in certain states and throughout Europe. A large part of the program will be devoted to local use, with periodic travel news of a regional nature. Certain locales also promote through outdoor advertising local stations that carry information of interest to travelers.

Road maps, especially those provided through travel clubs, can also be used effectively for en route information dissemination. Areas of interest, publicly provided attractions, and location of lodging facilities are just a few of the items found on travel club maps. Some clubs also provide, along with maps, booklets that supply more detailed information about communities such as history and available activities.

INTERPRETATION

Much of the preceding discussion focuses on providing information in various forms, with the intent of increasing length of stay in the community or capturing additional market share. Assuming that some aspect of the program works successfully and more visitors are coming to the community to visit points of interest, the next step in increasing length of stay and visitor enjoyment is to provide interpretation. Whereas information dissemination is useful for increasing awareness and use, or redistributing use (Brown and Hunt, 1969; Lucas, 1981; Roggenbuck and Berrier, 1982; Deasy and Greiss, 1966), interpretation is intended to inform, entertain, educate, and provide a frame of reference for some site. For example, a community with a historic district is just anther community with a bunch of old buildings unless the significance and value to the community of those buildings is conveyed to the visitor.

Warren (1986) lists six important goals of an interpretive program:

1. To enhance visitor appreciation for the natural and cultural heritage of an area illustrated by its processes, events, personalities and other resources around which sites are established

2. To stimulate in visitors the desire to leave the world a place of significant interest

3. To stimulate in visitors the desire to learn more about their heritage

4. To stimulate a desire to search for objective truth, to dispel myth, and to take a reasoned, balanced view of things

5. To instruct visitors on how to enjoy resources with minimal impact

6. To explain policies to visitors that might otherwise be confusing

Interpretation includes naturalist talks, publications, and other facilities and services provided to help people enjoy and understand the natural and cultural resources of the areas they visit. Effective interpretation requires a working knowledge of clientele groups for whom the messages are directed so that appropriate means can be used to arouse interest and effectively transmit knowledge.

In an effort to establish cooperative public/private relationships, the USDA-Forest Service has experimented with providing trained naturalists to privately owned and operated resort businesses in close proximity to a National Forest, with the intent of increasing visitor enjoyment through interpretive services. The Forest Service believes its management practices will be more appreciated once people begin to understand the complex relationships existing in natural areas. The resort operators benefit by having another activity available to their clientele. The experiment to date has been successful to the extent that there are not enough naturalists to meet the demand, an indication that interpretation is an important part of an area's attraction package.

Binks (1989) lists three main characteristics for effective community tourism interpreters:

1. Be responsive to community needs

2. Contribute to community development

3. Be able to get the community involved in providing ancillary interpretive services

There is no reason to expect community interpreters to be aware of all the aspects of their job, which is why it is necessary to provide training for them. Specific items included in the training involve:

1. Impressing upon them an understanding of the community they are working with, including the social, cultural, and economic factors that affect the community

2. Understanding the various dimensions involved in a sense of place, enabling the interpreter to address the community's relationship with its environment and heritage

3. Understanding how the community functions, how it is structured and how various groups relate to each other

4. Understanding the various approaches to promoting community action, the role of the facilitator and campaigner, as well as the extent to which one should be involved in various tourism issues.

5. Appreciating the emphasis on process rather than product

6. Appreciating their value and skills as an interpreter and how best to utilize those skills

7. Understanding their own limitations and where and who to go to for assistance

In a sense, community tourism interpreters are more than simple pieces of an overall tourism development program. Since they spend most of their time on the front line dealing directly with visitors, they need to know what is being planned in the community, who is doing the planning, and who should become involved in the overall planning process. Interpreters are a direct link between the tourists and those who are developing programs for improving or expanding the community's tourism base.

Interpreters and their programs exist as an integral component of community tourism development not only because they provide information and education programs on behalf of the community to its visitors, but because through interpretation opinions, knowledge and behavior of tourists can be positively influenced. Credible sources attempt to persuade visitors to behave sensitively to the physical and social environment they

find themselves in and inform them of key resource issues affecting not only the visitors but the community as well (Stokowski, 1990). Pearce (1984) finds that tourists, even when questioned immediately after a trip, are only able to recall selected bits of information presented during a tour. However, the experience has an emotional impact on the visitors, with positive changes noted for tourist's arousal level, sense of control, and emotional satisfaction. Interpretation is an important part of the package for achieving those positive changes.

Community tourism interpretation involves telling the community's most interesting or significant stories to residents and visitors. It encourages awareness of and pride in the natural and cultural heritage of the community and its people. A key to successful community tourism development is the ability of the community to share itself with visitors. Sharing its heritage and resources is part of the development package. Interpretation allows the sharing to take place by establishing intimacy with guests.

VISITOR SERVICES

Interpretation is a visitor service, but the extent of needed visitor services is much broader. Assuming the community is successful in attracting tourists, the next step is to manage the inflow of visitors. Managing visitors should be viewed as implementing a system that enhances visitor experiences, while at the same time reducing negative social impacts for community residents. Crowds attending festivals or events may overwhelm a community's public services system. Fighting, rioting, and vandalism are not intended outputs of what festival organizers had planned on being an enjoyable experience for visitors and local residents alike, but unfortunately there are numerous examples where that is exactly what happened. Preventing such occurrences enhances the experience for all those attending the event. Even normal amounts of tourism can tax a community's public services, which is why it is important to implement a visitor services plan as part of the community's tourism development effort.

A visitor services plan requires a community to assess its police, health services, maintenance, and sanitation department capabilities. Are there adequate levels of security personnel for crowd control and is there enough medical staff on duty to handle emergencies are just two of the questions that should be addressed before permits are issued for special events. How will litter be collected? In one of our example communities, the staff of the information center were also expected to clean up after the holiday celebration, leaving the center closed during a high use day. This is an example of not having an adequate visitor services plan in place. Obviously, the public sector cannot be expected to handle all visitor services, so there must be some coordination between the public and private sectors defining responsibilities. Simple services such as having enough personnel to answer visitors questions are often neglected during times of heavy use. If the community is experiencing an increase in the number of international visitors, it makes sense to have a directory of qualified volunteer interpreters to assist in an emergency. Inattention to what appear to be minor details is probably one of the most common mistakes a community makes when developing tourism. Instead of providing an exhaustive checklist of all the items communities should address when establishing a visitor service plan, the reader is referred to the publication Tourism USA (see references cited) for a broad overview of what should be considered during this stage of tourism planning.

FUNDING AND DEVELOPMENT ASSISTANCE

Funding sources for community development differ by country, state and region. They also differ in purpose. The following discussion focuses on funding sources available in one state in the United States, Wisconsin. Although some of these sources are not available in other states or communities in other countries, the discussion provides an overview of some of the programs available or that can be initiated. Funding sources can be grouped into two categories: Community Development and Enhancement of Existing Business Community.

Community Development

Community development programs are not usually tourism-specific. That is, they are intended to be utilized for the broad purpose of community economic development. Tourism is one form of community economic development and can be the main impetus for requesting assistance. Funding sources are available from the federal, state, or local government. The primary source of federal public funding assistance, especially in larger communities, is Community Development Block Grants (CDBGs). They are the largest government funding source available for community development revitalization (infrastructure development or improvement). Communities eligible for CDBGs must have populations exceeding 50,000 and be eligible to receive entitlement direct from the federal government. CDBG monies have been used to assist in the development of municipal sports and recreational facilities benefiting both residents and tourists. Although CDBGs are a major source of public works funding, the money available for these programs was reduced significantly during the 1980s (Matulef, 1988).

Many other U.S. federal programs indirectly assist tourism development efforts. The Farmers Home Administration (FHMA) provides funds primarily for agriculture based businesses although other businesses, especially in rural areas, can apply for loans as well. Most likely to receive support are those businesses which have an agriculture connection (e.g., farm stay operations).

The Housing and Urban Development (HUD) agency has a program to guarantee loans to local governments to acquire or rehabilitate property critical in stimulating industrial, commercial, or residential land developments. Normally these funds are provided contingent on receiving CDBG funds which can be used as collateral to guarantee the loan. Historic district revitalization programs are one type of tourism development that may qualify for HUD funding.

The Economic Development Administration (EDA) funds primarily manufacturing-based developments, but businesses that can demonstrate new job creation also qualify for assistance. The Small Business Administration (SBA) provides educational programs which improve access to SBA loan guarantees, aiding in business creation, retention, and expansion. Even though the SBA does not have a directed tourism development program, they have provided guaranteed loans for motels, water parks, restaurants, campgrounds, and other businesses that fall into the tourism/recreation category.

The state of Wisconsin has its own community economic development programs providing primarily development assistance. There are nine regional planning commissions in the state, with a total staff of twenty-five. Assistance includes proposal packaging for fund requests from federal and state agencies, business recruitment efforts which includes maintaining lists and descriptions of available sites and buildings, planning for industrial parks and infrastructure improvements, and collection and provision of statistical data needed for community business recruitment efforts.

The University of Wisconsin-Cooperative Extension Service is a jointly funded federal/state education institution which serves each county in the state. County offices are staffed by agents specializing in agriculture, youth development, and community resource development. Community resource development agents work with individuals, businesses, government agencies, and other organizations, and serve as catalysts for community development. One major service is the community economic analysis program. This program helps community leaders assess their current economic situation and development potential, and identify specific opportunities available to improve the local business environment. The agents also provide education and research necessary to address local opposition or apathy toward economic development. County agents are directly linked to the resources of the University of Wisconsin system, and utilize faculty expertise to address local problems. Similar university-based extension programs are available in every state within the U.S.

Funding for community development is available through state-authorized local funding options. This is accomplished by establishing Tax Incremental Financing (TIF) districts which issue Industrial Revenue Bonds. These bonds, which are exempt from federal taxes, can be used to retain existing industry, protect the health, safety, and welfare of state residents, and revitalize central business districts of municipalities. Currently there are over 350 TIF districts in Wisconsin.

Enhancement of the Existing Business Community

Community business enhancement includes business creation, retention and expansion. The primary Wisconsin state agency responsible for many programs with this goal is the Department of Development (DOD). The department employs consultants who work directly with businesses, community officials, local development organizations, and other state agencies. Consulting services include assessing appropriateness of local, state, and federal financing options in accordance with the current and future needs of a business or community, providing information to companies contemplating a move to Wisconsin, and assisting communities in becoming more attractive to businesses. DOD programs provide three different sources of funding:

1. The Wisconsin Housing and Economic Development Authority (WHEDA) has a business development bond program which provides low cost financing for business expansion through issuing tax exempt industrial revenue bonds. Businesses qualifying for this program must have annual sales under $3.5 million or be a first-time farmer. Financing is available to purchase or improve land, buildings, or equipment.

2. The Linked Deposit Loan (LiDL) program provides below-market interest rates on commercial loans to business that are more than 50-percent owned and controlled by women or minorities, with gross annual sales of less than $500,000.

3. The Business Energy Fund (BEF) program provides low-cost financing to small- and medium-sized businesses or projects that result in lowering energy consumption. Borrowers may choose a cash rebate of up to 25 percent of the cost of improvements or an interest rate subsidy which can effectively lower commercial loan rates to as low as 3 percent over a five-year period.

The UW-Cooperative Extension system is also involved in business enhancement. It operates a network of Small Business Development Centers which offer assistance to new or existing small businesses. Services include one-on-one counseling, product evaluation, product development and testing, business feasibility analysis, workshops, demonstration of new technologies and processes, federal and state fund procurement assistance, and data banks.

The Service Corps of Retired Executives (SCORE) is a Small Business Administration program. The SCORE program utilizes retired executives to provide counseling for new and existing small businesses. This is a volunteer program with retired executives available for small business counseling.

DEVELOPMENT ORIENTATIONS

The above discussion on funding sources deals primarily with assistance available for individual businesses. Sometimes the best source of assistance is provided by other businesses. How a community visually presents itself to visitors is more a function of how the local business community, with assistance from public agencies, organizes itself rather than how an individual business develops.

Communities can choose to develop in a number of ways. Normally the types of resources currently in place direct the development orientation. The development model chosen can determine not only the level of tourist activity but also the extent to which sociocultural change may take place. Lew (1989) studies the effects of three types of community development orientations: conservation, image centered, and economic. Conservation or historic development, which requires restoration of storefronts to a particular time period or reflects local cultural traditions, generally results in substantial local citizen involvement and acceptance of the tourism industry. It serves to preserve a high degree of authenticity and projects a clear sense of place. For these reasons, local residents exhibit more pride in their community and are willing to share that feeling with visitors. As the development proceeds and the authenticity becomes more apparent, government involvement, driven by resident pressure, intensifies as local ordinances are needed to preserve the theme projected by the historic redevelopment effort. Business impacts, including new business start up, is substantial, further reinforcing the success of the historic development orientation. The market area served by these types of communities is substantial but not as large as for the image development orientation.

Numerous examples of historic restoration and preservation done for purposes other than tourism development, but now which attract many tourists wishing to experience the "Old World" can be found throughout Europe. Some of the more interesting cities, their history, main tourism attractions and the type of planning undertaken for tourism can be found in Jansen-Verbeke (1988).

Image development communities project a mass image which is clearly defined and recognized. Communities located on a waterfront can utilize this resource as a central theme for redevelopment efforts. Similarly, western themes, as represented by Jackson Hole, Wyoming use their location as the backdrop for thematic development of the business district. These types of thematic development may not be truly representative of the community, and nearby attractions (e.g., national parks) become the draw to the area with the community serving as the service hub for the attractions. Image developments are driven more by the local business community than by the citizenry. Sense of place is not as strong due to the created image of the community rather than the restoration of an authentic period in the community's life. Market area served is usually higher than for conservation development, and is a function of the drawing power of the primary attraction(s) located close to the community. In a sense, conservation communities become attractions and image communities can become attractions but are not the main reason for the original selection of the development orientation. Image or thematic development usually results in less community pride and local involvement in the tourism industry. Perceived sociocultural impacts from tourism are higher but because of tourism's importance to the economic well-being of the community, development is rarely reversed.

Economic development communities are not generally tourism-centered. Instead, they are concerned more with revitalizing a community's retail district. The market area served by these communities is the smallest of the three orientations, with local residents as primary customers. Government controls and regulation are limited, and it is usually left up to the businesses to decide what is appropriate. Because of this, any later attempt to tap into the tourism market becomes problematic as no identifiable image is supported or projected. Rural communities which serve as regional shopping areas are most prone to this type of development orientation.

The selection of a development orientation can be difficult. The highest level of conflict occurs when residents struggle with a choice between a conservation or image orientation. Determining the appropriate type of development for an area depends on the level of public support for tourism development, resources and attractions currently in place, level of government involvement and the size of the expected market. Newer communities without an older retail district or strong cultural traditions may find that an image orientation is the best approach if tourism development is desired. The potential for conflict increases, however, when all the resources needed for either conservation or image development are present. Planning for conflict resolution requires all potential trade-offs and problems be clearly understood and articulated. Citizen involvement representative of all interest groups is a must in order for the community to be comfortable with the development orientation it has chosen.

CONCLUSION

Community tourism development is an extremely difficult task and differs markedly from the development process in place at the national or regional level. The main reason for this is that all the impacts associated with tourism development occur first and with the greatest intensity at the community level. How communities organize themselves determines both how successful the tourism industry becomes and the type(s) of tourism products presented to visitors.

This chapter begins with some examples of problems faced by communities when attempting to increase their number of visitors, then discusses how community-based tourism organizations can help manage the industry. Throughout the chapter, whether the discussion centers on marketing, delineating development zones, or securing sources of assistance, the common thread is community involvement. This chapter does not convey that message if sections are extracted and presented separately. It works best if presented in its entirety and with relationships to previous chapters internalized. At this point, the reader should be able to return to the examples presented at the beginning of this chapter and discuss how each community could have solved its problems.

EXECUTIVE SUMMARY

Communities that are just beginning their experiment with tourism development must keep in mind that, similar to any other industrial expansion, tourism brings with it change, and the process used to managing change determines the success of the experiment.

Successful tourism development requires a thorough review of resources in place, both physical and human.

Some of the more common problems inhibiting successful community tourism development include establishing industrial legitimacy for tourism, recognizing opportunities that for most local people are not viewed as anything special, failure to cooperate, communicate, and compromise with internal and external interest groups, and lack of any ongoing tourism based community awareness programs.

Since any community has a myriad of interest groups involved in providing services, controlling, or managing some aspect of tourism, there should be a separate organization established to deal only with tourism-related issues. Five key functions of this organization include: communication—dealing directly with other local groups or businesses involved in hosting tourists; research and data collection—becoming the storehouse for information on tourism; education and training—including conducting

community tourism-based awareness campaigns and identifying or conducting training programs intended to improve skill or hosting levels of community residents; promotion—based on research directly to target markets; and budget and finance—must have a source of revenues for operating the organization.

Basic micro-level requirements necessary to conduct a preliminary tourism development planning exercise are an inventory or area attractions, visitor profile analysis, and delineation of use zones.

Basic macro-level requirements necessary for tourism development at the community level include a set of travel attractors, community, and access corridors.

Access includes physical and communications, most commonly promotion, advertising, and marketing activity within an identified market area. However, en route and impulse advertising can be very effective at low cost.

Interpretation conceptually is a service and not a form of advertising/promotion. As such, its purpose is different, but if done correctly it can do more to increase experience satisfaction and consequently length of stay, positive referral and understanding about physical and social relationships in the destination than much more expensive advertising programs.

Numerous funding and assistance programs are available at the community level. Although the number and type available differ throughout the world, one common characteristic is that most are often overlooked because they are seen as dedicated to some other industry even though most tourism development efforts would qualify under the broad-based criteria used to identify program recipients.

Different community development options lead to different levels of success and impacts. Generally speaking, historic preservation efforts have the advantage of sustained tourism growth with a moderate level of associated sociocultural impacts. Image development, characterized by a somewhat arbitrary or artificially created theme can generate higher levels of tourism than communities using the historic preservation approach. However, they also generate higher levels of sociocultural impacts. The economic or unplanned type of development generates the most visitation in the shortest period of time but runs the risk of high sociocultural impacts and short development cycles.

REFERENCES

Allen, L., P. Long, R. Perdue, and S. Kieselbach. 1988. The Impact of Tourism Development on Residents' Perceptions of Community Life. *Journal of Travel Research* 27(1):16–21.

Binks, G. 1989. Interpreters in the Community. In D.L. Uzzel, ed. *Heritage Interpretation*. Vol. 1: *The Natural and Built Environment* (190–200). New York: Belhaven Press.

Blank, E. 1989. *The Community Tourism Industry Imperative; The Necessity, The Opportunity and Its Potential*. State College Pa.: Venture Publishing, Inc.

Brown, P. and J. Hunt. 1969. The Influence of Information Signs on Visitor Distribution and Use. *Journal of Leisure Research* 1:79–83.

Clarke, A. 1981. Coastal Development in France: Tourism as a Tool for Regional Development. *Annals of Tourism Research* 8(3):447–461.

Deasy, G. and P. Greiss. 1966. Impact of a Tourist Facility on its Hinterland. *Annals, Association of American Geographers* 56:290–306.

Ehrlich, T. 1970. *Specialized Trip Distribution Study, Metropolitan Recreation*. Washington, D.C.: Urban Transportation Center, Consortium of Universities.

Fridgen, J. 1984. Environmental Psychology and Tourism. *Annals of Tourism Research* 11:19–39.

Gartner, W. and J. Shen. 1992. The Impact of Tiananmen Square on China's Tourism Image. *Journal of Travel Research* 30(4):47–52.

Gartner, W. and D. Verbyla. 1986. Utilization of an Externally Directed Microcomputer System. *Journal of Park and Recreation Administration* 4(2):76–82.

Gunn, C. 1982. Destination Zone Fallacies and Half-Truths. *Tourism Management* 3(4):263–269.

Hultsman, W. 1988. Applications of a Touch Sensitive Computer in Park Settings: Activity Alternatives and Visitor Information. *Journal of Park and Recreation Administration* 6:1–13.

Jansen-Verbeke, M. 1988. *Leisure, Recreation and Tourism in Inner Cities: Explorative Case Studies*. Katholieke Universiteit Nijmegen: Geografisch en Planologisch Instituut.

Jordan, J. 1980. The Summer People and the Natives: Some Effects of Tourism in Vermont Vacation Village. *Annals of Tourism Research* 7(1):34–55.

Levin, J. 1988. CVBs: How They Get You Where They Want You. *Meetings and Conventions:* 125–140.

Lew, A. 1989. Authenticity and Sense of Place in the Tourism Development Experience of Older Retail Districts. *Journal of Travel Research* 27(4):22.

Lucas, R. 1981. Redistributing Wilderness Use through Information Supplied to Visitors. USDA-Forest Service Paper # INT-277. Missoula, Mont: Intermountain Forest and Range Experiment Station.

Matulef, M. 1988. Community Development: A National Perspective. *American City and Country* (September/October).

McIntosh, R., C. Goeldner, and J.R. Ritchie. 1995. *Tourism: Principles, Practices and Philosophies*. 7th ed. New York: John Wiley and Sons, Inc.

Murphy, P. 1985. *Tourism: A Community Approach*. New York: Methuen.

Murphy, P. 1988. Community Driven Tourism Planning. *Tourism Management* 9(2):96–104.

Northwest Regional Planning Commission. 1989. *Tourism Resource Directory for Northwest Wisconsin*. Spooner, Wis.

Pearce, D. 1989. *Tourist Development*. New York: Longman Scientific and Technical.

Pearce, P. 1984. "Tourist Guide Interaction. *Annals of Tourism Research* 11:129–146.

Perdue, R. 1986. The Influence of Unplanned Attraction Visits on Expenditures by Travel-Through Visitors. *Journal of Travel Research* 25(1):14–19.

Roggenbuck, J. and D. Berrier. 1982. A Comparison of the Effectiveness of Two Communication Strategies in Dispersing Wilderness Campers. *Journal of Leisure Research* 14(1982): 77–89.

Rosenow, J., and G. Pulshipher. 1979. *Tourism: The Good, the Bad, and the Ugly*. Lincoln, Nebr.: Century Three Press.

Scott, D., C. Schewe, and D. Frederick. 1978. A Multi-Brand/Multi-Attribute Model of Tourist State Choice. *Journal of Travel Research* 17: 23–29.

Stokowski, P. 1990. The Rhetoric of Interpretation: More than a Set of Techniques. *Journal of Park and Recreation Administration*. 27:45–48.

Stringer, P. 1984. Socio-environmental Psychology of Tourism. *Annals of Tourism Research* 11:151–154.

United States Department of Commerce. 1986. *Tourism USA: Guidelines for Tourism Development*.

Warren, H. 1986. "What" Comes before "How." in G. E. Machlis, ed. *Interpretive Views*, pp 41–46. Washington, D.C.: National Parks and Conservation Association.

Demand/Supply

The title of Part IV is reversed from what one normally encounters in the literature. It is often assumed, as in Say's law, that supply creates demand. The meaning of Say's Law can be encapsulated by using a line from a popular American movie entitled *Field of Dreams*. In the movie, a farmer carves a baseball playing field out of a cornfield, and when asked why, the answer is "If you build it they will come." "They" refers to the ghosts of famous baseball players from summers past, but since the movie became a box office success, millions of tourists have made their way to the legendary baseball field.

While examples of this relationship can be found in tourism (for example, see religious attractions in Chapter 9), there must exist some deeper reason for travel than simply because something exists somewhere else. In other words, the demand for a travel experience exists before the supply of attractions. Part IV addresses the demand for, and then supply development of tourism attractions.

Chapter 8 is the more theoretical of the two chapters in Part IV as the understanding of human behavior is not an exact science. It is generally accepted that every person is a unique individual sharing some common traits with a group but reserving some behavior unto him/herself. It is the identification of common traits that allows motivations for travel to be discerned and the travel decision process to be modeled. Common traits can also be used to identify cultures; this is the basis for the discussion of tourist, residual, and host culture interactions and implications contained in this chapter. Finally the chapter addresses how travelers are beginning to be identified by the type of development orientation they prefer to find at a destination. Tourism professionals call this "alternative forms of tourism".

Chapter 9 discusses supply or attraction development, building on the information contained in Chapter 8 by discussing some of the principles of attraction development that are considered necessary for success. It also delves deeper into the management decisions that drive the attraction development process. Although some of the information in this chapter is technically oriented, it is meant to avoid the "if you build it they will come" trap; it matters where an attraction is built, who it is built for, and what techniques are used to determine if it will generate a profit.

Although much of this chapter relates directly to private attraction development, it devotes a section to valuation of publicly provided attractions. Accountability for public expenditures has led to increased pressure to place some economic value on publicly provided attractions. That issue is addressed not only from the standpoint of the different techniques for estimating value, but also some of the problems encountered when decisions are based solely on economics.

Traveler Behavior

*High-risk recreation is on the increase, as shown at Dead Horse
Point State Park, Utah.
Photo by Carolyn Phelps*

Learning Objectives

Understand that internal and external triggering
mechanisms influence someone to select travel as a
desirable activity.

•

Explore the relationship between needs, wants, values
and motives to the travel decision process.

•

Review various consumer decision models relevant to
the travel decision process.

•

Compare a spatial travel model to a sociocultural one,
and distinguish which one is relevant to
understanding the impacts tourism generates.

•

Review reasons why alternative forms of tourism are
becoming more popular travel options.

INTRODUCTION

Principles of tourism development comprise both a supply- and demand-side dimension. The study of traveler behavior constitutes the demand side, as tourism research often focuses on who does what. Visitor profiles have been a staple of tourism research for many years. Although it is imperative that businesses understand the underlying demographic and geographic characteristics of their consumers, it is equally important to understand why they choose one product over another. Some of the psychographic market segmentation studies discussed in Chapter 10 attempt to understand the basic motivating influences culminating in a decision to leave home temporarily. Dann (1977) refers to these influences as "push" factors. Something in the human psyche is sending messages expressed in terms of wants to the individual, informing him/her of a psychological disequilibrium that can only be corrected through a travel experience.

Understanding "push" factors constitutes this chapter. It begins with a discussion of some basic concepts underlying the travel decision process. It then moves into a review of some of the models proposed to understand the movement of people through space and time. Finally, it discusses emerging forms of tourism and some of the barriers that prevent people from traveling. This demand-side approach is necessary to fully understand the tourism development process.

NEED AROUSAL

Kotler (1982) identifies three stages in what he calls "need arousal." In the first stage, external or internal stimulation triggers a predisposition to some product class. The second stage is considering needs that can be met through purchase of an item in the product class. In the third stage, these recognized needs activate wants.

Triggering Factors

External and internal stimuli can trigger the desire to travel. Internal stimuli are brought on by recognition of something lacking in everyday life. People raised in a seaside community who find themselves living inland may long to hear the soothing movement of the surf against the beach. Alternatively, a person's interest in downhill skiing may cause them to consider a trip to mountainous terrain. It may be something as simple as boredom with the daily routine which predisposes a person to read the weekly

TERRORISM AND TOURISM: CASE STUDY IN EGYPT

Travelers have been called a fickle lot. They have been accused of changing their minds as frequently as Joe Boxer would have everyone change their underwear. As shown in Maslow's hierarchy of needs (Figure 8.1), if lower order needs are not met, travel does not happen. The 1989 Tiananmen Square incident in Beijing, and the 1988 terrorist bomb attack on a Pan Am jet over Lockerbie, Scotland, both resulting in dramatic drops in visitation to China and Europe respectively, reinforced the need to satisfy lower order needs, especially safety and security, before travel to any area is seriously considered. When a country relies on mass tourism for a major portion of its export earnings, any disruption to the tourist flow can derail the economy. Government foes know this all to well, and increasingly target tourists in order to destabilize the government. Egypt is an excellent case in point.

Egypt was one of the first destinations to be packaged for mass tourism. Thomas Cook led the first tour group to the country in 1863. Mark Twain, writing in *Innocents Abroad,* describes the group's visit to the Pyramids in great detail, including an unflattering portrayal of some of the group members' actions. Since the mid 1800s, the number of tourists to Egypt has steadily increased with downturns only during periods of war. Major growth occurred in two periods. During the 1960s, annual percentage increases of 25+ were routinely recorded. The rate of increase dropped to the international average in the 1970s, but in the 1980s, after the signing of a peace treaty with

Israel, percentage increases again hit the 20+ figure.

1992 was the peak year for international visitation to Egypt, exceeding 3.2 million visitors who stayed over 22 million nights and spent over $2.4 billion. It was also the year that terrorists began to target tourists. Islamic fundamentalists, advocating a return to classical Islamic rules of societal behavior, received organizational assistance from forces outside the country, and with this help were able to recruit rural people who had become disenchanted with the present system. Over a period of 22 months from 1992 to 1994, there were 127 incidents of terrorism directed at tourists. Nine tourists were killed and 60 were injured. The attacks were mostly confined to Upper Egypt. Since 1994, there have been only three additional attacks. However, the bloodiest attack yet occurred in 1996.

Considering the number of tourists killed compared to the number of visitors, the chance of becoming a victim is estimated to be one in 500,000+, a rather insignificant chance unless, of course, you happen to be the one caught in the wrong place at the wrong time. In spite of the low probability of encountering terrorism, visits to Egypt dropped by 22 percent in 1993 and continued to free-fall in 1994, when numbers dropped an additional 12 percent. More telling, however, is that tourist nights and revenues dropped even more significantly, with declines of 19 and 42 percent respectively from 1992 to 1993. People were still coming to Egypt, but those who visited left

(continued on next page)

early and spent less than their colleagues in 1992 and before. Given that the probability of becoming a victim of terrorism was so small, why did large numbers of tourists stop coming to Egypt?

Enormous media exposure is one explanation. International coverage of what appeared to be a well organized attempt to unseat the government caused many people to reassess their safety and security needs. When some governments issued traveler advisories warning that travel to Egypt could be hazardous, many potential tourists opted for other, ostensibly safer destinations.

The government of Egypt, for the most part caught off guard by the terrorist attacks and resulting decline in visitation, reacted with some significant counter-terrorist programs. Through the Egyptian media, the extent of terrorism in the country was constantly downplayed. The international media largely chose to ignore what the Egyptian media was saying, so apart from some regional coverage this message was not receiving exposure in major markets. Of more importance was the military led counter-terrorist activities initiated by the government, coupled with programs to improve rural lifestyles through expanding economic opportunities and infrastructure investment. The government anti-terrorist task force even places agents on Nile cruises and at significant attractions in rural areas. The decline in the number of reported incidents has led to a rebound in visitors to the country. Estimates place 1995 numbers at close to 2.5 million. Given the current rate of growth, 1996 numbers should challenge the record year of 1992, although the recent attack in Cairo may alter this prediction.

Egypt is not the only country or region to suffer economically from attacks against tourists. Algeria, although not as dependent on tourism as Egypt, is almost without visitors now because of a number of attacks against foreign nationals. Florida also suffered when some renegade citizens targeted tourists because they were viewed as easy victims. Terrorism and tourism show a high degree of negative correlation. Travelers' behavior in response to real or perceived terrorist threats is a concern for many countries as tourism moves ever higher on the list of priority exports.

Source: Wahab, S. 1995. Egyptian Tourism and Terrorism. Paper presented at the Security and Risks in Travel and Tourism Conference. Mid-Sweden University, Ostersund, Sweden, 9-11 June.

Social

For many of the world's citizens, physiological and safety and security needs have been sufficiently achieved to allow for a tourism industry to develop. Poverty and hunger are still widespread, but the advantaged of any country are able to travel for pleasurable purposes. Much of that travel fulfills social needs.

Social needs are defined as love and belonging. Traveling with or visiting friends and relatives fall into this category of need fulfillment. Travel that strengthens, reinforces, or reestablishes interpersonal relationships meets a social need. When territorial instincts of animals give way to a sense of societal responsibility, social needs are being met. Much of today's travel fulfills social needs in some form, and forms the basis of a tourism industry.

Esteem

Esteem relates to the need for recognition within one's social or professional group. Once people feel the need to belong has been achieved, they may begin to position themselves within the group. High status within the group is achieved through group consensus, formal or informal. Title or position (e.g., vice president) within a group confers some measure of worth to the group. Academics may strive for recognition by publishing in scholarly journals, thereby establishing themselves as an expert in a certain area. "Keeping up with the Jones's" fuels consumption in the developed world and is a direct result of meeting esteem needs.

Travel fulfills esteem needs in different ways. Business travelers may not prefer to be "frequent flyers," but a certain status is associated with business travel. Similarly, travel for pleasurable purposes may be an important recognition factor in certain social groups. Having the economic means to engage in pleasure travel may set an individual apart from the social milieu. Although status and prestige are important needs, as discussed in more detail later, they are not always internalized or expressed by individuals as primary travel motivators. This may be partly due to the need for the recognition to come from the social or professional group rather than from the individual claiming ownership of those qualities.

Self-Actualization

Self-actualization is the highest need on Maslow's hierarchy. An individual achieves self actualization when he/she undertakes actions that provide internal satisfaction regardless of social consequences or acceptability. Education for the sake of acquiring knowledge instead of professional or social esteem is a form of self actualization. Travel provides opportunities to learn about different cultures, social organizations, ecosystems, humanity's role in a global society, and so on. Travel undertaken purely for the individual's self fulfillment is a form of self actualization.

Much has been written and discussed about what is refererred to as "alternative forms of travel." Ecotourism is probably the most popular of these alternative forms (see Chapter 4). Although alternative forms of travel are discussed in more depth later in this chapter, it is important to understand that they are not really new forms of travel, but ostensibly travel with a heavy dose of value and meaning. From a marketing perspective they can be viewed as trips emphasizing self-actualization needs.

Wants

Once needs have been triggered by some stimuli, wants become identifiable. Needs are not product-specific; they can be fulfilled in many different ways. A need for love and belonging can be realized through travel

with a friend or it can be achieved by inviting the same friend out to dinner. In either case, love and belonging needs are satisfied. Wants can be
satisfied by the attributes inherent in a specific product class. If the love
and belonging need is intense with respect to a certain friend, it may be
only be satisfied through a trip to an exotic destination where the relationship between the individuals must by necessity be one of dependency.
Travel is the product class containing the attributes of exotic location, different culture, currency, and customs, leading to a close and personal dependency relationship. These same attributes may not be available in other
products, leading to the selection of travel as the only product able to meet
the needs and wants of the couple.

From a tourism development perspective, understanding needs fulfilled by travel is insufficient for developing product image and destination
attributes. Want fulfillment may be a more important factor in the decision process of where to go and what do than needs satisfied. Probably the
best approach to understating wants is to examine motives, or expressions
of wants.

MOTIVES

Research on motives is an understandably difficult task. The underlying
motive for tourism is generally physical escape, which brings with it psychological escape (Grinstein, 1955; Crompton, 1979). Further investigation reveals that different people have different motives. While this is not
an especially profound statement, it implies that people may have more
than one motive for choosing a particular type of trip, and that different
groups may have different motivations associated with their choice of the
same destination.

A large body of knowledge has been accumulated with respect to motivations for recreation use of wilderness areas. While those using wilderness areas may or may not be tourists, the research provides insights into
the various motives associated with a particular type of destination and
recreation choice. Stankey and Schreyer (1987) examine a long list of
studies which identify some motivational patterns, separating the motives
into three categories: activity-centered, patterns of participation, and background characteristics.

Activity-Centered Tourism

Wilderness areas are commonly used for hiking, fishing, camping, hunting, and other outdoor recreational activities requiring a natural resource
base. Temporary escape is an oft-cited motive for choosing to engage in

these activities. Related to temporary escape are the motives of relaxation, solitude, challenge, exercise, and the desire to engage in these activities within an intimate or closed social group. Even though people choose different activities within the same setting, they often express the same motivations as reasons for doing so (Brown, 1981).

Wahab (1975) identifies five activity-centered types of tourism: cultural, recreational, sport, health, and conference. Smith (1989), building on Wahab's typology, accepts recreational and cultural, but adds ethnic, historical, and environmental. Other researchers add to Smith's list of activity-centered types of tourism. McIntosh et al. (1995) include business tourism, and Woodside et al. (1988) focus on urban tourism.

Ethnic Tourism

Ethnic tourism involves travel to learn, study, and become immersed or in other ways involved with a group of people that differ in custom, habits, traditions, and lifestyles from the visitor. For example, farm stays such as those offered to package tour visitors to New Zealand, involve close interaction with hosts. A network of working farm operators have organized to offer visitors a glimpse of farm life, usually accomplished through an overnight stay on a working farm. Guests learn about the farm operation by observing or in some cases directly engaging in farm chores. Meals are taken with the family, allowing for the establishment of interpersonal relationships. A sharing of beliefs and attitudes between host and guest often results. In addition to learning about how the farm operates, guests glimpse the lifestyles of their hosts. An underlying characteristic of ethnic tourism is the focus on learning more about different cultures. Some of this may be accomplished by observing cultural expressions through traditional dance, festivals or ceremonies. Sweet (1990) describes the attempts of a Pueblo Indian community in the southwestern United States to control the level of host/guest interaction. Village ritual dances, an important cultural reinforcement, are available for tourist viewing but only under strict conditions. Tourists not abiding by the rules are humiliated into compliance or asked to leave by tribal police. Most visitors applaud the level of control, feeling they are privileged to observe ancient rites.

Cultural Tourism

Travel to view and occasionally experience vanishing lifestyles constitutes cultural tourism. Whereas ethnic tourism involves a degree of immersion in an exotic lifestyle, cultural tourism provides opportunities to experience what life might have been like during a previous time. Reconstructed colonial villages, such as Colonial Williamsburg in the United States, relive some aspects of early life for the benefit of tourists. Living historical farms are also examples of lifestyles which are no longer practiced but still remembered. Mackinac Island, Michigan is an excellent example of cultural tourism. This community has developed a tourism industry by replicating a lifestyle of resort opulence which occurred during the late 1800s in the United States. Attention to detail, including the prohibition of motor vehicles on the island (emergencies excluded), and period store fronts, is one of the reasons for this community's success.

A major difference between ethnic and cultural tourism is the size of the attraction base. Ethnic tourism relies on existing exotic cultures which in total are vanishing. However, as societies evolve, the cultural tourism attraction base enlarges as more lifestyles become relics of the past.

Historical Tourism

Museums, monuments, historic sites, man-made structures, and other physical reminders of past events constitute the visual remnants of previous civilizations or significant periods in history. Visiting places commemorating past glories or human tragedies provides a deeper understanding of present day civilization's antecedents. Auschwitz concentration camp is not only a tourism attraction, but also serves to remind visitors of human genocidal tendencies. Monuments in Washington, D.C. instruct visitors of the origins of an attempt, still not realized, to form a multicultural, pluralistic society. History is often summarized for visitors through entertaining interpretive programs (e.g., light and sound shows), allowing a great deal of history to be absorbed in a short time. Any travel made primarily to visit places of historical interest constitutes historical tourism.

Environmental Tourism

Ethnic tourism's attractive power is related to the degree of cultural difference between hosts and guests. Environmental tourism relies on the uniqueness of an ecosystem to attract tourists. For example, the Galapogos Islands are home to one-of-a-kind animal species. That uniqueness sets them apart from other ecosystems, and is one of the reasons tourism activity on the islands has increased. Although early environmental tourism was associated with exploring unique ecosystems, declining environmental quality and increasing urbanization have generated interest in many different aspects of man's role as an environmental steward. Rural communities, especially in the United States, are beginning to initiate natural resource based programs such as promoting nonconsumptive use of wildlife, restoring prairies, and placing more emphasis on environmental education programs. Even though much of this is done without regard to its appeal to tourists, it has generated interest from residents and visitors alike. The importance of the environment to tourism can be seen by the increasing number of conferences focused on the environment and tourism in recent years. Even government-sponsored tourism conferences which focus on marketing include sessions on ecotourism possibilities as complements to the tourism attraction base. As society continues to misuse natural resources, ecosystem supply will shrink, leading to an increase in their attraction value.

Recreational Tourism

Recreation opportunities are prominently displayed in tourism advertising. Skiing, swimming, fishing, golfing, white-water rafting, relaxing on a sunny beach, and tennis are a few examples of recreation offerings intended to stimulate interest in the destination. Recreation activity is not limited to outdoor interests, as man-made entertainment centers (e.g., Atlantic City) are also included under recreational tourism, as are non-participatory activities (e.g., attending sporting events). With a trend toward decreasing leisure time, time spent on indoor and non-participatory type of recreational activities should increase. Those likely to increase will require little time commitment to learn skills and can be packaged for easy entry.

Health Tourism

Some of the earliest large tourism developments are located at natural hot springs. Bath, England is one of the most famous providing warm mineral baths to urban dwellers, ostensibly to ward off diseases resulting from city life. Ironically, a piece of classic literature (Ibson, Easton Press Edition, 1979) depicts the economic importance of hot springs to a local community. When the spring is discovered to be polluted, the purveyor of the news is ostracized and discredited by members of his family and the community. Fear of losing tourist revenue overrides social responsibility. Although intended to be a discourse on social morality, the play addresses issues facing the tourism industry today.

Other forms of health tourism include trips to weight reduction institutions, alcohol or drug rehabilitation centers, or simply moving to a new location during certain times of the year to avoid unhealthy climatic conditions. Very little information exists in the tourism literature about the magnitude of health tourism.

Sport Tourism

Smith includes sport tourism under recreational, and whether this is a separate category depends on how sports are classified. Attending sporting events, engaging in commercial recreation activities (e.g., golfing), or participating in non-commercial outdoor recreation activities can all be considered aspects of sport tourism. With enormous increases in salaries for professional sports personalities throughout the world, reflecting a societal love affair with professional sporting events, sport tourism will probably develop its own cadre of researchers, resulting in further classification.

Conference Tourism

Attendance at conferences, seminars, workshops, and conventions has steadily grown in the last decade. It is estimated to be a $40 billion industry in the U.S. (*Meeting and Convention Magazine*, 1990). Maintaining a competitive advantage requires a constant search for new methods of operation and sources of income. Trade associations, educational organizations, and special interest groups use conferences to maintain membership by providing information dissemination, sales, and increasing product awareness services.

Business Tourism

Although attending conferences, if part of business activity, can be considered business tourism, there is a great deal of individual travel. Sales activity probably constitutes the majority of individual business travel, although public relations, scientific data collection, and consulting services also qualify.

Urban Tourism

Traveling for cultural entertainment or escape from rural life are the primary reasons identified for visiting urban areas. Although there is much overlap between urban tourism and the other activity types of tourism discussed, it is included as a separate category to underscore the problem with inferring motives from activities. Museums, sporting events, ethnic communities, business activity, medical facilities, etc. are all present in large urban areas. Focusing on activity types may not provide much information about why the destination was selected.

Activities engaged in by tourists are only one way of inferring motives for participation. Selecting a package tour that focuses heavily on visiting historical sites might imply that educational motives are dominating the decision process. But as the work of Stankey and Schreyer (1987) indicates, multiple motives may be actually involved. From a marketing standpoint, it is important to understand the types of trips that are being selected if only to identify travel trends. However, specific motives tourists have for choosing one company over another may be the type of information operators need to stay in business.

Patterns of Participation

Tourists engaging in one of the activity-centered types of tourism probably have different motives which may be expressed through the way they engage in the activity. Patterns of participation can be discerned for a particular activity, such as hunting for deer with a firearm or a bow, or with respect to tourist services demanded.

Although most research on motivations is at the individual level, the family, the predominant social group engaged in pleasure travel, should be considered as the decision-making body (Crompton, 1981). Different spousal influences (i.e., husband dominant, wife dominant, joint) should manifest different motivations for activity preference and destination selection. Existing literature suggests that as income increases, the decision moves from wife dominant to joint to husband dominant (Nichols and Snepenger, 1988). Focusing on target markets using income as a delineator, motivations should be studied with respect to who is most likely to make a vacation decision.

Cohen (1972) categorizes travelers by their demand for travel services. Two categories, each with two subcategories, constitute his patterns of participation.

Institutionalized

Institutionalized tourism is mass tourism's cardiovascular system. It comprises all the interconnected tourism services which allow mass tourism to exist. Travel agents, commercial transportation, accommodations, food service, and tour wholesalers are a few of the operational services required to move large numbers of people. Cohen describes institutionalized tourists as traveling within an "environmental bubble." The "bubble" protects tourists from having to come into contact with a foreign way of life. Intermediaries are depended upon to handle all transactions, thus insulating visitors from host cultures. Institutionalized tourists are classified according to the amount of travel services they utilize.

Organized Mass Tourist   The organized mass tourist, almost exclusively, purchases a package tour. A packaged tour generally has a fixed itinerary with stops at familiar and known sites, includes a guide and all transportation, lodging, and food services. Emphasis is placed on collecting sites with short stops at any one site common. The appeal of a packaged tour, especially for novice international travelers is the ostensibly hassle-free, all inclusive package of services. Travelers do not have to obtain their own visa, learn host customs, speak the local language or decide where to stay or what to see. The organized mass tourist's reliance on package tours make this group the heaviest users of travel services.

Individual Mass Tourist   This group relies heavily on travel service providers but not to the same extent as the organized mass tourist. This tourist uses packaged tours, but generally chooses those allowing a measure of freedom. Some individual mass tourists package their own trips. They use travel service operations extensively, but they may rely more on a travel agent to secure transportation and lodging for them rather than purchasing a preplanned trip. Packages which include transportation and lodging only appeal to the individual mass tourist. Destination choices are still the familiar and known, but length of stay in any one place is usually longer. As the cultural distance between home and destination increases, the individual mass tourist will rely more on travel service operators and become more inclined to move into the organized mass tourist category by purchasing an all-inclusive packaged tour.

Non-Institutionalized

Non-institutionalized tourists are the antithesis of mass tourists. Although they sometimes rely on travel service operators for transportation, lodging, etc., they plan their own trips and select the services they need once they arrive at the destination. An avoidance of mass tourism destinations is characteristic of non-institutionalized tourists. Non-institutionalized tourists are classified as either explorers or drifters.

Explorer   Explorers pursue new travel experiences. They tend to avoid the familiar and seek novelty. They are also more apt to select locally provided services. There is much more interaction between explorers and the host society, but cultural immersion does not take place. Explorers' behavior would tend to identify them as risk-takers. They may also be more experienced travelers, comfortable with and able to understand and utilize travel service operators to the minimum extent required.

Drifter   A drifter moves from place to place, generally with no planned itinerary, and becomes immersed in the local culture. If they use travel services, they are the same utilized by the indigenous population. Instead of hotels, the drifter prefers to rent a room from a local family. They also avoid main tourist areas, preferring the company of local people over that of tourists. The drifter is the only one of the four groups completely removed from the protection of the "environmental bubble." Often the drifter becomes a temporary employee to earn sufficient income to continue traveling.

Although very little motivational research has been published comparing Cohen's four types of tourists, patterns of participation for travel services indicate that substantial motivational differences exist between them. Some of those motivational differences may be discerned by reviewing travelers' background characteristics.

BACKGROUND CHARACTERISTICS

Travel motivations are also related to an individuals' socioeconomic or psychological circumstances, which Stankey and Schreyer (1985) call background characteristics. Market segmentation, as discussed in Chapter 10, attempts to differentiate between consumers based on products purchased. Psychographic segmentation, especially, reveals hidden psychological traits held by one group of users versus another. Normally, psychographic segmentation is the first step in a process to identify members of a group. After psychological traits have been determined, further analysis reveals what specific characteristics members of each group have in common.

Prior experience is a commonly used background characteristic when exploring motivations for travel. Marketers use the term "heavy half" to describe product consumers that in aggregate make up less than 50 percent of total purchasers, but consume more than 50 percent of the product. The "heavy half" is the basis for the "20/80 rule," which simply means that 20 percent of all consumers of a particular product purchase or use 80 percent of the product. These "heavy half" consumers are more discriminating and more educated about their choice of product. For example, Schreyer et al. (1984) find that prior river running experience is related to motives and choice of a river to engage in the activity. Prior experience affects future decisions about why and where someone choses to recreate.

Race is also being increasingly recognized as a determinant of travel and destination choice. In the United States, Hispanic populations are the fastest growing minority group, expected to number 35 million by the year 2000. Irwin et al. (1990) investigates differences between Mexican-American and Anglo campers on a minimally developed campground in New Mexico. They find differences in use to be related to subcultural characteristics, concluding that cultural group affiliation can be a determinant of recreation choice.

Although background characteristics affecting travel choice and activity preference are related to motivations, most of the work to date is descriptive, with little theoretical support for the noted differences. In an attempt to encapsulate descriptive findings, three background characteristic categories are proposed: demographic, marginality, and ethnicity.

Demographic

Age, sex, education, income, and occupation, among others, make up the demographic category. Demographics are popular background characteristics used for understanding motives because they are easily measured and compared. Almost all visitor profile studies analyze demographic differences between user groups. Whenever motives for destination or activity selection are reported, they are most often based on demographic differences. From a marketing standpoint, this makes sense as advertisers and promoters want to know who they are targeting with a certain message.

Marginality

Motives may change based on exposure to the product. Marginality refers to the level of past experience with the product. Frequent travelers may have different motives for destination selection than novice travelers. If Maslow's hierarchy of needs categorization is operational, then motives would be expected to change as lower-order needs are fulfilled and higher-order needs are sought. Fulfilling higher-order needs may actually be associated with multiple motives, as more needs are being met through a single product purchase. For example, under-represented population groups (i.e., minorities) may not be as motivated to travel, having little previous opportunity due to lower economic standing than other population groups. As under-represented populations achieve a measure of economic parity, it should not be assumed they will have the same motives pushing them to the same destinations as experienced travelers.

Ethnicity

Ethnicity assumes the existence of subcultural groups with unique values and norms different from those of mass culture. Subcultures form social organizations with shared values. Choice of activity or destination conforms to the traditional values of the group, and motivations for destination selection is related to group values rather than the values of mass culture. Ethnic group members may be found in areas frequented by other members of the subculture which serve to support their subcultural identity. Motives may be more socially dependent than activity or demographically determined.

VALUES

Values are entwined with beliefs, in that they reside within one's belief system and result in expressed attitudes and ultimately behavior (Lessig, 1976). Whereas motives may explain why a person decides on a specific

Family reunions remain a strong travel motivator.
Photo by the author

course of action, values can influence motives. Values can be perceived as bundles of beliefs related to either how a person prefers to live or directs their immediate behavior. Rokeach (1968) labels preferred long-term belief bundles as terminal values, and those affecting immediate behavior as instrumental values. Examples of terminal values are social prestige, emotional tranquility, intellectual attainment, societal contributor, and interesting life. Instrumental values affecting daily decisions may be aggressive, peaceful, intellectual, caring, and logical. Pitts and Woodside (1986) conduct value segmentation analysis with a group of potential travelers, finding substantial differences between why certain groups patronized one attraction over another. Differences relate to both terminal and instrumental values. They argue that terminal values guide product class selection, and instrumental values guide brand selection. Their work on the importance of values in the travel decision process has implications for a set of decision models, multi–attribute attitude models, and their relationship with the travel decision process.

DESTINATION CHOICE

The basic premise determining whether an individual chooses one destination over another is utility maximization. Utility maximization is the economic basis for allocating scarce resources (e.g. money) between travel and all other goods. Once a decision to travel is made, an individual is stating in economic terms that travel is a good which, when purchased, increases his/her overall utility. Destination choice, then, is intended to maximize utility from the product class (travel) selected. Obviously, individuals can choose more than one destination over time, or even include many destinations in one trip, but for every separate decision made, only one destination can be selected. The question of how destinations are selected has been the focus of many tourism studies. Although the travel selection process is viewed from an individual perspective, it does not exclude joint or family decisions. Even when more than one individual is involved in decision making, the process resembles that of the individual, with important attributes reflecting a utility compromise position rather than utility maximization for the individual.

Multi-Attribute Attitude Models

If we accept values as bundles of beliefs, the travel decision model can be conceptualized as proceeding from beliefs to a product evaluation stage. Products are evaluated in terms of how each one provides for the reinforcement of favorable or unfavorable beliefs. The third stage evaluates the importance (salience) an individual places on each belief with respect to its presence in each product. Product selection is the one that maximizes an individual's utility. Graphically, Figure 8.2 presents this process. A more elaborate decision-making model has been developed by Schmoll (1977). This model, in Figure 8.3, includes the various factors that are considered

Figure 8.2 Utility Maximization
Process

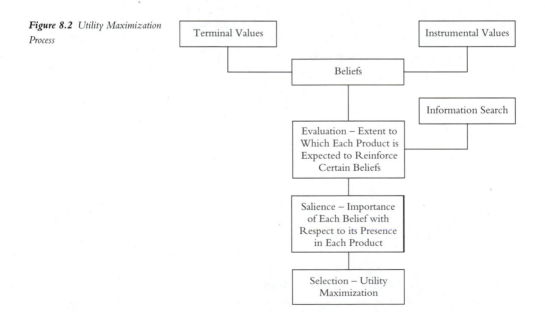

I. Travel Stimuli

II. Personal and Social Determinants of Travel Behaviour

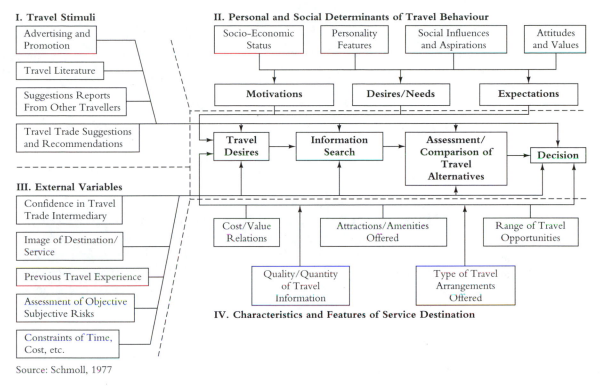

Source: Schmoll, 1977

Figure 8.3 *Schmoll's Travel Decision Process Model*

in a trip decision and that enter into the product-evaluation stage. In a sense, it identifies the numerous product attributes one may consider in the evaluation stage. However, the basic process identified in Figure 8.2 remains the same.

A number of conceptual models have been proposed to quantify part or all of this process. This family of models is called multi-attribute attitude models. Bruno and Wildt (1975) evaluate five different models: Linear Compensatory Model with Weighted Components, Linear Compensatory, Maximin, Maximax, and Power.

Linear Compensatory Model with Weighted Components

This is one of the most commonly used choice models, as it allows one to evaluate the importance of each product attribute. Mathematically, the model is represented:

$$Aij = \sum_{k=1}^{K} Cik\, Bijk$$

where:

     Aij = individual i's attitude toward brand j,

     Bijk = individual i's evaluation of brand j on a specific attribute k

     Cik = individual i's importance of attribute k.

The key term in the Linear Compensatory Model with Weighted Components is Cik, which allows for weighting of attributes with respect to their importance to an individual. This model has also been termed the perceived return (Wilkie and Pessemier, 1973) or "valence" model (Bilkey, 1953), which recognizes both the positive and negative influence of product attributes in the decision process. An individual or decision-making body determines all the attributes they wish to maximize from a travel experience. They then evaluate each destination with respect to how much of each attribute can be obtained from travel to each one. Since some attributes are more important than others, the model assumes that decision-makers are able to "weight" or prioritize each of the attributes. Once this internal 'weighting" procedure is completed, the chosen destination is the one with the highest internal score. If decision-makers have not had previous experience with the destination, the concept of destination image is an important contributor to attribute valuation. How image enters into the process is detailed in Chapter 11.

Linear Compensatory Model

In the Linear Compensatory Model, all attributes are weighted equally. The individual does not evaluate the importance of each attribute. Mathematically, the model is depicted:

$$Aij = \sum_{k=1}^{K} Bijk$$

Notice the absence of the Cik term which appears in the Linear Compensatory Model with Weighted Components. This is a simpler model to use since attribute importance is not considered. The ranking or the summation of the ratings for all attributes of the product determines choice. The product with the highest total attribute score is the one the model predicts will be purchased.

Minimax Model

Although the name may be somewhat misleading, this model assumes that individuals evaluate products in terms of how well product attributes meet minimum standards. It assumes that individuals assess all product attributes equally. Those products which do not possess certain attributes, or have them in short supply, are eliminated from further consideration. Minimax Models are noncompensatory, and do not consider attribute salience. For a brand to be selected, it must first meet minimum acceptable standards for all considered attributes. The brand with the maximum minimum attribute evaluations is preferred. Minimax Models are similar to perceived risk or minimum loss models. An individual's objective is to reduce the chance of loss (risk) from product selection. The product meeting minimum standards on all considered attributes is the one expected to minimize loss.

Maximax Model

The inverse of the Minimax Model is the Maximax Model. Again, the model is noncompensatory, as attribute importance is not considered. The product receiving the highest evaluation on any one attribute is considered to be the optimal choice. Maximax models are similar to what is termed perceived return strategies. The product chosen is the one expected to maximize return to the individual, or the product with the highest single attribute rating.

Power Model

The Power Model ranks and evaluates attributes in terms of importance to the individual. The process involves determining attribute importance. Product preference order is based on the evaluations of the most important attributes. If a tie occurs, the next most important attribute is considered. Power Models differ from Maximax Models due to the inclusion of an attribute importance evaluation step. A product selected using a Maximax Model is the one with the highest ranking for a product attribute. Power Models follow the same process, with the exception of an evaluation stage where all product attributes are evaluated in terms of individual importance and then ranked. For example, a selected destination must first have the most important attribute in sufficient supply which equals or exceeds, all other destinations. As the decision-maker moves down the list of important attributes, the destination perceived as having a preferred attribute in greater supply than another will be chosen.

Which model works best? Bruno and Wildt (1985) argue that all the models, with the exception of Maximin, predict choice fairly accurately. However, each model simulates different attitude structures of the individual. It is probable that different groups of travelers have different attitude structures. Some may view travel as essential to their emotional well-being, others as important to professional career development. One model would probably not predict destination selection for both groups equally well.

Linear Compensatory Models with Weighted Components involving an attribute evaluation and importance ranking process are the most frequently used destination-choice models. The advantage of these models is the logic of rational choice, derived from economic theory. Rational decisions require an evaluation of expected outcomes, leading to a utility maximization solution. The evaluation process implies the existence of perfect information. Perfect information does not mean that all outcomes are known, but that all consumers have access to the same information. The intangible nature of tourism products, inability to pretest before purchase, different experience levels with the tourism product, and different value systems underlying choice invalidate the perfect information assumption. In the absence of perfect information, different destination selection processes are the norm rather than the exception. As research on motivations for travel continues, the search for a "grand decision theory" will be abandoned and replaced by more specific models related to more refined and narrowly defined groups of travelers.

Spatial Model of Travel

The above discussion focuses on one aspect of traveler behavior—the destination selection process. Other models cover the act of traveling from pre-trip planing to post-trip reflection. One of the early trip models explaining recreation behavior is segmented based on spatial characteristics (Clawson and Knetsch, 1966). Five distinctive phases are identified for the total recreation experience: Anticipation, Travel To, On Site, Travel From, and Recollection. These five stages form the building blocks for most of the travel behavior models of today.

Anticipation

As noted above, a decision to travel begins with a recognition of an unmet need in the home environment which only a travel experience can satisfy. The Anticipation stage begins with a recognition of this need and involves all aspects of pre-trip planning necessary to make the trip a reality. Push/pull factors are important determinants of destination selection, and evaluation of those factors takes place primarily in the Anticipation phase.

Travel To

The act of physically moving from the home environment to the place(s) where the travel experience takes place constitutes the Travel To stage. This phase can be short, consisting of a one-day excursion, or may involve long-haul travel to foreign destinations. Generally, as the Travel To stage increases in proportion to the total trip length, the Anticipation stage also increases in duration. More pre-trip planning is required to lessen the economic risk associated with long-haul excursions. The importance of the Travel To stage is implicitly recognized in community tourism system models in the linkage between the community attraction complex and tourist generating markets.

One of the primary differences between most consumer goods and tourism products is an inverted channel of distribution. In tourism, goods do not flow to tourists, but tourists move to where the tourism product is produced (see Chapter 10). The role filled by travel intermediaries (e.g., travel agents, tour wholesalers) and transportation providers (e.g., airlines, rail carriers) is important to understanding the entire tourism development process. Most people agree that tourists do not travel simply to fly in airplanes or stay in hotels. However, the act of traveling accounts for the highest percentage of total trip expenditures (McIntosh et al., 1995). Understanding both supply and demand aspects of transportation allows for a clearer picture of transportation's impacts on tourism development. For example, in the United States, domestic tourism, and to an extent regional flows of international tourists, have been impacted by deregulation of the airline industry. The 1978 Cannon Kennedy Pearson Act set up a schedule phasing out price and route regulations for the domestic air industry in the country. Although critics argue over the effects of deregulation, some trends are apparent. Prices for competitive routes, which are also the most popular, have generally declined in real dollar terms. Unpopular routes have experienced real price increases and in some cases have been eliminated. In areas where real prices have risen or routes have been eliminated, tourism has suffered through the increase in price or through the elimination of one transportation linkage.

Another important aspect of tourism development included in the Travel To stage is en route communication. The nature and extent of en route communication is explained in more detail in Chapter 6. How rigid and inflexible travelers are on their way to an ultimate destination is important for areas which are not considered primary destinations, but have the potential to provide supplemental experiences to the traveler.

On Site

What people do while on site constitutes the satisfaction phase of travel. Even if people have multiple destinations on a single trip, the sum of those experiences usually determines the level of satisfaction or dissatisfaction with the entire trip. Satisfaction is a function of the Anticipation stage. Information search and image evaluation in the Anticipation stage determines expectations. On site experiences are measured against preconceived expectations, resulting in a measure of trip satisfaction. It is in the On Site stage where many components of the tourism industry come together. Accommodations, food service, attractions, shopping opportunities, and hospitality services are all involved in meeting tourists' expectations. While the On Site experience may not constitute even half the time or expense involved in the other stages of travel, it will for the most part determine satisfaction for the whole trip.

Visitor profile studies are the most common type of On Site research conducted. Where visitors originate, how old they are, what they do while on site, how much money they make, etc., are included in almost all visitor profile studies. Also included in many of these studies is an examination of user satisfaction. Satisfaction is believed to be related to motives influencing destination choice and expectations of the visit. This is the direct link to the Anticipation stage. Satisfaction also depends on the individual as different individuals have different satisfaction levels even though conditions at the destination remain the same (Stankey and Schreyer, 1985).

Travel From

The forgotten stage of travel behavior is Travel From. For domestic travel, especially by private motor vehicle, the choice of return routes may significantly differ from routes selected to travel to a destination. Even in-

Wider choice of transportation options has led to more "off-road" travel.
Photo by the author

ternational travel on commercial air carriers allowing open jaw or stopover tickets potentially influences tourism development through the act of returning home, although one could argue that sites visited on the journey home are part of the On Site stage since experiences are still being collected. As mentioned, much of the tourism literature deals with specific destination selection. Some studies (for example, Hunt et al., 1972) recognize the importance of multiple destination selection but do not indicate whether they are part of the Travel To or Travel From stage of travel. Motivations for destination selection may also differ between the various stages. If motivations influence the decision to leave home, is the home environment acting as a pull factor for return, or are push factors (motivations) more important? If, as has been suggested, travel springs from a desire or need to change place and pace, then once that need has been satisfied, is there a counter balancing need to recover equilibrium through a return home? While some of these questions may appear to be academic musings, their application to how we provide tourism products is direct. If people differ in their needs and motivations for each stage of the trip, the type of products provided and level of services demanded will differ. Choice of accommodation, food service, and level of shopping activity may all be influenced by the stage of travel a person is in. In the absence of any systematic research on the issue, the influence on tourism development is unknown.

Recollection

Clawson and Knetsch (1966) argue that the Recollection phase is the most important part of the travel experience. It usually occurs once an individual has returned home, although it can begin at any time after travel has begun. This stage may be very short if the individual is a frequent traveler, or may cover a much longer period, occurring when pictures or slides of the trip are processed, memorabilia is stored, souvenirs become part of the home environment, and experiences are shared with friends. Organic images based on visitation replace pre-trip images and satisfaction is assessed. Satisfaction and dissatisfaction are evaluated with respect to time and monetary costs. A new stage of Anticipation may begin as part of the Recollection stage, especially if the travel was extremely rewarding. New experiences such as travel to unique locations may have longer lasting memories than travel to familiar places.

All stages of the travel experience are interconnected. It is not always possible to delineate points where one stage ends and another begins. Although segmenting travel into various stages simplifies analysis of traveler behavior, ignoring the linkages between all stages provides only a myopic view of the total experience.

Sociocultural Model of Traveler Behavior

The previous model is spatially oriented, as it consists of different stages a tourist passes through on a trip. Each stage is identified by a series of actions that takes place in a different geographic setting. A sociocultural model of tourist behavior is independent of place, although place is not entirely removed from consideration, since by definition travel requires movement from one place to another. The focus shifts, however, from what a person does in one place to how they act, and interact with others, in psychological space.

Jafari (1987) proposes a model of tourist behavior built on the concept of cultural change. The basic premise is that during the course of a trip, individuals shed the culture of their home environment and assume a tourist culture. How this happens and the resulting implications for tourism development are discussed below. Jafari's model contains six main components with eight sub-components. The entire model is displayed in Figure 8.4. The six main components are: Corporation, Emancipation, Animation, Repatriation, Incorporation, and Omission.

Corporation

The Corporation stage consists of the individual's ordinary or home environment life. It is what the travel industry calls the market. Most people adapt to the norms and standards set by the community in which they live, recognizing and following accepted forms of behavior. As ordinary life continues, a state of imbalance occurs for many people. Some correct the imbalance through a change in daily activity, while others require a change of place. Motivations linked to unmet needs in the home environment lead to a recognition of travel as a means of restoring balance. When

Figure 8.4 Jafari's Tourist Model

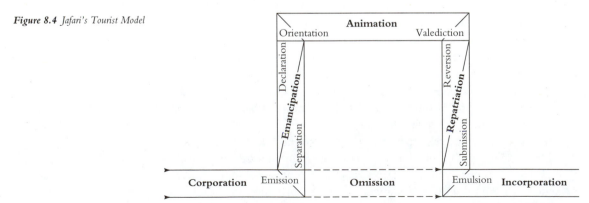

Source: Jafari, 1987

this happens, people enter into the sub-component phase of Emission. The travel decision process, outlined above, is the mental part of Emission, and the physical part consists of pre-trip preparations. Purchasing airline tickets, tuning the car, stopping mail delivery, packing suitcases, and setting timer lights for the house are all examples of physical activities that may be undertaken in preparation for a trip.

Emancipation

In the Emancipation process, an individual becomes physically and mentally removed from the bonds of ordinary life. The home culture in which they exist for most of the year becomes less important as the transformation into a tourist and a tourist culture begins. There are two sub-components of the Emancipation stage. First, separation occurs when the traveler physically moves beyond the boundaries of the home environment. Physical boundaries may be defined as community borders or, in the case of international travel, the point when the person leaves his/her country. The Separation component is not as important to the individual as it is to the travel industry. Travel services become important once physical separation has occurred. More important to the traveler is the Declaration sub-component. Declaration is a psychological act, internal but not always recognized by the individual, when touristhood begins. Changing from a suit and tie to a loud floral shirt may signify to the traveler and those around him/her that a transformation to the tourist culture has begun. The norms and standards existing in ordinary life, are being shed as a search for new norms and standards begins. Whereas Separation is physical removal from ordinary life, Declaration is psychological removal. The time Declaration takes to occur depends on the individual. For some it is instantaneous. Winter-weary college students leaving for tropical climates during spring break may dress in beach wear before they have even entered the car. Their refusal to take along any winter clothes is a formal declaration of emancipation from ordinary life. Others may resist the transformation. Jet travel can move someone from a snowy winter environment in the morning to a tropical beach environment by afternoon. It may take days for certain individuals to shed their long pants, socks, and shoes and become part of the beach crowd. Separation and Declaration complement each other. Separation serves to remind the individual of the growing distance between themselves and home, and Declaration signifies the shrinking distance between the individual and the tourist culture, or in Jafari's words, non-ordinary life.

The further a person enters into the Declaration stage, the more his/her normal patterns of behavior change. Spending constraints may temporarily vanish. Credit cards may be used more extensively. Expenses occurring in non-ordinary life do not always have to be paid in non-ordinary life, but in another place, another time, and another culture.

Animation

Once the individual has arrived at the destination he or she enters into the stage of Animation. The home or ordinary life culture assumes a backdrop or residual position. The dominant culture is the one other tourists already at the destination practice. Acceptable behavior is passed on from tourist to tourist through the process of Orientation. The traveler soon learns the norms and standards of the tourist culture by observing other tourists. Prior experience with the destination influences the extent of the Orientation phase. Novice visitors normally take longer to adjust than frequent visitors. What remains of the home culture is relegated to a residual role serving to remind the tourist of the psychological distance between what they have become and what they were. The travel industry at the destination recognizes and caters to the tourist culture. Ordinary consumerism, rejected during the Declaration phase of Emancipation, is further weakened. Credit cards become the normal means of payment rather than the exception.

Many of the social impacts of tourism development discussed in Chapter 5 can be explained by examination of the two cultures in place at a tourist destination. The tourist culture is anti-structural in that it rejects norms and standards operating in ordinary life. At the same time, a more structured ordinary life culture exists for local residents. While one group is engaging in hedonistic activity, the other is trying to maintain certain behavioral standards. Conflict occurs when the separate cultures clash. Attempts have been made to reduce negative social impacts by imposing rules and regulations affecting conduct. Signs prohibiting nude swimming, off road camping, or loud noises after eleven p.m., are all examples of attempts to introduce structure into a culture that promotes rejection of structure. More often than not they fail.

The last sub-component of Animation is Valediction. As the end of the vacation approaches, the residual culture, which for the most part has been dormant, reasserts itself. Preparations for return begin. Flight reservation are confirmed, vacation clothes packed and the last pictures taken. There may be one last spontaneous embrace of the tourist culture before final descent back to ordinary life. A last minute shopping spree or a final evening out with new-found friends may take place. Many organizations at their annual convention implicitly recognize the importance of a last fling by staging a final banquet or dance on the last evening. This serves to bond an organization's members to the tourist culture created by the annual convention, and encourages members to attend next year.

Repatriation

Returning to where the journey began constitutes the Repatriation stage. Similar to the transformation that took the traveler from ordinary to non-ordinary life, a reverse process begins. Reversion as a sub-component of Repatriation is the physical process of return. Boarding an airplane, putting luggage in the car, and checking under the bed at the hotel to make sure nothing is left behind are all physical acts that reaffirm the return to ordinary life. Submission is a complementary sub-component which serves to psychologically reaffirm the resurrection of the individual that existed in ordinary life. There are visible signs of submission, such as changing clothes to conform to those worn by members of the home environment. Week-old beards are shaved or the novel which was begun on the trip to the destination is now revisited. The residual culture which served as a backdrop while journeying through the Animation stage and resurrected during Valediction, fully reasserts itself. Memories contain episodes of what is now considered silly or foolish behavior, but which did not appear so while they were taking place. Reminders of all the credit card charges may also surface. At the same time, psychological markers of Animation appear; the tourist culture is remembered as existing in another time and place and more often than not viewed as something worth recapturing. Similar to the Travel From stage of the spatial model, little is known of the marketing implications of Repatriation. How long it lasts, if different groups of people are affected differently, when it begins to take effect, how spending patterns change, and how total trip satisfaction is affected by what occurs during Reparation, are for the most part untouched areas of study.

Incorporation

Incorporation consists of full physical and mental immersion into ordinary life. The sub-component of Emulsion represents the time it takes to become completely absorbed back into ordinary life. This may depend on the length of trip, time until next departure, or events which took place in ordinary life during the time away. Physical markers of Emulsion may include adjusting to time differences resulting in interrupted sleeping patterns, work which has piled up on the desk, or a garden overgrown with weeds. The tourist culture existing in non-ordinary life assumes a backdrop position. Statements like: "It's hard to believe two days ago we were in Caracas, it seems like ages ago," reinforce the distance between the tourist culture and the home culture. The ease with which a person moves back into ordinary life is not known. It is generally believed that pleasure travel increases productivity by restoring psychological balance. It is entirely possible that a depression state is created through Emulsion, reducing productivity in the short run until full Incorporation takes place. The extent and nature of travel on one's work productivity is a subject deserving further investigation.

Incorporation is also the stage where what happened during non-ordinary life has its greatest impact. Credit card charges are dealt with, a predictable and set lifestyle is restored, and memories of the trip are processed. Trip satisfaction evaluation occurs, similar to the processes outlined in the Recollection phase of the previous model. The strength of the experienced tourist culture is assessed against the costs of Incorporation, resulting in a decision to continue the life of the tourist at some future date. The growth in tourism over the last twenty years would appear to reinforce the strength of the tourist culture as a necessary element of life able to withstand the physical and psychological cost of admission even if only for a short time.

Omission

Life continues in the home environment while the individual is away. This is represented by the Omission stage of the model. The extent of the Omission stage is equal to the distance between Emission and Emulsion. Theoretically, as Omission lengthens, re-entry or culture shock associated with the return home increases. What happens to the traveler during Omission is not lost but temporarily ignored or set aside to be dealt with after full Incorporation.

Model Implications

Most of the research focusing on tourists has taken place while they are in either the Corporation stage or in Animation but not both. Research on potential tourists needs, preferences, images of destinations, expectations, and so on is usually conducted in the market or Corporation stage. Potential tourists are in ordinary life and act according to their ordinary life culture. Since all tourism emanates from a base of Corporation, market based research is justified on that basis. However, services packaged for tourists based on research conducted while they are in ordinary life ignore the implications of non-ordinary life or the existence of a tourist culture. Should the motivations leading to travel, services demanded, or attractions deemed important at the destination be expected to remain the same once a person has become a tourist and joined the tourist culture?

Other studies focus on tourists once they have entered the Animation stage. Again, visitor profiles are an example of this type of work. A large segment of recreation/travel research has been concerned with what people do, think, and how they act once on site. However, this has not been compared to similar work on the same group of people while they were in ordinary life. "Two sets of independent research, on two different groups of people, in two dichotomous worlds cannot support an argument on the tourist, let alone form a basis for the implementation of planning and marketing schemes" (Jafari, 1987:156).

If Jafari's model is operational, the implications for the tourism industry are critical. Each component of the sociocultural model represents a certain stage in the psychological transformation of the individual. Motivations for engaging in different activities can change. Services demanded may shift. The when, why, and where of social and environmental impacts may be related not only to the physical presence of tourists but to their psychological states as well. At the present time, a cohesive study of the tourist does not exist. What is known about tourist behavior has evolved from a series of case studies. As tourism intensity increases, tourism developments come under increasing pressure to control the negative impacts while continuing to provide the needed economic benefits. A greater understanding of the tourist and the sociocultural implications of tourism is required.

ALTERNATIVE FORMS OF TOURISM

The inclusion of a section on alternative forms of tourism in this chapter is predicated on the historical beginning of the movement. Mass tourism developed concurrently with the economic and technological growth in western societies after World War II. The same processes that allowed for the development of an urban industrial society provided the means for larger numbers of people to travel. Cohen (1987) contends that alternative tourism has its roots in two contemporary ideological views: alternative tourism as a reaction to modern consumerism, and alternative tourism as a reaction to the exploitation of the third world.

The growth of mass tourism has been made possible by the growth of associated industries (e.g. accommodations, transportation) dedicated to moving and hosting travelers. With growth and technological advances has come a drop in the real price of travel, allowing more people the opportunity to travel. Since early travel contained a high degree of travail, the modern travel industry has attempted to offer an experience based on less rigor, less time, and more comfort. In doing this, cultures have been commoditized, attractions trivialized and contrived, and experiences prepackaged. In other words, the authentic travel experiences of the past, which also had high time and money costs, have vanished in favor of the easy and safe. Those who reject mass tourism in favor of alternative forms of tourism are seen as members of a counterculture, rejecting the consumer society that prepackages products for convenience rather than quality. Although alternative forms of tourism are now becoming mainstream, they may have had their roots in the counterculture lifestyles exhibited by the youth of the western societies in the 1960s and 1970s.

Colonies as sources of raw material and labor for the developed world have become politically and socially incorrect. However, many critics claim the systems of dependency developed during the colonial period remain in place today, further widening the gap between developed and developing countries. Mass tourism, with its reliance on businesses owned and managed by members of the developed world, is viewed by some as the utilization of developing countries' land base and host societies as pleasure colonies. Alternative tourism is a rejection of this exploitation and attempts to develop a type of tourism more responsive to host societies needs.

Even though the antecedents of alternative tourism are important from a development perspective, they do not define what alternative tourism really is. The name "alternative forms of tourism" is a catch-all phrase for types of tourism that have been called soft path, people-to-people, small-scale, integrated tourism, and green tourism, among others. Ecotourism is probably the most prevalent name attached to alternative forms of tourism, as discussed in Chapter 4. The International Academy for the Study of Tourism (1990) identifies three elements of alternative forms of tourism which reveal its human dimension:

1. More sensitive and sympathetic to host communities and their total habitat

2. More cognizant of the tourists and the quality of their experience

3. More rewarding for people involved in the operational structure of tourism

Butler (1990) provides a more thorough comparison between mass tourism and alternative forms of tourism. His comparison has four main headings: General Features, Tourist Behavior, Basic Requirements, and Tourism Development Strategies, with examples provided under each category (Table 8.1).

General Features

Mass tourism is characterized by rapid development, with the emphasis on economic returns and less consideration to environmental and social impacts. Historically, mass tourism leads to unplanned and uncontrolled growth and development. Focus is on quick growth rather than sustain-

TABLE 8.1 Comparison of "Hard" and "Soft" Tourism

	Mass Tourism	Green Tourism
General Features	Rapid development	Slow development
	Big strides	Small steps
	Maximizes	Optimizes
	Socially, environmentally inconsiderate, aggressive	Socially, environmentally considerate, cautious
	Uncontrolled	Controlled
	Unplanned	Planned
	Without scale	In scale
	Short-term	Long-term
	Special interests	Total interests
	Remote control	Local control
	Unstable	Stable
	Sectoral	Holistic
	Price conscious	Value conscious
	Quantitative	Qualitative
	Growth	Development
Tourist Behavior	Large groups	Singles, families, and friends travel
	Little time	Much time
	Rapid transportation	Appropriate (also slow!) transportation
	Fixed program	Spontaneous decisions
	Tourists directed	Tourists decide
	Imported life style	Local life style
	Sights	Experiences
	Comfortable and passive	Demanding and active
	Little or no mental preparation	Some mental preparation
	No foreign language	Language learning
	Feeling of superiority	Open-minded approach
	Shopping	Bring presents
	Souvenirs	Memories, new knowledge
	Snaps and postcards	Photography, drawings, paintings
	Nosey	Tactful
	Loud	Quiet
Basic Requirements	Retention of peak holiday periods	Staggered holiday periods
	Untrained labor force—no career structure	Further education for labor force
	Publicity cliches	Tourist "education"
	Hard selling	Heart selling
	Tourism as economic panacea	Alternatives to and in tourism sought

(continued)

TABLE 8.1	(Continued)	
	Mass Tourism	*Green Tourism*
Tourism Development Strategies	Development without planning	First plan, then develop
	Project-led schemes	Concept-led schemes
	District level planning only	Regional coordination of district plans
	Scattered development	Concentrated development
	Building outside existing settlements	Development within existing settlements
	Intensive development in areas of finest landscapes	Fine landscape conserved
	New building and new bed capacity	Re-use existing buildings—better utilization of bed capacity
	Building for speculative unknown future demand	Fixed, limited development
	Tourism development everywhere	Development only in suitable places and where local services already exist
	Development by outside developers	Native developers only
	Employent primarily for non-natives	Employment according to local potential
	Development only on economic grounds	Discussion of all economic, ecological, and social issues
	Farming declines, labor force into tourism	Farm economy retained and strengthened
	Community bears social costs	Developer bears social costs
	Traffic "plan" favors cars	Traffic "plan" favors public transport
	Capacity for high seasonal demand	Capacity for average seasonal demand
	"Natural" and historical obstacles removed	"Natural" and historical obstacles retained
	Urban architecture	Vernacular architecture
	High technology and mechanized tourist installations	Selective mechanized development— "low-tech" development favored

Source: Butler, 1990, quoting Lane and Krippendorf

able development. Alternative tourism is much more slow to develop due to the intensive planning required to sustain growth. It is much more sensitive to local needs, especially environmental and social, and views economic returns in a long-term perspective.

Tourist Behavior

Large groups intent on collecting sites, souvenirs, and maintaining distance between tourists and locals characterize tourist behavior in mass tourism. Generally, the agenda for visiting attractions is fixed, with little time spent at any one place. In mass tourism, tourists move quickly into and out of areas. Tourist behavior in an alternative form of tourism is characterized by smaller groups with longer lengths of stay in an area, attempts to communicate with the host society in their language, and activities in keeping with the norms and standards of the host society.

Basic Requirements

Mass tourism usually comes in waves, resulting in seasonal fluctuations. Extensive promotion and publicity are used to increase demand. Multinational companies predominate, and local populations are offered low paying occupations with little chance of career advancement. Alternative forms of tourism can occur at any time and off season is appealing to many, as fewer numbers of other tourists will be encountered. Local ownership of tourist-related business is encouraged and local populations to a greater extent determine how resources are utilized.

Tourism Development Strategies

Extensive unplanned development is the norm rather than the exception in mass tourism. Areas with the most scenic resources are heavily developed, often changing the character of the area. Much of the development is undertaken by non-locals. Traditional industries (e.g., agriculture) decline, and tourism assumes the dominant form of development. Alternative tourism requires extensive initial planning with greater reliance on local labor, and local sources of capital in line with locally promulgated regulations. Tourism assumes a complementary industrial role emphasizing the importance to continuing traditional lifestyle patterns. Existing resources (e.g., buildings) are used and renovated when necessary rather than relying on new construction.

Butler (1990) also identifies the possible implications of alternative forms of tourism on the social, economic, and environmental impacts (Table 8.2). As expected, the overall economic impacts are negative due to fewer numbers of tourists, although since they stay longer, there is the opportunity for per capita spending to increase. In terms of the environmental and social impacts, there are still some negative effects, since only in the total absence of tourism will social and environmental impacts be nonexistent. However, in some cases alternative forms of tourism (i.e., ecotourism) have helped preserve ecosystems (see Chapter 4).

From the above discussion, it would seem that mass tourism is an inherently bad development option, and alternative forms of tourism are better; this is not always the case. Most of the criticism directed at mass tourism developments arises because of the unplanned nature of the development. Alternative forms of tourism are a reaction to the impacts spawned by unplanned developments, or as discussed in Chapter 1, a form of adaptancy to deal with tourism development's problems. As will be dis-

TABLE 8.2 Possible Implications of Alternative Tourism			
	Impacts		
	Social	*Environmental*	*Economic*
Tourists			
Numbers	Positive	Positive	Negative
Behavior	Questionable	Slightly positive	Negative
Location	Negative	Negative	Negative
Time	Positive	Negative	Positive
Contact	Negative	N/A	Neutral
Similarity	Negative	Slightly negative	Positive
Resource			
Fragility	Neutral	Negative	Neutral
Uniqueness	Neutral	Negative	Neutral
Capacity	Neutral	Slightly positive	Neutral
Economy			
Sophistication	Positive	Neutral	Negative
Leakage	Slightly positive	Neutral	Negative
Political			
Local control	Positive	Unknown	Neutral
Planning extent	Slightly negative	Unknown	Neutral

Source: Butler, 1990

cussed in Chapter 12, there are ways to plan and manage for mass tourism which make alternative forms of tourism less likely to be viewed as substitutes and more likely to be seen as different development options. To date, they appear to be acceptable development options for certain ecosystems and cultures.

Butler (1990) also mentions that the flow of development is always unidirectional. Tourism can proceed from an alternative form into mass tourism, and many times there is pressure to do so, but it can not retreat from mass tourism to an alternative form of tourism. Demand for alternative forms of tourism is on the increase (Ingram and Durst, 1989). Whether this is due to the root causes identified by Cohen is irrelevant when the consequences of market demand are considered. With increasing demand for alternative forms of tourism, tourism developments will be dedicated to providing alternative travel experiences. How they are planned and managed will be an important area of tourism development research in the future.

BARRIERS TO TRAVEL

Most of this chapter has been devoted to understanding the push factors leading to a travel decision. Pull factors are generally viewed from a supply-side dimension. The force of attractions in a destination area is generally viewed as exerting a pull response on the individual. Chapter 9 deals with the issue of pull from an attraction development perspective, and Chapter 11 examines destination image as a component of the pull factor. There is also another pull force that must be considered, the pull of the home environment can be viewed as a barrier to travel. All the constraints to travel can also be considered factors influencing travel. Reverse their direction and more travel results.

Money

Probably the most commonly recognized barrier to travel is money. Travel, especially pleasure travel, is demand-elastic. Demand-elastic goods may be considered luxury goods and the higher the demand elasticity, the more volatility in purchase patterns. Travel competes with other luxury goods for a share of an individual's or family's budget. How travel compares to other luxury goods (e.g., jewelry, luxury automobiles, fashionable clothes) is not known. What is known is that during times of economic depression, the amount of travel declines. There is also evidence to suggest that after prolonged recessions, travel does not immediately assume a position of prominence in the consumer basket of goods and services. Durable goods (e.g., automobiles, refrigerators, home remodeling) may be the first items purchased after a recession, while travel assumes a secondary role in the budget allocation process. Gartner and Hunt (1987) tracked travel to the state of Utah over a twelve-year period encompassing two recessions in the United States. Total travel to the state of Utah did not exceed pre-recession levels until some years after the recession was over. As the recession period lengthened, the time required to reach pre-recession periods also lengthened. Although this study has certain limitations, it suggests that travel, as a luxury good, assumes a secondary role to the purchase of many other goods and services.

Time

Another of the most commonly recognized constraints or barriers is the amount of time available for travel. Into the 1980s one of the more routinely heard reasons for increasing levels of tourism was more leisure time. Shorter work weeks, union contracts guaranteeing paid vacation, a greater emphasis on recreation and leisure were all factors resulting in increasing the amount of time allocated for pleasurable pursuits. This trend was reversed in the 1980s and has continued into the 1990s. Work weeks have increased, and less vacation time is taken even when it is still available. The ramifications of this trend on travel is mixed. Shorter but more frequent vacations appear to be more common. Domestic tourism may be the beneficiary of this trend, as international travel is generally longer in duration. Pent-up demand may also be building, and may exert itself after retirement age is reached. Shorter leisure time availability is assumed to negatively affect the demand for travel, but the consequences of less leisure time on different types of travel options is still relatively unknown.

Certain societal trends may affect the amount of leisure time available for travel. Year-round school is in place in some areas, and is being considered in many more. The effect of year-round school with periodic short break periods, may serve to smooth out the annual heavy vacation periods found in many countries. Seasonality for travelers will be reduced, but many destination areas dependent on climatic condition will still be faced with seasonal fluctuations in demand. Whether reducing seasonal movements of people will shift vacation preferences to other areas at other times is also unknown.

Health

People have historically traveled for health reasons. During the plague in Europe, it was felt a trip to the country or seaside would lessen the chance of contagion. Health is also a barrier to travel. Poor health limiting mobility or the fear of inadequate health services at the destination reduce willingness to venture far from home. To a great extent, the travel industry has taken steps to overcome the health obstacle. Barrier-free accommodations and attractions are now commonplace. Medical facilities are being found in more remote locations than ever before. Credit card companies provide emergency medical assistance and tour operators make arrangements with local facilities and physicians for service if needed. One disturbing health trend, especially for many tropical developing countries, is the resurgence of malaria. Drug-resistant strains are appearing at a much more frequent rate than ever before, often frustrating the ability of the medical community to compensate by developing new drugs. Overpopulation and weakening domestic economies throughout the world have also led to lax or nonexistent sanitation practices, increasing the incidence of cholera, hepatitis, and other human waste-borne disease.

Referring back to Maslow's hierarchy of needs, it is possible to predict the consequences of these trends. During the late 1970s and continuing today, terrorist attacks in Europe, South America, The Middle East, etc., did more to slow the flow of international tourism than any other cause, including recession and perceived fuel shortages. If people refuse to travel to certain areas because they do not feel safe, then it can be surmised that safety and security needs are important travel indicators. Health concerns may spark the same reaction as terrorism, as many potential travelers opt for an alternative destination that allows this lower order need to be realized.

Family Life Cycle

There are certain stages in a family life cycle that are more conducive to travel than others. Those stages are generally related to the presence or absence of the two main barriers to travel, time and money. Singles or couples without children may have more discretionary time and money than families with children. Time and money are most likely to be in short supply during formative family years, which may also correspond to the career development years of one or both parents. As families mature and careers become established, time may exert less influence than money, especially if parents are paying for college educations for their children. Indirect evidence of the influence of the family life cycle on vacation patterns is found in Dybka (1987). American vacations to Europe, considered both time and money intensive, occurs more frequently for the 21–30 age group and the 51+ age group. More travel to close proximity destinations (e.g., Caribbean, Canada, and within the U.S.) occurs during the intervening years. Although this study does not examine family composition as a travel determinant, the years where long-haul, expensive travel occurs closely parallel ages before families are formed or after families have matured.

The travel industry, to an extent, has recognized the monetary constraints imposed on families. Hotels and motels often do not charge additional fees if children under a certain age share a room with their parents. Child-care services are provided for couples wishing to spend a night away from the children. Even some of the new casinos in the midwestern United States are entering into cooperative relationships with large child-care companies to provide their services at the casino.

Others

There are many other reasons people decide not to travel. For every product, there are groups or segments which purchase it at a higher rate than others. Some people have purchased it in the past but it is no longer part of their consideration set, and some people have no desire to purchase it or have never done so. Some people do not travel because they do not consider it enjoyable. Others have had no experience traveling, possibly due to their economic status. They may not even be able to consider travel as part of the basket of goods and services available to them.

Barriers to travel will continue to exert a strong pull component, keeping potential travelers at home. As long as travel remains a luxury good subject to demand-elasticity, individuals will decide how best to spend discretionary time and money. Removing barriers whenever possible, such as through the development of barrier-free access, will increase overall demand for travel, but other barriers are beyond the present abilities of the travel industry to overcome.

Economic conditions will continue to be the major factor in the travel decision process. Through the 1990s, prevailing conditions of moderate growth and low interest rates are predicted to continue. With respect to the effects on travel trends, the outlook is mixed. Interest rates affect currency valuation, especially in the developed world. A developed country with high interest rates, such as Germany during the early 1990s, will see more international currency flow into it to purchase financial instruments (e.g., bonds). This has the effect of raising the value of the Deutsche Mark against other countries' currency. The higher a country's currency value with respect to some other country, the more products are imported and the less exported. Since international tourism is an export for the tourist receiving country, low currency values translate into increased tourist flows.

Low interest rates also affect consumer groups in different ways. Much has been written about the mature (over 50 years of age) market in the developed world, especially with respect to the total wealth they hold. Many people in the upper age brackets have relatively low living expenses. Mortgage costs, college education, and other high-ticket items have either been eliminated or are on the decline. Earnings have peaked, leaving the mature market with high levels of discretionary spending. Since many people in this category invest in interest bearing accounts (e.g., certificates of deposit), persistent low interest rates will erode the spending power of the group.

On the other hand, for consumers in the debt accumulation period of their lives, refinancing loans such as home mortgages can free up substantial money for other uses. Members of the tourism industry that follow these trends will likely shift marketing programs to rely less heavily on those people losing discretionary income from low interest rates and intensify efforts to attract consumers that have benefitted from the trend.

Conclusion

Travel demand is a difficult concept to operationalize. There are countless success stories where advertising or promotional programs have resulted in substantial increases in visitation. Similarly, there are numerous successful tourism developments that obviously have certain desirable attributes in sufficient supply. What those attributes might be and how people evaluate them with respect to internal motives, wants, and values is still an untapped field. An analogy to understanding tourism demand and traveler behavior can be found in the research surrounding superconductors. Physicists can achieve superconductivity results in controlled laboratory settings. They even know that certain materials are better superconductors under varying conditions than others. These results have been recorded and replicated. What they don't know is why or how it occurs. If it is difficult to figure out why physical, inanimate properties behave the way they do under certain conditions, it is even more difficult to determine why individuals travel and how they choose destinations.

Later in this book market segmentation is discussed, detailing a process for grouping individuals with certain traits together. The information in this chapter is the basis for much of that work commonly referred to as psychographic or benefit segmentation.

The study of traveler behavior, however, extends beyond direct applications to marketing and destination development. Understanding the movement into new forms of tourism (e.g., alternative forms of tourism) provides insight into societal trends reflecting a generation's lifetime of experiences. Future tourism is as much a part of what we know about our present travelers as are the experiences now being acquired by the next centuries' wandering hordes. In that sense, traveler behavior is an ever changing field of study and opportunity for scientists, tourism industry practitioners, host societies, and travelers themselves. If the ultimate goal is to understand the complexities of the individual travel decision process, leading to enlightened destination development, traveler behavior is an important part of the development equation.

EXECUTIVE SUMMARY

Using Maslow's need hierarchy, it is possible to categorize travel behavior by needs fulfilled. Once the first two basic needs are met, travel begins to assume a more important role in a person's life.

Understanding needs fulfilled through travel is not sufficient for understanding the travel decision process. Wants, expressed through motives, are much more important factors in the decision to travel.

Travel motivations can be assigned to three categories: activity-centered, patterns of participation, and background characteristics. Activity-centered motives allow for tourism to be classified into broad based groupings such as ethnic, cultural, recreation, business, etc. Patterns of participation can be used to group travelers by demand for services. Background characteristics allow for various types of segmentation (i.e., demographic, psychographic) to be used to explain reasons for travel and destination selected.

There are numerous types of consumer decision models available for explaining purchase behavior. The most commonly used, including touristic products, is termed Linear Compensatory with Weighted Components. This model assumes product attributes are weighted according to their importance, which then allows for different products to be compared according to the degree each one contains some or all of the most important attributes. Products (destinations) selected for purchase possess more of the important attributes, according to their assigned value, than all other products (destinations).

Various models exist to depict the entire travel process. The first of these is a spatial model which describes various trip stages in which an individual would find him/herself, including what happens in each stage. Each stage is differentiated by physical, geographical separation from the last stage. Recently, a sociocultural trip model describing various psychological states a person passes through with relationship to cultures encountered has been offered to explain what happens to an individual as a result of physical separation from home.

Alternative forms of tourism, such as ecotourism, are becoming increasingly popular. Three factors determine what can be classified as an alternative form of tourism: rejection of mass tourism, meaning small group size, longer lengths of stay, and close interaction with host societies; experiences provided are more sympathetic to hosts and their habitats (i.e., less intrusive, more sustainable); and, more rewarding for people involved in providing touristic goods and services (i.e., more direct economic impact to local providers).

Barriers to travel can be considered as an inverse pull component serving to keep people in their home community. The most common barriers encountered in the literature include, money, time, health and family life cycle. Monitoring current trends for certain segments of society with respect to each barrier can help determine when a barrier ceases being a home pull component and becomes a home push or attraction pull opportunity.

REFERENCES

Bilkey, W. 1953. A Psychological Approach to Consumer Behavior Analysis. *Journal of Marketing* 17:18–25.

Brown, P. 1981. Psychological Benefits of Outdoor Recreation, 13–17. In J.R. Kelly, ed. *Social Benefits of Outdoor Recreation*. Washington, D.C.: U.S. Department of Agriculture, Forest Service.

Bruno, A., and A. Wildt. 1975. Toward Understanding Attitude Structure: A Study of the Complimentarity of Multi-Attribute Attitude Models. *Journal of Consumer Research* 2:137–145.

Butler, R. 1990. Alternative Tourism: Pious

Hope or Trojan Horse? *Journal of Travel Research* 28(3): 40–45.

Clawson, M., and J. Knetsch. 1966. *Economics of Outdoor Recreation*. Baltimore: Johns Hopkins Press.

Cohen, E. 1972. Toward a Sociology of International Tourism. *Social Research* 39:164–182.

Cohen, E. 1987. "Alternative Tourism"—A Critique. *Tourism Recreation Research* 12(2):13–18.

Crompton, J. 1979. Motivations for Pleasure Vacation. *Annals of Tourism Research* 6(4):408–424.

Dann, G. 1977. Anomie, Ego Enhancement and Tourism. *Annals of Tourism Research* 4:184–194.

Dybka, J. 1987. A Look at the American Traveler: The U.S. Pleasure Travel Market Study. *Journal of Travel Research* 25(3):2–4.

Gartner, W., and J. Hunt. 1987. An Analysis of State Image Change over a Twelve-Year Period (1971–1983). *Journal of Travel Research* 26(2):15–19.

Grinstein, A. 1955. Vacations: A Psycho-Analytic Model. *International Journal of Psycho-Analysis* 36 (3):177–185.

Hunt, J., P. Brown, and A. Kinzler. 1972. *Utah Motor Vehicle Travel 1971–1972*. Logan, Utah: Institute for the Study of Outdoor Recreation and Tourism, Utah State University.

Ibsen, H. 1979 [1886]. *An Enemy of the People*. Norwalk, Conn.: Easton Press Edition.

Ingram, D., and P. Durst. 1989. Nature-Oriented Tour Operators: Travel to Developing Countries. *Journal of Travel Research* 28(2):11–15.

International Academy for the Study of Tourism. 1990. Theoretical Perspectives on Alternative Forms of Tourism. *Journal of Travel Research* 28(3):39.

Irwin, P., W. Gartner and C. Phelps. 1990. Mexican-American/Anglo Cultural Differences as Recreation Style Determinants. *Leisure Sciences* 12:335–348.

Jafari, J. 1987. Tourism Models: The Sociocultural Aspects. *Tourism Management* 8(2):151–159.

Kotler, P. 1982. *Marketing for Non-Profit Organizations*. Englewood Cliffs, N.J.: Prentice-Hall Inc.

Lessig, V. 1976. Measurement of Dependencies Between Values and Other Levels of the Consumer's Belief Space. *Journal of Business Research* 83:227–239.

Livy. 1978 [circa 24 B.C.], *History of Early Rome*. Norwalk, Conn.: Easton Press Edition.

1990 Market Study. 1990. *Meeting and Convention Magazine* November:21–33.

Maslow, A. 1954. *Motivation and Personality*. New York: Harper and Row.

McIntosh, R., C. Goeldner, and B. Ritchie. 1995. *Tourism: Principles, Practices, and Philosophy*. 7th ed. New York: John Wiley and Sons.

Nichols, C. and D. Snepenger. 1988. Family Decision Making and Tourism Behavior and Attitudes. *Journal of Travel Research* 26(4):2–6.

Pitts, R., and A. Woodside, 1986. Personal Values and Travel Decisions. *Journal of Travel Research* 25(1):20–25.

Rokeach, M. 1968. *Beliefs, Attitudes and Values*. San Francisco: Josey-Bass, Inc.

Schmoll, G. 1977. *Tourism Promotion*. London: Tourism International Press.

Schreyer, R., D. Lime, and D. Williams. 1984. Characterizing the Influence of Past Experience on Recreation Behavior. *Journal of Leisure Research* 16(1):131–149.

Smith, V. 1989. *Hosts and Guests*. 2nd ed. Philadelphia: University of Pennsylvania Press.

Stankey, G. and R. Schreyer. 1987. Attitudes Toward Wilderness and Factors Affecting Visitor Behavior: A State-of-Knowledge Review. 246–293. *Proceedings-National Wilderness Research Conference 1985: Issues, State-of-Knowledge, Future Directions*. Ogden, Utah: Intermountain Research Station.

Sweet, J. 1990. The Portals of Tradition: Tourism in the American Southwest. *Cultural Survival Quarterly* 14(2):6–8.

Wahab, S. 1975. *Tourism Management*. London: Tourism International Press.

Wilkie, W. and E. Pessemier. 1973. Issues in Marketing's Use of Multi-Attribute Attitude Models. *Journal of Marketing Research* 10:428–441.

Woodside, A., B. Pearce, and M. Waldo. 1988. Urban Tourism: An Analysis of Visitors to New Orleans and Competing Cities. *Journal of Travel Research* 27(3):22–30.

CHAPTER NINE

Attraction Development

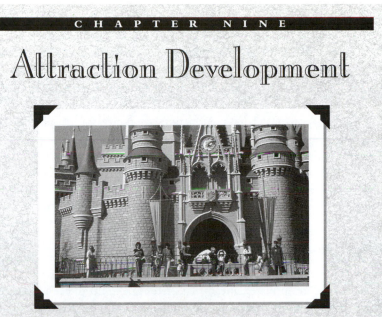

*Cinderella's Castle at Disney World in Orlando, Florida, a
premier private-sector attraction.
Photo by the author*

Learning Objectives

Understand that attractions form the pull component of the
push/pull equation and that attraction types can be grouped into
eleven different categories.

•

Examine the basic principles of attraction development.

•

Examine the principles of feasibility analysis for attractions.

•

Review factors that must be considered in any attraction
location decision.

•

Review concepts and methods used to identify and delineate
a trade area.

•

Examine different location decision models.

•

Review benefit or revenue/cost-analysis procedures including
selection of an appropriate interest or discount rate.

•

Review techniques, and the issues surrounding the use of them,
to value publicly held attractions.

INTRODUCTION

Attractions form the core of the tourism experience. They are the counter-balancing part of the demand/supply or push/pull equation addressed in the previous chapter. Attractions are the reason people travel to a particular destination. Hotels/motels, restaurants, souvenir shops, etc., all depend on the existence of at least one primary destination attraction. The primary attraction can be a stand-alone operation or the conglomeration of many smaller attractions into a unified whole. Understanding relationships between different types of attractions is an important part of attraction development.

Attractions are not easy to categorize. They come in all shapes and sizes, appeal to different groups, have diverse ownership, and present different opportunities and problems to developers and members of the host society. Amusement parks, water parks, resorts, nature-based parks (public and private), mega-malls, etc., make up the broad category of attractions. Not all attractions are compatible with each other and the beginning point of any attraction development program is to understand the unique features of the area (e.g. natural, sociocultural), and work within given limitations. Not all successful attraction developments have used this approach, but these are generally large mega-developments that create their own community to support their attraction.

Getz (1991) offers a model depicting the supply side of the tourism industry where attractions constitute the primary reason for the existence of tourism related businesses (Figure 9.1). Without attractions of some type, a tourism industry of any note cannot exist.

This chapter begins with a brief overview of the types of attractions most commonly discussed in the tourism literature. It then summarizes the basic principles that should be considered for successful attraction development. The remainder of the text, which constitutes the core section, discusses the various externalities affecting attraction development and analytical techniques to value private and public sector attractions.

TYPES OF ATTRACTIONS

Almost anything can be an attraction. The determining factor in attraction development is not what exists or can be built, but how the attraction is managed, where the attraction is located, who it is an attraction for, how it is interpreted, and what significance it has for local residents and visitors.

Attraction types can be grouped into eleven different categories. Many types of attractions can be allocated to more than one category,

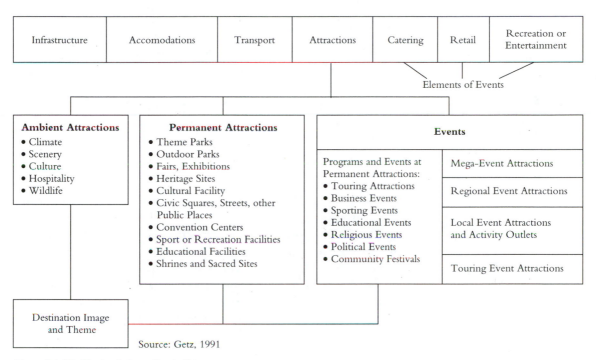

Figure 9.1 *The Tourism Industry Supply Side*

which helps them draw from diverse markets. However, for the purposes of classification, the characteristics which exert the strongest pulling power determine the category. For example, recreation activities fall into many different categories and are not included as a separate category in the list below. This does not mean they are unimportant; rather, the following categories should be examined with respect to what resources make an attraction amenable to various activity types.

The reader will note striking similarities between the different types of tourism described in the previous chapter and the attraction categories below. Say's Law that supply creates demand can be restated as supply categorizes demand, meaning that it is often easier to name something intangible (i.e., travel motivations) after a tangible characteristic (predominant site feature or activity). Thus, the following list is brief, as many of the explanations in the previous chapter to define types of tourism are sufficient to describe attraction types.

1. Natural—Natural resource characteristics such as dominant land or water features, flora and fauna, and their respective climates form either the main characteristics or supply supporting features of most attractions. Because of their attraction appeal, unique natural resource characteristics are often in the public domain in order to protect them from major transformational development. Private attractions, which rely more on built environments, often require particular climatic characteristics for success. For example, Disney properties are located in areas with season-extending climates. Their large capital outlays in a physical plant require sufficient season length to maximize return on investment.

2. Business—Large metropolitan areas are the centers of business tourism activity. The conglomeration of manufacturing, financial services, government, and individuals which collectively form large markets make metropolitan areas attractions for business tourism. For example, a supporting infrastructure of accommodations and food service operations, together with publicly supported convention centers, has led to a growth in conference business in metropolitan areas. Rural areas, although less important as centers of business activity, have begun to actively seek the convention/conference aspect of business tourism. Large and small resort operations are increasingly active in attracting this market segment. The combination of rural surroundings with an aesthetically appealing natural resource base adds an element of pleasure activity to convention/conference business tourism.

3. Historic—Relics of the past, whether they are remains of built environments or places where significant events took place, can be an attraction. Some sites may require restoration or preservation before becoming an attraction, but the key element determining success is interpretation. Sites from early history or prehistory need grounding, such as an explanation of their significance and relationship to modern-day life. Interpretation that both entertains and educates is necessary for a historical attraction to have strong appeal. Colonial Williamsburg, Virginia, and Gettysburg, Pennsylvania are two examples where interpretation of period living and historical events respectively has resulted in major historical attractions. For more information on interpretation, refer to Chapter 7.

4. Ethnic/Cultural—The way different people live, work, play, and worship comprise ethnic/cultural attractions. Many cultures do not see the uniqueness of their life as an attraction for other people. While this perception may be changed, the presentation of an ethnic/cultural attraction must be undertaken with sensitivity. Ethnic/cultural uniqueness, if it is offered as an attraction, must be

given the same protection as other attractions, subject to transformational change, as sustainable development will only be possible if the attraction remains relatively intact.

5. Friends and Relatives—Reinforcing personal relationships is described as a major tourism motivator in Chapter 8. There is no conscious effort made to develop friends and relatives attractions; however, recognizing their drawing power is important for the development of ancillary attractions. Attractions in close proximity to a friend or relative attraction market may initiate special programs to induce visitors to bring along their guests.

6. Medical—Health spas were some of the first medical centers recognized as tourist attractions. Resort health centers are now more common, treating a wide variety of ailments. Advances in medical science have led to specialized diagnostic and treatment centers with worldwide reputations. The Mayo Clinic in Rochester, Minnesota, is an example where a large tourism industry has developed to handle the influx of domestic and international patients and accompanying persons to the clinic.

7. Special Events—Special events such as annual festivals or infrequent mega-events (e.g., Olympics) serve as important short-term attractions. However, as generators of repeat visitation or destination awareness, they perform poorly. Mega-events, with the television exposure they receive, are viewed as destination promotions. However, as Ritchie and Smith (1991) discovered even the exposure received from hosting a Winter Olympics does not translate into significant destination awareness. Awareness decay begins shortly after the event is over and media exposure ceases.

   Special events are most useful as attractors when they showcase community values. Events which reinforce the image(s) destination residents wish to project serve the twofold purpose of enhancing image development efforts and increasing local pride in the community.

8. Government—Regional or national capitals are attractions because of the location of governmental headquarters. Governments have a tendency to glorify their accomplishments by building monuments, museums, and other symbols of their potency. Capitals, then, generate attraction appeal through the business of governments and by offering built attractions for tourists.

9. Parks—Many of the publicly provided parks are included in the natural resource category. Private-sector parks are much different and

rely mostly on a built environment for their attraction appeal. The most obvious of the private sector parks are the amusement or theme parks. Theme parks have grown into self-sufficient community attraction complexes, offering a range of services found in any destination community. This evolution of theme parks into resort complexes poses interesting dilemmas for destination development. The enclave approach separates tourists from community residents, and little if any cultural contact results. While social impacts may be less from enclave development, economic impact may also be reduced, especially if the attraction utilizes sources outside of the local area for needed goods. It can be argued that theme parks which rely on mass tourism markets for income are better suited to enclave development, as little if any beneficial cultural contact results from mass tourism developments. The enclave approach also allows for intensive site planning, reducing the spread of development and lessening the chances for widespread environmental impact to occur.

On the other hand, successful theme park development often leads to other economic activity outside of the enclave, resulting in development spread. This development spread is often not controlled by intensive site planning and indirectly the well planned and managed theme park can cause major environmental and sociocultural impacts from development outside its borders. Development spread is explored in more detail in Chapter 12.

10. Religious—Religious attractions are the most difficult to discuss from a development perspective. It is not necessarily the types of facilities constructed to host tourists that pose the most difficulty, but rather how religious attractions come into being. Most attraction developments start with a base of support, such as an area's natural resources, proximity to markets, or the presence of some other economic activity such as medical services or government. A religious attraction's base of support is the ethereal element of faith, and therefore is not predictable. Some of the more famous religious attractions include Mecca, the birthplace of Mohammed; Rome, the seat of power for the Catholic Church; and Salt Lake City, the headquarters of the Mormon religion (see Hudman and Jackson, 1992).

The first appearance of the Virgin Mary to a group of children in Medjugorje, Bosnia Hercogovina, formerly Yugoslavia, on June 25, 1981, and every day thereafter touched off an unrivaled tourism boom for this heretofore unknown destination. Before the war in Bosnia Hercogovina, an average of 4,000 visitors a day poured into the town, and in the 1980s over 10 million visitors from all over the world descended on Medjugorje. Recent conversations with those monitoring development in Medjugorje indicate that the war in surrounding areas has had little impact on visitor numbers. The city has over 8,000 commercial beds, with additional developments in neighboring cities (Vukonic', 1992). Similar "visions" in Lourdes, France transformed a little village into a major tourism destination. Although religious attractions can be built and even themed (e.g., Bible World), there is no substitution for spontaneous appearances of religious figures in the impact these events have on tourism development in areas with no other noteworthy attraction base.

In a similar vein, famous people's birthplaces take on the appearance of shrines. Presidential homesteads such as Jimmy Carter's in Plains, Georgia not only literally put Plains on the map, but is the home of the Carter Presidential Library, a major tourist attraction for the area. One of the best examples of this phenomenon is Graceland, the home of Elvis Presley outside of Memphis, Tennessee. The number of visitors to Presley's mansion rival figures for some of the more popular religious sites.

11. Other Built Attractions—Zoos, aquariums, sports arenas, and so on could all make up separate categories. They are grouped together in this category for simplicity and because they all require facility construction. Simply because they are grouped together in one category does not detract from their attraction potential. Many urban areas are beginning to rely more heavily on built attractions to complement already-existing business tourism.

PRINCIPLES OF ATTRACTION DEVELOPMENT

This section discusses the sequential stages of attraction development, beginning with a thorough understanding of what currently exists. Secondly, it offers an assessment approach for the attractions identified in Step one and finally an attraction mix strategy is formulated.

Inventory

Attractions are not always easy to identify, especially in the absence of obvious natural or man-made features. Therefore, the first step in attraction development is to inventory all existing and potential attractions. A potential attraction is one that may already exist but has not been previously recognized as an attraction. For example, the northern lights (aurora borealis) are common sights above the 45th parallel. Visitors from areas where the Northern Lights are not visible may not know they exist, and even if they do, they may not be aware of the time or conditions most likely for them to appear. Hence, the problem is not only in marketing the natural occurence as an attraction, but in providing the right type of information/interpretation for the visitor to fully appreciate the phenomonen.

Attraction inventory is not always an easy task, usually requiring a great deal of time and the assistance of many people in order to list the entire range of attractions available. Attractions should be inventoried by category such as those described above; Figure 9.2 shows a sample attraction inventory worksheet.

Assessment

Once attractions are inventoried, they should be evaluated. The Tourism Center at the University of Minnesota (1991) identifies five criteria for evaluating attractions.

Quality

Tourists, like other consumers, seek value for their money. Product quality determines value. High attraction quality goes beyond competent customer assistance, neat and pleasing facilities, and efficient operations to include natural and sociocultural resource protection. Maintaining the quality of an area's resource base sets the stage for the projection of quality services for all aspects of destination services.

Many private-sector organizations provide quality assessment of attractions by rating and evaluating member businesses. However, for those attractions which are not affiliated with a larger organization, quality assessment must be done at the local level. Local groups must also assess attraction quality in terms of integration with community resource values. A through review of service quality is undertaken in the next chapter.

Authenticity

Authenticity reflects a "sense of place." Tourists may have limited experience with a destination, and what they perceive exists may be acquired from many different sources. Actual visitation results in new perceptions. Attractions offered to tourists represent the perceived authenticity of the destination. Many successful communities rely almost exclusively on built attractions such as casinos, water parks, and so on. However, when a decision is made to move in the direction of built attractions that are not integrated within the sociocultural or natural resource base of the area, the destination moves into a higher risk category. Destinations relying exclu-

CULTURAL or HISTORIC Attraction	Attraction exists (✓) or number	Area has potential to develop the attraction in			Description/Notes/Problems
		1 yr?	3 yrs?	5 yrs?	
Archaeological Sites Art Galleries Antique and Craft Shops Battlefields Birthplaces or Homes of Famous People					
Burial Grounds Ceremonial Dances Churches Conservatories Costumed Events					
Covered Bridges Early Settlements Ethnic Celebrations Ethnic Restaurants or Grocery Stores Exhibits					
Famous Historical Buildings Flumes Folk Art Collections Ghost Towns Historic Building Tours					
Historic Railroads Indian Culture Landmarks Lumber Camps Mansions					
Memorials Mines Missions Monuments Museums					
Native Folklore Newsworthy Places Old Forts Pioneer Churches Pioneer Homes					
Re-Enactments of Historical Events Ruins Special "Nationality" Days Theaters (Stage Productions, Film) Trains					
Victorian Buildings And, What Else?					

Overall Assessment of Cultural/Historic Attractions

Excellent		Average		Poor	Score
5	4	3	2	1	

Source: Tourism Center, Minnesota Extension Service, 1991

Figure 9.2 *Inventory of Cultural/Historic Attractions*

sively on non-authentic built attractions must constantly evaluate competitors, as these attractions are easily substitutable. To prosper, non-authentic attractions must constantly change, improve product quality, adjust to market trends, and be heavily budgeted for promotion and marketing. They are also more likely to undergo rapid development transformation as they respond to market trends. Countering the risk assumed by a development strategy that emphasizes non-authentic attractions is the financial reward that comes from catering to a mass market.

Development of authentic attractions is more compatible with alternative forms of tourism and a sustainable development strategy. Authenticity represents what currently exists; cultural, historical, and natural resources form the foundation of establishing authenticity. Almost every area has something already in place that cannot be replicated elsewhere. The trick is to realize what those resources are and present them to visitors as representative of the area's sense of place. Too much development or too rapid development changes what exists and by definition changes authenticity. Authenticity becomes transitory and subject to interpretation.

Examples of authentic attractions are theme communities which represent the ethnic heritage of the residents. Integration with existing commercial activity may also lead to the development of authentic attractions. Farm stays, roadside fruit and vegetable stands, tours of processing facilities, and farm tours which offer agricultural education as an attraction are all examples of integrating authentic attractions with existing commercial activity. As discussed in Chapter 7, community development strategies affect the type and level of social impacts that result as well as the magnitude of the economic returns. In general terms, the farther removed from an authentic attraction the destination community becomes, the greater the potential for higher levels of sociocultural impacts, but also for higher economic returns.

Uniqueness

As more destinations seek to develop a tourism attraction base, uniqueness will become even more important. As discussed, travel brings a change of place and pace. Replicating what exists in the market or in other destinations does not offer anything new to the tourist. As destinations complete their attraction inventory, they probably find a wide range of attraction development options. Finding the right mix of attractions which provides the perception of an unique experience is the challenge. Uniqueness entices people to visit. Once tourists arrive, other attractions which may not be part of the uniqueness attraction mix are still necessary to provide activity options.

Uniqueness is somewhat related to authenticity, as what is authentic about a community and its natural/sociocultural resource base can be the key element for uniqueness. However, non-authentic attractions can also be used to develop uniqueness. For example, over time with its casino development, Las Vegas, Nevada has become the gambling center of the United States. However, the use of non-authentic built attractions to establish uniqueness poses a higher risk.

Activity Expansion

All attractions require activity options. It is one thing to promote the unique natural resource base of the area, but once people arrive they must have something to do on or with the resource. Even sightseeing requires the development of a transportation infrastructure (e.g., roads, trails) to move people through an area. The more activity options, the greater the opportunity for increasing length of stay and economic returns. The key question when considering activities for certain attractions is if they are compatible with the attraction and serve to maintain the sociocultural and environmental integrity of the area. This question is pertinent to different types of attraction development, including those which are initially non-authentic and rely on large-scale facility development. If the answer to this question is no, a community consensus must be established before proceeding with development.

Drawing Power

Attraction drawing power is measured in terms of visitors. Where they come from, how far they travel, and by what means of transportation are all considerations when assessing the drawing power of attractions. Drawing power for existing attractions is most easily measured using visitor profile studies. Determining drawing power for planned or potential attractions requires a feasibility study, which will be discussed later in this chapter.

Attractions should be grouped into primary and secondary categories. Simply using drawing power in the form of visitor numbers as a determinant for primary or secondary classification may be misleading. Many times the most visited attractions are secondary or supporting attractions. This is most likely to occur in metropolitan areas where the attraction may be business travel. During breaks in business activity it is not unusual for people to visit local attractions. The local attraction may not have enough appeal to initiate travel to the area, but it is important in providing a menu of options available to visitors. In the case where primary attractions may not be readily recognized, they are best identified from visitor surveys rather than from turnstile head counts. Primary attractions help destinations distinguish their uniqueness and identity. Identifying primary attractions also assists in developing an image promotion strategy.

Attraction Mix

Once attractions are inventoried and assessed, an attraction mix strategy can be developed. Two concepts help identify the right attraction mix: Organic Bunching and Thematic Appeal.

Organic Bunching

Grouping together like attractions is termed organic bunching. The idea behind organic bunching is to create a synergistic effect. The best way to describe what happens when like attractions are grouped together is to use the example of limited access highway exits and the presence of fast food restaurants. If one fast food restaurant is located at an exit, most likely others are found in close proximity. The exception are tollways which sell exclusive food service rights to one restaurant chain. By grouping like restaurants together, total traffic is greater than the sum of what each one could attract by itself. Some restaurants attract a disproportionate share of the traffic, and they benefit more from organic bunching than the rest;

Grand Hotel on Mackinac Island, Michigan, a resort attraction. Photo by the author

however, this discrepancy is due more to brand acceptance and corporate marketing strategy, as even the weak restaurant will have more potential customers than it could attract if it were the only choice available.

Tourism attraction development can also benefit from the synergy of organic bunching. One old building is an old building. Ten old buildings is a historic district. Grouping together supporting attractions, or in some cases single entities which by themselves would not even be considered an attraction, can create the synergy needed to form a primary attraction complex. Whenever an attraction exists that is so unique that compatibility with others is not possible, it should be segregated. The Grand Hotel on Mackinac Island, Michigan is an example of a unique property which is a primary attraction in and of itself. Its appeal would not be enhanced by having accommodations of lesser quality built next to it. The development strategy employed by the Grand Hotel is to separate it from the rest of the businesses in town by a green belt area which further emphasizes the uniqueness of the attraction. One of the best examples of organic bunching and synergy is around Orlando, Florida, the location of Disney World. Disney World created its own attraction package and made sure that sufficient land space was acquired to separate it from other attractions. On the periphery, however, numerous other attractions not only benefit from the traffic coming to Disney World, but serve to complement the region's attraction package (Fodness, 1990). All regional attractions benefit from this symbiotic relationship by having access to a larger market without bearing the burden of single entity promotion. An attraction mix strategy should identify those attractions which would benefit from the principle of organic bunching.

Thematic Appeal

With the success enjoyed by Disney properties, many private- and public-sector attractions are adopting a theme approach. Theme parks remain the leader in creating an atmosphere of escape and fantasy. The fundamental idea behind theme park development is psychologically transforming the individual to a different place and time, including places of make believe or fantasy (Milman, 1988). However, psychological transformation is not a prerequisite for theming. For example, public attractions are embracing the concept, as evidenced by museums staging special exhibitions of impressionist paintings or aquariums and zoological gardens developing south seas or safari habitats. Almost any attraction can be themed, including entire communities. The idea behind theming is uniqueness. Themes provide a basic identity for an attraction which can be supported through an image development strategy. Themes can range from the fantasy land of Disney to the more subdued theme of an early lumber town's authentic restoration. Themes can also be integrated into the existing lifestyle of local residents. For many small rural communities this may be the best approach, as when tourism development is integrated into local economic and social lifestyles, it functions as simply one of the local industries rather than the predominant exchange earner.

FEASIBILITY ANALYSIS

Attraction development inevitably involves an economic analysis of performance. Justifying the continuation of an existing attraction or estimating potential economic contributions of a proposed attraction involves some estimate of costs and benefits. The type of economic analysis performed depends on attraction ownership. Private sector attractions are concerned about the bottom line. Will the attraction provide a return on investment, and if so, how much? Public sector attractions, although not as concerned about return on investment, are increasingly under pressure to justify their present state, or lack thereof, of operational value. Many times value measures are used for budget allocation purposes.

The topic of feasibility analysis has been addressed in other parts of this book. For example, Chapter 10 discusses market and situation analyses which should be performed to identify the strengths, weaknesses, opportunities, and threats for existing business. In this chapter, the focus is on new entrants into the market. Specifically, what does a potential attraction have to consider before allocating capital resources to development? When public sector attractions are considered, the focus shifts to various techniques utilized to assess value.

Morrison (1989:89) defines a feasibility analysis as "a study of the potential demand for and economic feasibility of a business or other type of organization." In other words, will the business make money?

A series of questions direct the feasibility analysis:

1. What product will be developed? Tourism attractions are experiential products, and a thorough understanding of the product must precede any attempt to define the market.

2. Who comprises the market? After defining the product, it is necessary to determine who is attracted to the product. Is it one developed for children, adults, or seniors?

3. Where is the market located? The expected drawing power of the attraction determines the market area. Part of determining drawing

power is identifying any competing attractions between the proposed attraction and the market. Uniqueness increases market area. A complete answer to this question requires an assessment of whether the attraction is expected to be of the primary or secondary variety. Remember, secondary attractions rely on the existence of a primary attraction for their market.

4. How large is the market? Once a market area and potential customers are identified, secondary data sources such as Census Bureau statistics can be used to estimate the total size of the potential market. Market estimates should include, in addition to absolute size, income differentials. How many potential customers have incomes in the range necessary for travel to the area?

5. Is the market likely to grow, shrink, or stay the same? Again using census data, it is possible to estimate the future size of the market. In the case of a secondary attraction, future markets will be determined either by growth in the area of the primary attraction market or be a function of the changing size of the market currently in place.

Location

After the above questions have been addressed, suitable sites for attraction location can be considered. There are two different types of location analysis that must be performed. The first is a regional location decision, and the second involves specific site selection. The first decision, involving the region in which to locate, should be easy to answer. For example, if downhill skiing is identified as the primary activity to be offered, the range of options becomes limited to those areas with sufficient annual snowfall, or cold temperatures for snow-making, to have a season of sufficient length to meet revenue objectives. Areas become even more limited if the planned attraction must exist in a synergistic relationship with other similar attractions. However, if the attraction is of such magnitude that it is expected to be a resort destination providing sufficient services to be a stand-alone operation, then the range of options is much wider.

Assuming that the attraction is not large enough to be a stand-alone operation, then the location analysis decision includes investigating each possible area's market base with respect to current supply/demand situations. Although models exist for determining an area's demand potential with respect to current supply, most deal with retail store location and for the most part assume customers are familiar with the products offered. Some of these models are presented later, but their use for attraction location decisions is constrained by the nature of the tourism product. Since

PLANNED DEVELOPMENT OF CANCUN

Cancun, Mexico is a planned development, the product of a government agency and its policy of active intervention in the development of the country's tourism industry. The planning that went into the Cancun development is a direct result of bad experiences with Mexico's oldest and largely unplanned resort area of Acapulco. A review of the planning process used to develop Cancun provides an interesting case study of planning for mass tourism to achieve broad socioeconomic goals.

Acapulco is Mexico's oldest international resort center and for years one of its most affluent. Operating as a domestic retreat, it began to receive international attention during the late 1940s. Since little was known about tourism's dark side, little resort planning took place in Acapulco. Infrastructure and housing capacity were overwhelmed by the rapid growth of Acapulco (population increases averaging 15 percent annually). Slums sprang up on the hills overlooking Acapulco Bay, and the bay itself became a cesspool of untreated sewage. It was not an example of mass tourism at its best.

In 1974, the Mexican government created FONATUR (Fondo Nacional de Fomento al Turismo). It has broad development responsibilities with resources to support its activities. Its primary functions include identifying sites for future resort development, assisting the development of Mexican tourist businesses through loan programs, providing regular and oversight responsibility for existing developments, and purchasing land to initiate plans for future developments. Funded by oil revenues and World Bank loans, FONATUR began an aggressive period of resort expansion during the 1970s.

Site selection of FONATUR–planned resorts was based on two primary goals: 1) New resorts should be located in areas suffering from high unemployment with limited opportunities to develop alternative industries; and 2) resort development should serve as a catalyst for other development opportunities such as agriculture, handicrafts, and industry.

Previous resort-site selection work undertaken during the 1960s by the Bank of Mexico identified the Cancun area as possessing significant tourism resources with limited opportunity to develop other industries but tourism. Cancun is located in the Quintana Roo state, which at the time was Mexico's least populated state with the population concentrated in few small urban areas. It was also one of Mexico's poorest states. One of the reasons for its relatively low population and poor standard of living was the absence of any suitable soil (shallow limestone) for agriculture or oil reserves, Mexico's two largest industries.

The selection of Cancun also avoided an earlier problem Mexico had experienced with the resort development of Ixtapa on the Pacific coast. Land needed for Ixtapa was acquired by the Mexican government in a process simply described as eminent domain. Although people were paid individually and collectively for their land, many were not able to handle the displacement. Money did not compensate people for the loss of place that resulted when Ixtapa was built. Cancun, on the other hand, had less than 200 residents, mostly fishermen, so even if displacement problems occurred they were on a much smaller scale.

FONATUR entered into the development phase of Cancun with four main objectives: to increase employment opportunities, increase the number of the country's resorts and hopefully the number of tourists to Mexico, increase foreign exchange earnings through tourism, and act as a catalyst for additional regional development. It is the first and last objectives that deserve some attention.

There is no doubt employment in the area has increased. Since the beginning of construction in 1971 under the guidance of IN-FRATUR, FONATUR's predecessor, over 10,000 hotel rooms have been built with the ability to host over 2,000,000 visitors annually. Given that there were less than 200 residents in the area before development, new migrants from all parts of Mexico descended on Cancun. Included in the development plans were a workers' city with low-cost housing and other necessary services. Given the rate of development in and around Cancun, some question whether the workers' city is sufficient to handle the area's growth. Still, the situation experienced in Acapulco has yet to arise. The second objective, increasing regional development opportunities, must also be analyzed. The Cancun development has increased regional development opportunities but not so much as expected in the areas of agriculture, handicrafts, and other industry. What has increased is the number of small resort centers operating outside of the Cancun development zone. It is this ancillary development, or development spread, that poses threats to environmentally sensitive areas along Mexico's Caribbean coast. Some of the measures taken in Cancun, such as centralized sewage treatment centers, planned hotel zones, etc., are being defeated by development spread.

Most of the press Cancun has received has been positive. However, new criticisms continue to surface. Some claim that draining the lagoons around the hotel zone for development is an ecological disaster. Inadequate sewage treatment facilities are blamed for polluting the ground water. Still other critics point out that pre-development claims for the number of visitors and foreign exchange earnings the project was expected to accrue have not been realized. In spite of the criticism, one must look at how and why the project was planned and the information available to the planners at the time.

Cancun was built to diversify Mexico's resort offerings. Development plans were an attempt to avoid identified problems experienced at other resorts. The early site selection stage was based on social as well as economic criteria. For those reasons alone, the Cancun development is worthy of praise. Regardless of whether all the objectives have been achieved, it is important that the next generation of resort developments learn from the lessons of Cancun as it appears to have learned from the lessons of its predecessors.

Sources: Frueh, Susanne. 1986. Problems in a Tropical Paradise: The Impact of International Tourism on Cancun, Mexico. Unpublished M.S. thesis, University of South Carolina.
Gormsen, E. 1982. Tourism as a Development Factor in Tropical Countries: A Case Study of Cancun, Mexico. Applied Geography and Development 19:46-63.

tourism products are more experiential than most products, it is possible for a new attraction which supply/demand analysis calculates to be saturated to move into an area and still do well. Success may be more a factor of intangible considerations than for other types of businesses. However, the supply/demand analysis determines if a discrepancy exists, and if there is room in the area for an attraction similar to the others currently located there, or if success will depend more heavily on brand identification through product differentiation. Techniques available to estimate supply/demand relationships are discussed in more detail later in this chapter.

Supply/demand is just one of the factors that an attraction must consider in its location decision. Others may be just as critical and affect both region of location and site selection. Specific site selection does not work well for a business with a large trade area. Instead, Smith (1983) suggests using an aggregate-area approach focusing on the potential for development within a region rather than for a specific site. With that in mind, what follows is a sampling of the more important factors to consider when selecting a region for attraction location.

Transportation

Industrial location analysis heavily emphasizes transportation access. Bulky manufactured products generally have two options—highway or rail. Depending on the size and relative value of a manufactured product, adequate access to transportation facilities may not be enough. Costs generally increase with distance traveled to market, and many manufacturers choose to locate their manufacturing plant near large markets. An advertisement in the on-board magazine of Northwest Airlines (January 1991) touts Tennessee as a prime industrial plant location due to lower than average wage rates and situation within one day's driving distance of over 76% of the U.S. population (Figure 9.3). Although transportation is an important consideration for attraction location decisions, it is not as critical as for other industrial products. Remote locations do not pose as much of a problem for attractions as they did before the development of limited access highways and the expansion of air travel. Since the customer comes to the attraction, location analysis should identify the different transportation modes serving the area and, more importantly, the cost of using available transportation. Attractions not located in close proximity to major population centers must investigate air travel options and availability of rental cars. Deregulation of the airline industry throughout the world has made this a somewhat more difficult task with prices and routes in a constant state of flux. Attraction locations near major airline hubs or within short driving distance of major population centers are less at risk for sales decline

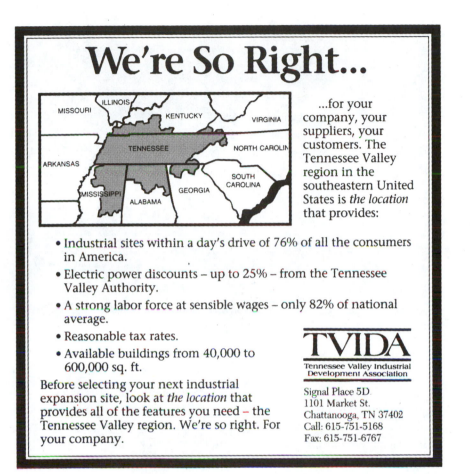

Figure 9.3 *Promoting Location Features Important for the Industry*

due to poor transportation access. As will be discussed later, when gravity models are presented, attractions located in remote areas requiring major commitments of time to reach them must develop a strong product image to overcome time/distance factor constraints.

Land Use and Costs

Land use and costs differ markedly from one region to another. For example, certain areas of the U.S. have extensive tracts of land in public ownership. This does not always preclude private development, but it makes the process of acquiring land for attraction development more time-consuming and tends to restrict certain development options. Many western U.S. ski resorts obtain special use permits enabling them to develop ski

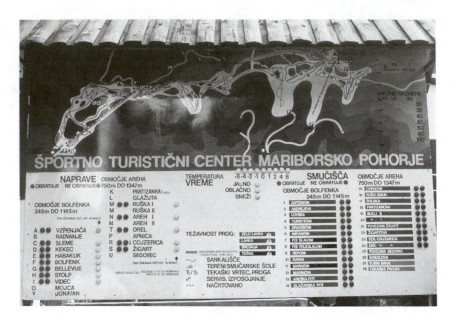

runs and construct service operations on public land. However, the process of obtaining additional permits or developing new areas can literally take decades. Even existing operations must continue to meet standards identified in the special use permit to continue operating on publicly held lands.

Land costs are also an important consideration. Generally, land prices reflect current uses and resource abundance. In the north midwestern United States, where resort attractions rely on locally available recreation opportunities, land costs may be considered reasonable, especially when compared to prices in Hawaii or Florida. Land price therefore reflects seasonality and resource availability. Larger resort attractions providing developed recreation opportunities generally use extensive tracts of land and must carefully select and design for certain uses in order to maximize the revenue generating ability of the facility. As a general rule, where land prices are high, attraction development will be more intensive, provide more services, and be priced at such a level that only the top end of the market will be potential customers.

Government

Government policies determine not only ownership of attractions but types of services that can be provided. Some countries exclude foreign ownership of land. Multinational companies operating within these countries generally enter into joint-venture arrangements or provide management services which include use of the corporate name. It has already been mentioned how government ownership of land can control attraction development, but even on private land government policies affect operations. For example, since many attractions, especially resorts, use extensive areas of land, environmental impact statements or assessments may be required. Local governments may also impose restrictions on land use and the types of services that can be provided. For example, the sale of alcoholic beverages may be subject to local regulation. A thorough investigation of the numerous ways government policies affect land use and attraction operations could constitute a separate text. Any attraction development planning team should include an expert on government laws and regulations (national, regional, and local) before reaching a final location decision.

Infrastructure

Large attractions such as resorts may be required to develop their own infrastructure when local systems are either nonexistent or inadequate. Obviously this can greatly increase costs, as land may have to be purchased for a lagoon sewage treatment system or new transportation corridors may have to be developed. In more urbanized areas, local communities will often absorb the cost of infrastructure improvements to create a greater economic base for local employment and income opportunities. Attractions locating in remote areas may not have the luxury of a community partner. Even when an attraction is built in an area with existing attractions sharing a certain infrastructure, capacity limits may require additional capital expenses to increase the system or limit the size of the development. Costs of infrastructure improvement, or in some cases development, may greatly affect a location decision.

Safety, Security, and Health Services

One may view police and health services as part of an area's infrastructure, but because of the remote locations of many attractions, it may be necessary to hire and train an internal security and health staff. Rural communities may not have sufficient resources or respond quickly enough to problems occurring at the attraction complex. Locating in an established destination area generally avoids this problem, as more often than not a community develops concurrently with the growth in attractions that would be able to provide these services.

Suppliers

Attractions must also consider the type of supplies they need. Suppliers may be required for maintenance of the physical plant and equipment, food, etc. Again, when an attraction is located in a destination area, often the existing community can supply many of these services. However, locating in remote areas increases costs since services such as laundry, if the attraction has an accommodations component, must be done in-house, requiring not only investment in a laundry building, but equipment and maintenance to keep the operation running. Food suppliers may cause the most problems for remote locations with less frequent fresh food deliveries. Inventory control is critical for operations that do not have quick access to food suppliers.

Financial

Probably one of the most difficult tasks for a new attraction is obtaining financing. Large corporations can use their leverage and credit rating for new ventures, but entrepreneurs often have difficulty raising capital for development. Attractions are considered risky ventures by many financial institutions, and without substantial collateral financing may be almost impossible to obtain from traditional financial institutions. If the proposed attraction location is within an established destination area, there is a higher probability that local financial institutions will be knowledgeable about the business and be able to analyze an attraction business plan. New ventures in remote locations outside of an established destination area may be forced to use venture capital markets for land acquisition and development.

Labor

An adequate supply of quality labor is essential for successful attraction operations. Successful attractions rely heavily on quality service, which usually requires a higher staff-to-client ratio than for other businesses. In developing countries, an educational system providing trained employees for the hospitality component of the tourism industry may not be in place. Some of the social impacts resulting from low level positions for indigenous peoples is discussed in Chapter 5. Attractions are no different from other hospitality businesses (e.g., restaurants) in that they suffer from high employee turnover rates, causing increased costs for training new hires. Also, as previously discussed (Chapter 3), location in certain areas can cause inflationary impacts for local goods and services including labor. Since labor may be a major portion of attraction operation expenditures, careful consideration of available labor supply in an area, skill level, and relative wage rates should be part of the location decision process.

Determining Trade Area

The factors discussed above should all be considered when selecting a region for attraction location. However, it is difficult to place statistical weights on any of the factors. It is up to the organization to determine which one of the factors limits probability of success and which are not considered impediments. Much of the information needed to assess factor importance can be drawn from a marketing plan which is preceded by addressing the questions posed at the beginning of the feasibility analysis section. Assuming that the organization is able to delineate a regional area that has the potential to meet its marketing and growth objectives, the next step is to select a site. This is a difficult task because attractions generally have a larger market area than other types of businesses. Much of the site selection literature focuses on retail business operations which for the most part offer tangible products. For example, a hardware store sells products that are interchangeable with those sold by other similar establishments. Research shows that a hardware store or similar retail outlet has a limited market area and site selection is an extremely important factor affecting long-term success.

One of the tactics retail establishments use to enlarge market areas is to develop brand loyalty, usually by franchising with chain organizations. The chain's buying power and supportive advertising is intended to establish name recognition for its retail outlets. Even with increased name recognition and brand affiliation, retail outlets still have relatively limited market areas.

Attractions, even those with brand name affiliation such as corporate resorts or theme parks, have an extremely difficult time defining their market area. Again, the nature of the tourism product makes it difficult to use retail location decision models for specific site selection. In fact, many factors that increase retail sales, such as location along heavily traveled corridors, work against attraction sales. Attraction market areas may be as large as the world or as small as one population center. In the case of mega-resorts, specific site selection is much less important than regional location. Since mega-resorts provide for most recreational opportunities through on site facility construction, only those regions with easy access and the right climate for the recreational opportunities offered are initially selected for consideration. Resorts with a more limited market area should spend more time on selecting the right site.

Even though retail location decision models are limited for use in site selection, for large attractions, there are times that modified versions of the models may be helpful. For smaller attractions, especially those in the secondary attraction category, retail location decision models may be more useful. The following discussion explains some of the more common models applicable to attraction location decisions, especially with respect to determining an effective trade area.

Supply/Demand

Delineation of a trade area is the first step in site selection. Reference has been made to understanding supply/demand considerations for attraction location. This entails estimating demand for the type of activities to be offered by the attraction with respect to available supply of similar attraction products in the area chosen for location consideration. If the attraction relies on supporting outdoor recreational activities, secondary data may be available to estimate future demand for those activities. For example, in the United States each state receiving money from the Federal Land and Water Conservation Fund for facility construction purposes must have completed a Statewide Comprehensive Outdoor Recreation Plan (SCORP). Included in each SCORP document are demand projections for selected outdoor recreation activities. Methods used to estimate demand vary by state, but in some cases demand for each activity is estimated by region. Attraction developers can use this information to determine which areas of a state are currently deficient in providing certain opportunities and which activities are expected to increase in popularity. Attractions providing or offering access to certain recreation activities deemed to be in short supply will be better able to select sites which appear to provide excess demand capacity. Using SCORP data to choose a location, however, does not guarantee success because the various methods used to estimate future demand may not be the most accurate. Also, because other factors such as market-area economic cycles, customer acceptance of the product, changing lifestyles, and level and quality of service affect not only future demand but amount of current sales, demand estimates should be used only as a guide to identifying possible attraction locations.

Demand estimates, whatever their source, only estimate future activity based on current situations. New products do not lend themselves to future demand estimation. For example, video recording and playback systems were not available during the 1960s; therefore accurate predictions of sales were not possible until they had been offered to the public and consumer acceptance occurred. Since many new attractions incorporate design elements that were unknown even a few years ago, demand estimates using historical data may be misleading. New products can create their own demand—Say's Law—and some successful attractions are testaments to Say's Law in action. If the attraction product is unique, innovative, and strategically located, demand will follow.

Normal Curve

One of the simplest location decision models used by retailers is the normal curve method, discussed in detail in Thompson (1982) and Ghosh and McLafferty (1987). Using existing properties, researchers can determine how large of a market area is served by a similar establishment. The procedure requires selecting a sample of customers patronizing similar establishments and plotting their home residence on a map. In this way, the proportion of customers traveling to the store from various distances can be determined. From the data, distance decay curves can be estimated (see Figure 9.4). As the distance between a particular business and one's home residence increases, probability of patronizing that establishment decreases. Of course, other factors can influence the distance decay curve, such as the image of the establishment, size of the population base, and location relationship to complimentary businesses. As a store's image increases, the market area expands. As population increases, market area contracts, and as the number of complimentary businesses in close proximity to each other increases, market area expands. These factors explain why many successful

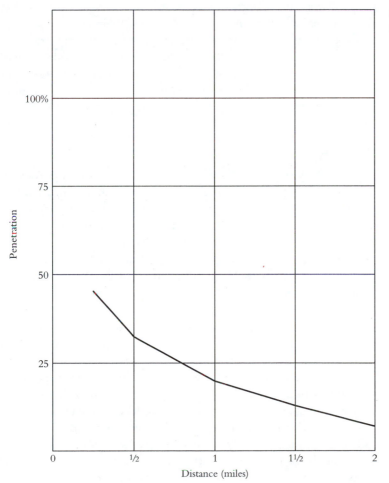

Figure 9.4 *Sample Normal Formula Curve for a Supermarket*

Source: Thompson, 1982

retail outlets are chain stores (image) and why certain businesses can saturate a market with numerous retail outlets. It also helps explain the widespread acceptance of shopping malls where synergistic effects of grouping complementary establishments occur.

Although the above discussion focuses on using normal curve analysis for retail establishment location, it also applies to attraction location. Most retail establishments locate in close proximity to their market or trade area. When the attraction is considered secondary, the size of its market area is a function of the drawing power of the primary attraction. Normal curve analysis may then be employed to choose a prime location for the secondary attraction given the drawing power and location of the primary attraction.

This is not the case, however, with primary attractions such as resorts. In fact, for most resorts to be successful, they must locate at a substantial distance from the market. Even resorts which are located within a few miles of major urban centers do not draw their business from the surrounding community but rather from tourists visiting the urban area. This is not to say that distance decay curves are not operational, but that they probably take on a different form. Since no data could be found using normal curve analysis for resort location decisions, it is not possible to determine what the shape of the distance decay curve might look like.

Analog

Analog systems are sales based. The procedure calls for estimating sales average per sub area. Sub areas are geographic units which, when aggregated, define total trade area. An underlying assumption for analog models is that the farther a customer travels to a particular establishment, the more he/she tends to purchase at one time. Identifying sales per sub area helps choose locations expected to generate maximum sales. Attractions might find analog methods useful because length of stay may be influenced by economic distance (costs associated with traveling to the attraction) and physical distance.

Data collection requirements are more difficult and costly than for normal curve analysis. In addition to determining where customers are coming from, on site expenditure data also must be collected. This makes it difficult to use analog analysis, as most existing attractions do not share this information with a possible competitor. Occasionally, secondary data may be available, possibly at the regional level, containing enough information on visitation and expenditure patterns to use analog methods. Whether secondary or primary data is used, care must be exercised to ensure that the sample chosen accurately reflects the entire population of users. For attractions, this would generally require a data collection program be established for one entire use season.

Step 1. *Regression model*

$$MS = b_0 - b_1x_1 + b_2x_2 - b_3x_3 + b_4x_4$$

Figure 9.5   *Forecasting Sales by Analog Regression Method*

MS	=	market share of analog store in zone
x_1	=	distance separating zone from store (miles)
x_2	=	size of store (100 square feet)
x_3	=	size of nearest competitor (100 square feet)
x_4	=	percentage of homes that are owner-occupied

Step 2. *Market share forecast for zone 23*

$$MS = b_0 - b_1(1.2) + b_2(650) - b_3(600) + b_4(68)$$
$$= .069$$

Step 3. *Weekly sales forecast for zone 23*

Weekly sales = MS × per capita sales potential × population in zone
= .069 × 21.08 × 1948
= \$2,833

Step 4. *Sum forecasts of all zones*

Step 5. *Adjust forecast for sales from outside trade area*

Source: Ghosh and McLafferty, 1987

Once sales data is collected, a concentric circle map is constructed delineating market zones. Information is then tabulated according to population within each zone and sales generated. Figure 9.5 provides an example of how this is done. Resulting information provides not only demarcation of trade areas but sales per sub unit. Using analog procedures for more than one site location can help determine alternative sites with the highest sales potential. Since analog analysis provides sales information, it can also be used to direct marketing and promotional efforts.

Multiple Regression

Multiple regression attempts to measure the influence of many factors, termed variables, on the drawing power of an attraction. With normal curve, there is no attempt to determine what influences a customer's choice of attraction except distance, which is an implicit factor built into the model. Also, since normal curve models are performance snapshots, there is no way to determine if certain conditions change what influence they may have on visitation. Multiple regression, on the other hand, can be used to determine the influence of as many variables as the analyst chooses on some preselected measure of performance. The analog model described above is a form of multiple regression, however its functional form is preset.

The basic multiple-regression model is an equation of the following form:

$$Y = b0 + b1X1 + b2X2 + \ldots bnxn$$

where Y (dependent variable) equals some preselected performance measure; X1 to Xn (independent variables) equals factors or variables chosen by the analyst and assumed to affect Y; b0 equals a calculated parameter which measures Y in the absence of any value for the independent variables (b0 is also referred to as the intercept term or the point where a straight line passes through the Y axis); b1 to bn(regression coefficients) equals the relative influence of each independent variable on the dependent variable.

Although the multiple-regression equation may appear to be a difficult analytical procedure, almost all computer-based statistical programs include regression models which make the computational task quite simple. The difficult task is data collection. Some of the important assumptions are that data be from a random sample of the population with variables included in the analysis measured, at least, at the interval level. Descriptive categorical data, nominal or ordinal level, are not appropriate for use in regression unless a conversion through the use of dummy variables is undertaken. For readers unfamiliar with levels of measurement or terms such as regression coefficients, explanations in statistical program manuals or the numerous research method texts available should provide enough information to use regression models.

The simplest multiple-regression models are linear, meaning that Y, the dependent variable, changes at a constant rate for every unit change in X. In other words, if sales is the dependent variable and the analysis determines that distance affects sales, then for every mile of increasing distance between attraction location and home residence of customers, there will be a corresponding increase or decrease in sales. Regressions are not always linear, but in the social sciences they are the most widely used because of their simplicity, and little information exists to expect variable associations to be anything but linear.

There are four steps required to use multiple regression. First, the analyst must select the dependent and set of independent variables to be used. The dependent variable is usually selected first, and then a set of independent variables thought to influence the dependent variable are selected. Secondly, data collection is undertaken. The use of primary data is recommended, although secondary data may be used as long as the assumptions of a random sample and level of measurement are not violated. The third step is to analyze the data and perform internal validity checks which are measures of model adequacy. This is the most difficult of the four steps, and those unfamiliar with regression analysis should consult a statistician for assistance.

The fourth step is to interpret the results. Statistical output identifies which variables are significantly influencing the dependent variable. Using a predetermined significance level, usually .05 in the social sciences, only those independent variables which meet the significance criterion are assumed to be important predictor variables and are retained in the final equation.

Although multiple regression is a more complex procedure than normal curve methods, it yields more useful data to aid in the location decision. It can help identify the factors most important for attraction success in certain areas. These factors are probably not the same for different regions. For example, the importance of regional image can be used as a variable in the equation. In situations where destination image is strong, the influence of distance may be less important. This may mean the effective trade area for a new attraction would be larger in one region than another. Also, the model allows for simulation analysis in the sense that different scenarios can be used to predict the effect on the performance variable. The flexibility, precision output, and myriad uses of regression analysis often justify the time, expense, and skill required to use it.

Fesenmaier and Roehl (1986) utilize regression analysis to evaluate the potential for campground development in Texas. Although their study is not intended to analyze the success potential of a particular site, they determine site characteristics associated with successful locations. Using the number of developed campgrounds per county as the dependent variable, they investigate the influence of various social and natural resource factors present in each county on the number of developed campgrounds (Figure 9.6). Location in areas with easy transportation access, close proximity to federal recreation areas, and lake access are some of the variables found to significantly contribute to success (Table 9.1). They also find some areas of the state could support additional campground operations. Although their work focuses on campgrounds, the analytical procedure they use is transferable to other attraction location decisions.

Gravity Models

Gravity models forecast magnitude of travel to a region based on its relative attractiveness with respect to some population center. Gravity models used today in social science research all have their roots in Newton's physical law of planetary attraction: the attraction between any two bodies is directly proportional to the masses of the two bodies and in inverse proportion to the square of the distance between them. For location analysis purposes, it is important to analyze the relative attractiveness of all regions being considered against each other. A two-region comparison equation would take the form:

$$V(1)/V(2) = A(1)/A(2)/[D(2)/D(1)]2,$$

Figure 9.6 *Variables Used to Estimate Success Potential of Campground Location*

Variable	Definition
Dependent LNCOMDEV[a]	The natural log of the number of developed campsites offered by commercial campgrounds, per county.
Independent BLACK[b]	Percentage of 1980 county population identified as Black by the 1980 Bureau of Census.
HISPANIC[b]	Percentage of 1980 county population identified as Hispanic by the 19890 Bureau of Census.
LNCPOP[b]	The natural log of the 1980 county population.
LNREGPOP[b]	The natural log of the total population of counties adjacent to the particular county.
NATURAL REGION (1)GULF[c]	Whether or not the county was located in the Gulf Coast natural resource area.
(2)HILLS[c]	Whether or not the county was located in the Texas Hill County natural resource area.
(3)MTS[c]	Whether or not the county was located in the mountain natural resource area.
(4)PINE[c]	Whether or not the county was located in the Pine Forest natural resource area.
(5)WEST[d]	Whether or not the county was located west of the 100th meridian.
LNWAREA★	The natural log of the surface acreage of lakes and reservoirs per county.
LNPUBDEV[a]	The natural log of the number of developed campsites offered by not-for-profit operations per county.
NATPFR[d]	The presence of a National Park, Forest or Recreation area within the county.
IHWAY[d]	Whether or not an interstate highway enters the particular county.
MULTI[d]	Whether or not a four-lane highway other than interstates enters the particular county.

Source: Fesenmaier and Roehl, 1986.
[a]TORIS (1984)
[b]U.S. Department of Commerce (1980)
[c]TORP (1975)
[d]compiled by author
★*Texas Almanac and Industrial Guide* (1981)

where V(1) and V(2) are the proportions of visitors from a general trade area attracted to regions 1 and 2; A(1) and A(2) are the relative attractiveness weights for regions 1 and 2; and D(1) and D(2) are distances from the center of the trade area for regions 1 and 2. Equation unknowns are measures of attractiveness for each of the regions and distance from center of trade area. Because of the unknowns in the equation, gravity models usually require some other analytical techniques be performed before they can be fully implemented. For example, measure of relative attractiveness can

TABLE 9.1   Results of Multiple–Regression Analysis
for Campground Location

Variable	Regression Coefficient	Beta Coefficient	Prob > F
Intercept	−2.28		0.00
LNCPOP	0.29	0.17	0.00
GULF	1.36	0.14	0.00
HILLS	1.03	0.13	0.01
LNWAREA	0.15	0.26	0.00
NATPER	2.01	0.21	0.00
IHIWAY	0.89	0.18	0.00
LNPUBDEV	0.20	0.18	0.00
Multiple R	0.638		
F Value	23.84		
Prob>F	0.0001		
d.f.	7,244		

Source: Fesenmaier and Roehl, 1986

be any one of a number of variables such as number of recreation opportunities in the region, number of guest rooms available, or even a measure of the touristic image of the region. Regression analysis can be used to determine the value of performance measures for each region which can then be used as a proxy for attraction. Since regression provides an approximation of the relative contribution of many variables on the preselected performance variable, it is a good candidate for determining attractiveness. Distance from the center of the trade area also must be determined. Using normal curve or analog methods, trade areas can be delineated. The mean value for distance traveled to each region can be used as the value for distance from center. Once these values are determined, a breaking point can be estimated. The breaking point is where the relative attractiveness of the two regions is equal (Converse, 1949). Repeating the procedure for all regions considered as possible resort locations results in further delineation of the trade area for every competing region with respect to all others and helps the analyst determine the attractiveness of each one.

Although gravity models have proven their ability to be effective in forecasting travel patterns (Smith, 1989), data and expertise requirements may make them expensive and time-consuming. The first step is to define the size of each region. Examples of regional delineation methods are provided in Chapter 3. Once all the regions to be analyzed are defined, a common measure of attraction must be obtained. Using some readily available regional characteristics such as number of lodging units available may be one option. Generally, the number of units in an area is a reflection of the area's ability to draw visitors, and in that case would be a good proxy for attractiveness. However, if one large poorly performing accommodation facility is located in the area, attractiveness could be overstated by simply using number of lodging units available. Also, it is possible that more attractive areas may not be accessible due to infrastructure deficiencies. In this case, using only available lodging units would understate the attraction potential of the area.

Most tourism-related examples of gravity models are in the field of recreation, and usually measure the attractiveness of a particular park or group of parks (Baxter and Ewing, 1981; Stynes et al., 1985). The lack of studies for other types of attraction location may be due to the proprietary nature of commissioned research or the lack of knowledge or perceived difficulty regarding the usefulness of the approach. Depending on the sophistication needed to develop an attractiveness variable, gravity models may be an expensive undertaking. On the other hand, attraction development is usually a very expensive proposition. Because of the accuracy of forecasting output generated, gravity models should be considered as one of the available techniques for location decision assistance.

BENEFIT/COST ANALYSIS

Almost all the location decision models discussed above provide information on trade area magnitude and expected visitation to the destination area from each sub unit in the trade area. Although it is almost impossible to accurately predict the amount of sales a new attraction locating in an area will capture, due in large part to variability between operations and the large number of variables affecting success, it is important to estimate expected revenues. Only by estimating revenues can the final part of the location decision be completed.

At the beginning of the chapter, the various factors affecting a location decision were discussed. Assuming that a regional area is chosen and various areas within the region analyzed for feasibility, then the next step is to select a specific area for attraction development. At this point, benefit/cost analysis becomes important. Benefit/cost analysis is a ratio measure of the relative benefits accruing to the attraction developer versus costs of development and operations.

In the public sector, benefits may be much harder to quantify as the organization responsible for the development may not be profit-motivated. Social welfare or benefits for a wide range of people underscore the development mission of many public sector organizations. In fact, since most public sector operations do not generate a profit, benefit/cost analysis is inverted to cost/benefit analysis and the focus is on cost-effectiveness rather than revenue maximization.

In the case of private sector operations, the emphasis is on profit and benefits are defined as revenue accruing to the owners of the operation. Revenues may be substituted for benefits and a revenue/cost analysis performed.

Revenues

Revenues are defined as the sum of all sales accruing to the attraction operation. Depending on the type of attraction, revenues may flow from many different sources. For a resort, lodging operations will generally be the largest single revenue generator, followed by food service, although user fees for golf, tennis, and gift sales may also be significant revenue sources. It is the task of the analyst to estimate all sources of revenues on an annual basis for the expected life of the operation. As previously mentioned, estimating revenues is a difficult task. Some of the location decision models discussed above also forecast use, and these estimates may form the basis for revenue projections. For an attraction that has many different revenue sources, it may be easiest to project revenues for the primary activity and assume that all other sources contribute in direct proportion to sales from the lead sector. For example, a resort with lodging, restaurants, golf, and tennis as revenue sources may find it easier to use the following method to measure total revenue. If occupancy is estimated at 60 percent annually (100 room resort) with the average number of guests per room estimated to be 2.2, and 20 percent of all guests use the golf course, then golf course revenues are predicted by the following equation:

$$Y = 132(.2)(x),$$

where Y equals revenue; 132 is the number of people available to use the golf course on any given day [$100 \times .6 (2.2)$]; (20 percent) is the estimated proportion of all guests who will golf; and x equals average green fees. Similar estimates are made for each revenue generating operation of the resort, resulting in annual total revenue estimates.

Costs

Costs are broken down into two categories, fixed and variable. Fixed costs are those that must be paid regardless of whether the resort has any customers. Any cost that is not related to use levels is fixed. For example, debt service tied to development costs, equipment or real estate leases, and management fees may all be considered fixed costs. In the long run, however, all fixed costs become variable costs. A real estate lease may be for a three-year period. When the lease period has elapsed, a decision is made whether to renew or pursue other options. At this point, real estate lease contracts become variable costs. Of course, filing for protection under bankruptcy laws makes all costs variable in nature.

Variable costs are a product of use. As soon as the attraction opens for business, there will be variable costs. Front desk, housekeeping, food service, and laundry are just a few of the expenses resort attractions encounter when they begin to accept guests. Although it is possible to estimate variable cost per guest, it is not an advisable method for determining total variable costs because of indivisibility constraints. One service person should be able to serve more than one guest. However, after a certain guest load, additional help will be required. Variable costs per guest will initially decline until an indivisibility constraint is encountered. After a certain point, guest services will suffer if additional help is not secured. At the point where the addition of one more guest causes an increase in hiring, variable costs will cease to decline on a per guest basis and begin to increase. Variable costs are best calculated based on expected use rates similar to how revenues are estimated. If the resort expects a 60-percent annual occupancy rate, variable costs should be estimated for all operations based on this figure.

Timeframe

There are two time periods that must be decided upon before benefit (revenue)/cost ratios can be computed. The first is based on the business cycle of the operation. Since most attractions are subject to seasonality constraints, it is best to use annual estimates of costs and revenues. This ensures that low as well as high seasons of use be included. Even attractions that operate continuously throughout the year may have low and high periods due to consumer preferences. Most businesses, including those in the tourism industry, operate on an annual cycle. Therefore, total revenues and costs should be projected on an annual basis.

The second timeframe consideration is much more complex as it involves an estimate of the attraction's life expectancy. Benefit/cost ratios are static in the sense that they provide a snapshot picture of expected performance based on estimates made during a specific time period. There are many factors affecting future success, including many not controllable by the attraction operator. The more years included in the revenue/cost streams, the higher likelihood of measurement error. Economic predictions of revenues and costs based on some historical time period lose their potency the further one is removed from the time period of estimation. However, some costs occur on a regular basis over a long time period. Land acquisition costs may be paid over a twenty-year time period on a land contract or fee simple deed with a lending institution holding the note. The amount of money required for long-term debt service is part of the cost stream in revenue/cost analysis. Although there is no agreement on how many years is appropriate to estimate costs and revenues, anything over ten years is pushing the credibility of economic projections. Often long-term debt service continues after ten years. For most purposes, assuming no large balloon payments after ten years, a ten-year projection should be sufficient. If the revenue/cost ratio is not greater than one using a ten-year planning period, there is little likelihood the project will eventually become a success. A ten-year period is a long time to carry a non-producing operation.

Assuming annual periods are selected for estimating revenues and costs and the life of the attraction is set at ten years, a revenue/cost stream can be displayed such as the one in Table 9.2. The last part of the analysis is to discount all revenues or costs into present value terms. Although estimates of future value are as easy and as valid as bringing all dollar estimates into present value terms, it is intuitively easier to assess performance with respect to present values. To bring all dollar estimates of costs and revenues into present value terms requires the selection of an appropriate discount rate.

TABLE 9.2   Ten-Year Revenue/Cost Stream (in thousands)

Year	Revenue	Cost
0	0	750
1	100	80
2	200	80
3	250	80
4	275	80
5	260	80
6	270	200 (renovation)
7	275	90
8	260	90
9	270	90

Discount Rate

A dollar today is worth more than a dollar in some future time period. This statement is the basis on which financial institutions operate. Interest charged for the use of someone else's money is the price paid to rent an amount of money for a specific time period. Discounting uses an appropriate rate of interest to express dollar values in some future time period in terms of their present purchasing power. Remember that in Table 9.2 a hypothetical stream of revenues and costs is presented for the entire life of the attraction. Costs and revenues occur at different times and not at the same magnitude. Usually development costs are front-heavy, meaning that a large portion occur before the attraction is even open for business. Even in a situation where the development organization has a strong credit rating, it is unlikely that all development costs can be mortgaged. Financial institutions usually require a large down payment. Since revenues start accruing in a future time period, it is important to determine if the projected revenue stream is large enough to offset future costs of debt management and operations plus initial development costs. Bringing all revenues and costs into present dollar values for comparison purposes provides a means to assess attraction feasibility. To do this, a discount rate must be chosen.

The choice of an appropriate discount rate is related to the risk of the venture. Certain investments such as U.S. Treasury bonds or bank deposits carry a low rate of interest because they are low risk. These investments are backed by the U.S. government. Other investments such as stocks generally provide higher returns if the economy grows. They can also provide large losses if the economy stagnates or declines. Still higher rates are available from investing in corporate notes, often referred to as "junk bonds." The high return from these investments only occurs if the corporation backing the notes performs well. They are some of the highest risk investments available because in the case of bankruptcy they are low on the creditor payment list.

Interest rates are comprised of three components. The first is the pure rate which in the U.S. is the rate for U.S. Treasury bonds during times of full employment and zero inflation. This is very difficult to determine since there has never been a time when these conditions prevailed. However, most economists use a figure from two to four percent for the pure rate. The second component is the rate of inflation, which is easily determined as it is one of the statistics reported on a monthly basis by most governments. The third component is the risk rate, which is dependent on the type of business operation. Attractions, primarily because of their status as a luxury good with performance highly subject to prevailing economic conditions, are considered risky ventures.

The correct rate of discount can vary, but should be higher than interest rates assigned to the safest ventures, but less than those available for "junk bonds." Different discount rates can easily be used for comparison purposes and to simulate performance under different market conditions.

Present Value Calculation

Once a discount rate is chosen, all dollar values can be converted into present value terms. The formula used for this purpose is:

$$V_0 = \frac{V_N}{(1 + i)n}$$

where Vo equals present value; V_N equals value in year N; i equals discount or interest rate; and n equals number of years of discounting. Applying this formula to the revenue/cost stream of Table 9.2 with a discount rate of 5 percent, results in the present value amounts displayed in Table 9.3. Adding up all present values for costs and revenues and dividing total revenues by total costs yields a revenue/cost ratio of 1.68. For the project to be considered feasible, the R/C ratio must be greater than 1. The same analysis can be completed for all areas being considered for site selection, and the one with the highest R/C ratio should be the one selected for site development.

Some of the factors affecting revenues and cost projections for each site include land acquisition costs, availability of labor and wage rates, size of trade area and projected demand, government regulations restricting

TABLE 9.3 Present Value Amounts of Revenues/Cost Over a 10 Year Period (in Thousands) Using a Discount Rate of 5%

Year	Revenue	Cost
0	0	750
1	95.24	76.19
2	181.82	72.73
3	215.52	68.96
4	225.41	65.57
5	203.12	62.50
6	201.50	149.25
7	195.03	63.83
8	175.67	60.81
9	174.19	58.06
PV	1,667.50	1,427.90
R/C = 1.68		

size and type of development, and capital acquisition costs. Because of these factors, it is important to analyze each area with respect to each one of the location decision factors addressed above. Only through this comprehensive process will a usable revenue/cost ratio be produced and a site chosen which provides the best opportunity for success.

The usefulness of revenue/cost ratios is not restricted to site selection. Assuming that investors can receive a rate of interest for an alternative investment in which they feel as secure as for the attraction. That rate of interest then becomes the discount rate to be used in revenue/cost calculations for the attraction. If the resulting r/c ratio is less than one, then the alternative investment would provide a higher return and investors should reconsider investing in attraction development. The use of revenue/cost methodology for this purpose is considered an opportunity analysis.

Another approach is to use the present value formula to determine the internal rate of return. The internal rate of return is the discount rate which makes the present value of revenues equal to the present value of costs. Figuring out the internal rate of return requires that all costs except those occurring at the start of the cost stream be set at zero. This is easily done by subtracting each year's costs from expected revenues. Costs incurred as a result of initial development are plugged into the present value formula as the value of V_N. The discount rate, i, is an unknown which, once determined, is the discount rate needed to offset all costs. If market interest rates exceed the discount rate, greater returns can be obtained by some other form of investment.

Revenue/cost ratios are extremely helpful when deciding among various investment options, development opportunities, or simply estimating the chances for a successful venture. They do not work well when public investment decisions are being made. Most public attractions (e.g., national parks) come into being as a result of the political process which is rarely, if ever, based on an economic analysis. This is not to say that economic impacts are not considered, but rather that they are just one aspect, and usually a minor one, of a much broader political agenda. Even if an economic feasibility analysis was not part of the initial attraction designation process, public attractions still come under pressure to show economic value. It is this pressure which has spawned numerous methodological techniques to estimate the value of publicly provided attractions.

VALUE OF PUBLIC ATTRACTIONS

Publicly provided attractions are not generally viewed as income generators. Even if their primary purpose is to protect a rare ecosystem, they also provide user experiences not normally available through the private sector.

The economic importance of public-sector attractions should not be lightly dismissed, however, as they provide opportunities for the private sector to either develop supporting attractions in close proximity to the public attraction, or facilities (e.g., accommodations) for people drawn to the public attraction. The extent that public-sector attractions contribute to the tourism industry is discussed in Chapter 6. The fact that public attractions do not directly generate a high revenue stream by no means reduces their overall tourism value.

Funding for public sector attractions is continually debated. Some argue that public attractions compete against the private sector and most if not all should be privatized. Even when resources are one of a kind (e.g., Grand Canyon), initiatives to allow private development on those lands periodically arise. The debate over how public lands should be used in the United States has its roots in early settlement policies. When the United States began its westward expansion in the mid 1800s, government policy to encourage settlement of the frontier was liberal and generous. This is evident by review of the Homestead Act of 1862 and other legislation that transferred public land into private ownership. (For an excellent review of United States western land policy see Stegner, 1982.) This trend was reversed in 1897 with the passage of the Forest Reserve Act (Organic Act) which designated large tracts of forested land, primarily in the western United States, as forest reserves. Charges of land "lock up" resulted and continue today wherever public resources are viewed as being used in an economically inefficient manner.

Historically the value of public resources has been determined by estimating the market value for commodities (e.g., timber, fisheries) obtained from the resource. Economic valuation of non-consumptive uses has only recently received attention and is labeled "amenity valuation" (Shafer et al., nd). Because of the antipathy toward public ownership of resources and the need to justify taxpayer support of those resources, methods to determine their economic value have received a great deal of attention in recent years. What follows is a review of some of those techniques.

Unit Day Values

One of the first attempts to assign values to recreation activities is contained in U.S. Senate Document 97 (Ad Hoc Water Resources Council, 1964). A Recreation Day was defined as a visit by one individual to a recreation development site for all or a reasonable portion of a 24-hour day. Types of recreation were defined as general, consisting of those activities attractive to the majority of recreationists and requiring some facility development (e.g., camping), or specialized with low intensity of use levels which may involve significant personal expense (e.g., hunting). Unit day values for general recreation days were worth $.50–1.50, with specialized ranging from \$2.00–6.00 in 1964. The purpose of assigning unit day values was to incorporate recreation values along with market based commodity values (e.g., kilowatt hours) into benefit estimates of federal development projects. Unit day values were purely an arbitrary measure of recreation value and did not have an extensive research foundation. All an analyst had to do was to estimate the number of general and specialized recreation days for a site and multiply by an appropriate dollar value. The result was the value of the site as an attraction.

Travel Cost

Simple Travel Cost

Cesario (1969), using methodology originally developed by Clawson (1959) and Clawson and Knetsch (1966), utilizes travel costs as a proxy for determining recreation values of publicly provided attractions. Travel cost methodology assumes people who visit a site value it at a level equal to or exceeding the cost of travel to the site. It also assumes people will continue to visit the site until the marginal cost of the next visit exceeds the marginal value of the experience obtained from visitation. If economic theory holds, each additional trip would have less value to the individual as marginal utility from consumption declines with each additional unit purchased. For example, if a trip to the Grand Canyon cost an individual \$500, the experience must be worth at least that much to the visiting individual. Assuming that the individual would have paid up to \$1100 in travel expenses for the visit, they would receive a benefit of \$600, or the difference between what a person values the experience at and what it costs to visit. This value above actual cost is termed consumer surplus. Even though the consumer surplus of \$600 exceeds total travel costs of \$500, this does not mean the individual will take another trip to the Grand Canyon. The marginal value to the individual from a second trip may be less than the \$500 in travel costs, and consequently another destination with higher marginal value may be selected.

Travel cost methodology requires a demand curve for visitation to the site be estimated. A simple equation for the demand curve is

$$V = a + bT$$

where V equals visitation rates, T equals travel costs, and a and b are coefficients to be fitted by a regression model. The coefficient b should have a negative value, representing decreased visitation as travel costs increase. Data requirements for estimating the demand function include origin of visitors to the site, estimate of travel costs from each zone of origin (travel costs can be estimated for people living within certain distance zones, e.g.,

50 miles), and population of each zone. From this information the percentage of people (usually expressed as percent per 1,000 people) from
each zone who travel to the site can be estimated. Normally the population zones are defined as concentric circles surrounding the attraction (see
Figure 9.7). Total visitation can be computed by taking the per capita visitation rate and multiplying by total population for each zone. If data are
accurate and the model functions according to the above equation, the
percentage of visitors per zone will decrease as distance between site and
zone increases assuming travel costs increase as distance from site increases.

Calculating the value of the site requires the area under the demand
curve, determined by the equation $V = a + bT$, be determined. For someone unfamiliar with calculating the area under a curve, a mathematician
schooled in calculus could supply the necessary expertise. Since a demand
curve is a price/quantity relationship, area can be converted into monetary
units. The average cost per trip for all visitors is then calculated and sub-
tracted from the value for the area under the curve. The difference is total
consumer surplus or the value of the site.

The simple travel-cost methodology is not without its critics. Its faults
have been pointed out by Mendelssohn and Markstrom (1988) and Harris
et al. (1988). Some of the concerns include the assumption of homogene-
ity of people between zones (i.e., people have similar socioeconomic characteristics regardless of zone residence), model usefulness after a certain
distance is exceeded, only the site visit has value as people will not experi-

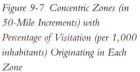

Figure 9-7 Concentric Zones (in 50-Mile Increments) with Percentage of Visitation (per 1,000 inhabitants) Originating in Each Zone

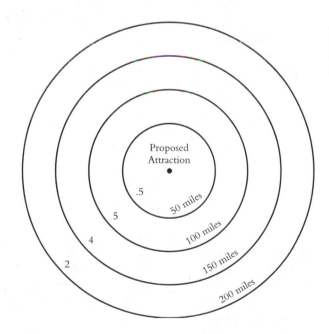

ence any value from the trip itself, the determination of benefit allocation between multiple destinations on one trip, and cost distribution between members of a group who travel together.

Multiple-Site Travel Cost

The multiple-site travel-cost model was developed to assess the influence of substitute sites on single-site valuation. Visitation to any one site is subject to the availability of other sites with similar characteristics. Consequently, an individual's marginal value from visiting a substitute site may be higher than that which would have been achieved from a second visit to the site being valued. Mendelssohn and Markstrom (1988) propose a site demand equation to deal with this problem, of the form

$$V = a + bT + cW + dP,$$

where V = visitation rates, T = travel costs to the site, W = some measure of socioeconomic characteristics of visitors, P = travel costs to alternative sites and a, b, c, and d are coefficients to be fitted by a regression model. This model would be used to estimate a demand equation for each type of site which, when aggregated, would provide the value for a system of sites. Adding or subtracting a site could also be evaluated by the addition or subtraction of a demand equation for the particular type of site. In a sense, the multiple-site travel-cost model is a way of measuring the effects of a regional system of attractions or the synergistic impact of developing a group of attractions.

Hedonic Price Method

Tourism products, because of their intangible nature, are purchased based on a subjective evaluation of the attributes represented by the product. The Hedonic Price method uses the market value of tangible products (e.g. housing) as a proxy measure for the value of intangible products. It has been used in recreation research to determine the value of environmental attributes. For example, if the method is functional, the price of a house in a highly valued environment will cost more than one in an area with less desirable environmental characteristics. The difference in price between two similar houses in different locations is the value of the environmental quality. The Hedonic Price method requires data be collected on market price of the tangible good and the presence and level of the intangible environmental attributes in close proximity to the tangible product. A statistical model is used to estimate environmental value, such as multiple linear regression of the form

$$V = a + bX1 + cX2 + \ldots zXn + e,$$

where V = market value of the tangible product, X1 to Xn are some measure of the environmental attributes, and a....z are coefficients to be fitted by the regression model.

Gartner et al. (1996), using a Hedonic Price method approach, attempt to measure the differences in property value of houses in a recreation area in northern Michigan with respect to location to selected natural resource characteristics. Using different regression equations to compensate for the political region of house location, it is found that some natural resource characteristics did significantly influence the perceived value of a house. In particular, evidence suggests that locating on certain size lakes and in close proximity to ski areas increases the value of housing. However, locations adjacent to tracts of public land reduce the value of housing. Using the Hedonic Price Method in this example, the attraction of public lands could be viewed as having negative value which underscores some of the difficulties with the model. Should public land attraction value estimates be a function of only those people with houses close by, or is it more appropriate to value these attractions based on visitor estimates of value? Travel cost models may be more appropriate estimates of public attractions value from a tourism perspective than Hedonic Price methods.

Other concerns with Hedonic Price methods include the assumptions inherent in the approach. It is not always possible for someone to live where they want. Job availability, which may be determined by proximity to markets, often precludes someone from purchasing a house in a highly valued environment. Even when environmental quality does influence business location decisions, the extent of development may alter the environmental quality of the area, reducing the value of the previously sought after environmental attributes. In that case, people will be locked into an area more likely because jobs are available rather than because they place high value on its environmental attributes.

Finally, Hedonic Price methods, since they involve a comparison between market-priced goods, cannot be measured at the ratio level which is a requirement for total valuation purposes. Although differences in value can be expressed in monetary terms, for total valuation of the environmental attributes to be determined, a zero starting point must be obtained. If housing was solely valued on its environmental attributes, a house located in an area with no environmental quality would have a value of zero. This is, if not impossible, almost impossible to find. While Hedonic Price methods can determine the difference in value between a product which has more of some attributes than others, there may still exist a similar product with an even smaller supply of the environmental attributes being measured. In that case, value estimates would increase. If a similar site with none of the environmental attributes being measured cannot be located, then there is no zero point and total value cannot be determined. Hedonic Price methods, however, are useful for determining how specific site characteristics may affect market value.

Contingent Valuation Methods

Contingent Valuation (CV) methods assess economic value changes under different policy scenarios. The two main CV methods are Willingness to Pay (WP) and Willingness to Accept (WA). Willingness to Pay involves an individual's expressed economic reaction to avoid a detrimental policy change or capture the benefits from a perceived advantageous change. Willingness to Accept is the economic incentive it would take to satisfy an individual who is unable to capture or avoid the effect of a policy change. Either method requires that affected individuals be informed and are able to comprehend the impacts, real or imaginary, of a proposed policy change.

Value estimates of the policy change are estimated by selecting a sample of the population expected to be affected by the change. A survey is administered to the sample population which elicits monetary estimates of either accepting, avoiding, or being able to benefit from the change. An average WP or WA is derived, which when generalized to the entire population of users, provides a total economic estimate of the change. Most often WP and WA estimates are derived for a very specific policy change such as the loss of an opportunity presently provided (e.g., deer hunting in parks), but it has the potential to be used on an even broader scale. For example, allowing major facility development on a public attraction that is presently offering only dispersed types of recreation activities is a policy change that can be economically assessed using CV methods. In this way, the value of public attractions can be assessed for different management options.

Concerns with using CV methods generally fall into two categories. First, do affected individuals understand the implications of the policy change and are they able to assess that change in economic terms within the time frame allowed for survey completion? Second, will people provide accurate measures of what the change means to them or, fearing that the policy change may become reality, do they over- or underestimate value in an attempt to bias the decision? In other words, since people are only asked to provide value estimates and are not required to actually enter into a cash transaction, are the results accurate representations of reality? A thorough theoretical discussion of the concerns surrounding the use of CV methods can be found in Hoehn and Swanson (1988).

Other Concerns with Public-Sector Attraction Development

Amenity valuation techniques have high political value but as discussed, all have inherent problems. Even if a method acceptable to all was developed there still remains the question of how the information will be used. If only those public attractions with the highest economic value receive budgetary support, only one type of tourism will be offered to users of public resources. Mass tourism will dominate, as the more users there are, the higher the economic value. A healthy attraction mix requires different attractions of varying development levels. Already there are some signs mass tourism overuse of public attractions (e.g., national parks) is degrading the environmental and psychological values recognized as worthy of protection (Lime, 1995).

Another concern deals not with the level of development on public attractions but for whom the attractions are developed. The private sector responds to market demand, real or potential, and builds attractions they believe will be profitable. Marketing strategies and techniques determine how the attraction is built and what audience it is built for. Historically, public agencies have not been driven by the same market forces and build attractions compatible with their mission. The problem is not with the mission of the agencies but the type of people who implement the mission.

Irwin et al. (1990), investigating user preferences for two different subcultures camping in a minimally developed campground, finds significant differences between the groups. Hispanic campers, comprised almost exclusively of a Mexican-American subculture, are not necessarily as satisfied with the facility as Anglo campers. In particular, Mexican-Americans would have preferred additional facility development. Some of those facilities are found in the region but are not frequented by the Mexican-American subculture, partially due to site restrictions on party size. Mexican-Americans recreate in an extended family group which by its very size could not be accommodated given existing use restrictions at the more developed sites. Therefore, a less desirable substitute site had to be found.

Generally, campgrounds and other public attractions in the United States are built according to directions obtained from a manual. The research for establishing development guidelines has been collected over a number of years, but comes primarily from the dominant user group. This group, with roots in Northern Europe, is Caucasian. Facilities have been designed by and built for the white subculture. Subcultures not in the mainstream have either ignored publicly provided attractions or used those that are less desirable but able to accommodate their unique sociocultural differences. Discrimination in the provision of publicly provided attrac-

Secondary or supporting attractions can provide a certain ambiance to a community.
Photo by the author

tions, subtle and probably not deliberate, is nonetheless real. Future attraction development, especially those on public lands, must recognize the multicultural composition of the population they serve. Facilities designed to meet the needs of minority subcultures may not have as much economic value, utilizing some of the valuation methods described above, as those designed for the predominant subculture. This poses an interesting question. Is the search for methods to value public attractions a form of economic discrimination against a country's minority populations?

CONCLUSION

Attractions form the supply side of tourism. They provide the "pull" which, when matched to a compatible "push," brings people into an area. There are numerous types of attractions, but in terms of "pull" they can be grouped simply into two categories. Primary attractions, either stand-alone operations or a grouping of similar sites, facilities, etc., are the reason people travel. They can be as ostentatious as a theme park or as subtle as a community of people. Secondary attractions rely on the existence of primary attractions for their market, but contribute to the overall attraction complex by increasing activity options for visitors.

Attraction development is a complex and involved process. Although there are some attraction principles which should be followed, applying those principles requires subjective judgment, detailed data gathering, and sophisticated analytical techniques. As competition for tourists increases, the time spent analyzing attraction-development opportunities should be paid back in the form of a long-term viable operation.

Attraction development is more than simply acquiring a piece of land and transforming it into something that appeals to tourists. Although this chapter deals more with the economics and feasibility of attraction development, it should be considered with respect to what has already been discussed in other parts of this book. Questions relating to how a proposed attraction fits into the sociocultural character of the area or what types of environmental changes may occur are just as important as a revenue/cost analysis. Certain techniques can reduce the economic risk associated with attraction development; however, if the destination area changes to the point where it loses its "pull," then each one of the attractions, no matter how well planned, will also suffer. The majority of this chapter deals with the attraction development process at the firm or single entity level, but successful development requires not only an understanding of micro management issues but also how each piece fits into the overall attraction development complex.

One should also be aware that attraction development is not the exclusive domain of the private sector. As public budgets come under greater scrutiny, there is increased pressure to demonstrate that public attractions have value. Some of the more popular valuation techniques are discussed here, as well as the difficulties and concerns surrounding the public attraction value issue. Planners and developers should consider a mix of public and private attractions if the goal is to create an attraction complex.

EXECUTIVE SUMMARY

Attractions are the pull of the push/pull equation. Eleven different attraction categories are identified, each appealing to specific groups. Most areas rely on the existence of some tangible attributes to support the development of specific types of tourism, with the notable exception to this statement being religious sites, usually developed after a vision has appeared, and for which no amount of pre-development planning is possible.

There are three basic attraction development principles, each with its own set of operational factors. The three principles are firstly to identify attractions in place or potential for new attractions, secondly to perform a quality assessment of each one, and finally to determine an appropriate attraction-mix strategy.

Organic bunching, the grouping of like attractions, can lead to a synergistic effect, producing more visitors than the sum of the drawing power of like attractions operating as single attractions. Similarly themed developments can lead to increased visitation, although it can also lead to a high risk/high return development strategy.

Some of the more important factors to be

considered when selecting a region for attraction location include: transportation, especially with respect to available modes and costs of each one, land use possibilities and associated land costs, government policies affecting type of attraction proposed, infrastructure conditions, safety/security/health concerns, supplier availability and access, access to financial markets, and adequate supply of the right type of labor.

Site selection methods for an attraction vary by category (i.e., primary vs. secondary), but all require that an effective trade or market area be the first consideration. As the attraction becomes more complex and market area increases, the usefulness of site selection models decreases.

Evaluating attraction feasibility requires rev-

enue/cost ratios be considered. Projected revenue and costs must be estimated, put into a time series stream, an appropriate discount rate selected and, reduced to present value estimates.

Public attractions are not subjected to the same type of revenue/cost analyses as private sector attractions because they are not set up to yield a monetary return on investment, but instead are intended to maximize social welfare. Because of the pressure to subject public attractions to monetary worth estimates, a number of methods have been developed to determine their economic value. None of them are fully accepted as the nature of public attractions does not lend itself to accurate estimates of public value.

REFERENCES

Ad Hoc Water Resources Council. 1963. *Evaluation Standards for Primary Outdoor Recreation Benefits*. Washington D.C.: Senate Document 97, Supplement No. 1.

Baxter, M. and G. Ewing. 1981. Models of Recreational Trip Distribution. *Regional Studies* 15:327–344.

Cesario, F. Jr. 1969. Operations Research in Outdoor Recreation. *Journal of Leisure Research* 1(1):33–50.

Clawson, M. 1959. *Methods of Measuring the Demand for and Value of Outdoor Recreation*. Resources for the Future, Reprint #10.

Clawson, M. and J. Knetsch. 1966. *The Economics of Outdoor Recreation*. Baltimore: Johns Hopkins Press.

Converse, P. 1949. New Laws of Retail Gravitation. *Journal of Marketing* 14:379–384.

Fesenmaier, D. and W. Roehl. 1986. Locational

Analysis in Campground Development Decisions. *Journal of Travel Research* 24(3):18–22.

Fodness, D. 1990. Consumer Perceptions of Tourism Attractions. *Journal of Travel Research* 28(4):3–9.

Gartner, W., D. Chappelle, and T.C. Girard. 1996. National Resource Characteristics Influence on Property Value: Case Study in Northern Michigan. *Journal of Travel Research* (in press).

Gartner, W. and D. Holecek. 1983. Economic Impact of an Annual Tourism Industry Exposition. *Annals of Tourism Research* 10(2):199–212.

Getz, D. 1991. *Festivals, Special Events, and Tourism*. New York: Van Nostrand Reinhold.

Ghosh, A. and S. McLafferty. 1987. *Location Strategies for Retail and Service Firms*. Lexington, Mass.: Lexington Books.

Harris, C., H. Tinsley, and D. Donnelly. 1988.

Research Methods for Public Amenity Resources Valuation: Issues and Recommendations, 201–218. In *Amenity Resources Valuation: Integrating Economics with Other Disciplines*. G. Peterson, B. Driver, and R. Gregory, eds. State College, Pa.: Venture Publishing.

Hoehn, J. and C. Swanson. 1988. Toward a Satisfactory Model of Contingent Valuation Behavior in a Policy Context. In *Amenity Resource Valuation: Integrating Economics with Other Disciplines*. G. Peterson, B. Driver, and R. Gregory, eds. State College, Pa.: Venture Publishing.

Hudman, L. and R. Jackson. 1992. Mormon Pilgrimage and Tourism. *Annals of Tourism Research* 19(1):107–121.

Irwin, P., W. Gartner, and C. Phelps, 1990. Mexican-American/Anglo Cultural Differences as Recreation Style Determinants. *Leisure Sciences* 12:335–348.

Lime, D. 1995. Congestion and Crowding at Recreation Sites. *Trend Tracker, 4th International Outdoor Recreation and Tourism Trends Symposium*. Tourism Center, University of Minnesota.

Mendelssohn, R. and D. Markstrom. 1988. The Use of Travel Cost and Hedonic Methods in Assessing Environmental Benefits, 159–166. In G. Peterson, B. Driver, and R. Gregory eds. *Amenity Resources Valuation: Integrating Economics with Other Disciplines*. State College Pa.: Venture Publishing.

Milman, A. 1988. Market Identification of a New Theme Park: An Example from Central Florida. *Journal of Travel Research* 26(4):7–11.

Morrison, A. 1989. *Hospitality and Travel Marketing*. New York: Delmar Publishers Inc.

Ritchie, B. and B. Smith. 1991. The Impact of a Mega-Event on Host Region Awareness: A Longitudinal Study. *Journal of Travel Research* 29(2): 16–22.

Shafer, E., R. Carline, R. Guldin, and H. Cordell. n.d. Economic Amenity Values of Wildlife—Six Case Studies in Pennsylvania. Submitted to Environmental Management for publication consideration.

Smith, S. 1983. *Recreation Geography*. New York: Longman Scientific and Technical.

Smith. S. 1989. *Tourism Analysis*. New York: Longman, Scientific & Technical.

Stegner, W. 1982. *Beyond the Hundredth Meridian: John Wesley Powell and the Second Opening of the West*. Lincoln, Nebr.: University of Nebraska Press.

Stynes, D., D. Spotts, and J. Strunk. 1985. Relaxing Assumptions of Perfect Information in Park Visitation Models. *Professional Geographer* 37(1):21–28.

Thompson, J. 1982. *Site Selection*. New York: Lebhar-Friedman Books.

Tourism Center, University of Minnesota. 1991. *Rural Tourism Development*. St. Paul, Minn.: Minnesota Extension Service.

Vukonic′, B. 1992. Medjugorje's Religion and Tourism Connection. *Annals of Tourism Research* 19(1):79–91.

PART V

Implementation

The last section of this book consists of three chapters: Marketing, Image, and Planning. The inclusion of a marketing chapter in a text on tourism development is predicated on the fact that many areas are currently active tourism destinations and need continued tourist activity to support their economic base. The marketing chapter provides some of the tools needed to maintain a healthy tourism-based economy. Similarly a chapter on image is included because tourism, more than any other economic activity, relies on the amorphous and intangible attributes of a destination to create a perceptual product. How these attributes are projected determines the types of tourists attracted and the types of tourism activities demanded. Understanding the image formation process can help host societies develop the type of tourism they are most comfortable providing.

A chapter on planning may seem an odd addition to a section called implementation. Throughout this book planning has been in the shadow of many of the subjects discussed. However, it is the process of planning which allows existing destinations to react to changing trends and provides the structure for new areas to develop. Without planning, successful implementation of a sustainable tourism development strategy is possible but not probable. The chapter on planning also serves the purpose of synthesizing many of the previous discussions found throughout the text, and in that regard serves as a concluding chapter.

Tourism Marketing

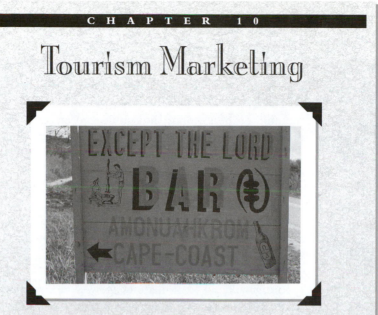

Cultural connotation or astute marketing?
Photo by the author

Learning Objectives

Review product life-cycle theory and its relationship
to tourism marketing.

•

Examine differences between tourism products and
other goods.

•

Review processes for developing a marketing plan.

•

Examine aspects of target marketing and techniques
used to identify markets.

•

Review the research process and its relationship to
tourism.

•

Examine the different categories of tourism research,
research methods commonly used, and setting of a
research mix strategy.

•

Explore three critical marketing issues of the 1990s—
strategic alliances, customer service, and cyberspace
marketing.

INTRODUCTION

The American Marketing Association defines marketing as the "process of planning and executing conception, pricing, promotion and distribution of ideas, goods, and services to create exchanges that satisfy individual and organizational objectives" (Lewis and Chambers, 1989) There are numerous texts on the principles of marketing that define it in many different ways. Simply put, marketing is a concept which, when applied successfully, forms a bridge between a producer and a market. The ultimate goal of marketing activities is to initiate consumer purchases for the producer's goods. Obviously, the more successful a marketing program becomes, the more product consumption takes place.

With the increasing number of travelers during the last decade, tourism marketing is sometimes viewed as an easy task. After all, there should be enough tourists for everyone, and if increases in tourism are any indication, tourism marketing has been very successful. That is not necessarily the case. While success can be measured in terms of increased visitors, revenues, employment, number of businesses, or in many other ways, growth does not always imply success. Growth must be directed and planned if it is to proceed without major surprises.

One reason for including a marketing chapter in a tourism development text is that once a decision to pursue tourism as an economic development option is made, failure to employ marketing strategies can lead to unplanned and uncontrolled consequences. This applies at all levels of development from the individual business to national initiatives. An important aspect of marketing often overlooked is that it is not an after-the-fact exercise. In other words, it is not something that is pursued after facilities are constructed, but something that should be undertaken before decisions are made about what products will be developed. In this sense, it operates as a planning technique and can help direct development. Even when facilities are already in place, marketing techniques can be used to help decide what course of action, including re-development, should be pursued.

This chapter begins with a review of product life-cycle theory and its implications for marketing and development, discusses the differences between marketing tourism products versus other goods, explores the fundamentals of developing a marketing plan, discusses target marketing techniques, reviews the importance of marketing research with a section on commonly utilized research methods, and concludes with a discussion of some of the critical marketing issues of the 1990s.

PRODUCT LIFE CYCLES

Wasson (1974) develops a product life-cycle curve (see Figure 10.1) that with few modifications can be applied to all products, including tourism. There are five stages, starting with market development or product introduction and proceeding through increasing levels of growth until market saturation results and eventually product decline. The reader will remember that Chapter 1 briefly discusses Butler's product life-cycle curve. The concept used by both Butler and Wasson is the same, but in this section the discussion is more detailed and related to marketing.

Another way of viewing product life cycles is from a supply/demand perspective. Stage one in Wassan's product life cycle is a period where supply exceeds demand. There are very few producers in this stage, and product acceptance receives high priority. Marketing programs in this stage are concerned with establishing distribution channels and developing brand identity. Deep discounts are offered to distributors and consumers in an attempt to create product demand. Profits are non-existent during the introductory stage, and the producer must have deep pockets in order to establish product identity. Little competition exists as consumer acceptance of the product has not yet been proved. One factor determining the

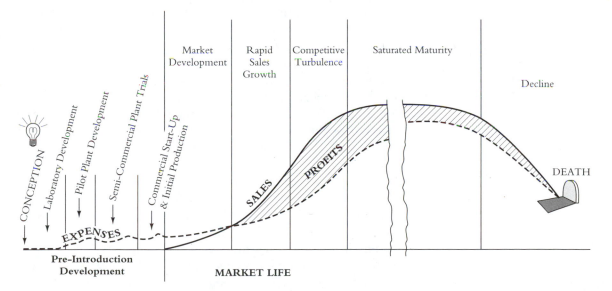

Source: Wasson, 1974

Figure 10.1 *The Full Product Life Cycle*

time it takes to establish product identity is complexity. The more complex the product, the more education required to learn how to use and enjoy the product. Product complexity is therefore a factor determining time duration for stage one.

International travel, especially to developing countries, is generally more complex than domestic travel. For example, for residents of the U.S. travel within the country is quite easy (assuming one has enough money to travel). Transportation systems are well established, no visas or passports are required for travel between the states, and culture shock is not a barrier although one could argue that in certain parts of the U.S. distinctly different cultures do exist. Travel outside the U.S. by a U.S. citizen requires more time be spent in the trip-planning process, especially for securing appropriate documents. This is one reason many international travelers prefer to use the services of a tour broker as a means of reducing product complexity.

Stage two is a period of rapid growth. Distribution channels are established and consumers fully accept the product. Demand exceeds supply in stage two, leading to increased sales and excess profits which induces more firms to enter the market. Not only does demand exceed supply, but demand increases at an increasing rate. This relationship can be shown mathematically by drawing lines tangential to the product life cycle curve. The slope of the lines will increase during the rapid growth stage, indicating incremental changes in demand are increasing. In other words, if a firm has a 20-percent increase in demand for its product in one reporting period, periods will show an average increase greater than 20 percent. As long as the marginal increase in demand for one period exceeds the increase in demand for the preceding period, then a firm is still in stage two or the rapid growth portion of the product life cycle. During stage two there is an emphasis on a production orientation as profits can be augmented by turning out additional products. Discount pricing is discontinued and product prices are established at a point approximating unitary elasticity in an attempt to maximize revenue. Marketing is focused on establishing brand identity to offset expected expanding levels of competition. As competition grows, discount pricing may be used as a means of eliminating marginal firms, but most of this activity takes place in stage three, where supply once again exceeds demand.

Wasson characterizes stage three as one of competitive turbulence. More firms start to produce the product, owing to the perception that excess profits exist. Demand for the product still exceeds supply during stage three, but the marginal increase in demand is declining. Again, mathematically this can be shown by comparing the slopes of tangential lines to the product life-cycle curve. If the slope of a line is less than the one in a preceding period, it indicates that the product life cycle has now moved into stage three. Marginal increases in demand are now less than those in a pre-ceding period. Obviously, there may still be fluctuations in demand due to such factors as seasonality, but over the long run marginal increases will show a downward movement. Analysis of demand changes must be based on comparable periods.

Since stage three is marked by the entry of additional producers, those firms that are to survive must switch from a production to a consumer orientation. In this stage, marketing takes on greater urgency and research becomes a critical component of any marketing plan. Understanding consumer needs and wants, identifying viable market segments, and providing additional service programs are all indicators of a switch to a consumer orientation. The latter half of stage three is characterized by widespread business failure in those firms that do not adopt a consumer orientation. Excess profits that induce the entry of additional firms have disappeared and business losses become the rule for most firms rather than the exception. The market is becoming saturated with product, and only those firms that understand their customer base and build brand loyalty will remain in business.

Stage four is characterized by flat demand. A product is considered mature, indicating that little room for growth remains. Although demand has stopped increasing, producers can still capture additional market share by invading their competitor's territory. This is sometimes done by introducing what appear to be new products. Beer provides an excellent example of how this may be done. For years, U.S. beer sales for the industry as a whole have been flat. In an attempt to capture competitor's market share, "new" types of beer have been introduced. These product introductions are based on market research of beer drinkers indicating consumer willingness to cut down on calorie consumption as the country's beer drinkers aged and ostensibly became more health conscious. However, the perception that drinking low-calorie beer did not fit with the macho image developed of beer drinkers over the years posed an acceptance problem for the new product. One beer company overcame this problem by using retired athletes, an age group that many beer drinkers could relate to, to promote the product. The result was a shift in demand from one type of beer to another. Overall industry sales did not improve significantly, but market share between the large producers did shift, forcing the leading companies to introduce their own brand of low calorie beer and undertake aggressive marketing campaigns to protect brand loyalty. Today the same companies are promoting an "ice" brewed beer which is higher in alcohol and contains as many calories, or more, as regular beer. Shuffling of the beer cans is once again underway.

Firms surviving into stage four have aggressive research and promotion programs constantly searching for any extra advantage to increase their market share at the expense of their competitors. New entries into the market are rare and price competition further reduces the opportunity for excess profits.

Eventually, products may slip into stage five, characterized by demand decline. Supply exceeds demand and retrenchment is the rule. Survival depends on firmly embracing a consumer orientation and adding additional services, new products, or redesigning to augment existing product attributes. The time it takes to enter stage five is different for each product and depends on such factors as technological change rendering a product obsolete, new product introductions as in the beer example, and the nature of the product in terms of it being a necessity or luxury good.

Even in the extreme case where it appears there is no longer a use for the product, one economic axiom prevails: "the last iceman always survives." After the introduction of electric and gas refrigeration, ice delivery was no longer needed. Refrigeration was accomplished by simply plugging in a refrigerator rather than purchasing a new block of ice every few days. Technological advances were blamed for the disappearance of the iceman. However, the last iceman developed specialty services, supplying blocks of ice for summer parties or moving into the ice sculpture business. The market is not large, but it exists, and since it is a specialty service prices charged can offset costs of operation and still generate a profit.

Product life-cycle approaches to analyzing product acceptance and longevity are intuitively easy to comprehend. However, the simplicity embodied in the approach is an oft cited criticism. Critics maintain that not all products follow life cycles as described above. External factors (e.g., technology), management decisions, availability or creation of substitutes, consumer taste shifts, or government legislation can all affect a product's life cycle (Cooper, 1989). While this is undoubtedly true, there is no way to plan for some of the exogenous factors that affect product appeal. Life-cycle theory allows marketing planning to proceed based on stages occurring in normal product life which can be modified if and when an exogenous influence occurs.

At this point, or perhaps sooner, the reader may ask how the product life cycle affects tourism. Is tourism the exception to the product life cycle? Won't it always be in a growth mode? The answer is that although tourism has shown significant increases in growth over the last 20 years, there is reason to expect that it is entering stage three. Competition is increasing for available tourists and more destinations are positioning themselves for tourism. Those that will be successful will adopt a consumer orientation and use all aspects of marketing for delivery and modification of their tourism products. The remainder of this chapter explores different marketing strategies and ideas, which, if adopted, will help separate a firm's product(s) from the clutter of tourism products now available.

However, a review of the major differences between touristic products and other goods is presented as background.

TRADITIONAL MARKETING VS. TOURISM MARKETING

Four conditions are necessary for marketing to occur: two or more parties (usually buyer and seller) with unmet needs, a desire and ability to satisfy each other's unmet needs, communication between parties, and something to exchange (Berkowitz et al., 1989). It is the nature of the something to exchange that makes tourism marketing different from that of tangible products.

Figure 10.2 lists the various characteristics of consumable items with emphasis on the differences between goods and services. Since tourism products fall into the services category the comparison is valid. Intangibility, instantaneous creation and consumption, perishability, and heterogeneity are the characteristics of the tourism product(s) most often encountered in the literature.

All products can be viewed as containing tangible and intangible attributes. A basketball can be said to have the tangible attribute of shape in that it is of a certain size to conform with collegiate or professional specifications. It may also have intangible qualities represented by color or celebrity endorsement. The tourism product is more often than not an amorphous mass of experiences entirely subjective and therefore of an intangible nature. It is usually thought of as produced and consumed, while

Characteristic	Goods	Services
Product	Tangible	Intangible
Ability to Measure	Objective	Subjective
Customer Perception	Standardized/What You See	Must be Consumed to Evaluate
Form	Manufactured	Created
Time Interval	Available Before & After	Almost Instantaneous
Shelf Life	Days to Years	Zero (perishable)
Possession	Utilitarian/Finite	Memories/Forever
Place	Product to Consumer	Customer to Product
Delivery	Consistent	Heterogeneity/Variable
Unit Definition	Precise	General
Product Flexibility	Limited	Broad
Pricing	Cost Basis	Limited Cost Basis
Marketing	Traditional/External	Nontraditional/Largely Internal

Figure 10.2 *Differences Betweeen Goods and Services*

Source: Adapted from Lewis, 1988

at the same time ceasing to exist as soon as consumed and remaining only as an experience.

Traditional products are primarily located on the tangible end of the spectrum. After manufacture they are packaged, distributed, and made available for consumer inspection. The consumer can generally try out the product prior to purchase. Since tourism products are produced and consumed at the same time, they are not available for inspection prior to purchase. This difference requires producers to promise performance characteristics which builds certain expectations. It is the molding of experience expectations, usually through image formation, that is critical in tourism product development. The smaller the difference between expectations and experience, the more likely a tourist is to be satisfied. Therefore, tourism product development, using image formation principles discussed in the next chapter, must be done so that the product is at least as desirable as competing products but not to the point that consumer expectations cannot be fully realized.

Product delivery is probably the most difficult part of any marketing program. Consumers may not realize the importance of this aspect of marketing, as the number and types of consumer goods available can often overwhelm the unsophisticated shopper. An example of this can be easily illustrated by a trip to a supermarket. The number of different brands, package sizes, and shelf space taken up by certain brands are often equated with consumer acceptance. While consumer acceptance is an ingredient in securing shelf space, it ranks second to dealer or distributor acceptance. For every product displayed, there are numerous competing products that fail to achieve dealer or distributor acceptance and are not available for consumer inspection. Failure to secure shelf space often deals a death blow to a new product. Some products are never even considered by dealers and distributors, especially if the producer fails to recognize the vagaries and complexities of the distribution system with which they are faced. For example, the failure of the Soviet system was in large part due to an inefficient distribution system for basic consumer goods. Although low agricultural production was also blamed for helping bring about Peristroika, even in times of good production, agricultural products often perished before they could be made available to consumers. Failure to secure or develop an efficient distribution system can destroy even the best products.

In the case of tourism, distribution channels are inverted. Instead of mass-producing goods in one location and then using distribution channels to deliver the product to where consumers live, tourists must be brought from many different locations to the point of production. Points of production are destinations. Since all destinations are different, it is impossible to guarantee product consistency in terms of achieving similar experiences. Actually, this may be one of the benefits for tourism developers in that since numerous products exist, there is low probability of exhausting all sought-after experiences. On the down side, since pleasure tourism is a luxury good relying on the existence and use of consumers' discretionary income, it is relatively easy for consumers to shut off the flow of dollars. There are little or no costs accrued by the consumer from eliminating or changing distribution channels.

Distribution of tourism products is a complex, involved process. A simple example outlining what a tourist might have to do for a two-week vacation illustrates the process. Assuming our tourist is flying to a destination, airline tickets must be purchased. The act of searching for the best fare coinciding with the vacation period constitutes the use of one distribution channel. Normally a travel agent fills the role of facilitator in the ticket purchasing process. Securing accommodations at the destination may require yet another distribution channel. Travel agents may or may not be able to book accommodations, but many times this is handled directly between the individual and the accommodation provider. Obtaining a rental car may require the use of a third distribution channel. Depending on what the tourist wants to do on site, more distribution channels will be utilized. Obtaining theater tickets, hiring a fishing guide, attending a sporting event, and so on all require some effort to arrange. There have been corporate attempts in the past to streamline the distribution process for the consumer, but they have been short-lived. One of the more celebrated involved United Airlines, Westin Hotels and Hertz Rental car company, which were consolidated into a new company named Allegis. The idea was simply to provide one-stop shopping for the three most frequently purchased travel services. Taking this scenario to its ultimate conclusion, one could envision a tourist arriving at the airport, checking in their luggage, flying to the destination on one airline, stepping into a waiting rental car after deplaning, and arriving at the hotel shortly before their luggage is delivered to their room. Conceptually, the idea had potential to revolutionize existing distribution channels, but it never really got off the ground. Investment financiers realized the company was more valuable when sold in parts rather than as a package and before the operation was six months old it collapsed due to a sell off of the individual assets.

The closest the tourism industry has come to streamlining the distribution process is through the use of tour operators. Tour operators recognize the complexity of travel product distribution and extensively package products. Packages often include transportation, lodging, meals, and occasionally entrance and guide fees. The number of travelers using tour operators ballooned during the 1970s and 1980s. Tour brokers cater to mass markets or use a low volume/high cost/high value approach to offset packaging costs.

MEETING PLANNER

The convention and meeting planning business has grown dramatically in the last ten years. Estimates place the number of people attending a meeting or conference outside the home community at more than 100 million in 1990 with an annual growth rate greater than ten percent. Expenditures, estimated at over $40 billion in 1990, were growing at a faster rate than attendance. Due to the enormous size of the market, the Wisconsin Convention and Visitor Bureau (WCVB) in cooperation with the Wisconsin Department of Tourism (WDOT) commissioned a study from faculty at the University of Wisconsin-Stout to determine the potential of increasing market share from the Northern Illinois region. Because meeting planners are recognized as the most influential people for site selection, the study concentrated on determining directly from meeting planners site requirements necessary to hold meetings of various sizes and the perceptions they held of various cities in Wisconsin as potential sites for their next meeting.

During the first three weeks of April 1990, a telephone survey was administered to 3,114 meeting planners, whose phone numbers were obtained from a subscription list to a major meeting planner magazine, located in the Northern Illinois region, including Chicago. A total of 1,274 usable surveys were obtained, with the non-response group consisting of inactive meeting planners (determined by using a preliminary screening question), no answer after three attempts, and refusals. Each usable survey contained, inter alia, information about specific meeting and convention needs, site attributes sought for a meeting location, and perception of selected Wisconsin cities as possible meeting sites.

Service and site attributes identified by meeting planners as most important, listed in priority order, were location, accessibility, quality of meeting space, quality of guest rooms, and price (for attendees). Services and attributes deemed important but not critical were cost of meeting space, airport transportation, restaurant, size of hotel, and free parking, Services and attributes not considered important were recreational facilities and a national sales contract. Not surprisingly, suburban and downtown hotels were most preferred, followed by resorts (surprising considering the low importance placed on recreational facilities), and airport hotel and conference centers. Cruise ships were preferred by only slightly over two percent of the meeting planners. Only three Wisconsin cities were perceived as being able to meet the needs of the meeting planners: Milwaukee, Lake Geneva (well-known convention and resort center), and Madison.

During the course of the three-week telephone survey, any meeting planner indicating an immediate desire to package a meeting in Wisconsin was given designation as a "hot lead" (approximately 10 percent), with their name immediately forwarded to the Wisconsin Convention and Visitor Bureau, who then sent them a special package (designed and funded by WDOT) of information on conducting meetings in Wisconsin. Other meeting planners indicating the desire to consider Wisconsin in the future were designated as potentials (approximately 60 percent). The remainder were classified as probably not. Both hot leads and potentials were put in a database with accompanying statistics on desired services. The database was then delivered to the WCVB which made it available to any Wisconsin city requesting the information. Each city also had access to the meeting planner packages prepared by WDOT.

The cooperative approach to this study and follow-up marketing strategy was well conceived, packaged, and administered. However, one fatal flaw was inherent in the design. No conversion study evaluating the effectiveness of the effort was ever undertaken. Even though it was recommended, it failed to materialize when the individual at the WCVB most influential in conceiving the idea and bringing the partnership together accepted a position in another state. The leadership void was never filled and to date no one knows definitively how many new meetings were held in Wisconsin as a result of the study and subsequent marketing activity.

Source: Davies, R. 1991. The Formulation of a Meeting and Convention Planning Model of Wisconsin Cities Utilizing the Evoked Set of Constructs. Master's Thesis in Hospitality and Tourism, University of Wisconsin-Stout.

Depending on the type of destination, new and unknown or developed and recognized, selling the product takes on different strategies. In the beginning stages, personal selling is most common. Palmer and Stull (1991) define personal selling as persuasive personal communication designed to help customers buy products that fulfill their wants and needs. There are two types of personal selling which can be simply described as either operating at the macro or micro level. Macro level personal selling involves convincing a distributor to sell your product. If the product is a destination, promoters would attempt to convince a travel intermediary to publicize or package the destination. Since personal selling is a costly proposition, most travel-related personal selling is done at the macro level. The most common form of macro selling consists of destination suppliers working with tour operators or wholesalers to include the destination in their offering. Destination suppliers, therefore, do not come in direct contact with the potential traveler but rely on their personal selling skills to have the tour packager sell it for them. Making personal selling work requires identification of decision makers and focusing time and effort on those people.

For example, Davies (1992) conducts a study intended to assist the state of Wisconsin increase its share of the convention and meeting business market. The state decided on a personal selling approach appealing directly to the people who make site location decisions. However, since the number of people who have that role is large, it was necessary to first qualify the market before direct personal selling could take place. The initial step was to focus on a geographical area. The northern Illinois area was chosen due to its close proximity to the state of Wisconsin and its large population in and around Chicago. A list of subscribers to the trade magazine *Convention and Meeting Planners* was obtained from the publisher. A telephone survey was then administered to all subscribers on the list. The purpose of the telephone survey was to identify those meeting planners with a propensity or willingness to plan meetings in Wisconsin, type and size of meetings normally arranged, services and facilities required, and awareness of possible Wisconsin meeting sites. After convention and meeting planners were qualified, they received a specially prepared brochure from the state travel office featuring Wisconsin communities able to meet convention planners' needs. Lists of qualified planners were also made available to the same Wisconsin cities for more direct personal selling. This approach was deemed to be the most cost-efficient as it reduced the time and expense involved in personal selling by making sure that only those convention and meeting planners that were qualified received personal attention.

Micro-level personal selling consists of selling directly to consumers. For destination communities it takes place once the visitor has arrived in the destination. Personal selling can almost be confused with quality service at this point and when it is most effective it is impossible to tell the two apart. The ability to inform guests of the different activities available to them in the area constitutes a personal selling approach that benefits the entire community. Personal selling also takes place in each establishment where tourists are found. The hotel lounge increases sales through the professionalism and advice its waitstaff provides. This type of personal selling and its relationship to customer service is covered in depth later in this chapter.

Advertising, viewed by many as the means to product acceptance, is affected by the type of product(s) offered for sale. Advertising methods can be either of a non-comparative or comparative nature. Non-comparative advertising is intended to increase product awareness and brand identification with comparative advertising used to establish product attribute superiority over a similar brand from another manufacturer. Comparative advertising works best when the objective is to increase market share by displacing a competitor's brand(s) (Rogers and Williams, 1989). Destination advertising has focused almost exclusively on developing distinctive place images and is rarely of the comparative variety. However, industry-specific products (e.g., hotel rooms) benefit more from comparative advertising. Since it is most effective when growth in specific product sales is negligible, it may become more utilized as competition increases and demand flattens, a situation increasingly experienced by the accommodations sector.

Sales promotion refers to marketing activities used to supplement other forms of promotion. This may include the use of coupons, (e.g., "two-for-one" packages) or any other type of incentive program where discount pricing seeks to increase sales during a specific time period. Sales promotions are especially useful during historically slow sales periods. Tourism, with its perishable products, uses sales promotion programs extensively. Most of the major destinations in the world and their respective businesses suffer through annual seasonal slow periods; most sales promotions occur during this period. For example, U.S. visitors to Europe find promotional discounts (e.g., free companion tickets) offered by airlines during winter months in the northern hemisphere. The expected seasonal slowdown in sales is countered by low prices, effectively increasing airline load factors.

Pricing products to maximize returns is probably the most difficult part of marketing. From a theoretical economics perspective, pricing is straightforward. Keynesian economics tells us that there is a price quantity relationship. A normal demand curve is downward sloping, indicating that for successively lower prices there is increasing quantity of the good demanded. Does this relationship hold true for tourism goods and services? The answer is more complex than a simple yes or no. For example, if a consumer is in the market for a new car and he/she already knows brand and model with options that they want to purchase, economic wisdom dictates that the dealership receiving that person's business is the one that can deliver the car at the lowest price. This assumption holds true if other intangibles are not considered, such as the dealership's reputation for service, or if a personal relationship exists between buyer and seller. However, with tourism no two products are alike. Different suppliers, including destinations, provide different experiences. Since the tourism product cannot be tested prior to purchase, price is a relative concept. Two important characteristics of price in this respect are what the price is telling the customer and what price stratagems are available to the producer. One might argue that prices are not set to tell the customer anything more but what a service or good costs. This may be the case in a purely competitive environment where there is no inherent difference between one company's product and its competitors. Tourism does not fit well into the category of perfect competition, and price is often used to inform the consumer as much about the product as a brochure might. Some of the information implicitly contained in price may include prestige or status value, level of service expected, and type of experience offered.

One other important aspect of price from a consumer's perspective is price elasticity of demand. High-priced or luxury goods tend to have higher price elasticities of demand. This means as the price of travel increases or when incomes are restricted, as may occur during recessionary periods with a decline in real income, less travel is purchased. The reasoning behind this is that there is a certain threshold of normal goods required to maintain a particular living standard. Items such as food, mortgages, and local transportation expenses usually receive first priority for purchase.

However, after a certain income level is attained, less and less of the budget, on a percentage basis, is spent on staples and more is allocated to superior goods. This relationship causes superior good providers to adjust their pricing policy during periods of real income change. In this sense, prices charged may be subject to market conditions uncontrollable by the supplier or producer of tourism goods and services.

From a producer's perspective, the price to charge is one that maximizes revenue. Again, elasticities are important determinants of price. If the price charged is in the inelastic portion of a consumer's demand curve, an increase in price results in an increase in revenue. Figure 10.3 graphically displays this relationship. Assuming a normal downward sloping demand curve with a current price of P_1, there will be a corresponding quantity purchase of Q_1. If P_1 is in the consumer's inelastic portion of the demand curve, an increase in price to P_2 results in less quantity purchased, but this reduction still provides more revenue to the producer. Total revenue is determined by multiplying price times quantity, which is the shaded area under the demand curve bounded by the points P_1, A, Q_1 for our initial situation and P_2BQ_2 for our terminal solution in Figure 10.3. The shaded area P_2BQ_2 is greater than P_1AQ_1, resulting in increased revenue. The opposite holds true if we are initially operating in the elastic portion of the demand curve. Figure 10.4 displays this situation. At an initial price of P_3, equilibrium is reached at point C, where quantity Q_3 is purchased. An increase of price to P_4 moves us to a new equilibrium point

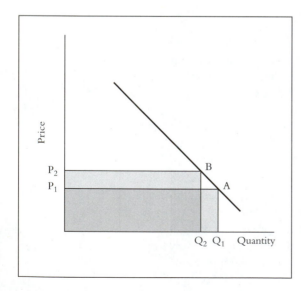

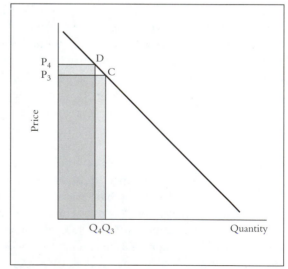

Figure 10.3 *Relationship of Elasticity to Revenue when Operating in the Inelastic Portion of the Demand Curve*

Figure 10.4 *Relationship of Elasticity to Revenue when Operating in the Elastic Portion of the Demand Curve*

of D where quantity Q_4 is purchased. The reduction in quantity purchased reduces total revenue which again can be calculated by determining the area under the demand curve bounded by the points P_3CQ_3, and P_4DQ_4. The area P_4DQ_4 is less than the area P_3CQ_3, resulting in less revenue to the producer. The point where revenue is maximized is called the point of unitary elasticity. Any change in price up or down from this point results in less revenue.

How do producers know where they are on the demand curve? Unfortunately there are no hard and fast rules indicating whether and when price should be changed. Knowledge of the current market helps to an extent. If present consumers have moderate levels of disposable income, recessionary periods usually result in fewer sales as less disposable income is available for the purchase of superior goods. Price discounting and special promotions would be most beneficial during this time. If the present user group has high levels of disposable income, superior goods should maintain current price levels during recessionary periods. Knowledge of current users is a must for pricing to be most effective in generating maximum revenues.

There are other factors for producers to consider, such as competition for the same market, production costs, and image. Image is important because pricing levels provide informational as well as transactional costs. If prices are set to provide information about expected experience levels, it may be more important to hold the line on prices during periods of decline and absorb what are hopefully short-term losses rather than send a perceptual message through discount pricing of declining expected experiences.

There are many types of pricing strategies that an individual firm can employ. Meidan (1989) lists and describes eight of the most common methods along with their advantages and disadvantages. A thorough discussion of each one of these methods is beyond the scope of this book. However, for the reader interested in microeconomic pricing strategies, Meidan's article should be reviewed.

It should be clear from the above discussion that tourism products differ significantly from most other tangible products. Understanding the differences is the first step in developing a viable marketing plan.

DEVELOPING A MARKETING PLAN

Planning is one of the primary keys to success but also one of the most difficult tasks involved in marketing. One of the reasons for this is that planning is seldom viewed as directly linked to sales.

A well-thought-out and prepared marketing plan achieves two major objectives. First, it provides the organization with a vision. Second, planning allows the organization to identify problems impeding attaintment of the long-term goals and identifies solutions to the problems.

Planning goals is directly related to the organization's mission statement. Different types of organizations (e.g. public, private, profit, non-profit) have different mission statements influencing planning goals. Regardless of the nature of the organization, each marketing plan starts with three questions that must be addressed before the plan is acceptable: Where am I now? Where do I want to be? How do I get from where I am to where I want to be? (Wahab et al., 1976). Morrison (1989) expands these three questions to include: How do we make sure we get there? and How do we know if we got there? (Figure 10.5). In the process of answering these ostensibly simple questions, a situational analysis must be conducted, marketing objectives set, promotional and pricing strategies devised, and an evaluation/monitoring program implemented. The situational analysis is the first step, and it begins with an assessment of the product.

Figure 10.5 Morrison's Marketing Model

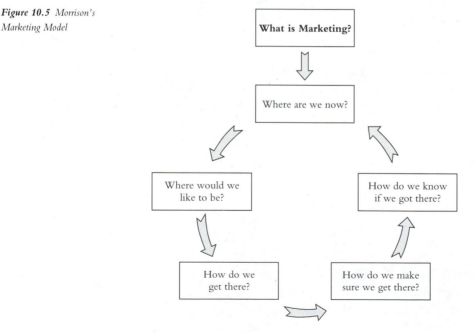

Source: Morrison, 1989

Product Analysis

An integral component of any marketing plan is a product analysis. Because tourism products are highly experiential, even though some aspects of the product offerings are tangible, it is important to analyze the location, structure (intangible vs. tangible), image, and quality of the product(s) offered.

If the organization represents more than a single business or industry group, product analysis takes an entirely different approach. For example, if the organization represents a community, the first step in product analysis is an inventory of the area's tourism resources or attractions. This is discussed earlier in this book, but is important to remember that the type of organization determines the nature of the tourism product analysis.

Once the initial product analysis step is finished, an analysis of the environmental setting in which the product is offered should be completed. Environmental setting includes an assessment of existing or projected economic conditions, laws and regulations affecting product offering, and technology considerations. An example of new technology coupled with changing legislation resulting in major impacts on a specific product is that of transportation in the United States. The development of an interstate highway network combined with an emerging airline industry reduced the demand for rail travel in the United States in the late 1940s. Today, rail transportation accounts for less than one percent of all passenger miles. Legislation initially intended to protect the development of an airline industry and then later legislation intended to make it more competitive had far-reaching impacts on types of transportation used and ultimately accessibility to tourism attractions.

The establishment of the Civil Aeronautics Board (CAB) in 1938 was a direct attempt to support the formation of a new industry. The CAB was in charge of issuing operating authority, controlling rates, route entry and exit, and aspects of how different airline companies interacted with each other. In addition, the CAB had complete control over foreign entry into U.S. ports, and all aspects of air safety. The underlying reason for regulating rates and routes was to ensure that a competitive airline industry comprised of many carriers, was established. In 1958, the Federal Aviation Administration was formed and assumed the safety functions previously relegated to the CAB. In 1978, the Cannon Kennedy Pearson Act effectively deregulated the airline industry and phased out the function of the CAB. In 1982, free entry and exit of routes was permitted, and in 1983 fares were completely deregulated and could be set at any level by any carrier. On January 1, 1985, the CAB ceased to exist. The reason for the airline deregulation act of 1978 was exactly the same for the 1938 regulatory act—competition. Deregulation of the airline industry initially resulted in much lower prices for many air travelers due to the increasing amount of competition for routes and passengers. From the mid 1970s to the mid 1980s, air travel gained passenger-mile percentage points compared to all other forms of transportation. This increase in air travel as a preferred transportation mode was at the expense of private motor vehicle travel and businesses serving those travelers. Although private motor vehicles still account for the majority of total passenger miles (over 80 percent) there was a five-percentage point drop from the mid 70s to the mid 80s in this type of transportation (Table 10.1). Since a 0.1 percent drop translates into approximately 1.2 billion passenger miles, the effects of new legislation and changing technology have far-reaching economic impacts.

Market Analysis

Once the product is identified, a market analysis which focuses on determining what market segments exist, size, and buying power of each segment is in order. Analysis helps determine consumers' needs and present use patterns. With this information, an organization can identify target markets for its products and provide data needed for developing the marketing mix.

Consumer Analysis

Closely related to market analysis is consumer analysis. Once current users are identified, further analysis is conducted with current and potential users to determine how product attributes are perceived. At this stage,

TABLE 10.1   Percentage of Total Passenger Miles for All Modes of Transportation Travel Years 1976–77 to 1983–84.

Year	Motor	Air	Bus	Rail
76–77	86.7	11.5	1.4	0.4
77–78	86.3	12.2	1.2	0.3
78–79	85.2	13.4	1.1	0.3
79–80	84.1	14.4	1.2	0.3
80–81	84.6	13.5	1.6	0.3
81–82	84.5	13.1	2.1	0.3
82–83	81.2	16.1	2.4	0.3
83–84	81.5	15.9	2.2	0.4

Source: Winterbottom and Gartner, 1985

image type research is most important. How consumers perceive the tourism product(s) offered ultimately determines long-term potential for growth and development. Other types of data collected include behavior and behavior profiles of consumers which can be used to monitor consumer changes over time and modify present tourism product(s) for more accurate positioning with respect to identified target markets.

Competitor Analysis

A tourism organization's/business' competitive position is determined after analysis of competitors products and markets served. The goal of a competitor analysis is to uncover consumer segments that fit the profile of users for your product(s) that are not now being served by another producer. A complementary goal is to uncover consumer segments that are not currently being served well by your competitors. From this information an opportunity analysis results.

Opportunity Analysis

An opportunity analysis is simply an exercise to determine strengths and weaknesses. Information obtained from the preceding steps is assembled and subjected to further analysis to determine opportunities. There are different techniques employed to identify opportunities. One of the most commonly used by all types of business is termed SWOT. SWOT is an acronym for Strengths, Weaknesses, Opportunities and Threats. It involves assembling all the information from the preceding analyses (i.e., potential strengths, weaknesses, opportunities, and threats as they relate to products offered and the position of a particular organization) and organizing them into a matrix. The analysis proceeds by matching items in each category against items in each other category. This process allows a business to determine where its products may have a comparative advantage against a competitor's and vice versa. It allows a business to focus on its products currently holding a competitive edge, determine which products should be eliminated, or what types of product positioning will be necessary to create a comparative advantage for some of its products. In a sense, SWOT is a futuring process which helps business focus on core strengths and identify areas of its business which need further attention. For a more complete review of the technique, refer to Bryson (1990).

Setting Objectives

Established objectives become the basis for developing a marketing strategy. There should be more than one marketing objective spanning different time periods. Longer-term objectives, generally exceeding five years, are termed strategic objectives as they identify the most important elements needed to be attained for long-term product viability. Objectives focus the organization and provide vision and direction. They are intended to answer the question "Where do we want to go?"

Budgets

Budgets provide the fuel for the organization to meet its stated objectives. There are two approaches to budgeting with respect to marketing objectives, bottom up or top down. Top down uses the budget to determine marketing objectives. Many publicly funded tourism organizations work with a set budget and must fit their objectives into this framework. How they determine the appropriate amount is an arbitrary and highly political process. Competitive forces such as the next door neighbor's budget may do as much to determine the size of the budget as anything else. Economic approaches such as determining the amount of taxes returned to the region as a result of additional economic activity generated through the marketing program are also considered. These "Return on Investment" (ROI) approaches are being examined more closely by politicians and department heads as justification for public expenditures.

Unfortunately, ROI methods often assume that any additional increases are due to the marketing program, or worse yet, that all taxes generated in the region through tourism activity, should be included in the ROI analysis. There are methods to measure the increase in travel or expenditures to a particular region as a result of special promotions. These are called conversion studies and are explained in more depth later in this chapter. Aside from special promotions, it is almost impossible to measure the total effect of all aspects of a large public (e.g., NTO) organization's tourism efforts. However, it is not unusual to attend regional tourism meetings and be informed that public tourism dollars are being repaid at figures as high as 50:1! A quick review of the material in Chapter 3 shows how insupportable these statements are. An argument for showing even higher ROI ratios to those who calculate all tourism tax receipts and compare them to the organization's tourism budget is to suggest eliminating all public funds for tourism marketing activities. If just one tourist spends one dollar in the state and no money is allocated for tourism marketing, the percentage of taxes returned to the region is divided by the region's total tourism budget. The result would be infinity, as any number divided by zero is infinity. Therefore, ROI approaches infinity if there are no public tourism marketing dollars allocated! This discussion is not meant to advocate the elimination of publicly funded tourism development programs; rather, it is used to show the abuses of using ROI estimates to justify public tourism marketing programs. ROI only has real meaning where the organization is profit-motivated, understands marginal revenues and costs, and has procedures in place for tracking revenues and costs.

Bottom-up budgeting occurs when objectives are established first and the costs of obtaining each objective is determined. For a private sector operation, product pricing reflects the cost of meeting each related objective. Single-service providers are the type of organizations most likely to utilize bottom-up budgeting. This type of budgeting is more complex, as each budget item relates to a specific marketing objective.

Evaluation

Once the above steps have been completed, the tourism organization (public or private) will have embarked on a marketing campaign. Tourism marketing should be viewed as a dynamic process requiring continual monitoring in order to make adjustments and changes as dictated by the marketplace or the organization itself. Depending on the nature of the organization, monitoring can include periodic examination of sales, costs, consumer attitudes, preferences, and behavior. The specific objectives determine the type of monitoring required.

TARGET MARKETING

Much of the above discussion has focused on developing a plan that is market-specific; that is, it is directed at a specific group of actual or potential consumers. To do this requires identifying target markets. Target marketing classifies people according to their perceived predisposition to purchase an organization's tourism product(s). There are many different ways to identify target markets. The process is referred to as segmentation, and involves breaking large markets into more manageable ones. The basic ideas behind market segmentation are:

1. Market segmentation assumes segment heterogeneity. That is, people within a segment act in a similar manner when presented with product choices. Heterogeneity can be determined with respect to person specific variables (e.g., demographics, psychographics, etc.), situational variables (e.g., types of products purchased at home versus those purchased on vacation), or an interaction of the two.

2. Business can introduce new products, modify existing ones, or change the product mix to capture product heterogeneity.

3. Business will do so if the expected return exceeds the cost of any shift in product modification (Green and Krieger, 1991).

Numerous methods have been used to segment markets. For simplicity, they can be categorized under four main headings: geographic, demographic, psychographic, and combinations. Before discussing the characteristics of each segmentation approach, it is important to understand what makes a segment useful for marketing purposes. Three conditions must be met:

1. Each member of a segment must have one trait that links all members of the segment together and which is absent for all excluded members. In other words, there must be some common binding characteristic that can be identified for each segment which makes it unique.

2. Each segment must be substantial. There must be enough members with a common characteristic to make the segment large enough for marketing purposes. Although there is no optimum size that must be achieved before marketing commences, the general rule of thumb is as profit margins for the goods offered decline, there must be a corresponding increase in the size of the segment.

3. Each segment must be exploitable. Exploitable in this sense refers to some way of reaching members of the segment in order to expose them to the marketing program. Without a means to reach a segment, there is no way to use marketing techniques to increase their purchase of the product.

The reason for segmentation is simply to reduce large populations into smaller ones that can then be targeted for specific marketing programs. There are a myriad of segmentation possibilities. Populations can be segmented by hair color, amount of touring experience, annual household income, music preferences down to specific artists, and so on. In fact, segmentation can be taken to the extreme where each individual, because of each person's inherent uniqueness, becomes a segment. Obviously, segmenting too far violates the condition of substantiality noted above. On the other hand, there may be a tendency not to segment enough, and exploitable characteristics are left uncovered. Generally, marketers employ segmentation principles often without fully understanding that they are doing so. As tourism has grown, technology advanced, and competition for the travelers' dollars has increased, segmentation has received more attention from academic researchers as well as practitioners. The types of segmentation discussed below have all evolved to become more complex and interdependent. Although these various categories are treated as separate types of segmentation, few practical uses of segmentation rely on only one type.

Geographic

Geographic segmentation is simply the process of grouping potential consumers into discernable geographic locations of residence. For example, rural areas possessing plentiful natural resources often view close urban areas as their geographic market. This very simple type of segmentation has worked well for years. Northern Wisconsin enjoys plentiful lakes, streams, forests, and mild summer climates. Historically, the markets for northern Wisconsin tourism-related businesses have been from the large urban area of Chicago, Illinois and to a lesser extent Minneapolis/St. Paul, Minnesota. Upstate New York and the Poconos in Pennsylvania appeal to urban residents in New York City and Philadelphia, as do many of the beach areas along the Atlantic coast. Similarly, seaside resorts throughout Europe attract many visitors from the closest major European capital. The reason for the early success of resorts in these locations is in large measure due to contrast and location. Contrast in natural resource base as well as population base appeal to many people living in an urban area. For many, a trip to the woods, mountains, or beaches is a refreshing change of pace from everyday life. At the same time that these resort areas offer an appealing contrast, they are also located less than a day's travel from their market area. Since in the past long distance modes of transportation (e.g., air travel) were more expensive and/or time-consuming, nearby resort areas were preferred vacation destinations and simple geographic segmentation was adequate. Advertising could be simply directed at the closest urban area and increases in advertising expenditures could be used to either further penetrate the market or to initiate new campaigns in other geographically close markets.

Geographic segmentation achieves popularity because it is relatively easy to use. The extent to which people organize themselves leads to membership in a geographical group based on some arbitrary characteristic. These groups become recognizable due to their residence preference and can be easily utilized for geographic segmentation purposes.

Early tourism image studies differentiated geographic markets based on perceptions of offered products. Hunt (1971) and Crompton (1979) are among the first to recognize that different regions held different perceptions of the same destination. More recently, Ritchie and Smith (1991) note regional variations in response to awareness of Calgary, Canada as a result of Calgary hosting the 1988 Olympics.

Another example can be found in an image study conducted by Gartner et al. (1983), who analyze people's perceptions of an outdoor recreation activity (downhill skiing) in one destination area (Utah) in an attempt to identify geographic markets most likely to be favorably disposed to an advertising campaign focusing on downhill skiing. Their findings reveal that many geographically closer areas held lower perceptions of downhill-skiing opportunities in Utah compared to some more distant markets. A marketing campaign directed at the distant market, coupled with expanded direct air service from a major carrier, resulted in increased travel to Utah for the purpose of downhill skiing. In this case, airline deregulation resulting in increased access and lower air fares presented an opportunity for geographic segmentation to be combined with a form of psychographic (image) segmentation, resulting in increased market share.

Geographic segmentation has evolved over the years and moved beyond the simple "location, location, location" decision process. Developing in close proximity to urban areas is no longer essential to success. Increasing competition, changing technology, population shifts, longer work weeks, and other forces constantly change the nature of the tourism industry. Simplistic geographic segmentation based on location to market is no longer enough of an edge for successful tourism development.

Demographic

Demographic segmentation groups potential consumers by socioeconomic characteristics. Age, income, race, and gender are all different types of characteristics that can be employed for demographic segmentation. Figure 10.6 lists the various socioeconomic characteristics most commonly employed for demographic segmentation.

Age has been one of the most commonly used characteristics to denote segments with numerous descriptive names given to groups of people falling into certain age categories. For example, the term "Baby Boomers" has almost instant recognition within the United States referring to the group of people born shortly after World War II. Similarly, the older travel market (more than 50 years) has been defined as the senior market (Shoemaker, 1989; Vincent and de los Santos, 1980), gray market (Supernaw, 1985), and mature market (Lazer, 1985; Allen, 1981). In reality, the

Figure 10.6 *Most Common Variables Used in Demographic Segmentation*

Race

Age

Income (Single & Family)

Household Size

Number of Children Under 18 in Household

Marital Status

Education

Occupation

older market comprises many separate markets whose only common characteristic is age. Attempts to further segment within age groups using other demographic characteristics has led to what popular culture refers to as DINKS, an acronym for "double income no kids."

Demographic segmentation is similar to geographic segmentation in terms of ease of use. Just as society organizes itself into geographical units, it also collects data on the number of people with specific demographic characteristics. Census data can reveal the number belonging to each demographic group with respect to their geographical affiliation. Morrison (1989) refers to this type of segmentation as geodemographic segmentation. While researchers continue to use demographics for segmentation purposes, there is an accepted notion that demographics alone do not provide sufficient information to make each segment exploitable.

Psychographic

Psychographic segmentation attempts to classify markets based on observed behavior, expressed interests, motivations and attitudes, or a host of other related psychological characteristics. It has quickly become the area of segmentation receiving the most attention in the literature, owing in great part to the seemingly endless ways of psychologically classifying groups of people. It is not possible here to present even a representative sample of the vast work completed in this area. Instead, a selected sample is reviewed to provide the reader with some idea of the different types of psychographic segmentation published.

One of the earliest studies addressing psychographic segmentation in tourism is Plog's (1974) Allocentric-Psychocentric approach to classification. Plog contends that people exhibit certain psychological traits in their travel behavior and choice of destination. For the U.S. population, the number of people with similar traits is distributed along a normal curve (Figure 10.7). At each extreme, at least three deviations from the mean, are the Allocentrics and Psychocentrics. Allocentrics are in part characterized by heavy activity levels, in search of the new, exotic or relatively unexplored areas, less concerned about many of the services provided by the tourism industry and less likely to become repeat customers. Travel for them becomes an opportunity to stress their individuality, explore new horizons and test the limits of their psyche. Psychocentrics, on the other hand, prefer the traditional or accepted destinations, have low activity levels and prefer brand-name services resulting in repeat business. The extent of their travels is limited to the familiar, and their quest for adventure almost nonexistent. Since both the Allocentric and Psychocentric markets are very small, targeting either group is difficult and can be risky. Larger populations are found in the near Allocentric/Psychocentric groups, with

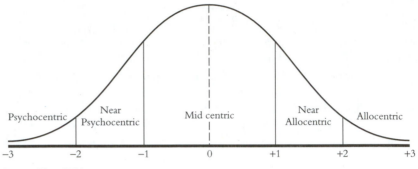

Figure 10.7 *Distribution of Psychographic Segments*

Source: Plog, 1974

both exhibiting similar characteristics to their named cousins, but the extremes of behavior and destination preference are less pronounced. The largest group of travelers is classified as Mid-Centrics. Midcentrics are often family-oriented, prefer moderate levels of activity and are willing to pay a fair amount for travel services. Whereas Allocentrics may be willing to pay more for less services if those services are found in exotic locations, Mid Centrics are more value-conscious consumers that forego the exotic for the comfortable.

Plog also discovers that income may mask the effect of group identification. If only observed travel behavior is used to determine group affiliation, then low income can mistakenly classify Allocentric psychological types into the Psychocentric group simply because the individual is financially unable to reveal their true group identity through destination choice. Although not addressed, other travel constraints (e.g., time, family life cycle) may also serve to mask a person's true psychological travel profile.

Some of the problems noted above can occur in any type of psychological segmentation. There is even some reason to suggest that primary data collection efforts used to reveal psychological profiles may be flawed depending on when data is collected. For example, Chapter 8 discusses a psychological model of traveler behavior. The main premise is that people enter and immerse themselves into different cultures when they travel. They are affected by the host culture, but more importantly they join a new tourist culture that exists solely in their chosen destination. This new tourist culture, if it is significantly different than their residual culture, may result in different feelings, attitudes, and behavior being expressed. Is it reasonable to assume, then, that psychological profiles completed while a person is a member of one culture will be similar to those completed while a part of a different culture? Although there is no evidence to support this proposition, there is also no evidence to reject it at this point.

Other notable psychographic segmentation tourism research includes VALS. VALS means values and lifestyles, and was originally developed at SRI International. It is a way of classifying people by means of psychological profiles with respect to certain demographic characteristics. This is a form of what Morrison (1989) refers to as two-stage segmentation. VALS groups people into nine life-style segments, such as Belongers, Achievers and Emulators. Although SRI's use of VALS was not tourism-related, Shih (1986) applies the basic principles to a data set collected to track the progress of Pennsylvania's tourism marketing program. He found VALS to be extremely useful for media selection, as different lifestyle groups have different media patterns. He also discovers that the majority of visitors to Pennsylvania could be assigned to three of the nine life-style groups. These were the groups VALS methodology indicated would be attracted to the state based on the type of marketing campaign conducted. VALS has much wider applications for tourism research and marketing than those discussed here, and is one of the different types of psychographic segmentation receiving increasing attention. As with most forms of psychographic segmentation, there are some problems with VALS that do not exist with either geographic or demographic segmentation. First, members of each lifestyle group are not exclusively tied to that group. An individual may exhibit certain life-style tendencies when purchasing pleasure travel and altogether different behavior when purchasing some other product. People may also shift into different groups during different periods of their life. Although people shift geographical affiliation and demographic characteristics throughout life as well, there are data collection systems in place supported by government that track these shifts. No such database exists for VALS or many other similar types of psychographic segmentation, thereby requiring expensive data collection efforts be conducted on a regular basis to track changes.

In another example, Mazanec (1992) experiments with a neural network approach to describing psychographic market segments. Neural network models, using the concepts of pattern recognition which form the base of artificial intelligence systems, work by identifying consumer segments without prior determination of the benefits sought. Once benefit segmentation is completed, each segment can be compared to the level of benefits present in the destination. Marketing efforts can be directed at those segments with the highest purchasing power who are also most likely to have their vacation expectations met by the touristic products available in the destination. Neural network models are still in the experimental stage for marketing purposes, but they hold great promise for fine tuning marketing efforts directed at psychologically based market segments.

Combination

Demographic and geographic segmentation becomes more refined and revealing when combined with psychographic forms of segmentation. Segmentation can be done in single stage, two-stage or multistage approaches (Morrison, 1989). What works best depends on how refined the researcher wants the final groups to be. One common method of two-stage segmentation involves an initial a priori approach where the researcher pre-selects the segment to be analyzed and then uses another form of segmentation to identify group differences between members of the first segment. Shoemaker (1989) provides an example of this approach by initially segmenting the entire travel market into two groups, those over and those under 50 years of age. This a priori segmentation effectively limited and focused the next stage. Conducting a form of psychographic segmentation, Shoemaker further groups the over 50 traveling segment into three categories which he labels "Family Travelers," "Active Resters," and "Older Set." Separate marketing activities could then be directed at only those segments deemed to be potential consumers of the specific tourism product(s) offered.

RESEARCH

Finding the answers to the questions directing the marketing plan begins with market research. The question "where are we now?" embodies: How well are the present set of goods and services provided received by the market?; what are competitors offering?; what are the met and unmet needs of present consumers?; and what other opportunities exist within the market? Market research is an ongoing process involving reassessment of chosen strategies in order to determine how well they are meeting stated objectives. Not all research is expensive to conduct, and many organizations may be surprised to find they have all the information they need to answer many of the questions at their fingertips. For example, lodging or resort properties have information on where the present group of users originates, length of stay, and possibly purpose of visit contained on guest registration cards. Public recreation agencies requiring permits for certain types of activities or registration for camping have similar types of information already available to them. This is the type of information needed to help answer the question "Where are we now?"

Other sources of information on market trends, including changing customer tastes, are available in trade or academic journals or through papers presented at conferences. Research data can also be purchased, or in some cases obtained free of charge, from a variety of research organizations including trade associations, national tourist offices, airline carriers, hotel companies, international and regional tourism organizations and public recreation agencies.

Market research is done in different ways, utilizing many different techniques. However, whatever types are selected, the following topical areas must be investigated: product analysis, market analysis, consumer analysis, competitor analysis, and opportunity analysis. Whether the researcher utilizes primary or secondary data to address these topics, there is a process which, if followed, organizes the task and makes a more useful end product.

Research Process

The research process can be broken down into a series of interrelated steps:

1. **Problem Identification.** What is the problem in need of research? What does the researcher hope to uncover in the ensuing investigation? If the problem is too large and unmanageable, research efforts will be wasted. For example, if market share is decreasing, it is best to start with a part of the problem and proceed to solve it by assembling pieces. If visitation declined by ten percent last year yet competitors' sales increased, it would be best to start with a competitor analysis and investigate whether the decline was due to increased competition brought on by new pricing or promotional strategies. If no concrete answers can be found, a product analysis may indicate if the problem is internal to the operation (e.g., poor service).

2. **Conduct a review of related information.** This step is sometimes referred to as a literature review. It involves collecting and systematically analyzing any information pertinent to the identified problem. Other peripherally-related research may provide clues to why the problem exists. Information can be compiled from published sources or may be acquired through meetings or interviews with others in a similar situation.

3. **Develop methods of analysis.** How will the research be conducted? In this step, the researcher decides if primary data will be collected and how that will be done (e.g., telephone interviews, mail survey). If step 2 uncovers useful sources of secondary data, their value to the

research problem at hand can be determined. If primary data collection is deemed necessary, a sample population will be identified, sample size set, and time frame for data collection established. Methods of analysis include selecting an appropriate analysis technique. How will the results be analyzed and presented?

4. Data Collection. This step requires data be collected in a useable form for analysis. If surveys are used, they must be designed, pretested, modified, and delivered to the sample population. Data collection must be done in a systematic manner. If no structure is imposed on the sampling frame, then results can be seriously biased. For example, if a business wants to know more about its present users but there are definite peak periods of use, sampling only during off times will not provide an accurate picture of the typical customer. Sampling must be set up so that it proportionally replicates actual use patterns.

5. Data Analysis. Data is analyzed using the techniques identified in the Methods step. This should only be considered a preliminary round of data analysis, as initial output may indicate further analysis on the data set is required to attain the research objectives. Other analytical techniques may be necessary to fully address the research problem specified in step 1.

6. Results Interpretation. What do the results indicate? All steps in the research process are critical as they form a hierarchy of investigation, but the interpretation of results will provide direction for management decisions. Interpretation should be consistent and relate to stated objectives but also refer back to what was uncovered during the literature review. Do the results support trends identified in previous research or do they signify a new direction? Action recommendations will follow from the interpretation.

7. Report Writing. The final step is to disseminate the information through report-writing and publication. If the researcher is part of a private sector enterprise, the report may be considered proprietary and available only to staff. If the research is not considered proprietary, a suitable publication outlet should be found. Innovation in research, and eventually product offering, builds on other research. Whether the intent is to form a theoretical body of knowledge or implement a new course of action, research results need to be shared with others who can utilize the information for specific purposes. Knowledge builds on knowledge, and report writing is a concrete form of knowledge acquisition.

Types of Research

As organizations increase in size, the financial resources available for research also increase. However, the types of research undertaken are usually limited by organizational mission statements. Coalition organizations (e.g., hospitality groups) generally sponsor research which is of some use to all members of the organization. Focusing on particular products is usually a concern at the firm level. While the types of research that are normally conducted are a function of the size and mission of the sponsoring organization, the following discussion focuses on research primarily useful to larger organizations. These types of research techniques can be assembled into four broad categories: assessment, monitoring, product positioning, and forecasting.

Assessment

The primary purpose of most assessment research is to determine the effectiveness, in terms of increased sales, of promotional programs and provide information to decision-makers about the program's value. The most common form of assessment research is a conversion study. The main focus of conversion studies is to estimate the percentage of inquires to a specific promotional campaign that resulted in actual sales (for public organizations, sales are synonymous with visitation). This usually requires some form of primary data collection using surveys administered to a sample of the population of inquirers responding to the specific promotional campaign. The two most common forms of data collection methods are mail surveys and telephone interviews, both producing similar results with telephone interviews best at reducing data collection time.

Conversion studies have been criticized on several grounds. Care must be exercised in selecting the sample, non-response bias must be controlled, and those people who had previously decided to purchase the product (e.g., travel to the region) before exposure to the promotion must be factored out of the sample (Silberman and Klock, 1986). Sometimes conversion studies have also been used to collect data for other purposes such as visitor profile information. While this has intuitive advantages such as solving two problems with one data collection effort, thereby reducing cost, it has not proved to be a practical or advisable technique (Perdue and Botkin, 1988). Most conversion research is undertaken by public organizations attempting to justify the use of public money for promotion. They are also of benefit to private organizations where concurrent advertising programs are being conducted and the organization wishes to evaluate each one separately.

Monitoring

Monitoring is probably the most common type of research conducted by the public sector. Depending on the research design, monitoring-focused research can also be used for product positioning purposes. Monitoring's intent is to initially establish baseline information regarding visitor profiles or visitor impacts, and then through periodic studies update the information. Economic impact studies are a form of monitoring research, and due to their significant political relevance are in high demand.

Many times organizations want more information about visitors than provided through economic impact studies. Types of visitor information desired include origin, length of stay, activity preference, party size, and so on. There have been many techniques utilized to collect information on visitors. Surveys conducted en route, at attractions (intercept), and port of entry/exit are the most common. Some techniques employ a diary survey format to track not only expenditures but also visitation patterns for the entire length of stay. Gartner and Hunt (1988) use a technique termed a front end, which, when combined with a diary instrument can overcome some of the bias problems inherent in the use of a diary survey technique.

Recently a "trip index" model originally developed by Pearce and Elliott (1983) used to estimate length of stay in an area has been modified by Uysal and McDonald (1989) to provide visitor profile information and segment travelers into groups useful for marketing purposes. This is an example of a monitoring type study also being used for product positioning purposes.

Product Positioning

Product positioning is the marketing art of identifying unique product characteristics for a particular consumer group(s) and developing promotional messages for that group. Most of the product positioning research is of the market segmentation variety. One of the problems with market segmentation for product positioning is the inability to adequately measure the existence of close economic substitutes. For example, market segmentation may reveal that significant numbers of potential visitors exist in a previously untargeted, geographically close market. However, destinations further away may be in a better position to capture that market due to the presence of better and cheaper access. Economic distance is therefore lower for the distant destination. The geographically closer destination must identify and promote product attributes which are not present in the destination with lower economic distance. Successful product positioning requires knowledge of competitor's products with respect to attributes sought by visitors in order to delineate and market comparative advantages. This type of product positioning research is receiving increasing attention.

No one model or technique has been universally accepted for product positioning research. Scott et al. (1978) use discriminant analysis techniques to measure touristic attributes most sought by travelers to Massachusetts. Similar discriminant analysis work is conducted by Phelps (1986) to identify tourist images of Menorca. Goodrich (1978) and Gartner (1989) use multidimensional scaling techniques to describe tourist images of different destinations (see next chapter). Other studies using different statistical techniques for product positioning purposes are performed by Embacher and Buttle (1989), who use repertory grid analysis, and Calantone et al. (1987), using correspondence analysis. Because of the many different research designs used in product positioning studies, this type of research remains a fruitful area for researchers and organizations looking for a decisive edge in an increasingly competitive tourist market.

Forecasting

The primary function of forecasting research is to predict future tourist flows (sales) to an area (business). Accurate predictions are necessary to plan investment decisions. Unfortunately, accurate predictions are difficult if not impossible to make due to the influence of exogenous factors. Who could have predicted the oil embargo of 1973 and the turmoil it caused for the tourism industry? Even with many of the problems inherent in forecasting, costs associated with not forecasting are high and may lead to erroneous measures of future demand, seriously affecting development decisions.

Inaccurate forecasts affect more than the tourism industry. Transportation systems may not be upgraded in time to handle traffic increases, resulting in congestion, resident irritation, and visitor substitution of destinations. Community support services (e.g., medical), which serve residents as well as visitors, may be overwhelmed, with unexpected increases in demand. The consequences of not forecasting are such that attempts to find accurate forecasting techniques continue.

Many methods, both quantitative and qualitative, have been utilized for forecasting. Regression, time series, Delphi, judgment-aided, gravity, and trip-generation models have all been used with varying degrees of success (Box and Jenkins, 1970; Ellis and Van Doren, 1983; Freund and Wilson, 1974; Swart et al., 1978; and Wander and Van Erden, 1980). The quantitative methods (e.g., regression, gravity) appear to be more useful for short-run forecasting, with the qualitative methods (e.g., Delphi, executive judgment) more applicable for long-range forecasts. The likelihood of unpredictable change increases as the forecasting time frame lengthens, decreasing the value of past data as an accurate predictor of future events. Uysal and Crompton (1985) suggest combining quantitative and qualitative methods to improve forecasting models.

Research Mix

The four categories of research discussed above provide the core of information required to guide marketing plans. However, all four types do not need to be conducted simultaneously. Because of the costs involved in collecting primary data, it is necessary to develop a research plan that prioritizes needs and budgets expenditures over time.

Monitoring research, especially economic impact information, has high value for public organizations due to its political significance. Different techniques for assessing economic impact exist, and once baseline economic impact measurements are completed, low-cost barometers can be constructed and updated using secondary data.

The types of monitoring research that profile visitors are extremely important for understanding present visitor patterns, but also for product positioning efforts. Visitor profile analyses conducted periodically can be used to gauge the effectiveness of promotion and advertising efforts in terms of meeting specific objectives (e.g., increasing length of stay). Disadvantages of visitor profile studies are primarily in terms of cost, since the reliance on primary data collection efforts tends to make this type of research expensive.

Product positioning research should be conducted after sufficient baseline information is available. In the increasingly competitive travel market, this type of research provides the greatest opportunity to identify appropriate attraction development for specific market segments which have the greatest potential for increasing travel market share. Monitoring type research, as previously mentioned, can provide some initial information for product positioning purposes, and it may be possible to combine the two to decrease overall research costs. For example, market-segmentation studies are relatively easy to perform with data collected through visitor profile research. However, experimental research designs provide the best opportunity to explore new positioning possibilities. Product positioning should be an integral component of the research mix because of its potential to increase market share through the identification of new markets, help direct marketing efforts, and guide facility development.

Ideally, assessment type research such as conversion studies should follow new product positioning strategies. To be most useful, this type of research should be completed after specific new markets are identified and promotional programs are planned, developed, and implemented for those markets. This approach would not only determine the value of a new positioning strategy but could also be used to pretest various positioning strategies to select the one with the greatest chance of success.

Once information on current users is known, forecasting research should begin since certain factors may affect one market more than another. It is important to understand present markets in order to make necessary adjustments when conditions change. For example, previous economic downturns due to increasing oil prices were regional in nature. Other sectors of the economy continued to grow at the same time as those that were oil-dependent declined. If visitor profile studies indicated that a primary market was heavily dependent on one industry, then forecasting research methodologies can take that into consideration. Failure to understand present markets could lead to forecasting research that is unable to predict some of the exogenous factors affecting regional travel behavior.

Forecasting research, which can be complex and costly, does not have to be conducted on an annual basis. Assuming there is little change in a particular market's economy, predictive values may be accurate for an extended period. If exogenous shocks do occur, dramatically altering travel flows, it would be wise to conduct additional forecasting research shortly after the event to avoid the consequences of over investment in attraction development.

Each category of research has its advantages and disadvantages, summarized in Figure 10.8 along with comparison of cost, level of complexity, purpose, expected outputs, and planning recommendations. Planning recommendations place the highest priority on conducting monitoring-type research followed by product positioning, assessment, and finally forecasting.

Marketing Issues of the 1990s

The previous discussion discussed creating an effective marketing plan backed by focused research. However, following the above steps is no guarantee of marketing success. New strategies and technology create new challenges and opportunities. The last section of this chapter deals with a few of the marketing issues that are crucial to the provision of recreation products and services in the 1990s. The three that are highlighted are strategic alliances, customer service, and cyberspace technology.

Strategic Alliances

Companies have always found ways to compete and cooperate often at the same time. During the 1980s, corporate buyouts were a common method of reducing competition or acquiring new product lines, often unrelated to the core business. Another common method used to expand into new areas was joint ventures. Joint ventures occur when two or more firms realize that they do not have the resources or willingness to assume the risk of a new business operation. Instead they cooperate and share risk by

Research Category	Methods	Primary Purpose(s)	Complexity & Cost	Planning Recommendation
Assessment	Conversion Modified Travel Cost	Evaluate promotion and advertising efforts	Models have been developed, reducing complexity. Cost is low for primary data collection efforts.	Should follow product positioning research and be used to evaluate new promotions and advertising.
Monitoring	Impact Studies (primarily economic) Barometers Indices Visitor Profiles	Establish baseline information and periodic updates. Budget justification.	Existing models keep complexity low. Costs low if an already developed model is used and secondary data are available. Exception for visitor profile analysis, which has relatively low complexity but high cost due to the collection of primary data.	Top priority. Needed to establish baseline information and should be completed before other research.
Product Positioning	Multidimensional Scaling Repertory Grid Discriminant Analysis Correspondence Analysis	Identify new markets and opportunities to increase travel flow from established markets. Uncover new strategies and products for promotion and advertising.	Complexity is high because many of the models are still experimental. Requires collecting primary data, making costs high.	Follows initial monitoring research and should continue annually in order to investigate new markets.
Forecasting	Time-Series Delphi Judgment Aided Focus Groups Gravity/Trip Generation	Provide information on future travel patterns for investment and planning decisions.	Complexity can be high. Experimental models are still being tested. Qualitative methods have higher cost because of the requirements of soliciting opinions and information from consumer panels. Quantitative methods have lower cost depending on the availability of secondary data.	Do not need to be conducted annually, but should be undertaken more frequently when exogenous factors change rapidly.

Figure 10.8 Research Selection Criteria Matrix

pooling resources. Sometimes joint ventures are the only development option as cash-poor countries without a formal private sector insist that they
be one of the partners in any new development. Their contribution may
take the form of land or many times simply operating permission. This was
the case in the People's Republic of China during the early days of hotel
construction in the 1970s. Critics of joint ventures cite conflicting management policies and the formation of a separate, formal, highly structured,
joint operating authority as drawbacks to these arrangements. Recently
there has been a move to less rigid strategic alliances as a way to overcome
some of the problems inherent in traditional joint-venture arrangements.

Many reasons have been offered for the increase in strategic alliances
during the 1990s, but at the heart of all the reasons is the increasing pace of
globalization. Yochelson (1992) cites four reasons for this trend. First, the
global distribution of economic power is achieving parity between nations.
The United States is no longer the preeminent global economic force with
its powerful domestic market. Newly emerging economies in Asia, the economic prowess of Japan, and strengthening of economic linkages in Europe
have evened out the global economic playing field. Second, due to technological change, especially in communications and information processing,
international competition is becoming more intense. Third, the demise of
centrally planned economies has led to a reliance on market forces to establish global economic order. Fourth, national governments that establish
trade and investment policies are increasingly in a reactive mode. The pace
of change, technological, social, and economic, is proceeding at such a rapid
rate that policy-making bodies are being forced to change and adjust long
held policies in order not to lose economic and political control.

Many businesses, aware that they are not big or powerful enough to
direct change, have entered into strategic alliances to benefit from the
change taking place. These alliances take on many different shapes and
forms. It is imperative that management carefully consider their options as
strategic alliances tend to be unstable and often fail.

Gates (1993) identifies some of the key reasons companies may enter
into a strategic alliance:

1. Need for a local partner to gain access to a new market

2. Overcome limitations such as finances or technological ability

3. Foster creativity outside the parent firm's bureaucratic structure

4. Share risk inherent in new product or technology development

One of the key characteristics of a successful strategic alliance is the
formation of a less-than-formal separate management board. While this

board should be able to develop recommendations for operations, it should not be able to dictate policy. Rigid control reduces creativity and injects another layer of bureaucracy, one of the things a strategic alliance attempts to avoid. Because of the reliance on a loose management structure, strategic alliances should be built on trust rather than formal operating guidelines. This is probably one of the most difficult things for a company to accept, especially if it has invested heavily in the alliance.

Tourism strategic alliances are most visible within the airline industry. Deregulation and mergers have moved some carriers into the mega category which means others, primarily small national carriers, have to compete against resources that almost surpass some countries' Gross National Products. The only way for these carriers to stay aloft is to enter into strategic alliances with some of the larger airlines (Go and Hedges, 1994).

One of the most successful strategic alliances is the Northwest/KLM partnership, originally begun in 1989. KLM Royal Dutch Airlines over the years has taken a larger equity interest in Northwest Airlines. Many critics questioned the move as Northwest hovered on the brink of bankruptcy in 1992-3. However, due to employee concessions in exchange for part ownership, debt restructuring, limited competition at its major hubs, and an improving economy, Northwest posted record earnings in 1994-5. Part of the turnaround is credited to the strategic alliance with KLM. Once receiving respective government approval, the airlines entered into a code-sharing agreement for selected transatlantic flights which allows each of them to market the other's flights. This allows KLM access to the U.S. domestic market through Northwest hubs in Memphis, Detroit, and Minneapolis. Northwest gained access to KLM's hub in Amsterdam. In addition to code-sharing, baggage transfer services have been consolidated, as has ticketing. Synchronized scheduling has also reduced the wait for passengers connecting through one of the hubs to another destination. A total of 350 cities in over 80 countries on six continents is available to Northwest/KLM passengers.

For Northwest, one of the advantages gained in the strategic alliance was access to Europe, Africa, and the Middle East. For KLM, access to the U.S. domestic market and western Asia was a prime consideration. In addition, both airlines realize cost savings through sharing of baggage handling, ticketing and other services. For the passenger, advance seating worldwide, access to each other's airport clubs, expanded destination options for frequent flyers, and relatively seamless service are advantages gained from choosing either airline.

One of the key considerations in choosing a strategic alliance is the extent service will be improved for the customer. If that is a primary consideration, any number of businesses can enter into strategic alliances. For example, MISR travel services in Egypt is one of the in-country tour operators that has established a strategic alliance with companies operating Nile Cruises. A customer in Cairo wishing to take a Nile Cruise from Aswan to Luxor need only pay MISR for the service. On the day of departure, a MISR representative takes the customer to the airport in Cairo and checks him/her in. Upon arrival in Aswan, another MISR representative picks up the customer at the airport and proceeds to the cruise ship where he/she is preregistered. At this point, services are transferred to the cruise company. Upon arrival in Luxor, another MISR representative contacts the customer with a schedule for departure and return to Cairo. The process of representatives meeting the flight is repeated, including transfer to a Cairo hotel for one night and transportation to the airport the next day for final departure if needed. The service is seamless, payment is to one agency, and the customer is free to enjoy the journey without the hassle of additional payment, securing taxi rides, etc.

Initially, strategic alliances may be considered for many of the reasons (risk and cost-sharing) mentioned previously. However, if the company is part of the tourism industry, economic reasons alone are not the sole determinant of success or failure. Customer service and convenience is a big part of the equation. Customer service is rapidly becoming an important product differentiation strategy in the 1990s and is the focus of our next marketing issue.

Customer Service

Customer service, also known as service quality, has its roots in product life-cycle theory. The reader will remember that as products mature, producers must switch from a production to a consumer orientation. This is especially critical for tourism goods and services, as the product is untestable prior to purchase and consumption. Purdue (1995a) defines service quality as the extent to which the service delivered exceeds customer service expectations. While this is something that many providers implicitly recognize today, it is only recently that the academic and professional community have begun to operationalize the concept and develop strategies for measuring and improving service quality. Perdue's (1995b) work provides a review of the evolution of the service quality construct, strategies for communicating with guests, evaluation techniques, and service failure recovery strategies.

Service quality became a separate issue during the late 1970s as the first spate of articles establishing service as different from tangible products was published. It became obvious that traditional product marketing strategy could not be easily transferred to service marketing for many of the same reasons identified earlier in Figure 10.2. This line of inquiry continued into the 1980s, where service quality clearly emerged as a central con-

cept of overall product marketing. In the latter half of the 1980s many different measures of service quality were presented and in the early 90s, with the concept firmly established, the focus has shifted to return on investment from service quality improvements and recovery strategies from service failures.

Making the quality service concept work for a business requires that a communication strategy be in place. In other words, it is extremely difficult to determine the success or failure of your program if your customers are not talking to you. The first requirement is that customers must believe that complaining will make a difference. A process for reacting to customer complaints must be in place, with the customers aware of how to initiate the process. Timing is a critical component of the process. If the intent is to deal with the problem before the customer departs, then surveys, the most common method of collecting service quality assessment data, are rather useless. However, if the intent is to monitor departmental quality, a continuous tracking system is needed. One technique that can be used for continuous tracking and possible complaint remedy is to use television survey systems. They are activated when the guest turns on the in-room television, and if the guest desires, he/she can receive immediate attention to their problem. Another technique that has been used with varying degrees of success is employee incident reports, where employees identify service problems as part of their regular duties. However, to make this type of system functional, employees should not view it as a means to spy on other employees or punish employees for service mistakes. It should be used as a self-help educational system with rewards for uncovering service quality problems.

Once a service-quality-data collection system is in place, there must be some way to categorize and assign attribute weights to customer complaints. Not all complaints threaten the viability of the operation and indeed some are unfounded and not valid.

Bartol and Martin (1991) identify eight dimensions of quality that should be constantly monitored:

1. Performance—how well is the service performed and received by guests? How much time people have to wait in line or how efficiently requests are handled are two key indicators of performance.

2. Features—are there any unique or different features, no matter how minor, that set your attraction apart from your competitors?

3. Reliability-do you consistently deliver what you promise?

4. Conformance—are all products of equally consistent quality? Do they reflect value for price?

5. Durability—will the product last? In tourism, where the product is an experience, durability can be defined as providing long-term, satisfying memories.

6. Serviceability—how well does the staff serve its guests? Are complaints handled in a respectful and helping manner? Are staff knowledgeable and able to provide information requests? Is there an organization commitment to providing the highest level of service available?

7. Aesthetics—does the attraction look well maintained and provide a feeling of comfort to its guests? This is one of the quality elements which will provide distance between competitors.

8. Perceived quality—do guests perceive the product to be of high quality? Perceptions do not always match reality. Management perceptions of quality may differ from guest perceptions of quality. It is the latter whose perceptions matter.

Once the dimensions have been disaggregated into related attributes and measured, they can be compared. Figure 10.9 shows an example of how this is done. This method combines complaint data with other forms of consumer data and competitor information. From this assessment it becomes clearer what must be done to improve service levels.

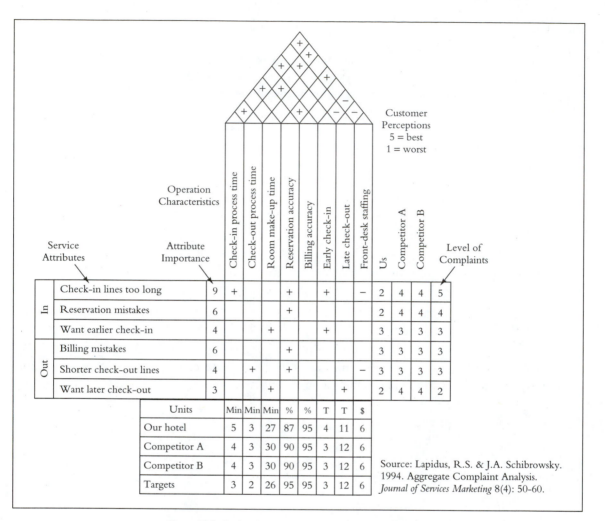

Figure 10.9 *Quality Service Matrix*

Finally, in spite of precautions, it is still possible to fail to provide expected levels of service. Periodically it is necessary to review service quality systems and change them when appropriate. The first thing to remember is that most people do not complain but prefer to pass bad service experiences on to other people in their circle of acquaintances. Therefore, user-friendly systems to elicit complaints are required. Constant review of new methods, choosing what appears appropriate for your business, and constant evaluation once the systems are in place is necessary.

Having achieved a user-friendly complaint system, the next step is to provide immediate resolution of the problem. Once the complaint is de-

termined to be valid (in case no determination can be made or the problem stems from some misunderstanding, the customer is always given the
benefit of the doubt), the customer should receive a sincere apology, be
offered adequate compensation or a fair solution, and treated in a manner
consistent with a caring company searching for a reasonable solution to
the problem.

Bartol and Martin (1991) recommend initiating a quality control program, incorporating many of the techniques discussed above, but put into
an assessment framework. Their program consists of:

1. A Total Quality Control (TQC) or Total Quality Management
    (TQM) program. TQC or TQM programs are approaches that
    emphasize an organization wide commitment to the provision of
    quality service. The program must be integrated into all departments
    and be a part of the organization's philosophy as expressed in its
    mission statement. The TQC or TQM approach aims at producing
    zero defects or complaints and requires a commitment from all levels
    of management. Quality should be a factor in performance evaluations.

2. Service audit. A service audit is a form of management by wandering
    around. Observations of group, unit, or individual performance com-
    prise a service audit. It is similar to the idea behind employee
    incident reports discussed above.

3. Human resource management. This begins by hiring the most
    qualified people for the job. Investing in training sessions for new as
    well as continuing employees improves skill, quality control levels,
    and creates a feeling that the organization is investing in its people.

4. Quality circles. Groups of employees who work together should
    meet on a regular basis and discuss methods to solve problems or
    initiate new quality programs. Quality circles should not be
    management-driven but work best when the employees are allowed
    to solve their own work related problems. Costs can be reduced and
    pride in providing quality service can result as employees feel
    ownership of the programs they help create.

5. Quality assurance through structure. The quality of an attraction can
    be portrayed in its structural design. Aesthetically blending
    architectural design in order for the attraction to have an aesthetic
    appeal also gives it an identity. Poorly designed attractions project an
    aura of poor quality and lack of attention to detail.

6. Acceptance sampling. Sampling the quality of goods produced is
    needed for quality control. Tourist attractions can apply this method

by surveying a sample of guests. Guest experience is the product produced and the only people who can evaluate experience quality are the guests. This is related to complaint surveys discussed above, but is more inclusive as it also includes an assessment of the total experience provided, including physical or mental stimulation/relaxation achieved, not simply those attributes that are directly affected by person to person interaction.

Cyberspace

Tourism marketing, as well as other product marketing, will be greatly transformed in the latter half of the 1990s. The vehicle behind the transformation is the internet or computer superhighway and its related companion, the World Wide Web (WWW). At the moment, the technology is entering a rapid acceptance stage and no one is exactly sure how it will all work out. What is sure is that many companies, large and small, are beginning to explore different uses of the technology for product marketing. Before discussing some of the tourism marketing applications related to use of this technology, some basic background is necessary.

The internet is a collection of computer networks that by using the same protocol are able to communicate with each other. The early uses of the internet consisted primarily of electronic mail or e-mail, as it has come to be known. Since the development of the internet was funded by the United States National Science Foundation, access was virtually free for academic and government users. As the use of the internet grew, so did the need to exchange information. Some of the information was in the form of large databases which were unable to be transferred using standard internet protocol. In 1989 a physicist, Tim Bernes-Lee, wrote a Hyper-Text Transfer Protocol (HTTP) and the HyperText Markup Language (HTML) which allowed large databases and video to be sent electronically. Additionally, it allowed for linkages with other computers and databases, thereby creating searchable files, enhanced data bases, and other aggregated files to be presented as one program. This system is now known as the World Wide Web (WWW).

The WWW allows any computer to become an access station. In other words, to access the information superhighway a person needs a computer, a modem for access to the highway, and a feeder system usually called a server which is analogous to a side or service road to a main highway. Server systems are now common and offered, at a fee, for public use. Once a person has all three pieces they can visit any stop on the WWW, and with some minor construction of their own become a WWW destination.

Current estimates of internet users is approximately 30 million, with the number expected to be ten times that by the turn of the century. Over 500 new web sites open each week (Majewski, 1995). Given current and expected future use, a major problem for marketing using this technology is how one finds what he/she is looking for. Software developers are quickly answering that question by providing systems called browsers that can be used to search, using key words, for selected access sites. Searches can be conducted by subject, key words, or simply by "surfing the net."

Hawkins (1995) has identified some current tourism-related marketing uses of the technology. They include individual companies (hotels, rental cars, tour operators) that have established their own home page and market their products directly to the consumer. Destinations, either individually or collectively, are appearing at increasing frequency. Many countries, states, and communities have home pages linked to other information containing all their travel literature in a retrievable, electronic format. Airline reservation systems are making user-friendly versions of their schedules available to potential customers. Even some large trade associations such as the National Tour Association are making the technology available to their members, thus creating a network of suppliers, packagers, and destinations.

One major advantage of the new technology is the ability to transmit video and graphics. Thus, a potential customer now has the opportunity to view different destinations through their home page, examine airline schedules, and search for special packages available through some of the tour operators. If someone is interested in packaging their own trip, this is becoming increasing possible as street maps, events, unique or unusual sites, supplier contacts, and almost any travel-related service can be made available through links with a home page. It is even possible to access bulletin boards where information on different destinations can be obtained from experienced travelers. Since this type of destination image formation is one of the most powerful agents (see next chapter under solicited organic), the technology has the ability to dramatically alter how we pick destinations for a visit. New 3D technology will make it possible for a user to view destinations or even activity options from different angles. For example, virtual reality systems will allow someone to experience "synthetic" hang-gliding or see the Temple of Karnak from above without leaving their home. All the options now or soon to be available of internet/web technology have even led to predictions that travel will decline as a result of the sensory stimuli now accessible from the privacy of one's home.

What does all this mean? Will travel decline or will easy access to electronic images of places stimulate travel to experience firsthand what was first glimpsed in cyberspace? Can electronic images replicate reality? For the present, tourism industry analysts are not viewing communication technology as a threat, but they do recognize it is rapidly changing how business is conducted.

With all the advances in the last couple years, there are still some obstacles remaining before the internet/web technology becomes more widely accepted. One of the first is speed of delivery. Presently, depending on time of day, access to sites and transmission of data, especially video and graphics, can be very slow. Users of a subscription service pay for online time so slowness equals cost. Increasing bandwidth capability is the answer, and this is being done, but as technology advances, bandwidth remains an obstacle to quick growth. Security still remains an issue, especially when direct sales are involved. New security software systems to prevent someone from accessing an electronic conversation and pirating sensitive information, such as credit card numbers, is being quickly developed. Electronic surveillance, something rarely discussed, is a concern for many users. Machlis (1995) discusses the possibility of electronic footprints allowing someone, legally or illegally, to track a customer's actions. Implications of this abuse are potentially damaging to the growth of the system.

Given so many unknowns about future use and marketing possibilities of the cyberspace technology, what can be said with some degree of certainty? First, technological obstacles such as bandwidth and security are easily solved and will remain short-term problems. Second, cash poor companies or small developing countries will have the same opportunity to access large markets as large companies. The cost of developing a home page and related, linked documents, is relatively minor. They will level out the playing field between the large and small users to an extent. Third, service will become increasingly important. Fast information will lead to fast expectations. Electronic companies will still have to provide high levels of customer service to set them apart from all the other cyberspace purveyors. Fourth, electronic surveillance will become more of a concern, especially if abuses become known and/or law enforcement tests their limits of use with the technology. Fifth, directing someone to a specific home page will remain a serious marketing issue even with the development of user-friendly searchable systems. Marketing via other media to make people aware of a particular home page address will continue to be a strategy employed during the technologies' high acceptance/growth stages.

Cyberspace marketing has arrived and it will become a part of almost every tourism-dependent company's marketing plan. For the foreseeable future, it will remain simply one aspect of an overall marketing effort using different media. For small businesses, it will most likely become a proportionally larger share of the marketing media mix than for larger, more diversified companies. Regardless, the internet/web is not ready to displace other parts of a marketing mix, but it has arrived as an important component of them.

CONCLUSION

Marketing can be simply defined as the process of forming a bridge between producer and consumer. The complexity of operationalizing the concept makes marketing more of an art than a science. Compounding the problem are the differences between tourism products and other goods. Most marketing strategies are based on the production of goods in a central location which are then delivered through various distribution channels to consumers. Since tourism goods are produced and consumed simultaneously, with the consumer traveling to the point of production, tourism marketing has become a separate area of study.

This chapter began by reviewing the concept of product life cycles and their relevance to tourism. All indications point to a situation where tourism will continue to grow but not at the same rate experienced during the last 20 plus years. Adopting a consumer orientation to the production and delivery of tourism goods requires attention to marketing. This is true whether the intent is to increase sales (visitation) or simply manage present markets.

The key to successful marketing is to develop a plan to internalize and incorporate the elements of a situation analysis into a marketing mix. The information needed to complete a situation analysis can be obtained from research conducted systematically, purposefully, and following a structured process.

Attention to the key issues of the 90s is critical to success. As globalization accelerates, strategic alliances become more useful and should be carefully studied. Customer service (service quality) will be increasingly used to differentiate between similar travel products. Cyberspace will open up new marketing opportunities with success dependent on manipulating the technology to suit the needs of a particular business and its clientele.

Marketing is just one of the implementation tools in the process of tourism development. The following chapters take implementation a step further into the arena of image development and finally into overall development planning. However, marketing stands out as a key ingredient of tourism development. It can take place in the absence of any overall development plan, but works best when integrated into a plan. It should not be viewed as simply a pro-growth tool. When used constructively, it can help businesses and public organizations deliver the types of products compatible with an area's range of resources. In that sense, it becomes a tool of implementation rather than a cause of overdevelopment.

EXECUTIVE SUMMARY

Tourism is entering a more mature stage of the product life cycle, characterized by increasing competition and lower rates of growth indicating the need for producers to adopt a consumer orientation to the production and delivery of goods and services.

Many differences exist between tourism products and other goods which greatly affects how they are marketed. The most important of these are an inverted distribution channel, production and consumption occurring simultaneously, reliance on personal selling skills, especially at the tour wholesaler end, and increasing use of sales and promotions to even out slow sales periods.

Travel is a luxury good, located in the elastic portion of an individual's demand curve, meaning the more important and intensive marketing becomes, especially during recessionary periods.

Marketing plans should be set to answer specific questions including: Where are we now, Where do we want to be, How do we get there, and How do we know when we get there?

Developing a marketing plan requires a thorough analysis of product, market, consumer, competition, and opportunities.

Target marketing can employ many different market segmentation strategies, the most common being a combination of the three main categories—demographic, geographic, and psychographic.

Market research involves a seven-step process from the identification of a research problem through data collection, analysis, and report of findings.

Research categories to be considered in any marketing plan include: assessment (how did we do), monitoring (how have things changed), product positioning (where would we like to be), and forecasting (trends). Establishing the right research mix depends on many factors, including type of organization (public or private), finances available, and objectives of the marketing plan.

Critical tourism marketing issues of the 1990s include strategic alliances, customer service, and cyberspace marketing. Strategic alliances, even though they have a high failure rate, are becoming more attractive due to globalization pressures. Customer service (quality service) is becoming one of the primary ways to differentiate tourism products. Cyberspace marketing using the Internet and World Wide Web is growing rapidly, and although cyberspace marketing techniques are still evolving, there is no doubt they are becoming an increasingly important part of any marketing plan.

REFERENCES

Allen, C. 1981. Measuring Mature Markets. *American Demographics* Vol. 3 (March):13–17.

Bartol, K. and D. Martin. 1991. Management. New York: McGraw-Hill, Inc.

Berkowitz, E., R. Kernin, and W. Rudelius. 1989. *Marketing*. 2nd ed. Boston: Irwin.

Box, G. and M. Jenkins. 1970. *Time Series Analysis: Forecasting and Control*. San Francisco: Holden Day.

Bryson, J. 1990. Strategic Planning for Public and Non-Profit Organizations: A guide to strengthening and sustaining organizational achievement. San Francisco: Jossey-Bass Publishers.

Calantone, R., C. di Benedetto, A. Hakam, and D. Bojanic. 1987. Multiple Multinational Tourism Positioning Using Correspondence Analysis. *Journal of Travel Research* 28(2):25–32.

Cooper, C. 1994. Product Lifecycle, pp. 341–345. In *Tourism Marketing and Management Handbook*. S. Witt and L. Moutinho, eds. Hertfordshire: Prentice Hall.

Crompton, J. 1979. An Assessment of the Image of Mexico as a Vacation Destination and the Influence of Geographical Location Upon that Image. *Journal of Travel Research* 17(4):18–23.

Davies, R. 1991. The Formulation of a Meeting and Convention Planning Model of Wisconsin Cities Utilizing the Evoked Set of Constructs. M.S. Thesis, Menomonie, WI: University of Wisconsin-Stout.

Ellis, B. and C. Van Doren. 1966. A Comparative Evaluation of Gravity and System Theory Models for Statewide Recreational Travel Flow. *Journal of Regional Sciences* 6(2):57–70.

Embacher, J. and F. Buttle. 1989. A Repertory Grid Analysis of Austria's Image as a Summer Vacation Destination. *Journal of Travel Research* 27(3):3–7.

Freund, J., and R. Wilson. 1974. An Example of a Gravity Model to Estimate Recreational Travel. *Journal of Leisure Research* 6(summer):241–256.

Gartner, W. 1989. Tourism Image: Attribute Measurement of Tourist State Choice Using Multidimensional Scaling Techniques. *Journal of Travel Research* 28(2):16–20.

Gartner, W., G. Cadez, J. Winterbottom, and J. Brockley. 1983. *Image of Utah*. Logan, Utah: Institute of Outdoor Recreation and Tourism, Utah State University.

Gartner, W. and J. Hunt. 1988. A Method to Collect detailed Tourist Flow Information. *Annals of Tourism Research* 15(1):159–165.

Gates, S. 1993. *Strategic Alliances: Guidelines for Successful Management*. New York: The Conference Board.

Go, F. and A. Hedges. 1994. Strategic Alliances, pp. 183–187. In *Tourism Marketing and Management Handbook*. S. Witt and L. Moutinho, eds. Hertfordshire: Prentice Hall.

Goodrich, J. 1978. A New Approach to Image Analysis Using Multidimensional Scaling. *Journal of Travel Research* 16:10–13.

Green, P., A. Krieger. 1991. Segmenting Markets with Conjoint Analysis. *Journal of Marketing* 55(October 1991):20–31.

Hawkins, D. 1995. Travel Marketing on the Internet. Paper presented at the 1995 meeting of the International Academy for the Study of Tourism. Cairo, Egypt.

Hunt, J. 1971. Image—A Factor in Tourism. Unpublished Ph.D. dissertation, Fort Collins, Co.: Colorado State University.

Lazer, W. 1985. Inside the Mature Market. *American Demographics*. March:24–25.

Lewis, R. and R. Chambers. 1989. *Marketing Leadership in Hospitality*. New York: Van Nostrand Reinhold.

Machlis, G. 1995. Presentation in the session Information Superhighway: Plethora of Uses, Possible Abuses. *4th International Outdoor Recreation and Tourism Trends Symposium*. St. Paul, Minn. Tourism Center, University of Minnesota.

Majewski, T. 1995. The Information Superhighway: Plethora of Uses, Possible Abuses,

Trend Tracker, 4th International Outdoor Recreation and Tourism Trends Symposium. St. Paul, MN. Tourism Center, University of Minnesota.

Mazanec, J. 1992. Classifying Tourists into Market Segments: A Neural Network Approach. *Journal of Travel and Tourism Marketing* 1(1):39–59.

Meidan, A. 1994. Pricing, pp. 354–358. In *Tourism Marketing and Management Handbook.* S. Witt, and L. Moutinho, eds. Hertfordshire: Prentice Hall.

Morrison, A. 1989. *Hospitality and Travel Marketing.* Albany, New York: Delmar Publishers Inc.

Palmer, D. and Stull. 1991. *Principles of Marketing.* 2nd ed. Cincinnati, OH: South Western.

Pearce, D. and J. Elliott. 1983. The Trip Index. *Journal of Travel Research* 22(1):6–9.

Perdue, R. 1995a. Quality Service for Tourism: Measurement and Evaluation. Presentation notes. *1995 Annual Conference of the Travel and Tourism Research Association.* Acapulco, Mexico.

Perdue, R. 1995b. Communication Strategies for Identifying and Resolving Consumer Complaints in Tourism Service Settings. Presentation notes: *1995 Annual Conference of the Travel and Tourism Research Association.* Acapulco, Mexico.

Perdue, R. and M. Botkin. 1988. Visitor Survey versus Conversion Study. *Annals of Tourism Research* 15(1):76–87.

Phelps, A. 1986. Holiday Destination Image— The Problem of Assessment: An Example Developed in Menorca. *Tourism Management* 7(3):168–180.

Plog, S. 1974. Why Destinations Rise and Fall in Popularity. *The Cornell Hotel and Restaurant Administration Quarterly* 14(4):55–58.

Ritchie, J., and B. Smith. 1991. The Impact of

A Mega-Event on Host Region Awareness: A Longitudinal Study. *Journal of Travel Research* 30(1):3–10.

Rogers, J. and T. Williams. 1989. Comparative Advertising Effectiveness: Practitioners' Perceptions Versus Academic Research Findings. *Journal of Advertising Research* 29(Oct./Nov.):22–37.

Scott, D., C. Schewe, and D. Frederick. 1978. A Multi-Brand/Multi-Attribute Model of Tourist State Choice. *Journal of Travel Research* 17(1):23–29.

Shih, D. 1986. "VALS as a Tool of Tourism Market Research: The Pennsylvania Experience." *Journal of Travel Research* 24(4):2–11.

Shoemaker, S. 1989. Segmentation of the Senior Pleasure Travel Market. 1989. *Journal of Travel Research* 27(3):14–21.

Silberman, J., and M. Klock. 1986. An Alternative to Conversion Studies for Measuring the Impact of Travel Ads. *Journal of Travel Research* 24(4):12–16.

Supernaw, G. 1985. Battle for the Gray Market, pp. 287–290. In TTRA Sixteenth Annual Conference Proceedings, Salt Lake City, Utah.

Swart, W., T. Var, and E. Gearing. 1970. Operations Research Application to Tourism. *Annals of Tourism Research* 1(Winter):33–51.

Uysal, M. and C. McDonald. 1989. Segmentation by Trip Index. *Journal of Travel Research* 27(3):38–42.

Uysal, M., and J. Crompton. 1985. An Overview of Approaches Used to Forecast Tourism Demand. *Journal of Travel Research* 23(4):7–15.

Vincent, V., and G. de los Santos. 1980. Winter Texans: Two Segments of the Senior Travel Market. *Journal of Travel Research* 29(1):9–12.

Wahab, S., and L. Crampon, and L. Rothfield. 1976. *Tourism Marketing*. London: Tourism International Press.

Wander, A., and D. Van Erden. 1980. Estimating the Demand for International Tourism Using Time Series Analysis. In D. Hawkins, ed. Washington, D.C.: George Washington University.

Wasson, R. 1974. *Dynamic Competitive Strategy & Product Life Cycles*. St. Charles, Ill.: Challenge Books.

Winterbottom, J., and W. Gartner. 1985. A Comparison of Tourism Transportation Modes from 1976–1984, pp. 155–163. *Proceedings of the 1985 National Outdoor Recreation Trends Symposium* II. Coordinated by the Department of Parks, Recreation and Tourism Management, Clemson University.

Yochelson, J. 1993. Foreword. *When Businesses Cross International Borders: Strategic Alliances and Their Alternatives*. H. James and M. Weidenbaum. London: Praeger.

Image Development

Country images can be portrayed through everyday occurrences, like these sheep being herded in New Zealand.
Photo by the author

Learning Objectives

Explore the different components of image.

•

Review the travel decision process with respect to the different components of image.

•

Examine the image formation process with respect to the variables or cost, credibility, and market penetration.

•

Review characteristics of images, such as how quickly they can be changed.

•

Discuss an image formation mix that should be considered once destination image objectives are decided.

•

Review various image assessment methods.

INTRODUCTION

Image as a factor in the travel decision process has been extensively studied. People hold perceptions of different destination areas which, when assessed and evaluated, become a key component of site selection. The image formation process is more important to tourism than to other industries. As addressed in the previous chapter, tourism products are an amorphous mass of experiences which are produced and consumed at the same time. There is no opportunity to sample the product prior to purchase. All consumer goods have attributes associated with the physical product that are evaluated prior to purchase. Tourism is no different in this regard. However, almost all consumer goods are available for attribute evaluation prior to purchase; tourism is the exception. If the family trip to Spain is not what was expected there is no money-back guarantee. This is not to say that there is no recourse for trips that are misrepresented or for services received which are less than those advertised. However, if the image one has of a destination differs markedly from reality in a way that lessens the enjoyment of the experience, the rule of thumb is caveat emptor.

Because of the importance of image in the travel decision process, marketeers spend a great deal of time, effort, and expense in presenting images of a destination that will hopefully appeal to an identified target market. Image formation is an involved process and with few exceptions destination images do not change quickly.

The image formation process constitutes the nucleus of this chapter. The chapter begins with a theoretical overview of the different components of image and their relationship to the travel decision process. Finally, different techniques for developing images and methods used to measure held images are presented.

IMAGE DEFINED

Crompton (1979) defines image as the sum of beliefs, impressions, ideas, and perceptions that people hold of objects, behaviors, and events. Mayo (1973) refers to images as simplified impressions. Images that people hold are a way of organizing the different stimuli received on a daily basis and help make sense of the world in which we live. Boulding (1956) defines image as the feelings we have of anything that is cognizant. Embodied in image development are the concepts of attitude, behavior, and motives. An attitude is the learned disposition people acquire regarding responses to objects, events, and people. Behavior is a response to some external stimuli and is dependent on attitudes. Attitudes may be viewed as the product of motives that lead to a predisposition for some specific type of behavior. Developed images appeal to certain motives that may manifest themselves in destination selection, the behavior element or the response. Motives are the most important internal variable as they selectively filter external input.

Image Components

Destination image(s) are made up of three distinctly different but hierarchical interrelated components: cognitive, affective, and conative. The interrelationship of these components ultimately determines predisposition for visitation.

Cognitive

Scott (1965) defines the cognitive image component as an evaluation of the known attributes of the product or an understanding of the product in an intellectual way. Boulding (1956) describes the cognitive component as images derived from fact. In other words, the cognitive component may be viewed as the sum of beliefs and attitudes of the object leading to some internally accepted picture of its attributes. It is how we perceive a product's inherent qualities. The amount of external stimuli processed about the object has a great deal to do with the formation of a cognitive image.

Monrovia, the capital of Liberia, has a cognitive image to many people based simply on its location in a West African country. Some people's cognitive image of Monrovia may have been formed by travel to the city, whereas others may not even know Monrovia is located in Liberia. In that case, the cognitive image of Monrovia may be subject to the image of another city or nation located in another part of the world. One might argue that one person's image is more accurate than another if it is based on more factual information such as that acquired from previous travel. However, in tourism all cognitive images are more or less based on perceptual fact rather than reality. It is the process of forming cognitive images that is important in creating destination awareness. This process will be explained later in the chapter.

Affective

The affective component of image is related to motives in the sense that it is how a person values the object under consideration. It is the "feelings" we hold about any object. Motives determine what we wish to obtain from the object, which then affects the object's valuation. It is easier to evaluate images of activities than it is of places. For example, if we consider Monrovia an exotic city with diverse cultures and our travel motives are predisposed to learning about and experiencing different cultural lifestyles, Monrovia will be valued more highly as a travel destination than cities which may offer cultures with which we are familiar. If, on the other hand, media reports have made us aware of civil unrest in Monrovia, travel motivations which place high importance on safety and security may make us value Monrovia less. It is only when travel to a particular place is considered do motivations impact on the affective component of image. If travel is not possible due to various other reasons, the affective component is much similar to attitudes or the cognitive component of image. The affective component becomes important when a decision to travel is actually being considered.

Conative

The conative component of image is analogous to behavior because it is the action component. After processing external and internal stimuli about a destination, a decision is made whether or not to travel to the area. This act is the conative component. Its relationship to the other image components is direct in that it depends on images developed during the cognitive stage which are assessed during the affective stage. Together, the three components of image form the travel decision process which is developed in more depth in the next section.

THE TRAVEL DECISION PROCESS

Unlimited wants and limited means is an axiom of economic theory. The economic beast wishes to consume at a rate which never quite satiates its hunger. Given limited means, how does the tourist, our economic beast, decide which destination to purchase? Again economic theory tells us that he/she will purchase items which maximize his/her utility given the constraints imposed by scarce resources. In other words, he/she will purchase the destination which provides the greatest satisfaction given the amount of money, time, and other factors allocated for travel.

The process of choosing a destination depends initially on needs expected to be fulfilled from travel and the opportunity of overcoming certain barriers to travel. Assuming the travel decision process involves a family vacation, the process can be depicted through the following simplified example.

The Travail family includes a husband and wife decision-making unit with a contributing subcommittee comprised of two children. In the process of deciding where to go, the first decision involves what types of outcomes are expected from the vacation. Is the intent to form a more cohesive family unit with activities engaged in by all members of the family?

Is the plan to find something for each family member in which they may pursue their own self-actualization needs? Is the purpose to provide opportunities for massive stimuli overload? Whatever the objective of the vacation, it is usually decided before a destination is selected. Destinations which appear to satisfy the major objective of the vacation form what has been described as an awareness set. Woodside and Ronkainen (1980) define the awareness set as all the destinations a consumer might consider for visitation within a specified time period. The cognitive component of image is critical in moving a destination into a decision-making unit's awareness set. What one knows or believes one knows about a destination determines whether it is viewed as meeting the vacation objective.

The second stage in the decision-making process is now reached by the Travail family. Additional information may be sought which can modify the cognitive component of image as new facts change perceptions of certain destinations. At this stage, barriers to travel may eliminate certain destinations from the awareness set. After checking the bank balance and amount of time available for the vacation, the decision-making unit removes some destinations from consideration. The removed destinations may still have an extremely high image in terms of satisfying the vacation objective, but they are not possible due to other factors. Destinations removed at this stage but retaining high image value move into the future set. Destinations in the future set will continue to appear for future trip consideration until vacation objectives change.

All remaining destinations in the awareness set are now scrutinized more closely and evaluated in terms of value to be derived from visitation. Narayana and Markin (1975) describe the decision process at this point as one of disaggregation. Three additional destination sets are formed: inert, inept, and evoked. The inert set consists of destinations that are neither valued positively or negatively. The affective image component stage has failed to value these destinations positively in terms of completely satisfying the vacation objective. The valuation may not be negative, but failure to value positively at this stage results in rejection. These destinations may or may not appear in future travel decision deliberations. The inept set consists of travel destinations that do not fare well during the valuation stage and are rejected from present and most probably future consideration. What remains is an evoked set which consists of those destinations which appear to meet the vacation objective and are affordable in terms of both money, time, and other considered travel constraints.

Howard (1963, 18) defines the evoked set as "the collection of brands the buyer actually considers in his or her purchase decision process." The size of the evoked set is smaller than the awareness set, and may actually be smaller than the future, inept, and inert sets. Studies by Thompson and Cooper (1979) and Woodside and Sherrel (1977) establish that the evoked set is very small, consisting of approximately only three destinations, although Woodside and Sherrel believe the evoked set increases as propensity to travel increases. Campbell (1969) also argues for a small evoked set, finding few buyers with as many as seven brands in the set, with evoked set size not influenced by awareness set size. The size of the evoked set is important because it indicates that any new destination entering into the evoked set normally requires that one be removed. Developing an effective destination image requires knowledge of the destinations already in the evoked set of the target market, and their image characteristics. Armed with this information, destination promoters can develop a tourism image which emphasizes attributes where a comparative advantage exists, eventually replacing a destination currently in the evoked set.

The Travails now reach a decision point. They must choose one destination over another. Each destination has something different to offer and each has a different price associated with its selection. Economic theory tells us that the final selection will be the one destination that serves to maximize the decision-making unit's utility or, in other words, the benefits derived from the travel experience. When comparing destinations, the decision-making unit assesses the attributes of each destination in terms of the cost of each attribute package. Summation of the attributes and their relative importance is equivalent to destination utility. For a review of the different techniques used to evaluate product attributes, refer to Chapter 8.

Obviously most people do not actually sit down and attempt to place numerical values on the attributes of each destination, but they mentally follow the above process to arrive at a decision. One destination finally elicits a behavioral response which is the cognitive image component and emerges from the evoked set as the preferred vacation site (Figure 11.1).

Since it is not possible to "test drive" each destination and assess the extent each one possesses a certain attribute, the decision-making unit proceeds based on their mental construct of what each destination has to offer. Therefore, destination image becomes extremely important in the final selection. The process of forming an image in prospective clients' minds is a key ingredient of tourism development. The next section explores the image formation process.

IMAGE FORMATION

We all hold images of places. When asked to provide a mental picture of a place, most people are able to respond. Even if someone is not familiar with a place (i.e., it is not in their awareness set), further information about the country or area of the world in which it is located should elicit a

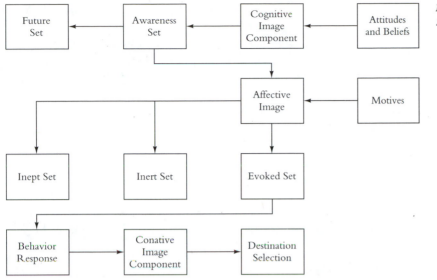

Figure 11.1 Destination
Selection Process

response. Understanding the way in which images of places are formed is part of the destination development process.

Gunn (1972) was among the first to break the image formation process into component parts. He envisions images as being formed either on an induced or organic level. He argues induced image formation is a function of the marketing and promotion efforts of a destination area or business. Pictures, as well as the written material regional organizations produce and disseminate attempt to form images in the minds of prospective travelers. These images may be projected to people through the media via paid advertisements, or directly to individuals assumed to be predisposed to travel to the area.

Organic images emanate from sources not directly associated with any development organization. News reports, movies, newspaper articles and other ostensibly unbiased sources of information generate organic images of places. The underlying difference between an induced image and an organic one is the control that people in the destination area have over how the image is presented. Induced images are presented by destination promoters and project what the destination offers to travelers. Organic images are not directly controlled by destination promoters, but are some other entity's projection of what exists there.

Phelps (1986) contends that images are formed on two levels, primary and secondary. Secondary image formation results from any information received from another source. Primary image formation results from actual visitation. In a sense, Phelps groups both Gunn's induced and most of the organic image formation agents into one type, and separates actual visitation into a distinctly different form of image formation.

Why is it important that we worry about nomenclature when we know that people are constantly being bombarded with information that in some way or another results in images being formed? If we can isolate the different ways that images are formed, image change can be monitored, new attempts to change images can be initiated, and effective ways to project images can be undertaken.

Using Gunn's image typology as a starting point, it is possible to view the image formation process as a continuum consisting of eight distinctly different components. The stages often operate concurrently, forming an image in the mind of the prospective traveler that is individually distinct. In other words, an individual's perceptual filters form an independent image unique to the person but with features shared by others.

Overt Induced I

Beginning at the induced end of the continuum, the first image formation agent is termed Overt Induced I. Overt Induced I agents consist of traditional forms of advertising. By using television, print media, brochures, billboards, and so on, destination promoters attempt to form particular images in the minds of prospective travelers. The person receiving the message is not confused by who is delivering it. It is a blatant attempt by the destination to construct an image of the salient attributes of the destination in the minds of the targeted audience. Depending on the type of medium chosen, the cost of reaching an individual may be very low although total cost can be quite expensive.

Television advertising generally carries the highest price tag, with total cost based on program viewership. With the expansion of cable television systems and the special interest programming found on many of these channels, it is possible to more effectively target markets using television advertising.

Radio advertising can also be an effective means to develop an area image. Due to the generally limited range of radio, it is most effective when used to develop a local image. A major problem in using radio is that the lack of visuals prevents the emotional side of an image from being fully developed. It is used primarily to deliver information rather than to construct elaborate mental pictures.

Brochures, a staple of almost every tourism-related business and community, are necessary to increase awareness and reinforce existing images. Brochures, as well as guide books and information booklets, are usually sent in response to some request for additional information, indicating that an image of the area has already been formed and further elaboration of that image is needed. Often the request originates after exposure to some destination advertisement, predisposing a decision-maker to request more information from the destination. Etzel and Wahlers (1985) refer to the information produced and sent to inquirers as Destination Specific Travel Literature (DSTL). Unlike television and radio advertising where the viewer or listener is part of a captive audience (most people do not switch channels simply to avoid advertisements although remote controls have increased the propensity to do just that), brochures must be selected by the person engaging in information search behavior. Brochures sent to travel agencies for distribution, may be more important than DSTL in developing images. However, the exposure brochures receive is extremely limited. Gilbert and Houghton (1991) find that a travel agent's clients spend, on the average, 54 seconds scanning racks for suitable brochures.

Billboards, although considered by many to be an eyesore, can be very effective when strategically placed and used to present an image which contrasts with the recipient's home environment. Depictions of pleasant, uncrowded, natural environments may be extremely effective when presented to commuters trapped in rush hour traffic in urban areas. Similarly, warm weather destination area promoters may be able to use billboards effectively during the middle of winter in northern locations.

Other types of commonly used Overt Induced I image formation agents include print media such as special interest magazines. The advantage of special interest publications is that readership profiles are generally available to advertisers and specific images which would appeal to the magazine's subscribers can be presented.

Overt Induced I image formation agents have the advantage of being able to achieve widespread coverage as well as targeting specific markets. However, they suffer from low credibility. People are constantly subjected to advertisements for all types of products. Many of the touted product attributes are not always as good as the advertisements lead one to believe. It does not take too many experiences with products that fail to meet expectations before the consumer becomes skeptical about what they are told. Tourism advertising is no exception. People may even be more dubious about some of the projected images of destinations simply because of the cost involved in trying the product.

Countering this low credibility problem is the extent of market penetration. Using traditional forms of advertising, it is possible to reach many people. However, the cost of reaching those people can be very high even though cost per individual contact may be low. Unfortunately for advertisers, it is not possible to pay for only x amount of viewers. Destination promoters choosing traditional forms of advertising are subject to indivisibility constraints. If one million people are expected to view a television program, it is not possible to only advertise to one-half million people.

The destination must come up with the amount necessary to reach all one million before it becomes possible to use that medium.

Most of the tourism Internet and Web technology uses described in the preceding chapter fall into the Overt Induced I category. Home pages identify the producer, although producing the page is much less costly than traditional forms of advertising. At the moment, however, informing a potential customer that a home page exists and its address is becoming more involved as other forms of advertising are often used to direct someone to a site on the Web. As the technology gains more users, this will become increasingly problematic.

Overt Induced II

Overt Induced II image formation agents consist of information received or requested from tour operators, wholesalers, and organizations which have a vested interest in the travel decision process but are not directly associated with any particular destination. Tour operators act as gatekeepers of information, and the type of information they distribute contributes to the images people hold about certain areas (McLellan and Noe, 1983; Bitner and Booms, 1982; Murphy, 1983). A major function of tour operators is to create attractive destination images for the places to which they arrange tours. Destination promoters work with tour operators to select images to be presented, but since tour operators are interested in increasing their business, only certain images are passed on to their clientele. This may lead to unrealistic portrayals of place, and result in images a destination's host society does not support or desire.

Destination area promoters have some control over the images tour operators present. Most non-resident tour operators must register in the country in which they are doing business and are subject to pressure, subtle or direct, to project specific destination images. However, realistic images are not always projected and because of the credibility tour operators have with their clients, this source of image formation may surpass the importance of all the Overt Induced I forms of image formation, especially in countries where foreign travel is heavily dependent on package tours. Countering the high credibility is lower market penetration. Independent tour operators or wholesalers do not have the resources to fully utilize mass market I types of image formation agents, and most concentrate on specialty markets.

Covert Induced I

Proceeding along the image formation continuum, the next component is termed Covert Induced I. It consists of developing destination images using traditional forms of advertising, as in Overt Induced I; however the image is now projected through a second–party spokesperson. The use of a second party tends to mask attempts by destination promoters to directly influence the audience, hence the use of the adjective covert. Covert Induced I types of image formation are a direct attempt to eliminate some of the problems of low credibility inherent in the Overt Induced I image formation agents. Second-party spokespeople are generally chosen based on name recognition and credibility. Credibility is improved, but the tradeoff is in terms of increasing cost, as the second party spokesperson is usually compensated for his or her time and audience recognition factor. The second-party spokesperson approach works best when specific products are advertised, but it can also be used for tourism image development if the second party has positive, high recognition value.

A recognizable spokesperson attracts attention to the endorsed product using their attractive and likeable qualities to differentiate their advertisement from the clutter of other advertising messages (Atkin and Block, 1983). Credibility is enhanced whenever the advertised product has a high psychological or social risk (Friedman and Friedman, 1979), which may be the case with long-haul international travel. The use of a second party does not affect market penetration, as it uses the same advertising strategy as that used in Overt Induced I.

Covert Induced II

The fourth component of image formation is termed Covert Induced II. The person influenced by this agent should not be aware that destination promoters are directly involved in developing the projected image. Covert Induced II agents take the form of ostensibly unbiased articles, reports, and stories about a particular place, delivered by someone with high credibility that apparently has no vested interest in the destination. Familiarization (FAM) trips are generally the vehicle used to achieve Covert Induced II types of image formation. Travel writers for newspapers, magazines, or specific activity groups may be invited to participate in an all-expenses paid trip to some area or business operation to sample their offering. The end result is that writers facing deadline pressure often write about their most recent travel experience. This type of advertisement is a form of image development which may be very useful in reaching identified target markets. FAM trips are also held for tour brokers and operators in an attempt to develop favorable images in their minds which will then be passed on to their clients, resulting in increased visitation.

Credibility rises as the image is now projected by a source that does not appear to have any connection with the destination except through visitation. Cost is less than with other forms of induced image formation, as only expenses related to the writer's visit are covered, with production and distribution costs of the image development effort borne by the publication purchasing the writer's work. The increase in credibility and reduction in cost is somewhat offset by a decline in market penetration. For the image formation effort to be useful, the intended audience must be exposed to the report, article, etc. that has been produced. This requires that a reader be predisposed to learn more about the featured area or specific activity. There is no captive audience in this type of image formation.

The destination area has less control over the published travel account, as it has no veto power over what is written. Thus, the type of image projected may not match the type of image residents of the destination area wish to be presented. However, Covert Induced II types of image formation provide a relatively low-cost means to develop destination images, albeit with some risk. For example, resort areas and small communities with limited advertising and promotion funds may find that FAM trips for carefully selected participants are an effective way to develop their tourism image. Some newspapers and magazines refuse to allow their travel writers to participate in an expenses-paid FAM trip in order to avoid accusations of biased reporting which may also affect other aspects of their operation.

Autonomous

The fifth image component is termed Autonomous. It consists of independently produced reports, articles, films, documentaries, and so on about specific places. There are two sub-components in the Autonomous category: news and popular culture.

The most common form of Autonomous image formation agents are television news stories. The destination area has no control over what appears in the story, and its image is subject to someone else's interpretation. Byerly (1985) reports that the average American child spends 27,000 hours watching television before graduation from high school. This compares to only 18,000 hours in a classroom during the same period of time. This exposure to television is a prime source of image formation. News stories, because of their apparently unbiased approach, are assumed to have major impacts on tourism image development. If the event reported is of major consequence, there is an opportunity for image change in a relatively short period of time.

For example, Gartner and Shen (1992) study the impact of Tiananmen Square on the People's Republic of China's (PRC) tourism image. A study assessing the mature markets image of the PRC was conducted prior to Tiananmen Square. One year after the incident, which was reported with live coverage by every major news station in the free world, the study was repeated, using essentially the same sample population and an identical survey instrument.

The study analyzes 22 activity and attraction attributes grouped into five categories. Interestingly, even though most of the attributes showed declines in impressiveness ratings, only seven out of 22 were significantly lower, at the .05 level of probability. The researchers also investigate image change for ten tourism services. Again, even though all ten declined in absolute value terms, only four were significantly different. Significant differences were noted for services that were most likely to be important to tourists, such as safety and security, receptiveness of local people to tourists, and pleasant attitudes of service personnel. Survey respondents did not view services affecting the efficient movement of people (e.g., on time arrivals and departures, inland transportation) as changing as much, but thought people to people relationships suffered as a result of Tiananmen Square. In conclusion, the Autonomous image formation agents changed the PRC's tourism image in the short run, but the nature of the change was more related to how visitors perceived the provision of touristic services rather than the country's activity or attraction base.

Roehl (1990) provides another example of what can happen as a result of major news coverage. He investigates changes in travel agents' attitudes after Tiananmen Square. Many agents advocated trade and military restrictions after the conflict. As attitudes are related to image formation, especially in the cognitive state, future travel to the PRC may depend not only on images held of touristic attitudes, but attitudes toward the host government.

Other studies also support the influence of Autonomous image formation agents. The U.S. Travel Service (1977), now the U.S. Travel and Tourism Administration, in a study investigating foreigners' perceptions of the United States, concludes that many images are based on news reports and movies that depicted violence in the country. The Pacific Travel News (1984), reports that U.S. citizens' images of Korea are primarily derived from the popular television series *M.A.S.H.,* and represent an image of Korea more than thirty years outdated.

The Autonomous image formation agent, because of its high credibility and high market penetration, may be the only agent capable of changing and area's image dramatically in a short period of time. One of the reasons may be the lack of information people have of destinations that are far removed from their home residence. If people form images based on little acquired information, they are more susceptible to change when massive amounts of information are processed in a relatively short period of time. It is not possible, given the high cost of induced image formation agents, to quickly and effectively counter perceptions and images the autonomous agents project.

The above studies provide evidence supporting the importance of news reporting as Autonomous image formation agents. Unfortunately, as news events unfold, destination promoters can do very little to control the images reporters portray. Even when authoritative governments censor news reports, it only serves to lend credibility to what has already been presented. Destination images damaged as a result of a major news event, however, can still be salvaged to some extent. Milo and Yoder (1991) examine the process of news coverage during a major event and identify opportunities for destination promoters to control the impact of the event on touristic image.

At the start of a major news event, broadcast media request little local support for news coverage except through affiliate stations. After the event, however, independent reporters seek follow up stories and local officials are often asked to provide assistance. During this phase of news coverage, image damage control can be initiated. It is also possible that the effect of negative autonomous change agents, although significant in the short term, may not be an important factor in long-term image change. Thurstone (1967) contends that in the absence of any reinforcing information, images may revert back to those held before the exogenous shock.

Popular culture also portrays images of people and places. Increased travel to Australia occurred shortly after the release and subsequent box office success of *Crocodile Dundee*. The film's star, Paul Hogan, also became a tourism spokesperson for the country. Other forms of popular culture (e.g. documentaries, sitcoms) also play a role in destination image formation. Although the effects of popular culture on image formation have not been thoroughly studied, there is enough anecdotal evidence to suggest a strong relationship. Many states in the U.S. have even organized film promotion offices to encourage companies to select locations in the state for their movies, television shows, etc.

Unsolicited Organic

The sixth image component is termed Unsolicited Organic. It consists of unrequested information received from individuals who have visited an area or believe they know what exists there. People receive information on areas on a regular basis in conversation over coffee, at dinner with friends, during business meetings, or in any place or setting where the topic shifts to world politics or simply places recently visited. The person receiving the information does not request it and therefore the credibility factor is only moderate. However, since it comes from an acquaintance, it may carry a higher level of credibility than information received from any of the induced agents. Low market penetration counters the higher level of credibility, as only those people exposed to the message are affected; individual communication is much less pervasive than mass media. However, if the information is about a destination that has received relatively little exposure through the induced or autonomous agents, then unsolicited organic information can be a very important source of image formation. Cost of Unsolicited Organic image formation is nonexistent unless one considers the indirect cost to the destination from an unfavorable report.

Solicited Organic

The seventh component is termed Solicited Organic. It consists of requested information received from a knowledgeable source, generally one's friends or relatives. Because of the nature of the information flow, someone responding to a specific information request, the credibility factor is very high. Solicited information is often used to move a destination from the awareness set into the inert, inept, or evoked set. It may also be used to help select a destination from the evoked set. The Solicited Organic component is very important when a person is in an information search mode. This stage of image formation is also referred to as "word of mouth" advertising. Market penetration is very low, however, because as more people are contacted for information, a point is reached where people provide information that simply reinforces that received from others. Stutman and Newell (1984) refer to this as acquiring salient beliefs. When the point where substantial reinforcement of previously stated beliefs is reached, the information seeker analyzes the information, evaluates it in terms of their own beliefs, assesses motivations, and finally decides which set to move the destination into. Although there is no direct cost to the destination area for this stage of image formation, the experience the destination provides is critically important in forming positive salient beliefs about travel to the area. In the long run, in the absence of any negative Autonomous image formation, the Solicited Organic component is the most critical determinant of an area's economic tourism health.

Organic

The final component of image formation is simply termed Organic, and consists of actual visitation after which a new destination image is formed in the minds of the visitor. A visitor holding a new image returns to the image formation cycle as a distributor of information in the unsolicited and solicited organic components.

Many studies have been conducted of image change as a result of visitation. Gyte (1988) conducts a study using student visitors to Tunisia as the sample population. He reports a number of reversed images of the Tunisian environment as a result of visitation. Prior to visitation, Tunisia

Images should be built around recognizable strengths, as with the Renaissance Center in downtown Detroit, Michigan.
Photo by the author

was perceived as rough and vivid. After visitation, images changed to smooth and drab.

Khan (1991) investigates the image of tourism activities and attractions in Wisconsin between groups of visitors and non-visitors. For almost every evaluated activity and attraction, post-trip images are more impressive than pre-trip images. Similarly, Shen (1989) finds that for the American mature traveler to China, 7 of 32 tested attributes had significantly improved post-trip images and only one attribute significantly declined in impressiveness.

Phelps (1986) compares images held by first time visitors to Menorca with those held by returning visitors. Some of the findings reveal that although there were differences between groups, some first-time visitors held images of Menorca similar to the repeat visit group. Further investigation reveals that a majority of those in the first-time group having similar images to the repeat visitation group had substantial contact with members of the repeat visitor group prior to visiting Menorca. This contact fits into the Unsolicited and Solicited Organic component of image formation and underscores the importance of those two image formation agents. Figure 11.2 provides a summary of all the image formation agents compared against cost, market penetration, and credibility.

DESTINATION IMAGE CHARACTERISTICS

Having examined the different ways in which destination images are formed, the following are some principles that more or less guide those interested in developing and manipulating images:

1. Touristic images change slowly; the larger the entity the more slowly the image changes.

    The rate of image change is inversely related to the complexity of the system. This is as true of complex ecosystems as it is of socially and politically structured entities (e.g., nations, cities, communities). A tourism image is made up of many different parts, including the natural resource base in which activities take place, the sociocultural system that governs the provision and type of touristic services, and the man-made structures that serve the needs of tourists and may also provide some of the attractions.

    Boulding (1956) suggests that information affecting images can cause three effects. In the first instance, received information is not in conformity with held beliefs, setting up a situation of cognitive dissonance. The individual attempts to avoid the incoming information,

Figure 11.2 *Image Formation*
Agents

Image Change Agent	Credibility	Market Penetration	Destination Cost
OVERT INDUCED I			
Traditional forms of advertising, (e.g., brochures, T.V., radio, print, billboard, etc.)	Low	High	High
OVERT INDUCED II			
Information received from tour operators, wholesalers	Medium	Medium	Indirect
COVERT INDUCED I			
Second-party endorsement of products via traditional forms of advertising	Low/Medium	High	High
COVERT INDUCED II			
Second-party endorsement through apparently unbiased reports (e.g., newspaper travel section articles)	Medium	Medium	Medium
AUTONOMOUS			
New and popular culture: documentaries, reports, news stories, movies, television programs	High	Medium/High	Indirect
UNSOLICITED ORGANIC			
Unsolicited information received from friends and relatives	Medium	Low	Indirect
SOLICITED ORGANIC			
Solicited information received from friends and relatives	High	Low	Indirect
ORGANIC			
Actual visitation	High	—	Indirect

thereby reducing the dissonance. If enough information can be avoided, the image remains essentially unaffected. In the second instance, the information keeps coming and cannot be avoided, resulting in a gradual image change. In the third instance, enough new information is received to result in a general reassessment of the image previously held, and leads to an entirely new image. The key element, then, in image change is the amount and extent of new information which contrasts to the image currently held. Autonomous image change agents, if constant and prolonged, will eventually be unavoidable, causing an image shift. Induced image formation agents can also have the same effect, but because of their low credibility rating take longer to affect change.

Gartner and Hunt (1987) study touristic image change for the state of Utah over a 12 year period. Evidence links increased visitation to an improved state image, although Utah's image did not improve dramatically with respect to its nearest competitors. The image of the region in which Utah is situated had also improved, leading to the conclusion that an improvement in a larger entity, the intermountain region of the United States, benefits all states within the region.

Crompton (1979), Cumings (1983), and Kotler (1982) provide further evidence of the relatively long time factor involved in changing touristic images. In the absence of any major news event causing an individual to process massive amounts of information quickly, destination image will remain relatively constant in the short run.

2. Induced image formation attempts must be focused and long-term.

As a result of the time it takes to change an image, any induced image formation programs must be long-term. If destination promoters have scarce financial resources that fluctuate on an annual basis, and the image change effort is on again off again, they would be better off focusing on improving their product and utilizing the organic image formation agents for promotion. Images tend to have stability and as discussed above, in the absence of any major autonomous impacts take years to shift. Therefore, consistency is a requirement for long-term image change using induced formation agents.

Consistency should not be confused with repetition of the same message. Exposure to the same advertisement can result in a diminishing marginal rate of effectiveness (Schumann et al., 1990). Six exposures to the same commercial may be the point at which diminishing returns occur (Grass and Wallace, 1969). Consistency in this case refers to the planned long-term delivery of a message that has at its core a common theme (image) without always using the same vehicle to deliver the message.

3. The smaller the entity in relation to the whole, the less of a chance to develop an independent image.

This rule has its exceptions and generally they relate to distance from market and strength of brand image. Hunt (1971), in one of the earliest tourism image studies, finds that distance from one's permanent residence to destination was a factor in the image held of the destination. The further one lives from the destination, the less likely one is to have a clear image of it. Crompton's (1979) study on images of Mexico lends further support to Hunt's earlier conclusions.

Khan (1991), studying the image of Wisconsin's tourism regions and comparing those images to the prevailing state image, finds with very few exceptions that regional image matches state image. The subjects in Khan's study are residents of states surrounding Wisconsin. These findings lend further support to the strength of brand image, in this case a state image, overpowering images of smaller entities located within the state.

A brand, as defined by Okoroafo (1989), is a name, design, symbol, or combination of these used to identify a service or product. A state, or in the case of international tourism a country, provides brand identification for image development. Slogans such as "I Love New York," "Akwaaba (you are welcome—Ghana)" or "Say Yes to Michigan" all create a point of reference and create a perception based on the images evoked from these brand identification statements. Brand identification does not rule out a strong independent image at the community or regional level, but the establishment of that image is more important in localized areas and less distinct the farther one is removed from the community. Communities or regions can use this to their advantage, however, as they may be able to piggyback on a strong brand image in their advertising and promotion.

There are exceptions where a smaller entity has such a strong image that it overpowers the larger area. This may be the case where the only opportunity for developing an image is through the autonomous agents. For example, if the results of the U.S. Travel Service study which finds non-residents' images of the United States are a function of news and movies depicting violence in the country are extended, it would not be unlikely to find that images of certain states are related more to images held of its cities. In this case, cities receiving the exposure are considered the brand against which the other areas in the state are evaluated.

4. To be effective, image change depends on an assessment of present images.

Changing an image depends on knowing what images prospective travelers now hold and initiating efforts to reinforce existing images or move images in a new direction. Image change efforts are essentially wasted if baseline data establishing present image position is not known. Understanding images held by target markets is essential to avoid moving the image into a position held by an able and strong competitor. Methods to assess presently held images are discussed later in this chapter.

IMAGE MIX

The selection of the right image formation agents to build a desired touristic image depends on many factors. The first is the amount of money budgeted for image development. Many small communities are unable to use expensive induced formation agents. Focusing on quality service, unique attraction packages, and lower-cost image-formation agents may be the wisest choice for cash poor rural communities.

A second concern is the characteristics of the target market. If the travel decision-making body comprises a family unit, induced image formation agents may be a top priority. Gitelson and Crompton (1983) find family groups more likely to use media sources for information acquisition than singles. They also find that college-educated individuals are more likely to use destination-specific literature (DSTL).

Other demographic characteristics need to be considered. Capella and Greco (1987) find that people over 60 years of age are more inclined to rely on Solicited Organic image formation agents, as families and friends greatly influenced this group's destination selection. Some print media (i.e., magazines and newspapers) are also important information sources for this group. Age is also a factor in determining credibility ratings of various companies (Weaver and McCleary, 1984), and further investigation may show a relationship between age and different types of image formation agents.

Timing also has to be considered. Van Raaij and Francken (1984) find Overt Induced I sources of image formation to be important information sources early in the decision process. Overt Induced II sources enter into the information search process at a later stage. Throughout the information acquisition period, Solicited Organic sources are used at the same rate.

Finally, the type of image(s) to be projected must be addressed. If a strong brand image already exists, less money and effort will be required to develop a local area image which is consistent with the dominant brand image. On the other hand, if a strong unique image independent or counter to the prevailing brand image is to be projected, all image formation agents should be considered as important contributors. For a small entity to establish an image different from the prevailing brand image requires that a large number of tourists be hosted to justify the expense and time involved in forming a unique image. Consequently, mass tourism markets must be developed. Small-scale tourism developments using alternative forms of tourism should avoid widespread use of induced-formation agents and rely primarily on the organic types to develop their touristic image. In this way, the type of images formed are consistent with the type of experiences offered.

Deciding on the right image formation mix for a community, region, or larger entity is not an easy process. Although the field has produced some case studies which indicate the types of formation agents that work best with specific groups or in certain instances, more work needs to be done before the theoretical aspects of image mix can become fully operational.

IMAGE ASSESSMENT METHODS

There are numerous studies assessing tourists' images of destinations. Essentially, each method evaluates individuals' perceptions of attributes present in varying degrees within a destination. Some methods compare attributes across destinations, thereby identifying comparative advantages and disadvantages. Almost every method assumes some knowledge of the key attributes of the destination as a starting point, although when comparing different destinations it may be more important to test for brand strength than the presence of any particular attribute. Since image measurement is not necessarily a measure of reality, some attributes of a destination not present to any great degree may still be perceived as abundant.

Computer advances have made statistical computation of data much faster and simpler. It is no longer necessary to understand how data is manipulated as much as it is to be able to interpret findings. The following discussion on different methods that can be employed to study destination images does not delve into the details of analysis except where absolutely necessary for understanding basic principles. It assumes the person employing these statistical techniques has access to computer consulting services or is able to utilize the many statistical computing packages available.

Factor Analysis

Data collection is the most important step for any analytical procedure, as output is dependent on input. The saying "garbage in, garbage out" is especially relevant in image research. How do we know the attributes being measured are really the most salient attributes for destination image identification? For example, Berlin (1987) identifies attributes related to a camping experience, asking users of two campgrounds on the Chippewa National Forest in Minnesota to evaluate those attributes in terms of their importance in achieving a desired experience. Attributes identified for analysis are primarily related to the enjoyment of outdoor recreation (e.g., rest, relaxation, quiet). The campgrounds are dissimilar in terms of facility development and primary activities available. Activities and facility development in one campground are primarily related to fishing, and in the other primary activities are more of a passive nature (e.g., hiking, primitive camping, etc.), with limited, rustic facilities provided. Study results reveal that attributes valued by both groups are essentially the same. Can it be assumed, then, that the sites are substitutes for each other, or do people initially select one campground over another based on facility development allowing for specific activities, and then proceed to achieve similar benefits from the experience? Misspecification of attributes can lead to results that do not differentiate between groups or destinations in terms of preferred or valued attributes.

Attributes for measurement can be identified through an inventory assessment of the tourism products currently offered to tourists. If tourists are attracted to an area's natural resource base, then attributes related to those resources should be assessed. Since tourism is a people-to-people industry, attributes of the hospitality component should also be included. Receptiveness to tourists, quality of services provided, and sociocultural appeal are a few of the hospitality attributes that should be assessed in an image study. Impressiveness of attractions should also be included. The number and type of attributes to be included in any data collection effort is initially a function of the inventory assessment, and then the amount of time required to complete and return any survey instrument. When using factor analysis, the number of attributes measured is dependent on acceptable survey length, as the procedure allows for data reduction of many variables into a few manageable image factors. This is one of the major advantages of utilizing programs such as factor analysis for image research.

For use in factor analysis, attributes should be measured using scaling techniques that provide for interval level measurement. The requirement of interval level measurement is necessary to develop the second half of the first step, the construction of a covariance matrix. The simplest type of scales are one interval used in dichotomous choice questions. The one interval is naturally equal to itself, thereby satisfying interval level measurement requirements. More complex scales, sometimes referred to as Likert scales (Likert, 1932), assess degrees of agreement or disagreement with a statement. For example, using a five-point Likert scale with response choices listed as Strongly Agree, Agree, Neutral, Disagree, or Strongly Disagree, individuals are asked to check the choice that most accurately reflects their opinion of a statement such as "National Parks in Tanzania are some of the most beautiful in the world." A series of statements using the same scale are presented to the respondent encompassing the entire range of attributes to be measured.

A more commonly used version of the Likert scale called a semantic differential scale, was developed by Osgood, Suci and Tannenbaum (1957). Semantic differential scales are anchored on each end by bipolar adjectives. Very Impressive, Very Unimpressive; Very Hot, Very Cold; Very Receptive, Very Unreceptive are a few examples of bipolar adjectives that have been used in tourism research to measure attributes. The scale generally consists of five to seven intervals which are assumed for analytical purposes to be equal intervals, thus satisfying the interval level measurement criterion (Figure 11.3).

Once data are collected, the other steps in Factor Analysis can be followed, resulting in the reduction of all the original variables into "factors." Factors can then be used to reveal the underlying image attributes of a destination.

Cluster Analysis

Cluster analysis is another statistical procedure providing data reduction capabilities. Starting with a data set, cluster analysis allows the researcher to be able to reduce the number of original variables into relatively homogenous groups. Aldenderfer and Blashfield (1984) list five steps necessary to perform cluster analysis: 1. Select a sample to be clustered. 2. Define a set of variables on which to measure the entities in the sample. 3. Compute the similarities in the entities. 4. Use a cluster analysis method to create groups of similar entities. 5. Validate the resulting cluster solution. Cluster analysis is similar to factor analysis in terms of application. One noticeable difference between the two, and also between cluster analysis and multidimensional scaling (discussed below), is how output is represented. Cluster analysis allows the researcher to build a picture of variable similarity. This is called a dendogram because it takes a tree form (Figure 11.4). The researcher observes how variables combine or cluster, and can stop the clustering algorithm whenever he/she feels sufficient data reduction has been

Figure 11.3 *Examples of Bipolar Adjective Semantic Differential Scales*

Very Impressive/Impressive/Neutral/Unimpressive/Very Unimpressive

-----X(1)-------X(2)----X(3)------X(4)----------X(5)------

Very Hot/ Hot/ Neutral/ Cold/ Very Cold

--X(1)---X(2)--X(3)--X(4)----X(5)--

Very Receptive/ Receptive/ Neutral/ Unreceptive/ Very Unreceptive

-----X(1)--------X(2)-----x(3)-----x(4)-----------x(5)------

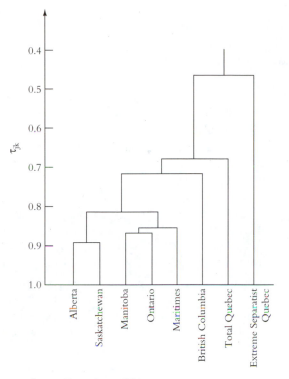

Figure 11.4 *Comparison of Canadian Provinces on 13 Self-Reported Attributes*

Source: Romesburg, 1984

achieved. Cluster analysis is the preferred data reduction technique for combining attribute scores when no a priori information exists to the underlying attribute structure. For a more detailed review of cluster analysis, refer to Romesburg (1984).

Multidimensional Scaling (MDS)

Multidimensional scaling operates in a similar manner to factor and cluster analysis in that it seeks to uncover some hidden structure in the data. When used for image research, attributes that are perceived similarly tend to group together. One added advantage of multidimensional scaling is that output can be graphically displayed (at least through three dimensions), which makes it especially appealing for destination comparison. Not only can measured attributes be displayed in dimensional space, but the position of selected destinations are also displayed. Data can be collected in such a manner that a visual inspection of the graphical display reveals which destinations have the closest relationship to each attribute. This allows the researcher to not only focus on specific attribute strengths

IMAGE ANALYSIS TECHNIQUES

Factor analysis is a statistical analysis technique generally used for data reduction. It assumes that the variables measured are able to be combined into more aggregate level variables, sometimes called source variables. If the focus is on image identification using attribute measurement procedures, for factor analysis to work attributes must be able to be condensed into fewer attributes that separate and link individual attributes together. For example, assume members of a sample population are asked to rate the impressiveness of forty selected attributes of a destination. A simple correlation analysis between the variables provides some evidence as to which variables are perceived similarly. Factor analysis can then be used to examine whether a smaller subset of variables can explain some of the observed correlations. Assuming that the forty variables are indeed able to be combined into a small subset of five factors, the researcher can use the results for exploratory or continuing analysis purposes.

Exploratory purposes consist of examining the various attribute groupings, comprising the five factors, and determining some underlying linkage between members in each group. Once the common denominator for each group is found they are named and become the image characteristics of the destination. These factors can also be used in further statistical tests. Assume one is interested in testing for significant destination image differences between two groups, those who have visited the destination and those who have not. Tests for significant differences between each group are performed for each of the five factors. This is a much simpler procedure then testing for sig-

nificant differences between each group and every attribute. Instead of forty separate tests for significant difference only five need to be performed.

Kim and Mueller (1978) describe four steps required to perform factor analysis:;1. data collection and preparation of the relevant covariance matrix, 2. extraction of the initial factors, 3. rotation to a terminal solution and interpretation, and 4. construction of factor scales and use in further analysis. For readers unfamiliar with Factor Analysis a primer text on the subject, such as Kim and Mueller, is recommended. Since an explanation of the procedure is beyond the scope of this text only one half of the first step, data collection, will be discussed in depth.

Uddin (1988), investigating the state of Utah's touristic image, uses factor analysis to identify the main components of that image. Data were collected from a nonresident sample on the perception of 22 image attributes. Using principal components analysis and varimax rotation, seven factors are constructed. The first factor, which Uddin names parks, consists of variables directly related to the visitation or non-consumptive enjoyment of Utah's natural resources base. The second factor, named activity, comprises variables that contained either a consumptive component (e.g., fishing, hunting) or recreational activity (e.g., skiing). The third component is labeled culture, and contains variables such as shopping, museums, symphony, and so on. The fourth component is named nightlife, and contains variables related to late-night city activities. There are also three other factors consisting of one variable each. These variables do not show high factor loading scores for any of the other factors, but are considered unique variables (Figure 11.5).

In addition to identifying the main components of Utah's image factor, scales assess differences in images between groups. Image differences were investigated between those who had visited the state versus those who had not. The parks and culture factors were perceived as more impressive by those who had visited the state, whereas the activity and winter temperature (single variable factor) were not viewed any differently. The nightlife factor was considered more impressive by the group without previous tourism experience in Utah and liquor laws (single variable factor) were considered less restrictive by the non-visitation group. In addition, people residing in different geographical regions also held different impressions of the various factors, leading to the conclusion that regions around the country have different perceptions of the same destination. These findings, although not impossible to obtain using other methods, are made simpler with the data reduction capabilities of factor analysis.

Gartner (1989), using multidimensional scaling techniques and the same data set as Uddin, assesses the competitive position of four western U.S. states (Montana, Colorado,

Utah, Wyoming) with respect to 15 attributes. The results in two dimensions are displayed in Figure 11.6. The closeness in terms of euclidean distance between a state and any attribute represents the extent to which that attribute is considered present in a state and viewed positively by visitors to the state. The only exception is the attribute liquor, which was measured on a different scale, and closeness in this case represents an attribute that is perceived as more restrictive and less impressive. After reviewing attribute clustering, the axes were rotated orthogonally (denoted by the dashed lines) to more accurately separate attributes for dimensional analysis. The two dimensions chosen to represent the clustering were social group affiliation (dimension 1) and natural/cultural based (dimension 2). Results indicated that two states, Wyoming and Montana, were perceived by the sample population as sharing a common image, which was heavily influenced by both states' natural resource base. Colorado also had a natural-resource-based image, but it was also viewed as a state providing opportunities for resident and visitor interaction. Utah was perceived as slightly less open in terms of social interaction, had restrictive liquor laws, and possessed more of a culturally-based image with impressive cities.

of each destination, but by searching for attribute clustering, hidden, unspecified attributes can also be uncovered. This becomes clearer in the specific example below and in the case study. It is the ability to display attribute proximity to destinations which makes MDS so appealing to tourism image researchers.

Multidimensional scaling refers to a class of statistical techniques that measure proximities. This proximity is simply a mathematical number expressing similarity or dissimilarity between variables. Proximities are easiest to visualize through spatial output which is possible in two and three di-

Factor 1 (PARKS)		Factor 2 (ACTIVITY)		Factor 3 (CULTURE)		Factor 4 (NIGHTLIFE)	
UTNTPARK	.83	UTFISH	.87	UTSYMPH	.75	UTNCLUBS	.79
UTSTPARK	.81	UTHUNT	.85	UTMUSEUM	.73	UTNIGHT	.71
UTNATFOR	.76	UTBOAT	.74	UTSHOP	.57	UTSHOWS	.65
UTHISTOR	.69	UTSKIING	.56	UTCULTUR	.56		
UTSIGHT	.55	UTCAMP	.56	UTCITIES	.50		
				RECEPTUT	.37		

THREE INDEPENDENT ITEMS:

1. LIQURUT

2. STEMPUT

3. WTEMPUT

Source: Uddin, 1988

Figure 11.5   *Components of Utah's Tourist Image as Yielded by Composite Factor Analysis*

mensions. Even though many MDS programs allow for analysis through six dimensions, spatial examination is lost after three, which is why the majority of examples confine themselves to only two or three dimensions.

There are four steps required to perform MDS analysis:

1. Collect data on attributes and objects.

2. Using an appropriate MDS program, analyze the data set.

Figure 11.6 *Multidimensional Scaling Output for State Position Relative to Tourism Product(s)*

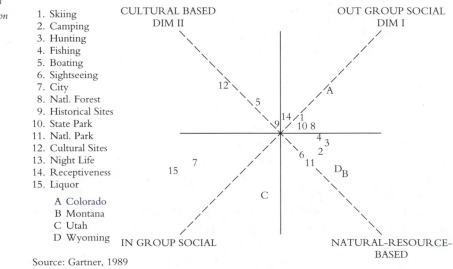

1. Skiing
2. Camping
3. Hunting
4. Fishing
5. Boating
6. Sightseeing
7. City
8. Natl. Forest
9. Historical Sites
10. State Park
11. Natl. Park
12. Cultural Sites
13. Night Life
14. Receptiveness
15. Liquor

A Colorado
B Montana
C Utah
D Wyoming

Source: Gartner, 1989

3. After obtaining a spatial plot, interpret the output.

4. Test for dimensional validity.

For image research purposes, the first step is accomplished by selecting a sample population to evaluate different destinations (objects) in terms of selected attributes. The selection and measurement of attributes can be accomplished in the same manner that data is collected for factor or cluster analysis. However, since the focus is often on destination comparison, the sample population is asked to evaluate each image attribute with respect to each destination. Scales constructed to measure attributes will be the same for each of the destinations to be compared. Factor and cluster analysis can also be used to compare destinations, but it requires that factors be exactly the same for each destination and factor scales be used in another statistical procedure to determine differences between destinations. MDS bypasses the need to construct factor scales and does not involve other statistical procedures for comparison purposes. The drawback, however, is that MDS does not have the same rigid statistical grounding as factor or cluster analysis and the interpretation of underlying attributes is more subjective.

Once data is collected, one of the many computer-based statistical programs can be used for analysis. No attempt is made here to assess the various programs used for MDS; instead the reader is referred to Green and Rao (1972) or Kruskal and Wish (1978) for an in-depth discussion of the various options. Once data are analyzed, the researcher moves from the realm of objective analysis to one much more subjective. A visual inspection of the output is conducted and proximity of attributes to destinations is reviewed. The closer an attribute is to a destination, the more that destination is perceived to contain the attribute. Clustering of attributes is also inspected, and any underlying trait that links the attributes together determined. Since this step is highly subjective, the researcher must have some intimate knowledge of the tourism appeal of the destinations analyzed. Questions to be asked at this point include: Why do certain attributes cluster together? Why do some destinations appear to be perceived differently in terms of attribute clusters? What common link can there be between attribute clusters and specific destinations?

Usually, spatial output is normalized with an x-y axis separating some of the attributes and destinations. This separation is entirely arbitrary without any intuitive meaning, and the researcher can rotate the axis in an orthogonal or oblique manner, whichever works best, to obtain a better visual clustering of the attributes. Finally, the output is subjected to a validity test, referred to as goodness of fit or stress (Kruskal and Wish, 1978). Stress tests help determine the appropriate number of dimensions needed to obtain statistically reliable results. There is no hard and fast rule as to what stress value is required before the analyst chooses a different dimension. In fact, the need to display output visually, in two or three dimensions often overrides an ambiguous stress value, which indicates the analysis may be tighter if a higher dimension is used.

Goodrich (1978) is one of the first tourism researchers to use MDS procedures for image analysis. He compares nine destination regions on ten touristic attributes, asking each respondent to rate the degree to which each destination contains each attribute. Respondents are also asked to rate the similarity/dissimilarity of each paired combination of destinations. Similarity/dissimilarity results are subjected to a multidimensional scaling program, INDSCAL. There appeared to be a clustering of destinations based on affiliation with the United States. With one exception, all non-U.S. destinations clustered together, and all U.S. destinations were found in another cluster. All destinations were considered warm weather, tropical, or semi-tropical.

The second step requires attribute (variable) perceptions be added to the analysis. In two dimensions, the underlying attributes resulting from the analysis are entertainment (dimension 1) and culture/lifestyle (dimension 2). The U.S. destinations were clustered to the extreme end of dimension 1, indicating respondents viewed them as having more facilities for shopping, water sports, golfing, and tennis. The non-U.S. destinations, with one exception, were at one end of dimension 2, which indicated that they were perceived as having fewer historical and cultural attractions. Although Goodrich's study was exploratory in nature and was based on a small, very localized sample, results indicate that the multidimensional scaling approach is able to establish perceptual differences between destinations based on their affiliation with home country (possibly indicating

Sometimes the most powerful images are the simplest. Photo by the author

the existence of brand image) and amount of touristic attributes offered by the various countries.

The spatial analysis and graphical output afforded by the use of MDS allows destinations to view their position with respect to any other destination in terms of attribute strengths. Dimensional interpretation provides for a more subjective view of each destination's image. The underlying attributes which are used to name dimensions are an amalgamation of measured attributes, and help a destination identify its image strengths with respect to two composite attributes. Although data reduction is achieved, the value of individual attributes is not lost for specific marketing purposes.

CONCLUSION

The image formation process is critical to tourism marketing, promotion, and development. For most products, image formation can be a section within a much larger chapter on marketing. The reason it has its own chapter in this text is due to the nature of the tourism product. Tourism, probably more than any other product, is purchased after an evaluation of attributes a destination possesses where the touristic activity is expected to take place. Since it is not possible to pre-test the tourism product, attribute evaluation is a function of destination image. The types of images projected can direct the development process, as some images appeal to certain groups, increasing demand for specific activities and the type of development necessary (mass/alternative) to accommodate visitors. Images presented can also be a source of pride for local residents or represent loss of local control over the type of tourism being offered.

Understanding the image formation process does not guarantee more local involvement in the type of tourism a community or region is developing. However, it does provide the knowledge needed to direct development. Image formation principles, once understood and used correctly, at least allow the image formation process to proceed on a predictable path. However, there are also some "wild card" events which even the best prepared image development specialists are not able to control. Even so, understanding the consequences of "wild card" events can help steer the image development process back on track sooner than would otherwise happen through neglect or ignorance. The information contained in this chapter, from the importance of image in the travel decision process, to the image formation process, to how image(s) is(are) measured provides the basics for understanding image and its relationship to the tourism development process.

EXECUTIVE SUMMARY

Three main image components are identified as cognitive, affective, and conative. Cognitive is the fact component, and consists of information we know or believe to be true. The affective component is related to motives and determines how we value any object being considered. The conative component is analogous to behavior, and becomes important when we decide to buy something or select a travel destination.

The travel decision process consists of a series of stages where destinations are evaluated, saved for future consideration, discarded, or retained for further evaluation and consideration. The final set, termed an evoked set, consists of a very small group of destinations which are affordable and appear to meet the expectations of the evaluative body. From this set comes the destination of choice.

The image formation process can be separated into discrete influences which, upon interacting, form an individualistic impression or image of place. One way to view these influences is with respect to the variable of cost, credibility of message delivered, and market penetration. Induced image formation agents can be characterized as high cost and low credibility with high market penetration. Organic agents are characterized by low cost, high credibility but low market penetration. The most effective are termed Autonomous, and usually consist of news or popular culture (e.g., movies) resulting in rapid yet usually short-term image change.

Destinations images, for the most part, can be characterized by:

1. Resistance to rapid change

2. Requiring a focused and long-term image change strategy if induced formation agents are used

3. Subject to image(s) held of larger entities of which the destination is only a small part

4. Requiring knowledge of current place image(s) before any image modification is undertaken

It is important to select the right mix of image formation agents to use. Generally, the constraints determining what is available include financial resources, image formation objectives, and speed of image change desired.

Image-assessment techniques are common, and most use a series of scales to determine held images which are then aggregated into some explanatory variables. These data-reduction techniques allow for many different image dimensions to be explored.

REFERENCES

Aldenderfer, M., and R. Blashfield. 1984. *Cluster Analysis*. Quantitative Applications in the Social Sciences. Newbury Park, Calif: A Sage University Paper, #44.

Atkin, C. and M. Block. 1983. Effectiveness of Celebrity Endorsers. *Journal of Advertising Research* 23 (Feb./March):57–61.

Berlin, N. 1987. User Characteristics and Benefit Segmentation of Two Campgrounds on the Chippewa National Forest. Logan, Utah: Institute of Outdoor Recreation and Tourism, Utah State University.

Bitner, J., and H. Booms. 1982. Trends in Travel and Tourism Marketing: The Changing Structure of Distribution Channels. *Journal of Travel Research* 20(4):39–44.

Boulding, K. 1956, *The Image—Knowledge in Life and Society*. Ann Arbor, Mich.: University of Michigan Press.

Byerly, C. 1985. *Media and Sexism—An Instructional Manual for Secondary School Teachers*. Olympia: Washington Office of the State Superintendent of Public Instruction.

Campbell, B. 1969. The Existence of Evoked Set and Determinants of its Magnitude in Brand Choice Behavior. Unpublished Doctoral Dissertation, Columbia University.

Capella, L., and G. Greco. 1987. Information Sources of Elderly for Vacation Decisions. *Annals of Tourism Research* 6(4):148–151.

Crompton, J. 1979. An Assessment of the Image of Mexico as a Vacation Destination and the Influence of Geographical Location Upon that Image. *Journal of Travel Research* 17(4):18–23.

Cumings, B. 1983. Korean-American Relations: A Century of Contact and Thirty-Five Years of Intimacy, pg. 237. In *New Frontiers in American-East Asian Relations*. W.J. Cohen, ed. New York: Columbia University Press.

Etzel, M., and R. Wahlers. 1985. The Use of Requested Promotional Material by Pleasure Travelers. *Journal of Travel Research* 23(4):2–6.

1984. Evaluating Korea. *Pacific Travel News*. February:38–40.

Friedman, H. and L. Friedman. 1979. Endorser Effectiveness by Product Type. *Journal of Advertising Research* 19(Oct./Nov.):63–71.

Gartner, W. 1989. Tourism Image: Attribute Measurement of State Tourism Products Using Multidimensional Scaling Techniques. *Journal of Travel Research* 28(2):16–20.

Gartner, W., and D. Hunt. 1987. An Analysis of State Image Change Over a Twelve Year Period (1971–1983). *Journal of Travel Research* 26(2): 15–19.

Gartner, W., and J. Shen. 1992. The Impact of Tiananmen Square on China's Tourism Image. *Journal of Travel Research* 30(4):47–52.

Gilbert, D., and P. Houghton. 1991. An Exploratory Investigation of Format, Design, and Use of U.K. Tour Operator's Brochures. *Journal of Travel Research* 30(2):20–25.

Gitelson, R., and J. Crompton. 1983. The Planning Horizon and Sources of Information Used by Pleasure Vacationers. *Journal of Travel Research* 21(3):2–7.

Goodrich, J. 1978. A New Approach to Image Analysis through Multi-Dimensional Scaling. *Journal of Travel Research* 16:10–13.

Grass, R., and W. Wallace. 1969. Satiation Effects of Television Commercials. *Journal of Advertising Research* 9(Sept.):3–8.

Green, P., and V. Rao. 1972. *Applied Multidimensional Scaling: A Comparison of Approach and Algorithms*. New York: Holt, Rinehart and Winston.

Gunn, C. 1972. *Vacationscape: Designing Tourist Regions*. Austin, Tex.: Bureau of Business Research, University of Texas.

Gyte, D. 1988. *Tourist Cognition of Destination: An Exploration of Techniques of Measurement and Representation of Images of Tunisia*. Nottingham: Department of Geography, Trent Polytechnic.

Howard, J. 1963. *Marketing Management*. Homewood, Ill.: Irwin Publishing Company.

Hunt, J. 1971. Image—A Factor in Tourism. Unpublished Doctoral dissertation. Colorado State University, Fort Collins, Colo.

Khan, S. 1991. Nonresidents' Perceptions of Wisconsin's Tourism Regions. Unpublished M.S. Thesis, Menomonie, WI: University of Wisconsin-Stout.

Kim, J., and C. Mueller. 1978. Introduction, *Factor Analysis; What it is and How to do it*. Newbury Park, Calif.: Sage Publications.

Kotler, P. 1982. *Marketing for Non-Profit Organizations*. Englewood Cliffs N.J.: Prentice Hall.

Kruskal, J., and M. Wish. 1978. *Multidimensional Scaling*. Quantitative Applications in the Social Sciences. Newbury Park, CA: Sage University Paper #11.

Likert, R. 1932. *A Technique for the Measure of Attitudes*. Archives of Psychology #140, New York: Columbia University Press.

Mayo, E. 1973. Regional Images and Regional Travel Behavior, pp. 211–217. *Proceedings of the Fourth Annual Travel Research Association Conference*. Salt Lake City, Utah.

McLellan, R. and F. Noe. 1983. Source of Information and Types of Messages Useful to International Tour Operators. *Journal of Travel Research* 8(3):27–30.

Milo, K. and S. Yoder. 1991. Recovery from Natural Disaster: Travel Writers and Tourist Destinations. *Journal of Travel Research* 30(1):36–39.

Murphy, P. 1983. Perception of Attitudes of Decision-Making Groups in Tourist Centers. In *The Image of Destination Regions*. M. Stabler, ed. New York: Croom Helm, Inc.

Narayana, C., and R. Markin. 1975. Consumer Behavior and Product Performance: An Alternative Conceptualization. *Journal of Marketing* 39:1–6.

Okoroafo, S. 1989. Branding in Tourism, pp. 23–26. In S.F. Witt, ed. *Tourism Marketing and Management Handbook*. New York, N.Y.: Prentice Hall.

Osgood, C., G. Suci, and P. Tannenbaum. 1957. *The Measurement of Meaning*. Urbana, Ill: University of Illinois Press.

Phelps. A. 1986. Holiday Destination Image: The Problem of Assessment; An Example Developed in Menorca. *Tourism Management* 7(3):168–180.

Roehl, W. 1990. Travel Agents Attitudes Toward China After Tiananmen Square. *Journal of Travel Research* 29(2):16–22.

Romesburg, H. 1984. *Cluster Analysis for Researchers*. Belmont, CA: Lifetime Learning Publications.

Schumann, D., R. Petty, and S. Clemon. 1990. Predicting the Effectiveness of Different Strategies of Advertising Variation: A Test of the Repetition-Variation Hypotheses. *Journal of Consumer Research* 17(Sept.):192–202.

Scott, W. 1965. Psychological and Social Correlates of International Images. In *International Behavior: A Social-Psychological Analysis*. H. Kelman, ed. New York: Holt, Rinehart and Winston.

Shen, J. 1989. Tourism Image of China as perceived by the American Mature Traveler. Unpublished M.S. Thesis, Menomonie, WI: University of Wisconsin-Stout.

Stutman, R. and S. Newell. 1984. Beliefs versus Values: Salient Beliefs in Designing A Persuasive Message. *The Western Journal of Speech Communication* 48(Fall 1984):362–372.

Thompson, J. and P. Cooper. 1979. Attitudinal Evidence on the Limited Size of Evoked Set of

Travel Destinations. *Journal of Travel Research* 17(3):23–25.

Thurstone, L. 1967. The Measurement of Social Attitudes. Chapter 2, in *Readings in Attitude Theory and Measurement*. M. Fishbein, ed. New York: John Wiley and Sons, Inc.

Uddin, Z. 1988. Determinants of the Components of a State's Tourist Image and their Marketing Implications. Unpublished Ph. D. dissertation, Utah State University.

United States Travel Service. 1977. *International Market Reviews of Selected Major Tourism Generating Countries*. Washington, D.C.: U.S. Department of Commerce.

Van Raaij, W., and D. Francken. 1984. Vacation Decision, Activities and Satisfactions. *Annals of Tourism Research* 11(1):101–112.

Weaver, P., and K. McCleary. 1984. A Market Segmentation Study to Determine the Appropriate Ad/Model Format for Travel Advertising. *Journal of Travel Research* 23(1):12–16.

Woodside, A. and J. Clokey. 1974. Multi-Attribute Multi-Brand Models. *Journal of Advertising Research* 14(5):33–40.

Woodside, A., and D. Sherrell. 1977. Traveler Evoked Set, Inept Set, and Inert Sets of Vacation Destinations. *Journal of Travel Research* 16(1):14–18.

Woodside, A., and I. Ronkainen. 1980. Vacation Travel Planning Segments: Self Planning vs. User of Motor Clubs and Travel Agents. *Annals of Tourism Research* 7(3):385–394.

Development Planning Revisited

Tourism integrated into the community of Vienna, Austria.
Photo by the author

Learning Objectives

Review reasons for engaging in tourism planning and examine related tourism planning goals.

•

Examine the process used for developing an effective tourism plan.

•

Review the concept of sustainable development, with special attention to the operational characteristics required to transform it from a concept to a workable definition.

•

Understand that mass tourism developments are not inherently unsustainable, but do require careful pre-development planning in order to avoid many undesirable impacts.

•

Explore the concept of integrated development and review some economic and social welfare theory which supports an integrated approach.

•

Review the public involvement process with special attention to the theory of stakeholder analysis.

INTRODUCTION

Tourism development planning is a process for orderly change. Development in any shape or form means change. Reacting to change is more or less damage control. Planning, although not avoiding conflict over change, can reduce the level of animosity and disarray associated with a system in crisis. Planning, then, should be viewed in the context of anticipating change and be concerned with the future implications of current decisions. A tourism development plan is an outline of future events and their potential impacts. Unplanned development, or short-term planning which does not anticipate the future, will almost surely lead to a division of people, organizations, and institutions that must be in agreement for quality development (Gunn, 1988).

Although planning for tourism development is an oft-cited concept, it has been poorly operationalized, partially due to the ideological foundations of the society in which planning takes place. Market-based economies rely on the private sector and elements of capitalism for economic growth and development. Planning in that context is often viewed as limiting individual property rights. In centrally planned economies where the state holds all property rights, well formulated plans may fail to produce expected results because of the absence of individual incentives. To be effective, planning involves a commitment from diverse interest groups. A compromise position which respects individual rights to capital but also recognizes collective rights to a community, must be found. Opening up the planning process to as many people as possible removes the feeling of restrictiveness, allowing everyone—developers, government officials, concerned citizens, etc.—to assume ownership of the plan and become part of the process of directing change.

This final chapter reviews some of the reasons planning is assuming a greater role in the tourism development process, covers some of the elements found in successful plans, and concludes with suggestions for planning at the individual and community levels. Sustainable development, a concept still in search of an operational definition, is discussed in the context of planning for small-scale tourism as well as for mass markets.

REASONS FOR PLANNING

Throughout this book, elements of planning have been presented and discussed. Many factors make tourism development planning imperative for orderly and acceptable growth. Some of the more critical factors are presented below.

Impacts

Tourism development produces economic, sociocultural, and environmental impacts. Focusing on only one type of impact furnishes an unrealistic portrayal of the full range of impacts a development activity generates. Any change has the potential to create desirable and undesirable consequences. At the same time, a change one group views as beneficial may be seen as disruptive or undesirable by another. Planning allows for the full range of impacts to be identified, analyzes who will and who will not benefit from the proposed development, and outlines a process for organized development.

Economic impacts, in terms of how much money will be generated, are almost always provided in a development plan. If the development is a private sector operation, the focus is on sales generated as shown in an initial feasibility analysis. Often estimates are also made of economic impact on the community or region in which the project will be located, or, in the case of national accounts, potential foreign exchange earnings. Depending on the magnitude and location of the proposed development, environmental impact statements or assessments may also be required. Countries have developed procedures for assessing the environmental impacts from many different types of development projects. Slowly, many countries have also come to realize that development also brings with it sociocultural change. Methods to assess sociocultural impacts, similar to those used for environmental analyses, have lately received some attention. All three types of impacts deserve attention in any development plan.

Industry Fragmentation

Tourism, unlike other economic activities, is still searching for an industrial definition. Chapter 1 discusses some of the different definitions of tourism and tourist activity. One of the problems in trying to define a phenomenon like tourism is the structural foundation on which it rests. On any one trip a tourist may utilize the services of a hotel, restaurant, transportation company, retail shopping outlets, private and public attractions, and a host of other related service vendors. Each separate business, agency, or bureau providing touristic services is allied with its respective organization. Tourism development planning, to be effective, requires cooperation between all service providers. The fact that they may have different missions and operational objectives makes the task more difficult. Effective planning requires recognition of the complexity involved in touristic activity and establishes a process where the needs of each service provider is reconciled with the needs of all others and the host community. This makes tourism development planning a much larger and more difficult task than planning undertaken with a specific purpose (e.g., marketing).

Competition

Reference to product life-cycles (see Chapter 10) underscores the need for more effective planning. Whenever a product is in stage 2 or 3, where the majority of tourism products currently find themselves, a shift from a production to a consumer orientation must occur to survive. More producers appearing in stage 2 to capture some of the profits from excess demand effectively reduces individual firm profits and increases competition. Planning is needed to develop the types of products demanded by consumers, identify specific markets, and establish a framework for continual product assessment and market change.

Improve Interrelationships

Since tourism involves and affects many different businesses, public and private agencies, and associations, as well as members of the host community, effective development planning requires input from each group. Planning should not be viewed as a confrontational exercise but an opportunity for involvement from each interest group and an exchange of concerns and ideas. Development planning helps identify the type and source of future problems and allows everyone interested to understand the long-term implications of the plan. In this context, planning should be viewed as proactive management.

Development Spread

Unplanned tourism development has a tendency to spread from its point of origin along a path of least economic resistance. Consumer goods producers have a tendency to locate close to their market with respect to transportation cost. This tendency does not necessarily hold for tourism products, although transportation cost is a factor. The larger the development becomes, the more likely it is to develop its own transportation access and locate closer to the resource which constitutes the primary attraction. Initially, the first developments will appear in the area with the highest amenity or attraction values. As increasing levels of development occur, spread from the core resource results. In coastal areas, this spread occurs up and down the coastline, and in mountainous terrain it is most likely to happen along major access routes. Primary reasons for this spread are the density and costs of development in the core area. As development continues to increase, the core area may actually shift to another area of high intensity development.

Certain patterns can be associated with certain types of development. For example, Smith (1991) studies the patterns of beach development in Asia and Australia, identifying eight development stages. The first stage has no tourism, but there may be some type of indigenous settlement in place. The second stage sees the discovery of the area by tourists, most likely domestic, and is apparent through the construction of seasonal homes. Stage three occurs when the first hotel is built, quickly followed by additional development leading to an identifiable resort area (stage 4). As tourist numbers increase, a business area is established (stage 5), followed by the spread of hotels into inland areas (stage 6). Major transformation occurs at this point, as the once rural beach resort finds it has become an urban resort (stage 7); eventually, in the last stage, it evolves into a fully urbanized city resort. While not all beach resort areas follow this evolutionary cycle, the model provides some indicators for predicting development transformation and spread at least with beach development.

Underlying the process of development evolution and spread is the concept of land rent. Land rent is defined as "the economic return that accrues or should accrue to land for its use in production" (Barlowe, 1972, 157). The amount of land rent available from any one site is a function of production costs. For example, assume there are three possible locations for a new beachfront resort. All sites are assumed to have similar income generating power. However, each site differs from the others with respect to certain cost considerations. Cost differentials may include better access, less development regulations to contend with, prices for labor, and lower development costs due to a favorable topographical situation. As shown in Figure 12.1, cost differences are reflected in average cost (AC) and marginal cost (MC) curves. Once fixed costs and variable costs are determined, the optimum operating point is where the marginal cost curve intersects the marginal revenue (MR) curve which in Figure 12.1 is the line CD. Total returns are equal to the rectangle ACDF, or average price per unit sold multiplied by total number of units sold. Land rent is the shaded area in the diagram, BCDE, which represents total returns minus total cost. The site chosen for development is the one with the highest land rent. Therefore, understanding production cost factors helps predict areas most likely to be impacted by development spread as development proceeds along the path of least economic resistance.

Development spread may not be entirely supply-side-driven. Movements of urban dwellers to suburbia, which occurred at high rates during the last three decades, is a product of urban congestion, crime, and the desire for people to live in more rural, country settings. Eventually, the sub-

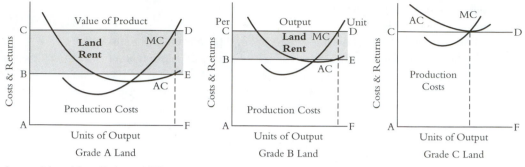

Source: Adapted from Barlowe, 1972

Figure 12.1 *Illustration of the Effects Differences in Land Quality Have Upon the Amounts of Land Rent which Accrue to Three Grades of Land*

urbs become as crowded as the city which was left behind, leading to another move outward away from the new city. Tourists may react in a similar manner. As the destination core becomes increasingly crowded, developers may intuitively pick up on the demand for less crowded experiences similar to those available when the core area was less developed. Development spread is met with acceptance by tourists, represented by patronage, and another round of development and development spread begins.

PLANNING GOALS

In order to contend with some of the problems associated with unplanned development, researchers and practitioners have searched for a set of goals that drive the planning process. Tourism planning goals have been identified by McIntosh et al. (1995) as:

1. Providing a framework for raising the living standard of the people through the economic benefits of tourism

2. Developing an infrastructure and providing recreation facilities for visitors and residents alike

3. Ensuring types of development within visitor centers and resorts that are appropriate to the purposes of those areas

4. Establishing a development program consistent with the cultural, social, and economic philosophy of the government and the people of the host country or area

5. Optimizing visitor satisfaction

The first four goals deal with maintaining the cultural or environmental integrity of the area in which tourism will take place. Host societies and the land on which they live are most at risk from unplanned tourism development. Establishing development goals which put the providers of the tourism experience, including private sector operations which exist via tourist expenditures, first recognizes that planning involves as many members of the local community as possible. Optimizing visitor satisfaction, which is necessary if tourism is to succeed in an area, should be a product of the type of tourism a host society wishes to offer. In a sense, the above goals require a planning process that reviews what an area has to offer in the way of a tourism experience, assesses local resource needs, and provides a product that represents local values and is in demand by visitors.

The above goals are primarily operative at the community or local level. National or regional level goals are much broader and usually emphasize economic development. The problems associated with increasing levels of development, although addressed at higher levels, are left up to the destination areas to solve.

TOURISM PLANNING PROCESS

Almost every tourism text has a chapter or section on the planning process. With the emphasis placed on the need for organized planning, it is surprising to travel and see so many unplanned development projects. While individual facilities may be well planned and managed, there appears to be a lack of coordination between the various interest groups involved in tourism development. Integrated development planning is still the exception rather than the rule. One of the major reasons for this is the enormous time commitment in developing a workable plan. Private sector operations, especially the capital intensive types, are usually in the forefront of planning simply because they have the resources to make it a priority item. However, relying on the private sector to formulate a tourism plan that incorporates the goals discussed above is risky. Profit motivations may override the need to incorporate as many elements of society as possible in developing a plan for the entire community.

Tourism planning intensifies and becomes more critical when it becomes a local issue. Since most national development strategies are concerned with how tourism fits into the overall economic development plan for a country, national tourism offices become marketing organizations although they can and do provide technical development assistance to local communities. Planning intensity, however, should increase at the local level as the community becomes the destination and the receiver of the various impacts generated through tourism. The following planning process, although presented so that it can be adopted at any level, should be viewed as a means of empowering communities with the techniques of initiating tourism development planning.

1. Establish a funding source for tourism development planning. Most tourism development planning processes start with defining the system, developing leadership, inventorying attractions, or uncovering market profiles of present visitors. All these approaches are useful and can begin the planning process, but one problem exists with each one—who is going to do it. Many small communities rely on a Chamber of Commerce for leadership. This approach has merit as the economic benefits of tourism activity do accrue to local businesses. However, Chambers of Commerce are established to represent businesses, and decisions made by this group may not reflect interests of other segments in the community. For effective and involved planning to take place, a separate professional tourism organization is needed and this can only happen if a funding source dedicated to tourism development planning is established. There are many approaches that can be used to establish a funding source (see Chapter 7), but almost every one requires some government action. Government leadership in setting up a funding source for tourism development planning accomplishes two things. First, it recognizes tourism development as a priority item which is supported by policy. Second, it removes the element of interest group bias from the process as government in democratic countries is considered a representative body for everyone. Not all communities have recognized the need for government planning assistance, and many have left tourism development initiatives entirely up to the private sector. The opposite may also be true, as in some developing countries the private sector may be weak or insignificant with government in control of planning and development.

2. Create a Tourism Organization. A separate tourism organization is needed if tourism development is expected to be one of the leading economic development agents in a community. The organization should include as many representatives from different interest groups as possible. Business leaders, government officials, concerned citizens, academicians, and others in the community should be afforded an opportunity to belong to the tourism organization. The ideal size of a tourism organization depends on the emphasis placed on tourism development. Hirner et al. (1986) propose a comprehensive

organizational structure comprised of numerous subcommittees (Figure 12.2). It should be kept in mind that this is an idealistic organizational structure. However, even at the small community level, the proposed model can be used as an aid in devising an effective tourism organization. As the size of the organization grows, the need for a funding source to accomplish all subcommittee tasks becomes apparent.

3. Analyze the present situation. This is a very large and important task. It not only requires an assessment of the present market situation but, at the local level, a review of physical and social resource limits. Linkages between private and public sector organizations must be established. Legal and political constraints and opportunities must be identified. Accomplishing these tasks is what makes the formation of a tourism organization imperative. A present situation analysis can be viewed from a supply/demand perspective. What allows or prevents tourism development from succeeding in an area constitutes supply-side considerations. Understanding present or potential tourists constitutes the demand side. Figure 12.3 lists some of the various supply/demand factors that must be analyzed in order to understand the present situation.

4. Set objectives. Local or community-level objectives may be more focused on community expectations from tourism rather than simply increasing dollar flows. For example, they may specifically address in-frastructure improvement, better or increased access to recreation areas, or an increase in certain quality of life aspects. Setting objectives allows two things to happen. It provides concrete direction for the chosen alternative (explained below) and a benchmark for measuring success. Objectives, especially in the early stages of a tourism development plan, should be readily obtainable. Success feeds off success. Unrealistic expectations can easily destroy all the hard work that has gone into the planning process.

5. Develop alternative strategies. There are many approaches to attain stated objectives, but only a few of them will work given the present situation. Different strategies should be developed and discussed. Not all are readily apparent, but if enough are proposed, a few will eventually emerge as the most likely to accomplish identified objectives.

6. Select a preferred alternative. Each alternative should be analyzed against data gathered during the situation analysis phase. Some which are promising will prove unworkable. It is possible that elements of

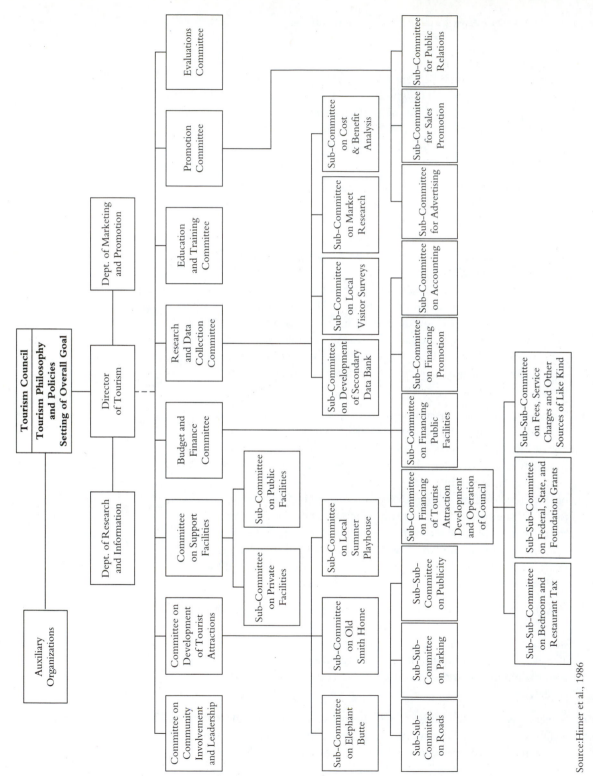

Source: Hirner et al., 1986

Figure 12.2 *Tourism Organizational Structure (Sample)*

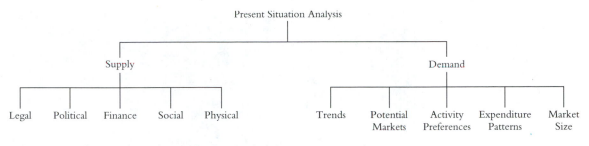

Figure 12.3 *Supply/Demand Considerations in a Situation Analysis*

one will be combined with another to form a better alternative. Deciding on a preferred alternative requires consensus be reached between members of the organization. A helpful technique during this stage is to develop a matrix with the alternatives listed across the top, and criteria which relate to what was uncovered during the present situation analysis stage listed down the side (Figure 12.4). Numerical values can then be assigned to each alternative depending on how well it meets each criterion. Alternatives with the highest numerical scores can then be subjected to a further round of debate and analysis, with one eventually being selected for implementation.

Sample Criteria	Alternative #1	Alternative #2	Alternative #3	Alternative #4
Funding Availability				
Politically Acceptable				
Physical Resource Availability				
Social Resource Availability				
Consistent with Known Market Trends				
Overall Ability to Meet Objectives				
Directed at Target Market				

Key: 10 = High Priority
          0 = No Probability

Figure 12.4   *Matrix of Alternatives Weighted Against Criteria Used to Select a Preferred Alternative*

Aerial photos of Traverse City, Michigan from 1950 and 1980, showing temporal development in a tourism-development community. Photo by Michigan State University, Department of Resource Develpment

7. Implement the preferred alternative. Once a preferred alternative is selected, it must be implemented. Responsibilities are assigned, programs needed to implement are established, and resources are made available to carry out the task. This is the action component of a tourism plan, and moves the plan from the drawing board to the field. Unfortunately, many tourism development plans begin with step 7 and in spite of this, some do succeed. However, the odds are decidedly against this occurring on a regular basis. Planning is a risk adverse strategy. When dealing with public resources, both financial and human risk should be minimized.

8. Monitor and evaluate. Planning is a dynamic process. The hard work that is required to develop a workable plan continues even after the preferred alternative is implemented. How well is the preferred alternative working, and are there any unforeseen obstacles are just two of the questions that must be addressed during this step. Care should be taken, however, not to continually attempt to "fine tune" a development plan. When things are not proceeding according to the plan, the entire process must be reviewed. Were the data collected during the present situation analysis inaccurate? Were the outputs specified in the objectives unrealistic? Were the criteria selected for alternative evaluation appropriate? Should the criteria have been weighted to reflect those deemed most important? These are just a few of the questions that should be asked during the evaluation stage. If so, the plan will become a dynamic instrument directing development.

Planning Example

The planning process is most likely to break down when more than one jurisdictional unit is involved. The Lake George basin in the Adirondack Mountains of upper New York state is an example of this problem. Lake George has been a popular resort area and second home location for over 100 years. Its natural beauty, proximity to large numbers of people, and relatively easy access are some of the reasons for its popularity. Water quality has been debated, monitored, and regulated for as long as the area has been frequented by visitors, but during the 1970s and 80s, with increased use came increased concern over declining water quality. Over time, water quality became recognized as a basin-wide issue involving multi-county and multi-municipality participation in the planning process. A task force representing every municipality, lakeowner association, and special interest group convened to deal with the problem. A total of 110 recommendations were presented to protect the water quality of the basin (*A Sense of Place: Tourism, Development and the Environment,* 1992). The planning committee reviewed these recommendations, subjected them to a public hearing process, and implemented preferred alternatives. Convening special task forces comprised of representatives from all interest groups is a means of dealing with ecosystem issues where one managing authority is not in control. It is a way of refining the public participation process.

This task was not easy. One could argue that attempts to organize multi-jurisdictional groups have been made as long as water quality issues have been identified and it was only when water quality decline became apparent to the majority of residents that action was taken. However, as successes continue to occur in community-wide cooperation, proactive multi-jurisdictional planning groups should become more common.

Tourism Master Plan

Conceptually, the planning process described above is functional and workable given the resources and desire to engage in a proactive approach to tourism development. Where it often breaks down is after objectives are determined and alternatives discussed, in the implementation phase. Who does what, when, and how are overriding concerns that must be addressed in order to achieve an optimal solution. Tourism development planning in its basic form is no different than constructing a new skyscraper or building a high-speed transportation system. Certain things (e.g., ordering and having materials delivered at the right time) must be organized in order for the task to be accomplished.

Baker (1990) takes this concept and develops an objective tree for tourism planning (Figure 12.5). It begins with the establishment of a primary goal which is then defined in terms of objectives. Objectives are accomplished through task completion. Personnel can be assigned to each one of the tasks, and timelines established for completion. Eventually, the goal is accomplished. The objective tree approach is flexible enough that different goals, objectives, and tasks can be accommodated. It is simply an architect's view of how the plan will be implemented and can serve as a guide for any level of tourism development planning.

The tourism planning process is a requirement if one of the overriding goals is to implement a sustainable approach to development. Understanding what sustainable means will help in setting plan objectives.

SUSTAINABLE DEVELOPMENT

Sustainable development concerns grew out of the rapid exploitation of the earth's environment for economic gain. Realization that short-term gains were coming at the expense of long-term losses for future genera-

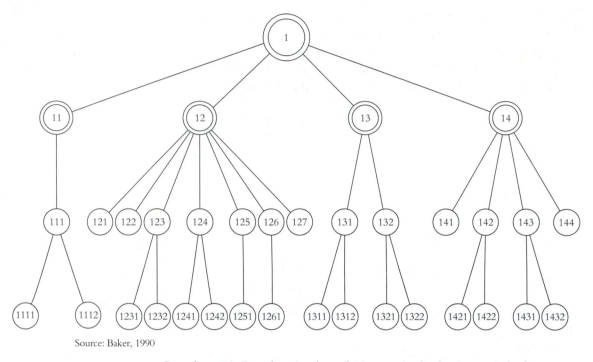

Source: Baker, 1990

Example: 1. Expand provinces' contribution to national and socioeconmic development
          11. Increase foreign exchange earnings   14. Reduce cost burden on investors
         111. Increase number of foreign visitors,   144. Increase infrastructure where
              length of stay, and expenditures   investment potential is high
        1111. Increase and upgrade services and
              infrastructure

Figure 12.5 *The Objective Tree for a Tourism Development Master Plan*

tions began to reshape global development strategy. Dragicevic (1991) traces concerns over sustainable development and the environmental consequences of development to the late 1950s. These early warnings, generally ignored until the World Conservation Strategy of 1980 (IUCN, 1980) and the Bruntland report of 1987 (UN, 1987), called for a global sustainable development strategy. This strategy encompasses all potentially exploitative economic development activities including tourism. Since these early conferences where the concept of sustainable development was recognized, numerous other communiqués and charters have been drafted and submitted to various national governments and world bodies. One of the most recent is the Charter on Sustainable Tourism from the World Conference on Sustainable Tourism. The main points of the Charter are contained in Figure 12.6.

In spite of all the attention it has received, sustainable development remains a concept searching for a clear definition. Pearce and Turner

Main Points of the Charter

The following is a summary of some of the main points of the charter, which has been sent to the United Nations Commission on Sustainable Development.

✔Tourism development shall be based on criteria of sustainability, which means that it must be ecologically sound in the long term, economically viable, as well as ethically and socially equitable for the local communities.

✔The sustainable nature of tourism requires that it should integrate the natural, cultural and human environments. It must respect the fragile balances that characterize many tourist destinations, in particular small islands and environmentally sensitive areas.

✔Tourism must consider its effects on cultural heritage and traditional elements, activities and dynamics of each local community. These elements must at all times play a central role in the formulation of tourism strategies, particularly in developing countries.

✔Sustainable development means the solidarity, mutual respect, and participation of all players implicated in the process, especially those indigenous to the locality. This must be based on efficient cooperation mechanisms at all levels: local, national, regional and international.

✔Governments and authorities shall promote actions for integrating the planning of tourism with environmental non-government organizations (NGOs) and local communities.

✔Measures must be developed to permit a more equitable distribution of the benefits and burdens of tourism. This implies a change in consumption patterns and the introduction of ecologically honest pricing. Governments and multilateral organizations are called on to abandon subsidies that have negative effects on the environment.

✔Environmentally and culturally vulnerable spaces, both now and in the future, shall be given special priority in the matter of technical cooperation and financial aid for sustainable tourism development. Similarly, special treatment should be given to spaces that have been degraded by obsolete and high-impact tourism models.

✔Government, authorities, and NGOs with responsibility for tourism and the environment shall promote and participate in the creation of open networks for information, research, dissemination, and transfer of appropriate tourism and environmental knowledge and technology.

✔There is a need to support and promote feasibility studies, vigorously-applied scientific field-work, tourism demonstration projects within the framework of sustainable development, the development of programmes in the field of international cooperation, and the introduction of environmental management systems.

Source: World Tourism Organization (WTO)

Figure 12.6   *United Nations Commission on Sustainable Development Main Points of Sustainable Development Charts*

(1990, 24) propose the following definition: "sustainable development, or growth, involves maximizing and optimally distributing the net benefits of economic development, so far as these can be achieved, while establishing and reaffirming the conditions of security under which the services and qualities of natural resources can be maintained, restored, or improved into the foreseeable future." Originally focused on environmental concerns, the concept has been broadened to include socioeconomic and cultural phenomena.

Inskeep (1991, 459–467) includes in his book a draft of "An Action Strategy for Sustainable Development" which was presented at the Globe 90 Conference on Sustainable Development by the Tourism Stream Action Strategy Committee. Suggestions to achieve sustainable development in the paper are directed at governments, tourists, and tourism industry operators. While it is risky to paraphrase the advice given by many international experts, the basic premise is that all groups involved in tourism should become more aware of developments' environmental and sociocultural impacts, and strive to reduce the by-products of tourism activity. Statements as to how this can be achieved are included in the report. While the advice provided by the committee, if adopted, would result in less intrusive forms of tourism development, there is still no clear definition as to what sustainable development is and how sustainable developments change over time to accommodate population increases or increasing tourism demand.

A major difficulty in operationalizing the concept of sustainable development is determining what is sustainable. Assume two different development strategies as depicted in Figure 12.7. Strategy A is sustained growth or growth occurring at a constant rate. Strategy B is no growth with the level of development held constant. Each strategy may or may not be sustainable with respect to environmental or sociocultural impacts. A sustained growth strategy may be sustainable if it utilizes existing excess resource capacity. For example, increases in tourism may result from adding a different product mix to that currently available. The use of abandoned rail tracks for biking/hiking activities or the development of a farm-stay program may result in increased tourism activity without any further exploitation of local resources. On the other hand, a no growth strategy may not be sustainable if consumer trends and tastes change, resulting in decreased travel to the area and a declining quality of life for local residents due to economic losses. In order to more fully understand

Figure 12.7 *Sustained Development Growth vs. No Growth*

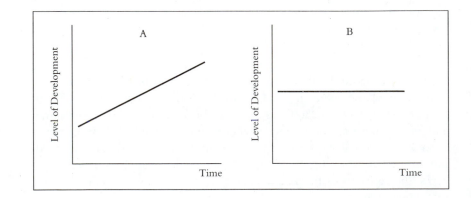

what makes sustainable development possible, a more thorough analysis of the concept is in order.

McIntyre and Hetherington (1992) outline the key elements of a sustainable development policy. They begin with the essence of the concept, or what it is intended to accomplish. Basically, sustainable development is stewardship of the air, water, and land, and is sensitive to people's values and visions. A workable sustainable development policy generally contains three key elements: activities, requirements, and outputs.

Activities

The most common types of tourism activities representative of sustainable development are nature or ecotourism, and cultural tourism. Nature tourism may be represented by back-country hiking, canoe trails, and other ecologically sound recreation activities. Nature tourism does not have to be non-consumptive as long as the resources consumed are renewable in the short term. In this respect, activities such as regulated hunting, fishing, mushroom and wild berry picking pursuits are sustainable. Cultural tourism may include performing and visual arts, ethnic customs, handicrafts, and indigenous peoples' way of living that is freely but not necessarily without a charge, presented to tourists. Any culturally based activity that enhances community esteem and provides for social exchanges between diverse peoples can be included in culturally sustainable tourism. If a cultural activity moves into the realm of staged authenticity and no longer serves the purpose of reinforcing cultural values, it moves beyond sustainable. Other activities that provide economic benefits to local people and do not degrade the environmental or cultural integrity of the land or people are considered sustainable.

Requirements

Sustainable development demands active planning. The requirements for it to work include knowledge of tourism's impacts on the natural and cultural environments of the area. In order to accomplish this, information from all segments of society must be solicited. It is critical that the public involvement process is directed at uncovering the interrelationships between the area's natural and cultural resources and its economic and social well being. A major goal of sustainable development is to ensure that the economic and social benefits from tourism are distributed as equitably as possible throughout all segments of the community. Without active public involvement, decision makers are only guessing that this goal is being achieved. Planning is also necessary to ensure that whenever negative impacts, perceived or real, are encountered there exists a framework to address the problems.

ECOTOURISM, SUSTAINABLE DEVELOPMENT, SUSTAINABLE TOURISM: SOME REACTIONS FROM THE FIELD

Sustainable development is more of a concept than anything else. While at its very core it deals with maintaining some economic activity related to tourism without any undue detrimental changes on the natural or cultural environment, operationalizing the concept is open to wide interpretation. Members of the academic community have been debating the meaning of sustainable development and its related terms such as ecotourism for years. There is yet no consensus on what it really means, let alone how to implement a sustainable development policy. What may be enlightening for some is to see how academics and practitioners, all hooked to a tourism electronic bulletin board accessible by subscription on the Internet, responded to one person's reaction to the marketing piece distributed for a conference being staged to teach ecotourism marketing methods. The conference brochure stated: "Ecotourism, also known as low-impact or sustainable tourism, refers to nature, adventure, and cultural tourism. With the coming of the baby boomers, 76 million strong, the experience of Ecotourism will provide destinations that offer excitement and mystique, personal growth, social aspects, or physical fitness."

Among the statements the person beginning the discussion offered were: "Tourism operators of all stripes see a new niche, really an old one, to which they can give established tourism a new spin. If you are going to harness 76 million baby boomers and restructure existing tourism for the Ecotourism market, then what becomes of the low impact help-the-protected-area type of tourism used to draw clients to such workshops?" (Bryan Farrell)

A selection of some of the responses to this statement follow:

"Where exactly has the eco part of the word gone? Given that a variety of tourism ventures have often included some appreciation/enjoyment of natural features, I understand the confusion and I understand the desire to jump on the increasingly popular and profitable ecotourism bandwagon . . . is ecotourism primarily a conservation and "sustainable development" initiative or is ecotourism primarily a new marketing opportunity?" (Constance Russell)

"Experiences which exploit nature (flora or fauna) can be counterproductive to that ideal and miss out on ecotourism's potential as environmental education . . . An adequate definition of ecotourism must also include educational concerns." (Constance Russell)

"At least the environmental and cultural impact of mass tourism is more concentrated—and thus more governable—compared to individual tourists' impacts." (Tom Selanniemi)

"I am convinced more than ever that ecotourism is simply a form of mass tourism in its early *stages* . . . the important issue is how can we make tourism, in general, more environmentally and socially benign?" (John Crotts)

"Eco-tourism—ego-tourism—a new product for the market where some gain ego enhancement" . . . Peter Murphy stated. . . . . Disney is a sustainable tourism product. There is much to justify this view." (Chris Ryan)

"I found where workers in the field were trying to establish sustainable development indicators so that development situations could be closely monitored and analyzed, something needed desperately in sustainable tourism" (Bryan Farrell)

". . . success is directly related to the match between the true objective of ecotourism and the strong local feelings of retaining culture and control." (Thomas Iverson)

". . . the greatest need for sustainable tourism is to identify specific approaches and tools to be applied to tourism development scenarios such that one could say "that is a sustainable tourism development. . . . In the search for actionable concepts perhaps the most important principle I found was that perfection was not necessary: Levels achieved are preferable to extremes not attained." (Brad Wellstead)

". . . it is wrong to belittle the concepts of ecotourism/sustainable tourism, but rather we need to examine why they have evolved and the implications that they have on the expectations/behaviors/and evaluations of consumers. It could be that product changes have occurred, but those changes may be in the form of the consumer's view rather than in fundamental 'real' changes." (Rick Perdue)

"What are the politics of sustainability? . . . Sustainability implies long term, but we all know that politics are short-term oriented . . . the next election or the next poll." (Frederic Dimanche)

"Sustainable development is the development of strategies to ensure the long term success of one's tourism product . . . how then can 'we' sustain it? Do guests sustain the tourism product through conscious choices or does the host society sustain their product through planning, subsidies, etc.?" (Daren Bloomquist)

"Most of us "haoles" or "outsiders" who visit XXXXX wish that it could be left pristine and untouched, yet the burgeoning population requires some form of economic development. I can't help but feel that if XXXX handbooks had been available years ago that an ecotourism-based private sector might be flourishing right now. Instead there is widespread corruption, virtually no private sector and a huge bloated government sector" (Thomas Iverson)

"Could it be that the best chance for sustainability is relative obscurity, difficult access, and poor marketing?" (Brian Hill)

The above comments demonstrate a wide range of reactions to the concepts of sustainable development, sustainable tourism, and ecotourism. Comments range from outright despair with little hope of ever achieving something approaching sustainability, to arguments suggesting that operational standards need to be developed, and others suggesting that people first need to decide for whom sustainability applies. What most contributors to the discussion would most likely agree on is that there is not now nor is there likely to be any universally-agreed-to definition of sustainability and its related forms. Rather, there needs to be a case-by-case discussion as to what it means in a particular context, and that planning frameworks incorporating the concept's various meanings are needed before irreversible development takes place.

Source: Trinet bulletin board—A medium of discussion between tourism researchers and scholars, (21 Sept–5 Oct, 1995).

A planning framework developed by Draper and Driscoll (1991) to solve some of the problems related to sustainable development involves social dilemma theory. They maintain that tourism development has historically been one-sided, with developers focusing on self interest leading to unchecked development. The theory underlying this trend (i.e., tragedy of the commons) is discussed in Chapter 3. Problems can be mitigated on the basis of either structural or behavioral solutions. A structural solution is one which changes the reward system for those who either cooperate or defect from the preferred outcome. For example, if development occurs in a fragile ecosystem, restrictions on development can be imposed. The use of zoning is one method of restricting development. Alternatively, if a developer presents a plan to maintain the environmental integrity of an area which includes some public land, the public property can be converted to private property, allowing the developer to reap economic returns from environmental protection. The idea behind structural change is once a decision has been made about the type of development appropriate for an area, the regulatory incentives/disincentives can be used to achieve the desired result.

Behavioral changes do not use regulatory power but instead rely on social values such as altruism, group norms, social responsibility, and such to produce the desired result. A key component affecting behavioral change is education. As mentioned above, one of the requirements for sustainable development is knowledge about tourism's impact on the natural and cultural environment. As more information becomes available regarding these impacts, the opportunity to affect behavioral change increases.

Achieving sustainable development likely involves the use of both structural and behavioral changes. A systems model showing how the process works is presented in Figure 12.8. Again, the interrelationships between the economic, social, and environmental systems must be understood. This requirement mandates an active community planning process.

Outputs

Assuming sustainable development is achievable, what are the expected outputs? They are the same as embodied in the tourism planning goals discussed above. The protection and enhancement of the natural and cultural environment of an area is most important, while maintaining or increasing the level of economic returns. If this can be accomplished, the quality of life for residents of the host community will increase and visitor satisfaction will be enhanced. Ancillary outputs such as infrastructure improvement and an increased supply of recreation and cultural facilities for residents and guest will also result.

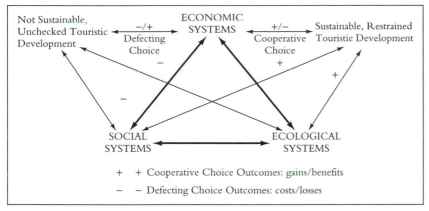

Figure 12.8 *A Systems Model of Touristic Development Trade-Offs*

Source: Draper and Driscoll, 1991

Bramwell (1991) proposes techniques for achieving sustainable development:

1. Assessment of capacity—an assessment of the maximum tourist load the environment can tolerate before deteriorating

2. Transport Management—to lessen the stress of congestion and its effect on host communities, a plan consisting of parking strategies, signpost routes, traffic restriction and such should be implemented

3. Marketing and Information—a plan to market only those areas not considered sensitive and likely to loose critical resource values through land use change

4. Conservation and adaption—minimization of visitor wear and tear through continued resource management

5. Design and control of development—tourism developments designed to blend with the existing environment

6. Involving the local community—a forum for continued local input should be established

Sustainable development strategies are still in the experimental stage. For example, an operational model (Figure 12.9) has been developed for Costa Rica. It integrates economics, agriculture, water resources, mining, tourism, energy, urbanization, and science (Quesada-Mateo and Solis-Rivera, 1990) Because of the recent attempts to define and operationalize the sustainable development concept, few workable examples are available.

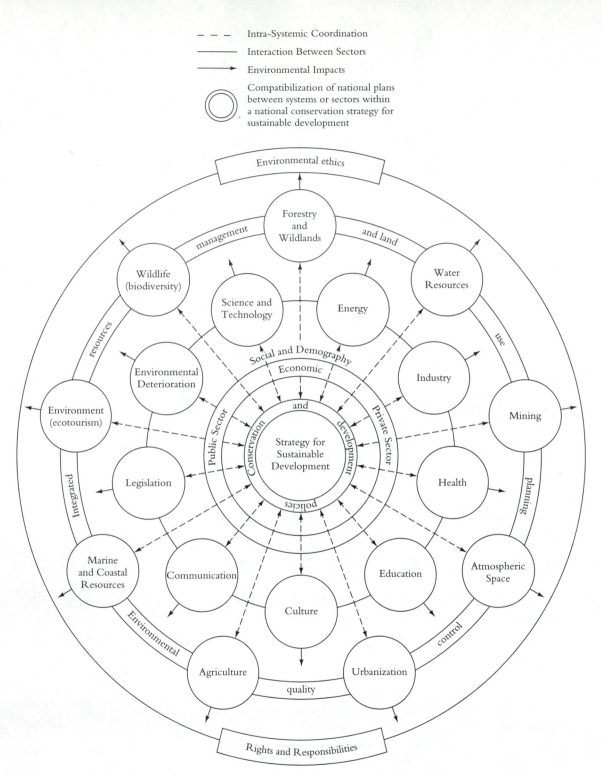

Source: Quesada-Mateo and Solis-Rivera, 1990

Figure 12.9 *An Integrated Systems Approach Methodology for Planning National Conservation Strategies for Sustainable Development: An Example from Costa Rica*

PLANNING FOR MASS TOURISM

Sustainable tourism development is a reaction to the consequences of un-planned mass tourism developments. The principles of sustainable development are the same as those embodied in the concept of alternative forms of development. As such, they are one and the same. This poses an interesting dilemma. Should mass tourism developments which generate substantial amounts of economic earnings be rejected? The answer is no for many reasons. Since mass tourism developments have enormous economic potential, they will be continually sought after by countries in need of foreign exchange. They are also in demand by tourists. Consider the advantage of cost. Mass tourism developments make their money on volume. Profit margins can afford to be small as long as volume remains high. Tourists benefit through lower prices, and developers, managers, and host community residents benefit through a constant flow of money. Eliminating mass tourism destinations is neither economically feasible nor desirable.

The key to developing mass tourism destinations is, once again, planning. First, it must be recognized that mass tourism is not an evil but an opportunity. It is ideally suited to urban areas where the infrastructure needed to handle large amounts of people is already in place. It is also ideally suited for resort destination areas. The same principles used for sustainable development can be applied to mass tourism destinations, but with the understanding that major transformation will occur. Where it occurs is a planning challenge. It may be acceptable to allow certain ecosystems which are deemed in adequate supply to be transformed by major development. Fragile or scarce ecosystems should still be protected.

Planned destination areas, sometimes called enclave developments, are ideal for hosting large amounts of people in a relatively small area, thus concentrating and making possible the management of impacts. Criticisms of enclave developments, especially in developing countries, focus on the expatriation of earnings and the lack of significant host/visitor contact. The problem of social alienation between the groups will probably never be adequately solved, but careful planning and management can increase the flow of economic returns to residents of host communities.

There is some evidence to reject the goal of social exchange as beneficial when dealing with mass tourism development. A study by Allen et al. (1988) showed less community acceptance for tourism as the level of tourism development and the number of tourists arriving increased. Planning for mass tourism development must recognize that trade-offs in impacts will have to be made. It may be possible to offer both mass tourism in the way of enclave development, and a community-based alternative form of tourism which is more host/guest interactive. Planning for enclave development should concentrate on the full range of structural and behavior change agents required to reduce as much as possible the undesirable impacts of this type of development.

INTEGRATED DEVELOPMENT

Tourism development works best when it is fully integrated into the economic base of an area. When it is only one of a group of industrial activities, the economy will be diversified and less susceptible to major economic fluctuations. For example, if tourism declines because of a shortage of fuel for transportation, a tourism-dependent community will be harder hit than one which also has an agricultural or manufacturing base. Major losses in one industry can be cushioned by stable or increasing demand for the products produced by other sectors. Even when demand for all locally produced products declines, the total economic loss is a weighted average of the losses from all industrial activity. An economic diversification strategy is a form of risk avoidance; in other words, an economic insurance policy. In addition to reducing the chances for major economic losses, a diversification strategy can almost always produce more economic and social benefits than a single industry, even if that single industry is experiencing an economic boom. This can be shown by reference to production theory.

Production is a function of the combination of fixed and independent variables. A production equation may take the form: $Y = f(X1....Xf, Xf + 1 ...... Xt)$ where Y = production, $X1...Xf$ are fixed inputs and $Xf + 1 .... Xt$ are a set of variable inputs. The production function produced by this equation is shown in Figure 12.10. Notice that the production curve increases rapidly, begins to level off and then declines as inputs are increased. This is due to the law of diminishing returns. For example, assume the equation represents corn production. Nitrogen is one of the variable inputs needed to produce corn. However, excessive levels of nitrogen can stunt or kill the corn plant. After a certain amount of nitrogen is applied to the land, any additional amounts will have deleterious effects and reduce the harvest, hence the law of diminishing returns.

Tourism is also subject to a production function. Some of the variable inputs include land and labor. As inputs increase, more land may be converted from other uses and be used for tourism development. Diminishing returns can occur in many ways. Increasing levels of development may change the market for the product, leading to an eventual decline in visitation. If the production function represents quality of life outputs rather

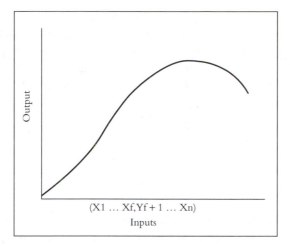

Figure 12.10 Production
Function

than economic returns, diminishing returns can be viewed from an environmental or social degradation aspect. In either case, production, no matter how it is measured, will eventually reach the point of diminishing returns and decline with increasing levels of inputs.

Assume there is a choice between two types of industrial outputs such as tourism and agriculture. Each one has a separate production function as depicted in Figure 12.11. If one of the variable inputs is in short supply, such as land, and is needed by both activities, then a decrease in the use of that input by one of the activities can lead to an increase in output by the other. If the one using most of the input is operating in the diminishing-

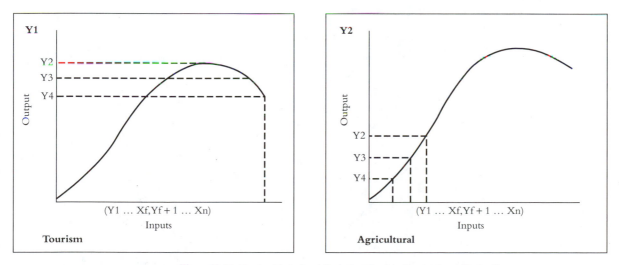

Figure 12.11 *Tourism/Agricultural Production Function Showing Input Trade-offs*

returns portion of the curve, then a reallocation of the input from the one producing diminishing returns to the other will boost production for both. For example, if tourism output is at Y4, production can be increased by reallocating some of the limiting input to the other activity. Tourism production increases to a level shown by the point Y3 and agricultural output also increases.

The last question to be asked is what is the optimal allocation of the inputs between the two activities? This is shown in Figure 12.12. Since individuals will choose to purchase a combination of products which will put them on their highest utility curve, the same logic applies to the allocation of productive inputs. The diagonal lines in Figure 12.12 are called iso-revenue or iso-value product lines. The further the line is from the origin, the more revenue generated. The curved line is called an iso-cost line and represents input costs. Anywhere along the iso-cost line, the total cost of the inputs used in production remains the same. Inputs are now allocated between the two production activities is such a way that if one values an input at a higher rate than another, it will be sold to the one which places the highest value on it. Production is maximized for both where the iso-revenue curve is tangential to the iso-cost line. This is also the point where the marginal value product of each variable input in use by each production activity divided by the price of the input is equal for all the inputs. In equation form this optimal production point is where:

Figure 12.12 *Combination of Two Goods that Produce Higher Revenue*

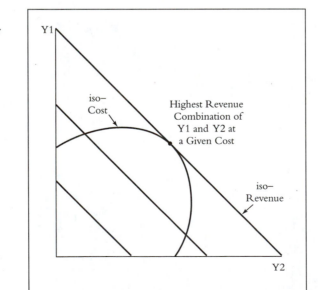

$$MVPX1Y1/PX1 = MVPX1Y2/PX1 = MVP\ X2Y1/PX2 =$$
$$MVP\ X2Y2/PX2.....MVP\ XnY1/PXn = MVPXnY2/PYn = 1.$$

Production theory supports the need for a diversified area economy from an economics perspective. Intuitively it is also applicable when social welfare and not economic returns are considered. Assuming the primary goal of tourism development is to provide an increase in the quality of life for host communities, allocation of inputs is still maximized where the marginal value products of the inputs are equal among uses. The trick is to define marginal value product in non-economic terms. For example, the input labor is not used efficiently when all jobs are tied to one industry. Not all people are equally happy working in tourism, agriculture, or any other industrial activity. When people are presented with options, they can allocate their labor time in order to provide them with the highest intrinsic as well as economic return. Similarly, the use of land for only one activity does not provide enough diversity of uses to satisfy residents or visitors. Open space, wild areas, agricultural land, and clean air and water are as much a part of the tourism package as structural developments.

Recognizing diversity makes as much sense from a social welfare perspective as it does from an economic point of view leads to a better and more useful allocation of resource inputs in an area. Planning for tourism development should be directed at trying to find the optimal production point for all an area's inputs. Unfortunately, no clear answer to how this is done is currently available. There are examples where tourism has stepped in to prop up an area's economy due to declining demand for traditional products. In Cyprus, an economic downturn from a decline in mineral production and the closing of foreign military bases has been offset by an increase in tourism (Witt, 1991). Similarly, in Jamaica, foreign exchange earnings from tourism have lessened the economic gap resulting from a decline in bauxite production (Din, 1988). The extent to which tourism can offset losses in other sectors is a function of resource substitutability. Tourism should not be viewed as an easy or even preferable substitute for all other industries, but if some resources can be easily converted to other uses, it can be viewed as an economic insurance policy.

PUBLIC INVOLVEMENT

Throughout this chapter, and indeed throughout the book, heavy emphasis has been placed on public involvement in the tourism development and planning process. While it is easy to say this must be done, obtaining public involvement that represents all impacted groups is much harder to realize. Involving affected groups in the planning process is often referred to as strategic planning with stakeholders. Freeman (1984) defines a stakeholder as any group affected by or who can affect the future of a corporation. For tourism development the definition can be broadened to include the future of a community. Recognizing that one business or one group's decision affects other groups in the community is the beginning stage of strategic planning through stakeholders.

Stakeholder analysis requires that planners recognize and identify groups that can be considered stakeholders, understand the goals and criteria each stakeholder uses to evaluate the planning process, and construct strategies to deal with each stakeholder (Bryson and Roering, 1987). Rowe et al. (1986) propose a "force-field" analysis to more fully understand stakeholder analysis. Basically it involves reviewing past stakeholder positions and then identifying assumptions stakeholders will bring to the bargaining table for the issues to be resolved. Two categories of assumptions are identified: supporting or driving force assumptions, and resisting or constraining force assumptions. Supporting or driving force assumptions are those considered in favor of the planner's position and constraining force assumptions pose threats or danger to the desired outcome. Both sets of assumptions are assigned subjective weights with respect to importance and support for the planner's position. Supporting and resisting assumptions for each stakeholder are then arrayed in a grid format with each one paired against its closest counterpart. A simple summation of importance weights provides the planner with some idea of the probability for success or failure of the proposed initiative. One problem inherent in the discussion so far is that stakeholder groups are assumed to have equal political power. Obviously this is an unrealistic assumption. Once the stakeholder analysis process is completed, two different strategies to deal with unequal political power can be utilized. These strategies are referred to as a cooperative linkage model or gaming theory model. The stakeholder analysis leading to these two different strategies is outlined in Figure 12.13.

The cooperative linkage model recognizes unequal political power exists between stakeholders and uses the interrelationships between groups to influence the outcome. It involves linking groups with common goals and shared interests, thereby creating a temporary mega-stakeholder group. The new stakeholder group uses its power to counter adverse assumptions or develops compromise alternatives which effectively lead to new supporting assumptions in favor of the planning initiative. The key to success for the cooperative linkage model is in finding supporting assumptions which bind different stakeholders together and isolates stakeholders holding important adverse assumptions. Accomplishing this task requires planners have both the time and political savvy to act as change agents and

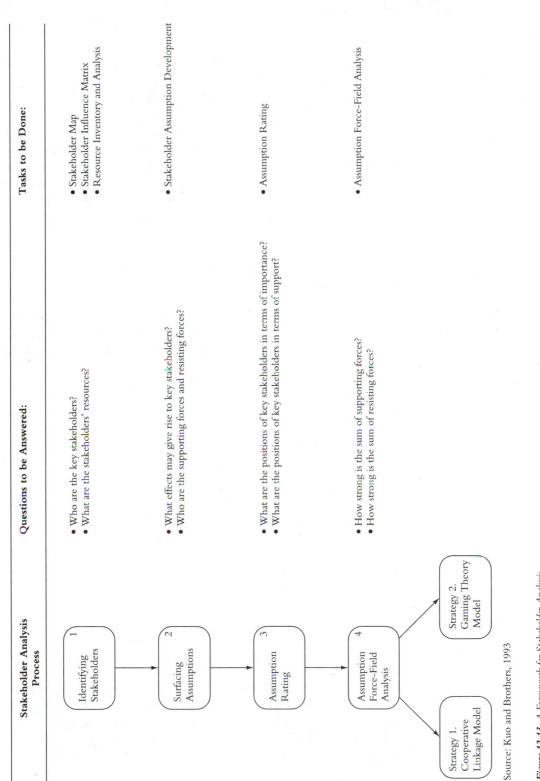

Stakeholder Analysis Process

Questions to be Answered:

Tasks to be Done:

1 Identifying Stakeholders

- Who are the key stakeholders?
- What are the stakeholders' resources?

- Stakeholder Map
- Stakeholder Influence Matrix
- Resource Inventory and Analysis

2 Surfacing Assumptions

- What effects may give rise to key stakeholders?
- Who are the supporting forces and resisting forces?

- Stakeholder Assumption Development

3 Assumption Rating

- What are the positions of key stakeholders in terms of importance?
- What are the positions of key stakeholders in terms of support?

- Assumption Rating

4 Assumption Force-Field Analysis

- How strong is the sum of supporting forces?
- How strong is the sum of resisting forces?

- Assumption Force-Field Analysis

Strategy 1. Cooperative Linkage Model

Strategy 2. Gaming Theory Model

Source: Kuo and Brothers, 1993

Figure 12.13 *A Framework for Stakeholder Analysis*

resource personnel for the key stakeholders identified as critical members of the new cooperative stakeholder group.

The gaming theory model comes into play when two powerful stakeholders hold divergent views on the proposed initiative. There are two different strategies each stakeholder may adopt. One is to negotiate. Negotiation results in a compromise position which neither group fully supports but is willing to accept because of fear of losing some control over the outcome. Another strategy is to "play hardball." When one group feels it has sufficient political clout to carry its position, it may refuse to negotiate. The outcome then favors one group's position entirely over the other. However, if this strategy is used, adversarial proceedings may be initiated with a solution imposed by an outside body such as the judiciary. Since the legal process may take years to resolve and the outcome is apt to be a win/lose situation, negotiation may be a more desired outcome for both groups.

The stakeholder analysis process which identifies supporting and adverse assumptions forms the basis for negotiation. One clue to the probable success of a negotiated outcome is the importance placed on what can be considered emotion or principle based assumptions. The more emotion- or principle-based assumptions there are, the less of a chance for a negotiated settlement with an increasing probability for a court imposed decision.

Stakeholder analysis provides an option to resolve some of the issues surrounding any tourism development plan. As one option, it may lead to more public involvement in the planning process, a goal that has been emphasized throughout this text. At the very least it allows assumptions both in favor and against any plan to surface and be dealt with in a structured and strategic manner. While every planner must consider the political system in which he/she operates, no plan will be met with complete acceptance by every segment of society. Success in planning requires as much, and in some cases more, attention be paid to the political process as to the numbers derived in a feasibility analysis.

CONCLUSION

The process of planning for tourism development remains a difficult but not impossible task. As the potential long-term economic and social costs of inappropriate development increase, the planning process must become more intensive. Searching for the optimal allocation of resources between competing uses is the challenge. The key to successful tourism development at any level is careful planning. Much early tourism planning was site- and facility-specific. It is only recently that the impacts of tourism development on the natural resource base and indigenous populations have become more easily known and recognized. With this knowledge has come a call for more integrative and involved planning. Tourism planning should not be done in a vacuum. As many affected groups as possible should be involved in deciding the type of tourism that is right for their community. While this has become one of the supports of a sustainable development platform, there are still different opinions over how this goal can be achieved.

This chapter discusses much of the current thinking regarding tourism development planning, sustainable development as a concept, and the process of public involvement. Even if the substantial percentage increases in new tourists experienced during the 1970s and 1980s are not realized during the 1990s, there is no indication that tourism demand will decrease. New tourism developments have the decided advantage of learning from the mistakes of the past, but their success will be invariably tied to the planning process they utilize. Tourism planning should be viewed as a proactive process entwined within the indigenous political process, requiring each affected group to make their best case for what they want to offer tourists. Only when this has been achieved can a tourism destination area be said to have accomplished their own form of sustainable development.

EXECUTIVE SUMMARY

Numerous reasons exist for engaging in tourism planning. Some of the more critical ones include the types of impacts created through development, fragmented nature of the tourism industry with little organizational cohesiveness, and the increasing levels of competition between individual businesses and destinations.

To be effective, planning goals must involve and include issues affecting local environmental and social subsystems, reconciled as much as possible to the needs of the private sector.

Local tourism planning is an involved process which begins with the establishment of a funding source for a tourism organization which should be empowered to organize efforts to review the present situation, set development objectives, develop alternative strategies for meeting the objectives, select a preferred alternative, and help implement and monitor the changes brought by the chosen development option.

Sustainable development is still a concept in search of a workable definition. For most people it means use without resource abuse or degradation. If it is to become an operational concept, it must be integrated into the planning process and contain certain elements including activity, requirements, and options components.

Mass tourism, often criticized as unsustainable, can be a sustainable development if planners recognize that major transformation usually occurs, host/guest interactions are not a top priority, large volumes of people must be handled by efficient transportation and waste management systems, and ancillary impacts such as development spread are anticipated and managed.

Economic and social welfare theory shows

that a diversification plan with tourism as one option is a preferred development strategy.

Public involvement can be enhanced by a stakeholder analysis. One of two alternative strategies, cooperative linkage or gaming theory, can be chosen based on the results of the stakeholder analysis. Regardless of the strategy chosen, the chances of a negotiated settlement decline as the number of emotion or principle based assumptions increases.

REFERENCES

A Sense of Place: Tourism, Development, and the Environment. Videocassette, Brookline, Mass.: Umbrella Films.

Allen, L., P. Long, R. Perdue, and S. Kieselbach. 1988. The Impact of Tourism Development on Resident's Perceptions of Community Life. *Journal of Travel Research* 27(1):16–21.

Baker, I. 1990. The Objective Tree in Tourism Planning. *Journal of Travel Research* 28(4):33–36.

Barlowe, R. 1972. *Land Resource Economics: The Economics of Real Property.* Englewood Cliffs, N.J.: Prentice Hall.

Bramwell, B. 1991. Sustainability and Rural Tourism Policy in Britain. *Tourism Recreation Research* 16(2):49–51.

Bryson, J. and W. Roering. 1987. Applying Private-Sector Strategic Planning in the Public Sector. *Journal of the American Planning Association* 53(1): 9–22.

Din, K. 1988. Social and Cultural Impacts of Tourism. *Annals of Tourism Research* 15(4):563–566.

Dragicevic, M. Towards Sustainable Development. *Proceedings of the 1991 AIEST Conference: 29–62.* St-Gall, Switzerland: AIEST.

Draper, D. and A. Driscoll. 1991. Development Dilemmas: Enhancing Sustainable Development Through Cooperative Choices. *Proceedings of the AIEST Conference.* St-Gall, Switzerland.

Freeman R. 1984. *Strategic Management: A Stakeholder Approach.* Marshfield, MA: Pitman Publishing, Inc.

Gunn, C. 1988. *Tourism Planning.* New York: Taylor & Francis.

Hirner, K., G. Weaver, C. Colton, G. Gillespie, and B. Cox. 1986. *Tourism USA—Guidelines for Tourism Development.* University of Missouri and U.S. Travel and Tourism Administration, Department of Commerce.

Inskeep, E. 1991. *Tourism Planning: An Integrated and Sustainable Development Approach.* New York: Van Nostrand Reinhold.

IUCN. 1980. *World Conservation Strategy: Living Resource Conservation for Sustainable Development.* Gland, Switzerland: IUCNR, UNEP.

Kuo, J. and G. Brothers. 1993. *Stakeholder Analysis: An Application to Public Provision of Recreation Opportunities.* Chapel Hill, NC: Department of Parks, Recreation and Tourism Management, North Carolina University.

McIntosh, R., C. Goeldner, and B. Ritchie. 1995. *Tourism: Principles, Practices, and Philosophies.* New York: John Wiley and Sons, Inc.

McIntyre, G. and A. Hetherington. 1992. *Sustainable Tourism Development: Guidelines for Local Planners.* Bainbridge Island, Wash.: Meta-Link, Inc.

Pearce, D and R. Turner. 1990. *Economics of*

Natural Resources and the Environment. Hemel Hempstead, U.K.: Harvester, Wheatsheaf, cited in Dragicevic, 1991.

Quesada-Mateo, C., and V. Solis-Rivera. 1990. Sintesis ECODES by Dr. Carlos A. Quesada, p.307, Memoria (Congreso de Conservacion para el Desarrollo Sostenible: 1st., San Jose, Costa Rica). Carlos A. Quesada-Mateo y Vivienne Solis-Rivera MIRENEM, 1990.

Rowe, A., R. Mason, and K. Dickel. 1986. *Strategic Management: A Methodological Approach.* Reading, Mass.: Addison-Wesley Publishing Company.

Smith, R., 1991. Beach Resorts: A Model of Development Evolution. *Landscape and Urban Planning* 21:189–210.

UN. 1987. *Our Common Future.* The World Commission on Environmental and Development. Oxford: Oxford University Press.

Witt, S. 1991. Tourism in Cyprus: Balancing the Benefits and Costs. *Tourism Management* 12(1):37–46.

Index